Moral Philosophy:
A Reader

Moral Philosophy:
A Reader

Fourth Edition

Edited by

Louis P. Pojman

and

Peter Tramel

Hackett Publishing Company, Inc.
Indianapolis/Cambridge

Dedicated to the memory of
Louis P. Pojman (1935–2005)

Printed in the United States of America

20 19 18 17   4 5 6 7 8

For further information, please address:
  Hackett Publishing Company, Inc.
  P.O. Box 44937
  Indianapolis, IN 46244–0937

  www.hackettpublishing.com

Cover design by Brian Rak and Abigail Coyle
Interior design by Dan Kirklin

Library of Congress Cataloging-in-Publication Data

Moral philosophy: a reader / edited by Louis P. Pojman and
    Peter Tramel. —4th ed.
              p. cm.
      ISBN 978-0-87220-962-6 (pbk.) — ISBN 978-0-87220-963-3 (cloth)
        1. Ethics—Textbooks. I. Pojman, Louis P.   II. Tramel, Peter, 1965–
        170—dc22   2009010450

The paper used in this publication meets the minimum requirements of American National Standard
for Information Sciences—Permanence of Paper for Printed Library Materials, ANSI Z39.48–1984.
∞

Contents

Preface to the Fourth Edition   vii
General Introduction: What Is Moral Philosophy?   ix

I.   What Is Morally Right Conduct?
    Introduction: Plato's Moral Philosophy   1
    1. Plato: What Is Right Conduct?   2

II.   Moral Relativism vs. Moral Objectivism
    Introduction   19
    2. Herodotus: Custom Is King   20
    3. Thomas Aquinas: Natural Law   21
    4. Ruth Benedict: Cultural Relativism   33
    5. Louis P. Pojman: A Defense of Ethical Objectivism   38
    6. Gilbert Harman: A Defense of Ethical Relativism   53

III.   Ethics and Egoism
    Introduction   60
    7. Plato: Why Should I Be Moral?   60
    8. Thomas Hobbes: Egoism as the Beginning of Morality   69
    9. Ayn Rand: A Defense of Ethical Egoism   79
    10. James Rachels: A Critique of Ethical Egoism   86
    11. Howard Kahane: Sociobiology, Egoism, and Reciprocity   94

IV.   Value: What Is the Good?
    Introduction   111
    12. Plato: The Good and the Allegory of the Cave   114
    13. Jeremy Bentham: Classical Hedonism   120
    14. Friedrich Nietzsche: Beyond Good and Evil   123
    15. G. E. Moore: The Good Is Not Natural   131
    16. Robert Nozick: The Experience Machine   141
    17. W. D. Ross: Value Pluralism   143
    18. Derek Parfit: What Makes Someone's Life Go Best?   148

V.   Utilitarian Ethics
    Introduction   156
    19. John Stuart Mill: Utilitarianism   158
    20. John Hospers: Rule-Utilitarianism   164
    21. Bernard Williams: A Critique of Utilitarianism   175

22. Sterling Harwood: Eleven Objections to Utilitarianism   186
23. Brad Hooker: Ideal Code Utilitarianism   200

VI. Deontological Ethics
     Introduction   216
     24. Immanuel Kant: The Foundations of Ethics   218
     25. Melissa Bergeron and Peter Tramel: Rightness as Fairness:
         Kant's Categorical Imperative   238
     26. W. D. Ross: What Makes Right Acts Right?   261
     27. William Frankena: A Reconciliation of Ethical Theories   271
     28. T. M. Scanlon: A Contractarian Ethics   279

VII. Virtue Ethics
     Introduction   299
     29. Aristotle: Virtue Ethics   301
     30. Bernard Mayo: Virtue and the Moral Life   312
     31. William Frankena: A Critique of Virtue-Based Ethics   316
     32. Alasdair MacIntyre: The Nature of the Virtues   323
     33. Jonathan Bennett: The Conscience of Huckleberry Finn   339
     34. Rosalind Hursthouse: Virtue and Emotion   348

VIII. Morality and Religion
     Introduction   356
     35. Plato: The Euthyphro Problem   359
     36. Bertrand Russell: A Free Man's Worship   361
     37. James Rachels: God and Morality Are Incompatible   366
     38. C. Stephen Layman: God and the Moral Order   377
     39. Peter Byrne: God and the Moral Order: A Reply to Layman   388

IX. Applied Ethics
     Introduction   395
     40. Judith Jarvis Thompson: The Trolley Problem   397
     41. Peter Singer: Famine, Affluence, and Morality   412
     42. Onora O'Neill: Kantian Ethics and World Hunger   421
     43. John T. Noonan Jr.: Abortion Is Morally Wrong   434
     44. Mary Anne Warren: The Personhood Argument in Favor
         of Abortion Rights   439
     45. John Rawls: Fifty Years after Hiroshima   444
     46. Michael Walzer: Supreme Emergency   450
     47. Thomas Nagel: War and Massacre   463

Preface to the Fourth Edition

Since the first edition in 1993, this anthology has done much good service in introductory ethics courses. I remember admiring it as I chose it for a primary text in the first such courses I taught—well before I had the good fortune to meet and work with its inventor, Louis Pojman. Out of respect for its long-standing success, I have tried in this, the first edition of *Moral Philosophy: A Reader* under my stewardship, to obey the physicians' ancient precept: "First, do no harm."

I have thus preserved Louis's division of the text into his General Introduction followed by topical sections. However I have made a number of changes in the selections, primarily in the interest of updating the volume, and I have accordingly revised, and in some cases replaced, the section introductions.

The new selections for this edition include: Gilbert Harman, selection from *The Nature of Morality;* G. E. Moore, selection from *Principia Ethica;* Brad Hooker, selection from *Ideal Code, Real World;* Melissa Bergeron and Peter Tramel, "Rightness as Fairness: Kant's Categorical Imperative"; T. M. Scanlon, selection from *What We Owe to Each Other;* Rosalind Hursthouse, selection from *On Virtue Ethics;* James Rachels, "God and Human Attitudes"; C. Stephen Layman, "God and the Moral Order"; Peter Byrne, "God and the Moral Order: A Reply to Layman"; Judith Jarvis Thomson, "The Trolley Problem"; Onora O'Neill, selection from *Matters of Life and Death;* John Rawls, "Fifty Years after Hiroshima"; Michael Walzer, selection from *Just and Unjust Wars;* and Thomas Nagel, "War and Massacre."

General Introduction

What Is Moral Philosophy?

> We are discussing no small matter, but how we ought to live.
>
> (Socrates in Plato's *Republic*)

What is it to be a moral person? What is the nature of morality, and why do we need it? What is the good, and how shall I know it? Are moral principles absolute or simply relative to social groups or individual decision? Is it in my interest to be moral? Is it sometimes in my best interest to act immorally? How does one justify one's moral beliefs? What is the basis of morality? Which ethical theory provides the best justification and explanation of the moral life? What is the relationship between morality and religion?

These are some of the questions that we shall be looking at in this book. We want to understand the foundation and structure of morality. We want to know how we should live.

The terms 'moral' and 'ethics' come from Latin and Greek respectively (*mores* and *ethos*), deriving their meaning from the idea of custom. Although philosophers sometimes use these terms interchangeably, it is useful to have a clearer conceptual scheme. In this work I shall use 'morality' to refer to certain customs, precepts, and practices of people and cultures. This is sometimes referred to as 'positive morality.' I shall use 'moral philosophy' to refer to philosophical or theoretical reflection on morality. Specific moral theories issuing from such philosophical reflection I shall call 'ethical theories,' in line with a common practice. 'Ethics' I shall use to refer to the whole domain of morality and moral philosophy, since they have many features in common. For example, they both have to do with values, virtues, and principles and practices, though in different ways. I shall refer to specific moral theories as 'ethical theories,' in line with a common practice.

Moral philosophy is the systematic endeavor to understand moral concepts and justify moral principles and theories. It undertakes to analyze such concepts as 'right,' 'wrong,' 'permissible,' 'ought,' 'good,' and 'evil' in their moral contexts. Moral philosophy seeks to establish principles of right behavior that may serve as action guides for individuals and groups. It investigates which values and virtues are paramount to the worthwhile life or society. It builds and scrutinizes arguments in ethical theories, and it seeks to discover valid principles (e.g., 'Never kill innocent human beings') and the relationship between those principles (e.g., 'Does saving a life in some situations constitute a valid reason for breaking a promise?').

Morality as Compared with Other Normative Subjects

Moral precepts are concerned with norms; roughly speaking, they are concerned not with what is, but with what ought to be. How should I live my life? What is the right thing to do in this situation? Should one always tell the truth? Do I have a duty to report a coworker whom I have seen cheating our company? Should I tell my friend that his spouse is having an affair? Is premarital sex morally permissible? Ought a woman ever to have an abortion? Morality has a distinct action-guiding or *normative* aspect,[1] an aspect it shares with other practical institutions, such as religion, law, and etiquette.

Moral behavior, as defined by a given religion, is often held to be essential to the practice of that religion. But neither the practices nor precepts of morality should be identified with religion. The practice of morality need not be motivated by religious considerations. And moral precepts need not be grounded in revelation or divine authority—as religious teachings invariably are. The most salient characteristic of ethics—by which I mean both philosophical morality (or morality, as I will simply refer to it) and moral philosophy—is that it is grounded in reason and human experience.

To use a spatial metaphor, secular ethics are horizontal, omitting a vertical or transcendental dimension. Religious ethics have a vertical dimension, being grounded in revelation or divine authority, though generally using reason to supplement or complement revelation. These two differing orientations will often generate different moral principles and standards of evaluation, but they need not. Some versions of religious ethics, which posit God's revelation of the moral law in nature or conscience, hold that reason can discover what is right or wrong, even apart from divine revelation.

Morality also has much in common with law. And, not surprisingly perhaps, some people make the mistake of equating the two. After all, laws can promote well-being and social harmony, and can resolve conflicts of interest, just as morality can.

Yet there are crucial differences. Ethics may judge certain laws to be immoral without denying that they are valid laws. Laws may permit slavery, for example, or unjust discrimination. An anti-abortion advocate may believe laws permitting abortion to be immoral.

It is possible, too, that under some circumstances the requirements of law may be at odds with the requirements of ethics. Consider the reply given by a trial lawyer when asked what he would do if he discovered that a client had committed a murder some years back for which another man had been convicted and would soon be executed: The lawyer said it was his legal obligation to keep this information confidential and that, if he divulged it, he would be disbarred.[2] Might not a lawyer in this situation also have a moral obligation to save an innocent man from being executed? And might it not override a legal or moral obligation to preserve his client's confidentiality?

Not all aspects of morality are covered by law. While it is generally agreed, for example, that lying is usually immoral, there is no general law against it. (There are, to be sure, laws against lying in certain circumstances: while under oath, for example, or on an income-tax return.)

Sometimes college newspapers publish advertisements for "research assistance," where it is tacitly understood that the companies involved will aid and abet plagiarism. The publication of such ads is legal, but it is doubtful that it is morally correct.

In 1963, thirty-nine people in Queens, New York, watched from their apartments for some forty-five minutes while an assailant beat up and finally killed a woman, Kitty Genovese; they did nothing to intervene, not even calling the police. These people broke no law, but they were very likely morally culpable for not calling the police or otherwise coming to the aid of the victim.

Even if it were thought desirable to have laws which governed all aspects of morality, this would prove impractical. In 1351 King Edward III of England promulgated a law against treason that made it a crime merely to think homicidal thoughts about the king. For reasons easy to imagine, this law proved unenforceable. Once an act has been committed, of course, intention plays a crucial role in determining its legal character. But intention alone, intention that is not acted upon, remains outside the reach of law.

The mere fact that it is impractical to have laws against bad intentions, however, does not mean such intentions are not bad, are not morally wrong. Suppose I buy a gun with the intention of killing Uncle Charlie, but never get a chance to act on that intention (say, Uncle Charlie moves to Australia). Though I have committed no crime, I have committed a moral wrong.

How else does morality differ from law? To begin with, we might say that law is enforced by sanctions[3] that restrict a violator's liberty (for example, by imprisonment or fines), whereas morality does not rely on these sanctions. Morality does rely, however, on what we might call "moral sanctions," primarily those of conscience and reputation. (By morality, remember, we mean morality not motivated by religious considerations.)

Morality differs, too, from etiquette and custom, which concern form and style, rather than the essence of social existence. Etiquette determines what is polite behavior rather than what behavior is, in a deeper sense, right. Custom represents society's decision as to how we are to dress, greet one another, eat, celebrate festivals, dispose of the dead, and carry out social transactions.

Whether we greet others with a handshake, a bow, a hug, or a kiss on the cheek will differ in various cultures and social systems. People in England hold their fork in their right hand. In other countries, people hold a fork in their right hand or left hand or whichever hand a person feels like holding it. In India, people typically eat without a fork. They simply use the forefingers of the right hand.

None of these practices has any moral superiority. Etiquette helps social transactions flow smoothly, but it is not the substance of those transactions. The observance of custom graces our social existence, but it is not what social existence is about.

At the same time, it can be wrong to disregard etiquette and custom. A cultural crisis recently developed in India when some Americans went to the beaches clad in skimpy bathing suits. This was found highly offensive, though there is nothing intrinsically wrong with wearing skimpy bathing suits or, for that matter, with wearing none at all. Especially when one is a guest in someone else's home or country, however, ignoring or displaying contempt for such customs can be more than merely rude; it can be morally wrong. In the example just given, we might say it was not the wearing of the bathing suits but a kind of insensitivity that was wrong.[4]

Law, etiquette and religion are all important institutions, but each has limitations. The limitation of the law is that we can not have a law against every social malady, nor can we enforce every desirable rule. The limitation of etiquette is that it does not get to the heart of what is of vital importance for personal and social existence. Whether or not one eats with one's fingers pales in signifi-cance compared with whether or not one is honest or trustworthy or just. Etiquette is a cultural *invention*, but morality claims to be a *discovery*.

The limitation of the religious injunction is that it rests on authority, and we are not always sure of or in agreement about the credentials of the authority or on how the authority would rule in ambiguous or new cases. Since religion is founded not on reason but on revelation, we cannot use reason to convince someone who does not share our religious views that our view is the right one. I hasten to add that when moral differences are caused by fundamental moral principles, it is unlikely that philosophical reasoning will settle the matter. Often, however, our moral differences turn out to be rooted in world views, not moral principles. For example, antiabortion and pro-choice advocates often agree that it is wrong to kill innocent persons, but differ on the facts. The antiabortion advocates may hold a religious view that states that the fetus has an eternal soul and thus possesses a right to life, while the pro-choice advocates may deny that anyone has a soul and hold that only self-conscious, rational beings have a right to life.

In summary, morality distinguishes itself from law and etiquette by going deeper into the essence of rational existence. It distinguishes itself from religion in that it seeks reasons, rather than authority, to justify its principles. The central purpose of moral philosophy is to secure valid principles of conduct and values that can be instrumental in guiding human actions and producing good character. As such, it is the most important activity known to humans, for it has to do with how we are to live.

Domains of Ethical Assessment

It might seem at this point that ethics concerns itself entirely with rules of conduct based solely on an evaluation of acts. However, the situation is more complicated than this. Most ethical analysis falls into one or some of the following four domains:

Domain	Evaluative terms	
1. Action (the act)	permissible	not permissible

obligatory   optional   wrong

neutral   supererogatory

2. Consequences	good, bad, neutral
3. Character	virtuous, vicious, neutral
4. Motive	good, evil, neutral

Let us examine each of these domains.

(1) *Action.* The most common classification of acts may be as obligatory, optional, or wrong.

(i) An obligatory act is an act morality requires you to do, an act it is not permissible for you to refrain from doing.

(ii) A wrong act is an act you have an obligation, or duty, to refrain from, an act you ought not to do, an act it is not permissible to do.

(iii) An optional act is an act which it is neither obligatory nor wrong to do. It is not your duty to do it; neither is it your duty to not to do it.

Theories which place the emphasis on the nature of the act are called 'deontological' (from the Greek word for "duty"). These theories hold that there is something inherently right or good about such acts as truth telling and promise keeping and something inherently wrong or bad about such acts as lying and promise breaking. The most famous of these systems is Kant's moral theory, which we shall study in Part VI.

(2) *Consequences.* We said above that lying is generally seen as wrong and telling the truth is generally seen as right. But consider this situation. You are hiding in your home an innocent woman named Laura, who is fleeing gangsters. Gangland Gus knocks on your door, and when you open it, he asks if Laura is in your house. What should you do? Should you tell the truth or lie? Those who say that morality has something to do with consequences of actions would prescribe lying as the morally right thing to do.

Those who deny that we should look at the consequences when considering what to do when there is a clear and absolute rule of action will say that we should either keep silent or tell the truth. When no other rule is at stake, of course, the rule-oriented ethicist will allow the foreseeable consequences to determine a course of action. Theories which focus primarily on consequences in determining moral rightness and wrongness are called 'teleological' ethical theories (from the Greek *telos,* meaning "goal-directed"). The most famous of these theories is utilitarianism, which we shall study in Part V.

(3) *Character.* While some ethical theories emphasize principles of action in themselves and some emphasize principles involving consequences of action, other theories, such as Aristotle's ethics, emphasize character or virtue. According to Aristotle, it is most important to develop virtuous character, for if and only if we have good people can we ensure habitual right action. Although the virtues are not central to other types of moral theories, most moral theories include the virtues as important. Most reasonable people, whatever their notions about ethics, would judge that the people who watched Kitty Genovese being assaulted lacked good character. Different moral systems emphasize different virtues, to varying degrees. We shall study virtue in Part VII.

(4) *Motive.* Finally, virtually all ethical systems, but especially Kant's, accept the relevance of motive. It is important to the full assessment of any action that the intention of the agent be

taken into account. Two acts may be identical, and one judged morally culpable, the other not. Consider John's pushing Joan off a ledge, causing her to break her leg. In situation (A) he is angry and intends to harm her. In situation (B) he sees a knife flying in her direction and intends to save her life. In (A), what he did was clearly wrong. In (B), he did the right thing.

By contrast, two acts may get opposite results and, on the basis of intention, be judged equally good. Imagine two soldiers trying to cross enemy lines ill order to communicate with an ally. One is captured through no fault of his own, and the other succeeds. In a full moral description of any act, motive will be taken into consideration as a relevant factor.

In this work we will examine several fundamental questions in moral philosophy. In Part I, beginning with a selection from Plato's *Republic*, we look at the question, "What is morally right conduct?" In this classical discussion we find embedded many of the questions to be examined later in this book: "Is morality objectively valid?" Why should I be moral?" "What is the nature of morality?"

In Part II we examine the question "Are moral principles valid relative to cultural or individual approval, or are they objectively and universally valid?"

In Part III we inquire into the relationship of morality to self-interest. Why should I be moral even when it is not in my interest to be so? Or is it really in my interest always to be moral? Or is morality simply enlightened self-interest, in a manner that precludes altruism?

In Part IV we examine the nature of value. Are there any intrinsic, objective values, or are all values subjective, simply objects of desire?

In Parts V–VII we examine major ethical theories in the history of Western moral philosophy. In Part V we look at utilitarianism, beginning with a selection from John Stuart Mill's classic work *Utilitarianism*. In Part VI we examine

Kant's deontological ethics, beginning with a selection from his *Grounding for the Metaphysics of Morals*. Part VII considers virtue ethics, beginning with Aristotle's classic formulation in his *Nicomachean Ethics*.

In Part VIII we turn to the relationship of ethics to religion. Are all moral principles based on divine commands, or are they autonomous, having independent validity? And, whatever our answer to that question, does secular morality have the resources sufficient to motivate compliance with moral reasons, or does morality need the support of divine sanctions?

Finally, in Part IX we turn to a few topics in applied ethics. Is it worse to do a bad thing than to permit a bad thing to happen? Are those of us with more than enough resources to keep ourselves alive morally obliged to help those without, such as those whose lives are threatened by famine? If so, how much must we give up? Is abortion morally permissible? If so, under what circumstances? In war, are there ever situations in which it would be permissible, or at least less wrong than any other alternative, to torture or to target innocent civilians? This last question takes us back to the first, but with the addition of incredibly high stakes.

It is to be hoped that these readings will stimulate you to do your own thinging on each of the major questions raised in the study of moral philosophy. The challenge is as exciting as it is important, for, to quote Socrates, "We are discussing no small matter, but how we ought to live."

Notes

1. Webster's Collegiate Dictionary defines *normative* as "of, or relating or conforming to or prescribing norms or standards."

2. This question was asked, and this reply was given, in the television program *Ethics in America* (PBS, 1989).

3. A sanction is a mechanism for social control, used to enforce society's standards. It may consist of rewards or punishment, praise or blame, approbation or disapprobation.

4. Although Americans pride themselves on tolerance and awareness of other cultures, customs and etiquette can be a bone of contention. A friend of mine tells of an experience early in his marriage. John and his wife were hosting their first Thanksgiving meal. He had been used to small celebrations with his immediate family, whereas his wife had been used to grand celebrations. He writes, "I had been asked to carve, something I had never done before, but I was willing. I put on an apron, entered the kitchen, and attacked the bird with as much artistry as I could muster. And what reward did I get? [My wife] burst into tears. In *her* family the turkey is brought to the *table*, laid before the [father], grace is said, and *then* he carves! 'So I fail patriarchy,' I hollered later. 'What do you expect?'" (from John Buehrens and Forrester Church, *Our Chosen Faith* [Beacon Press, 1989], p. 140.)

PART I

What Is Morally Right Conduct?

Introduction: Plato's Moral Philosophy

Plato (427–347 B.C.) lived in Athens, the great Greek democratic city-state, in the aftermath of its glory under Pericles. He was Socrates' disciple and the founder of the first school of philosophy, the Academy. In his dialogues, and especially in the *Republic*, from which our first selection, as well as selections III.7 and IV.12, are taken, he sets forth and develops some of the ideas of his teacher, Socrates.

Socrates (470–399 B.C.) is the father of moral philosophy, the first philosopher in the Western tradition to raise fundamental questions about the nature of morality: "What is justice?" "What is virtue?" "Can virtue be taught?" "What is the good life?" "Why should I be moral?" "Is morality more than mere convention?" In our first two selections Socrates deals with two central questions, "What is justice or right conduct?" and "Why should I be moral (or just)?"

The *Republic* is a classic dialogue on political philosophy, centering on the nature of goodness and of the good life. Although the Greek idea of *justice* has some different connotations from our concept of morally right conduct, it is close enough to our concept to be serviceable in pro-

moting an understanding of the central features of moral philosophy.

The dialogue takes place around the year 422 B.C., in the Athenian home of Cephalus, an elderly, prosperous businessman. Socrates is in his 40s. Those present, besides Cephalus and his son, Polemarchus, include two of Plato's brothers, Glaucon and Adeimantus, and the sophist Thrasymachus. Socrates is the narrator.

In the initial discussion Cephalus defines justice or right conduct as telling the truth and paying back what one has borrowed. Socrates quickly dismisses this definition with a telling counterexample. Polemarchus then takes over from his father and, citing the poet Simonides, argues that right conduct is to give each man what is due him: doing good to one's friends and evil to one's enemies. This undergoes modifications under analysis but is finally rejected as inadequate. At this point Thrasymachus jumps in and vehemently argues that justice is that which promotes the interest of the stronger: Might makes right. As the argument proceeds, Thrasymachus changes his thesis to claim that injustice is more profitable than justice and is the way to happiness.

Reprinted from *Plato's Republic*, trans. G. M. A. Grube (Indianapolis: Hackett Publishing Company, 1974), by permission of the publisher.

1

What Is Right Conduct?

PLATO

So we went to the home of Polemarchus, and there we found Lysias and Euthydemus, the brothers of Polemarchus, also Thrasymachus of Chalcedon, Charmantides of Paiania, and Cleitophon the son of Aristonymus. Polemarchus's father Cephalus was also in the house. I thought he looked quite old, as I had not seen him for some time. He was sitting on a seat with a cushion, a wreath on his head, for he had been offering a sacrifice in the courtyard. There was a circle of seats there, and we sat down by him.

As soon as he saw me Cephalus welcomed me and said: Socrates, you don't often come down to the Piraeus to see us. You should. If it were still easy for me to walk to the city you would not need to come here, we would come to you, but now you should come more often. You should realize that, to the extent that my physical pleasures get feebler, my desire for conversation, and the pleasure I take in it, increase. So be sure to come more often and talk to these youngsters, as you would to good friends and relations.

I replied: Indeed, Cephalus, I do enjoy conversing with men of advanced years. As from those who have travelled along a road which we too will probably have to follow, we should enquire from them what kind of a road it is, whether rough and difficult or smooth and easy, and I should gladly learn from you what you think about this, as you have reached the point in life which the poets call "the threshold of old age,"[1] whether it is a difficult part of life, or how your experience would describe it to us.

Yes, by Zeus, Socrates, he said, I will tell you what I think of old age. A number of us who are more or less the same age often get together in accordance with the old adage.[2] When we meet, the majority of us bemoan their age: they miss the pleasures which were theirs in youth; they recall the pleasures of sex, drink, and feasts, and some other things that go with them, and they are angry as if they were deprived of important things, as if they then lived the good life and now were not living at all. Some others deplore the humiliations which old age suffers in the household, and because of this they repeat again and again that old age is the cause of many evils. However, Socrates, I do not think that they blame the real cause. For if old age were the cause, then I should have suffered in the same way, and so would all others who have reached my age. As it is, I have met other old men who do not feel like that, and indeed I was present at one time when someone asked the poet Sophocles: "How are you in regard to sex, Sophocles? Can you still make love to a woman?" "Hush man, the poet replied, I am very glad to have escaped from this, like a slave who has escaped from a mad and cruel master." I thought then that he was right, and I still think so, for a great peace and freedom from these things come with old age: after the tension of one's desires relaxes and ceases, then Sophocles' words certainly apply, it is an escape from many mad masters. As regards both sex and relations in the household there is one cause, Socrates, not old age but the manner of one's life: if it is moderate and contented, then old age too is but moderately burdensome; if it is not, then both old age and youth are hard to bear.

I wondered at his saying this and I wanted him to say more, so I urged him on by saying: Cephalus, when you say this, I don't think most people would agree with you; they think you endure old age easily not because of your manner of life but because you are wealthy, for the wealthy, they say, have many things to encourage them.

What you say is true, he said. They would not agree. And there is something in what they say, but not as much as they think. What Themistocles said is quite right: when a man from Seriphus[3] was insulting him by saying that his high reputation was due to his city and not to himself, he replied that, had he been a Seriphian, he would not be famous, but neither would the other had he been an Athenian. The same can be applied to those who are not rich and find old age hard to bear—namely, that a good man would not very easily bear old age in poverty, nor would a bad man, even if wealthy, be at peace with himself. . . .

It surely is, said I. Now tell me this much [Cephalus], What is the greatest benefit you have received from the enjoyment of wealth?

I would probably not convince many people in saying this, Socrates, he said, but you must realize that when a man approaches the time when he thinks he will die, he becomes fearful and concerned about things which he did not fear before. It is then that the stories we are told about the underworld, which he ridiculed before—that the man who has sinned here will pay the penalty there—torture his mind lest they be true. Whether because of the weakness of old age, or because he is now closer to what happens there and has a clearer view, the man himself is filled with suspicion and fear, and he now takes account and examines whether he has wronged anyone. If he finds many sins in his own life, he awakes from sleep in terror, as children do, and he lives with the expectation of evil. However, the man who knows he has not sinned has a sweet and good hope as his constant companion, a nurse to his old age, as Pindar too puts it. The poet has expressed this charmingly, Socrates, that whoever lives a just and pious life

Sweet is the hope that nurtures his heart,
companion and nurse to his old age,
a hope which governs the rapidly changing
  thoughts of mortals.

This is wonderfully well said. It is in this connection that I would say that wealth has its greatest value, not for everyone but for a good and well-balanced man. Not to have lied to or deceived anyone even unwillingly, not to depart yonder in fear, owing either sacrifices to a god or money to a man: to this wealth makes a great contribution. It has many other uses, but benefit for benefit I would say that its greatest usefulness lies in this for an intelligent man, Socrates.

Beautifully spoken, Cephalus, said I, but are we to say that justice or right[4] is simply to speak the truth and to pay back any debt one may have contracted? Or are these same actions sometimes right and sometimes wrong? I mean this sort of thing, for example: everyone would surely agree that if a friend has deposited weapons with you when he was sane, and he asks for them when he is out of his mind, you should not return them. The man who returns them is not doing right, nor is one who is willing to tell the whole truth to a man in such a state.

What you say is correct, he answered.

This then is not a definition of right or justice, namely, to tell the truth and pay one's debts.

It certainly is, said Polemarchus interrupting, if we are to put any trust in Simonides.

And now, said Cephalus, I leave the argument to you, for I must go back and look after the sacrifice.

Do I then inherit your role? asked Polemarchus.

You certainly do, said Cephalus laughing, and as he said it he went off to sacrifice.

Then do tell us, Polemarchus, said I, as the heir to the argument, what it is that Simonides stated about justice which you consider to be correct.

He stated, said he, that it is just to give to each what is owed to him, and I think he was right to say so.

Well now, I said, it is hard not to believe Simonides, for he is a wise and inspired man, but what does he mean? Perhaps you understand him, but I do not. Clearly he does not mean what we were saying just now, that anything he has deposited must be returned to a man who is not in his right mind; yet anything he has deposited is owing to him. Is that not so?—Yes.

But it is not to be returned to him at all if he is out of his mind when he asks for it?—That's true.

Certainly Simonides meant something different from this when he says that to return what is owed is just.

He did indeed mean something different, by Zeus, said he. He believes that one owes it to one's friends to do good to them, and not harm.

I understand, said I, that one does not give what is owed or due if one gives back gold to a depositor, when giving back and receiving are harmful, and the two are friends. Is that not what you say Simonides meant?—Quite.

Well then, should one give what is due to one's enemies?

By all means, said he, what is in fact due to them, and I believe that is what is properly due from an enemy to an enemy, namely, something harmful.

It seems, I said, that Simonides was suggesting the nature of the just poetically and in riddles. For he thought this to be just, to give to each man what is proper to him, and he called this what is due.—Surely.

Then by Zeus, I said, if someone asked him: "Simonides, what does the craft[5] which we call medicine give that is due, and to whom?" What do you think his answer would be?

Clearly, it is the craft which prescribes medicines and food and drink for our bodies.

And what does the craft which we call cooking give that is due and fitting, and to whom?—It adds flavor to food.

Very well. What, and to whom, does that craft give which we would call justice?

It must follow from what was said before, Socrates, that it is that which benefits one's friends and harms one's enemies.

He means then that to benefit one's friends and harm one's enemies is justice?—I think so.

And who is most capable of benefiting his friends and harming his enemies in matters of health and disease?—A physician.

And who can do so best when they are sailing and heading into a storm?—A pilot.

What about the just man? In what activity and what task is he most able to benefit his friends and harm his enemies?—In waging war and in alliances, I think.

Very well. Now when people are not ill, my dear Polemarchus, the physician is no use to them?—True.

Nor is the pilot when they are not sailing?—That is so.

So to people who are not fighting a war the just man is useless?—I do not think so at all.

Justice then is useful also in peace time?—It is.

And so is farming, is it not?—Yes.

For the producing of a harvest?—Yes.

And the cobbler's craft too?—Yes.

I think you would say for getting shoes?—Certainly.

Well then, what is it which justice helps one to use or acquire in peace time?—Contracts, Socrates.

By contracts you mean dealings between people, or something else?—That is what I mean.

Is the just man a good and useful associate in a game of checkers, or is the checkers player?—The checkers player.

And for putting together bricks and stones, is the just man a better and more useful associate than the builder?—Not at all.

In what kind of dealings then is the just man a better associate than the builder or the musician, as the musician is better than the just man in matters of music?—In money matters, I think.

Except perhaps, Polemarchus, when money is to be used, for whenever one needs to buy or sell a horse together, I think the horse breeder is a more useful associate. Is that not so?—Apparently.

And when one needs to buy a boat, the shipbuilder or the captain of a ship?—So it seems.

In what joint use of silver and gold is the just man a more useful associate than the others?

—Whenever one needs to deposit it and keep it safe.

You mean whenever there is no need to use it, but to keep it?—Quite so.

So it is whenever money is not being used that justice is useful?—I'm afraid so.

And whenever one needs to keep a pruning knife safe, but not to use it, justice is useful both in associations and in private. When you need to use it, however, it is the craft of vine dressing that is useful.—So it seems.

You will agree then that when one needs to keep a shield or a lyre safe and not use them, justice is a useful thing, but when you need to use them, it is the hoplite's or the musician's craft which is useful.—That necessarily follows.

So with all other things, justice is useless in their use, but useful when they are not in use.—I fear so.

In that case, my friend, justice is not a very important thing if it is only useful for things not in use. Let us, however, investigate the following point: is not the man most capable of landing a blow in a fight, be it boxing or any other kind, also the most capable of guarding against blows?—Certainly.

And the man most able to guard against disease is also the man most able to inflict it unnoticed?—So it seems.

Further, the same man is a good guardian of a camp who is also able to steal the plans of the enemy and be aware of their actions?—Quite so.

Whenever a man is a good guardian of anything, he is also a good thief of it.—Apparently.

If then the just man is good at guarding money, he is also good at stealing it.—So our argument shows.

The just man then has turned out to be a kind of thief. You may well have learned this from Homer, for he likes Odysseus's maternal grandfather Autolycus, and at the same time he says that he excelled all men in thieving and perjury. It follows that justice, according to you and Homer and Simonides, appears to be a craft of thieving, of course to the advantage of one's friends and to the harm of one's enemies. Is this not what you meant?

No, by Zeus, he said, I don't any longer know what I meant, but this I still believe to be true, that justice is to benefit one's friends and harm one's enemies.

When you say friends, do you mean those whom a man believes to be helpful to him, or those who are helpful even if they do not appear to be so, and so with enemies?

Probably, he said, one is fond of those whom one thinks to be good and helpful to one, and one hates those whom one considers bad and harmful.

Surely people make mistakes about this, and consider many to be helpful when they are not, and often make the opposite mistake about enemies?—They do.

Then good men are their enemies, and bad people their friends?—Quite so.

And so it is just and right for these mistaken people to benefit the bad and harm the good?—It seems so.

But the good are just and able to do no wrong?—True.

But according to your argument it is just to harm those who do no wrong.

Never, Socrates, he said. It is the argument that is wrong.

It is just to harm the wrongdoers and to benefit the just?

That statement, Socrates, seems much more attractive than the other.

Then, Polemarchus, for many who are mistaken in their judgment it follows that it is just to harm their friends, for these are bad, and to benefit their enemies, who are good, and so we come to a conclusion which is the opposite of what we said was the meaning of Simonides.

That certainly follows, he said, but let us change our assumption; we have probably not defined the friend and the enemy correctly.

Where were we mistaken, Polemarchus?

—When we said that a friend was one who was thought to be helpful.

How shall we change this now? I asked.

Let us state, he said, that a friend is one who is both thought to be helpful and also is; one who is thought to be, but is not, helpful is thought to be a friend but is not. And so also with the enemy.

According to this argument then, the good man will be a friend, and the bad man an enemy. —Yes.

You want us to add to what we said before about the just, namely, that it is just to benefit one's friend and harm one's enemy; to this you want us to make an addition and say that it is just to benefit the friend who is good and to harm the enemy who is bad?

Quite so, he said. This seems to me to be well said.

But, I said, is it the part of the just man to harm anyone at all?

Why certainly, he said, those who are bad and one's enemies.

Do horses become better or worse when they are harmed?—Worse.

Do they deteriorate in their excellence as dogs or as horses?—As horses.

And when dogs are harmed, they deteriorate in their excellence as dogs, not in that of horses? —Necessarily.

Shall we not say so about men too, that when they are harmed they deteriorate in their human excellence?—Quite so.

And is not justice a human excellence?—Of course.

Then men who are harmed, my friend, necessarily become more unjust.—So it appears.

Can musicians, by practising music, make men unmusical?—Not possibly.

Or can teachers of horsemanship, by the practice of their craft, make them into non-horsemen?—Impossible.

Well then, can the just, by the practice of justice, make men unjust? Or, in a word, can good men, by the practice of their virtue, make men bad?—They cannot.

It is not the function of heat to cool things, but the opposite?—Yes.

Nor of dryness to make things wet but the opposite?—Quite so.

And it is not the function of the good to harm people, but the opposite?—It seems so.

And the just man is good?—Certainly.

It is not then the function of the just man, Polemarchus, to do harm to a friend or anyone else, but it is that of his opposite, the unjust man?—I think that you are entirely right, Socrates.

If, then, anyone tells us that it is just to give everyone his due, and he means by this that from the just man harm is due to his enemies and benefit due to his friends—the man who says that is not wise, for it is not true. We have shown that it is never just to harm anyone.—I agree.

You and I, I said, will therefore together fight anyone who tells us that Simonides said this, or Bias or Pittacus or any other of our wise and blessed men.—Yes, and I am quite willing to join that fight. . . .

While we were speaking Thrasymachus often started to interrupt, but he was restrained by those who were sitting by him, for they wanted to hear the argument to the end. But when we paused after these last words of mine he could no longer keep quiet. He gathered himself together like a wild beast about to spring, and he came at us as if to tear us to pieces.

Polemarchus and I were afraid and flustered as he roared into the middle of our company: What nonsense have you two been talking, Socrates? Why do you play the fool in thus giving way to each other? If you really want to know what justice is, don't only ask questions and then score off anyone who answers, and refute him. You know very well that it is much easier to ask questions than to answer them. Give an answer yourself and tell us what you say justice is. And don't tell me that it is the needful, or the advantageous, or the beneficial, or the gainful, or the useful, but tell me clearly and precisely what you mean, for I will not accept it if you utter such rubbish.

His words startled me, and glancing at him I was afraid. I think if I had not looked at him before he looked at me, I should have been speechless. As it was I had glanced at him first when our discussion began to exasperate him, so I was able to answer him and I said, trembling: do not be hard on us, Thrasymachus, if we have erred in our investigation, he and I; be sure that we err unwillingly. You surely do not believe that if we were searching for gold we would be unwilling to give way to each other and thus destroy our chance of finding it, but that when searching for justice, a thing more precious than much gold, we mindlessly give way to one another, and that we are not thoroughly in earnest about finding it. You must believe that, my friend, for I think we could not do it. So it is much more seemly that you clever people should pity us than that you should be angry with us.

When he heard that he gave a loud and bitter laugh and said: By Heracles, that is just Socrates' usual irony. I knew this, and I warned these men here before that you would not be willing to answer any questions but would pretend ignorance, and that you would do anything rather than give an answer, if anyone questioned you.

You are clever, Thrasymachus, I said, for you knew very well that if you asked anyone how much is twelve, and as you asked him you warned him: "Do not, my man, say that twelve is twice six, or three times four, or six times two, or four times three, for I will not accept such nonsense," it would be quite clear to you that no one can answer a question asked in those terms. And if he said to you: "What do you mean, Thrasymachus? Am I not to give any of the answers you mention, not even, you strange man, if it happens to be one of those things, but am I to say something which is not the truth, or what do you mean?" What answer would you give him?

Well, he said, do you maintain that the two cases are alike?

They may well be, said I. Even if they are not, but the person you ask thinks they are, do you think him less likely to answer what he believes to be true, whether we forbid him or not?

And you will surely do the same, he said. Will you give one of the forbidden answers?

I shouldn't wonder, said I, if after investigation that was my opinion.

What, he said, if I show you a different answer about justice from all these and a better one? What penalty do you think you should pay then?

What else, said I, but what is proper for an ignorant man to pay? It is fitting for him to learn from one who knows. And that is what I believe I would deserve.

You amuse me, he said. You must not only learn but pay the fee.

Yes, when I have the money, I said.

We have the money, said Glaucon. If it is a matter of money, speak, Thrasymachus, for we shall all contribute for Socrates.

Quite so, said he, so that Socrates can carry on as usual: he gives no answer himself, and then, when someone else does give one, he takes up the argument and refutes it.

My dear man, I said, how could one answer, when in the first place he does not know and does not profess to know, and then, if he has an opinion, an eminent man forbids him to say what he believes? It is much more seemly for you to answer, since you say you know and have something to say. Please do so. Do me that favor, and do not begrudge your teaching to Glaucon and the others.

While I was saying this, Glaucon and the others begged him to speak. It was obvious that Thrasymachus was eager to do so and earn their admiration, and that he thought he had a beautiful answer, but he pretended that he wanted to win his point that I should be the one to answer. However, he agreed in the end, and then said: "There you have Socrates' wisdom; he himself is not willing to teach, but he goes around learning from others, and then he is not even grateful."

When you say that I learn from others you are right, Thrasymachus, said I, but when you say that I am not grateful, that is not true. I show what gratitude I can, but I can only give praise. I have no money, but how enthusiastically I praise when someone seems to me to speak well is something you will realize quite soon after you have given your answer, for I think you will speak well.

Listen then, said he. I say that the just is nothing else than the advantage of the stronger. Well, why don't you praise me? But you will not want to.

I must first understand your meaning, said I, for I do not know it yet. You say that the advantage of the stronger is just. What do you mean, Thrasymachus? Surely you do not mean such a thing as this: Poulydamas, the pancratist athlete, is stronger than we are; it is to his advantage to eat beef to build up his physical strength. Do you mean that this food is also advantageous and just for us who are weaker than he is?

You disgust me, Socrates, he said. Your trick is always to take up the argument at the point where you can damage it most.

Not at all, my dear sir, I said, but tell us more clearly what you mean.

Do you not know, he said, that some cities are ruled by a despot, others by the people, and others again by the aristocracy?—Of course.

And this element has the power and rules in every city?—Certainly.

Yes, and each government makes laws to its own advantage: democracy makes democratic laws, a despotism makes despotic laws, and so with the others, and when they have made these laws they declare this to be just for their subjects, that is, their own advantage, and they punish him who transgresses the laws as lawless and unjust. This then, my good man, is what I say justice is, the same in all cities, the advantage of the established government, and correct reasoning will conclude that the just is the same everywhere, the advantage of the stronger.

Now I see what you mean, I said. Whether it is true or not I will try to find out. But you too, Thrasymachus, have given as an answer that the just is the advantageous whereas you forbade that answer to me. True, you have added the words "of the stronger."

Perhaps, he said, you consider that an insignificant addition!

It is not clear yet whether or not it is significant. Obviously, we must investigate whether what you say is true. I agree that the just is some kind of advantage, but you add that it is the advantage of the stronger. I do not know. We must look into this.—Go on looking, he said.

We will do so, said I. Tell me, do you also say that obedience to the rulers is just?—I do.

And are the rulers in all cities infallible, or are they liable to error?—No doubt they are liable to error.

When they undertake to make laws, therefore, they make some correctly and make others incorrectly?—I think so.

"Correctly" means that they make laws to their own advantage, and "incorrectly" not to their own advantage. Or how would you put it?—As you do.

And whatever laws they make must be obeyed by their subjects, and this is just?—Of course.

Then, according to your argument, it is just to do not only what is to the advantage of the stronger, but also the opposite, what is not to their advantage.

What is that you are saying? he asked.

The same as you, I think, but let us examine it more fully. Have we not agreed that, in giving orders to their subjects, the rulers are sometimes in error as to what is best for themselves, yet it is just for their subjects to do whatever their rulers order. Is that much agreed?—I think so.

Think then also, said I, that you have agreed that it is just to do what is to the disadvantage of the rulers and the stronger whenever they unintentionally give orders which are bad for themselves, and you say it is just for the others to obey their given orders. Does it not of necessity follow, my wise Thrasymachus, that it is just to do the opposite of what you said? The weaker are then ordered to do what is to the disadvantage of the stronger.

Yes by Zeus, Socrates, said Polemarchus, that is quite clear.

Yes, if you bear witness for him, interrupted Cleitophon.

What need of a witness? said Polemarchus. Thrasymachus himself agrees that the rulers sometimes give orders that are bad for themselves, and that it is just to obey them.

Thrasymachus maintained that it is just to obey the orders of the rulers, Polemarchus.

He also said that the just was the advantage of the stronger, Cleitophon. Having established those two points, he went on to agree that the stronger sometimes ordered the weaker, their subjects, to do what was disadvantageous to themselves. From these agreed premises it follows that what is of advantage to the stronger is no more just than what is not.

But, Cleitophon replied, he said that the advantage of the stronger is what the stronger believes to be of advantage to him. This the weaker must do, and that is what he defined the just to be.

That is not how he stated it, said Polemarchus.

It makes no difference, Polemarchus, I said. If Thrasymachus now wants to put it that way, let us accept it. Tell me, Thrasymachus, was this what you intended to say justice is, namely, that which appears to the stronger to be to his advantage, whether it is so or not? Shall we say that this is what you mean?

Not in the least, said he. Do you think that I would call stronger a man who is in error at the time he errs?

I did think you meant that, said I, when you said that the rulers were not infallible but were liable to error.

You are being captious, Socrates, he said. Do you call a man a physician when he is in error in the treatment of patients, at the moment of, and in regard to this very error? Or would you call a man an accountant when he makes a miscalculation at the moment of, and with regard to this miscalculation? I think that we express ourselves in words which, taken literally, do say that the physician is in error, or the accountant, or the grammarian. But each of these, insofar as he is what we call him, never errs, so that, if you use language with precision—and you want to be precise—no practitioner of a craft ever errs. It is when the knowledge of his craft leaves him that he errs, and at that time he is not a practitioner of it. No craftsman, wise man, or ruler is in error at the time that he is a ruler in the precise sense. However, everyone will say that the physician or the ruler is in error. Take it then that this is now my answer to you. To speak with precision, the ruler, insofar as he is a ruler, unerringly decrees what is best for himself, and this the subject must do. The just then is, as I said from the first, to do what is advantageous to the stronger.

Very well, Thrasymachus, said I. You think I am captious?

You certainly are, he said.

And you think that it was deliberate trickery on my part to ask you the questions I did ask?

I know it very well, he said, but it will not do you any good, for I would be well aware of your trickery; nor would you have the ability to force my agreement in open debate.

I would not even try, my good sir, I said, but in order to avoid a repetition of this, do define clearly whether it is the ruler in the ordinary or the precise sense whose advantage is to be pursued as that of the stronger.

I mean, he said, the ruler in the most exact sense. Now practice your trickery and your captiousness on this if you can, for I will not let any statement of yours pass, and you certainly won't be able to.

Do you think, I said, that I am crazy enough to try to shave a lion or trick Thrasymachus?

You certainly tried just now, he said, though you are no good at it.

Enough of this sort of thing, I said. But tell me: is the physician in the strict sense, whom you mentioned just now, a moneymaker or one who treats the sick? Tell me about the real physician.—He is one who treats the sick, said he.

What about the ship's captain? Is he, to speak correctly, a ruler of sailors or a sailor?—A ruler of sailors.

We should not, I think, take into account the fact that he sails in a ship, and we should not call him a sailor, for it is not on account of his sailing that he is called a ship's captain, but because of his craft and his authority over sailors.—True.

And there is something which is advantageous to each of these, that is: patients and sailors?—Certainly.

And is not the purpose of a craft's existence to

seek and secure the advantageous in each case? —That's right.

Now is there any other advantage to each craft, except that it be as perfect as possible?—What is the meaning of that question?

It is this, said I. If you asked me whether our body is sufficient unto itself, or has a further need I should answer: "It certainly has needs, and for this purpose the craft of medicine exists and has now been discovered, because the body is defective, not self-sufficient. So to provide it with things advantageous to it the craft of medicine has been developed." Do you think I am correct in saying this or not?—Correct.

Well then, is the craft of medicine itself defective, or is there any other craft which needs some further excellence—as the eyes are in need of sight, the ears of hearing, and, because of this need, they require some other craft to investigate and provide for this?—is there in the craft itself some defect, so that each craft requires another craft which will investigate what is beneficial to it, and then the investigating craft needs another such still, and so ad infinitum? Or does a craft investigate what is beneficial to it, or does it need neither itself nor any other to investigate what is required because of imperfections? There is in fact no defect or error of any kind in any craft, nor is it proper to any craft to seek what is to the advantage of anything but the object of its concern; it is itself pure and without fault, being itself correct, as long as it is wholly itself in the precise sense. Consider this with that preciseness of language which you mentioned. Is it so or otherwise?—It appears to be so.

The craft of medicine, I said, does not seek its own advantage but that of the body.—Yes.

Nor does horse breeding seek its own advantage but that of horses. Nor does any other craft seek its own advantage—it has no further need— but that of its object.—That seems to be the case.

And surely, Thrasymachus, the crafts govern and have power over their object.

He agreed, but with great reluctance at this point.

No science of any kind seeks or orders its own advantage, but that of the weaker which is subject to it and governed by it.

He tried to fight this conclusion, but he agreed to this too in the end. And after he had, I said: Surely no physician either, insofar as he is a physician, seeks or orders what is advantageous to himself, but to his patient? For we agreed that the physician in the strict sense of the word is a ruler over bodies and not a moneymaker. Was this not agreed?

He said yes.

So the ship's captain in the strict sense is a ruler over sailors, and not a sailor?—That has been agreed.

Does it not follow that the ship's captain and ruler will not seek and order what is advantageous to himself, but to the sailor, his subject.

He agreed, but barely.

So then, Thrasymachus, I said, no other ruler in any kind of government, insofar as he is a ruler, seeks what is to his own advantage or orders it, but that which is to the advantage of his subject who is the concern of his craft; it is this he keeps in view; all his words and actions are directed to this end.

When we reached this point in our argument and it was clear to all that the definition of justice had turned into its opposite, Thrasymachus, instead of answering, said: Tell me, Socrates, do you have a nanny?

What's this? said I. Had you not better answer than ask such questions?

Because, he said, she is letting you go around with a snotty nose and does not wipe it when she needs to, if she leaves you without any knowledge of sheep or shepherds.

What is the particular point of that remark? I asked.

You think, he said, that shepherds and cowherds seek the good of their sheep or cattle, whereas their sole purpose in fattening them and looking after them is their own good and that of their master. Moreover, you believe that rulers in the cities, true rulers that is, have a different attitude towards their subjects than one has towards sheep, and that they think of anything else, night and day, than their own advantage. You are so far from understanding the nature of justice and the just, of injustice and the unjust, that you do not realize that the just is really another's good, the advantage of the stronger and the ruler, but for the inferior who obeys it is a personal injury. Injustice on the other hand exercises its power over those who are truly naive and just, and those over whom it rules do what is of advantage to the other, the stronger, and, by obeying him, they make him happy, but themselves not in the least.

You must look at it in this way, my naive Socrates: the just is everywhere at a disadvantage compared with the unjust. First, in their contracts with one another: wherever two such men are associated you will never find, when the partnership ends, the just man to have more than the unjust, but less. Then, in their relation to the city: when taxes are to be paid, from the same income the just man pays more, the other less; but, when benefits are to be received, the one gets nothing while the other profits much; whenever each of them holds a public office, the just man, even if he is not penalized in other ways, finds that his private affairs deteriorate through neglect while he gets nothing from the public purse because he is just; moreover, he is disliked by his household and his acquaintances whenever he refuses them an unjust favor. The opposite is true of the unjust man in every respect. I repeat what I said before: the man of great power gets the better deal. Consider him if you want to decide how much more it benefits him privately to be unjust rather than just. You will see this most easily if you turn your thoughts to the most complete form of injustice which brings the greatest happiness to the wrongdoer, while it makes those whom he wronged, and who are not willing to do wrong, most wretched. This most complete form is depotism; it does not appropriate other people's property little by little, whether secretly or by force, whether public or private, whether sacred objects or temple property, but appropriates it all at once.

When a wrongdoer is discovered in petty cases, he is punished and faces great opprobrium, for the perpetrators of these petty crimes are called temple robbers, kidnappers, housebreakers, robbers, and thieves, but when a man, besides appropriating the possessions of the citizens, manages to enslave the owners as well, then, instead of those ugly names he is called happy and blessed, not only by his fellow-citizens but by all others who learn that he has run through the whole gamut of injustice. Those who give injustice a bad name do so because they are afraid, not of practicing but of suffering injustice.

And so, Socrates, injustice, if it is on a large enough scale, is a stronger, freer, and more powerful thing than justice and, as I said from the first, the just is what is advantageous to the stronger, while the unjust is to one's own advantage and benefit.

Having said this and poured this mass of close-packed words into our ears as a bathman might a flood of water, Thrasymachus intended to leave, but those present did not let him, and made him stay for a discussion of his views. I too begged him to stay and I said: My dear Thrasymachus, after throwing such a speech at us, you want to leave before adequately instructing us or finding out whether you are right or not? Or do you think it a small thing to decide on a whole way of living, which, if each of us adopted it, would make him live the most profitable life?

Do I think differently? said Thrasymachus.

You seem to, said I, or else you care nothing for us nor worry whether we'll live better or worse, in ignorance of what you say you know. Do, my good sir, show some keenness to teach us. It will not be without value to you to be the benefactor of so many of us. For my own part, I tell you that I do not believe that injustice is more profitable than justice, not even if one gives it full scope and does not put obstacles in its way. No, my friend. Let us assume the existence of an unjust man with every opportunity to do wrong, either because his misdeeds remain secret or because he has the power to battle things through; nevertheless, he does not persuade me that injustice is more profitable than justice. Perhaps some other of us feels the same, and not only I. Come now, my good sir, really persuade us that we are wrong to esteem justice more highly than injustice in planning our life.

And how, said he, shall I persuade you, if you are not convinced by what I said just now? What more can I do? Am I to take my argument and pour it into your mind?

Zeus forbid! Don't you do that, but first stick to what you have said and, if you change your position, do so openly and do not deceive us. You see now, Thrasymachus—let us examine again what went before—that, while you first defined the true physician, you did not think it necessary later to observe the precise definition of the true shepherd, but you think that he fattens sheep, in so far as he is a shepherd, not with what is best for the sheep in mind, but like a guest about to be entertained at a feast, with a banquet in view, or again a sale, like a moneymaker, not a shepherd. The shepherd's craft is concerned only to provide what is best for the object of its care; as for the craft itself, it is sufficiently provided with all it needs to be at its best, as long as it does not fall short of being the craft of the shepherd. That is why I thought it necessary for us to agree just now that every kind of rule, as far as it truly rules, does not seek what is best for anything else than the subject of its rule and care, and this is true both of public and private kinds of rule. Do you think that those who rule over cities, the true rulers, rule willingly?—I don't think it, by Zeus, I know it, he said.

Well, but Thrasymachus, said I, do you not realize that in other kinds of rule no one is willing to rule, but they ask for pay, thinking that their rule will benefit not themselves but their subjects. Tell me, does not every craft differ from every other in that it has a different function? Please do not give an answer contrary to what you believe, so that we can come to some conclusion.

Yes, that is what makes it different, he said.

And each craft benefits us in its own particular way, different from the others. For example, medicine gives us health, navigation safety while sailing, and so with the others.—Quite so.

And the craft of earning pay gives us wages, for that is its function. Or would you call medicine the same craft as navigation? Or, if you wish to define with precision as you proposed, if the ship's captain becomes healthy because sailing benefits his health, would you for that reason call his craft medicine?—Not at all, he said.

Nor would you call wage-earning medicine if someone is healthy while earning wages?—Certainly not.

Nor would you call medicine wage-earning if someone earns pay while healing?—No.

So we agree that each craft brings its own benefit?—Be it so.

Whatever benefit all craftsmen receive in common must then result clearly from some craft which they pursue in common, and so are benefited by it.—It seems so.

We say then that if the practitioners of these crafts are benefited by earning a wage, this results from their practicing the wage-earning craft.

He reluctantly agreed.

So this benefit to each, the receiving pay, does not result from the practice of their own craft, but if we are to examine this precisely, medicine provides health while the craft of earning provides pay; house building provides a house, and the craft of earning which accompanies it provides a wage, and so with the other crafts; each fulfills its own function and benefits that with which it is concerned. If pay is not added, is there any benefit which the practitioner gets from his craft?—Apparently not.

Does he even provide a benefit when he works for nothing?—Yes, I think he does.

Is this not clear now, Thrasymachus, that no craft or rule provides its own advantage, but, as we have been saying for some time, it procures and orders what is of advantage to its subject; it aims at his advantage, that of the weaker, not of the stronger. That is why, my dear Thrasymachus, I said just now that no one willingly wants to rule, to handle and straighten out the affairs of others. They ask for pay because the man who intends to practice his craft well never does what is best for himself, nor, when he gives such orders, does he give them in accordance with his craft, but he pursues the advantage of his subject. For that reason, then, it seems one must provide remuneration if they are to be willing to rule, whether money or honor, or a penalty if he does not rule.

What do you mean, Socrates? said Glaucon. I understand the two kinds of remuneration, but I do not understand what kind of penalty you mean, which you mention under the heading of remuneration.

Then you do not understand the remuneration of the best men, I said, which makes them willing to rule. Do you not know that the love of honor and money are made a reproach, and rightly so? —I know that.

Therefore good men will not be willing to rule for the sake of either money or honor. They do not want to be called hirelings if they openly receive payment for ruling, nor, if they provide themselves with it secretly, to be called thieves. Nor will they do it for honor's sake, for they have no love for it. So, if they are to be willing to rule, some compulsion or punishment must be brought to bear on them. That is perhaps why to seek office willingly, before one must, is thought shameful. Now the greatest punishment is to be ruled by a worse man than oneself if one is not willing to rule. I think it is the fear of this which makes men of good character rule whenever they do. They approach office not as something good or something to be enjoyed, but as something necessary because they cannot entrust it to men better than, or even equal to, themselves. In a city of good men, if there were such, they would probably vie with each other in order not to rule, not, as now, in order to be rulers. There it would be quite clear that the nature of the true ruler is not to seek his own advantage but that of his subjects, and everyone, knowing this, would prefer to receive benefits rather than take the trouble to benefit others. In this matter I do not at all

agree with Thrasymachus that the just is the advantage of the stronger, but we will look into this matter another time. What seems to me of greater importance is what Thrasymachus is saying now, namely, that the life of the unjust man is to be preferred to that of the just. Which will you choose, Glaucon, and which of our views do you consider the more truly spoken?

I certainly think that the life of the just is more profitable.

You have heard, said I, all the blessings of the unjust life which Thrasymachus enumerated just now?

I heard, said he, but I am not convinced.

Do you want us to persuade him, if we could find the means to do so, that what he says is not true?

Of course I want it, he said.

If we were to oppose him, I said, with a parallel set speech on the blessings of the just life, then another speech from him in turn, then another from us, we should have to count and measure the blessings mentioned on each side, and we should need some judges to decide the case. If, on the other hand, we investigate the question, as we were doing, by seeking agreement with each other, then we can ourselves be both the judges and the advocates.—Quite so.

Which method do you prefer? I asked.—The second.

Come then, Thrasymachus, I said, answer us from the beginning. You say that complete injustice is more profitable than complete justice?

I certainly do say that, he said, and I have told you why.

Well then, what about this: you call one of the two a virtue and the other a vice?—Of course.

That is, you call justice a virtue, and injustice a vice?

Is that likely, my good man, said he, since I say that injustice is profitable, and justice is not?

What then?—The opposite.

Do you call being just a vice?—No, but certainly high-minded foolishness.

And you call being unjust low-minded?—No, I call it good judgment.

You consider the unjust then, Thrasymachus, to be good and knowledgeable?

Yes, he said, those who are able to carry injustice through to the end, who can bring cities and communities of men under their power. Perhaps you think I mean purse-snatchers? Not that those actions too are not profitable, if they are not found out, but they are not worth mentioning in comparison with what I am talking about.

I am not unaware of what you mean, I said, but this point astonishes me: do you include injustice under virtue and wisdom, and justice among their opposites?—I certainly do.

That makes it harder, my friend, and it is not easy now to know what to say. If you had declared that injustice was more profitable, but agreed that it was a vice or shameful as some others do, we could have discussed it along the lines of general opinion. Now, obviously, you will say that it is fine and strong, and apply to it all the attributes which we used to apply to justice, since you have been so bold as to include it under virtue and wisdom. —Your guess, he said, is quite right.

We must not, however, shrink from pursuing our argument and looking into this, so long as I am sure that you mean what you say. For I do not think you are joking now, Thrasymachus, but are saying what you believe to be true.

What difference, said he, does it make to you whether I believe it or not? Is it not my argument you are refuting?

No difference, said I, but try to answer this further question: do you think that the just man wants to get the better of the just?

Never, said he, for he would not then be well mannered and simple, as he is now.

Does he want to overreach a just action?[6]

Not a just action either, he said.

Would he want to get the better of an unjust man, and would he deem that just or not?

He would want to, he said, and he would deem it right, but he would not be able to.

That was not my question, said I, but whether the just man wants and deems it right to outdo not a just man, but an unjust one?—That is so.

What about the unjust man? Would he deem it right to outdo the just man and the just action?

Of course he does, he said, since he deems it right to get the better of everybody.

So the unjust man will get the better of another unjust man or an unjust action and he will strive to get all he can from everyone?—That is so.

Let us put it this way, I said. The just man does not try to get the better of one like him but of one unlike him, whereas the unjust man overreaches the like and the unlike?—Very well put.

The unjust man, I said, is knowledgeable and good, and the just man is neither?—That is well said too.

It follows, I said, that the unjust man is like the knowledgeable and the good, while the just man is unlike them?

Of course that will be so, he said, being such a man he will be like such men, while the other is not like them.

Good. Each of them has the qualities of those he is like?—Why not?

Very well, Thrasymachus. Now you speak of one man as musical, of another as unmusical?—I do indeed.

Which is knowledgeable and which is not?

Of course the musical man is knowledgeable, the unmusical is not.

What he has knowledge of he is good at,[7] and he who has no knowledge is bad?—Yes.

Is not the same true of the physician?—The same.

Do you think, my dear sir, that any musician, when tuning his lyre, desires, in the tightening and relaxing of the strings, to do better than another musician or deems it right to get the better of him?—I don't think so.

But he wants to do better than a nonmusician?—Necessarily.

What of a physician? When prescribing food or drink, does he want to do better than another medical man or action?—Certainly not.

But better than the nonmedical?—Yes.

In matters involving any kind of knowledge or

ignorance, do you think that any expert would wish to achieve more than any other expert would do or say, rather than, in respect to the same action, achieve the same as anyone like himself?—Well, perhaps it must be as you say.

What about the nonexpert? Does he not want to outdo the expert and the nonexpert equally? —Perhaps.

The man with knowledge is wise?—I agree.

And the wise is good?—I agree.

So the good and wise does not wish to get the better of one like himself, but of the unlike and opposite?—Apparently.

But the bad and ignorant would want to get the better of his like and his opposite?—So it appears.

Now Thrasymachus, I said, we found that the unjust man tries to get the better of both those like and those unlike him. Did you not say so?—I did.

Yes, and the just man will not get the better of his like, but of one unlike him?—Yes.

The just man then, I said, resembles the wise and good, while the unjust resembles the bad and ignorant?—It may be so.

Further, we agreed that each will be such as the man he resembles?—We did so agree.

So we find that the just man has turned out to be good and wise, and the unjust man ignorant and bad.

Thrasymachus agreed to all this, not easily as I am telling it, but reluctantly and after being pushed. It was summer and he was perspiring profusely. And then I saw something I had never seen before: Thrasymachus blushing. After we had agreed that justice was virtue and wisdom, and injustice vice and ignorance, I said: Very well, let us consider this as established, but we also said that injustice was powerful, or don't you remember, Thrasymachus?

I remember, he said, but then I am not satisfied with what you are now saying. I could make a speech about it, but if I should speak I know that you would say I am delivering a public oration. So either allow me to speak or, if you want to ask

questions, ask them, and I will say "very well," and nod yes and no, as one does to old wives' tales.

Don't ever do that, I said, against your own opinion.

Just to please you, he said, since you won't let me speak. What else do you want?

Nothing at all, said I. If you will do this, do it. I will ask my questions.—Ask them then.

I am asking what I asked before, so that we may proceed with our argument about the relation of justice and injustice in an orderly way. It was said that injustice is more powerful and stronger than justice. But now, I said, since justice is wisdom and virtue, it will easily be shown to be also stronger than injustice which is ignorance; nobody could still not know that. However, I do not want to state this thus simply, Thrasymachus, but to look into it in some such way as this: would you say that it is unjust for a city to undertake to enslave other cities unjustly and hold them in subjection, having enslaved many cities to its power?

Of course, he said, this is what the best city will do, the most completely unjust.

I understand that this was your argument, I said, but let me examine this point: will the city which has become stronger than another achieve this power without justice, or must it do so with the help of justice?

If what you said just now stands—that justice is wisdom—with the help of justice, but if things are as I stated them, with injustice.

I am delighted, Thrasymachus, that you do not merely nod yes or no, but that you answer in a very fine manner.

I am doing it to please you, he said.

You are doing well. Now please me also by answering this question: do you think that a city, an army, a band of robbers or thieves, or any other body of men which engages unjustly upon a common course, could achieve anything if they wrong one another?—No indeed.

What if they do not wrong one another? Would they not achieve more?—Certainly.

Yes, for injustice, Thrasymachus, causes factions and hatreds and fights with one another, while justice brings a sense of common purpose and friendship. Is that not so?—Be it so, to agree with you.

You are doing well my good friend. Tell me this: if it is the result of injustice to bring hatred wherever it occurs, then its presence, whether among free men or slaves, will make them hate each other and quarrel, and be unable to achieve any common purpose?—Quite so.

What if it occurs between two men? Will they not be at odds, hate each other, and be hostile to each other as well as to the just?—They will be.

Does injustice, my good sir, lose this capacity for dissension when it occurs within one individual, or will it preserve it intact?

Let it be preserved intact, he said.

It seems to follow that injustice, wherever it occurs, be it in a city, a family, an army, or anything else results in making it incapable of achieving anything as a unit because of the dissensions and differences it creates, and, further, it makes that unit hostile to itself, to its every enemy, and to the just. Is that not so?—Quite.

Even in one individual it has the same effect, which follows from its nature. First, it makes that individual incapable of achievement because he is at odds with himself and not of one mind. It makes him his own enemy, as well as the enemy of the just, does it not?—It does.

The gods too, my friend, are just.—Be it so.

So the unjust man is also an enemy of the gods, while the just man is their friend.

Bravely enjoy your feast of words, he said. I will not oppose you, to avoid unpopularity in this company.

Come then, said I, complete the feast for me by answering as you are now doing. The just are shown to be wiser and more able in action, while the unjust are not even able to act together, for surely, when we speak of a powerful achievement by unjust men acting in common, we are altogether far from the truth. They could not have kept their hands off each other if they had been completely bad, but clearly they had some justice which forbade them to wrong each other and their enemies at the same time. It was this which enabled them to do what they did. They started on their unjust course being half evil with injustice, for those who are completely evil and completely unjust are also completely incapable of achievement. I can see that this is so, and not as you at first assumed.

We must now examine whether the just also live a better life than the unjust and are happier, a point which we deferred for later investigation. I think it is clear even now that they are, yet we must look into this further, for the argument concerns no casual topic, but one's whole manner of living.—Look into it, then.

I am looking, said I. Do you think there is such a thing as the function of a horse?—I do.

And would you define the function of a horse, or of anything else, as to do that which can be done only, or be done best, by means of it?

I do not understand your question, he said.

Put it like this: is it possible to see by any other means than the eyes?—Certainly not.

Further, could you hear by any other means than the ears?—Not possibly.

Then we are right to say that these are the functions of eyes and ears?—Quite so.

Further, would you use a dagger or a carving knife to trim the branches of a vine, or many other instruments?—Of course.

But you would not do it as well with any other instrument as with a pruning knife which was made for the purpose?—That is true.

Then shall we put it that this is the function of a pruning knife?—We shall.

Now I think you will understand my recent question better, when I inquired whether the function of each thing is to do that which it alone can perform, or perform better than anything else could.—I understand, he said, and I think that is the function of each.

Very well, said I. Does each thing to which a

particular task is assigned also have its excellence? Let us go over the same ground again. We say that the eyes have a particular task?—Yes.

They also have their own excellence?—They have.

The ears, too, have a function?—Yes.

So they have their excellence?—That too.

Is that not the case with all other things?—It is.

Moreover, could the eyes perform their function well if they did not possess their own excellence or virtue, but their own vice instead?

How could they? he said. You mean blindness instead of sight?

Whatever their virtue is, for I am not now asking that, but whether any agent performs its function well by means of its own excellence or virtue, or badly through its own badness or vice. —What you say is true.

So the ears, too, deprived of their own virtue, would perform their function badly.—Quite so.

And we could say the same about all other things?—I think so.

Come now, consider this point next: There is a function of the soul which you could not fulfill by means of any other thing, as for example: to take care of things, to rule, to deliberate, and other things of the kind; could we entrust these things to any other agent than the soul and say that they belong to it?—To no other.

What of living? Is that not a function of the soul?—It most certainly is.

So there is also an excellence of the soul?—We say so.

And, Thrasymachus, will the soul ever fulfill its function well if it is deprived of its own particular excellence, or is this impossible?—Impossible.

It is therefore inevitable that the bad soul rules and looks after things badly and that the good soul does all these things well.—Inevitable.

Now we have agreed that justice is excellence of the soul, and that injustice is vice of soul?—We have so agreed.

The just soul and the just man, then, will live well, and the unjust man will live badly.—So it seems, according to your argument.

Surely the one who lives well is blessed and happy, and the one who does not is the opposite.—Of course.

So the just man is happy, and the unjust one is wretched.—So be it.

It profits no one to be wretched, but to be happy.—Of course.

And so, my good Thrasymachus, injustice is never more profitable than justice.

Let that be your banquet of words, he said, at the feast of Bendis, Socrates.

Given by you, Thrasymachus, I said, after you became gentle and ceased to be angry with me. Yet I have not had a good banquet, but that was my fault, not yours. I seem to have behaved as gluttons do, snatching at every dish that passes them and tasting it before they have reasonably enjoyed the one before. So I, before finding the answer to our first enquiry into the nature of justice, let that go and turned to investigate whether it was vice and ignorance or wisdom and virtue. Another argument came up after, that injustice was more profitable than justice, and I could not refrain from following this up and abandoning the previous one so that the result of our discussion for me is that I know nothing; for, when I do not know what justice is, I shall hardly know whether it is a kind of virtue or not, or whether the just man is unhappy or happy.

Notes

1. The phrase occurs several times in Homer (e.g., *Iliad* 22, 60). It refers to old age as the threshold on leaving life.

2. The old saying that like consorts with like.

3. Seriphus was a small island of little importance.

4. It should be kept in mind throughout the *Republic* that the Greek word *dikaios* and the noun *dikaiosyne* are often used, as here, in a much wider sense than our word "just" and "justice" by which we must usually translate them. They then mean "right" or "right-

eous," i.e., good conduct in relation to others, and the opposite, *adikia*, then has the general sense of wrong-doing.

5. By *technê*, here translated "craft," Socrates refers to any art or craft which requires special knowledge. The word "art" has been avoided in the translation because it implies for us other factors than knowledge, and it is knowledge alone which Socrates has in mind. He then proceeds to equate "justice" with such a *technê*, as implying the knowledge of how to behave, on the well-known Socratic belief that virtue is knowledge.

6. *pleon echein* or *pleonexia*, literally "to have more," comes to mean "to outdo, to overreach, to do better than." Now there is one right note to strike in music and the musician has the necessary knowledge to do so. He will want to do this, but he will not want to do better than another musician with the same knowledge, which would be absurd. So the just man, if justice is a *technê*, a matter of knowledge, will have the knowledge to do the right thing, and cannot want to do better than that, so he will not desire to outdo another just man with the same knowledge.

7. As before, the craftsman with sufficient knowledge is good at his craft, and his virtue or excellence as a craftsman depends on, in a sense is, that knowledge. Socrates assumes throughout that *dikaiosyne* or "justice" in the sense it is here used is also a matter of knowledge, a *technê*. So the notion of "being good at one's craft" being a matter of knowledge is broadened to "being good is a matter of knowledge," i.e., the famous Socratic paradox that "virtue" (*aretê*) is knowledge.

PART II

Moral Relativism vs. Moral Objectivism
Introduction

Is morality completely relative solely to individual choice or cultural approval, or are there universally valid moral principles?

Ethical relativism maintains that all moral principles are valid relative to cultural or individual choice. It denies that there are any independently justified moral principles. It is to be distinguished from *moral skepticism*, the view that there are no valid moral principles at all (or at least none that we can be confident about). There are two forms of ethical relativism: (1) *subjectivism*, which views morality as a personal decision ("Morality is in the eyes of the beholder") and (2) *conventionalism*, which views moral validity in terms of social acceptance. Opposed to ethical relativism are various theories of *ethical objectivism*. All forms of objectivism affirm the universal validity of some moral principles. The strongest form, *moral absolutism*, holds that there is exactly one right answer to every question. "What should I do in situation *x*?" whatever that situation be, and that a moral principle can never be overridden—even by another moral principle.

A weaker form of objectivism sees moral principles as universally valid but not always applicable. That is, moral principle A could be overridden by moral principle B in a given situation, and in other situations there might be no right answer. We turn to our readings. First we have the Greek historian Herodotus' classic description of cultural variation. After that we turn to St. Thomas Aquinas's classic defense of Natural Law, a universal law that is based on universal human nature to promote the common good. This law is eternal, ultimately based on the divine law, and is discoverable by reason. In turn, it constitutes the basis for civil law. Next we turn to Ruth Benedict's defense of moral relativism in which she argues that morality depends on the particular cultures and contexts in which people find themselves. Fourth, Louis Pojman argues against moral relativism and in favor of moral objectivism. Finally, Gilbert Harman argues for a form of moral relativism according to which our moral obligations are relative to the agreements we make and our reasons for entering into those agreements.

2

Custom Is King

HERODOTUS

Herodotus (485–430 B.C.*), a Greek, the first Western historian, in this brief passage from his* Histories *illustrates cultural relativism and may suggest
that ethical relativism is the correct view ("culture is
king").*

Thus it appears certain to me, by a great variety of proofs, that Cambyses was raving mad; he
would not else have set himself to make a mock of
holy rites and long-established usages. For if one
were to offer men to choose out of all the customs in the world such as seemed to them the
best, they would examine the whole number, and
end by preferring their own; so convinced are
they that their own usages far surpass those of all
others. Unless, therefore, a man was mad, it is
not likely that he would make sport of such matters. That people have this feeling about their
laws may be seen by very many proofs: among
others, by the following. Darius, after he had got
the kingdom, called into his presence certain
Greeks who were at hand, and asked—"What he
should pay them to eat the bodies of their fathers
when they died?" To which they answered, that
there was no sum that would tempt them to do
such a thing. He then sent for certain Indians, of
the race called Callatians, men who eat their fathers, and asked them, while the Greeks stood by,
and knew by the help of an interpreter all that
was said—"What he should give them to burn
the bodies of their fathers at their decease?" The
Indians exclaimed aloud, and bade him forbear
such language. Such is men's wont herein; and
Pindar was right, in my judgment, when he said,
"Custom is the king o'er all."

Herodotus, *The Histories of Herodotus,* trans. George
Rawlinson (New York: Appleton, 1859).

3

Natural Law

THOMAS AQUINAS

The Roman Catholic Dominican monk Thomas Aquinas (1225–1274) is considered by many to be one of the three or four greatest philosophers and the greatest philosopher of religion in Western thought. He was born near the Italian town of Aquino, the son of the Count Aquino. While at the University of Naples, much to the horror of his aristocratic parents, he decided to join the Dominicans, a mendicant (begging) order of monks, considered by many to be a hotbed of religious fanatics. Because he was stubborn, deliberate, methodical, slow and portly, his fellow students thought him stupid and unkindly gave him the nickname "The Dumb Ox." His teacher at the University of Cologne, Albertus Magnus, however, saw great promise in the youth and declared, "You call him a Dumb Ox; I tell you the Dumb Ox will bellow so loud his bellowing will fill the world." Among his great works are Summa Contra Gentiles *(On the Truth of the Catholic Faith against the Gentiles) and* Summa Theologica *(Summation of Theology) from which the present selection is taken.*

In this selection Aquinas argues that there is a universal natural law, morally binding on all human beings, because it is based on reason, which in turn participates in eternal law. It is unchangeable, possessed by all human beings, and the sole basis of all valid positive law, i.e., what legislatures enact. The purpose of this natural or moral law is to promote the common good. The first principle of natural law is that "good should be done and promoted, and evil is to be avoided." All other principles are based on this basic principle. Unjust positive "laws," being immoral, are not true laws. So civil disobedience can be warranted.

Reprinted from A. Pegis, ed., *Basic Writings of Saint Thomas Aquinas* (New York: Random House, 1948), by permission.

The highly formal structure of the Summa Theologica *consists of a number of Questions, each divided into a number of Articles. An Article proceeds by (1) asking a question, (2) raising objections to the thesis Aquinas will argue for, (3) offering a general statement of Aquinas's position (beginning with the phrase "On the contrary" and "I answer," and finally (4) replying to the objections raised. When Aquinas refers to "the Philosopher," he means Aristotle; to "the Apostle," St. Paul.*

Question 90
On the Essence of Law

We have now to consider the extrinsic principle of acts. Now the extrinsic principles inclining to evil is the devil, of whose temptation we have spoken. But the extrinsic principle moving to good is God, Who both instructs us by means of His law, and assists us by His grace. Therefore, in the first place, we must speak of law; in the second place, of grace. Concerning law, we must consider (1) law itself in general; (2) its parts. Concerning law in general, three points offer themselves for our consideration: (1) its essence; (2) the different kinds of law; (3) the effects of law. Under the first head there are four points of inquiry: (1) Whether law is something pertaining to reason; (2) concerning the end of law; (3) its cause; (4) the promulgation of law.

First Article
Whether Law Is Something
Pertaining to Reason?

We proceed thus to the First Article:
Objection 2. In the reason there is nothing else but power, habit, and act. But law is not the power

itself of reason. In like manner, neither is it a habit of reason, because the habits of reason are the intellectual virtues, of which we have spoken above. Nor again is it an act of reason, because then law would cease when the act of reason ceases; for instance, while we are asleep. Therefore law is nothing pertaining to reason.

Obj. 3. Further, the law moves those who are subject to it to act rightly. But it belongs properly to the will to move to act, as is evident from what has been said above. Therefore law pertains not to the reason but to the will, according to the words of the Jurist: *Whatsoever pleases the sovereign has the force of law.*

On the contrary, It belongs to the law to command and to forbid. But it belongs to reason to command, as was stated above. Therefore it is something pertaining to reason.

I answer that, Law is a rule and measure of acts whereby man is induced to act or is restrained from acting; for *lex* [law] is derived from *ligare* [to bind], because it binds one to act. Now the rule and measure of human acts is the reason, which is the first principle of human acts, as is evident from what has been stated above. For it belongs to the reason to direct to the end, which is the first principle of all matters of action, according to the Philosopher [Aristotle]. Now that which is the principle in any genus of numbers is the rule and measure of that genus: for instance, unity in the genus of numbers, and the first movement in the genus of movements. Consequently, it follows that law is something pertaining to reason.

Reply to Obj. 2. Just as, in external acts, we may consider the work and the work done—for instance, the work of building and the house built—so in the acts of reason we may consider the act itself of reason, i.e., to understand and to reason, and something produced by this act. With regard to the speculative reason, this is first of all the definitions; secondly, the proposition; thirdly, the syllogism or argument. And since the practical reason also makes use of the syllogism in operable matters, as we have stated above and as the philosopher teaches, hence we find in the . . . prac-

tical reason something that holds the same position in regard to operations, as, in the speculative reason, the proposition holds in regard to conclusions. Such universal propositions of the practical reason that are directed to operations have the nature of law. And these propositions sometimes are under our actual consideration, while sometimes they are retained in the reason by means of a habit.

Reply to Obj. 3. Reason has its power of moving from the will, as was stated above; for it is due to the fact that one wills the end, that the reason issues its commands as regards things ordained to the end. But in order that the volition of what is commanded may have the nature of law, it needs to be in accord with some rule of reason. It is in this sense that we should understand the saying that the will of the sovereign has the force of law; otherwise the sovereign's will would savor of lawlessness rather than of law.

Second Article
Whether Law Is Always Directed
to the Common Good?

Objection 1. It would seem that law is not always directed to the common good as to its end. For it belongs to law to command and to forbid. But commands are directed to certain individual goods. Therefore the end of law is not always the common good.

Obj. 2. Further, law directs man in his actions. But human actions are concerned with particular matters. Therefore law is directed to some particular good.

Obj. 3. Further Isidore[1] says: *If law is based on reason, whatever is based on reason will be a law.* But reason is the foundation not only of what is ordained to the common good, but also of that which is directed to private good. Therefore law is not directed only to the good of all, but also to the private good of an individual.

On the contrary, Isidore says that *laws are enacted for no private profit, but for the common benefit of the citizens.*

I answer that, As we have stated above, law belongs to that which is a principle of human acts, because it is their rule and measure. Now as reason is a principle of human acts, so in reason itself there is something which is the principle of human acts, so in reason itself there is something which is the principle in respect of all the rest. Hence to this principle chiefly and mainly law must needs be referred. Now the first principle in practical matters, which are the object of the practical reason, is the last end: and the last end of human life is happiness or beatitude. Consequently, law must needs concern itself mainly with the order that is in beatitude. Moreover, since every part is ordained to the whole as the imperfect to the perfect, and since one man is a part of the perfect community, law must needs concern itself properly with the order directed to universal happiness. Therefore the Philosopher, in the above definition of legal matters, mentions both happiness and the body politic, since he says that we call those legal matters just *which are adapted to produce and preserve happiness and its parts for the body politic* [*Ethics* V.1]. For the state is a perfect community, as he says in the *Politics* I.

Now, in every genus, that which belongs to it chiefly is the principle of the others, and the others belong to that genus according to some order toward that thing. Thus fire, which is chief among hot things, is the cause of heat in mixed bodies, and these are said to be hot in so far as they have a share of fire. Consequently, since law is chiefly ordained to the common good, any other precept in regard to some individual work must needs be devoid of the nature of a law, save in so far as it regards the common good. Therefore every law is ordained to the common good.

Reply Obj. 1. A command denotes the application of a law to matters regulated by law. Now the order to the common good, at which law aims, is applicable to particular ends. And in this way commands are given even concerning particular matters.

Reply Obj. 2. Actions are indeed concerned with particular matters, but those particular matters are referable to the common good, not as to a common genus or species, but as to a common final cause, according as the common good is said to be the common end.

Reply Obj. 3. Just as nothing stands firm with regard to the speculative reason except that which is traced back to the first indemonstrable principles, so nothing stands firm with regard to the practical reason, unless it be directed to the law end which is the common good. Now whatever stands to reason in this sense has the nature of law.

Third Article
Whether the Reason of Any
Man Is Competent to Make Laws?

Obj. 1. It would seem that the reason of any man is competent to make laws. For the Apostle [Paul] says (Rom. 2:14) that *when the Gentiles, who have not the law, do by nature those things that are of the law, . . . they are a law to themselves.* Now he says this of all in general. Therefore anyone can make a law for himself.

Obj 2. Further, as the Philosopher says, *the intention of the lawgiver is to lead men to virtue.* But every man can lead another to virtue. Therefore the reason of any man is competent to make laws.

On the contrary, Isidore says, *A law is an ordinance of the people, whereby something is sanctioned by the Elders together with the Commonality.* Therefore not everyone can make laws.

I answer that, A law, properly speaking, regards first and foremost the order to the common good. Now to order anything to the common good belongs either to the whole people, or to someone who is the representative of the whole people. Hence the making of a law belongs either to the whole people or to a public person who has care of the whole people; for in all other matters the directing of anything to the end concerns him to whom the end belongs.

Reply Obj. 1. A law is in a person not only as in one who rules, but also, by participation, as in one that is ruled. In the latter way, each one is a law to himself, in so far as he shares the direction that he receives from one who rules him. Hence the same biblical text goes on: *Who show the work of the law written in their hearts (Rom. 2:15).*

Reply Obj. 2. A private person cannot lead another to virtue efficaciously, for he can only advise; and if his advice be not taken, it has no coercive power, such as the law should have in order to prove an efficacious inducement to virtue, as the philosopher says. But this coercive power is vested in the whole people or in some public person to whom it belongs to inflict penalties. Therefore the framing of laws belongs to him alone.

Question 91
On The Various Kinds of Law

First Article
Whether There Is an Eternal Law?

Objection 1. It would seem that there is no eternal law. For every law is imposed on someone. But there was not someone from eternity on whom a law could be imposed, since God alone was from eternity. Therefore no law is eternal.

Obj. 2. Further, promulgation is essential to law. But promulgation could not be from eternity. Therefore no law can be eternal.

On the contrary, Augustine[2] says, *that Law which is the Supreme Reason cannot be understood to be otherwise than unchangeable and eternal.*

I answer that, Law is nothing else but a dictate of practical reason emanating from the ruler who governs a perfect community. Now it is evident, granted that the world is ruled by divine providence, that the whole community of the universe is governed by the divine reason. Therefore the very notion of the government of things in God, the ruler of the universe, has the nature of a law. And since the divine reason's conception of things is not subject to time, but is eternal, according to Prov. 8:23, therefore it is that this kind of law must be called eternal.

Reply Obj. 1. Those things that do not exist in themselves exist in God, inasmuch as they are known and preordained by Him, according to Rom. 4:17: *Who calls those things that are not, as those that are.* Accordingly, the eternal concept of the divine law bears the character of an eternal law in so far as it is ordained by God to the government of things foreknown by Him.

Reply Obj 2. Promulgation is made by word of mouth or in writing, and in both ways the eternal law is promulgated, because both the divine Word and the writing of the Book of Life are eternal. But the promulgation cannot be from eternity on the part of the creature that hears or reads.

Second Article
Whether There Is in Us a Natural Law?

Objection 1. It would seem that there is no natural law in us. For man is governed sufficiently by the eternal law, since Augustine says that *the eternal law is that by which it is right that all things should be most orderly.* But nature does not abound in superfluities, as neither does she fail in necessaries. Therefore man has no natural law.

Obj. 2. Further, by the law man is directed, in his acts, to the end, as was stated above. But the directing of human acts to their end is not a function of nature, as is the case in irrational creatures, which act for an end solely by their natural appetite; whereas man acts for an end by his reason and will. Therefore man has no natural law.

On the contrary, the gloss on Rom. 2:14 *(When the Gentiles, who have not the law, do by nature those things that are of the law)* comments as follows: *Although they have no written law, yet they have the natural law, whereby each one knows, and is conscious of, what is good and what is evil. . . .* As we have stated above, law, being a rule and measure, can be in a person in two ways: in one way, as in him that rules and measures; in another way, as in that which is ruled and measured, since a thing is ruled and measured in so far as it partakes of the rule or measure. Therefore, since all things subject to divine providence are ruled and measured by the eternal law, as was stated above, it is evident that all things partake in some way in the eternal law, in so far as, namely, from its being imprinted on them, they derive their respective inclinations to their proper acts and ends. Now among all others, the rational creature is subject to divine providence in a more excellent way, in so far as it itself partakes of a share of providence, by being provident both for itself and for others. Therefore it has a share of the eternal reason, whereby it has a natural inclination to its proper act and end; and this participation of the eternal law in the rational creature is called the natural law. Hence the Psalmist, after saying (Ps. 4:5): *Offer up the sacrifice of justice*, and as though someone asked what the works of justice are, adds; *many say, Who shows us good things?* In answer to which question he says: *The light of Thy countenance, O Lord, is signed upon us.* He thus implies that the light of natural reason, whereby we discern what is good and what is evil, which is the function of the natural law, is nothing else than an imprint on us of the divine light. It is therefore evident that the natural law is nothing else than the rational creature's participation of the eternal law.

Reply Obj. 1. This argument would hold if the natural law were something different from the eternal law; whereas it is nothing but a participation thereof, as we have stated above.

Reply Obj. 2. Every act of reason and will in us is based on that which is according to nature, as was stated above. For every act of reasoning is based on principles that are known naturally, and every act of appetite in respect of the means is derived from the natural appetite in respect of the last end. Accordingly, the first direction of our acts of their end must needs be through the natural law.

Third Article
Whether There Is a Human Law?

Objection 1. It would seem that there is not a human law. For the natural law is a participation of the eternal law, as was stated above. Now through the eternal law *all things are most orderly*, as Augustine[2] states. Therefore the natural law suffices for the ordering of all human affairs. Consequently there is no need for a human law.

Obj. 2. Further, law has the character of a measure, as was stated above. But human reason is not a measure of things, but *vice versa*, as is stated in *Metaph.* x. Therefore no law can emanate from the human reason.

Obj. 3. Further, a measure should be most certain, as is stated in *Metaph.* x. But the dictates of the human reason in matters of conduct are uncertain, according to *Wis.* ix. 14: *The thoughts of mortal men are fearful, and our counsels uncertain.* Therefore no law can emanate from the human reason.

On the contrary, Augustine distinguishes two kinds of law, the one eternal, the other temporal, which he calls human.

I answer that, As we have stated above, a law is a dictate of the practical reason. Now it is to be observed that the same procedure takes place in the practical and in the speculative reason, for each proceeds from principles to conclusions, as was stated above. Accordingly, we conclude that, just as, in the speculative reason, from naturally known indemonstrable principles we draw the conclusions of the various sciences, the knowledge of which is not imparted to us by nature, but acquired by the efforts of reason, so too it is that from the precepts of the natural law, as from common and indemonstrable principles, the human reason needs to proceed to the more particular determination of certain matters. These particular determinations, devised by human reason, are called human laws, provided that the other essential conditions of law be observed, as was stated above. Therefore Tully[3] says in his *Rhetoric* that *justice has its source in nature; thence certain things came into custom by reason of their utility; afterwards these things which emanated from nature, and were approved by custom, were sanctioned by fear and reverence for the law.*

Reply Obj. 1. The human reason cannot have a full participation of the dictate of the divine reason, but according to its own mode, and imperfectly. Consequently, just as on the part of the speculative reason, by a natural participation of divine wisdom, there is in us the knowledge of certain common principles, but not a proper knowledge of each single truth such as that contained in the divine wisdom, so, too, on the part of the practical reason, man has a natural participation of the eternal law, according to certain common principles, but not as regards the particular determinations of individual cases, which are, however, contained in the eternal law. Hence the need for human reason to proceed further to sanction them by law.

Reply Obj. 2. Human reason is not, of itself, the rule of things. But the principles impressed on it by nature are the general rules and measures of all things relating to human conduct, of which the natural reason is the rule and measure, although it is not the measure of things that are from nature.

Reply Obj. 3. The practical reason is concerned with operable matters, which are singular and contingent, but not with necessary things, with which the speculative reason is concerned. Therefore human laws cannot have that inerrancy that belongs to the demonstrated conclusions of the sciences. Nor is it necessary for every measure to be altogether unerring and certain, but according as it is possible in its own particular genus.

Fourth Article
Whether There Was Any Need for a Divine Law?

We proceed thus to the Fourth Article:—

Objection 1. It would seem that there was no need for a divine law. For, as was stated above, the natural law is a participation in us of the eternal law. But the eternal law is the divine law, as was stated above. Therefore there is no need for a divine law in addition to the natural law and to human laws derived therefrom.

Obj. 2. Further, it is written (*Ecclus.* xv. 14) that *God left man in the hand of his own counsel.* Now counsel is an act of reason, as was stated above. Therefore man was left to the direction of his reason. But a dictate of human reason is a human law, as was stated above. Therefore there is no need for man to be governed also by a divine law. . . .

On the contrary, David prayed God to set His law before him, saying (*Ps.* cxix. 33): *Set before me for a law the way of Thy justifications, O Lord.*

I answer that, Besides the natural and the human law it was necessary for the directing of human conduct to have a divine law. And this for four reasons. First, because it is by law that man is directed how to perform his proper acts in view of his last end. Now if man were ordained to no other end than that which is proportionate to his natural ability, there would be no need for man to have any further direction, on the part of his reason, in addition to the natural law and humanly devised law which is derived from it. But since man is ordained to an end of eternal happiness which exceeds man's natural ability, as we have stated above, therefore it was necessary that, in addition to the natural and the human law, man should be directed to his end by a law given by God.

Secondly, because, by reason of the uncertainty of human judgment, especially on contingent and particular matters, different people form different judgments on human acts; whence also different and contrary laws result. In order, therefore, that man may know without any doubt what he ought to do and what he ought to avoid, it was necessary for man to be directed in his proper acts by a law given by God, for it is certain that such a law cannot err.

Thirdly, because man can make laws in those matters of which he is competent to judge. But man is not competent to judge of interior movements that are hidden, but only of exterior acts which are observable; and yet for the perfection of virtue it is necessary for man to conduct himself rightly in both kinds of acts. Consequently, human law could not sufficiently curb and direct interior acts, and it was necessary for this purpose that a divine law should supervene.

Fourthly, because, as Augustine says, human law cannot punish or forbid all evil deeds, since, while aiming at doing away with all evils, it would do away with many good things, and would hinder the advance of the common good, which is necessary for human living. In order, therefore, that no evil might remain unforbidden and unpunished, it was necessary for the divine law to supervene, whereby all sins are forbidden.

And these four causes are touched upon in *Ps.* cxix. 8, where it is said: *The law of the Lord is unspotted, i.e.,* allowing no foulness of sin; *converting souls,* because it directs not only exterior, but also interior, acts; *the testimony of the Lord is faithful,* because of the certainty of what is true and right; *giving wisdom to little ones,* by directing man to an end supernatural and divine.

Reply Obj. 1. By the natural law the eternal law is participated proportionately to the capacity of human nature. But to his supernatural end man needs to be directed in a yet higher way. Hence the additional law given by God whereby man shares more perfectly in the eternal law.

Reply Obj. 2. Counsel is a kind of inquiry, and hence must proceed from some principles. Nor is it enough for it to proceed from principles imparted by nature, which are the precepts of the natural law, for the reasons given above; but there is need for certain additional principles, namely, the precepts of the divine law. . . .

Question 94
The Natural Law

First Article
Whether the Natural Law Is a Habit?

We proceed thus to the First Article:—

Objection 1. It would seem that the natural law is a habit. For, as the Philosopher says, *there are three things in the soul—power, habit and passion.* But the natural law is not one of the soul's powers, nor is it one of the passions, as we may see by going through them one by one. Therefore the natural law is a habit.

Obj. 2. Further, Basil says that the *conscience or synderesis is the law of our mind,* which can apply only to the natural law. But *synderesis* is a habit, as was shown in the Fist Part. Therefore the natural law is a habit.

Obj. 3. Further, the natural law abides in man always, as will be shown further on. But man's

reason, which the law regards, does not always think about the natural law. Therefore the natural law is not an act, but a habit.

On the contrary, Augustine says that *a habit is that whereby something is done when necessary.* But such is not the natural law, since it is in infants and in the damned who cannot act by it. Therefore the natural law is not a habit.

I answer that, A thing may be called a habit in two ways. First, properly and essentially, and thus the natural law is not a habit. For it has been stated above that the natural law is something appointed by reason, just as a proposition is a work of reason. Now that which a man does is not the same as that whereby he does it, for he makes a becoming speech by the habit of grammar. Since, then, a habit is that by which we act, a law cannot be a habit properly and essentially.

Secondly, the term habit may be applied to that which we hold by a habit. Thus *faith* may mean *that which we hold by faith.* Accordingly, since the precepts of the natural law are sometimes considered by reason actually, while sometimes they are in the reason only habitually, in this way the natural law may be called a habit. So, too, in speculative matters, the indemonstrable principles are not the habit itself whereby we hold these principles; they are rather the principles of which we possess the habit.

Reply Obj. 1. The Philosopher proposes there to discover the genus of virtue; and since it is evident that virtue is a principle of action, he mentions only those things which are principles of human acts, viz., powers, habits and passions. But there are other things in the soul besides these three: *e.g.,* acts, as *to will* is in the one that wills; again, there are things known in the knower; moreover, its own natural properties such as immortality and the like, are in the soul.

Reply Obj. 2. Synderesis is said to be the law of our intellect because it is a habit containing the precepts of the natural law, which are the first principles of human actions.

Reply Obj. 3. This argument proves that the natural law is held habitually; and this is granted.

To the argument advanced in the contrary sense we reply that sometimes a man is unable to make use of that which is in him habitually, because of some impediment. Thus, because of sleep, a man is unable to use the habit of science. In like manner, through the deficiency of his age, a child cannot use the habit of the understanding of principles, or the natural law, which is in him habitually.

Second Article
Whether the Natural Law Contains
Several Precepts, or Only One?

We proceed thus to the Second Article:—

Objection 1. It would seem that the natural law contains, not several precepts, but only one. For law is a kind of precept, as was stated above. If therefore there were many precepts of the natural law, it would follow that there are also many natural laws.

Obj. 2. Further, the natural law is consequent upon human nature. But human nature, as a whole, is one; though, as to its parts, it is manifold. Therefore, either there is but one precept of the law of nature because of the unity of nature as a whole, or there are many by reason of the number of parts of human nature. The result would be that even things relating to the inclination of the concupiscible power would belong to the natural law.

Obj. 3. Further, law is something pertaining to reason, as was stated above. Now reason is but one in man. Therefore there is only one precept of the natural law.

On the contrary, The precepts of the natural law in man stand in relation to operable matters as first principles do to matters of demonstration. But there are several first indemonstrable principles. Therefore there are also several precepts of the natural law.

I answer that, As was stated above, the precepts of the natural law are to the practical reason what the first principles of demonstrations are to the speculative reason, because both are self-evident principles. Now a thing is said to be self-evident in two ways: first, in itself; secondly, in relation to us. Any proposition is said to be self-evident in it-self, if its predicate is contained in the notion of the subject; even though it may happen that to one who does not know the definition of the subject, such a proposition is not self-evident. For instance, this proposition, *Man is a rational being,* is, in its very nature, self-evident, since he who says *man says a rational being;* and yet to one who does not know what a man is, this proposition is not self-evident. Hence it is that, as Boethius says, certain axioms or propositions are universally self-evident to all; and such are the propositions whose terms are known to all, as, *Every whole is greater than its part,* and, *Things equal to one and the same are equal to one another.* But some propositions are self-evident only to the wise, who understand the meaning of the terms of such propositions. Thus to one who understands that an angel is not a body, it is self-evident that an angel is not circumscriptively in a place. But this is not evident to the unlearned, for they cannot grasp it.

Now a certain order is to be found in those things that are apprehended by men. For that which first falls under apprehension is *being,* the understanding of which is included in all things whatsoever a man apprehends. Therefore the first indemonstrable principle is that *the same thing cannot be affirmed and denied at the same time,* which is based on the notion of *being* and *not-being:* and on this principle all others are based, as is stated in *Metaph.* iv. Now as *being* is the first thing that falls under the apprehension absolutely, so *good* is the first thing that falls under the apprehension of the practical reason, which is directed to action (since every agent acts for an end, which has the nature of good.) Consequently, the first principle in the practical reason is one founded on the nature of good, viz., that *good is that which all things seek after.* Hence this is the first precept of law, that *good is to be done and promoted, and evil is to be avoided.* All other precepts of the natural law are based upon this; so that all the things which the practical reason naturally apprehends as man's good belong to the precepts of the natural law under the form of things to be done or avoided.

Since, however, good has the nature of an end, and evil, the nature of the contrary, hence it is that all those things to which man has a natural inclination are naturally apprehended by reason as being good, and consequently as objects of pursuit, and their contraries as evil, and objects of avoidance. Therefore, the order of the precepts of the natural law is according to the order of natural inclinations. For there is in man, first of all, an inclination to good in accordance with the nature which he has in common with all substances, inasmuch, namely, as every substance seeks the preservation of its own being, according to its nature; and by reason of this inclination, whatever is a means of preserving human life, and of warding off its obstacles, belongs to the natural law. Secondly, there is in man an inclination to things that pertain to him more specially, according to that nature which he has in common with other animals; and in virtue of this inclination, those things are said to belong to the natural law *which nature has taught to all animals*, such as sexual intercourse, the education of offspring, and so forth. Thirdly, there is in man an inclination to good according to the nature of his reason, which nature is proper to him. Thus man has a natural inclination to know the truth about God, and to live in society; and in this respect, whatever pertains to this inclination belongs to the natural law: *e.g.*, to shun ignorance, to avoid offending those among whom one has to live, and other such things regarding the above inclination.

Reply Obj. 1. All these precepts of the law of nature have the character of one natural law, inasmuch as they flow from one first precept.

Reply Obj. 2. All the inclinations of any parts whatsoever of human nature, *e.g.*, of the concupiscible and irascible parts, in so far as they are ruled by reason, belong to the natural law, and are reduced to one first precept, as was stated above. And thus the precepts of the natural law are many in themselves, but they are based on one common foundation.

Reply Obj. 3. Although reason is one in itself, yet it directs all things regarding man; so that

whatever can be ruled by reason is contained under the law of reason.

Fourth Article
Whether the Natural Law Is the Same in All Men?

We proceed thus to the Fourth Article:—

Objection 1. It would seem that the natural law is not the same in all. For it is stated in the *Decretals*[4] that *the natural law is that which is contained in the Law and the Gospel.* But this is not common to all men, because, as it is written (*Rom.* 10. 16), *all do not obey the gospel.* Therefore the natural law is not the same in all men.

Obj. 2. Further, *Things which are according to the law are said to be just,* as is stated in *Ethics* v. But it is stated in the same book that nothing is so just for all as not to be subject to change in regard to some men. Therefore even the natural law is not the same in all men.

Obj. 3. Further, as was stated above, to the natural law belongs everything to which a man is inclined according to his nature. Now different men are naturally inclined to different things—some to the desire of pleasures, others to the desire of honors, and other men to other things. Therefore, there is not one natural law for all.

On the contrary, Isidore says: *The natural law is common to all nations.*

I answer that, As we have stated above, to the natural law belong those things to which a man is inclined naturally; and among these it is proper to man to be inclined to act according to reason. Now it belongs to the reason to proceed from what is common to what is proper, as is stated in *Physics* i. The speculative reason, however, is differently situated, in this matter, from the practical reason. For, since the speculative reason is concerned chiefly with necessary things, which cannot be otherwise than they are, its proper conclusions, like the universal principles, contain the truth without fail. The practical reason, on the other hand, is concerned with contingent matters, which is the domain of human actions; and, consequently, although there is necessity in the common principles, the more we descend toward the particular, the more frequently we encounter defects. Accordingly, then, in speculative matters truth is the same in all men, both as to principles and as to conclusions; although the truth is not known to all as regards the conclusions, but only as regards the principles which are called *common notions.* But in matters of action, truth or practical rectitude is not the same for all as to what is particular, but only as to the common principles; and where there is the same rectitude in relation to particulars, it is not equally known to all.

It is therefore evident that, as regards the common principles whether of speculative or of practical reason, truth or rectitude is the same for all, and is equally known by all. But as to the proper conclusions of the speculative reason, the truth is the same for all, but it is not equally known to all. Thus, it is true for all that the three angles of a triangle are together equal to two right angles, although it is not known to all. But as to the proper conclusions of the practical reason, neither is the truth or rectitude the same for all; nor, where it is the same, is it equally known by all. Thus, it is right and true for all to act according to reason, and from this principle it follows, as a proper conclusion, that goods entrusted to another should be restored to their owner. Now this is true for the majority of cases. But it may happen in a particular case that it would be injurious, and therefore unreasonable, to restore goods held in trust; for instance, if they are claimed for the purpose of fighting against one's country. And this principle will be found to fail the more, according as we descend further toward the particular; *e.g.,* if one were to say that goods held in trust should be restored with such and such a guarantee, or in such and such a way; because the greater the number of conditions added, the greater the number of ways in which the principle may fail, so that it be not right to restore or not to restore.

Consequently, we must say that the natural law, as to the first common principles, is the same for all, both as to rectitude and as to knowledge. But

as to certain more particular aspects, which are conclusions, as it were, of those common principles, it is the same for all in the majority of cases, both as to rectitude and as to knowledge; and yet in some few cases it may fail, both as to rectitude, by reason of certain obstacles (just as natures subject to generation and corruption fail in some few cases because of some obstacle), and as to knowledge, since in some the reason is perverted by passion, or evil habit, or an evil disposition of nature. Thus at one time theft, although it is expressly contrary to the natural law, was not considered wrong among the Germans, as Julius Caesar relates.

Reply Obj. 1. The meaning of the sentence quoted is not that whatever is contained in the Law and the Gospel belongs to the natural law, since they contain many things that are above nature; but that whatever belongs to the natural law is fully contained in them. Therefore Gratian,[5] after saying that *the natural law is what is contained in the Law and the Gospel,* adds at once, by way of example, *by which everyone is commanded to do to others as he would be done by.*

Reply Obj. 2. The saying of the Philosopher is to be understood of things that are naturally just, not as common principles, but as conclusions drawn from them, having rectitude in the majority of cases, but failing in a few.

Reply Obj. 3. Just as in man reason rules and commands the other powers, so all the natural inclinations belonging to the other powers must needs be directed according to reason. Therefore it is universally right for all men that all their inclinations should be directed according to reason.

Fifth Article
Whether the Natural Law Can Be Changed?

We proceed thus to the Fifth Article:—

Objection 1. It would seem that the natural law can be changed. For on *Ecclus,* xvii. 9 (*He gave them instructions, and the law of life*) the *Gloss* says: *He wished the law of the letter to be written, in order to correct the law of nature.* But that which is corrected is changed. Therefore the natural law can be changed.

Obj. 2. Further, the slaying of the innocent, adultery, and theft are against the natural law. But we find these things changed by God: as when God commanded Abraham to slay his innocent son (*Gen.* xxii. 2); and when He ordered the Jews to borrow and purloin the vessels of the Egyptians (*Exod.* xii. 35); and when He commanded Osee to take to himself *a wife of fornications* (*Osee* i. 2). Therefore the natural law can be changed.

Obj. 3. Further, Isidore says that *the possession of all things in common, and universal freedom, are matters of natural law.* But these things are seen to be changed by human laws. Therefore it seems that the natural law is subject to change.

On the contrary, It is said in the *Decretals: The natural law dates from the creation of the rational creature. It does not vary according to time, but remains unchangeable.*

I answer that, A change in the natural law may be understood in two ways. First, by way of addition. In this sense, nothing hinders the natural law from being changed, since many things for the benefit of human life have been added over and above the natural law, both by the divine law and by human laws.

Secondly, a change in the natural law may be understood by way of subtraction, so that what previously was according to the natural law ceases to be so. In this sense, the natural law is altogether unchangeable in its first principles. But in its secondary principles, which, as we have said, are certain detailed proximate conclusions drawn from the first principles, the natural law is not changed, so that what it prescribes be not right in most cases. But it may be changed in some particular cases of rare occurrence, through some special causes hindering the observance of such precepts, as was stated above.

Reply Obj. 1. The written law is said to be given for the correction of the natural law, either because it supplies what was wanting to the natural law, or

because the natural law was so perverted in the hearts of some men, as to certain matters, that they esteemed those things good which are naturally evil; which perversion stood in need of correction.

Reply Obj. 2. All men alike, both guilty and innocent, die the death of nature; which death of nature is inflicted by the power of God because of original sin, according to *1 Kings* ii. 6: *The Lord killeth and maketh alive.* Consequently, by the command of God, death can be inflicted on any man, guilty or innocent, without any injustice whatever. In like manner, adultery is intercourse with another's wife, who is allotted to him by the law emanating from God. Consequently intercourse with any woman by the command of God is neither adultery nor fornication. The same applies to theft, which is the taking of another's property. For whatever is taken by the command of God, to Whom all things belong, is not taken against the will of its owner, whereas it is in this that theft consists. Nor is it only in human things that whatever is commanded by God is right; but also in natural things, whatever is done by God is, in some way, natural, as was stated in the First Part.

Reply Obj. 3. A thing is said to belong to the natural law in two ways. First, because nature inclines thereto: *e.g.,* that one should not do harm to another. Secondly, because nature did not bring with it the contrary. Thus, we might say that for man to be naked is of the natural law, because nature did not give him clothes, but art invented them. In this sense, *the possession of all things in common and universal freedom* are said to be the natural law, because, namely, the distinction of possessions and slavery were not brought in by nature, but devised by human reason for the benefit of human life. Accordingly, the law of nature was not changed in this respect, except by addition.

Notes

1. Isidore of Seville (ca. 560–636), Archbishop of Seville. He was the author of several theological works,

including *Sententiarum libri tres* and *De fide catholica*, which were highly influential in the Middle Ages.

2. Augustine: St. Augustine, Bishop of Hippo (354–430), one of the foremost Christian philosophers who taught that a divine illumination enlightened every soul with special knowledge of God. His most influential works are *Confessions* (400) and *On the City of God* (413–426).

3. Tully: Marcus Tullius Cicero (106–143 B.C.), Roman statesman, orator and Stoic philosopher, he set forth the early version of Natural Law.

4. Decretals: Papal epistles or decrees replying to some question on faith or authority.

5. Gratian (359–383), a Christian emperor who issued enactments against paganism.

4

Cultural Relativism

RUTH BENEDICT

Ruth Benedict (1887–1948) was a foremost American anthropologist who taught at Columbia University. She is best known for her book Patterns of Culture *(1935). Benedict views social systems as communities with common beliefs and practices which have become more or less well integrated patterns of ideas and practices. Like a work of art, a social system chooses which theme of its repertoire of basic tendencies to emphasize and then goes about to produce a holistic grand design favoring those tendencies. The final systems differ from one another in striking ways, but there is no reason to say that one system is better than another. What is considered normal or abnormal behavior depends on the choices of these social systems, or what Benedict calls the "idea-practice pattern of the culture."*

Benedict views morality as dependent on the varying histories and environments of different cultures. In this essay she assembles an impressive amount of data from her anthropological research of tribal behavior on an island in northwest Melanesia, from which she draws her conclusion that moral relativism is the correct view of moral principles.

Modern social anthropology has become more and more a study of the varieties and common elements of cultural environment and the consequences of these in human behavior. For such a study of diverse social orders primitive peoples fortunately provide a laboratory not yet entirely vitiated by the spread of a standardized worldwide civilization. Dyaks and Hopis, Fijians and Yakuts are significant for psychological and sociological

From "Anthropology and the Abnormal," by Ruth Benedict, in *The Journal of General Psychology* 10 (1934): 59–82, a publication of the Helen Dwight Reid Educational Foundation. Reprinted by permission of Heldref Publications.

study because only among these simpler peoples has there been sufficient isolation to give opportunity for the development of localized social forms. In the higher cultures the standardization of custom and belief over a couple of continents has given a false sense of the inevitability of the particular forms that have gained currency, and we need to turn to a wider survey in order to check the conclusions we hastily base upon this near-universality of familiar customs. Most of the simpler cultures did not gain the wide currency of the one which, out of our experience, we identify with human nature, but this was for various historical reasons, and certainly not for any that gives us as its carriers a monopoly of social good or of social sanity. Modern civilization, from this point of view, becomes not a necessary pinnacle of human achievement but one entry in a long series of possible adjustments.

These adjustments, whether they are in mannerisms like the ways of showing anger, or joy, or grief in any society, or in major human drives like those of sex, prove to be far more variable than experience in any one culture would suggest. In certain fields, such as that of religion or of formal marriage arrangements, these wide limits of variability are well known and can be fairly described. In others it is not yet possible to give a generalized account, but that does not absolve us of the task of indicating the significance of the work that has been done and of the problems that have arisen.

One of these problems relates to the customary modern normal-abnormal categories and our conclusions regarding them. In how far are such categories culturally determined, or in how far can we with assurance regard them as absolute? In how far can we regard inability to function socially as diagnostic of abnormality, or in how far is it necessary to regard this as a function of the culture?

As a matter of fact, one of the most striking facts that emerge from a study of widely varying cultures is the ease with which our abnormals function in other cultures. It does not matter what kind of "abnormality" we choose for illustration, those which indicate extreme instability, or those which are more in the nature of character traits like sadism or delusions of grandeur or of persecution, there are well-described cultures in which these abnormals function at ease and with honor, and apparently without danger or difficulty to the society. . . .

The most notorious of these is trance and catalepsy. Even a very mild mystic is aberrant in our culture. But most people have regarded even extreme psychic manifestations not only as normal and desirable, but even as characteristic of highly valued and gifted individuals. This was true even in our own cultural background in that period when Catholicism made the ecstatic experience the mark of sainthood. It is hard for us, born and brought up in a culture that makes no use of the experience, to realize how important a role it may play and how many individuals are capable of it, once it has been given an honorable place in any society. . . .

Cataleptic and trance phenomena are, of course, only one illustration of the fact that those whom we regard as abnormals may function adequately in other cultures. Many of our culturally discarded traits are selected for elaboration in different societies. Homosexuality is an excellent example, for in this case our attention is not constantly diverted, as in the consideration of trance, to the interruption of routine activity which it implies. Homosexuality poses the problem very simply. A tendency toward this trait in our culture exposes an individual to all the conflicts to which all aberrants are always exposed, and we tend to identify the consequences of this conflict with homosexuality. But these consequences are obviously local and cultural. Homosexuals in many societies are not incompetent, but they may be such if the culture asks adjustments of them that would strain

any man's vitality. Wherever homosexuality has been given an honorable place in any society, those to whom it is congenial have filled adequately the honorable roles society assigns to them. Plato's *Republic* is, of course, the most convincing statement of such a reading of homosexuality. It is presented as one of the major means to the good life, and it was generally so regarded in Greece at that time.

The cultural attitude toward homosexuals has not always been on such a high ethical plane, but it has been very varied. Among many American Indian tribes there exists the institution of the *berdache*, as the French called them. These men-women were men who at puberty or thereafter took the dress and the occupations of women. Sometimes they married other men and lived with them. Sometimes they were men with no inversion, persons of weak sexual endowment who chose this role to avoid the jeers of the women. The berdaches were never regarded as of first-rate supernatural power, as similar men-women were in Siberia, but rather as leaders in women's occupations, good healers in certain diseases, or, among certain tribes, as the genial organizers of social affairs. In any case, they were socially placed. They were not left exposed to the conflicts that visit the deviant who is excluded from participation in the recognized patterns of his society.

The most spectacular illustrations of the extent to which normality may be culturally defined are those cultures where an abnormality of our culture is the cornerstone of their social structure. It is not possible to do justice to these possibilities in a short discussion. A recent study of an island of northwest Melanesia by Fortune describes a society built upon traits which we regard as beyond the border of paranoia. In this tribe the exogamic groups look upon each other as prime manipulators of black magic, so that one marries always into an enemy group which remains for life one's deadly and unappeasable foes. They look upon a good garden crop as a confession of theft, for everyone is engaged in making magic to induce into his garden the productiveness of his neighbors'; therefore no secrecy in the island is so rigidly insisted upon as the secrecy of a man's harvesting of his yams. Their polite phrase at the acceptance of a gift is, "And if you now poison me, how shall I repay you this present?" Their preoccupation with poisoning is constant; no woman ever leaves her cooking pot for a moment untended. Even the great affinal economic exchanges that are characteristic of this Melanesian culture area are quite altered in Dobu since they are incompatible with this fear and distrust that pervades the culture. They go farther and people the whole world outside their own quarters with such malignant spirits that all-night feasts and ceremonials simply do not occur here. They have even rigorous religiously enforced customs that forbid the sharing of seed even in one family group. Anyone else's food is deadly poison to you, so that communality of stores is out of the question. For some months before harvest the whole society is on the verge of starvation, but if one falls to the temptation and eats up one's seed yams, one is an outcast and a beachcomber for life. There is no coming back. It involves, as a matter of course, divorce and the breaking of all social ties.

Now in this society where no one may work with another and no one may share with another, Fortune describes the individual who was regarded by all his fellows as crazy. He was not one of those who periodically ran amok and, beside himself and frothing at the mouth, fell with a knife upon anyone he could reach. Such behavior they did not regard as putting anyone outside the pale. They did not even put the individuals who were known to be liable to these attacks under any kind of control. They merely fled when they saw the attack coming on and kept out of the way. "He would be all right tomorrow." But there was one man of sunny, kindly disposition who liked work and liked to be helpful. The compulsion was too strong for him to repress it in favor of the opposite tendencies of his culture. Men and women never spoke of him without laughing; he was silly and simple and definitely crazy. Nevertheless, to the ethnologist used to a culture that has, in

Christianity, made his type the model of all virtue, he seemed a pleasant fellow. . . .

. . . Among the Kwakiutl it did not matter whether a relative had died in bed of disease, or by the hand of an enemy, in either case death was an affront to be wiped out by the death of another person. The fact that one had been caused to mourn was proof that one had been put upon. A chief's sister and her daughter had gone up to Victoria, and either because they drank bad whiskey or because their boat capsized they never came back. The chief called together his warriors, "Now I ask you, tribes, who shall wail? Shall I do it or shall another?" The spokesman answered, of course, "Not you, Chief. Let some other of the tribes." Immediately they set up the war pole to announce their intention of wiping out the injury, and gathered a war party. They set out, and found seven men and two children asleep and killed them. "Then they felt good when they arrived at Sebaa in the evening."

The point which is of interest to us is that in our society those who on that occasion would feel good when they arrived at Sebaa that evening would be the definitely abnormal. There would be some, even in our society, but it is not a recognized and approved mood under the circumstances. On the Northwest Coast those are favored and fortunate to whom that mood under those circumstances is congenial, and those to whom it is repugnant are unlucky. This latter minority can register in their own culture only by doing violence to their congenial responses and acquiring others that are difficult for them. The person, for instance, who, like a Plains Indian whose wife has been taken from him, is too proud to fight, can deal with the Northwest Coast civilization only by ignoring its strongest bents. If he cannot achieve it, he is the deviant in that culture, their instance of abnormality.

This head-hunting that takes place on the Northwest Coast after a death is no matter of blood revenge or of organized vengeance. There is no effort to tie up the subsequent killing with any responsibility on the part of the victim for the death of the person who is being mourned. A chief whose son has died goes visiting wherever his fancy dictates, and he says to his host, "My prince has died today, and you go with him." Then he kills him. In this, according to their interpretation, he acts nobly because he has not been downed. He has thrust back in return. The whole procedure is meaningless without the fundamental paranoid reading of bereavement. Death, like all the other untoward accidents of existence, confounds man's pride and can only be handled in the category of insults.

Behavior honored upon the Northwest Coast is one which is recognized as abnormal in our civilization, and yet it is sufficiently close to the attitudes of our own culture to be intelligible to us and to have a definite vocabulary with which we may discuss it. The megalomaniac paranoid trend is a definite danger in our society. It is encouraged by some of our major preoccupations, and it confronts us with a choice of two possible attitudes. One is to brand it as abnormal and reprehensible, and is the attitude we have chosen in our civilization. The other is to make it an essential attribute of ideal man, and this is the solution in the culture of the Northwest Coast.

These illustrations, which it has been possible to indicate only in the briefest manner, force upon us the fact that normality is culturally defined. An adult shaped to the drives and standards of either of these cultures, if he were transported into our civilization, would fall into our categories of abnormality. He would be faced with the psychic dilemmas of the socially unavailable. In his own culture, however, he is the pillar of society, the end result of socially inculcated mores, and the problem of personal instability in his case simply does not arise.

No one civilization can possibly utilize in its mores the whole potential range of human behavior. Just as there are great numbers of possible phonetic articulations, and the possibility of language depends on a selection and standardization of a few of these in order that speech communication may be possible at all, so the possibility of organized behavior of every sort, from the fashions of local dress and houses to the dicta of a

people's ethics and religion, depends upon a similar selection among the possible behavior traits. In the field of recognized economic obligations or sex tabus this selection is as nonrational and subconscious a process as it is in the field of phonetics. It is a process which goes on in the group for long periods of time and is historically conditioned by innumerable accidents of isolation or of contact of peoples. In any comprehensive study of psychology, the selection that different cultures have made in the course of history within the great circumference of potential behavior is of great significance.

Every society, beginning with some slight inclination in one direction or another, carries its preference farther and farther, integrating itself more and more completely upon its chosen basis, and discarding those types of behavior that are uncongenial. Most of those organizations of personality that seem to us most uncontrovertibly abnormal have been used by different civilizations in the very foundations of their institutional life. Conversely the most valued traits of our normal individuals have been looked on in differently organized cultures as aberrant. Normality, in short, within a very wide range, is culturally defined. It is primarily a term for the socially elaborated segment of human behavior in any culture; and abnormality, a term for the segment that that particular civilization does not use. The very eyes with which we see the problem are conditioned by the long traditional habits of our own society.

It is a point that has been made more often in relation to ethics than in relation to psychiatry. We do not any longer make the mistake of deriving the morality of our locality and decade directly from the inevitable constitution of human nature. We do not elevate it to the dignity of a first principle. We recognize that morality differs in every society, and is a convenient term for socially approved habits. Mankind has always preferred to say, "It is a morally good," rather than "It is habitual," and the fact of this preference is matter enough for a critical science of ethics. But historically the two phrases are synonymous.

The concept of the normal is properly a variant

of the concept of the good. It is that which society has approved. A normal action is one which falls well within the limits of expected behavior for a particular society. Its variability among different peoples is essentially a function of the variability of the behavior patterns that different societies have created for themselves, and can never be wholly divorced from a consideration of culturally institutionalized types of behavior.

Each culture is a more or less elaborate working out of the potentialities of the segment it has chosen. In so far as a civilization is well integrated and consistent within itself, it will tend to carry farther and farther, according to its nature, its initial impulse toward a particular type of action, and from the point of view of any other culture those elaborations will include more and more extreme and aberrant traits.

Each of these traits, in proportion as it reinforces the chosen behavior patterns of that culture, is for that culture normal. Those individuals to whom it is congenial either congenitally, or as the result of childhood sets, are accorded prestige in that culture, and are not visited with the social contempt or disapproval which their traits would call down upon them in a society that was differently organized. On the other hand, those individuals whose characteristics are not congenial to the selected type of human behavior in that community are the deviants, no matter how valued their personality traits may be in a contrasted civilization.

The Dobuan who is not easily susceptible to fear of treachery, who enjoys work and likes to be helpful, is their neurotic and regarded as silly. On the Northwest Coast the person who finds it difficult to read life in terms of an insult contest will be the person upon whom fall all the difficulties of the culturally unprovided for. The person who does not find it easy to humiliate a neighbor, nor to see humiliation in his own experience, who is genial and loving, may, of course, find some unstandardized way of achieving satisfactions in his society, but not in the major patterned responses that his culture requires of him. If he is born to

play an important role in a family with many hereditary privileges, he can succeed only by doing violence to his whole personality. If he does not succeed, he has betrayed his culture; that is, he is abnormal.

I have spoken of individuals as having sets toward certain types of behavior, and of these sets as running sometimes counter to the types of behavior which are institutionalized in the culture to which they belong. From all that we know of contrasting cultures it seems clear that differences of temperament occur in every society. The matter has never been made the subject of investigation, but from the available material it would appear that these temperament types are very likely of universal recurrence. That is, there is an ascertainable range of human behavior that is found wherever a sufficiently large series of individuals is observed. But the proportion in which behavior types stand to one another in different societies is not universal. The vast majority of individuals in any group are shaped to the fashion of that culture. In other words, most individuals are plastic to the moulding force of the society into which they are born. In a society that values trance, as in India, they will have supernormal experience. In a society that institutionalizes homosexuality, they will be homosexual. In a society that sets the gathering of possessions as the chief human objective, they will amass property. The deviants, whatever the type of behavior the culture has institutionalized, will remain few in number, and there seems no more difficulty in moulding the vast malleable majority to the "normality" of what we consider an aberrant trait, such as delusions of reference, than to the normality of such accepted behavior patterns as acquisitiveness. The small proportion of the number of the deviants in any culture is not a function of the sure instinct with which that society has built itself upon the fundamental sanities, but of the universal fact that, happily, the majority of mankind quite readily take any shape that is presented to them. . . .

5

A Defense of Ethical Objectivism

Louis P. Pojman

In this article I first analyze the structure of ethical relativism as constituted by two theses: the diversity thesis and the dependency thesis. Then I examine two types of ethical relativism: subjectivism and conventionalism, arguing that both types have serious problems. Next I indicate a way of taking into account the insights of relativism while maintaining an objectivist position. I outline two objectivist arguments. I conclude by suggesting some reasons why people have been misled by relativist arguments.

"Who's to Judge What's Right or Wrong?"

Like many people, I have always been instinctively a moral relativist. As far back as I can remember . . . it has always seemed to be obvious that the dictates of morality arise from some sort of convention or understanding among people, that different people arrive at different understandings, and that there are no basic moral demands that apply to everyone. This seemed so obvious to me I assumed it was everyone's instinctive view, or at least everyone who gave the matter any thought in this day and age.

—Gilbert Harman[1]

Ethical relativism is the doctrine that the moral rightness and wrongness of actions vary from society to society and that there are not absolute universal moral standards on all men at all times. Accordingly, it holds that whether or not it is right for an individual to act in a certain way depends on or is relative to the society to which he belongs.

—John Ladd[2]

Gilbert Harman's intuitions about the self-evidence of ethical relativism contrast strikingly with Plato's or Kant's equal certainty about the truth of objectivism, the doctrine that universally valid or true ethical principles exist.[3] "Two things fill the soul with ever new and increasing wonder and reverence the oftener and more fervently reflection ponders on it: the starry heavens above and the moral law within," wrote Kant. On the basis of polls taken in my ethics and introduction to philosophy classes over the past several years, Harman's views may signal a shift in contemporary society's moral understanding. The polls show a two-to-one ratio in favor of moral relativism over moral absolutism, with fewer than five percent of the respondents recognizing that a third position between these two polar opposites might exist. Of course, I'm not suggesting that all of these students had a clear understanding of what relativism entails, for many who said they were relativists also contended in the same polls that abortion except to save the mother's life is always wrong, that capital punishment is always wrong, or that suicide is never morally permissible.

Among my university colleagues, a growing number also seem to embrace moral relativism. Recently one of my nonphilosopher colleagues voted to turn down a doctoral dissertation proposal because the student assumed an objectivist position in ethics. (Ironically, I found in this same colleague's work rhetorical treatment of individual liberty that raised it to the level of a non-negotiable absolute.) But irony and inconsistency aside, many relativists are aware of the tension between their own subjective positions and their metatheory that entails relativism. I confess that I too am tempted by the allurements of this view and find some forms of it plausible and worthy of serious examination. However, I also find it deeply troubling.

In this essay I will examine the central notions of ethical relativism and look at the implications that seem to follow from it. Then I will present the outline of a very modest objectivism, one that takes into account many of the insights of relativism and yet stands as a viable option to it.

1. An Analysis of Relativism

Let us examine the theses contained in John Ladd's succinct statement on ethical (conventional) relativism that appears at the beginning of this essay. If we analyze it, we derive the following argument:

1. Moral rightness and wrongness of actions vary from society to society, so there are no universal moral standards held by all societies.
2. Whether or not it is right for individuals to act in a certain way depends on (or is relative to) the society to which they belong.
3. Therefore, there are no absolute or objective moral standards that apply to all people everywhere.

1. The first thesis, which may be called the *diversity thesis,* is simply a description that acknowledges the fact that moral rules differ from society to society. The Spartans of ancient Greece and the Dobu of New Guinea believe that stealing is morally right, but we believe it is wrong. The Roman father had the power of life and death (*just vitae necisque*) over his children, whereas we condemn parents for abusing their children. A tribe in East Africa once threw deformed infants to the hippopotamuses, and in ancient Greece and Rome infants were regularly exposed, while we abhor infanticide. Ruth Benedict describes a tribe in Melanesia that views cooperation and kindness as vices, whereas we see them as virtues. While in ancient Greece, Rome, China, and Korea parricide was condemned as "the most execrable of crimes," among Northern Indians aged persons, persons who were no longer capable of walking,

were left alone to starve. Among the California Gallinomero, when fathers became feeble, a burden to their sons, "the poor old wretch is not infrequently thrown down on his back and securely held while a stick is placed across his throat, and two of them seat themselves on the ends of it until he ceases to breathe."[4] Sexual practices vary over time and place. Some cultures permit homosexual behavior, while others condemn it. Some cultures practice polygamy, while others view it as immoral. Some cultures condone while others condemn premarital sex. Some cultures accept cannibalism, while the very idea revolts us. Some West African tribes perform clitoridectomies on girls, whereas we deplore such practices. Cultural relativism is well documented, and "custom is the king o'er all." There may or may not be moral principles that are held in common by every society, but if there are any, they seem to be few at best. Certainly it would be very difficult to derive any single "true" morality by observing various societies' moral standards.

2. The second thesis, the *dependency thesis,* asserts that individual acts are right or wrong depending on the nature of the society from which they emanate. Morality does not occur in a vacuum, and what is considered morally right or wrong must be seen in a context that depends on the goals, wants, beliefs, history, and environment of the society in question. As William G. Sumner says,

We learn the morals as unconsciously as we learn to walk and hear and breathe, and [we] never know any reason why the [morals] are what they are. The justification of them is that when we wake to consciousness of life we find them facts which already hold us in the bonds of tradition, custom, and habit.[5]

Trying to see things from an independent, noncultural point of view would be like taking out our eyes in order to examine their contours and qualities. There is no "innocent eye." We are simply culturally determined beings.

We could, of course, distinguish between a weak and a strong thesis of dependency, for the nonrelativist can accept a certain degree of relativity in the way moral principles are *applied* in various cultures, depending on beliefs, history, and environment. For example, Jewish men express reverence for God by covering their heads when entering places of worship, whereas Christian men uncover their heads when entering places of worship. Westerners shake hands upon greeting each other, whereas Hindus place their hands together and point them toward the person to be greeted. Both sides adhere to principles of reverence and respect but apply them differently. But the ethical relativist must maintain a stronger thesis, one that insists that the moral principles themselves are products of the cultures and may vary from society to society. The ethical relativist contends that even beyond environmental factors and differences in beliefs, a fundamental disagreement exists among societies. One way for the relativist to support this thesis is by appealing to an indeterminacy of translation thesis, which maintains that there is a conceptual relativity among language groups so that we cannot even translate into our language the worldviews of a culture with a radically different language.

In a sense we all live in radically different worlds. But the relativist wants to go further and maintain that there is something conventional about *any* morality, so that every morality really depends on a level of social acceptance. Not only do various societies adhere to different moral systems, but the very same society could (and often does) change its moral views over place and time. For example, the majority of people in the southern United States now view slavery as immoral, whereas one hundred and forty years ago they did not. Our society's views on divorce, sexuality, abortion, and assisted suicide have changed somewhat as well—and they are still changing.

3. The conclusion that there are no absolute or objective moral standards binding on all people follows from the first two propositions. Combining cultural relativism (*the diversity thesis*) with the *dependency thesis* yields ethical relativism in its classic form. If there are different moral principles from culture to culture and if all morality is rooted in culture, then it follows that there are no universal moral principles that are valid (or true) for all cultures and peoples at all times.

2. Subjectivism

Some people think that this conclusion is still too tame, and they maintain that morality is dependent not on the society but rather on the individual. As my students sometimes maintain, "Morality is in the eye of the beholder." They treat morality like taste or aesthetic judgments—person relative. This form of moral subjectivism has the sorry consequence that it makes morality a very useless concept, for, on its premises, little or no interpersonal criticism or judgment is logically possible. Suppose that you are repulsed by observing John torturing a child. You cannot condemn him if one of his principles is "torture little children for the fun of it." The only basis for judging him wrong might be that he was a hypocrite who condemned others for torturing. But suppose that another of his principles is that hypocrisy is morally permissible (for him); thus we cannot condemn him for condemning others for doing what he does.

On the basis of subjectivism Adolf Hitler and the serial murderer, Ted Bundy, could be considered as moral as Gandhi, so long as each lived by his own standards, whatever those might be. Witness the following paraphrase of a tape-recorded conversation between Ted Bundy and one of his victims in which Bundy justifies his murder:

Then I learned that all moral judgments are "value judgments," that all value judgments are subjective, and that none can be proved to be either 'right' or 'wrong.' I even read somewhere that the Chief Justice of the United States had written that the American Constitution expressed nothing more than collective value judgments. Believe it or not, I figured out for myself—what apparently the Chief Justice couldn't figure out for himself—that if the rationality of one value judgment was zero, multiplying it by millions would not make it one whit more rational. Nor is there any 'reason' to obey the law for anyone, like myself, who has the boldness and daring—the strength of character—to throw off its shackles. . . . I discovered that to become truly free, truly unfettered, I had to become truly uninhibited. And I quickly discovered that the greatest obstacle to my freedom, the greatest block and limitation to it, consists in the insupportable 'value judgment' that I was bound to respect the rights of others. I asked myself, who were these 'others'? Other human beings, with human rights? Why is it more wrong to kill a human animal than any other animal, a pig or a sheep or a steer? Is your life more to you than a hog's life to a hog? Why should I be willing to sacrifice my pleasure more for the one than for the other? Surely you would not, in this age of scientific enlightenment, declare that God or nature has marked some pleasures as 'moral' or 'good' and others as 'immoral' or 'bad'? In any case, let me assure you, my dear young lady, that there is absolutely no comparison between the pleasure I might take in eating ham and the pleasure I anticipate in raping and murdering you. That is the honest conclusion to which my education has led me—after the most conscientious examination of my spontaneous and uninhibited self.[6]

Notions of good and bad, or right and wrong, cease to have interpersonal evaluative meaning. We might be revulsed by the views of Ted Bundy, but that is just a matter of taste. A student might not like it when her teacher gives her an F on a test paper, while he gives another student an A for a similar paper, but there is no way to criticize him for injustice, because justice is not one of his chosen principles.

Absurd consequences follow from subjectivism. If it is correct, then morality reduces to aesthetic tastes about which there can be neither argument nor interpersonal judgment. Although many students say they espouse subjectivism, there is evidence that it conflicts with other of their moral views. They typically condemn Hitler

as an evil man for his genocidal policies. A contradiction seems to exist between subjectivism and the very concept of morality, which it is supposed to characterize, for morality has to do with *proper* resolution of interpersonal conflict and the amelioration of the human predicament (both deontological and teleological systems do this, but in different ways—see Parts V and VI of this anthology). Whatever else it does, morality has a minimal aim of preventing a Hobbesian state of nature (see Part III), wherein life is "solitary, poor, nasty, brutish, and short." But if so, subjectivism is no help at all, for it rests neither on social agreement of principle (as the conventionalist maintains) nor on an objectively independent set of norms that bind all people for the common good. If there were only one person on earth, there would be no occasion for morality, because there wouldn't be any interpersonal conflicts to resolve or others whose suffering he or she would have a duty to ameliorate. Subjectivism implicitly assumes something of this solipsism, an atomism in which isolated individuals make up separate universes. Subjectivism treats individuals like billiard balls on a societal pool table where they meet only in radical collisions, each aimed at his or her own goal and striving to do in the others before they themselves are done in. This atomistic view of personality is belied by the facts that we develop in families and mutually dependent communities in which we share a common language, common institutions, and similar rituals and habits, and that we often feel one another's joys and sorrows. As John Donne wrote, "No man is an island, entire of itself; every man is a piece of the continent."

Radical individualistic ethical relativism is incoherent. If so, it follows that the only plausible view of ethical relativism must be one that grounds morality in the group or culture. This form is called *conventionalism*.

3. Conventionalism

Conventional ethical relativism, the view that there are no objective moral principles but that all valid moral principles are justified (or are made true) by virtue of their cultural acceptance, recognizes the social nature of morality. That is precisely its power and virtue. It does not seem subject to the same absurd consequences which plague subjectivism. Recognizing the importance of our social environment in generating customs and beliefs, many people suppose that ethical relativism is the correct metaethical theory. Furthermore, they are drawn to it for its liberal philosophical stance. It seems to be an enlightened response to the sin of ethnocentricity, and it seems to entail or strongly imply an attitude of tolerance toward other cultures. Anthropologist Ruth Benedict says, that in recognizing ethical relativity, "We shall arrive at a more realistic social faith, accepting as grounds of hope and as new bases for tolerance the coexisting and equally valid patterns of life which mankind has created for itself from the raw materials of existence."[7] The most famous of those holding this position is the anthropologist Melville Herskovits, who argues even more explicitly than Benedict that ethical relativism entails intercultural tolerance.

> (1) If morality is relative to its culture, then there is no independent basis for criticizing the morality of any other culture but one's own.
> (2) If there is no independent way of criticizing any other culture, we ought to be *tolerant* of the moralities of other cultures.
> (3) Morality is relative to its culture. Therefore,
> (4) We ought to be *tolerant* of the moralities of other cultures.[8]

Tolerance is certainly a virtue, but is this a good argument for it? I think not. If morality simply is relative to each culture, then if the culture in question does not have a principle of tolerance, its members have no obligation to be tolerant. Herskovits seems to be treating the *principle of tolerance* as the one exception to his relativism. He seems to be treating it as an absolute moral principle. But from a relativistic point of view there is no more reason to be tolerant than to be intolerant and neither stance is objectively morally better than the other.

Not only do relativists fail to offer a basis for criticizing those who are intolerant, but they cannot rationally criticize anyone who espouses what they might regard as a heinous principle. If, as seems to be the case, valid criticism supposes an objective or impartial standard, relativists cannot morally criticize anyone outside their own culture. Adolf Hitler's genocidal actions, so long as they are culturally accepted, are as morally legitimate as Mother Teresa's works of mercy. If conventional relativism is accepted, racism, genocide of unpopular minorities, oppression of the poor, slavery, and even the advocacy of war for its own sake are as equally moral as their opposites. And if a subculture decided that starting a nuclear war was somehow morally acceptable, we could not morally criticize these people. Any actual morality, whatever its content, is as valid as every other, and more valid than ideal moralities—since the latter aren't adhered to by any culture.

There are other disturbing consequences of ethical relativism. It seems to entail that reformers are always (morally) wrong since they go against the tide of cultural standards. William Wilberforce was wrong in the eighteenth century to oppose slavery; the British were immoral in opposing *suttee* in India (the burning of widows, which is now illegal in India). The early Christians were wrong in refusing to serve in the Roman army or to bow down to Caesar, since the majority in the Roman Empire believed that these two acts were moral duties. In fact, Jesus himself was immoral in breaking the law of His day by healing on the Sabbath day and by advocating the principles of the Sermon on the Mount, since it is clear that few in His time (or in ours) accepted them.

Yet we normally feel just the opposite, that the reformer is a courageous innovator who is right, who has the truth, against the mindless majority. Sometimes the individual must stand alone with the truth, risking social censure and persecution.

As Dr. Stockman says in Ibsen's *Enemy of the People*, after he loses the battle to declare his town's profitable but polluted tourist spa unsanitary, "The most dangerous enemy of the truth and freedom among us—is the compact majority. Yes, the damned, compact and liberal majority. The majority has *might*—unfortunately—but *right* it is not. Right—are I and a few others." Yet if relativism is correct, the opposite is necessarily the case. Truth is with the crowd and error with the individual.

Similarly, conventional ethical relativism entails disturbing judgments about the law. Our normal view is that we have a prima facie duty to obey the law, because law, in general, promotes the human good. According to most objective systems, this obligation is not absolute but relative to the particular law's relation to a wider moral order. Civil disobedience is warranted in some cases where the law seems to be in serious conflict with morality. However, if moral relativism is true, then neither law nor civil disobedience has a firm foundation. On the one hand, from the side of the society at large, civil disobedience will be morally wrong, so long as the majority culture agrees with the law in question. On the other hand, if you belong to the relevant subculture which doesn't recognize the particular law in question (because it is unjust from your point of view), disobedience will be morally mandated. The Ku Klux Klan, which believes that Jews, Catholics, and Blacks are evil or undeserving of high regard, are, given conventionalism, morally permitted or required to break the laws which protect these endangered groups. Why should I obey a law that my group doesn't recognize as valid?

To sum up, unless we have an independent moral basis for law, it is hard to see why we have any general duty to obey it; and unless we recognize the priority of a universal moral law, we have no firm basis to justify our acts of civil disobedience against "unjust laws." Both the validity of law and morally motivated disobedience of unjust laws are annulled in favor of a power struggle.

There is an even more basic problem with the notion that morality is dependent on cultural acceptance for its validity. The problem is that the notion of a *culture* or *society* is notoriously difficult to define. This is especially so in a pluralistic society like our own where the notion seems to be vague with unclear boundary lines. One person may belong to several societies (subcultures) with different value emphases and arrangements of principles. A person may belong to the nation as a single society with certain values of patriotism, honor, courage, laws (including some which are controversial but have majority acceptance, such as the current law on abortion). But he or she may also belong to a church which opposes some of the laws of the state. He may also be an integral member of a socially mixed community where different principles hold sway, and he may belong to clubs and a family where still other rules are adhered to. Relativism would seem to tell us that where he is a member of societies with conflicting moralities, he must be judged both wrong and not-wrong whatever he does. For example, if Mary is a U.S. citizen and a member of the Roman Catholic Church, she is wrong (qua Catholic) if she chooses to have an abortion and not-wrong (qua citizen of the U.S.A.) if she acts against the teaching of the Church on abortion. As a member of a racist university fraternity, KKK, John has no obligation to treat his fellow Black student as an equal, but as a member of the university community itself (where the principle of equal rights is accepted) he does have the obligation; but as a member of the surrounding community (which may reject the principle of equal rights) he again has no such obligation; but then again as a member of the nation at large (which accepts the principle) he is obligated to treat his fellow with respect. What is the morally right thing for John to do? The question no longer makes much sense in this moral Babel. It has lost its action-guiding function.

Perhaps the relativist would adhere to a principle which says that in such cases the individual may choose which group to belong to as primary.

If Mary chooses to have an abortion, she is choosing to belong to the general society relative to that principle. And John must likewise choose among groups. The trouble with this option is that it seems to lead back to counter-intuitive results. If Murder Mike of Murder, Incorporated, feels like killing Bank President Ortcutt and wants to feel good about it, he identifies with the Murder, Incorporated society rather than the general public morality. Does this justify the killing? In fact, couldn't one justify anything simply by forming a small subculture that approved of it? Ted Bundy would be morally pure in raping and killing innocents simply by virtue of forming a little coterie. How large must the group be in order to be a legitimate subculture or society? Does it need ten or fifteen people? How about just three? Come to think about it, why can't my burglary partner and I found our own society with a morality of its own? Of course, if my partner dies, I could still claim that I was acting from an originally social set of norms. But why can't I dispense with the interpersonal agreements altogether and invent my own morality—since morality, on this view, is only an invention anyway? Conventionalist relativism seems to reduce to subjectivism. And subjectivism leads, as we have seen, to moral solipsism, to the demise of morality altogether.

Should one object that this is an instance of the *Slippery Slope Fallacy*,[9] let that person give an alternative analysis of what constitutes a viable social basis for generating valid (or true) moral principles. Perhaps we might agree (for the sake of argument, at least) that the very nature of morality entails two people making an agreement. This move saves the conventionalist from moral solipsism, but it still permits almost any principle at all to count as moral. And what's more, those principles can be thrown out and their contraries substituted for them as the need arises. If two or three people decide that they will make cheating on exams morally acceptable for themselves, via forming a fraternity "Cheaters Anonymous" at their university, then cheating becomes moral. Why not? Why not rape, as well?

However, I don't think you can stop the move from conventionalism to subjectivism. The essential force of the validity of the chosen moral principle is that it is dependent on *choice.* The conventionalist holds that it is the choice of the group, but why should I accept the group's silly choice, when my own is better (for me)? Why should anyone give such august authority to a culture of society? If this is all morality comes to, why not reject it altogether—even though one might want to adhere to its directives when others are looking in order to escape sanctions?

4. A Critique of Ethical Relativism

However, while we may fear the demise of morality, as we have known it, this in itself may not be a good reason for rejecting relativism. That is, for judging it false. Alas, truth may not always be edifying. But the consequences of this position are sufficiently alarming to prompt us to look carefully for some weakness in the relativist's argument. So let us examine the premises and conclusion listed at the beginning of this essay as the three theses of relativism.

1. *The Diversity Thesis.* What is considered morally right and wrong varies from society to society, so that there are no moral principles accepted by all societies.
2. *The Dependency Thesis.* All moral principles derive their validity from cultural acceptance.
3. *Ethical Relativism.* Therefore, there are no universally valid moral principles, objective standards which apply to all people everywhere and at all times.

Does any one of these seem problematic? Let us consider the first thesis, the diversity thesis, which we have also called cultural relativism. Perhaps there is not as much diversity as anthropologists like Sumner and Benedict suppose. One can also see great similarities between the moral codes of various cultures. E. O. Wilson has identified over a score of common features,[10] and before him

Clyde Kluckhohn has noted some significant common ground.

Every culture has a concept of murder, distinguishing this from execution, killing in war, and other "justifiable homicides." The notions of incest and other regulations upon sexual behavior, the prohibitions upon untruth under defined circumstances, of restitution and reciprocity, of mutual obligations between parents and children—these and many other moral concepts are altogether universal.[11]

Colin Turnbull's description of the sadistic, semidisplaced, disintegrating Ik tribe in Northern Uganda supports the view that a people without principles of kindness, loyalty, and cooperation will degenerate into a Hobbesian state of nature. But he has also produced evidence that underneath the surface of this dying society, there is a deeper moral code, from a time when the tribe flourished, which occasionally surfaces and shows its nobler face.

On the other hand, there is enormous cultural diversity, and many societies have radically different moral codes. Cultural relativism seems to be a fact, but even if it is, it does not by itself establish the truth of ethical relativism. Cultural diversity in itself is neutral between theories. For the objectivist could concede complete cultural relativism, but still defend a form of universalism; for he or she could argue that some cultures simply lack correct moral principles.[12]

On the other hand, a denial of complete cultural relativism (i.e., an admission of some universal principles) does not disprove ethical relativism. For even if we did find one or more universal principles, this would not prove that those principles had any objective status. We could still *imagine* a culture that was an exception to the rule and be unable to criticize it. So the first premise doesn't by itself imply ethical relativism, nor does its denial disprove ethical relativism.

We turn to the crucial second thesis, the dependency thesis. Morality does not occur in a vacuum; rather, what is considered morally right or wrong must be seen in a context, depending on the goals, wants, beliefs, history, and environment of the society in question. We distinguished a *weak* and a *strong* thesis of dependency. The weak thesis says that the application of principles depends on the particular cultural predicament, whereas the strong thesis affirms that the principles themselves depend on that predicament. The nonrelativist can accept a certain relativity in the way moral principles are *applied* in various cultures, depending on beliefs, history, and environment. For example, a raw environment with scarce natural resources may justify the Eskimos' brand of euthanasia to the objectivist, who in another environment would consistently reject that practice. The members of a tribe in the Sudan throw their deformed children into the river because of their belief that such infants *belong* to the hippopotamus, the god of the river. We believe that they have a false belief about this, but the point is that the same principles of respect for property and respect for human life are operative in these contrary practices. They differ with us only in belief, not in substantive moral principle. This is an illustration of how nonmoral beliefs (e.g., deformed children belong to the hippopotamus) when applied to common moral principles (e.g., give to each his due) generate different actions in different cultures. In our own culture the difference in the nonmoral belief about the status of a fetus generates opposite moral prescriptions. The major difference between pro-choicers and pro-lifers is not whether we should kill persons but whether fetuses are really persons. It is a debate about the facts of the matter, not the principle of killing innocent persons.

So the fact that moral principles are weakly dependent doesn't show that ethical relativism is valid. In spite of this weak dependency on nonmoral factors, there could still be a set of general moral norms applicable to all cultures and even recognized in most, which are disregarded at a culture's own expense.

What the relativist needs is a strong thesis of

dependency, that somehow all principles are essentially cultural inventions. But why should we choose to view morality this way? Is there anything to recommend the strong thesis over the weak thesis of dependency? The relativist may argue that in fact we don't have an obvious impartial standard from which to judge. "Who's to say which culture is right and which is wrong?" But this seems to be dubious. We can reason and perform thought experiments in order to make a case for one system over another. We may not be able to know with certainty that our moral beliefs are closer to the truth than those of another culture or those of others within our own culture, but we may be justified in believing that they are. If we can be closer to the truth regarding factual or scientific matters, why can't we be closer to the truth on moral matters? Why can't a culture be simply confused or wrong about its moral perceptions? Why can't we say that the society like the Ik which sees nothing wrong with enjoying watching its own children fall into fires is less moral in that regard than the culture that cherishes children and grants them protection and equal rights? To take such a stand is not to commit the fallacy of ethnocentrism, for we are seeking to derive principles through critical reason, not simply uncritical acceptance of one's own mores.

Many relativists embrace relativism as a default position. Objectivism makes no sense to them. I think this is Ladd and Harman's position, as the latter's quotation at the beginning of this article seems to indicate. Objectivism has insuperable problems, so the answer must be relativism. The only positive argument I know for the strong dependency thesis upon which ethical relativism rests is that of the indeterminacy of translation thesis. This theory, set forth by B. L. Whorf and W. V. Quine,[13] holds that languages are often so fundamentally different from one another that we cannot accurately translate concepts from one to another. But this thesis, while relatively true even within a language (each of us has an idiolect), seems falsified by experience. We do learn foreign languages and learn to translate across linguistic

frameworks. For example, people from a myriad of language groups come to the United States and learn English and communicate perfectly well. Rather than a complete hiatus, the interplay between these other cultures eventually enriches the English language with new concepts (for example, *forte / foible*, *taboo*, and *coup de grâce*), even as English has enriched (or "corrupted" as the French might argue) other languages. Even if it turns out that there is some indeterminacy of translation between language users, we should not infer from this that no translation or communication is possible. It seems reasonable to believe that general moral principles are precisely those things that can be communicated transculturally. The kind of common features that Kluckhohn and Wilson advance—duties of restitution and reciprocity, regulations on sexual behavior, obligations of parents to children, a no-unnecessary-harm principle, and a sense that the good should flourish and the guilty be punished—these and others constitute a common human experience, a common set of values within a common human predicament of struggling to survive and flourish in a world of scarce resources.[14] So it is possible to communicate cross-culturally and find that we agree on many of the important things in life. If this is so, then the indeterminacy of translation thesis, upon which relativism rests, must itself be relativized to the point where it is no objection to objective morality.

5. The Case for Moral Objectivism

If nonrelativists are to make their case, they will have to offer a better explanation of cultural diversity and why we should nevertheless adhere to moral objectivism. One way of doing this is to appeal to a divine law, and human sin, which causes deviation from that law. Although I think that human greed, selfishness, pride, self-deception, and other maladies have a great deal to do with moral differences and that religion may lend great support to morality, I don't think that a religious justification is necessary for the validity of moral principles. In any case, in this section I shall out-line a modest nonreligious objectivism, first by appealing to our intuitions and secondly by giving a naturalist account of morality that transcends individual cultures.

First, I must make it clear that I am distin-guishing moral *absolutism* from moral *objectivism*. The absolutist believes that there are nonover-rideable moral principles which ought never to be violated. Kant's system, or one version of it, is a good example. One ought never to break a promise, no matter what. Act utilitarianism also seems absolutist, for the principle, Do that act that has the most promise of yielding the most utility, is nonoverrideable. An objectivist need not posit any nonoverrideable principles, at least not in unqualified general form, and so need not be an absolutist. As Renford Bambrough put it,

To suggest that there is a *right* answer to a moral problem is at once to be accused of or credited with a belief in moral absolutes. But it is no more necessary to believe in moral absolutes in order to believe in moral objectivity than it is to believe in the existence of absolute space or absolute time in order to believe in the objectivity of temporal and spatial relations and of judgments about them.[15]

On the objectivist's account moral principles are what William Ross refers to as *prima facie* principles, valid rules of action which should gen-erally be adhered to, but which may be overridden by another moral principle in cases of moral con-flict. For example, while a principle of justice may generally outweigh a principle of benevolence, there are times when enormous good could be done by sacrificing a small amount of justice, so that an objectivist would be inclined to act ac-cording to the principle of benevolence. There may be some absolute or nonoverrideable princi-ples, but there need not be many or any for objec-tivism to be true.[16]

If we can establish or show that it is reasonable to believe that there is at least one objective moral principle which is binding on all people every-where in some ideal sense, we shall have shown that relativism is probably false and that a limited objectivism is true. Actually, I believe that there are many qualified general ethical principles which are binding on all rational beings, but one will suffice to refute relativism. The principle I've chosen is the following:

A. It is morally wrong to torture people for the fun of it.

I claim that this principle is binding on all ra-tional agents, so that if some agent, S, rejects A, we should not let that affect our intuition that A is a true principle but rather try to explain S's be-havior as perverse, ignorant, or irrational instead. For example, suppose Adolf Hitler doesn't accept A. Should that affect our confidence in the truth of A? Is it not more reasonable to infer that Adolf is morally deficient, morally blind, ignorant, or ir-rational than to suppose that his noncompliance is evidence against the truth of A?

Suppose further that there is a tribe of Hit-lerites somewhere who enjoy torturing people. The whole culture accepts torturing others for the fun of it. Suppose that Mother Teresa or Gandhi tries unsuccessfully to convince them that they should stop torturing people altogether, and they respond by torturing the reformers. Should this affect our confidence in A? Would it not be more reasonable to look for some explana-tion of Hitlerite behavior? For example, we might hypothesize that this tribe lacked a developed sense of sympathetic imagination which is neces-sary for the moral life. Or we might theorize that this tribe was on a lower evolutionary level than most *Homo sapiens*. Or we might simply conclude that the tribe was closer to a Hobbesian state of nature than most societies, and as such probably would not survive. But we need not know the cor-rect answer as to why the tribe was in such bad shape in order to maintain our confidence in A as a moral principle. If A is a basic or core belief for us, we will be more likely to doubt the Hitlerites' sanity or ability to think morally than to doubt the validity of A.

We can perhaps produce other candidates for membership in our minimally basic objective moral set. For example:

1. Do not kill innocent people.
2. Do not cause unnecessary pain or suffering.
3. Do not cheat or steal.
4. Keep your promises and honor your contracts.
5. Do not deprive another person of his or her freedom.
6. Do justice, treating equals equally and unequals unequally.
7. Tell the truth.
8. Help other people, at least when the cost to oneself is minimal.
9. Reciprocate (show gratitude for services rendered).
10. Obey just laws.

These ten principles are examples of the *core morality*, principles necessary for the good life. They are not arbitrary, for we can give reasons why they are necessary to social cohesion and human flourishing. Principles like the Golden Rule, not killing innocent people, treating equals equally, truth telling, promise keeping, and the like are central to the fluid progression of social interaction and the resolution of conflicts of which ethics are about (at least minimal morality is, even though there may be more to morality than simply these kinds of concerns). For example, language itself depends on a general and implicit commitment to the principle of truth telling. Accuracy of expression is a primitive form of truthfulness. Hence, every time we use words correctly we are telling the truth. Without this behavior, language wouldn't be possible. Likewise, without the recognition of a rule of promise keeping, contracts are of no avail and cooperation is less likely to occur. And without the protection of life and liberty, we could not secure our other goals.

A moral code or theory would be adequate if it contained a requisite set of these objective principles or the core morality, but there could be more than one adequate moral code or theory which contained different rankings of these principles and other principles consistent with *core morality*. That is, there may be a certain relativity to secondary principles (whether to opt for monogamy rather than polygamy, whether to include a principle of high altruism in the set of moral duties, whether to allocate more resources to medical care than to environmental concerns, whether to institute a law to drive on the left side of road or the right side of the road, and so forth), but in every morality a certain core will remain, though applied somewhat differently because of differences in environment, belief, tradition, and the like.

The core moral rules are analogous to the set of vitamins necessary for a healthy diet. We need an adequate amount of each vitamin—some humans more of one than another—but in prescribing a nutritional diet we don't have to set forth recipes, specific foods, place settings, or culinary habits. Gourmets will meet the requirements differently than ascetics and vegetarians, but the basic nutrients may be had by all without rigid regimentation or an absolute set of recipes.

Stated more positively, an objectivist who bases his or her moral system on a common human nature with common needs and desires might argue for objectivism somewhat in this manner:

1. Human nature is relatively similar in essential respects, having a common set of needs and interests.
2. Moral principles are functions of human needs and interests, instituted by reason in order to promote the most significant interests and needs of rational beings (and perhaps others).
3. Some moral principles will promote human interests and meet human needs better than others.
4. Those principles which will meet essential needs and promote the most significant interests of humans in optimal ways can be said to be objectively valid moral principles.
5. Therefore, since there is a common human nature, there is an objectively valid set of moral principles, applicable to all humanity.

This argument assumes that there is a common

human nature. In a sense, I accept a *strong dependency thesis*—morality *depends* on human nature and the needs and interests of humans in general, but not on any specific cultural choice. There is only one large human framework to which moral principles are relative.[17] I have considered the evidence for this claim toward the end of Section 4, but the relativist may object. I cannot defend it any further in this paper, but suppose we content ourselves with a less controversial first premise, stating that some principles will tend to promote the most significant interests of persons. The revised argument would go like this:

1. Objectively valid moral principles are those adherence to which meet the needs and promote the most significant interests of persons.
2. Some principles are such that adherence to them meets the needs and promotes the most significant interests of persons.
3. Therefore, there are some objectively valid moral principles.

Either argument would satisfy objectivism, but the former makes it clearer that it is our common human nature that generates the common principles.[18] However, as I mentioned, some philosophers might not like to be tied down to the concept of a common human nature, in which case the second version of the argument may be used. It has the advantage that even if it turned out that we did have somewhat different natures or that other creatures in the universe had somewhat different natures, some of the basic moral principles would still survive.

If this argument succeeds, there are ideal moralities (and not simply adequate ones). Of course, there could still be more than one ideal morality, from which presumably an ideal observer would choose under optimal conditions. The ideal observer may conclude that out of an infinite set of moralities two, three, or more combinations would tie for first place. One would expect that these would be similar, but there is every reason to believe that all of these would contain the set of core principles.

Of course, we don't know what an ideal observer would choose, but we can imagine that the conditions under which such an observer would choose would be conditions of maximal knowledge about the consequences of action-types and impartiality, second-order qualities which ensure that agents have the best chance of making the best decisions. If this is so, then the more we learn to judge impartially and the more we know about possible forms of life, the better chance we have to approximate an ideal moral system. And if there is the possibility of approximating ideal moral systems with an objective core and other objective components, then ethical relativism is certainly false. We can confidently dismiss it as an aberration and get on with the job of working out better moral systems.

Let me make the same point by appealing to your intuitions in another way. Imagine that you have been miraculously transported to the dark kingdom of hell, and there you get a glimpse of the sufferings of the damned. What is their punishment? Well, they have eternal back itches which ebb and flow constantly. But they cannot scratch their backs, for their arms are paralyzed in a frontal position, so they writhe with itchiness throughout eternity. But just as you are beginning to feel the itch in your own back, you are suddenly transported to heaven. What do you see in the kingdom of the blessed? Well, you see people with eternal back itches, who cannot scratch their own backs. But they are all smiling instead of writhing. Why? Because everyone has his or her arms stretched out to scratch someone else's back, and, so arranged in one big circle, a hell is turned into a heaven of ecstasy.

If we can imagine some states of affairs or cultures that are better than others in a way that depends on human action, we can ask what are those character traits that make them so. In our story people in heaven, but not in hell, cooperate for the amelioration of suffering and the production of pleasure. These are very primitive goods, not sufficient for a full-blown morality, but they give us a hint as to the objectivity of morality. Moral goodness has something to do with the ameliorating of suffering, the resolution of conflict, and the promotion of human flourishing. If our heaven is really better than the eternal itchiness of hell, then whatever makes it so is constitutively related to moral rightness.

6. An Explanation of the Attraction of Ethical Relativism

Why, then, is there such a strong inclination toward ethical relativism? I think that there are four reasons, which haven't been adequately emphasized. One is the fact that the options are usually presented as though absolutism and relativism were the only alternatives, so conventionalism wins out against an implausible competitor. At the beginning of this paper I referred to a student questionnaire that I have been giving for twenty years. It reads as follows: "Are there any ethical absolutes, moral duties binding on all persons at all times, or are moral duties relative to culture? Is there any alternative to these two positions?" Fewer than five percent suggest a third position and very few of them identify objectivism. Granted, it takes a little philosophical sophistication to make the crucial distinctions, and it is precisely for lack of this sophistication or reflection that relativism has procured its enormous prestige. But, as Ross and others have shown and as I have argued in this chapter, one can have an objective morality without being absolutist.

The second reason for an inclination toward ethical relativism is the confusion of moral objectivism with moral realism. A realist is a person who holds that moral values have independent existence, if only as emergent properties. The antirealist claims that they do not have independent existence. But objectivism is compatible with either of these views. All it calls for is deep intersubjective agreement among humans because of a common nature and common goals and needs.

An example of a philosopher who confuses objectivity with realism is the late J. L. Mackie, who rejects objectivism because there are no good arguments for the independent existence of moral values. He admits, however, that there is a great deal of intersubjectivity in ethics. "There could be agreement in valuing even if valuing is just something people do, even if this activity is not further validated. Subjective agreement would give intersubjective values, but intersubjectivity is not objectivity."[19] But Mackie fails to note that there are two kinds of intersubjectivity, and that one of them gives all that the objectivist wants for a moral theory. Consider the following situations of intersubjective agreement:

Set A

A1. All the children in first grade at School S would agree that playing in the mud is preferable to learning arithmetic.
A2. All the youth in the district would rather take drugs than go to school.
A3. All the people in Jonestown, British Guiana, agree that the Rev. Jones is a prophet from God, and they love him dearly.
A4. Almost all the people in community C voted for George Bush.

Set B

B1. All the thirsty desire water to quench their thirst.
B2. All humans (and animals) prefer pleasure to pain.
B3. Almost all people agree that living in society is more satisfying than living as hermits alone.

The naturalist contrasts these two sets of intersubjective agreements and says that the first set is accidental, not part of what it means to be a person, whereas the agreements in the second set are basic to being a person, basic to our nature. Agreement on the essence of morality, the core set, is the kind of intersubjective agreement more like the second kind, not the first. It is part of the essence of a human in community, part of what it means to flourish as a person, to agree and adhere to the moral code.

The third reason is that our recent sensitivity to cultural relativism and the evils of ethnocentricism, which have plagued the relations of Europeans and Americans with those of other cultures, has made us conscious of the frailty of many aspects of our moral repertoire, so that there is a tendency to wonder "Who's to judge what's really right or wrong?" However, the move from a reasonable cultural relativism, which rightly causes us to rethink our moral systems, to an ethical relativism, which causes us to give up the heart of morality altogether, is an instance of the fallacy of confusing factual or descriptive statements with normative ones. Cultural relativism doesn't entail ethical relativism. The very reason that we are against ethnocentricism constitutes the same basis for our being for an objective moral system: that impartial reason draws us to it.

We may well agree that cultures differ and that we ought to be cautious in condemning what we don't understand, but this in no way need imply that there are not better and worse ways of living. We can understand and excuse, to some degree at least, those who differ from our best notions of morality, without abdicating the notion that cultures without principles of justice or promise keeping or protection of the innocent are morally poorer for these omissions.

A fourth reason which has driven some to moral nihilism and others to relativism is the decline of religion in Western society. As one of Dostoevsky's characters has said, "If God is dead, all things are permitted." The person who has lost religious faith feels a deep vacuum and understandably confuses it with a moral vacuum, or he or she finally resigns to a form of secular conventionalism. Such people reason that if there is no God to guarantee the validity of the moral order, there must not be a universal moral order. There is just radical cultural diversity and death at the end. But even if there turns out to be no God and no immortality, we still will want to live happy, meaningful lives during our fourscore years on earth. If this is true, then it matters by which principles we live, and those which win

out in the test of time will be objectively valid principles.

In conclusion I have argued (1) that cultural relativism (the fact that there are cultural differences regarding moral principles) does not entail ethical relativism (the thesis that there are no objectively valid universal moral principles); (2) that the dependency thesis (that morality derives its legitimacy from individual cultural acceptance) is mistaken; and (3) that there are universal moral principles based on a common human nature and a need to solve conflicts of interest and flourish.

So "Who's to judge what's right or wrong?" We are. We are to do so on the basis of the best reasoning we can bring forth, and with sympathy and understanding.[20]

Notes

1. Gilbert Harman, "Is There a Single True Morality?" in *Morality, Reason and Truth*, eds. David Copp and David Zimmerman (Rowman & Allenheld, 1984).

2. John Ladd, *Ethical Relativism* (Wadsworth, 1973).

3. Lest I be misunderstood, in this essay I will generally be speaking about the validity rather than the truth of moral principles. Validity holds that they are proper guides to action, whereas truth presupposes something more. It presupposes Moral Realism, the theory that moral principles have special ontological status (see Part IX). Although this may be true, not all objectivists agree. R. M. Hare, for instance, argues that moral principles, while valid, do not have truth value. They are like imperatives which have practical application but cannot be said to be true. Also, I am mainly concerned with the status of *principles*, not theories themselves. There may be a plurality of valid moral theories, all containing the same objective principles. I am grateful to Edward Sherline for drawing this distinction to my attention.

4. Reported by the anthropologist Powers, *Tribes of California*, p. 178. Quoted in E. Westermarck, *Origin and Development of Moral Ideals* (London, 1906), p. 386. This work is a mine of examples of cultural diversity.

5. W. G. Sumner, *Folkways* (Ginn & Co., 1906), p. 76.

6. This is a paraphrased and rewritten statement of

Ted Bundy by Harry V. Jaffa, *Homosexuality and the Natural Law* (Claremont, CA: The Claremont Institute of the Study of Statesmanship and Political Philosophy, 1990), 3–4.

7. Ruth Benedict, *Patterns of Culture* (New American Library, 1934), p. 257.

8. Melville Herskovits, *Cultural Relativism* (Random House, 1972).

9. The fallacy of objecting to a proposition on the erroneous grounds that, if accepted, it will lead to a chain of states of affairs which are absurd or unacceptable.

10. E. O. Wilson, *On Human Nature* (Bantam Books, 1979), pp. 22–23.

11. Clyde Kluckhohn, "Ethical Relativity: Sic et Non," *Journal of Philosophy*, LII (1955).

12. Colin Turnbull, *The Mountain People* (New York: Simon & Schuster, 1972).

13. See Benjamin Whorf, *Language, Thought and Reality* (MIT Press, 1956); and W. V. Quine, *Word and Object* (MIT Press, 1960), and *Ontological Relativity* (Columbia University Press, 1969).

14. David Hume gave the classic expression to this idea of a common human nature when he wrote:

It is universally acknowledged that there is a great uniformity among the actions of men, in all nations and ages, and that human nature remains still the same, in its principles and operations. The same events follow from the same causes. Ambition, avarice, self-love, vanity, friendship, generosity, public spirit; these passions, mixed in various degrees, and distributed through society, have been, from the beginning of the world, and still are, the source of all the actions and enterprises which have ever been observed among mankind. Would you know the sentiments, inclinations, and course of life of the Greeks and Romans? Study well the temper and actions of the French and English: you cannot be much mistaken in transferring to the former most of the observations which you have made with regard to the latter. Mankind are so much the same, in all times and places, that history informs us of nothing new or strange in that particular. Its chief use is only to discover the constant and universal principles of human nature, by showing men in all varieties of circumstances and situations, and furnishing us with materials, from which we may form our observations, and become acquainted with the regular springs of human action and behavior. These records of wars, intrigues, factions, and revolutions, are so many collections of experiments by which the politician or moral philosopher fixes the principles of his science; in the same manner as the physician or natural philosopher becomes acquainted with the nature of plants, minerals, and other external objects, by the experiments which he forms concerning them. Nor are the earth, water, and other elements examined by Aristotle and Hippocrates more like to those which at present lie under our observation than the men described by Polybius and Tacitus are to those who now govern the world. *Essays, Moral, Political and Literary* (Longman, Green, 1875).

15. Renford Bambrough, *Moral Skepticism and Moral Knowledge* (London: Routledge & Kegan Paul, 1979), p. 33.

16. William Ross, *The Right and the Good* (Oxford University Press, 1931), p. 18f.

17. In his essay "Moral Relativism" in *Moral Relativism and Moral Objectivity* (Blackwell, 1996) by Gilbert Harman and Judith Jarvis Thomson, Harman defines moral relativism as the claim that "There is no single true morality. There are many different moral frameworks, none of which is more correct than the others." (p. 5) I hold that morality has a function of serving the needs and interests of human beings, so that some frameworks do this better than others. Essentially, all adequate theories will contain the principles I have identified in this essay.

18. I owe the reformulation of the argument to Bruce Russell. Edward Sherline has objected (in correspondence) that assuming a common human nature in the first argument begs the question against the relativist. You may be the judge.

19. J. L. Mackie, *Ethics: Inventing Right and Wrong* (Penguin, 1977), p. 22.

20. Bruce Russell, Morton Winston, Edward Sherline, and an anonymous reviewer made important criticisms on earlier versions of this article, issuing in this revision.

6

A Defense of Ethical Relativism

GILBERT HARMAN

Gilbert Harman is Stuart Professor of Philosophy at Princeton University. He is author of important works in many areas of philosophy, including epistemology, action theory, practical reason, and moral philosophy. In this selection, Harman defends a form of ethical relativism according to which our moral obligations are relative to agreements we make and to our reasons for entering into those agreements.

1. Moral Conventions

Hume says that some, but not all, aspects of morality rest on "convention." There is a convention in Hume's sense when each of a number of people adheres to certain principles so that each of the others will also adhere to these principles. I adhere to the principles in my dealings with the others because I benefit from their adherence to these principles in their dealings with me and because I think that they will stop adhering to these principles in their dealings with me unless I continue to adhere to the principles in my dealings with them. For example, two farmers have a convention of helping each other till their fields. Farmer A helps farmer B till his fields so that when it comes time to till farmer A's fields, farmer B will help farmer A. Each farmer benefits from this practice, which depends upon their expectation that the other will continue it.

Hume mentions other conventions of this sort, for example those that give rise to the

Reprinted by permission of the publisher from Gilbert Harman, *The Nature of Morality*, pp. 103–114. Copyright © 1977 by Oxford University Press.

institutions of money. Certain pieces of paper can be traded for goods only because they will be accepted in turn by others in exchange for their goods. The conventions of language provide another example, one which indicates that conventions may be extremely subtle and even impossible for an ordinary person to describe in any precise and explicit way.

Conventions are reached through a process of implicit bargaining and mutual adjustment. Two people rowing a boat will adjust their actions with respect to each other so that they pull at the same time. It does not matter what their rate is, as long as both row at the same rate. If one tries to row more quickly and the other tries to row more slowly, some sort of compromise will have to be reached.

Among the most important conventions, according to Hume, are those having to do with property. It is useful to each person that there should be a system of security regarding possessions. This system is entirely conventional; and until it develops, there is no such thing as property. Another important convention is the one that makes possible explicit contracts and promises. The convention is that, by using a certain form of words (or other sign), a person binds himself to do what he says he will do. The obligation to keep your promises therefore itself derives from a prior convention, according to Hume.

Hume says that the original motive to observe conventions is "natural" rather than moral, by which he means that it is a self-interested motive. Initially, each person continues to adhere to the conventional principles in his dealings with others so that they will continue to do so in their dealings with him. Eventually habits develop. Action in accordance with those principles becomes relatively automatic; it would be hard to change. Obligations based on those principles come to seem natural and obvious. According to Hume, these "natural" obligations will strike us as moral as soon as we reflect sympathetically on the usefulness of the relevant conventions to human society. For, as you will recall, Hume accepts a kind of ideal observer theory. In his view, moral judgments express feelings based on sympathy.

Hume himself does not think that everything about morality is conventional, although he thinks that much is. He holds that sympathy can lead us to approve or disapprove of some things apart from prior conventions—for example, we will approve of kindness to others even in a state of nature—and, in Hume's view, this is moral approval. But he would probably agree that moral *obligations* and *duties* depend on convention; in any event, I will assume in what follows that this is part of Hume's theory.

A more extreme theory than Hume's would treat every aspect of morality as conventional. For example, when Hume believes that a weak sympathy for others is built into people, it might be supposed instead that sympathy itself derives from a convention whereby people tacitly agree to respect each other at least to the extent of trying to feel sympathy for others. But we do not need to decide between Hume's theory and this more extreme version.

Hume's tacit convention theory of morality is a more specific version of the social custom theory. It has a number of advantages. For one thing, it provides a more specific account of the way in which morality involves social utility: certain rules are conventionally adopted because each person benefits from everyone else acting in accordance with those rules. We therefore expect rules to be adopted if they promote social utility in the sense that they are beneficial to all.

To take another example, [. . .] we do not normally assume that you are obligated to help someone when you know that he would not help you if the situation were reversed; we feel that to help such a person would be to do something that is above and beyond the call of duty, a generous act rather than something you are obligated to do. But this is just what we would expect given Hume's theory. There are reasons of self-interest for people to adopt a convention of *mutual* aid, but no obvious reasons of this sort to extend this convention to aid those who do not participate in the convention. So, given Hume's theory, we would not expect an obligation or duty to help the person who would not help you. On the other hand, sympathy would lead an observer to approve of your helping this person; so, given Hume's theory, it would be a good thing if you were to help him even though you are not obligated to do so.

We [are reluctant] to blame cannibals for eating human flesh, despite our abhorrence of their doing so and our view that it would be wrong for any of us to do so while visiting a society that practiced cannibalism. Given Hume's theory we might explain our own aversion to the eating of human flesh in the following way. We have a tacit convention in our society that we will respect each other as people. We will, in Kant's phrase, "treat people as ends," as if they were sacred and possessed a special kind of dignity. Furthermore, there are various conventional forms in which we have come to express our respect and we have therefore come to see it as demeaning to human dignity if persons are not treated according to these conventions. For example, if someone dies, we think it appropriate to hold a funeral and bury the body or perhaps cremate it. Given our current conventions, we will not eat the body. To do that would strike us as an insult to the memory of the person who has died. It would indicate a lack of respect for persons as persons. Our respect for people and our conventional habits of expressing that respect lead us automatically to reject the idea that we could eat human flesh; indeed, we have come to find the very idea disgusting.

Our reactions to the cannibals are complicated, however, because two moralities are relevant, theirs and ours. In judging the situation, we can simply appeal to our own morality: "Eating people is wrong!" But in judging the cannibals themselves, we must take their morality into account. We cannot simply blame them for what they do, because their moral understanding is not the same as ours. They see nothing wrong with eating people; and there is no obvious reason why they should. This makes it difficult for us to judge that it is wrong *of them* to eat human flesh. We do not feel comfortable in judging the cannibals themselves to be wrong. It does not seem right to say that each of them ought morally not to eat human flesh or that each of them has a moral duty or obligation not to do so. At best we might say that it ought not to be the case that they eat human flesh; but as we have seen before that is not the same sort of judgment at all. From our own point of view we can judge their acts and their situation, even their society and morality; but we cannot, it seems, judge *them*.

[. . . .] We are inclined to suppose that a person ought morally not to have done a particular thing only if we can also assume that he had a reason not to do it. We could not suppose that the cannibals ought morally not to eat human flesh unless we also supposed that they have a reason not to eat human flesh. The trouble is that we are presently assuming that they have no such reason, because their morality is not the same as ours. Given this assumption, we can make certain moral or evaluative judgments about the cannibals; for example, we can call them "ignorant savages." But we cannot correctly say of them that they are morally wrong to eat human flesh or that they ought morally not to do it.

2. Judging Outsiders

Now, it is very difficult to get a clear grasp on such examples just because it is not always clear when someone has a reason to do something and when he does not. To take a very different sort of example, Hitler, who had millions of people killed, was an extraordinarily evil man. In some sense we can say that he ought not to have killed those people and that what he did was wrong. Yet the following remarks are weak and even in some way odd: "It was wrong of Hitler to have ordered the extermination of the Jews." "Hitler ought morally not to have ordered the extermination of the Jews."

One might suppose that it is the enormity of Hitler's crime against humanity that makes such remarks seem too weak. He killed so many people; it would have been wrong of him to have killed only one. To say simply that it was wrong of him to have ordered the extermination of the Jews suggests that it was *only* wrong—that it is wrong only in the way in which murder is wrong. And, given what Hitler did, that is as if one were to say that it was *naughty* of Hitler to have ordered the extermination of the Jews.

This explanation, however, is not completely satisfactory. First of all, there are things we can say about Hitler without the same sort of oddity. Although it would be odd to say that it was wrong of Hitler to have acted as he did, it is not equally odd to say that what Hitler did was wrong. Similarly, there is no oddness in the remark, "What Hitler did ought never to have happened." That is not odd in the way that it is odd to say, "Hitler ought morally not to have ordered the extermination of the Jews." But, if the enormity of his crime makes the one remark odd, why doesn't it make the other remark as odd?

Another reason for doubting that the enormity of the crime, by itself, is the reason for the oddness in certain of these judgments is that we can make these very judgments about someone who has committed an equally enormous crime, at least if enormity is measured in numbers of people killed. For example, Stalin was also a mass murderer who ordered the purges of the thirties knowing that millions of people would be killed. Yet it is possible to think that Stalin was really only trying to do the right thing, that he hated the prospect of the purges, that he was however also alarmed at the consequences of not ordering the purges because he was afraid that the revolution was in danger of collapse. He found himself faced with a terrible choice and he opted for what he took to be the lesser of two evils. I am not suggesting that this is the truth about Stalin; it probably is not. I mean only that this is a possible view of Stalin. Of course, even someone taking such a sympathetic view of Stalin can suppose that Stalin was terribly mistaken. To take this view of Stalin is certainly not to condone Stalin's actions. It can never be right to order the deaths of millions of people like that, no matter what you hope to gain. Indeed, taking this view of Stalin, it is natural to say that it was wrong of Stalin to have ordered the purges; Stalin was morally wrong to have done so. The interesting question, then, is why is it not odd to say this about Stalin in the way that it is odd to say the same thing about Hitler. It cannot be the vast numbers of people killed that makes a difference, since vast numbers were killed by both men. And certainly the judgment that it was wrong of Stalin to have ordered the purges is not the judgment that it was *naughty* of him to have done so. Why then does it seem that if you say that it was wrong of Hitler to have done what he did you are saying something as odd and ridiculous as if you had said that it was naughty of Hitler to have done that.

Part of the answer has to do with our conception of the attitudes that we think Hitler and Stalin took toward their crimes, with the moral principles we think of them accepting, with our views of what they considered to be reasons for action. Hitler's attitude was in this respect much more extreme than Stalin's. Hitler is farther from us than Stalin is (or as Stalin is imagined to be in the view of him that I have sketched). Hitler is beyond the pale in a way that Stalin was not. Hitler was not just immoral, he was amoral, he was evil. Stalin was terrible and also, perhaps, evil; but he was not wholly beyond the reaches of morality as I have imagined him. We cannot but think of Hitler as beyond the reaches of morality or at least that part of morality that we invoke in judging him to be an evil man.

In saying that it was wrong of Hitler to have ordered the extermination of the Jews we would be saying that Hitler had a reason (every reason in the world) not to do what he did. But what is horrible about someone who did what he did is that he could not have had such a reason. If he was willing to exterminate a whole people, there was no reason for him not to do so: that is just what is so terrible about him. That is why it sounds too weak to say that it was wrong of him to do what he did. It suggests that he had a reason not to act as he did and we feel that any man who could have done what Hitler did must be the sort of man who would not have had a reason not to do it. Such a man is evil rather than wrong.

This is why it is odd to say that it was wrong of Hitler to have acted as he did but it is not odd to say that Hitler's act was wrong. The judgment that Hitler's act was wrong and the judgment that it never ought to have happened do not imply that Hitler had a reason not to do what he did. The fact that we feel that Hitler was not the sort of person who could have had such a reason does not undermine judgments of his *acts* in the way that it undermines certain judgments about *him*.

All this is explicable in Hume's tacit convention theory. Hitler, like the cannibals, is outside our morality, although in a different direction. We can judge his acts with reference to our morality, but not Hitler himself, since that would imply that he was someone who acknowledged the moral standards we use to judge him. To say, "It was wrong of Hitler" or "Hitler ought morally not to have done it" would imply that Hitler accepted the relevant moral conventions. But his actions show that he does not accept those conventions. He is therefore beyond the pale and an enemy of humanity.

There are other examples that confirm the same point. Consider judgments that we might make about Martians who felt no concern for us. Suppose that these Martians would not be deterred from a given course of action simply by the reflection that that course of action would harm some human being. These Martians would not treat such a consideration as any sort of reason. For them, the consideration would simply not tell against that course of action at all. In that case, we cannot say that it would be morally wrong of the Martians to harm us.

This is to disagree with Kant, who would say that, since a Martian is a rational being, it has a reason not to harm any of us, because we too are rational beings.[1] "The Martian would not agree to our harming it; so how can it agree to its harming us?" Kant believes that reflection of this sort can provide the Martian with motivation not to harm us. If Kant were right, there would be no need for moral conventions. We could make do with pure practical reason alone.

Now a defender of Hume's tacit convention theory will assume, plausibly, that Kant is mistaken about the powers of pure practical reason. When we first come across the Martians, they may well have no reason to be concerned about us at all, and, in that case, there are no moral constraints on them in their dealings with us. If they harm us, that is not a matter of morality or immorality, although it may well be a matter of war between the planets. If it turns out that there is no way for us to harm the Martians, so that they do not need to be concerned about us even for reasons of self-interest, then a morality that encompasses us and them may never develop.

On the other hand, if a conflict develops that is in neither their interest nor ours, we and they may try to arrive at conventions that would reduce or eliminate this sort of conflict. For example, we and they might adopt a convention of respect for each other as rational beings that would involve, among other things, trying to avoid actions that would harm other rational beings. In that case, there would be a morality encompassing us and them.

This is how a morality would arise from a state of nature, according to a tacit convention theory. Before any conventions were established, there would be no such thing as right and wrong; it would not make sense to judge what people morally ought or ought not to do. But once a group of people developed conventional patterns of action in order to avoid conflicts with each other, their actions could be judged with reference to those conventions. People who remained outside the relevant group and still in a state of nature could, however, not be so judged.

3. Conventional Aspects of Morality

One reason for thinking that morality has arisen like this, as the result of convention, is that certain elements in our actual moral views seem to reflect what would be the result of implicit bargaining and mutual adjustments between people of different powers and resources. For example, consider a point I have alluded to several times. In our morality, harming someone is thought to be much worse than helping someone. That is why we suppose that a doctor cannot cut up one patient in order to save five other patients by distributing the one patient's organs according to need. Now, this general principle about harming and not helping may seem irrational and unmotivated, but it makes sense if we suppose that our moral views derive from a tacit convention that arose among people of different wealth, status, and power. For, whereas everyone would benefit equally from a conventional practice of trying not to harm each other, some people would benefit considerably more than others from a convention to help those who needed help. The rich and powerful do not need much help and are often in the best position to give it; so, if a strong principle of mutual aid were adopted, they would gain little and lose a great deal, because they would end up doing most of the helping and would receive little in return. On the other hand, the poor and weak might refuse to agree to a principle of noninterference or noninjury unless they also reached some agreement on mutual aid. We would therefore expect a compromise. [For . . .] the expected compromise would involve a strong principle of noninjury and a much weaker principle of mutual aid—which is just what we now have. If our moral principles were not in this way a result of bargaining and adjustment, it would be hard to see why we would suppose that there is this moral difference between harming and not helping; and it would be hard to understand how our moral principles could be the result of bargaining and adjustment in this way unless they were derived from some sort of convention in Hume's sense. So, this aspect of our moral views is evidence in favor of Hume's tacit convention theory.

Now, it is important that Hume's theory is an *actual* convention theory. Duties and obligations are seen as deriving from actual, not hypothetical, conventions. Hume's theory is therefore to be distinguished from hypothetical agreement theories that say that the correct moral rules are those that people *would* agree to under certain conditons of equality. Hume's explanation of moral motivation requires his actual convention theory and does not work on any sort of hypothetical agreement theory. Hume says that we act morally first out of self-interest and then out of a habit of following certain conventional rules. We cannot in the same way explain why someone would be motivated to adhere to principles he *would have* agreed to adhere to in a position of equality.

Furthermore, the suggested explanation of the moral difference we recognize between harming and not helping depends on the assumption that our morality rests on an actual convention among people of different powers and resources. It is not easy to see how this aspect of our moral views could be explained by assuming that obligations depend on what we *would* agree to in a position of equality. For, in such a position, it seems likely that we would not agree to our present moral principles.

4. The Tacit Convention Theory and Kant's Theory

Finally, it should also be observed that the tacit convention theory follows important aspects of Kant's theory, even though it rejects one of Kant's key ideas. Kant argued that we must think of the principles of morality as principles that each of us legislates for himself and for others, whom we perceive as also legislating the same principles.[. . .] The tacit convention theory, like Kant's theory, sees moral principles as principles for which the source is both internal and external. They are principles legislated by others and by yourself. They represent the principles of a general will. Kant was wrong in thinking that these principles are determined by reason alone and therefore wrong to assume that they were universal. Nevertheless he was right to emphasize their objectivity and interpersonal character. The private principles of one person, which that person does not take to be shared by others, do not represent a normal case of moral principles. At best, they represent a limiting case. Morality is essentially social.

The tacit convention theory of morality is therefore not a version of pure externalism. It is a combination: internalism plus externalism. The principles that apply to you, according to this theory, are not simply whatever principles are conventionally accepted by the surrounding group; you must accept the conventions too. Otherwise they could not give you reasons to do things, and judgment about what you ought morally to do or about what it would be right or wrong of you to do could not be made with reference to those conventions. An amoral person can exist in the midst of others who share a common morality. But such a person can no more be judged in terms of other people's principles than can Hitler or the cannibals. If a Martian who does not care about human life decides to live in our midst but does not see any reason to accept our conventions, we cannot say correctly that the Martian is morally obligated not to harm us (although we can judge that it would be a bad thing if the Martians were to harm us). Similarly, it would be a misuse of language to say of hardened professional criminals that it is morally wrong of them to steal from others or that they ought morally not to kill people. Since they do not share our conventions, they have no moral reasons to refrain from stealing from us or killing us. (On the other hand, we can judge them enemies of society and can say that they ought to be hunted down and put into prison.)

Moralities are social. The are defined by the conventions of groups. But you belong to more than one group, and different groups have different conventions. Which conventions determine your moral obligations? They all do. Since you belong to a number of different groups, you are subject to a number of different moralities—the morality of your family, perhaps your school, a professional morality (your "business ethics"), the morality of your neighborhood, the various moralities of various groups of friends, the morality of your country, and finally, perhaps, a limited morality you share with most of humanity. These moralities will sometimes be in conflict, and give rise to a tragic situation in which you are faced with a conflict of loyalties. In that case, there is no clear moral solution to your problem. You must choose the group which is most important to you and act on its conventions.

There is a limiting case of morality in which the relevant "group" contains only one person. In that case, a person will be able to say he has certain moral obligations deriving from his personal principles and will not judge others to be similarly obligated (by his principles). For example, a pacifist may think that he morally ought not to participate in wars, although he will not make the same judgment about other persons. He will not say that it is wrong of them to participate, although he will certainly think that it is bad for everyone that they engage in wars. And there are many other cases in which a person imposes moral obligations and duties on himself without supposing that other persons are similarly obligated.

This represents a limiting case of morality rather than a central case (even though it may be a common case) because we normally think of a morality as a set of principles that can be used to judge more than one person and because . . . we think of morality as imposing external constraints on someone. Without objective external constraints, there would be no such thing as morality, as we ordinarily understand it, even if people adhered to their own personal principles. If there were only individual moralities, only sets of personal principles and no group conventions, morality as we normally think of it would not yet exist.

Note

1. Immanuel Kant (1724–1804), German philosopher and author of many important philosophical works, including the monumental *Critique of Pure Reason* and *The Groundwork of the Metaphysics of Morals*, from which Reading 24 is taken.

PART III

Ethics and Egoism

Introduction

Why should we be moral? That is, why should we be moral when it is in our self-interest to be immoral? Or is it always really in our interest to be moral, despite appearances to the contrary? Or is morality only generally in our best interest, so that we may have to decide whether to follow its commands when they become too burdensome?

Egoism is a challenge to morality. It comes in two main forms. The first form, call it "egoism proper," admits that morality consists of a set of objective, altruistic or other-regarding principles but simply denies that we ought always to be moral. If we have good reason to be selfish, we should be so. The egoist admits that sometimes it is in our interest to be moral but asks, "Why should I be moral when it is not in my interest to be so?" This is the kind of egoism with which

Thrasymachus seems to end up (reading I.1) and which Glaucon puts forth as the devil's advocate in our first selection.

The second form, call it "ethical egoism," *universalizes* the egoist principle, thus making it a moral principle: "Everyone ought always to act in his or her self-interest." In this way the question, "Why be moral?" does not arise. True morality is simply enlightened self-interest. Thomas Hobbes sets forth a contractual theory of ethical egoism in our second reading, and Ayn Rand espouses a more individualist version in our third reading. James Rachels sets out a comprehensive critique of ethical egoism in our fourth reading, and, finally, Howard Kahane develops a theory of egoism within the context of sociobiological thought, arguing for a morality based on reciprocity.

7

Why Should I Be Moral?

PLATO

Glaucon, Plato's older brother, uneasy with Socrates' reply to Thrasymachus (see reading I.1), asks Socrates whether justice is good in itself or only a necessary evil. Glaucon sets forth the hypothesis that egoistic power seeking and pleasure seeking con-

Reprinted from *Plato's Republic,* trans. G. M. A. Grube (Indianapolis: Hackett Publishing Company, 1974), by permission of the publisher.

stitute the ideally good life. However, the hypothesis continues, reason alerts us that others might seek the same power, which would greatly interfere with our freedom and result in a state of chaos in which no one was happy. Therefore, we must compromise our quest for power and unmitigated pleasure. Morality constitutes this compromise. As a mutually agreed-upon set of restrictions aimed at preventing others from prospering at our expense, morality has no intrinsic but only instrumental value.

To illustrate his hypothesis Glaucon relates a myth of Gyges, a sheperd who discovers a ring that enables him to become invisible. Gyges uses the ring to attain the highest reaches of power and pleasure. Glaucon asks whether it is not plausible to suppose that we all would do likewise? Then he offers a thought experiment that compares the life of the seemingly just (but unjust) man who is the epitome of success with that of the seemingly unjust (but just) man who is the epitome of failure. Which would we choose?

In the second part of this reading, we have highlights of Socrates' solution to this question, Why should I be moral?

We enter the dialogue where we left off in selection I.1. Socrates has just shown that the type of egoism advocated by Thrasymachus is contradictory. Socrates is speaking.

When I had said this I thought I had done with the discussion, but evidently this was only a prelude. Glaucon on this occasion too showed that boldness which is characteristic of him, and refused to accept Thrasymachus's abandoning the argument. He said: Do you, Socrates want to appear to have persuaded us, or do you want truly to convince us that it is better in every way to be just than unjust?

I would certainly wish to convince you truly, I said, if I could.

Well, he said, you are certainly not attaining your wish. Tell me, do you think there is a kind of good which we welcome not because we desire its consequences but for its own sake: joy, for example, and all the harmless pleasures which have no further consequences beyond the joy which one finds in them?

Certainly, said I, I think there is such a good.

Further, there is the good which we welcome for its own sake and also for its consequences, knowledge for example and sight and health. Such things we somehow welcome on both counts.

Yes, said I.

Are you also aware of a third kind, he asked, such as physical training, being treated when ill, the practice of medicine, and other ways of making money? We should say that these are wearisome but beneficial to us; we should not want them for their own sake, but because of the rewards and other benefits which result from them.

There is certainly such a third kind, I said, but why do you ask?

Under which of these headings do you put justice? he asked.

I would myself put it in the finest class, I said, that which is to be welcomed both for itself and for its consequences by any man who is to be blessed with happiness.

That is not the opinion of the many, he said; they would put it in the wearisome class, to be pursued for the rewards and popularity which come from a good reputation, but to be avoided in itself as being difficult.

I know that is the general opinion, I said. Justice has now for some time been objected to by Thrasymachus on this score while injustice was extolled, but it seems I am a slow learner.

Come then, he said, listen to me also to see whether you are still of the same opinion, for I think that Thrasymachus gave up before he had to, charmed by you as by a snake charmer. I am not yet satisfied by the demonstration on either side. I am eager to hear the nature of each, of justice and injustice, and what effect its presence has upon the soul. I want to leave out of account the rewards and consequences of each. So, if you agree, I will do the following: I will renew the argument of Thrasymachus; I will first state what people consider the nature and origin of justice; secondly, that all who practice it do so unwillingly as being something necessary but not good; thirdly, that they have good reason to do so, for, according to what people say, the life of the unjust man is much better than that of the just.

It is not that I think so, Socrates, but I am perplexed and my ears are deafened listening to Thrasymachus and innumerable other speakers; I have never heard from anyone the sort of defense of justice that I want to hear, proving that it is better than injustice. I want to hear it praised for itself, and I think I am most likely to hear this from you. Therefore I am going to speak at length in praise of the unjust life, and in doing so I will show you the way I want to hear you denouncing injustice and praising justice. See whether you want to hear what I suggest.

I want it more than anything else, I said. Indeed, what subject would a man of sense talk and hear about more often with enjoyment?

Splendid, he said, then listen while I deal with the first subject I mentioned: the nature and origin of justice.

They say that to do wrong is naturally good, to be wronged is bad, but the suffering of injury so far exceeds in badness the good of inflicting it that when men have done wrong to each other and suffered it, and have had a taste of both, those who are unable to avoid the latter and practice the former decide that it is profitable to come to an agreement with each other neither to inflict injury nor to suffer it. As a result they begin to make laws and covenants, and the law's command they call lawful and just. This, they say, is the origin and essence of justice; it stands between the best and the worst, the best being to do wrong without paying the penalty and the worst to be wronged without the power of revenge. The just then is a mean between two extremes; it is welcomed and honored because of men's lack of the power to do wrong. The man who has that power, the real man, would not make a compact with anyone not to inflict injury or suffer it. For him that would be madness. This then, Socrates, is, according to their argument, the nature and origin of justice.

Even those who practice justice do so against their will because they lack the power to do wrong. This we could realize very clearly if we imagined ourselves granting to both the just and the unjust the freedom to do whatever they liked. We could then follow both of them and observe where their desires led them, and we would catch the just man redhanded traveling the same road as the unjust. The reason is the desire for undue gain which every organism by nature pursues as a

good, but the law forcibly sidetracks him to honor equality. The freedom I just mentioned would most easily occur if these men had the power which they say the ancestor of the Lydian Gyges possessed. The story is that he was a shepherd in the service of the ruler of Lydia. There was a violent rainstorm and an earthquake which broke open the ground and created a chasm at the place where he was tending sheep. Seeing this and marvelling, he went down into it. He saw, besides many other wonders of which we are told, a hollow bronze horse. There were window-like openings in it; he climbed through them and caught sight of a corpse which seemed of more than human stature, wearing nothing but a ring of gold on its finger. This ring the shepherd put on and came out. He arrived at the usual monthly meeting which reported to the king on the state of the flocks, wearing the ring. As he was sitting among the others he happened to twist the hoop of the ring towards himself, to the inside of his hand, and as he did this he became invisible to those sitting near him and they went on talking as if he had gone. He marvelled at this and, fingering the ring, he turned the hoop outward again and became visible. Perceiving this, he tested whether the ring had this power and so it happened: if he turned the hoop inwards he became invisible, but was visible when he turned it outwards. When he realized this, he at once arranged to become one of the messengers to the king. He went, committed adultery with the king's wife, attacked the king with her help, killed him, and took over the kingdom.

Now if there were two such rings, one worn by the just man, the other by the unjust, no one, as these people think, would be so incorruptible that he would stay on the path of justice or bring himself to keep away from other people's property and not touch it, when he could with impunity take whatever he wanted from the market, go into houses and have sexual relations with anyone he wanted, kill anyone, free all those he wished from prison, and do the other things which would make him like a god among men. His actions would be in no way different from those of the other and they would both follow the same path. This, some would say, is a great proof that no one is just willingly but under compulsion, so that justice is not one's private good, since wherever either thought he could do wrong with impunity he would do so. Every man believes that injustice is much more profitable to himself than justice, and any exponent of this argument will say that he is right. The man who did not wish to do wrong with that opportunity, and did not touch other people's property, would be thought by those who knew it to be very foolish and miserable. They would praise him in public, thus deceiving one another, for fear of being wronged. So much for my second topic.

As for the choice between the lives we are discussing, we shall be able to make a correct judgment about it only if we put the most just man and the most unjust man face to face; otherwise we cannot do so. By face to face I mean this: let us grant to the unjust the fullest degree of injustice and to the just the fullest justice, each being perfect in his own pursuit. First, the unjust man will act as clever craftsmen do—a top navigator, for example, or physician distinguishes what his craft can do and what it cannot; the former he will undertake, the latter he will pass by, and when he slips he can put things right. So the unjust man's correct attempts at wrongdoing must remain secret; the one who is caught must be considered a poor performer, for the extreme of injustice is to have a reputation for justice, and our perfectly unjust man must be granted perfection in injustice. We must not take this from him, but we must allow that, while committing the greatest crimes, he has provided himself with the greatest reputation for justice; if he makes a slip he must be able to put it right; he must be a sufficiently persuasive speaker if some wrongdoing of his is made public; he must be able to use force, where force is needed, with the help of his courage, his strength, and the friends and wealth with which he has provided himself.

Having described such a man, let us now in our argument put beside him the just man, simple as he is and noble, who, as Aeschylus put it, does not wish to appear just but to be so. We must take away his reputation, for a reputation for justice would bring him honor and rewards, and it would then not be clear whether he is what he is for justice's sake or for the sake of rewards and honor. We must strip him of everything except justice and make him the complete opposite of the other. Though he does no wrong, he must have the greatest reputation for wrongdoing so that he may be tested for justice by not weakening under ill repute and its consequences. Let him go his incorruptible way until death with a reputation for injustice throughout his life, just though he is, so that our two men may reach the extremes, one of justice, the other of injustice, and let them be judged as to which of the two is the happier.

Whew! My dear Glaucon, I said, what a mighty scouring you have given those two characters, as if they were statues in a competition.

I do the best I can, he replied. The two being such as I have described, there should be no difficulty in following the argument through as to what kind of life awaits each of them, but it must be said. And if what I say sounds rather boorish, Socrates, realize that it is not I who speak, but those who praise injustice as preferable to justice. They will say that the just man in these circumstances will be whipped, stretched on the rack, imprisoned, have this eyes burnt out, and, after suffering every kind of evil, he will be impaled and realize that one should not want to be just but to appear so. Indeed, Aeschylus's words are far more correctly applied to the unjust than to the just, for we shall be told that the unjust man pursues a course which is based on truth and not on appearances; he does not want to appear but to be unjust:

He harvests in his heart a deep furrow
from which good counsels grow.

He rules his city because of his reputation for justice, he marries into any family he wants to, he gives his children in marriage to anyone he wishes, he has contractual and other associations with anyone he may desire, and, beside all these advantages, he benefits in the pursuit of gain because he does not scruple to practice injustice. In any contest, public or private, he is the winner, getting the better of his enemies and accumulating wealth; he benefits his friends and does harm to his enemies. To the gods he offers grand sacrifices and gifts which will satisfy them, he can serve the gods much better than the just man, and also such men as he wants to, with the result that he is likely to be dearer to the gods. This is what they say, Socrates, that both from gods and men the unjust man secures a better life than the just. . . .

The Socratic Solution to the Problem of Why Be Moral?

Socrates has argued that the soul is made up of three parts: a rational part, a spirited part, and an appetitive or passionate part. Justice is defined as a harmony of the soul when each part fulfills its proper function—reason ruling, the spirit courageously serving reason, and the appetites living in temperance, being guided by reason. We join Socrates as he is discussing the relationship of the spirited part to the reasoning part.

These two parts will also most effectively stand on guard on behalf of the whole soul and the body, the one by planning, the other by fighting, following its leader, and by its courage fulfilling his decisions.—That is so.

It is this part which causes us to call an individual brave, when his spirit preserves in the midst of pain and pleasure his belief in the declarations of reason as to what he should fear and what he should not.—Right.

And we shall call him wise because of that small part of himself which ruled in him and made those declarations, which possesses the knowledge of what is beneficial to each part, and of what is to the common advantage of all three.—Quite so.

Further, shall we not call him moderate because of the friendly and harmonious relations between these same parts, when the rulers and the ruled hold a common belief that reason should rule, and they do not rebel against it?—Moderation, he said, is surely just that, both in the individual and the city.

And he will be just in the way we have often described.—Necessarily.

Now, I said, has our notion of justice become at all indistinct? Does it appear to be something different from what it was seen to be in the city?—I do not think so.

If any part of our soul still disputes this, we could altogether confirm it by bringing up common arguments.—What are they?

For example, concerning the city and the man similar to it by nature and training, if we had to come to an agreement whether we think that this man has embezzled a deposit of gold and silver, who, do you think, would consider him to have done this rather than men of a different type?—No one would.

And he would have nothing to do with temple robberies, thefts, or betrayals, either of friends in his private life, or, in public life, of cities?—Nothing.

Further, he would be in no way untrustworthy in keeping an oath or any other agreement.—How could he be?

Adultery too, disrespect for parents, neglect of the gods would suit his character less than any other man's.—Much less.

And the reason for all this is that every part within him fulfills its own function, be that ruling or being ruled?—Certainly that, and nothing else.

Are you still looking for justice to be anything else than this power which produces such men and such cities as we have described?—By Zeus, he said, not I.

We have then completely realized the dream we had when we suspected that, by the grace of god, we came upon a principle and mold of justice right at the beginning of the founding of our city.—Very definitely.

Indeed, Glaucon—and this is why it is useful—it was a sort of image of justice, namely, that it was right for one who is by nature a cobbler to cobble and to do nothing else, and for the carpenter to carpenter, and so with the others.—Apparently.

And justice was in truth, it appears, something like this. It does not lie in a man's external actions, but in the way he acts within himself, really concerned with himself and his inner parts. He does not allow each part of himself to perform the work of another, or the sections of his soul to meddle with one another. He orders what are in the true sense of the word his own affairs well; he is master of himself, puts things in order, is his own friend, harmonizes the three parts like the limiting notes of a musical scale, the high, the low, and the middle, and any others there may be between. He binds them all together, and himself from a plurality becomes a unity. Being thus moderate and harmonious, he now performs any action, be it about the acquisition of wealth, the care of his body, some public actions, or private contract.[1] In all these fields he thinks the just and beautiful action, which he names as such, to be that which preserves this inner harmony and indeed helps to achieve it, wisdom to be the knowledge which oversees this action, an unjust action to be that which always destroys it, and ignorance the belief which oversees that.—Socrates you are altogether right.

Very well, I said, we would then not be thought to be lying if we claim that we have found the just man, the just city, and the justice that is in them. —No, by Zeus, we would not.

Shall we say so then?—Yes, let us.

Let that stand then, I said. After this we must, I think, look for injustice.—Obviously.

Surely it must be a kind of civil war between the three parts, a meddling and a doing of other people's task, a rebellion of one part against the whole soul in order to rule it, though this is not fitting, as the rebelling part is by nature fitted to serve, while the other part is by nature not fit to serve, for it is of the ruling kind. We shall say, I think, that such things, the turmoil and the stray-ing, are injustice and license and cowardice and ignorance and, in a word, every kind of wickedness.—That is what they are.

If justice and injustice are now sufficiently clear to us, then so are unjust actions and wrongdoing on the one hand, just actions on the other, and all such things.—How so?

Because they are no different from healthy and diseased actions; what those are in the body, these are in the soul.—In what way?

Healthy actions produce health, diseased ones, disease.—Yes.

Therefore, just actions produce justice in a man, and unjust actions, injustice?—Inevitably.

To produce health in the body is to establish the parts of the body as ruler and ruled according to nature, while disease is that they rule and are ruled contrary to nature.—That is so.

Therefore, to produce justice is to establish the parts of the soul as ruler and ruled according to nature, while injustice means they rule and are ruled contrary to nature.—Most certainly.

Excellence then seems to be a kind of health and beauty and well-being of the soul, while vice is disease and ugliness and weakness.—That is so.

Then do not fine pursuits lead one to acquire virtue, ugly ones to acquire vice?—Of necessity.

It is left for us to enquire, it seems, if it is more profitable to act justly, to engage in fine pursuits and be just, whether one is known to be so or not, or to do wrong and be unjust, provided one does not pay the penalty and is not improved by punishment.

But Socrates, he said, this enquiry strikes me as becoming ridiculous now that justice and injustice have been shown to be such as we described. It is generally thought that life is not worth living when the body's nature is ruined, even if every kind of food and drink, every kind of wealth and power are available; yet we are to enquire whether life will be worth living when our soul, the very thing by which we live, is confused and ruined, if only one can do whatever one wishes, except that one cannot do what will free one from vice and injustice and make one acquire justice and virtue.

Ridiculous indeed. . . . Very well, I said. As we have come to this point in our discussion, let us take up again what was said at first, which has led us to this. It was said at some point that injustice was to the benefit of the completely unjust man who had a reputation for justice, was it not?—It certainly was.

Since we have fully agreed, I said, upon the effect of each, that is, of just and unjust behavior, let us now talk to the man who maintains this point of view.—How?

Let us in our argument fashion an image of the soul, so that he may understand the kind of thing he was saying.—What kind of image?

One of the kind that are told in ancient legends about creatures like the Chimera, Scylla, Cerberus, and many others in whose natures many different kinds had grown into one.—We are told of such creatures.

Fashion me then one kind of multiform beast with many heads, a ring of heads of both tame and wild animals, who is able to change these and grow them all out himself.

A work for a clever modeler, he said. However, as words are more malleable than wax and such things, take it as fashioned.

Then one other form, that of a lion, and another of a man, but the first form of all is much the largest, and the second, second.—That is easy and it is done.

Gather the three into one, so that they somehow grow together.—All right.

Model around them on the outside the appearance of being one, a man, so that anyone who cannot see what is inside but only the outside cover will think it is one creature, a man.—Done.

Let us now tell the one who maintains that injustice benefits this man, and that justice brings him no advantage, that his words simply mean that it benefits the man to feed the multiform beast well and make it strong, as well as the lion and all that pertains to him, but to starve and

weaken the man within so that he is dragged along whithersoever one of the other two leads. He does not accustom one part to the other or make them friendly, but he leaves them alone to bite and fight and kill each other.—This is most certainly what one who praises injustice means.

On the other hand, one who maintains that justice is to our advantage would say that all our words and deeds would tend to make the man within the man the strongest. He would look after the many-headed beast as a farmer looks after his animals, fostering and domesticating the gentle heads and preventing the wild ones from growing. With the lion's nature as his ally, he will care for all of them and rear them by making them all friendly with each other and with himself.—This is most definitely the meaning of him who praises justice.

What is said of justice is true in every way, and what is said on the other side is false, whether one examines it from the point of view of pleasure, of good repute, or of advantage; whereas he who condemns justice has nothing sound to say, and he does not know what he is condemning.—I don't think he does at all.

Let us then gently persuade him—he is not willingly wrong—by asking him: "My good sir, should we not say that beautiful and ugly traditions have originated as follows: the beautiful are those which subordinate the beastlike parts of our nature to the human, or perhaps we should say to the divine, while the ugly enslaves the gentler side to the wilder?" Will he agree or what?—He will agree if he takes my advice.

Can it benefit anyone, I said, to acquire gold unjustly if when he takes the gold he enslaves the best part of himself to the most vicious part? Or, if by taking the gold he should make a slave of his son or daughter in the house of wild and evil men, it would certainly not benefit him to acquire even a great deal of gold on those terms.

If then he enslaves the most divine part of himself to the most ungodly and disgusting part and feels no pity for it, is he not wretched and is he not accepting a bribe of gold for a more terrible death than Eriphyle when she accepted the necklace for her husband's life?—Much more, said Glaucon. I will answer for him.

Then do you think that licentiousness has long been condemned because in a licentious man that terrible, that big, that multiform beast is let loose more than it should be?—Clearly.

Obstinacy and irritability are condemned whenever the lion and snakelike part is increased and stetched disproportionately?—Surely.

Are luxury and softness condemned because the slackening and looseness of this same part produce cowardice?—Of course.

And do not flattery and meanness come when this same spirited part is subordinated to the turbulent beast which accustoms it from youth to being abused for the sake of money and the beast's insatiability, and to become an ape instead of a lion?—Certainly.

Why do you think the mechanical work of one's own hands is subject to reproach? Shall we say that it is so only when the best part of one's soul is naturally weak and cannot rule the animals within but pampers them and can learn nothing except ways to flatter them.—That is likely.

Therefore, in order that such a man be ruled by a principle similar to that which rules the best man, we say he must be enslaved to the best man, who has a divine ruler within himself. It is not to harm the slave that we believe he must be ruled, as Thrasymachus thought subjects should be, but because it is better for everyone to be ruled by divine intelligence. It is best that he should have this within himself, but if he has not, then it must be imposed from outside, so that, as far as possible, we should all be alike and friendly and governed by the same principle.—Quite right.

This, I said, is clearly the aim of the law which is the ally of everyone in the city, and of our rule over children. We should not allow them to be free until we establish a government within them, as we did in the city, fostering the best in them with what is best in ourselves and securing within the child a similar guardian and ruler, and then let him go free.—The law does make that clear.

How then and by what argument can we maintain, Glaucon, that injustice, licentiousness, and shameful actions are profitable, since they make a man more wicked, though he may acquire more riches or some other form of power?—We cannot.

Or that to do wrong without being discovered and not to pay the penalty is profitable? Does not one who remains undiscovered become even more vicious, whereas within the man who is discovered and punished the beast is calmed down and tamed; his whole soul, settling into its best nature, as it acquires moderation and justice together with wisdom, attains a more honored condition than a strong, beautiful, and healthy body, insofar as the soul is to be honoured more than the body.—Most certainly.

The man of sense then will direct all his efforts to this end; firstly, he will prize such studies as make his soul like this, and he will disregard the others.—Obviously.

Then, I said, he will see to his bodily condition and nurture it in such a way that he does not entrust it to the irrational pleasure of the beast, turn himself that way, and live on that level. It is not even health he aims at, nor does he consider it most important that he should be strong, healthy, or beautiful, unless he acquires moderation as a result, but he will cultivate harmony in his body for the sake of consonance in his soul.— That is altogether true, if he is truly to be a cultured man.

To the same end, there will be order and measure in his acquisition of wealth. He will not be panicked by the numbers of the crowd into accepting their idea of blessedness and increase his wealth without limit, and so have unlimited ills.— I do not think he will do so.

Looking to the government within, I said, he will guard against disturbances being caused there by too much wealth or too little, and he will direct, as far as he can, both the acquiring and spending of his possessions.—Very definitely.

He will have the same end in view as regards honors. He will share in, and willingly taste, those which he believes will make him a better man, but he will avoid both public and private honors which he believes will destroy the existing condition of his soul.

Note

1. Plato here seems to link his present more psychologically profound definition of justice and injustice as inner states of soul with the more external description of them in the first book. Clearly the unjust man who, in the argument with Thrasymachus, wanted to get the better of everybody is here the man whose appetitive part is out of control and rebels against the ruling reason. His antisocial conduct now follows from this.

Egoism as the Beginning of Morality

Thomas Hobbes

Thomas Hobbes (1588–1679), the greatest English political philosopher, gave classic expression to the idea that morality and politics arise out of a social contract. The son of a clergyman, born in Gloucestershire during the approach of the Spanish Armada, he was educated at Oxford University and lived through an era of political revolutions as a scholar and tutor (he was tutor to Prince Charles II of England).

In the Leviathan *(1651), from which our selection is taken, he develops a moral and political theory based on psychological egoism. Hobbes believed that we always act in our own self-interest, to obtain gratification and to avoid harm. However, we cannot obtain any of the basic goods because of the inherent fear and insecurity in an unregulated "state of nature," in which life is "solitary, poor, nasty, brutish and short." Because of this "war of every man against every man," we cannot relax our guard. There is little time to build or to cultivate the earth or to enjoy life, since our neighbor may be plotting to undo us. In this state of anarchy the prudent person concludes that it really is in everyone's self-interest to make a contract to sustain a minimal morality of respecting human life, keeping covenants made, and obeying the laws of the society. This minimal morality, which Hobbes refers to as "The Laws of Nature," is nothing more than a set of maxims of prudence. To insure that we all obey this covenant Hobbes proposes a strong sovereign state, the "Leviathan," to impose severe penalties on those who disobey the laws, for "covenants without the sword are but words."*

From the *Leviathan* (1651), edited by Louis P. Pojman.

Of the Natural Condition of Mankind As Concerning Their Felicity, and Misery

Men by Nature Are Equal

Nature hath made men so equal, in the faculties of the body, and mind; so that though there be found one man sometimes manifestly stronger in body, or of quicker mind than another; yet when all is reckoned together, the difference between man, and man, is not so considerable, as that one man can thereupon claim to himself any benefit, to which another may not pretend, as well as he. For as to the strength of body, the weakest has strength enough to kill the strongest, either by secret machination, or by confederacy with others, that are in the same danger with himself.

And as to the faculties of the mind, setting aside the arts grounded upon words, and especially that skill of proceeding upon general, and infallible rules, called science; which very few have, and but in few things; as being not a native faculty, born with us; nor attained, as prudence, while we look after somewhat else, I find yet a greater equality amongst men, than that of strength. For prudence, is but experience; which equal time, equally bestows on all men, in those things they equally apply themselves unto. That which may perhaps make such equality incredible, is but a vain conceit of one's own wisdom, which almost all men think they have in a greater degree, than the vulgar; that is, than all men but themselves, and a few others, whom by fame, or for concurring with themselves, they approve. For such is the nature of men, that howsoever they may acknowledge many others to be more witty, or more eloquent, or more learned; yet they will hardly believe there be many so wise as themselves; for they see their own wit at hand, and other men's at a distance. But this proveth rather that men are in that point equal, than unequal. For there is not ordinarily a greater sign of the equal distribution of any thing, than that every man is contented with his share.

From Equality Proceeds Fear

From this equality of ability, arises equality of hope in the attaining of our ends. And therefore if any two men desire the same thing, which nevertheless they cannot both enjoy, they become enemies; and in the way to their end, which is principally their own preservation and sometimes their enjoyment only, endeavor to destroy, or subdue one another. And from hence it comes to pass, that where an invader hath no more to fear, than another man's single power; if one plant, sow, build, or possess a convenient seat, others may probably be expected to come prepared with forces united, to dispossess, and deprive him, not only of the fruit of his labor, but also of his life, or liberty. And the invader again is in the like danger of another.

From Fear Proceeds War

And from this fear of one another, there is no way for any man to secure himself, so reasonable, as anticipation; that is, by force, or wiles, to master the persons of all men he can, so long, till he see no other power great enough to endanger him: and this is no more than his own preservation requireth, and is generally allowed. Also because there be some, that taking pleasure in contemplating their own power in the acts of conquest, which they pursue farther than their security requires; if others, that otherwise would be glad to be at ease within modest bounds, should not by invasion increase their power, they would not be able, long time, by standing only on their defense, to subsist. And by consequence,

such increase of dominion over men being necessary to a man's preservation, it ought to be allowed him.

Again, men have no pleasure, but on the contrary a great deal of grief, in keeping company, where there is no power able to over-awe them all. For every man desires that his companion should value him, at the same rate he sets upon himself: and upon all signs of contempt, or undervaluing, naturally endeavors, as far as he dares, (which amongst them that have no common power to keep them in quiet, is far enough to make them destroy each other), to extort a greater value from his contemners, by damage; and from others, by the example.

So that in the nature of man, we find three principal causes of quarrel. First, competition; secondly, fear; thirdly, glory.

The first, maketh men invade for gain; the second, for safety; and the third, for reputation. The first use violence, to make themselves masters of other men's persons, wives, children, and cattle; the second, to defend them; the third, for trifles, as a word, a smile, a different option, and any other sign of undervalue, either direct in their persons, or by reflection in their kindred, their friends, their nation, their profession, or their name.

Out of Civil States There Is Always War of Everyone against Everyone

Hereby it is manifest, that during the time men live without a common power to keep them all in awe, they are in that condition which is called war; and such a war, as is of every man, against every man. For war consists not in battle only or the act of fighting; but in a tract of time, wherein the will to contend by battle is sufficiently known: and therefore the notion of *time*, is to be considered in the nature of war; as it is in the nature of weather. For as the nature of foul weather, lies not in the shower or two of rain; but in an inclination thereto of many days together: so the nature of war, consists not in actual fighting; but in the known disposition thereto, during all the time there is no assurance to the contrary. All other time is PEACE.

The Problems and Inconvenience of Such a War

Whatsoever therefore occurs in a time of war, where every man is enemy to every man; the same occurs in the time, wherein men live without other security, than what their own strength, and their own invention shall furnish them withal. In such condition, there is no place for industry; because the fruit thereof is uncertain: and consequently no culture of the earth; no navigation, nor use of the commodities that may be imported by sea; no commodious building; no instruments of moving, and removing, such things as require much force; no knowledge of the face of the earth; no account of time; no arts; no letters; no society; and which is worst of all, continual fear, and danger of violent death; and the life of man solitary, poor, nasty, brutish, and short.

It may seem strange to some man, that has not well weighed these things; that nature should thus dissociate, and render men apt to invade, and destroy one another: and he may therefore, not trusting to this inference, made from the passions, desire perhaps to have the same confirmed by experience. Let him therefore consider with himself, when taking a journey, he arms himself, and seeks to go well accompanied; when going to sleep, he locks his doors; when even in his house he locks his chests; and this when he knows there be laws, and public officers, armed, to revenge all injuries shall be done him; what opinion he has of his fellow subjects, when he rides armed; of his fellow citizens, when he locks his doors; and of his children, and servants, when he locks his chests. Does he not there as much accuse mankind by his actions, as I do by my words? But neither of us accuse man's nature in it. The desires, and other passions of man, are in themselves no sin. No more are the actions, that proceed from those passions, till they know a law that forbids them: which till laws be made they cannot know: nor can any law be made, till they have agreed upon the person that shall make it.

It may perhaps be thought, there was never such a time, nor condition of war as this; and I believe it was never generally so, over all the world: but there are many places, where they live so now. For the savage people in many places of America, except the government of small families, the concord whereof depends on natural lust, have no government at all; and live at this day in that brutish manner, as I said before, Howsoever, it may be perceived what manner of life there would be, where there were no common power to fear, by the manner of life, which men that have formerly lived under a peaceful government, use to degenerate into, in a civil war.

But though there had never been any time, wherein particular men were in a condition of war one against another; yet in all times, kings, and persons of sovereign authority, because of their independency, are in continual jealousies, and in the state and posture of gladiators; having their weapons pointing, and their eyes fixed on one another; that is, their forts, garrisons, and guns upon the frontiers of their kingdoms; and continual spies upon their neighbors; which is a posture of war. But because they uphold thereby, the industry of their subjects; there does not follow from it, that misery, which accompanies the liberty of particular men.

In This State of War Nothing Is Unjust

To this war of every man, against every man, this also is a result; that nothing can be unjust. The notions of right and wrong, justice and injustice have there no place. Where there is no common power, there is no law: where no law, no injustice. Force, and fraud, are in war the two cardinal virtues. Justice, and injustice are none of the faculties neither of the body, nor mind. If they were, they might be in a man that were alone in the world, as well as his senses, and passions. They are qualities, that relate to men in society, not in solitude. It is consequent also to the same condition, that there be no property, no ownership, no *mine* and *thine* distinct; but only that to be every man's, that he can get; and for so long, as he can keep it. And thus much for the ill condition, which man be mere nature is actually placed in; though with a possibility to come out of it, consisting partly in the passions, partly in his reason.

The Passions Which Incline Men to Peace

The passions that incline men to peace are fear of death; desire of such things as are necessary to commodious living; and a hope by their industry to obtain them. And reason suggest convenient articles of peace, upon which men may be drawn to agreement. These articles, are they, which otherwise are called the Laws of Nature: whereof I shall speak more particularly, in the two following chapters.

Of the First and Second Natural Laws, and of Contracts

The Right of Nature

The Right of Nature, which writers commonly call *jus naturale*, is the liberty each man hath, to use his own power, as he will himself, for the preservation of his own nature; that is to say, of his own life; and consequently, of doing anything, which in his own judgment, and reason, he shall conceive to be the best means thereunto.

Liberty

By LIBERTY, is understood, according to the proper signification of the word, the absence of external impediments: which impediments, may oft take away part of a man's power to do what he would; but cannot hinder him from using the power left him, according as his judgment, and reason shall dictate to him.

A Law of Nature

A LAW OF NATURE, *lex naturalis*, is a precept or general rule, found out by reason, by which a man is forbidden to do that, which is destructive of his life, or taketh away the means of preserving the same; and to omit that, by which he thinketh it may be best preserved. For though they that speak of this subject, use to confound *jus*, and *lex*, *right* and *law:* yet they ought to be distinguished; because RIGHT, consisteth in liberty to do, or to forbear; whereas LAW, determines, and binds to one of them: so that law, and right, differ as much, as obligation and liberty; which in one and the same matter are inconsistent.

In the State of Nature Every Man Has a Right to Everything.

And because the condition of man, as has been shown in the precedent chapter, is a condition of war of every one against every one; in which case every one is governed by his own reason; and there is nothing he can make use of, that may not be a help unto him, in preserving his life against his enemies; it followeth, that in such a condition, every man has a right to every thing; even to one another's body. And therefore, as long as this natural right of every man to every thing endures, there can be no security to any man, how strong or wise soever he be, of living out the time, which nature ordinarily alloweth men to live. And consequently it is a precept, or general rule of reason, *that every man, ought to endeavor peace, as far as he has hope of obtaining it; and when he cannot obtain it, that he may seek, and use, all helps, and advantages, of war.* The first branch of which rule, contains the first, and fundamental law of nature; which is, *to seek peace, and follow it.* The second, the sum of the right of nature; which is, *by all means we can, to defend ourselves.*

The Second Law of Nature

From this fundamental law of nature, by which men are commanded to endeavor peace, is derived this second law; *that a man be willing, when others are so too, as far-forth, as for peace, and defense of himself he shall think it necessary, to lay down this right to all things; and be contented with so much liberty against other men, as he would allow other men against himself.* For as long as every man holds this right, of doing any thing he likes, so long are all men in the condition of war. But if other men will not lay down their right, as well as he; then there is no reason for any one, to divest himself of his: for that were to expose himself to prey, which no man is bound to, rather than to dispose himself to peace. This is that law of the Gospel; *whatsoever you require that others should do to you, that do ye to them.* And that law of all men, "What you do not want done to you, do not do to others."

Giving up a Right

To *lay down* a man's *right* to anything, is to *divest* himself of the *liberty*, of hindering another of the benefit of his own right to the same. For he that renounces, or passes away his right, gives not to any other man a right which he had not before; because there is nothing to which every man had not right by nature: but only stands out of his way, that he may enjoy his own original right, without hindrance from him; not without hindrance from another. So that the effect which redounds to one man, by another man's defect of right, is but so much diminution of impediments to the use of his own right original.

Right is laid aside, either by simply renouncing it; or by transferring it to another. By *simply* RENOUNCING; when he cares not to whom the benefit thereof redounds. By TRANSFERRING; when he intends the benefit thereof to some certain person, or persons. And when a man has in either manner abandoned, or granted away his right; then is he said to be OBLIGED, or BOUND, not to hinder those, to whom such right is granted, or abandoned, from the benefit of it: and that he *ought*, and it is his DUTY, not to make void that voluntary act of his own: and that such hindrance is INJUSTICE, and INJURY, as being "without right," the right being before renounced, or transferred. So that *injury*, or *injustice*, in the controversies of the world, is somewhat like to that, which in the disputations of scholars is called *absurdity*. For as it is there called an absurdity, to contradict what one maintained in the beginning: so in the world, it is called injustice, and injury, voluntarily to undo that, which from the beginning he had voluntarily done. The way by which a man either simply renounces, or transfers his right, is a declaration, or signification, by some voluntary and sufficient sign, or signs, that he does so renounce, or transfer; or has so renounced, or transferred the same, to him that accepts it. And these signs are either words only, or actions only; or, as it happens most often, both words, and actions. And the same are the BONDS, by which men are bound, and obliged: bonds, that have their strength, not from their own nature, for nothing is more easily broken than a man's word, but from fear of some evil consequence upon the rupture.

Some Rights Are Inalienable

Whensoever a man transfers his right, or renounces it; it is either in consideration of some right reciprocally transferred to himself; or for some other good he hopes for thereby. For it is a voluntary act: and of the voluntary acts of every man, the object is some *good to himself.* And therefore there be some rights, which no man can be understood by any words, or other signs, to have abandoned, or transferred. At first a man cannot lay down the right of resisting them, that assault him by force, to take away his life; because he cannot be understood to aim thereby, at any good to himself. The same may be said of wounds, and chains, and imprisonment; both because no benefit proceeds from such patience; as there is to the patience of suffering another to be wounded, or imprisoned: as also because a man cannot tell, when he seeth men proceed against him by violence, whether they intend his death or not. And

lastly the motive, and end for which this renouncing, and transferring of right is introduced,
is nothing else but the security of a man's person,
in his life, and in the means of so preserving life,
as not to be weary of it. And therefore if a man by
words, or other signs, seem to despoil himself of
the end, for which those signs were intended; he
is not to be understood as if he meant it, or that it
was his will; but that he was ignorant of how such
words and actions were to be interpreted.

The Contract

The mutual transferring of right, is that which
men call CONTRACT.

There is a different between transferring of
right to the thing; and transferring, or tradition,
that is delivery of the thing itself. For the thing
may be delivered together with the translation of
the right; as in buying and selling with ready-
money; or exchange of goods, or lands: and it
may be delivered some time after.

The Covenant

Again, one of the contractors, may deliver the
thing contracted for on his part, and leave the
other to perform his part as some determinate
time after, and in the meantime be trusted; and
then the contract on his part, is called PACT, or
COVENANT: or both parts may contract now, to
perform hereafter: in which cases, he that is to
perform in time to come, being trusted, his performance is called *keeping of promise*, or faith; and
the failing of performance, if it be voluntary, *violation of faith*.

When the transferring of right, is not mutual:
but one of the parties transferreth, in hope to
gain thereby friendship, or service from another,
or from his friends; or in hope to gain the reputation of charity, or magnanimity; or to deliver his
mind from the pain of compassion; or in hope of
reward in heaven, this is not contract, but GIFT,
FREE-GIFT, GRACE: which words signify one and
the same thing.

Signs of contract, are either *express,* or *by inference.* Express, are words spoken with understanding of what they signify: and such words are
either of the time *present,* or *past;* as, *I give, I
grant, I have given, I have granted, I will that this
be yours:* or of the future; as, *I will give, I will
grant:* which words of the future are called
PROMISE.

When Covenants of Mutual Trust Become Invalid

If a covenant be made, wherein neither of the
parties perform presently, but trust one another;
in the condition of mere nature, which is a condition of war of every man against every man,
upon any reasonable suspicion, it is void: but if
there be a common power set over them both,
with right and force sufficient to compel performance, it is not void. For he that performs first,
has no assurance the other will perform after;
because the bonds of words are too weak to bridle
men's ambition, avarice, anger, and other passions, without the fear of some coercive power;
which in the condition of mere nature, where all
men are equal, and judges of the justness of their
own fears, cannot possibly be supposed. And
therefore he which performs first, does but betray himself to his enemy; contrary to the right,
he can never abandon, of defending his life, and
means of living.

But in a civil estate, where there is a power set
up to constrain those that would otherwise violate
their faith, that fear is no more reasonable: and
for that cause, he which by the covenant is to
perform first, is obliged so to do.

The cause of fear, which maketh such a covenant invalid, must be always something arising
after the covenant made; as some new fact, or
other sign of the will not to perform: else it cannot make the covenant void. For that which could
not hinder a man from promising, ought not to be
admitted as a hindrance of performing.

Of Other Laws of Nature

The Third Law of Nature: Justice

From that law of nature, by which we are obliged to transfer to another, such rights, as being retained, hinder the peace of mankind, there followeth a third; which is this, *that men perform their covenants made:* without which, covenants are in vain, and but empty words; and the right of all men to all things remaining, we are still in the condition of war.

And in this law of nature, consists the fountain and origin of JUSTICE. For where no covenant has preceded, there has no right been transferred, and every man has right to everything; and consequently, no action can be unjust. But when a covenant is made, then to break it is *unjust:* and the definition of INJUSTICE is no other than *the not performance of covenant.* And whatsoever is not unjust, is *just.*

Justice and Injustice Come into Being with the Creation of the Commonwealth

But because covenants of mutual trust, where there is a fear of not performance on either part, as hath been said in the former chapter, are invalid; though the origin of justice be the making of covenants; yet injustice actually there can be none, till the cause of such fear be taken away; which while men are in the natural condition of war, cannot be done. Therefore before the names of just, and unjust can have place, there must be some coercive power, to compel men equally to the performance of their covenants, by the terror of some punishment, greater than the benefit they expect by the breach of their covenant; and to make good that propriety, which by mutual contract men acquire, in recompense of the universal right they abandon: and such power there is none before the erection of a commonwealth. And this is also to be gathered out of the ordinary definition of justice in the Schools: for they say, that *justice is the constant will of giving to every man his own,* and therefore where there is no *own,* that is, no property, there is no injustice; and where there is no coercive power erected, that is, where there is no commonwealth, there is no property; all men having right to all things: therefore where there is no commonwealth, there nothing is unjust. So that the nature of justice, consists in keeping of valid covenants: but the validity of covenants begins not but with the constitution of a civil power, sufficient to compel men to keep them: and then it is also that property begins. . . .

On the Duty to Submit to Arbitration

And because, though men be never so willing to observe these laws, there may nevertheless arise questions concerning a man's action; first, whether it were done, or not done; secondly, if done, whether against the law, or not against the law; the former whereof, is called a question *of fact;* the latter a question *of right,* therefore unless the parties to the question, covenant mutually to stand to the sentence of another, they are as far from peace as ever. This other to whose sentence they submit is called an ARBITRATOR. And therefore it is of the law of nature, *that they that are at controversy, submit their right to the judgment of an arbitrator.*

And seeing every man is presumed to do all things in order to his own benefit, no man is a fit arbitrator in his own cause; and if he were never so fit; yet equity allowing to each party equal benefit, if one be admitted to the judge, the other is to be admitted also; and so the controversy, that is, the cause of war, remains, against the law of nature.

For the same reason no man in any cause ought to be received for arbitrator, to whom greater profit, or honor, or pleasure apparently ariseth out of the victory of one party, than of the other: for he hath taken, though an unavoidable bribe, yet a bribe; and no man can be obliged to trust him. And thus also the controversy, and the condition of war remaineth, contrary to the law of nature.

And in a controversy of *fact*, the judge being to give no more credit to one, than to the other, if there be no other arguments, must give credit to a third; or to a third and fourth; or more: for else the question is undecided, and left to force, contrary to the law of nature.

These are the laws of nature, dictating peace, for a means of the conservation of men in multitudes; and which only concern the doctrine of civil society. There be other things tending to the destruction of particular men; as drunkenness, and all other parts of intemperance; which may therefore also be reckoned amongst those things which the law of nature hath forbidden; but are not necessary to be mentioned, nor are pertinent enough to this place.

A Rule by Which the Laws
of Nature May Be Examined

And though this may seem too subtle a deduction of the laws of nature, to be taken notice of by all men; whereof the most part are too busy getting food, and the rest too negligent to understand; yet to leave all men inexcusable, they have been contracted into one easy sum, intelligible even to the meanest capacity; and that is, Do *not that to another, which thou wouldest not have done to thyself;* which shows him that he has no more to do in learning the laws of nature, but, when weighing the actions of other men with his own, they seem too heavy, to put them into the other part of the balance, and his own into their place, that his own passions, and selflove, may add nothing to the weight; and then there is none of these laws of nature that will not appear unto him very reasonable.

The Laws of Nature Oblige in Conscience Always,
But in Effect Only When There is Security

The laws of nature oblige *in foro interno*, that is to say, they bind to a desire they should take place: but *in foro externo*, that is, to the putting them in

act, not always. For he that should be modest, and tractable, and perform all he promises, in such time, and place, where no man else should do so, should but make himself a prey to others, and procure his own certain ruin, contrary to the ground of all laws of nature, which tend to nature's preservation. And again, he that having sufficient security, that others shall observe the same laws towards him, observes them not himself, seeketh not peace, but war; and consequently the destruction of his nature by violence.

And whatsoever laws bind *in foro interno*, may be broken, not only by a fact contrary to the law, but also by a fact according to it, in case a man think it contrary. For though his action in this case, be according to the law; yet his purpose was against the law; which, where the obligation is *in foro interno*, is a breach.

The Laws of Nature Are Eternal

The laws of nature are immutable and eternal; for injustice, ingratitude, arrogance, pride, iniquity, acception of persons, and the rest, can never be made lawful. For it can never be that war shall preserve life, and peace destroy it.

The same laws, because they oblige only to a desire, and endeavor, I mean an unfeigned and constant endeavor, are easy to be observed. For in that they require nothing but endeavor, he that endeavoreth their performance, fulfilleth them; and he that fulfilleth the law, is just.

The Science of These Laws Is
The True Moral Philosophy

And the science of them, is the true and only moral philosophy. For moral philosophy is nothing else but the science of what is *good*, and *evil*, in the conversation, and society of mankind. *Good*, and *evil*, are names that signify our appetites, and aversions; which in different tempers, customs, and doctrines of men, are different: and divers men, differ not only in their judgment, on the sense of what is pleasant, and unpleasant to the taste, smell, hearing, touch, and sight; but also of what is conformable, or disagreeable to reason, in the actions of common life. Nay, the same man, in divers times, differs from himself; and one time praises, that is, calls good, what another time he dispraises, and calls evil: from whence arise disputes, controversies, and at last war. And therefore so long as a man is in the condition of mere nature, which is a condition of war, as private appetite is the measure of good, and evil: and consequently all men agree on this, that peace is good, and therefore also the way, or means of peace, which, as I have showed before, are *justice, gratitude, modesty, equity, mercy,* and the rest of the laws of nature, are good; that is to say; *moral virtues;* and their contrary *vices,* evil. Now the science of virtue and vice, is moral philosophy; and therefore the true doctrine of the laws of nature, is the true moral philosophy. But the writers of moral philosophy, though they acknowledge the same virtues and vices; yet not seeing wherein consisted their goodness; nor that they come to be praised, as the means of peaceable, sociable, and comfortable living, place them in a mediocrity of passions: as if not the cause, but the degree of daring, made fortitude; or not the cause, but the quantity of a gift, made liberality.

These dictates of reason, men used to call by the name of laws, but improperly: for they are but conclusions, of theorems concerning what conduces to the conservation and defense of themselves; whereas law, properly, is the word of him, that by right hath command over others. But yet if we consider the same theorems, as delivered in the word of God, that by right commandeth all things; then are they properly called laws.

Of the Causes, Generation, and Definition of a Commonwealth

The final cause, end, or design of men, who naturally love liberty, and dominion over others, in the introduction of that restraint upon themselves, in which we see them live in commonwealths, is the foresight of their own preservation, and of a more contented life thereby; that is to say, of getting themselves out from that miserable condition of war, which is necessarily consequent, as has been shown, to the natural passions of men, when there is no visible power to keep them in awe, and tie them by fear of punishment to the performance of their covenants, and observation of those laws of nature set down in the fourteenth and fifteenth chapters.

For the laws of nature, as *justice, equity, modesty, mercy,* and, in sum, *doing to others, as we would be done to,* of themselves, without the terror of some power, to cause them to be observed, are contrary to our natural passions, that carry us to partiality, pride, revenge, and the like. And covenants, without the sword, are but words, and of no strength to secure a man at all. Therefore notwithstanding the laws of nature, which every one hath then kept, when he has the will to keep them, when he can do it safely, if there be no power erected, or not great enough for our security; every man will, and may lawfully rely on his own strength and art, for caution against all other men. And in all places, where men have lived by small families, to rob and spoil one another, has been a trade, and so far from being reputed against the law of nature, that the greater spoils they gained the greater was their honor; and men observed no other laws therein, but the laws of honor; that is, to abstain from cruelty, leaving to men their lives, and instruments of husbandry. And as small families did then; so now do cities and kingdoms which are but greater families, for their own security, enlarge their dominions, upon all pretenses of danger, and fear of invasion, or assistance that may be given to invaders, and endeavor as much as they can, to subdue, or weaken their neighbors, by open force, and secret arts, for want of other caution, justly; and are remembered for it in after ages with honor.

The only way to erect a common power, which may be able to defend men from invasion of foreigners, and the injuries of one another, and thereby to secure them in such fruits of the earth and enable them to live contentedly; is to confer all their power upon one man or upon one assembly of men, to bear in their person; and every one to own, and acknowledge himself to be author of whatsoever he that so beareth their person, shall act, or cause to be acted, in those things which concern the common peace and safety; and therein to submit their wills, every one to common peace and safety; and therein to submit their will, every one to his will, and their judgment to his judgment. This is more than consent or concord; it is a real unity of them all, in one and the same person, made by covenant of every man with every man, in such manner, as if every man should say to every man, *I authorize and give up my right of governing myself, to this man, or to this assembly of men, on this condition, that thou give up thy right to him, and authorize all his actions in like manner.* This done, the multitude so united in one person, is called a COMMONWEALTH, in Latin CIVITAS.

This is the generation of the great LEVIATHAN or rather, to speak more reverently, of that *mortal god,* to which we owe under the *immortal God,* our peace and defense. For by this authority, given him by every particular man in the commonwealth, he hath the use of so much power and strength conferred on him, that by terror thereof, he is enabled to perform the wills of them all, to peace at home, and mutual aid against their enemies abroad. And in him consists the essence of the commonwealth; which, to define it, is *one person, of whose acts a great multitude, by mutual covenants one with another, have made themselves every one the author, to the end he may use the strength and means of them all, as he shall think expedient, for their peace and common defense.*

And he that carries this person, is called SOVEREIGN, and said to have *sovereign* power; and every one besides, his SUBJECT.

A Defense of Ethical Egoism

AYN RAND

Ayn Rand (1908–1982) wrote several philosophical novels, including The Fountainhead *(1943) and* Atlas Shrugged *(1959), from which this selection is taken. Her work sets forth a version of ethical egoism that she called "objectivism," the theory that rational beings ought to pursue their own happiness and that altruism and self-sacrifice are incompatible with rational morality. In this selection she criticizes altruistic morality ("the morality of sacrifice") and praises the morality of selfishness.*

". . . Yes, this *is* an age of moral crisis. Yes, you *are* bearing punishment for your evil. But it is not man who is now on trial and it is not human nature that will take the blame. It is your moral code that's through, this time. Your moral code has reached its climax, the blind alley at the end of its course. And if you wish to go on living, what you now need is not to *return* to morality—you who have never known any—but to *discover* it.

"You have heard no concepts of morality but the mystical or the social. You have been taught that morality is a code of behavior imposed on you by whim, the whim of a supernatural power or the whim of society, to serve God's purpose or your neighbor's welfare, to please an authority beyond the grave or else next door—but not to serve *your* life or pleasure. Your pleasure, you have been taught, is to be found in immorality, your interests would best be served by evil, and any moral code must be designed not *for* you, but *against* you, not to further your life, but to drain it.

"For centuries, the battle of morality was fought

From *Atlas Shrugged* by Ayn Rand. Published by Random House, Inc. Reprinted by permission of the executor of the Estate of Ayn Rand.

between those who claimed that your life belongs to God and those who claimed that it belongs to your neighbors—between those who preached that the good is self-sacrifice for the sake of ghosts in heaven and those who preached that the good is self-sacrifice for the sake of incompetents on earth. And no one came to say that your life belongs to you and that the good is to live it.

"Both sides agreed that morality demands the surrender of your self-interest and of your mind, that the moral and the practical are opposites, that morality is not the province of reason, but the province of faith and force. Both sides agreed that no rational morality is possible, that there is no right or wrong in reason—that in reason there's no reason to be moral.

"Whatever else they fought about, it was against man's mind that all your moralists have stood united. It was man's mind that all their schemes and systems were intended to despoil and destroy. Now choose to perish or to learn that the anti-mind is the anti-life.

"Man's mind is his basic tool of survival. Life is given to him, survival is not. His body is given to him, its sustenance is not. His mind is given to him, its content is not. To remain alive, he must act, and before he can act he must know the nature and purpose of his action. He cannot obtain his food without a knowledge of food and of the way to obtain it. He cannot dig a ditch—or build a cyclotron—without a knowledge of his aim and of the means to achieve it. To remain alive, he must think.

"But to think is an act of choice. The key to what you so recklessly call 'human nature,' the open secret you live with, yet dread to name, is the fact that *man is a being of volitional consciousness.* Reason does not work automatically; thinking is not a mechanical process; the connections of logic are not made by instinct. The function of your stomach, lungs or heart is automatic; the function of your mind is not. In any hour and issue of your life, you are free to think or to evade that effort. But you are not free to escape from your nature, from the fact that *reason* is your means of survival—so that for *you*, who are a human being, the question 'to be or not to be' is the question 'to think or not to think.'

"A being of volitional consciousness has no automatic course of behavior. He needs a code of values to guide his actions. 'Value' is that which one acts to gain and keep, 'virtue' is the action by which one gains and keeps it. 'Value' presupposes an answer to the question: of value to whom and for what? 'Value' presupposes a standard, a purpose and the necessity of action in the face of an alternative. Where there are no alternatives, no values are possible.

"There is only one fundamental alternative in the universe: existence or non-existence—and it pertains to a single class of entities: to living organisms. The existence of inanimate matter is unconditional, the existence of life is not: it depends on a specific course of action. Matter is indestructible, it changes its forms, but it cannot cease to exist. It is only a living organism that faces a constant alternative: the issue of life or death. Life is a process of self-sustaining and self-generating action. If an organism fails in that action, it dies; its chemical elements remain, but its life goes out of existence. It is only the concept of 'Life' that makes the concept of 'Value' possible. It is only to a living entity that things can be good or evil.

"A plant must feed itself in order to live; the sunlight, the water, the chemicals it needs are the values its nature has set it to pursue; its life is the standard of value directing its actions. But a plant has no choice of action; there are alternatives in the conditions it encounters, but there is no alternative in its function: it acts automatically to further its life, it cannot act for its own destruction.

"An animal is equipped for sustaining its life; its senses provide it with an automatic code of action, an automatic knowledge of what is good for it or evil. It has no power to extend its knowledge or to evade it. In conditions where its knowledge proves inadequate, it dies. But so long as it lives, it acts on its knowledge, with automatic safety and no power of choice, it is unable to ignore its own good, unable to decide to choose the evil and act as its own destroyer.

"Man has no automatic code of survival. His particular distinction from all other living species is the necessity to act in the face of alternatives by means of *volitional choice*. He has no automatic knowledge of what is good for him or evil, what values his life depends on, what course of action it requires. Are you prattling about an instinct of self-preservation? An *instinct* of self-preservation is precisely what man does not possess. An 'instinct' is an unerring and automatic form of knowledge. A desire is not an instinct. A desire to live does not give you the knowledge required for living. And even man's desire to live is not automatic: your secret evil today is that *that* is the desire you do not hold. Your fear of death is not a love for life and will not give you the knowledge needed to keep it. Man must obtain his knowledge and choose his actions by a process of thinking, which nature will not force him to perform. Man has the power to act as his own destroyer—and that is the way he has acted through most of his history.

"A living entity that regarded its means of survival as evil, would not survive. A plant that struggled to mangle its roots, a bird that fought to break its wings would not remain for long in the existence they affronted. But the history of man has been a struggle to deny and to destroy his mind.

"Man has been called a rational being, but rationality is a matter of choice—and the alternative his nature offers him is: rational being or suicidal animal. Man has to be man—by choice; he has to hold his life as a value—by choice; he has to learn to sustain it—by choice; he has to discover the values it requires and practice his virtues—by choice.

"A code of values accepted by choice is a code of morality.

"Whoever you are, you who are hearing me now, I am speaking to whatever living remnant is left uncorrupted within you, to the remnant of the human, to your *mind*, and I say: There *is* a morality of reason, a morality proper to man, and *Man's Life* is its standard of value.

"All that which is proper to the life of a rational being is the good; all that which destroys it is the evil.

"Man's life, as required by his nature, is not the life of a mindless brute, of a looting thug or a mooching mystic, but the life of a thinking being—not life by means of force or fraud, but life by means of achievement—not survival at any price, since there's only one price that pays for man's survival: reason.

"Man's life is the *standard* of morality, but your own life is its *purpose.* If existence on earth is your goal, you must choose your actions and values by the standard of that which is proper to man—for the purpose of preserving, fulfilling and enjoying the irreplaceable value which is your life.

"Since life requires a specific course of action, any other course will destroy it. A being who does not hold his own life as the motive and goal of his actions is acting on the motive and standard of *death*. Such a being is a metaphysical monstrosity, struggling to oppose, negate, and contradict the fact of his own existence, running blindly amuck on a trail of destruction, capable of nothing but pain.

"Happiness is the successful state of life; pain is an agent of death. Happiness is that state of unconsciousness which proceeds from the achievement of one's values. A morality that dares to tell you to find happiness in the renunciation of your happiness—to value the failure of your values—is an insolent negation of morality. A doctrine that gives you, as an ideal, the role of a sacrificial animal seeking slaughter on the altars of others, is giving you *death* as your standard. By the grace

of reality and the nature of life, man—every man—is an end in himself, he exists for his own sake, and the achievement of his own happiness is his highest moral purpose.

"But neither life nor happiness can be achieved by the pursuit of irrational whims. Just as man is free to attempt to survive in any random manner, but will perish unless he lives as his nature requires, so he is free to seek his happiness in any mindless fraud, but the torture of frustration is all he will find, unless he seeks the happiness proper to man. The purpose of morality is to teach you, not to suffer and die, but to enjoy yourself and love.

"Sweep aside those parasites of subsidized classrooms, who live on the profits of the mind of others and proclaim that man needs no morality, no values, no code of behavior. They, who pose as scientists and claim that man is only an animal, do not grant him inclusion in the law of existence they have granted to the lowest of insects. They recognize that every living species has a way of survival demanded by its nature, they do not claim that a fish can live out of water or that a dog can live without its sense of smell—but man, they claim, the most complex of beings, man can survive in any way whatever, man has no identity, no nature, and there's no practical reason why he cannot live with his means of survival destroyed, with his mind throttled and placed at the disposal of any orders *they* might care to issue.

"Sweep aside those hatred-eaten mystics who pose as friends of humanity and preach that the highest virtue man can practice is to hold his own life as of no value. Do they tell you that the purpose of morality is to curb man's instinct of self-preservation? It is for the purpose of self-preservation that man needs a code of morality. The only man who desires to be moral is the man who desires to live.

"No, you do not have to live; it is your basic act of choice; but if you choose to live, you must live as a man—by the work and the judgment of your mind.

"No, you do not have to live as a man: it is an

act of moral choice. But you cannot live as anything else—and the alternative is that state of living death which you now see within you and around you, the state of a thing unfit for existence, no longer human and less than animal, a thing that knows nothing but pain and drags itself through its span of years in the agony of unthinking self-destruction.

"No, you do not have to think; it is an act of moral choice. But someone had to think to keep you alive; if you choose to default, you default on existence and you pass the deficit to some moral man, expecting him to sacrifice his good for the sake of letting you survive by your evil. . . .

"This much is true: the most *selfish* of all things is the independent mind that recognizes no authority higher than its own and no value higher than its judgment of truth. You are asked to sacrifice your intellectual integrity, your logic, your reason, your standard of truth—in favor of becoming a prostitute whose standard is the greatest good for the greatest number.

"If you search your code for guidance, for an answer to the question: 'What *is* the good?'—the only answer you will find is *'The good of others.'* The good is whatever others wish, whatever you feel they feel they wish, or whatever you feel they ought to feel. 'The good of others' is a magic formula that transforms anything into gold, a formula to be recited as a guarantee of moral glory and as a fumigator for any action, even the slaughter of a continent. Your standard of virtue is not an object, not an act, nor a principle, but an *intention.* You need no proof, no reasons, no success, you need not achieve *in fact* the good of others—all you need to know is that your motive was the good of others, *not* your own. Your only definition of the good is a negation: the good is the 'non-good for me.'

"Your code—which boasts that it upholds eternal, absolute, objective moral values and scorns the conditional, the relative and the subjective—your code hands out, as its version of the absolute, the following rule of moral conduct: If *you* wish it, it's evil; if others wish it, it's good; if the motive of your action is *your* welfare, don't do it; if the motive is the welfare of others, then anything goes.

"As this double-jointed, double-standard morality splits you in half, so it splits mankind into two enemy camps: one is *you,* the other is all the rest of humanity. *You* are the only outcast who has no right to wish or live. *You* are the only servant, the rest are the masters, *you* are the only giver, the rest are the takers, *you* are the eternal debtor, the rest are the creditors never to be paid off. You must not question their right to your sacrifice, or the nature of their wishes and their needs: their right is conferred upon them by a negative, by the fact that they are 'non-you.'

"For those of you who might ask questions, your code provides a consolation prize and booby-trap: it is for your own happiness, it says, that you must serve the happiness of others, the only way to achieve your joy is to give it up to others, the only way to achieve your prosperity is to surrender your wealth to others, the only way to protect your life is to protect all men except yourself—and if you find no joy in this procedure, it is your own fault and the proof of your evil; if you were good, you would find your happiness in providing a banquet for others, and your dignity in existing on such crumbs as *they* might care to toss you.

"You who have no standard of self-esteem, accept the guilt and dare not ask the questions. But you know the unadmitted answer, refusing to acknowledge what you see, what hidden premise moves your world. You know it, not in honest statement, but as a dark uneasiness within you, while you flounder between guiltily cheating and grudgingly practicing a principle too vicious to name.

"I, who do not accept the unearned, neither in values nor in *guilt,* am here to ask the questions you evaded. Why is it moral to serve the happiness of others, but not your own? If enjoyment is a value, why is it moral when experienced by others, but immoral when experienced by you? If the sensation of eating a cake is a value, why is it an immoral indulgence in your stomach, but a moral goal for you to achieve in the stomach of others?

Why is it immoral for you to desire, but moral for others to do so? Why is it immoral to produce a value and keep it, but moral to give it away? And if it is not moral for you to keep a value, why is it moral for others to accept it? If you are selfless and virtuous when you give it, are they not selfish and vicious when they take it? Does virtue consist of serving vice? Is the moral purpose of those who are good, self-immolation for the sake of those who are evil? . . .

"Under a morality of sacrifice, the first value you sacrifice is morality; the next is self-esteem. When need is the standard, every man is both victim and parasite. As a victim, he must labor to fill the needs of others, leaving himself in the position of a parasite whose needs must be filled by others. He cannot approach his fellow men except in one of two disgraceful roles: he is both a beggar and a sucker.

"You fear the man who has a dollar less than you, that dollar is rightfully his, he makes you feel like a moral defrauder. You hate the man who has a dollar more than you, that dollar is rightfully yours, he makes you feel that you are morally defrauded. The man below is a source of your guilt, the man above is a source of your frustration. You do not know what to surrender or demand, when to give and when to grab, what pleasure in life is rightfully yours and what debt is still unpaid to others—you struggle to evade, as 'theory,' the knowledge that by the moral standard you've accepted you are guilty every moment of your life, there is no mouthful of food you swallow that is not *needed* by someone somewhere on earth—and you give up the problem in blind resentment, you conclude that moral perfection is not to be achieved *or desired*, that you will muddle through by snatching as snatch can and by avoiding the eyes of the young, of those who look at you as if self-esteem were possible and they expected you to have it. Guilt is all that you retain within your soul—and so does every other man, as he goes past, avoiding *your* eyes. Do you wonder why your morality has not achieved brotherhood on earth or the good will of man to man?

"The justification of sacrifice, that your moral-

ity propounds, is more corrupt than the corruption it purports to justify. The motive of your sacrifice, it tells you, should be *love*—the love you ought to feel for every man. A morality that professes the belief that the values of the spirit are more precious than matter, a morality that teaches you to scorn a whore who gives her body indiscriminately to all men—this same morality demands that you surrender your soul to promiscuous love for all comers.

"As there can be no causeless wealth, so there can be no causeless love or any sort of causeless emotion. An emotion is a response to a fact of reality, an estimate dictated by your standards. To love is to *value*. The man who tells you that it is possible to value without values, to love those whom you appraise as worthless, is the man who tells you that it is possible to grow rich by consuming without producing and that paper money is as valuable as gold.

"Observe that he does not expect you to feel a causeless fear. When his kind get into power, they are expert at contriving means of terror, at giving you ample cause to feel the fear by which they desire to rule you. But when it comes to love, the highest of emotions, you permit them to shriek at you accusingly that you are a moral delinquent if you're incapable of feeling causeless love. When a man feels fear without reason, you call him to the attention of a psychiatrist; you are not so careful to protect the meaning, the nature and the dignity of love.

"Love is the expression of one's values, the greatest reward you can earn for the moral qualities you have achieved in your character and person, the emotional price paid by one man for the joy he receives from the virtues of another. Your morality demands that you divorce your love from values and hand it down to any vagrant, not as response to his worth, but as response to his *need*, not as reward, but as alms, not as a payment for virtues, but as a blank check on vices. Your morality tells you that the purpose of love is to set you free of the bonds of morality, that love is superior to moral judgment, that true love transcends, forgives and survives every manner of evil in its object, and the greater the love the greater the depravity it permits to the loved. To love a man for his virtues is paltry and human, it tells you; to love him for his flaws is divine. To love those who are worthy of it is self-interest; to love the unworthy is sacrifice. You owe your love to those who don't deserve it, and the less they deserve it, the more love you owe them—the more loathsome the object, the nobler your love—the more unfastidious your love, the greater your virtue—and if you can bring your soul to the state of a dump heap that welcomes anything on equal terms, if you can cease to value moral values, you have achieved the state of moral perfection.

"Such is your morality of sacrifice and such are the twin ideals it offers: to refashion the life of your body in the image of a human stockyards, and the life of your spirit in the image of a dump. . . .

"Since childhood, you have been hiding the guilty secret that you feel no desire to be moral, no desire to seek self-immolation, that you dread and hate your code, but dare not say it even to yourself, that you're devoid of those moral 'instincts' which others profess to feel. The less you felt, the louder you proclaimed your selfless love and servitude to others, in dread of ever letting them discover your own self, the self that you betrayed, the self that you kept in concealment, like a skeleton in the closet of your body. And they, who were at once your dupes and your deceivers, they listened and voiced their loud approval, in dread of ever letting you discover that they were harboring the same unspoken secret. Existence among you is a giant pretense, an act you all perform for one another, each feeling that he is the only guilty freak, each placing his moral authority in the unknowable known only to others, each faking the reality he feels they expect him to fake, none having the courage to break the vicious circle.

"No matter what dishonorable compromise you've made with your impracticable creed, no matter what miserable balance, half-cynicism, half-superstition, you now manage to maintain, you still preserve the root, the lethal tenet: the belief that the moral and the practical are opposites. Since childhood, you have been running from the terror of a choice you have never dared fully to identify: If the *practical*, whatever you must practice to exist, whatever works, succeeds, achieves your purpose, whatever brings you food and joy, whatever profits you is evil—and if the good, the moral is the *impractical*, whatever fails, destroys, frustrates, whatever injures you and brings you loss or pain—then your choice is to be moral or to live.

"The sole result of that murderous doctrine was to remove morality from life. You grew up to believe that moral laws bear no relation to the job of living, except as an impediment and threat, that man's existence is an amoral jungle where anything goes and anything works. And in that fog of switching definitions which descends upon a frozen mind, you have forgotten that the evils damned by your creed were the virtues required for living, and you have come to believe that actual evils are the *practical* means of existence. Forgetting that the impractical 'good' was self-sacrifice, you believe that self-esteem is impractical; forgetting that the practical 'evil' was production, you believe that robbery is practical. . . .

"Accept the fact that the achievement of your happiness is the only *moral* purpose of your life, and that *happiness*—not pain or mindless self-indulgence—is the proof of your moral integrity, since it is the proof and the result of your loyalty to the achievement of your values. Happiness was the responsibility you dreaded, it required the kind of rational discipline you did not value yourself enough to assume—and the anxious staleness of your days is the monument to your evasion of the knowledge that there is no moral substitute for happiness, that there is no more despicable coward than the man who deserted the battle for his joy, fearing to assert his right to existence, lacking the courage and the loyalty to life of a bird or a flower reaching for the sun. Discard the protective rags of that vice which you called a virtue: humility—learn to value yourself, which means: to fight for your happiness—and when you learn that *pride* is the sum of all virtues, you will learn to live like a man.

"As a basic step of self-esteem, learn to treat as the mark of a cannibal any man's *demand* for your help. To demand it is to claim that your life is *his* property—and loathsome as such claim might be, there's something still more loathsome: your agreement. Do you ask if it's ever proper to help another man? No—if he claims it as his right or as a moral duty that you owe him. Yes—if such is your own desire based on your own selfish pleasure in the value of his person and his struggle.

10

A Critique of Ethical Egoism

James Rachels

James Rachels (1941–2003) was a professor of philosophy at the University of Alabama. He was an influential applied ethicist and the author of many articles and several widely read books on moral philosophy, including The End of Life: Euthanasia and Morality *(1986) and* The Elements of Moral Philosophy *(1986), from which the present essay is taken. In this succinct essay Rachels first distinguishes ethical egoism, the doctrine that it is always our duty to act exclusively in our self-interest, from psychological egoism, the doctrine that people always act out of their own perceived self-interest. He examines three arguments in favor of ethical egoism showing that each fails to support its conclusion, and then examines three arguments against the doctrine. He argues that only one of these is sound, but it is enough to invalidate ethical egoism.*

Is There a Duty to Contribute for Famine Relief?

Each year millions of people die of malnutrition and related health problems. A common pattern among children in poor countries is death from dehydration caused by diarrhea brought on by malnutrition. James Grant, executive director of the United Nations Children's Fund (UNICEF), estimates that about 15,000 children die in this way *every day*. That comes to 5,475,000 children annually. Even if his estimate is too high, the number that die is staggering.

For those of us in the affluent countries, this poses an acute moral problem. We spend money on ourselves, not only for the necessities of life but for innumerable luxuries—for fine automobiles, fancy clothes, stereos, sports, movies, and

Reprinted from *The Elements of Moral Philosophy* (New York: Random House, 1986) by permission of McGraw-Hill Publishing Company and the author.

so on. In our country, even people with modest incomes enjoy such things. The problem is that we *could* forgo our luxuries and give the money for famine relief instead. The fact that we don't suggests that we regard our luxuries as more important than feeding the hungry.

Why do we allow people to starve to death when we could save them? Very few of us actually believe our luxuries are that important. Most of us, if asked the question directly, would probably be a bit embarrassed, and we would say that we probably should do more for famine relief. The explanation of why we do not is, at least in part, that we hardly ever think of the problem. Living our own comfortable lives, we are effectively insulated from it. The starving people are dying at some distance from us; we do not see them, and we can avoid even thinking of them. When we do think of them, it is only abstractly, as bloodless statistics. Unfortunately for the starving, statistics do not have much power to motivate action.

But leaving aside the question of *why* we behave as we do, what is our *duty*? What *should* we do? We might think of this as the "common-sense" view of the matter: morality requires that we balance our own interests against the interests of others. It is understandable, of course, that we look out for our own interests, and no one can be faulted for attending to his own basic needs. But at the same time the needs of others are also important, and when we can help others—especially at little cost to ourselves—we should do so. Suppose you are thinking of spending ten dollars on a trip to the movies, when you are reminded that ten dollars could buy food for a starving child. Thus you could do a great service for the child at little cost to yourself.

Commonsense morality would say, then, that you should give the money for famine relief rather than spending it on the movies.

This way of thinking involves a general assumption about our moral duties: it is assumed that we have moral duties *to other people*—and not merely duties that we create, such as by making a promise or incurring a debt. We have "natural" duties to others *simply because they are people who could be helped or harmed by our actions.* If a certain action would benefit (or harm) other people, then that is a reason why we should (or should not) do that action. The common-sense assumption is that other people's interests *count,* for their own sakes, from a moral point of view.

But one person's common sense is another person's naive platitude. Some thinkers have maintained that, in fact, we have no "natural" duties to other people. *Ethical Egoism* is the idea that each person ought to pursue his or her own self-interest exclusively. It is different from Psychological Egoism, which is a theory of human nature concerned with how people *do* behave— Psychological Egoism says that people do in fact always pursue their own interests. Ethical Egoism, by contrast, is a normative theory—that is, a theory about how we *ought* to behave. Regardless of how we do behave, Ethical Egoism says we have no moral duty except to do what is best for ourselves.

It is a challenging theory. It contradicts some of our deepest moral beliefs—beliefs held by most of us, at any rate—but it is not easy to refute. We will examine the most important arguments for and against it. If it turns out to be true, then of course that is immensely important. But even if it turns out to be false, there is still much to be learned from examining it—we may, for example, gain some insight into the reasons why we *do* have obligations to other people.

But before looking at the arguments, we should be a little clearer about exactly what this theory says and what it does not say. In the first place, Ethical Egoism does not say that one should promote one's own interests *as well as* the interests of others. That would be an ordinary, unexceptional view. Ethical Egoism is the radical view that one's *only* duty is to promote one's own interests. According to Ethical Egoism, there is only one ultimate principle of conduct, the principle of self-interest, and this principle sums up *all* of one's natural duties and obligations.

However, Ethical Egoism does not say that you should *avoid* actions that help others, either. It may very well be that in many instances your interests coincide with the interests of others, so that in helping yourself you will be aiding others willy-nilly. Or it may happen that aiding others is an effective *means* for creating some benefit for yourself. Ethical Egoism does not forbid such actions; in fact, it may demand them. The theory insists only that in such cases the benefit to others is not what makes the act right. What makes the act right is, rather, the fact that it is to one's own advantage.

Finally, Ethical Egoism does not imply that in pursuing one's interests one ought always to do what one wants to do, or what gives one the most pleasure in the short run. Someone may want to do something that is not good for himself or that will eventually cause himself more grief than pleasure—he may want to drink a lot or smoke cigarettes or take drugs or waste his best years at the race track. Ethical Egoism would frown on all this, regardless of the momentary pleasure it affords. It says that a person ought to do what *really is* to his or her own best advantage, *over the long run.* It endorses selfishness but it doesn't endorse foolishness.

Three Arguments in Favor of Ethical Egoism

What reasons can be advanced to support this doctrine? Why should anyone think it is true? Unfortunately, the theory is asserted more often than it is argued for. Many of its supporters apparently think its truth is self-evident, so that arguments are not needed. When it *is* argued for, three lines of reasoning are most commonly used.

1. The first argument has several variations, each suggesting the same general point:

a. Each of us is intimately familiar with our own individual wants and needs. Moreover, each of us is uniquely placed to pursue those wants and needs effectively. At the same time, we know the desires and needs of other people only imperfectly, and we are not well situated to pursue them. Therefore, it is reasonable to believe that if we set out to be "our brother's keeper," we would often bungle the job and end up doing more mischief than good.

b. At the same time, the policy of "looking out for others" is an offensive intrusion into other people's privacy; it is essentially a policy of minding other people's business.

c. Making other people the object of one's "charity" is degrading to them; it robs them of their individual dignity and self-respect. The offer of charity says, in effect, that they are not competent to care for themselves; and the statement is self-fulfilling—they cease to be self-reliant and become passively dependent on others. That is why the recipients of "charity" are so often resentful rather than appreciative.

What this adds up to is that the policy of "looking out for others" is self-defeating. If we want to promote the best interests of everyone alike, we should *not* adopt so-called altruistic policies of behavior. On the contrary, if each person looks after his or her *own* interests, it is more likely that everyone will be better off, in terms of both physical and emotional well-being. Thus Robert G. Olson says in his book *The Morality of Self-Interest* (1965), "The individual is most likely to contribute to social betterment by rationally pursuing his own best long-range interests." Or as Alexander Pope said more poetically,

Thus God and nature formed the general frame
And bade self-love and social be the same.

It is possible to quarrel with this argument on a number of grounds. Of course no one favors bungling, butting in, or depriving people of their self-respect. But is this really what we are doing

when we feed hungry children? Is the starving child in Ethiopia really harmed when we "intrude" into "her business" by supplying food? It hardly seems likely. Yet we can set this point aside, for considered as an argument for Ethical Egoism, this way of thinking has an even more serious defect.

The trouble is that it isn't really an argument *for Ethical Egoism* at all. The argument concludes that we should adopt certain policies of action; and on the surface they appear to be egoistic policies. However, the *reason* it is said we should adopt those policies is decidedly *un*egoistic. The reason is one that to an egoist shouldn't matter. It is said that we should adopt those policies because doing so will promote the "betterment of society"—but according to Ethical Egoism, that is something we should not be concerned about. Spelled out fully, with everything laid on the table, the argument says:

1. We ought to do whatever will promote the best interests of everyone alike.
2. The interests of everyone will best be promoted if each of us adopts the policy of pursuing our own interests exclusively.
3. Therefore, each of us should adopt the policy of pursuing our own interests exclusively.

If we accept this reasoning, then we are not ethical egoists at all. Even though we might end up *behaving* like egoists, our ultimate principle is one of beneficence—we are doing what we think will help everyone, not merely what we think will benefit ourselves. Rather than being egoists, we turn out to be altruists with a peculiar view of what in fact promotes the general welfare.

2. The second argument was put forward with some force by Ayn Rand, a writer little heeded by professional philosophers but who nevertheless was enormously popular on college campuses during the 1960s and 1970s. Ethical Egoism, in her view, is the only ethical philosophy that respects the integrity of the individual human life. She regarded the ethics of "altruism" as a totally destructive idea, both in society as a whole and in

the lives of individuals taken in by it. Altruism, to her way of thinking, leads to a denial of the value of the individual. It says to a person: *your* life is merely something that may be sacrificed. "If a man accepts the ethics of altruism," she writes, "his first concern is not how to live his life, but how to sacrifice it." Moreover, those who would *promote* this idea are beneath contempt—they are parasites who, rather than working to build and sustain their own lives, leech off those who do. Again, she writes:

Parasites, moochers, looters, brutes and thugs can be of no value to a human being—nor can he gain any benefit from living in a society geared to *their* needs, demands and protections, a society that treats him as a sacrificial animal and penalizes him for his virtues in order to reward *them* for their vices, which means: a society based on the ethics of altruism.

By "sacrificing one's life" Rand does not necessarily mean anything so dramatic as dying. A person's life consists (in part) of projects undertaken and goods earned and created. To demand that a person abandon his projects or give up his goods is also a clear effort to "sacrifice his life." Furthermore, throughout her writings Rand also suggests that there is a *metaphysical* basis for egoistic ethics. Somehow, it is the only ethics that takes seriously the *reality* of the individual person. She bemoans "the enormity of the extent to which altruism erodes men's capacity to grasp . . . the value of an individual life; it reveals a mind from which the reality of a human being has been wiped out."

What, then, of the starving people? It might be argued, in response, that Ethical Egoism "reveals a mind from which the reality of a human being has been wiped out"—namely, the human being who is starving. Rand quotes with approval the evasive answer given by one of her followers: "Once, when Barbara Brandon was asked by a student: 'What will happen to the poor . . . ?'— she answered: 'If *you* want to help them, you will not be stopped.'"

All these remarks are, I think, part of one continuous argument that can be summarized like this:

1. A person has only one life to live. If we place any value on the individual—that is, if the individual has any moral worth—then we must agree that this life is of supreme importance. After all, it is all one has, and all one is.
2. The ethics of altruism regards the life of the individual as something one must be ready to sacrifice for the good of others.
3. Therefore, the ethics of altruism does not take seriously the value of the human individual.
4. Ethical Egoism, which allows each person to view his or her own life as being of ultimate value, *does* take the human individual seriously—in fact, it is the only philosophy that does so.
5. Thus, Ethical Egoism is the philosophy that ought to be accepted.

The problem with this argument, as you may already have noticed, is that it relies on picturing the alternatives in such an extreme way. "The ethics of altruism" is taken to be such an extreme philosophy that *nobody*, with the possible exception of certain monks, would find it congenial. As Ayn Rand presents it, altruism implies that one's own interests have *no* value, and that *any* demand by others calls for sacrificing them. If that is the alternative, then any other view, including Ethical Egoism, will look good by comparison. But this is hardly a fair picture of the choices. What we called the common-sense view stands somewhere between the two extremes. It says that one's own interests and the interests of others are both important and must be balanced against one another. Sometimes, when the balancing is done, it will turn out that one should act in the interests of others; other times, it will turn out that one should take care of oneself. So even if the Randian argument refutes the extreme "ethics of altruism," it does not follow that one must accept the other extreme of Ethical Egoism.

3. The third line of reasoning takes a somewhat different approach. Ethical Egoism is usually presented as a *revisionist* moral philosophy, that is, as a philosophy that says our common-sense moral views are mistaken and need to be changed. It is possible, however, to interpret Ethical Egoism in a much less radical way, as a theory that *accepts* common-sense morality and offers a surprising account of its basis.

The less radical interpretation goes as follows. In everyday life, we assume that we are obliged to obey certain rules. We must avoid doing harm to others, speak the truth, keep our promises, and so on. At first glance, these duties appear to be very different from one another. They appear to have little in common. Yet from a theoretical point of view, we may wonder whether there is not some hidden *unity* underlying the hodgepodge of separate duties. Perhaps there is some small number of fundamental principles that explain all the rest, just as in physics there are basic principles that bring together and explain diverse phenomena. From a theoretical point of view, the smaller the number of basic principles, the better. Best of all would be *one* fundamental principle, from which all the rest could be derived. Ethical Egoism, then, would be the theory that all our duties are ultimately derived from the one fundamental principle of self-interest.

Taken in this way, Ethical Egoism is not such a radical doctrine. It does not challenge common-sense morality; it only tries to explain and systematize it. And it does a surprisingly successful job. It can provide plausible explanations of the duties mentioned above, and more:

a. If we make a habit of doing things that are harmful to other people, people will not be reluctant to do things that will harm *us*. We will be shunned and despised; others will not have us as friends and will not do us favors when we need them. If our offenses against others are serious enough, we may even end up in jail. Thus it is to our own advantage to avoid harming others.

b. If we lie to other people, we will suffer all the ill effects of a bad reputation. People will distrust us and avoid doing business with us. We will often need for people to be honest with us, but we can hardly expect them to feel much of an obligation to be honest with us if they know we have not been honest with them. Thus it is to our own advantage to be truthful.

c. It is to our own advantage to be able to enter into mutually beneficial arrangements with other people. To benefit from those arrangements, we need to be able to rely on others to keep their parts of the bargains we make with them—we need to be able to rely on them to keep their promises to us. But we can hardly expect others to keep their promises to us if we are not willing to keep our promises to them. Therefore, from the point of view of self-interest, we should keep our promises.

Pursuing this line of reasoning, Thomas Hobbes suggested that the principle of Ethical Egoism leads to nothing less than the Golden Rule: we should "do unto others" *because* if we do, others will be more likely to "do unto us."

Does this argument succeed in establishing Ethical Egoism as a viable theory of morality? It is, in my opinion at least, the best try. But there are two serious objections to it. In the first place, the argument does not prove quite as much as it needs to prove. At best, it shows only that *as a general rule* it is to one's own advantage to avoid harming others. It does not show that this is *always* so. And it could not show that, for even though it may usually be to one's advantage to avoid harming others, sometimes it is not. Sometimes one might even *gain* from treating another person badly. In that case, the obligation not to harm the other person could *not* be derived from the principle of Ethical Egoism. Thus it appears that not all our moral obligations can be explained as derivable from self-interest.

But set that point aside. There is still a more fundamental question to be asked about the proposed theory. Suppose it is true that, say, contributing money for famine relief is somehow to one's own advantage. It does not follow that this is the only reason, or even the most basic reason, why doing so is a morally good thing. (For example, the most basic reason might be *in order to help the starving people.* The fact that doing so is also to one's own advantage might be only a secondary, less important, consideration.) A demonstration that one could *derive* this duty from self-interest does not prove that self-interest is the *only reason* one has this duty. Only if you accept an additional proposition—namely, the proposition that there is no reason for giving *other than* self-interest—will you find Ethical Egoism a plausible theory.

Three Arguments against Ethical Egoism

Ethical Egoism has haunted twentieth-century moral philosophy. It has not been a popular doctrine; the most important philosophers have rejected it outright. But it has never been very far from their minds. Although no thinker of consequence has defended it, almost everyone has felt it necessary to explain why he was rejecting it—as though the very possibility that it might be correct was hanging in the air, threatening to smother their other ideas. As the merits of the various "refutations" have been debated, philosophers have returned to it again and again.

The following three arguments are typical of the refutations proposed by contemporary philosophers.

1. In his book *The Moral Point of View* (1958), Kurt Baier argues that Ethical Egoism cannot be correct because it cannot provide solutions for conflicts of interest. We need moral rules, he says, only because our interests sometimes come into conflict. (If they never conflicted, then there would be no problems to solve and hence no need for the kind of guidance that morality provides.) But Ethical Egoism does not help to resolve conflicts of interest; it only exacerbates them. Baier argues for this by introducing a fanciful example:

Let B and K be candidates for the presidency of a certain country and let it be granted that it is in the interest of either to be elected, but that only one can succeed. It would then be in the interest of B but against the interest of K if B were elected, and vice versa, and therefore in the interest of B but against the interest of K if K were

liquidated, and vice versa. But from this it would follow that B ought to liquidate K, that it is wrong for B not to do so, that B has not "done his duty" until he has liquidated K; and vice versa. Similarly K, knowing that his own liquidation is in the interest of B and therefore, anticipating B's attempts to secure it, ought to take steps to foil B's endeavors. It would be wrong for him not to do so. He would "not have done his duty" until he had made sure of stopping B. . . .

This is obviously absurd. For morality is designed to apply in just such cases, namely, those where interests conflict. But if the point of view of morality were that of self-interest, then there could never be moral solutions of conflicts of interest.

Does this argument prove that Ethical Egoism is unacceptable? It does, *if* the conception of morality to which it appeals is accepted. The argument assumes that an adequate morality must provide solutions for conflicts of interest in such a way that everyone concerned can live together harmoniously. The conflict between B and K, for example, should be resolved so that they would no longer be at odds with one another. (One would not then have a duty to do something that the other has a duty to prevent.) Ethical Egoism does not do that, and if you think an ethical theory should, then you will not find Ethical Egoism acceptable.

But a defender of Ethical Egoism might reply that *he* does not accept this conception of morality. For him, life is essentially a long series of conflicts in which each person is struggling to come out on top; and the principle he accepts— the principle of Ethical Egoism—simply urges each one to do his or her best to win. On his view, the moralist is not like a courtroom judge, who resolves disputes. Instead, he is like the Commissioner of Boxing, who urges each fighter to do his best. So the conflict between B and K will be "resolved" not by the application of an ethical theory but by one or the other of them winning the struggle. The egoist will not be embarrassed by this—on the contary, he will think it no more than a realistic view of the nature of things.

2. Some philosophers, including Baier, have leveled an even more serious charge against Ethical Egoism. They have argued that it is a *logically inconsistent* doctrine—that is, they say it leads to logical contradictions. If this is true, then Ethical Egoism is indeed a mistaken theory, for no theory can be true if it is self-contradictory.

Consider B and K again. As Baier explains their predicament, it is in B's interest to kill K, and obviously it is in K's interest to prevent it. But, Baier says,

if K prevents B from liquidating him, his act must be said to be both wrong and not wrong—wrong because it is the prevention of what B ought to do, his duty, and wrong for B not to do it; not wrong because it is what K ought to do, his duty, and wrong for K not to do it. But one and the same act (logically) cannot be both morally wrong and not morally wrong.

Now, does *this* argument prove that Ethical Egoism is unacceptable? At first glance it seems persuasive. However, it is a complicated argument, so we need to set it out with each step individually identified. Then we will be in a better position to evaluate it. Spelled out fully, it looks like this:

1. Suppose it is each person's duty to do what is in his own best interests.
2. It is in B's best interest to liquidate K.
3. It is in K's best interest to prevent B from liquidating him.
4. Therefore B's duty is to liquidate K, and K's duty is to prevent B from doing it.
5. But it is wrong to prevent someone from doing his duty.
6. Therefore it is wrong for K to prevent B from liquidating him.
7. Therefore it is both wrong and not wrong for K to prevent B from liquidating him.
8. But no act can be both wrong and not wrong—that is a self-contradiction.
9. Therefore the assumption with which we started—that it is each person's duty to do what is in his own best interests—cannot be true.

When the argument is set out in this way, we can see its hidden flaw. The logical contradiction—that it is both wrong and not wrong for K to prevent B from liquidating him—does *not* follow simply from the principle of Ethical Egoism. It follows from that principle, *and* the additional premise expressed in step (5)—namely, that "it is wrong to prevent someone from doing his duty." Thus we are not compelled by the logic of the argument to reject Ethical Egoism. Instead, we could simply reject this additional premise, and the contradiction would be avoided. That is surely what the ethical egoist would want to do, for the ethical egoist would never say, without qualification, that it is always wrong to prevent someone from doing his duty. He would say, instead, that *whether one ought to prevent someone from doing his duty depends entirely on whether it would be to one's own advantage to do so.* Regardless of whether we think this is a correct view, it is, at the very least, a *consistent* view, and so this attempt to convict the egoist of self-contradiction fails.

3. Finally, we come to the argument that I think comes closest to an outright refutation of Ethical Egoism. It is also the most interesting of the arguments, because at the same time it provides the most insight into why the interests of other people *should* matter to a moral agent.

Before this argument is presented, we need to look briefly at a general point about moral values. So let us set Ethical Egoism aside for a moment and consider this related matter.

There is a whole family of moral views that have this in common: they all involve dividing people into groups and saying that the interests of some groups count for more than the interests of other groups. Racism is the most conspicuous example; it involves dividing people into groups according to race and assigning greater importance to the interests of one race than to others. The practical result is that members of the preferred race are to be *treated better* than the others. Anti-Semitism works the same way, and so can nationalism. People in the grip of such views will think, in effect: "*My* race counts for more," or "Those who believe in *my* religion count for more," or "*My* country counts for more," and so on.

Can such views be defended? Those who accept them are usually not much interested in argument—racists, for example, rarely try to offer rational grounds for their position. But suppose they did. What could they say?

There is a general principle that stands in the way of any such defense, namely: *We can justify treating people differently only if we can show that there is some factual difference between them that is relevant to justifying the difference in treatment.* For example, if one person is admitted to law school while another is rejected, this can be justified by pointing out that the first graduated from college with honors and scored well on the admissions test, while the second dropped out of college and never took the test. However, if *both* graduated with honors and did well on the entrance examination—in other words, if they are in all relevant respects equally well qualified—then it is merely arbitrary to admit one but not the other.

Can a racist point to any differences between, say, white people and black people that would justify treating them differently? In the past, racists have sometimes attempted to do this by picturing blacks as stupid, lacking in ambition, and the like. *If* this were true, then it might justify treating them differently, in at least some circumstances. (This is the deep purpose of racist stereotypes—to provide the "relevant differences" needed to justify differences in treatment.) But of course it is not true, and in fact there are no such general differences between the races. Thus racism is an *arbitrary* doctrine, in that it advocates treating some people differently even though there are no differences between them to justify it.

Ethical Egoism is a moral theory of the same type. It advocates that each of us divide the world into two categories of people—ourselves and all the rest—and that we regard the interests of those in the first group as more important than the interests of those in the second group. But each of us can ask, what is the difference between myself and others that justifies placing myself in this special category? Am I more intelligent? Do I

enjoy my life more? Are my accomplishments greater? Do I have needs or abilities that are so different from the needs or abilities of others? *What is it that makes me so special?* Failing an answer, it turns out that Ethical Egoism is an arbitrary doctrine, in the same way that racism is arbitrary.

The argument, then, is this:

1. Any moral doctrine that assigns greater importance to the interests of one group than to those of another is unacceptably arbitrary unless there is some difference between the members of the groups that justifies treating them differently.
2. Ethical Egoism would have each person assign greater importance to his or her own interests than to the interests of others. *But there is no general difference between oneself and others, to which each person can appeal, that justifies this difference in treatment.*
3. Therefore, Ethical Egoism is unacceptably arbitrary.

And this, in addition to arguing against Ethical Egoism, also sheds some light on the question of why we should care about others.

We should care about the interests of other people *for the very same reason we care about our own interests;* for their needs and desires are comparable to our own. Consider, one last time, the starving people we could feed by giving up some of our luxuries. Why should we care about them? We care about ourselves, of course—if *we* were starving, we would go to almost any lengths to get food. But what is the difference between us and them? Does hunger affect tham any less? Are they somehow less deserving than we? If we can find no relevant difference between us and them, then we must admit that if *our* needs should be met, so should *theirs.* It is this realization, that we are on a par with one another, that is the deepest reason why our morality must include some recognition of the needs of others, and why, then, Ethical Egoism fails as a moral theory.

11

Sociobiology, Egoism, and Reciprocity

HOWARD KAHANE

Howard Kahane, (1928–2001) was professor of philosophy at the University of Maryland Baltimore Country. He is the author of several works in philosophy, including Logic and Contemporary Rhetoric *and* Logic and Philosophy.

Egoists are right in insisting that it is rational to try to maximize one's own desires, but wrong in forgetting that most of us have strong desires favoring fair play, justice, and the like, whose satisfaction sometimes requires us to act contrary to egoistic principles. But when does this happen? And what are the principles of fair play and justice that we desire to satisfy? Recent sociobiological theories suggest answers to these questions based on ideas concerning reciprocal altruism and the evolution of moral and other regarding sentiments. Moral sentiments evolved, on this view, because of the tremendous benefits of cooperative behavior. That is why, for most of us, at any rate, playing the game fair and square means, roughly speaking, not taking advantage of others by making unfair agreements, and keeping (uncoerced) agreements, implicit as well as explicit, when others can be expected to do so in return. We see agreements as competitively fair *only if they treat all competitors in the same way and thus do not favor one party compared to others, and as* cooperatively fair *only if they distribute the benefits of cooperative ventures according to the time, wealth, effective effort, and so on, each party contributes. In addition, evolutionary forces have instilled in most of us a desire for retribution—a desire to strike back at those who betray us by failing to keep fair agreements—and sentiments of empathy, compassion, affection, and the like, that tend to motivate the keeping of fair agreements and the friendliness and trust that make for reasonably well functioning societies. Homo sapiens having evolved as an in-group–out-group social animal.*

It must not be forgotten that although a high standard of morality gives but a slight or no advantage to each individual man and his children over the other men of the same tribe, yet that an increase in the number of well-endowed men and an advancement in the standard of morality will certainly give an immense advantage to one tribe over another. . . . [T]he standard of morality and the number of well-endowed men will thus everywhere tend to rise and increase.

—Charles Darwin

Crito, we owe a cock to Aesculapius. Pay it and do not neglect it.

—Last utterance of Socrates
(as reported by Plato)

There has been a controversy started of late . . . concerning the general foundation of Morals; whether they be derived from Reason, or from sentiment; whether we attain the knowledge of them by chain of argument and induction, or by an immediate feeling and finer internal sense; whether, like all sound judgment of truth and falsehood, they should be the same to every rational intelligent being, or whether, like the perception of beauty and deformity, they be founded entirely on the particular fabric and constitution of the human species.

—David Hume

1. Egoism

If, as Hume claimed, morals come down to a matter of internal sentiments—to desires, feelings, and the like—then why should we ever do anything other than what we feel like doing at any given moment? Why act unselfishly, or according to alleged moral principles foisted on us from the "outside"? Why not, in other words, adopt the extreme form of *egoism* that tells us to act so as to maximize strictly selfish immediate desires and goals?

The reason we should not is that rejecting externally grounded moral standards does not make it rational to always satisfy immediate selfish appetites. For one thing, rationality requires *prudence*. Unselfish actions engaged in now often have large selfish payoffs later. An enlightened egoistic theory thus will allow, for example, giving an expensive gift to one's boss in the expectation of large returns later. And for another, rationality requires that we take account of all of our motivating sentiments, including the *altruistic*, unselfish, ones directed towards friends, mates, and close kin, in particular, offspring. It is very human indeed to want to sacrifice for our own children, siblings, and dear friends. So if egoism is to be a sensible, rational, theory, it must permit a certain amount of altruistic, unselfish, behavior.

In fact, if there were no relevant human sentiments other than the ones just described, being an egoist and being rational would amount to pretty much the same thing. They do not because there is a particular type of nonegoistic sentiment that rationality requires us to weigh in the balance, namely, the kind that leads us to favor *justice, retribution, loyalty, fair play*, and that sort of thing. A truly egoistic theory, after all, has to counsel against giving in to sentiments of this kind.

Of course, saying that we have sentiments favoring justice, fair play, or whatever, is a far cry from spelling out what this means in practice. What are the principles of fair play that seem intuitively right to most of us? How do we feel about retribution? Do we really desire this kind of striking back at transgressors? Is retribution any different from nasty old revenge? What, if anything, makes, or ought to make, a person feel *obligated* to sacrifice for others? What, in other words, do these moral sentiments of ours tell us to *do*, or not do?

The history of philosophy is chock full of answers to these questions, but unfortunately, the answers given by one philosopher generally conflict with what many others have claimed to have proved beyond a shadow of a doubt. Utilitarians, such as John Stuart Mill, tie moral obligation to human happiness, pleasure, or satisfaction. Our duty, according to utilitarians, is to produce the greatest possible amount of these goods, irrespective of how they are distributed. Animal rights advocates insist we also need to take account of the welfare of other sentient beings. Kantians argue that morality requires us always to treat other human beings as ends, never as means. Others claim that morality requires us always to act out of love for all human beings. Which, if any, of these seekers-after-truth should we believe?

Clearly, introspection is not irrelevant to any investigation of these questions. If it feels radically wrong, or right, maybe it is wrong, or right. But human beings are notoriously self-deceivers. We tend, for example, to overestimate the strengths of our other-regarding, altruistic, sentiments and to think of ourselves as a good deal more highminded than in fact we are. Looking into one's own psyche obviously needs to be complemented by other sorts of investigations. What, for instance (let's get to the point) does science have to say about the matter? Philosophers have always looked to the science of their day for guidance, and we are fortunate today in having the recently burgeoning science of evolutionary biology to consult. So before accepting any particular philosophical theory about the nature of human moral sentiments, not excluding the one to be presented here shortly, we ought at least to find out how it fits with what biologists tell is in the evolutionary cards. What could moral sentiments be like that have evolved in this world of tooth and claw?

2. Sociobiology and Reciprocity

To start with, we need to remember that *genes* are the basic units of natural selection, not species and certainly not individual organisms. Human beings, as all living things, thus can profitably be thought of as "gene survival machines."[1] Of course, genes do not produce behavior in any direct way; they just code for the production of complicated molecules in body cells, which in turn give us motivating interests (desires, perceived goals, and the like).

In everyday life, we often divide the actions typically engaged in by our fellows into those that are selfish—intended to benefit the actor—and those that are unselfish, designed to benefit others. Evolutionary biologists further divide the unselfish kind into those they call *kin altruistic*, intended to benefit close relatives, and those labeled *reciprocal altruistic*, designed to benefit others who can be expected to return the favor.

That we should be programmed to perform selfishly has an obvious evolutionary explanation. Gene survival machines need time to procreate, during which they have to survive and prosper. Similarly, that we engage in a great deal of kin altruism, in particular working hard to benefit our own children, makes good evolutionary sense. Close relatives harbor a nice portion of our own genes, and genetic success depends on our own genes being passed down through the next generation. Offspring well cared for obviously have a much better chance to win at the genetic game than those left to fend for themselves. The vital importance of kin altruism is the reason that the old saying about blood being thicker than water is so absolutely true.

But the widespread nature of reciprocal altruism in human populations needs a bit of explanation and discussion. In particular, why bother to reciprocate when we already have received our share of the benefits generated by a cooperative agreement? Why, to take a relatively trivial case, pay for goods already received, or for services already rendered? Where is the genetic payoff in this kind of honesty? Or, to put the question another way, how could moral sentiments motivating us to benefit nonkin, often at great sacrifice to ourselves, have evolved in this dog-eat-dog world? The answer is that they evolved because of the tremendous benefits of reciprocal altruistic behavior. Human beings are the cooperating animal par excellence,[2] and cooperation requires reciprocity. In most cases, two heads, or two pairs of hands, not to mention many, are much better than one. But scratching my back pays off for you, genetically speaking, only if I can be trusted to scratch your back in return. When cheating on reciprocal arrangements goes beyond a certain point, cooperative arrangements break down, and their vital benefits are lost. Morality is the oil that lubricates the machinery of cooperation, which makes possible the goods on which human life depends. The moral sentiments motivating us to keep bargains evolved because the actions they encourage have a greater average genetic payoff than behavior of the more selfish variety. In the long run, trustworthy cooperators win out in competition with those who cheat. (No wonder Socrates' last remark expressed his strong desire that a debt be repaid.)

Note, by the way, that cooperation pays off not just in the competitions that go on within societies but also with respect to conflicts between cultures. *Homo sapiens* has evolved as an in-group–out-group social animal. Victory in the genetic game depends not just on doing well within one's own society but also on the success of one's in-group vis-à-vis competing out-groups. It does a body little good to win out in competitions with compatriots if one's group as a whole loses out to other groups. Thus, to cite a famous case, the citizens of Carthage who were successful in competition with other Carthegenians became genetic losers when their whole society was wiped out by Roman legions.

So it isn't surprising that strong sentiments favoring group loyalty have evolved to the point, for instance, that individuals are willing to seriously risk their lives in time of war. Of course, risking life and limb in this way makes sense only when there is the morally required reciprocity of *trust*— when there is reasonable assurance that others also will do so. (Charles Darwin clearly understood this implication of his evolutionary theory; witness his remark that morality is an important element in the success of one tribe over others.)

We shouldn't forget, however, that the other human beings with whom we must cooperate in order to succeed in life are at the same time our most serious genetic competitors.[3] Indeed, this is very likely the most fundamental fact that needs to be kept in mind if we are to understand the human moral animal. *Success in life requires us to cooperate with our most serious genetic competitors!*

That is why, incidentally, it makes sense to speak of the *temptation* to sin. The cooperative side of our nature insists that we play the reciprocity game straight even when greater profits are to be made by cheating; the competitive side demands that we "defect" (a technical term) whenever doing so will maximize selfish interests. When (as in the case of saints) the cooperative side is totally in command, there is no temptation to cheat; when (as is regularly true only for sociopaths) the competitive side has exclusive sway, defection becomes automatic, temptation irrelevant.

Speaking of saints and sociopaths brings to mind the point that both, but especially saints, are bound to be rare in any human population. A society composed exclusively, or even on the whole, of one or the other cannot be *evolutionarily stable.* A group composed primarily of saints is bound to be invaded, sooner or later, by those programmed to clever cheating. A society made up chiefly of sinners will fail to hold its own against more diversely populated competing groups. Theory therefore suggests that most people in a society will fall somewhere in between these two extremes, an idea that is confirmed by even casual observations of *Homo sapiens* in action in everyday life. Virtually all of us are stocked with the stan-

dard sorts of sentiments, but we differ in their relative strengths—the reason, no doubt, some of us find it more difficult than do others to resist the temptation to renege on bargains when there is great profit to be had in doing so. (Because it is so important that our own reciprocal altruistic practices yield a satisfactory return on investment, one of life's chief tasks is to discover who among our fellows can be trusted and who cannot, so as to avoid dealings with the latter whenever possible. Finding a mate who will stick with us through thick and thin, and not be tempted away into greener pastures, is an important case in point. Betrayal of trust is one of life's most serious pitfalls.)

The point of all this talk about reciprocity and cooperation is that their evolution required a concurrent development of dispositions and sentiments making them viable. Sentiments do not evolve willy-nilly; they come into existence because animals stocked with them do better, genetically speaking, than those not so provisioned. The love and affection we feel for offspring, for example, make it more likely that we will engage in kin altruism when necessary rather than act selfishly.

What then are the chief sentiments associated with reciprocity and cooperation? Clearly, those such as affection, empathy, compassion, and the like, sentiments that tend to reduce the temptation to cheat on reciprocal arrangements. Fondness makes sacrifice easier, hate more difficult. Friends cooperate better, with less chicanery, than enemies, or even casual acquaintances. This is true, certainly, with respect to everyday cooperative agreements struck between in-group members; it is true in spades with respect to the societywide agreement, implied in group membership, not to betray one's fellows in conflicts with competing societies.

This brings to mind the point that evolutionary forces have produced not just specific sentiments, such as empathy and compassion, but also a general disposition to accept and find reasonable the customs and regulations of one's own in-group. Genetic success depends on working cohesively with one's compatriots, and it is difficult to do so with individuals who deviate greatly from accepted behavioral norms. Note, however, that this general disposition to conform often conflicts with specific sentiments favoring justice and fair play, not to mention those motivating us to seek personal gain.

Finally, before moving on to other matters, it needs to be noticed that in referring to theories of evolutionary biology we do not commit the fallacy David Hume railed against of inferring from what *is* the case—the way in which human beings in fact behave—to what *ought to be* the case, the way they ought to perform. The claim being made here is not that evolutionary theories *prove* anything about moral obligation but rather that they provide very good reasons for believing human beings on the whole are well supplied with sentiments tending to increase profitable cooperative activities, sentiments of the kind that have generally been regarded as moral. It would be a mistake to conclude after quick introspection, or without seriously considering the possibility of self-deception concerning one's true motives and intentions, that the cited biological theories are on the wrong track, just as it generally is a mistake to run afoul of theories confirmed by a great many diverse experiences in favor of conclusions that are more narrowly supported. Those who ignore what science tells us about human nature and adopt moral philosophies that fail to take appropriate account of what science says about our in-group–out-group nature, or that advocate unscientific, "goody-goody" theories obligating us to love and care for all of our fellows, do so at their peril. (We cannot, while hating the sin, love the sinner, nor do we genuinely wish to do so. Evolutionary forces have made sure of that.)

Even so, it would be a mistake to ignore everyday experiences, introspective or otherwise, that appear to contradict what science has to say. We need to weigh all of the evidence we can get on the matter. Those who examine their own psyches and find little that conforms to what has been or is about to be said concerning fair play and moral sentiments will have good, although certainly not conclusive, reason to be skeptical. But the experiences of this writer, at any rate, lend support to the idea that most of us, when we face up to it, do indeed, with exceptions here and there, pretty much conform to what evolutionary theory suggests about the nature of human moral nature.[4]

3. Nature Versus Nurture

Underpinning the evolutionary theories appealed to in this essay is the idea that human behavior, like all animal behavior, has a strong genetic component. This does not mean, of course, that human behavior is "hard wired." In particular, it does not mean that genes provide us with a stock of moral sentiments of various strengths that we then carry around, unaltered, throughout our lives. Genes do determine certain physical characteristics, for instance eye color, once and for all. But they do not determine once and for all how we will act in the various sorts of situations encountered in everyday life. Rather, they establish a range of possible responses within which environmental factors—conditioning—play a role. The mix of moral sentiments and dispositions we have at a given time in life thus depends both on our genetic endowment, given to us at the moment of conception, and on the experiences we have had up to that time.

Unfortunately, scientific understanding of the ways in which these hereditary and environmental forces interact is still in its infancy. We know certain gross sorts of generalities, for instance, that being raised in a neglectful or abusive family tends to reduce the strengths of moral sentiments such as compassion and empathy, thus reducing the likelihood that those of us raised in this sort of inhospitable environment will play the game fair and square. But we also know that there are lots of exceptions to this general rule and that many individuals brought up in this way turn out to be kind, caring, upstanding members of society. Finer-tuned theories about how nature and nurture interact are needed, and no doubt will be supplied in the future.

But it is crystal clear now that evolutionary theories concerning human moral behavior cannot be rejected simply because we know that environmental factors influence behavior. We can be quite sure that, as stated before, environment influences behavior only within a range laid down by genetic factors that have evolved over long periods of time, factors that evolved because individuals stocked with certain combinations of genes have won out over competitors endowed with different genetic mixes.

In a great many cases, the genetic component of behavior is obvious. No one supposes, for instance, that we can shape randomly chosen individuals into athletic or aesthetic geniuses merely by providing them with the right sorts of environment, any more than that we can turn them into 100-meter-dash champions simply by having them step onto the track in a pair of Reeboks or Nikes. We all know that it takes both natural talent and intense practice to produce high-caliber performances of this kind. Similarly, although the languages individuals speak depend on where and by whom they are raised, no one supposes that we can teach, say, dogs to speak Chinese simply by having them raised in a Chinese-speaking family. Which language a person speaks depends on all sorts of environmental factors, but the ability to learn any languages at all requires the sort of genes that human beings have but dogs, alas, lack.

Why, then, suppose that moral dispositions and sentiments are any different? Even if we still do not completely understand how heredity and environment interact to generate particular responses to moral situations, we do understand why evolutionary forces have provisioned *Homo sapiens* with a moral dimension—to enable us to gain the advantages of cooperative behavior. And we know a few modestly vague but still useful facts about the kinds of moral dispositions that evolutionary forces, shaped by environmental factors, are likely to produce in the general run of human beings. Philosophers ignore this knowledge at their peril.

4. Reciprocity and Morality: The Principles of Fair Play

Although sentiments such as affection and compassion certainly are important, perhaps even vital, to the evolution of complex reciprocal arrangements, they are not sufficient. What is required in addition is a general disposition, a genuine desire, to keep one's word—to be *trustable*. We can not be fond of everyone we deal with; bargains frequently need to be kept with people we hardly know, and even, sometimes, with enemies. A reciprocity of trust, generated in part by sentiments favoring the keeping of one's word, is required to get these sorts of arrangements off the ground.

But all agreements are not created equal. Some are a good deal fairer than others. We need to be able to tell, at least in some rough way, which bargains are *fair* and which are not. Fairness enters the picture because of the fact, insisted on before, that we have to cooperate so often with serious genetic rivals. (Bees, ants, and other social insects, cooperate with in-group members of the same caste without regard to fairness, but that is because, in effect, they are clones of each other and thus not genetic competitors.) Those who regularly get less than a fair share of the spoils of cooperative ventures, or do more than their share of service to the community as a whole, tend to be defeated by craftier competitors, and this is the reason we all have at least a modestly good sense of what counts as a *fair share* of the fruits of cooperative endeavors, or a fair share of our social duties, and why we usually try very hard not to get the short end of the stick. (Note, by the way, that even those intent on cheating need to know what constitutes a fair share. Most chicanery doesn't involve out-and-out thievery but rather just stacking the deck in one's favor.)

Life being as nasty as it is, however, we often need to take what we can get. Confronted with a choice, say, of less than a fair salary or none at all, prudence dictates knuckling under. But it always is better to garner a fair share if we can.

Of course, if a fair share is good, taking the whole pie would be even better, as would be doing less than one's share of community service. The genetic point behind the sentiments motivating us to resist this sort of temptation, moving us to settle for a fair share even when we might be able to get more, or to risk our necks in battle rather than letting buddies down, is the instability over very long periods of time of societies in which most people are motivated to cheat most of the time. Social life can and does limp along although we all cheat some of the time, and even though a few of us do most of the time, but it breaks down when most of us do so most of the time. Cooperation can stand only so much chicanery. Groups in which this sort of moral theft is more common tend, other things being equal, to lose out when competing with those in which it is less frequent. (Note that this is true with respect to private organizations and small groups as well as to whole societies.)

Most agreements are more or less of the explicit variety. The various parties indicate their acceptance of a contractual arrangement via the spoken or written word. But some are generated without explicit agreements being reached. Custom, for example, tends to generate agreements that are binding even though only implicit. Most everyday social obligations—to refrain from eating in certain public places, to give directions to strangers, to be civil when in public, and so on—very likely arose in this way and became explicitly voiced, those that have, only later.

Because cooperation takes place so often with genetic competitors, and because fair competition requires at least a modicum of cooperation (as it does, for example, in sporting competitions where all players must cooperate at least by conforming to the agreed-upon rules of the game), to be completely fair an arrangement has to be both *competitively* and *cooperatively fair.*

An agreement is generally thought to be *competitively fair* only if the terms of the agreement do not favor a particular competitor over others—only if they do not provide an advantage to one party as compared to others. We see the rules, for instance, that assign greater weights to some horses than to others in a horse race as not fair to the horses themselves (as opposed to owners or wagerers) for that very reason. We do not mind being unfair to horses in this way, but certainly would not think an Olympic marathon fair if the rules required human competitors to be treated in this unequal manner.

Although our basic intuitions concerning competitive fairness given to us by evolutionary forces are reasonably clear, particular cases often are hard to decide. Nature wants us, whenever possible, to play games in which, at the very least, we are not at a disadvantage compared to genetic competitors. But when is this the case? Would a rule permitting insider stock trading, for instance, be fair because it allows everyone, whether an insider or outsider, to engage in this activity? The answer to this kind of question is that there is no automatic answer. It all depends on what sorts of competitive games we wish to play. We say, in fact, that insider trading is unfair because a rule that permitted it would give a tremendous advantage to some speculators (insiders) over others (outsiders) and thus would discourage most people from playing the game. But we could just as well say that a stock market competition allowing this practice is not unfair, because it allows everyone, outsiders as well as insiders, to engage in insider trading if they can. (The rules of bridge are thought to be fair in allowing all players to remember which cards have been played by whom, and in what order, even though lots of players are not up to this task.) We say, in fact, that having much greater wealth to wager than market competitors is not unfair, because it treats everyone in the same way (allowing everyone with any amount of money to play the game). But we could just as well say that allowing this kind of play, although desirable for practical reasons, is unfair, because it gives a tremendous advantage to fat cats. Either way of speaking can be correct; what counts is that we understand what has moved us to talk in one way rather than the other.[5]

It sometimes is argued that there is indeed an objective way to decide whether, say, a marketplace that permits stock competitions between rich and ordinary players is or is not fair. On this view, what counts is that the rules of the game tend to make victory go to those whose winning "talents" are internal to the players. Fair stock market rules, for instance, should on the whole produce winners who best understand the underlying forces that produce high, or low, stock prices, or perhaps who best understand the "true value" of stocks because they know about the competitive chances of the corporations whose issues are being traded. So some would argue against the fairness of trading rules that reward the external talent of having more venture capital than most other players. (Note that certain championship poker competitions are designed to assure complete competitive fairness by providing each player with the same number of startup chips.)

But this way of looking at the matter does not always work. Take the case of two males competing for the hand of the same female. We do not generally think that such a contest is unfair just because one of the factors tipping the scales is the greater wealth of the victorious suitor. We see the external talent of having lots of money as very relevant indeed to the game of choosing a mate wisely. (At this point, we again need to avoid the temptation to be goody-goody!) The point is that fairness or unfairness is determined at least in part by what sorts of games we wish to play, and this often has to do with practical considerations involving external talents, such as money or status.

What, then, about the other sort of fairness—the cooperative variety? What makes an agreement cooperatively fair? The answer reflects the fact that cooperators typically also are competi-

tors. A fair division of profits or duties, therefore, must not favor some cooperators over others, which means that profits must be parceled out so as to be commensurate with input. That is why an arrangement is generally thought to be *cooperatively fair* only when its fruits are divided according to the various amounts of time, wealth, effective effort, and so on, each participant contributes. Equal input merits equal share of profits, greater input a greater share. (Whatsoever ye sow, ye also *ought* to reap.) All other ways of dividing profits allow some competing cooperators to gain an advantage over others simply by entering into fair agreements with them, and not because they are superior competitors. To reduce this possibility to a minimum, nature has instilled in us a strong desire to gain at least a fair share, as just described, of the benefits of cooperative ventures.

It is important at this point to remember that the sentiments we have been discussing are *universal*. The peoples of all cultures are motivated by empathy, affection, compassion, and the like, as well as by a sense of fair play. Philosophers and social scientists often justify the contrary claim—that moral sentiments are shaped almost exclusively by environmental forces—by pointing to their great diversity from one culture to another. But this neglects the fact that amidst the diversity there is a common base—the sentiments we have concentrated on here.[6]

5. Retribution and Revenge

But the cooperative sentiments discussed so far are not quite the whole story. Another mechanism has evolved to increase the likelihood of successful cooperation, namely, a desire to strike back at those who do not play the game straight. This desire takes several different forms, which need to be distinguished.

One way to strike back is to refuse to play cooperative games with those who cheat, thus depriving them of the benefits cooperation tends to generate. Another is to return chicanery with chicanery—to fight fire with fire. (Only suckers feel obligated to be honest with those who are dishonest.) But a better way, perhaps, is to exact retribution—to punish those who cheat on contractual arrangements.

Unfortunately, everyday uses of the term "retribution" tend to be rather ambiguous, not to mention vague. And, indeed, retribution often is confused with its cousin, revenge. By *retribution* we mean here harming individuals because they have failed to play the game fairly, by *revenge*, harming someone in return for being harmed. The two concepts obviously overlap; some cases of revenge also constitute retribution. But revenge often has nothing to do with retribution, as in cases where guilty parties strike back at those who, with justification, exact retribution.

Sentiments favoring retribution evolved, no doubt, because of their deterrence value. When those who are cheated tend to strike back, crime is much less likely to pay. But deterrence is generally not the principal motive—certainly not the only one—pushing us into punishing guilty parties. Rather, it is the strong desire most of us have that "justice be done." This powerful sentiment favoring retribution is entirely separate from a desire to deter sin, even though, as just remarked, it no doubt evolved because of its deterrent value (just as, for instance, the desire for sexual intercourse is separate from a desire for offspring, although the desire for sex evolved without doubt because it increases the likelihood of reproduction). Deterrence is forward looking. When we punish the guilty in order to deter others from committing crimes, we try to influence what happens in the future. Retribution, by contrast, is backward looking. When we punish the guilty in order to gain retribution, we do so because of what they have done in the past, not in order to influence the future. Of course, we often punish for both of these reasons.

Unfortunately, retribution recently has had a rather poor press, perhaps because retribution usually also constitutes revenge, and nonretributive cases of revenge generally, and rightly, are seen to be odious. Negative feelings about these nonretributive instances tend to rub off onto retributive cases. Another reason may be that the desire for retribution, as for revenge, is seen as a holdover from our uncivilized past, when our distant ancestors were mere beasts. Of course, those who see it this way generally forget that this can be said about all human sentiments. (Note, again, the tendency towards the goody-goody, reinforced in this case, perhaps, by an inclination to deny the relationship between human beings and other animals, an inclination that to this day moves many people to reject the theory of evolution itself.)

In any case, theory suggests, and everyday experience confirms, that most of us do indeed harbor a rather strong desire that the guilty be punished in order to achieve justice. The fact that we expended a good deal of effort to punish the leaders of Germany and Japan after World War II, even though history attests to the unlikelihood that tyrants can be deterred in this way, supports theory on this point, as do the cathartic feelings generated when justice is done—when the guilty receive their due. (Note in this vein the Judeo-Christian doctrine of a "life for a life, eye for an eye, [and] tooth for a tooth.")

6. Degrees of Friendliness

The sentiments of empathy, compassion, affection, and the like, mentioned before, tend to generate *friendships* between individuals, in particular when they engage in various kinds of reciprocal activities. Friends form a kind of small in-group within or overlapping larger groups, including the primary ones that we think of as societies. In fact, societies can be thought of as very large groups of friends, although not on average nearly as *friendly* as close friends often are.

Other things being equal, friends tend to win out when competing with groups of people held together merely by the prospect of personal gain, and this, no doubt, is one reason for the evolution of the sentiments that make friendships endure.

Friends tend to be loyal to one another in much the same way as are citizens of the same society, and for many of the same reasons. Friendliness makes it more likely that citizens will hang together rather than separately.

The more important the kinds of cooperative behavior that individuals, whether true friends or not, engage in, the greater the *degree of friendliness* that holds between them. But no mere amount of cooperation is sufficient by itself to make an association into a friendship (or a group into a society). What is lacking in the case of cooperating nonfriends is a concern for the other fellow, feelings of affection that lead to an increase in trustworthiness, a decrease in advantage taking, and a willingness to come to one another's aid in time of need. Nonfriends cooperate primarily for their own advantage; friends are also motivated by a sense of concern and loyalty.

Friendships, nevertheless, are kept going because of mutual advantage. They are, after all, based pretty much on reciprocity, as are most human associations (including, it is important to remember, the association between mates). Of course, unlike the case of merely commercial relationships, the reciprocity books do not need to balance between friends, because of the concern, mentioned before, friends have for one another. But when ledgers becomes seriously unbalanced, friendships fade, as they also often do when friends compete with one another for positions or mates. (Recall Aristotle's remark: "Ah, my friends, there are no friends," intended to convey the point that friendships have their limits.)

In any case, friendliness needs to be kept separate in our minds from the related concept of fairness. A person can be scrupulously fair in dealings with others, be motivated by a high regard for fair play, and yet be completely lacking in the sentiments of affection and concern that characterize friendships. Even so, fair reciprocity is always more likely when a desire to play the game fairly is wedded to a concern for the other fellow. It is always easier to cheat enemies than friends.

In short, sentiments that tend to cement friendships, coupled with those that incline us to favor fair play, and reinforced by a strong desire to strike back at transgressors, constitute a large part of the winning biological package that has produced modern *Homo sapiens* and our cooperative ecological niche. The other part, of course, is the sentiments that guide the competitive side of human nature. These two sides of our psyches frequently are in harmony, but occasionally they clash, in which case the competitive side may win out over the cooperative, the reason all of us, at least now and then, give in to the temptation to sin—to take advantage of the trust of others.

7. Fair Group Decision Procedures

Unanimity is the only fair procedure for arriving at the terms of a two-party cooperative venture. Allowing one party greater say than the other clearly would not be competitively fair. Unanimity also is the most practical procedure when just two people are involved. But it becomes less and less practical as the number of potential cooperators becomes larger and larger. Practical considerations thus often force the choice of a different sort of procedure, such as majority rule.

But what makes a decision procedure fair is the same no matter how large the group in question happens to be. Nor does the nature of the group have any relevance. What counts is that the procedural rules followed do not favor one person, or group of persons, over others. (This is the crucial ingredient because coming to group-wide agreements is almost always a competitive activity.) Majority rule, and even plurality rule, are therefore usually just as fair as the decision procedure requiring unanimity.

It is true, of course, that a fair *procedure* does not guarantee a fair *outcome*. Mistakes are bound to be made, and, what's more, human beings are far from being governed solely by altruistic or fairminded motives. There is, in fact, no fair decision procedure that can guarantee fair outcomes, although clearly, unanimity makes it a good deal harder for unprincipled operators to tyrannize others. Nor does a fair outcome prove anything about the fairness of a procedure. Accidents will happen, and, anyway, despots do on occasion rule in the common interest.

Speaking of despots again brings to mind the fact that we all are members—citizens—of that special kind of organization anthropologists think of as an *in-group*. We are in our bones an in-group–out-group animal. During the vast sweep of human evolution, most of the cooperative behavior engaged in by *Homo sapiens* was of the in-group variety. Most moral strictures, requiring truth telling, forbidding certain kinds of killings, and so on, very likely got started as in-group agreements that applied, therefore, primarily to one's fellows and not necessarily to the people over on the next hill. Out-group relationships tended to be governed by different sorts of agreements reached by one group vis-à-vis another and were more easily broken when the situation warranted. Today, primary in-groups—nations—usually contain millions or even hundreds of millions of members, and things have changed somewhat for that reason as well as because of the vast amount of international trade that has generated complicated intergroup agreements. But the rules still are different for intragroup interactions than for the international variety, and many more agreements are struck, *and kept*, between citizens of the same society than of different societies. Fair play wins out more often when we deal with compatriots than with the peoples of other lands.

Although, as just mentioned, unanimity is not a viable option where large groups, in particular large in-groups, are concerned, these groups nevertheless can, and generally do, achieve a kind of "meta" unanimity via the implicit or explicit agreement of all members to accept and abide by group-wide decisions, however they happen to be reached. Indeed, the failure of a society to obtain this sort of overarching agreement from a large majority of its citizens tends to sound the death knell of an in-group (as the recent collapse of the Soviet Union illustrated all too well).

Finally, it is worth noting that the problems discussed before (in section 4) concerning relevant "talents" sometimes arise when we attempt to spell out fair group decision procedures. We want victory in the passing of legislation to be achieved by those with the most compelling reasons and arguments, not the largest bankrolls, biggest megaphones, or strongest goons. Merely requiring that everyone has just one vote thus is not sufficient. The problem is to specify the other ways in which voters must be equal if a decision procedure is to be completely fair, and there is no automatic, or easy, way in which this can be done.

8. Fair Play in the Real World

Moral theorists often neglect the fact, remarked on a while back, that sentiments favoring fair play do not always override the other springs to action. Practical considerations of various kinds sometimes are more pressing. In wartime, the *common good* requires some citizens to sacrifice while others gain more than a fair share of the benefits. When a government manipulates interest rates to stimulate the national economy, some profit while others lose. (Reducing interest rates, for instance, tends to benefit borrowers more than the general run of the population while harming those dependent on returns from savings.)

But there often are ways in which this kind of unfairness can be rectified. Having chosen a free market economic system for practical reasons (say, to maximize the production of goods), a fair-minded electorate can at least partially rectify any resulting unfair distributions of wealth (such as profits garnered by economic barons at the expense of ordinary workers) via high taxes for the rich, or by a negative income tax benefiting those at the bottom of the heap. And burdens usually can be passed around so that the same citizens do not always suffer.

The trouble is that remedies of this kind often are not forthcoming; the same groups tend to bear the burdens, or benefits, and, worse, governments controlled by foolish, ignorant, or corrupt politicians frequently mete out gratuitous harms of various kinds. In addition, honest citizens who obey laws at some expense to themselves frequently find themselves at a competitive disadvantage compared to less scrupulous compatriots.

Although resignation from an unfair or corrupt golf or chess club is a simple matter, and alternatives generally are readily available, resigning from one's primary in-group is usually fraught with difficulties and regrets, and becoming a member of another society is neither automatic nor always possible. Emigration is not like moving from one social club, or job, to another. What, then, is the morally right response of citizens, say, in a democracy where the laws of the land have been enacted by means of reasonably fair procedures, to the various kinds of social unfairness most of us are subjected to in everyday life?

What, for instance, about obedience to laws or customs that are widely flouted? In two-person agreements and similarly in agreements struck between several parties, it is clear that the non-compliance of one party releases the other or others from any obligations accrued under the agreements. Doesn't it follow, then, because laws are just agreements struck between much larger numbers of people, that when most citizens in a society violate a particular law, others tend to be absolved from strict obedience to that statute? Doesn't the fact (and it is a fact) that most taxpayers cheat on their income taxes constitute a very good reason for others to do so? Being moral does not entail being a patsy! Similarly, doesn't the fact that governments often discriminate in the enforcement of laws, as, for example, local governments tend to do with respect to real estate assessments, justify others in not being scrupulous, say, about notifying authorities concerning improvements that have increased the values of their properties? Doesn't it make sense that in these sorts of cases the implicit social agreement to obey the laws of the land can be disregarded?

Of course, even if the answer to these questions is *yes*, a principle of proportionality surely is

in order stating roughly that the greater the unfairness, the larger the justified deviation from scrupulous obedience. The greater the number of people who cheat on taxes, and the more serious their chicanery, the more justified others are in doing so, and on a larger scale. (It follows, by the way, that in extreme cases in which whole groups of citizens, for example, racial or caste minorities, find themselves repeatedly on the short end of the stick, the moral force of the general agreement to obey fairly enacted laws is seriously eroded.)

Laws proscribing behavior not harmful to others, for example, statutes forbidding the use of marijuana or the viewing of pornographic movies in the privacy of one's own home, provide another interesting kind of case. As in the others just considered, the fact of widespread disobedience tends to absolve others of a duty to compliance. But there is another reason often cited for noncompliance, namely, the essentially private nature of behavior that does no harm to anyone else. Forbidding cigarette smoking in public is one thing—others may be harmed, or annoyed, by the smoke produced; making it illegal when done in private is something else altogether. Wherein this difference?

Perhaps the chief difference has to do with social usefulness, or rather its lack. To take one example, when tax laws are fairly enacted and enforced, and not often infringed, no excuse exists for noncompliance. But even when all of this is true with respect to a law forbidding, say, the private consumption of alcohol, there still is a reason for imbibing anyway, namely, the lack of a socially useful purpose for the law requiring us to refrain. Cheating on taxes when others do not provides an unfair competitive advantage to those who do and a correlative disadvantage to citizens who do not; smoking tobacco at home harms the competitive chances of no one else. The thought that private behavior of this kind is no one else's business is firmly rooted in the fact that it *is* no one else's business! (The contrary argument, based on the idea that private behavior often has public consequences, is not well taken, in particular because the remedy then is to legislate against the public offense. Millions drink; only some drink and then drive. Wherein the justice in punishing those who drink responsibly because some drink irresponsibly? Note, by the way, that virtually all private behavior may, on occasion, have public consequences. Does it make sense, to take just one such case, to legislate against the rejection of one lover by another on grounds that this may, and indeed often does, have harmful public consequences?)

No doubt there are many who will find the idea quite shocking that it sometimes is rational, and not unfair, to violate fairly enacted legislation. But those who do might consider their thoughts about the many such laws passed at one time or another that discriminate against racial minorities, or against an entire sex (usually female). They might also think about laws that prohibit private fornication between unmarried adults, or those proscribing perfectly ordinary kinds of sexual intercourse performed by married couples in their own bedrooms. Those still shocked might dwell on the countless pieces of legislation enacted by reasonably fair procedures that have made it illegal to practice any but a preferred religion, and the favored religion only in an orthodox manner, or on laws *requiring* the practice of a favored religion, or barring those who do not at least pretend to accept the official doctrine from most positions of consequence in society.

9. Fair Play in the Marketplace

It's true, as they say, that we don't live by bread alone. But it is also true that we don't live without bread. Economic interactions thus are at least as important as any others. But we should expect intuitions concerning fair play in the marketplace to be rather vague, and even somewhat ambiguous, because they were designed by evolutionary forces to handle fairly simple kinds of transactions that are quite different from the complicated cooperative interactions characteristic of today's economic arenas.

As in the case of any other sorts of activities, to be competitively fair, the rules of an economic game must treat all players in the same way, and to be cooperatively fair, must return profits (and losses!) according to share of input. And economic activities, just as any others, can be more, or less, friendly. Generally, but not always, more means better (because unfriendly competitions tend to be less efficient, and because friendly competitors are more likely to play the game straight, thus producing larger long-term profits).

Also, as in the case of every other sort of competitive activity, whether or not economic practices fall within the limits of fair play depends on what games it is we wish to play—on how friendly we desire competitions to be—or, to put the matter another way, on what sorts of advantage takings, if any, we want to permit. Remember that a game can be competitively fair even though advantage takings are permitted, provided that all players are allowed them equally.

At one time or another, the rules of economic games have allowed competitors to take advantage of opponent ignorance, foolishness, stupidity, misfortune, and vulnerable economic condition, and have even permitted players to completely shut others out of the game. There never has been a marketplace in which all of these kinds of advantage takings have been forbidden, but markets that endure for very long generally devise ways to ensure a certain amount of friendliness and, in particular, have tried to assure the adherence to fair contracts that is at the heart of intuitions concerning fair play.

Happily, marketplaces these days tend to be somewhat friendlier than those in existence even a few years ago. The principle of *caveat emptor* (let the buyer beware) has been seriously eroded, insider trading is illegal on most exchanges, and so on. But free markets, at any rate, still allow players to take advantage of certain kinds of competitor ignorance and, especially, of competitor economic distress. Forbidding the latter sort of advantage taking, say, by making it illegal either to buy goods cheaply from those overstocked or to sell items in short supply at higher prices, would go a long way towards rescinding the law of supply and demand on which free markets depend. In any case, deciding which sorts of unfriendly behavior to permit, and which to proscribe, usually is decided as much on the basis of practical as on fair-play considerations, and is, in fact, one of the serious matters fought over (as it should be) in the sociopolitical arena.

This is true also with respect to quite a few issues concerning cooperative fairness. As stated before, intuitions on the matter tend to be clear only for the simplest sorts of cases in which all parties contribute equally, or at least make the same sorts of contributions (as when one person invests a hundred dollars and another five hundred, or one supplies one-fourth of an inventory and the other three-fourths). We do, however, have a few other extremely vague but nevertheless relevant sentiments to draw on. They tell us, most of us at any rate, that the more effective, dangerous, odious, tedious, skillful, or unhealthy labor happens to be, other things being equal, the greater the slice of profits it deserves, just as more venturesome capital deserves a more handsome return than investments that are safer.

But these intuitions are primarily qualitative. They do not tell us, for example, how much more remuneration dangerous employment deserves than the more prosaic variety, or how to compare one sort of skillful work with another. How can we compare the labor value of an engineer to that of a shop steward, or of an assembly line worker to a chief executive officer? What about the efforts of a waiter as compared to a college professor? How much more valuable is the labor of a Mozart than of a composer of pop tunes? Is there a way to compare invested capital with expended labor? We know that something is wrong when, for example, American CEOs earn on average seventeen times more than their Japanese counterparts and hundreds, sometimes thousands, of times more than the general run of their employees, or when junk bond entrepreneurs earn thousands of times as much as average workers by putting together deals that enrich a few while destroying once-sound corporations. But we don't

know what precise figures would make things right. We have comparative antennae that function somewhat, but lack intuitions concerning quantitative standards in most cases.

In any event, the problem is compounded by the fact that there is no such thing as *the* value of labor or capital, irrespective of particular human evaluations. Values do not exist independently of *valuers*. The value of labor to an employer (a buyer of labor) is in what it produces, whereas to a laborer (a seller of labor) it is in the time and effort expended, and, unfortunately, the two evaluations generally do not coincide. (Note that similar remarks apply to the value of commodities other than labor and capital.)

Suppose, however, we could determine that the labor of the president of a corporation produces, say, fifty times as much profit as the efforts of an average worker, thus being fifty times as valuable to the buyers of labor. It still would not follow that the CEO in question deserves fifty times the salary of an average employee. For one thing, no person is an island. What someone accomplishes is due in large part to the knowledge, training, and opportunity provided by society as a whole, and some receive much greater benefits of this kind than others. And for another thing, money is only one kind of payment for services rendered. In the case of truly outstanding producers—the Aristotles, Newtons, and Monets of the world—fame, honor, power, or in extreme cases even immortality, may well constitute the major portion of their just deserts. (It is interesting how much it bothers lots of people, including this writer, that a genius like Mozart should have died at an early age without an understanding of his place in history—uncertain as to how long his music would survive his own demise.) Note also that ordinary workers tend to value their own labor just as highly as do outstanding producers.

Of course, plenty of economists have argued that free markets provide the best guide to the value of capital, labor, and, indeed, of goods in general. Their view, no doubt, does have the merit that it ties value to what actual John Does or Mary Roes are willing to pay. The trouble, if we overlook the fact that no completely free markets have ever existed, is that marketplaces reward not just skill, insight, knowledge, perseverence, productivity, and other relevant talents, but also "talents" such as economic and political power, thus generally running counter to intuitions concerning fair wages and fair return on investment. (Note, by the way, that in actual marketplaces, the most odious jobs are among the lowest paying, while pop music phenoms whose products are quickly forgotten—for instance, New Kids on the Block—frequently earn a great deal more in one year than do the vast majority of great artists and thinkers in a lifetime.)

Of course, a fair-minded electorate might opt for a modestly free market economy anyway. For one thing, moral considerations do not necessarily take precedence over all others; and for another, as mentioned before, the unfairness of a free marketplace can be rectified to some extent by offsetting devices (such as negative income taxes). Nevertheless, it is important to remember the difficulty of obtaining true competitive fairness in a free-market economy, given the power of great wealth and the human tendencies towards nepotism that tilt socioeconomic playing fields in favor of the rich and their offspring.

10. Rights Talk

According to the contractual way of looking at things that is being championed here, it is agreements, promises, that *obligate* people to act in certain ways. On this view, therefore, *rights* are derivative from agreements: my promise to do something for you generates my obligation to perform as promised and your right to have me do so. Talk of rights divorced from agreements, implicit or explicit, makes no sense from this contractual point of view. Of course, only those of us with a high regard for keeping fair agreements have any *reason* to satisfy the rights of others generated by our promises.

In the history of philosophy, and in particular in the present day, a contrary view has often been championed, at least implicitly, according to which there are "natural rights" that we all are obligated to respect. But natural rights theorists are confronted with serious problems that advocates often neglect. How, for example, do these abstract objects, *natural* rights, come into existence? If we suppose that there are such things, why should anyone accept the burden of satisfying them? The contractual view has fairly simple answers to these questions. Rights come into existence via fair promises that generate obligations. It makes sense for those who are fair-minded to respect the rights of others precisely because they are fair-minded—precisely because they harbor strong sentiments favoring trust and fidelity. On this view, no appeal needs to be made to alleged objective "natural rights" that automatically adhere to "persons" by virtue of their humanity, or to sentient beings because of their capacity to experience, or to suffer.

11. The Good Person

The chief point of this essay has been to describe a particular sort of contractual theory of moral obligation and to support selection of that theory by appeal, in particular, to recent theories put forth by evolutionary biologists. According to these theories, moral sentiments generally evolved primarily because they tended to foster increasingly complicated and beneficial cooperative activities. The moral person, it has been implied, is someone who keeps fair bargains—whose word can be trusted.

But it should be noted that most philosophers have thought of morality in a somewhat wider sense. They often speak of a noncontractual obligation to be charitable, or compassionate, and generally claim that we have a special obligation to care for our own children. On the view being championed here, we only have obligations of this sort if we have agreed to them, either explicitly or implicitly, as, for example, when the citizens of a society decide that parents will take care of their own children (not a universal practice, by the way).

However, there is a good reason, at least in the eyes of this writer, for restricting the term "moral" in the way it has been here. For the moral obligation individuals have to keep bargains that *they* have entered into draws on actions *they* have performed. In demanding that these bargains be kept, others can appeal to these actions. Morality, in this sense, is self-imposed, in that it stems from one's own actions. Demanding, say, that others be charitable, in the absence of their agreement to act in this way, constitutes an attempt to impose obligations "from the outside."

Of course, there is nothing wrong in using the term "moral" in a wider sense than is employed here, provided we pay attention to relevant differences. Thus, those who extend the term to cover the treatment of offspring need to notice that the sentiments motivating most of us to care for our own children differ greatly from those leading us, say, to repay a debt to a bank. We sacrifice for offspring because we care about their welfare, whether or not we have agreed to do so. We pay back bank loans because, having agreed to do so, we feel obligated to hold up our end of the bargain (and also, of course, because we may be forced to anyway and don't want to ruin our credit rating), not because we have any great desire to increase the profits of the bank. Similarly, we are motivated to give street people money, those of us who are, by feelings of compassion and empathy, whether or not we have agreed to benefit them (say, via societywide legislation), but pay telephone bills because we have agreed to do so (and don't want service cut off), not because we have any great love for AT&T.

The point is that there are at least three different sorts of sentiments motivating altruistic behavior that need to be distinguished, one from another, namely, those favoring the keeping of fair bargains, those, such as compassion, leading us to care about the welfare of others, including non-kin, and those inclining us to desire the best for our own flesh and blood. The first evolved to foster reciprocal-altruistic practices, the third for kin-altruistic reasons, and the second to increase the likelihood both of reciprocal and of kin altruism.

But when we restrict the concept of moral obligation just to cases in which bargains have been made, as has been done in this essay, another term is needed to cover the wider sense often employed by other theorists. One way to do this is to say that being fair-minded, having a general disposition to make and keep fair contracts, is only part of what it takes to be a *good person*—to have the respect of one's fellows. The scrooges of the world may scrupulously obey the law and honor contracts and still be thought of as rather miserable human specimens. It is their unfriendly, mean-spirited natures—their lack of compassion or empathy for others—that makes others see them as *bad* individuals. (The evolutionary reason for our seeing things in this way no doubt is related to the value of compassion, empathy, and the like, in fostering both kin- and reciprocal-altruistic practices. Of course, this doesn't change the fact that we desire them for their own sake.)

But being a more or less good person is quite different from being goody-goody. Goody-goody tends to be a pose. We cannot just hate the sin while loving the sinner, as some moral philosophies require. Universal love and forgiveness are not in the cards for human beings. The reason, as insisted on before, is that the cooperation we all must engage in usually has to take place with our most serious genetic competitors. So the very activities that (biologically speaking) generate the other-regarding sentiments so favored by goody-goody philosophers also are responsible for the limits placed on these emotions. The typical reasonably good person is a full-blooded human animal, capable of anger and hatred as well as love, not a one-dimensional cardboard figure. Good individuals have an *appropriate* stock of other-regarding sentiments and do not need to deny feelings of contempt, disdain, or hatred felt for slippery, mean-spirited, or ungenerous characters.

This writer has lacked respect for most of the leaders of his native land during the second half of the twentieth century, not just because they have so often violated the principles of fair play, but also because they have been so lacking in empathy or compassion for those at the bottom of the pecking order. They have, in other words, not been good people. The reader is urged not to conclude that my intent in espousing a theory of contractual fair play has been to champion a victor/vanquished morality. My utopia, in which better competitors always emerge victorious, definitely is not one in which those who attain great success stand on a Neitzschean height and grind the rest of us into the dust.

Notes

1. This expression seems to have been introduced by Richard Dawkins. See his excellent book *The Selfish Gene* (Oxford and New York: Oxford University Press, 1976). Three other excellent books on the sociobiological approach are Robert Trivers's *Social Evolution* (Menlo Park, Calif., Benjamin/Cummings, 1985); E. O. Wilson's *On Human Nature* (Cambridge, Mass., Harvard University Press, 1978); and Robert Axelrod's *The Evolution of Cooperation* (New York: Basic Books, 1984), in particular the chapter by W. D. Hamilton.

2. Not counting animals, such as bees and ants, that do not reproduce bisexually. Interestingly, E. O. Wilson's pioneering evolutionary biology treatise, *Sociobiology: The New Synthesis* (Cambridge, Mass.: Harvard University Press, 1975), deals primarily with the social insects.

3. We pass over, because irrelevant to the topic of moral obligation, the ongoing competitions with viruses, bacteria, and fungi that need to be won in order to achieve genetic success.

4. The theories concerning reciprocal and kin altruism on which this account is based are not without their detractors. See in particular R. C. Lewontin, L. Kamin, and S. Rose: *Not in Our Genes* (New York: Pantheon, 1984). But in the opinion of this writer, the tide of research is going against the naysayers. See, for instance, Katherine Milton's fascinating article "Diet and Primary Evolution," (*Scientific American*, August, 1993), in which she convincingly ties the evolution of cooperation and fair play to diet problems encountered in an arboreal environment.

5. Note the connection to the age-old philosophical conundrum about whether, when we have had to replace every part of a ship over the years, the resulting vessel is or is not the same ship as the original. We answer one way or the other depending on other considerations, for example on whom we want to have title to the reconstructed item. There is no way to answer questions of this kind without bringing external interests to bear.

6. It may be thought that these sentiments are not universal on grounds that systems completely unfair to whole groups of people—women, slaves, untouchables—often gain general acceptance, being perceived as fair even by many of those who are given the short end of the stick. But anyone who is tempted to accept this line of reasoning should notice that, first, the general tendency to favor whatever system one grows into enables some of those tyrannized to overlook the unfairness of their situations (self-deception is quite valuable when nothing can be done to rectify matters); second, many of those persecuted understand the nature of their predicament very well indeed, in spite of the fact that the society as a whole sees their condition as fair; third, the more privileged members of disadvantaged groups, for example, educated slaves, generally look on their situations more favorably than those less privileged; and, fourth, human beings, as most social animals, tend, rightly or wrongly (and no doubt very often wrongly), to see the dominance of some members of their in-group over others as justified by the superior qualities or performance of the privileged members. The point is that the acceptance, or pretense of acceptance, of unfair social arrangements as fair by large numbers of the oppressed merely proves their gullibility, or self-deception, or ignorance of nonmoral facts, not their lack of a sense of fairness of the kind discussed here, a point reinforced by the well-known fact that members of oppressed classes are notoriously picky about minor sorts of unfairnesses in their relationships with others who belong to oppressed classes. (That those who gain by unfair social arrangements so often tend to think their good fortune justified—even Aristotle tried to justify slavery—should produce no surprise. There is, after all, an evolutionary benefit in being able to justify a double standard when there is personal profit in doing so.)

PART IV

Value: What Is the Good?

Introduction

Morality is said to aim at the good, whether it is defined in terms of motives, actions, character, or consequences. This leads to an inquiry into Value.

What sort of things are valuable? The term 'value' (from the Latin *valere*, meaning "to be of worth") is highly elastic, being used sometimes narrowly as a synonym for 'good' or 'valuable' and sometimes broadly for the whole scope of evaluative terms, ranging from the highest good through the indifferent to the worst evil, comprising positive neutral as well as negative "values." In the narrow sense the opposite of 'value' is 'evil' or 'disvalue.' In a comprehensive value theory (sometimes referred to as *axiology*) the broader meaning of the word is used.

What Kinds of Goods Are There?

In reading III.7 (Plato's "Why Should I Be Moral?"), Socrates distinguishes three kinds of goods: (1) purely intrinsic good (of which simple joys are an example); (2) purely instrumental good (of which medicine and making money are examples); and (3) combination goods (such as knowledge, sight, and health), which are good in themselves and good as a means to further goods.

The essential difference is between intrinsic and instrumental goods. We consider some things good or worthy of desire (desirable) in themselves and other things good or desirable only because of their consequences. Intrinsic goods are good because of their nature—they are not derived from other goods; whereas instrumental goods are worthy of desire because they are effective means in reaching our intrinsic goods.

Money is the other example of an instrumental value. Few if any of us really value money for its own sake, but almost all of us value it for what it can buy. When we ask, What is money for? we arrive at such goods as food and clothing, shelter and automobiles, entertainment and education. But are any of these really intrinsic goods, or are they all themselves instrumental goods? When we ask, for example, What is entertainment for? what answer do we come up with? Most of us will come up with the answer of enjoyment or pleasure— Socrates' example of an intrinsic good. Can we further ask, What is enjoyment or pleasure for?

Are there any intrinsic values? Are there any entities whose values are not derived from anything else, which are sought after for their own sake, that are just good in themselves? Or are all values relative to desirers, instrumental to goals which are the creation of choosers? Those who espouse the notion of intrinsic value usually argue that pleasure is an example of an intrinsic value and that pain is an example of an intrinsic disvalue. It is just good to experience pleasure and bad to experience pain. Naturally, these philosophers admit that individual experiences of pleasure can be bad (because they result in some other disvalue—like a hangover after a drinking spree) and individual painful experiences can be valuable (e.g., having a painful operation to save one's life). The intrinsicalist affirms that pleasure just is better than pain. We can see this straight off. We don't need any arguments to convince us that pleasure is good or that gratuitous pain is intrinsically bad. Suppose we see a man torturing a child and order him to stop it at once. If he replies, "I agree that the child is experiencing great pain, but why should I stop torturing her?" we would suspect some mental aberration on his part.

The nonintrinsicalist denies that the above arguments have any force. The notion that the experience itself has any value is unclear. It is only by our choosing pleasure over pain that the notion of value gets off the ground. In a sense, all value is extrinsic or a product of choosing. Many existentialists, most notably Jean-Paul Sartre, believe that we invent our values by arbitrary choice. The freedom to create our values and so define ourselves is godlike and, at the same time, deeply frightening, for we have no one to blame for our failures but ourselves. "We are condemned to freedom." "Value is nothing else but the meaning that you choose. One may choose anything so long as it is done from the ground of freedom."[1]

What Things Are Good?

Philosophers divide into two broad camps: those of *hedonists* and *nonhedonists*. The hedonist (being derived from *hedon*, the Greek word for 'pleasure') asserts that all pleasure is good, that pleasure is the only thing good in itself, and that all other goodness is derived from this value. An experience is good in itself if and only if it provides some pleasure and to the extent that it provides pleasure. Sometimes this definition is widened to include the amelioration of pain, pain being seen as the only thing bad in itself. For simplicity's sake we will use the former definition, realizing that it may need to be supplemented by reference to pain.

Hedonists subdivide into (a) *sensualists* and (b) *satisfactionists*, the former equating all pleasure with sensual titillation and the latter with satisfaction or enjoyment, which may not involve sensuality. It is a pleasurable state of consciousness, such as one we experience after accomplishing a successful venture or receiving a gift. The opposite of (a), sensual enjoyment, is physical pain. The opposite of (b), satisfaction, is displeasure or dissatisfaction.

The Greek philosopher Aristippus (c. 435–356 B.C.) and his school, the Cyrenaics, espoused the sensualist position—that the only (or primary) good was sensual pleasure and that this goodness was defined in terms of its intensity.

Most hedonists since the third century B.C. fol-

low Epicurus (342–270 B.C.), who had a broader view of pleasure:

It is not continuous drinkings and revellings, nor the satisfaction of lusts, nor the enjoyment of fish and other luxuries of the wealthy table, which produce a happy life, but sober reasoning, searching out the motives for all choice and avoidance, and banishing mere opinions, to which are due the greatest disturbance of the spirit.[2]

The distinction between pleasure as satisfaction and as sensation is important, and failure to recognize it results in confusion and paradox. One example of this is the paradox of masochism. How can it be that the masochist enjoys (i.e., takes pleasure in) pain, which is the opposite of pleasure? "Well," the hedonist responds, "because of certain psychological aberrations, the masochist enjoys (qua *satisfaction*) what is painful (qua *sensation*)." He or she does not enjoy (qua *sensation*) what is painful (qua *sensation*). It could also be the case that there is a two-level analysis available to explain the masochist's behavior. On a lower or basic level he is experiencing either pain or dissatisfaction, but on a higher level he approves and finds satisfaction from that pain or dissatisfaction.

Nonhedonists divide into two camps: *monists* and *pluralists*. Monists believe that there is a single intrinsic value but that it is not pleasure. Perhaps it is a transcendent value, 'the Good,' which we do not fully comprehend but which is the basis of all our other values. This seems to be Plato's view. Pluralist nonhedonists generally admit that pleasure or enjoyment is an intrinsic good but add that there are other intrinsic goods as well, such as knowledge, friendship, freedom, love, conscientiousness, and life itself.

A hedonist like Jeremy Bentham (1748–1832) in our second reading argues that while these qualities are good, their goodness is derived from the fact that they bring pleasure or satisfaction. Such hedonists ask of each of the above-mentioned values, What is it for? What is knowledge for? If it gave no one any satisfaction or enjoyment, would it really be good? Why do we feel there is a significant difference between knowing how many stairs there are in New York City and whether or not there is life after death? We do not normally value knowledge of the first kind, but knowledge of the second kind is relevant for our enjoyment.

What are friendship and love for? the hedonist asks. If we were made differently and did not get any satisfaction out of love and friendship, would they still be valuable? Are they not highly valuable, significant instrumental goods because they bring enormous satisfaction?

Even moral commitment or conscientiousness is not good in itself, avers the hedonist. Morality is not intrinsically valuable but is meant to serve human need, which in turn has to do with bringing about satisfaction.

According to the hedonist, life is not intrinsically good. It is quality that counts. An ameoba or a permanently comatose patient has life but no intrinsic value. Only when consciousness appears does the possibility for value arrive. Consciousness is a necessary but not a sufficient condition for satisfaction.

The nonhedonist responds that this is counterintuitive. In our fifth reading Robert Nozick challenges those who would identify value with simple states like pleasure or satisfying experience. In our sixth reading W. D. Ross argues against hedonism and for value pluralism.

In our third reading Friedrich Nietzsche posits the will to power as the dominant value that humans, like all creatures caught up in the evolutionary struggle for survival, desire most. Genuine morality is based on the will to power, but there is a constant tendency on the part of the mediocre ("the herd") to invert morality and promulgate the passive virtues of self-denial, humility, tolerance, resignation, and pity.

In our final reading Derek Parfit explores three theories of "the good life": hedonism, desire for fulfillment, and objective lists. He illustrates the problems in each of these theories and suggests that the best life may consist in a combination of hedonism and objective lists.

Are Values Objective or Subjective?

Do we desire the Good because it is good or is the Good good because we desire it?

The objectivist holds that values are worthy of desire whether or not anyone actually desires them. They are somehow independent of us. The subjectivist holds, to the contrary, that values are dependent on desirers, relative to desirers.

The classic objectivist view on values (the absolutist version) is given by Plato (in our first reading), who taught that the Good was the highest form, ineffable, godlike, independent, and knowable only after a protracted education in philosophy. We desire the Good because it is good. The allegory of the cave gives us a picture of Plato's ideas.

In our fourth reading G. E. Moore argues that the Good is *sui generis*—i.e., utterly unique—and that its existence is independent of human or rational interest. Moore claims that the Good is a simple, unanalyzable quality like the color yellow, but one which must be known through the intuitions. Moore believes that a world with beauty is more valuable than one that is a garbage dump, regardless of whether there are conscious beings in those worlds. "Let us imagine one world exceedingly beautiful. Imagine it as beautiful as you can . . . and then imagine the ugliest world you can possibly conceive. Imagine it simply one heap of filth."[3] Moore asks us, even if there were no conscious being, no one who might derive pleasure or pain, in either world, wouldn't we want the first world to exist rather than the second?

Subjectivism treats values as merely products of conscious desire. A value is simply the object of interest. Values are created by desires, and they are valuable only to that degree to which they are desired: the stronger the desire, the greater the value. The difference between the subjectivist and the weak objectivist position (or mixed view) is simply that the subjectivist makes no normative claims about "proper desiring," judging all desires equal. Anything one happens to desire is, by definition, a value, a Good.

The objectivist responds that we can separate

the Good from what one desires. We can say, for example, Joan desires more than anything else to get into the Pleasure Machine, where she will experience unmitigated but mindless pleasures, but it is not good; or John desires more than anything else to join the Ku Klux Klan, but it is not good (not even for John). There is something just plain bad about the Pleasure Machine and the Klan even if Joan and John never experience any dissatisfaction on account of them.

On the other hand, suppose Joan does not want to have any friends and John does not want to know any history or science (beyond that which is necessary for his needs as a mud-wrestler). The objectivist would reply that it really would be an objectively good thing if Joan did have friends and that John knew something about history and science.

Is there a way to adjudicate the disagreement between the subjectivist and the objectivist?

We turn to Plato's vision of the Good as a transcendent reality.

Notes

1. Jean-Paul Sartre, *Existentialism and Human Emotions*, trans. Bernard Frechtman (Philosophical Library, 1957), pp. 23, 48f. "Value is nothing else but the meaning that you choose. . . . One may choose anything if it is on the grounds of free involvement."

2. Epicurus, "Letter to Manoeceus," C. Bailey (trans.), in W. J. Oates, ed., *The Stoics and Epicurean Philosophers* (Random House, 1940, p. 32).

3. G. E. Moore, *Principia Ethica* (Cambridge, 1903).

12

The Good and the Allegory of the Cave

PLATO

For Plato, values are objective realities that exist independently of knowers. We become good by knowing the Good. In a sense virtue is knowledge and vice is ignorance. No rational person would willingly do evil, for evil corrupts the soul. The Good is good for us, so we must know the Good if we would be happy. What is knowledge for Plato? To know, rather than merely to believe, is to apprehend eternal forms or ideas. The forms are objective, eternal, intangible, unchangeable, transcendent, universal, and absolute realities. To know that some particular object is beautiful is to understand the absolute form of beauty. There is a form or idea of justice, the form of

Reprinted from *Plato's Republic*, trans. G. M. A. Grube (Indianapolis: Hackett Publishing Company, 1974), by permission of the publisher.

equality, the form of courage, and so on. The highest form of all is the form of the Good in which all of the other forms participate. The task of each person or "soul," as Plato calls our inner person, is to perfect our selves by philosophical education to the point where we grasp the eternal forms.

In this classic passage from the Republic *Socrates argues that all of the moral and political virtues are centered in the Good and that only by knowing the Good can we achieve political harmony and harmony in the soul. He compares the Good to the sun, and then, using an allegory of the cave, argues that becoming virtuous consists in the soul's turning from looking at appearances to studying the eternal ideas.*

We join Socrates in the midst of a discussion of the virtues with Plato's brothers, Adeimantus and Glaucon.

Socrates, said Adeimantus, are these virtues not the most important subject of study? Is there anything still more important than justice, courage, self-control, and wisdom?

There is, I said, the Form of the Good is the greatest object of study, and that it is by their relation to it that just actions and the other things become useful and beneficial. You probably knew that I was about to say this and, besides, that our knowledge of it is inadequate. If we do not know the Good, even the fullest possible knowledge of others things is no help to us, any more than if we acquire any possession without the Good. Do you think there is any advantage to have acquired every kind of possession, if it is not good, or to have every kind of knowledge without that of the Good, thus knowing nothing beautiful or good? —No, by Zeus, I do not.

Furthermore, you certainly know that most people believe that pleasure is the Good, while the more enlightened believe it is knowledge. —Of course.

What about those who define the Good as pleasure? Are they less confused than others? Are not even they compelled to admit that there are bad pleasures?—Definitely

So then this is a subject of great and frequent controversies?—It is.

Further, is it not clear that in the case of just and beautiful things, many are content with what seems so, even if it is not, yet they act, acquire, and think on that basis; but when it comes to good things nobody is satisfied to acquire what seems to be so, but they seek things that really are good, and everybody in this case disdains appearances.—Quite so.

Every soul pursues the Good, and all its actions are done for its sake. The soul divines that it is something but is perplexed and cannot adequately grasp what it is, nor does it have about this the firm opinion which it has about other things, and because of this it misses the benefits, if any, even of those other things. Should we say that even the best men in the city to whom we entrust everything must remain in such darkness about so great and so important a subject? —Least of all.

If people do not recognize the Good, they are not likely to find a guardian who is able to recognize what is right and desirable in institutions and customs.—No doubt.

Our society will only be perfectly governed when such a man who knows the Good looks after it.

Necessarily, Adeimantus replied, but, Socrates, what is your own view of the Good? Is it knowledge, or pleasure, or something else?

What a man! I said. I knew all along that you would not be content with the views of the masses.

Well, Socrates, he said, it does not seem right to me to be able to tell the opinions of others and not one's own, especially for a man who has spent so much time as you have occupying himself with this subject.

Why? said I. Do you think it right to talk about things one does not know as if one knew them? Have you never noticed that opinions not based on knowledge are ugly things? The best of them are blind; or do you think that those who express a true opinion without knowledge are any different from blind people who yet follow the right road?—They are not different.

Do you want to contemplate ugly, blind, and crooked things when you can hear bright and beautiful things from others?

Here Glaucon broke in. By Zeus, Socrates, you must not give up now that you are in sight of the goal. We shall be satisfied if you discuss the Good in the same fashion as you did justice, moderation, and the other virtues.

I would like to do that, but I fear I shall not be able to do so, and that in my eagerness I shall disgrace myself and make myself ridiculous, but I am willing to tell you what appears to be the offspring of the Good and most like it, if that is agreeable to you.—Tell us.

We were speak of many beautiful things and many good things, and we define them in speech. —We do.

And beauty itself and Goodness itself, and so with all the things which we then classed as many; we now class them again according to one Form of each, which is one and which we in each case call that which is.—That is so.

And we say that the many things are the objects of sight but not of thought, while the Forms are the objects of thought but not of sight. —Altogether true.

With what part of ourselves do we see the objects that are seen?—With our sight.

And so things heard are heard by our hearing, and all that is perceived is perceived by our other senses?—Quite so.

Have you considered how very lavishly the maker of our senses made the faculty of seeing and being seen?—I cannot say I have.

Look at it this way: do hearing and sound need another kind of thing for the former to hear and the latter to be heard, and in the absence of this third element the one will not hear and the other not be heard?—No, they need nothing else.

Neither do many other senses, if indeed any, need any such other thing, or can you mention one?—Not I.

But do you not realize that the sense of sight and that which is seen do have such a need? —How so?

Sight may be in the eyes, and the man who has it may try to use it, and colours may be present in the objects, but unless a third kind of thing is present, which is by nature designed for this very purpose, you know that sight will see nothing and the colours remain unseen.—What is this third kind of thing?

What you call light, I said.—Right.

So to no small extent the sense of sight and the power of being seen are yoked together by a more honorable yoke than other things which are yoked together, unless light is held in no honor.—That is far from being the case.

Which of the gods in the heavens can you hold responsible for this, whose light causes our sight to see as beautifully as possible, and the objects of sight to be seen?—The same as you would, he said, and as others would; obviously the answer to your question is the sun.

And is not sight naturally related to the sun in this way?—Which way?

Sight is not the sun, neither itself nor that in which it occurs which we call the eye.—No indeed.

But I think it is the most sunlike of the organs of sense.—Very much so.

And it receives from the sun the capacity to see as a kind of outflow.—Quite so.

The sun is not sight, but is it not the cause of it, and is also seen by it?—Yes.

Say then, I said, that it is the sun which I called the offspring of the Good, which the Good begot as analogous to itself. What the Good itself is in the world of thought in relation to the intelligence and things known, the sun is in the visible world, in relation to sight and things seen.—How? Explain further.

You know, I said, that when one turns one's eyes to those objects of which the colors are no longer in the light of day but in the dimness of the night, the eyes are dimmed and seem nearly blind, as if clear vision was no longer in them. —Quite so.

Yet whenever one's eyes are turned upon objects brightened by sunshine, they see clearly, and clear vision appears in those very same eyes? —Yes indeed.

So too understand the eye of the soul: whenever it is fixed upon that upon which truth and reality shine, it understands and knows and seems to have intelligence, but whenever it is fixed upon what is mixed with darkness—that which is subject to birth and destruction—it opines and is dimmed, changes its opinions this way and that, and seems to have no intelligence.—That is so.

Say that what gives truth to the objects of knowledge, and to the knowing mind the power to know, is the Form of Good. As it is the cause of knowledge and truth, think of it also as being the object of knowledge. Both knowledge and truth are beautiful, but you will be right to think of the Good as other and more beautiful than they. As in the visible world light and sight are rightly considered sunlike, but it is wrong to think of them as the sun, so here it is right to think of knowledge and truth as Goodlike, but wrong to think of either as the Good, for the Good must be honored even more than they.

This is an extraordinary beauty you mention, he said, if it provides knowledge and truth and is itself superior to them in beauty. You surely do not mean this to be pleasure!

Hush! said I, rather examine the image of it in this way.—How?

You will say, I think, that the sun not only gives to the objects of sight the capacity to be seen, but also that it provides for their generation, increase, and nurture, though it is not itself the process of generation.—How could it be?

And say that as for the objects of knowledge, not only is their being known due to the Good, but also their reality being, though the Good is not being but superior to and beyond being in dignity and power. . . .

Next, I said, compare the effect of education and the lack of it upon our human nature to a situation like this: imagine men to be living in an underground cavelike dwelling place, which has a way up to the light along its whole width, but the entrance is a long way up. The men have been there from childhood, with their neck and legs in fetters, so that they remain in the same place and can only see ahead of them, as their bonds prevent them turning their heads. Light is provided by a fire burning some way behind and above them. Between the fire and the prisoners, some way behind them and on a higher ground, there is a path across the cave and along this a low wall has been built, like the screen at a puppet show in front of the performers who show their puppets above it.—I see it.

See then also men carrying along that wall, so that they overtop it, all kinds of artifacts, statues of men, reproductions of other animals in stone

or wood fashioned in all sorts of ways, and, as is likely, some of the carriers are talking while others are silent.—This is a strange picture, and strange prisoners.

They are like us, I said. Do you think, in the first place, that such men could see anything of themselves and each other except the shadows which the fire casts upon the wall of the cave in front of them?—How could they, if they have to keep their heads still throughout life?

And is not the same true of the objects carried along the wall?—Quite.

If they could converse with one another, do you not think that they would consider these shadows to be the real things?—Necessarily.

What if their prison had an echo which reached them from in front of them? Whenever one of the carriers passing behind the wall spoke, would they not think that it was the shadow passing in front of them which was talking? Do you agree? —By Zeus I do.

Altogether then, I said, such men would believe the truth to be nothing else than the shadows of the artifacts?—They must believe that.

Consider then what deliverance from their bonds and the curing of their ignorance would be if something like this naturally happened to them. Whenever one of them was freed, had to stand up suddenly, turn his head, walk, and look up toward the light, doing all that would give him pain, the flash of the fire would make it impossible for him to see the objects of which he had earlier seen the shadows. What do you think he would say if he was told that what he saw then was foolishness, that he was now somewhat closer to reality and turned to things that existed more fully, that he saw more correctly? If one then pointed to each of the objects passing by, asked him what each was, and forced him to answer, do you not think he would be at a loss and believe that the things which he saw earlier were truer than the things now pointed out to him?—Much truer.

If one then compelled him to look at the fire itself, his eyes would hurt, he would turn round and flee toward those things which he could see, and think that they were in fact clearer than those now shown to him.—Quite so.

And if one were to drag him thence by force up the rough and steep path, and did not let him go before he was dragged into the sunlight, would he not be in physical pain and angry as he was dragged along? When he came into the light, with the sunlight filling his eyes, he would not be able to see a single one of the things which are now said to be true.—Not at once, certainly.

I think he would need time to get adjusted before he could see things in the world above; at first he would see shadows most easily, then reflections of men and other things in water, then the things themselves. After this he would see objects in the sky and the sky itself more easily at night, the light of the stars and the moon more easily than the sun and the light of the sun during the day.—Of course.

Then, at last, he would be able to see the sun, not images of it in water or in some alien place, but the sun itself in its own place, and be able to contemplate it.—That must be so.

After this he would reflect that it is the sun which provides the seasons and the years, which governs everything in the visible world, and is also in some way the cause of those other things which he used to see.—Clearly that would be the next stage.

What then? As he reminds himself of his first dwelling place, of the wisdom there and of his fellow prisoners, would he not reckon himself happy for the change, and pity them?—Surely.

And if the men below had praise and honors from each other, and prizes for the man who saw most clearly the shadows that passed before them, and who could best remember which usually came earlier and which later, and which came together and thus could most ably prophesy the future, do you think our man would desire those rewards and envy those who were honored and held power among the prisoners, or would he feel, as Homer put it, that he certainly wished to be "serf to another man without possessions upon the earth"[1] and go through any suffering, rather than share their opinions and live as they do?—Quite so, he said, I think he would rather suffer anything.

Reflect on this too, I said. If this man went down into the cave again and sat down in the same seat, would his eyes not be filled with darkness, coming suddenly out of the sunlight?—They certainly would.

And if he had to contend again with those who had remained prisoners in recognizing those shadows while his sight was affected and his eyes had not settled down—and the time for this adjustment would not be short—would he not be ridiculed? Would it not be said that he had returned from his upward journey with his eyesight spoiled, and that it was not worthwhile even to attempt to travel upward? As for the man who tried to free them and lead them upward, if they could somehow lay their hands on him and kill him, they would do so.—They certainly would.

This whole image, my dear Glaucon, I said, must be related to what we said before. The realm of the visible should be compared to the prison dwelling, and the fire inside it to the power of the sun. If you interpret the upward journey and the contemplation of things above as the upward journey of the soul to the intelligible realm, you will grasp what I surmise since you were keen to hear it. Whether it is true or not only the god knows, but this is how I see it, namely, that in the intelligible world the Form of the Good is the last to be seen, and with difficulty; when seen it must be reckoned to be for all the cause of all that is right and beautiful, to have produced in the visible world both light and the fount of light, while in the intelligible world it is itself that which produces and controls truth and intelligence, and he who is to act intelligently in public or in private must see it.—I share your thought as far as I am able.

Come then, share with me this thought also: do not be surprised that those who have reached this point are unwilling to occupy themselves with human affairs, and that their souls are always pressing upward to spend their time there, for this is natural if things are as our parable indicates.—That is very likely.

Further, I said, do you think it at all surprising that anyone coming to the evils of human life from the contemplation of the divine behaves awkwardly and appears very ridiculous while his eyes are still dazzled and before he is sufficiently adjusted to the darkness around him, if he is compelled to contend in court or some other place about the shadows of justice or the objects of which they are shadows, and to carry through the contest about these in the way these things are understood by those who have never seen Justice itself?—That is not surprising at all.

Anyone with intelligence, I said, would remember that the eyes may be confused in two ways and from two causes, coming from light into darkness as well as from darkness into light. Realizing that the same applies to the soul, whenever he sees a soul disturbed and unable to see something, he will not laugh mindlessly but will consider whether it has come from a brighter life and is dimmed because unadjusted, or has come from greater ignorance into greater light and is filled with a brighter dazzlement. The former he would declare happy in its life and experience, the latter he would pity, and if he should wish to laugh at it, his laughter would be less ridiculous than if he laughed at a soul that has come from the light above.—What you say is very reasonable.

We must then, I said, if these things are true, think something like this about them, namely, that education is not what some declare it to be; they say that knowledge is not present in the soul and that they put it in, like putting sight into blind eyes.—They surely say that.

Our present argument shows, I said, that the capacity to learn and the organ with which to do so are present in every person's soul. It is as if it were not possible to turn the eye from darkness to light without turning the whole body; so one must turn one's whole soul from the world of becoming until it can endure to contemplate reality, and the brightest of realities, which we say is the Good.—Yes.

Education then is the art of doing this very thing, this turning around, the knowledge of how the soul can most easily and most effectively be turned around; it is not the art of putting the capacity of sight into the soul; the soul possesses that already but it is not turned the right way or looking where it should. This is what education has to deal with.—That seems likely.

Now the other so-called virtues of the soul seem to be very close to those of the body—they really do not exist before and are added later by habit and practice—but the virtue of intelligence belongs above all to something more divine, it seems, which never loses its capacity but, according to which way it is turned, becomes useful and beneficial or useless and harmful. Have you ever noticed in men who are said to be wicked but clever, how sharply their little soul looks into things to which it turns its attention? Its capacity for sight is not inferior, but it is compelled to serve evil ends, so that the more sharply it looks the more evils it works.—Quite so.

Yet if a soul of this kind had been hammered at from childhood and those excrescences had been knocked off it which belong to the world of becoming and have been fastened upon it by feasting, gluttony, and similar pleasures, and which like leaden weights draw the soul to look downward—if, being rid of these, it turned to look at things that are true, then the same soul of the same man would see these just as sharply as it now sees the things towards which it is directed. —That seems likely.

Notes

1. *Odyssey* 11, 489–90, where Achilles says to Odysseus, on the latter's visit to the underworld, that he would rather be a servant to a poor man on earth than king among the dead.

13

Classical Hedonism

JEREMY BENTHAM

Jeremy Bentham (1748–1832) was a British utilitarian (see Part V) and legal reformer. In this essay from An Introduction to the Principles of Morals and Legislation, *he argues that pleasure is the only intrinsic value and pain the only intrinsic evil. All other goods and evils derive from these two qualities. Moral rightness and wrongness are defined in terms of his hedonistic calculus, according to their consequences in producing pleasure and pain.*

Of the Principle of Utility

I. Nature has placed mankind under the governance of two sovereign masters, *pain* and *pleasure.* It is for them alone to point out what we ought to do, as well as to determine what we shall do. On the one hand the standard of right and wrong, on the other the chain of causes and effects, are fastened to their throne. They govern us in all we do, in all we say, in all we think: every effort we can make to throw off our subjection, will serve but to demonstrate and confirm it. In words a man may pretend to abjure their empire: but in reality he will remain subject to it all the while. The *principle of utility* recognizes this subjection, and assumes it for the foundation of that system, the object of which is to rear the fabric of felicity by the hands of reason and of law. Systems which attempt to question it, deal in sounds instead of sense, in caprice instead of reason, in darkness instead of light.

But enough of metaphor and declamation: it is not by such means that moral science is to be improved.

II. The principle of utility is the foundation of

Excerpted from *An Introduction to the Principles of Morals and Legislation* (1789).

the present work: it will be proper therefore at the outset to give an explicit and determinate account of what is meant by it. By the principle of utility is meant that principle which approves or disapproves of every action whatsoever, according to the tendency which it appears to have to augment or diminish the happiness of the party whose interest is in question: or, what is the same thing in other words, to promote or to oppose that happiness. I say of every action whatsoever; and therefore not only of every action of a private individual, but of every measure of government.

III. By utility is meant that property in any object, whereby it tends to produce benefit, advantage, pleasure, good, or happiness, (all this in the present case comes to the same thing) or (what comes again to the same thing) to prevent the happening of mischief, pain, evil, or unhappiness to the party whose interest is considered: if that party be the community in general, then the happiness of the community: if a particular individual, then the happiness of that individual.

Value of a Lot of Pleasure or Pain, How to Be Measured

I. Pleasures then, and the avoidance of pains, are the *ends* which the legislator has in view: it behoves him therefore to understand their *value.* Pleasures and pains are the *instruments* he has to work with: it behoves him therefore to understand their force, which is again, in other words, their value.

II. To a person considered *by himself,* the value of a pleasure or pain considered *by itself,* will be greater or less, according to the four following circumstances:

1. Its *intensity*.
2. Its *duration*.
3. Its *certainty* or *uncertainty*.
4. Its *propinquity* or *remoteness*.

III. These are the circumstances which are to be considered in estimating a pleasure or a pain considered each of them by itself. But when the value of any pleasure or pain is considered for the purpose of estimating the tendency of any *act* by which it is produced, there are two other circumstances to be taken into the account; these are,

5. Its *fecundity*, or the chance it has of being followed by sensations of the *same* kind: that is, pleasures, if it be a pleasure: pains, if it be a pain.

6. Its *purity*, or the chance it has of *not* being followed by sensations of the *opposite* kind: that is, pains, if it be a pleasure: pleasures, if it be a pain.

These two last, however, are in strictness scarcely to be deemed properties of the pleasure or the pain itself; they are not, therefore, in strictness to be taken into the account of the value of that pleasure or that pain. They are in strictness to be deemed properties only of the act, or other event, by which such pleasure or pain has been produced; and accordingly are only to be taken into the account of the tendency of such act or such event.

IV. To a *number* of persons, with reference to each of whom the value of a pleasure or a pain is considered, it will be greater or less, according to seven circumstances: to wit, the six preceding ones; *viz.*

1. Its *intensity*.
2. Its *duration*.
3. Its *certainty* or *uncertainty*.
4. Its *propinquity* or *remoteness*.
5. Its *fecundity*.
6. Its *purity*.

And one other; to wit:

7. Its *extent*; that is, the number of persons to whom it *extends*; or (in other words) who are affected by it.

V. To take an exact account then of the general tendency of any act, by which the interests of a community are affected, proceed as follows. Be-

gin with any one person of those whose interests seem most immediately to be affected by it: and take an account,

1. Of the value of each distinguishable *pleasure* which appears to be produced by it in the *first* instance.

2. Of the value of each *pain* which appears to be produced by it in the *first* instance.

3. Of the value of each pleasure which appears to be produced by it *after* the first. This constitutes the *fecundity* of the first *pleasure* and the *impurity* of the first *pain*.

4. Of the value of each *pain* which appears to be produced by it after the first. This constitutes the *fecundity* of the first *pain*, and the *impurity* of the first pleasure.

5. Sum up all the values of all the *pleasures* on the one side, and those of all the pains on the other. The balance, if it be on the side of pleasure, will give the *good* tendency of the act upon the whole, with respect to the interests of that *individual* person; if on the side of pain, the *bad* tendency of it upon the whole.

6. Take an account of the *number* of persons whose interests appear to be concerned; and repeat the above process with respect to each. *Sum up* the numbers expressive of the degrees of *good* tendency, which the act has, with respect to each individual, in regard to whom the tendency of it is *good* upon the whole: do this again with respect to each individual, in regard to whom the tendency of it is *good* upon the whole: do this again with respect to each individual, in regard to whom the tendency of it is *bad* upon the whole. Take the *balance*; which, if on the side of *pleasure*, will give the general *good tendency* of the act, with respect to the total number or community of individuals concerned; if on the side of pain, the general *evil tendency*, with respect to the same community.

VI. It is not to be expected that this process should be strictly pursued previously to every moral judgment, or to every legislative or judicial operation. It may, however, be always kept in view: and as near as the process actually pursued on these occasions approaches to it, so near will such process approach to the character of an exact one.

VII. The same process is alike applicable to pleasure and pain, in whatever shape they appear: and by whatever denomination they are distinguished: to pleasure, whether it be called *good* (which is properly the cause or instrument of pleasure) or *profit* (which is distant pleasure, or the cause or instrument of distant pleasure,) or *convenience,* or *advantage, benefit, emolument, happiness,* and so forth: to pain, whether it be called *evil,* (which corresponds to *good*) or *mischief,* or *inconvenience,* or *disadvantage,* or *loss,* or *unhappiness,* and so forth.

VIII. Nor is this a novel and unwarranted, any more than it is a useless theory. In all this there is nothing but what the practice of mankind, wheresoever they have a clear view of their own interest, is perfectly comformable to. An article of property, an estate in land, for instance, is valuable, on what account? On account of the pleasures of all kinds which it enables a man to produce, and what comes to the same thing the pains of all kinds which it enables him to avert. But the value of such an article of property is universally understood to rise or fall according to the length or shortness of the time which a man had in it: the certainty or uncertainty of its coming into possession: and the nearness or remoteness of the time at which, if at all, it is to come into possession. As to the *intensity* of the pleasures which a man may derive from it, this is never thought of, because it depends upon the use which each particular person may come to make of it; which cannot be estimated till the particular pleasures he may come to derive from it, or the particular pains he may come to exclude by means of it, are brought to view. For the same reason, neither does he think of the *fecundity* or *purity* of those pleasures.

Thus much for pleasure and pain, happiness and unhappiness, in *general.*

14

Beyond Good and Evil

FRIEDRICH NIETZSCHE

Friedrich Nietzsche (1844–1900) was a German philosopher and a forerunner of Existentialism. Descended through both of his parents from Lutheran ministers, Nietzsche was raised in a devout Christian home and was known as "the little Jesus" by his schoolmates. He studied theology at the University of Bonn and philology at Leipzig, becoming an atheist in the process. At the age of twenty-four he was appointed professor of classical philology at the University of Basel in Switzerland, where he taught for ten years until forced by ill health to retire. Eventually he became mentally ill. He died on August 25, 1900.

Nietzsche believes that the fundamental creative force that motivates all creation is the will to power. We all seek, not happiness, but to affirm ourselves, to flourish and dominate. Since we are essentially unequal in ability, intelligence, and imagination, it follows that the fittest will survive and be victorious in the contest with the weaker and the baser. Great beauty inheres in the struggle of the noble spirit ascending to his pinnacle on the trunks of lesser beings, including lesser human beings. But this process is hampered by Judeo-Christian morality, which Nietzsche labels "slave morality." Slave morality, which is the invention of the jealous priests, envious and resentful of the power and excellence of the noble spirit, makes us become meek and mild, so that we believe the lie that all humans have equal worth. He sometimes, as in our reading, refers to this as the ethics of "resentment."

Nietzsche's idea of an inegalitarian aesthetic-ethic assumes the thesis that "God is dead." God plays no vital role in our culture—except as a protector of the slave morality, including the idea of the equal worth of all persons. If we recognize that there is no rational

basis for believing in God, we will see that the whole edifice of slave morality must crumble and with it the notion of equal worth. In its place will arise the morality of the noble person based on the virtues of high courage, disciplined passion, pride, and intelligence, in the pursuit of affirmation and excellence.

We begin this section with Nietzsche's famous description of the madman who announces the death of God; we then turn to selections from Beyond Good and Evil, The Genealogy of Morals, *and* The Twilight of the Idols.

The Madman and the Death of God

Have you ever heard of the madman who on a bright morning lighted a lantern and ran to the marketplace calling out unceasingly, "I seek God! I seek God!"—As there were many people standing about who did not believe in God, he caused a great deal of amusement. Why! Is he lost? Said one. Has he strayed away like a child? said another. Or does he keep himself hidden? Is he afraid of us? Has he taken a sea-voyage? Has he emigrated?—the people cried out laughingly, all in a hubbub. The insane man jumped into their midst and transfixed them with his glances. "Where is God gone?" he called out. "I mean to tell you! *We have killed him,*—you and I! We are all his murderers! But how have we done it? How were we able to drink up the sea? Who gave us the sponge to wipe away the whole horizon? What did we do when we loosened this earth from its sun? Whither does it now move? Whither do we move? Away from all suns? Do we not dash on unceasingly? Backwards, sideways, forwards, in all directions? Is there still an above and below? Do we not stray, as through infinite nothingness? Does not empty space breathe upon us? Has it not become colder? Does not night come on continu-

Reprinted from *The Complete Works of Nietzsche*, ed. Oscar Levy, vols. 10 and 11 (New York: T. Foulis, 1910).

ally, darker and darker? Shall we not have to light lanterns in the morning? Do we not hear the noise of the grave-diggers who are burying God? Do we not smell the divine putrefaction?—for even Gods putrefy! God is dead! God remains dead! And we have killed him! How shall we console ourselves, the most murderous of all murderers? The holiest and the mightiest that the world has hitherto possessed has bled to death under our knife,—who will wipe the blood from us? With what water could we cleanse ourselves? What lustrums, what sacred games shall we have to devise? Is not the magnitude of this deed too great for us? Shall we not ourselves have to become gods, merely to seem worthy of it? There never was a greater event,—and on account of it, all who are born after us belong to a higher history than any history hitherto!"—Here the madman was silent and looked again at his hearers; they also were silent and looked at him in surprise. At last he threw his lantern on the ground, so that it broke in pieces and was extinguished. "I come too early," he then said, "I am not yet at the right time. This prodigious event is still on its way, and is travelling,—it has not yet reached men's ears. Lightning and thunder need time, the light of the stars needs time, deeds need time, even after they are done, to be seen and heard. This deed is as yet further from them than the furthest star,—*and yet they have done it!*"—It is further stated that the madman made his way into different churches on the same day, and there intoned his *Requiem aeternam deo.* When led out and called to account, he always gave the reply: "What are these churches now, if they are not the tombs and monuments of God?"— . . .

What Is Noble?

Every elevation of the type "man" has hitherto been the work of an aristocratic society and so it will always be—a society believing in a long scale of gradations of rank and differences of worth among human beings, and requiring slavery in some form or other. Without the *pathos of dis-* *tance,* such as grows out of the incarnated difference of classes, out of the constant outlooking and downlooking of the ruling caste on subordinates and instruments, and out of their equally constant practice of obeying and commanding, of keeping down and keeping at a distance—that other more mysterious pathos could never have arisen, the longing for an ever new widening of distance within the soul itself, the formation of ever higher, rarer, further, more extended, more comprehensive states, in short, just the elevation of the type "man," the continued "self-surmounting of man," to use a moral formula in a supermoral sense. To be sure, one must not resign oneself to any humanitarian illusions about the history of the origin of an aristocratic society (that is to say, of the preliminary condition for the elevation of the type "man"): the truth is hard. Let us acknowledge unprejudicedly how ever higher civilisation hitherto has *originated!* Men with a still natural nature, barbarians in every terrible sense of the word, men of prey, still in possession of unbroken strength of will and desire for power, threw themselves upon weaker, more moral, more peaceful races (perhaps trading or cattle-rearing communities), or upon old mellow civilisations in which the final vital force was flickering out in brilliant fireworks of wit and depravity. At the commencement, the noble caste was always the barbarian caste: their superiority did not consist first of all in their physical, but in their psychical power—they were more *complete* men (which at every point also implies the same as "more complete beasts").

Corruption—as the indication that anarchy threatens to break out among the instincts, and that the foundation of the emotions, called "life," is convulsed—is something radically different according to the organisation in which it manifests itself. When, for instance, an aristocracy like that of France at the beginning of the Revolution, flung away its privileges with sublime disgust and sacrificed itself to an excess of its moral sentiments, it was corruption:—it was really only the closing act of the corruption which had existed for centuries, by virtue of which that aristocracy had abdicated step by step its lordly prerogatives and lowered itself to a *function* of royalty (in the end even to its decoration and parade-dress). The essential thing, however, in a good and healthy aristocracy is that it should *not* regard itself as a function either of the kingship or the commonwealth, but as the *significance* and highest justification thereof—that it should therefore accept with a good conscience the sacrifice of a lesion of individuals, who, *for its sake,* must be suppressed and reduced to imperfect men, to slaves and instruments. Its fundamental belief must be precisely that society is *not* allowed to exist for its own sake, but only as a foundation and scaffolding, by means of which a select class of beings may be able to elevate themselves to their higher duties, and in general to a higher *existence:* like those sun-seeking climbing plants in Java—they are called *Sipo Matador,*—which encircle an oak so long and so often with their arms, until at last, high above it, but supported by it, they can unfold their tops in the open light, and exhibit their happiness.

To refrain mutually from injury, from violence, from exploitation, and put one's will on a par with that of others: this may result in a certain rough sense in good conduct among individuals when the necessary conditions are given (namely, the actual similarity of the individuals in amount of force and degree of worth, and their co-relation within one organisation). As soon, however, as one wished to take this principle more generally, and if possible even as *the fundamental principle of society,* it would immediately disclose what it really is—namely, a Will to the *denial* of life, a principle of dissolution and decay. Here one must think profoundly to the very basis and resist all sentimental weakness: life itself is *essentially* appropriation, injury, conquest of the strange and weak, suppression, severity, obtrusion of peculiar forms, incorporation, and at the least, putting it mildest, exploitation;—but why should one for ever use precisely these words on which for ages a disparaging purpose has been stamped? Even the organisation within which, as was previously sup-

posed, the individuals treat each other as equal—it takes place in every healthy aristocracy—must itself, if it be a living and not a dying organisation, do all that towards other bodies, which the individuals within it refrain from doing to each other: it will have to be the incarnated Will to Power, it will endeavour to grow, to gain ground, attract to itself and acquire ascendancy—not owing to any morality or immorality, but because it *lives,* and because life *is* precisely Will to Power. On no point, however, is the ordinary consciousness of Europeans more unwilling to be corrected than on this matter; people now rave everywhere, even under the guise of science, about coming conditions of society in which "the exploiting character" is to be absent:—that sounds to my ears as if they promised to invent a mode of life which should refrain from all organic functions. "Exploitation" does not belong to a depraved, or imperfect and primitive society: it belongs to the *nature* of the living being as a primary organic function; it is a consequence of the intrinsic Will to Power, which is precisely the Will to Life.— Granting that as a theory this is a novelty—as a reality it is the *fundamental fact* of all history: let us be so far honest toward ourselves!

Master and Slave Morality

In a tour through the many finer and coarser moralities which have hitherto prevailed or still prevail on the earth, I found certain traits recurring regularly together, and connected with one another, until finally two primary types revealed themselves to me, and a radical distinction was brought to light. There is *master-morality* and *slave-morality;*—I would at once add, however, that in all higher and mixed civilisations, there are also attempts at the reconciliation of the two moralities; but one finds still oftener the confusion and mutual misunderstanding of them, indeed, sometimes their close juxtaposition—even in the same man, within one soul. The distinctions of moral values have originated either in a ruling caste, pleasantly conscious of being different from the ruled—or among the ruled class, the slaves and dependents of all sorts. In the first case, when it is the rulers who determine the conception "good," it is the exalted, proud disposition which is regarded as the distinguishing feature, and that which determines the order of rank. The noble type of man separates from himself the beings in whom the opposite of this exalted, proud disposition displays itself: he despises them. Let it at once be noted that in this first kind of morality the antithesis "good" and "bad" means practically the same as "noble" and "despicable";—the antithesis "good" and "*evil*" is of a different origin. The cowardly, the timid, the insignificant, and those thinking merely of narrow utility are despised; moreover, also, the distrustful, with their constrained glances, the self-abasing, the doglike kind of men who let themselves be abused, the mendicant flatterers, and above all the liars:—it is a fundamental belief of all aristocrats that the common people are untruthful. "We truthful ones"—the nobility in ancient Greece called themselves. It is obvious that everywhere the designations of moral value were at first applied to *men,* and were only derivatively and at a later period applied to *actions;* it is a gross mistake, therefore, when historians of morals start with questions like, "Why have sympathetic actions been praised?" The noble type of man regards *himself* as a determiner of values; he does not require to be approved of; he passes the judgment: "What is injurious to me is injurious in itself"; he knows that it is he himself only who confers honour on things; he is a *creator of values.* He honours whatever he recognises in himself: such morality is self-glorification. In the foreground there is the feeling of plenitude, of power, which seeks to overflow, the happiness of high tension, the consciousness of a wealth which would fain give and bestow:—the noble man also helps the unfortunate, but not—or scarcely—out of pity, but rather from an impulse generated by the superabundance of power. The noble man honours in himself the powerful one, him also who has power over himself, who knows how to speak and

how to keep silence, who takes pleasure in subjecting himself to severity and hardness, and has reverence for all that is severe and hard. "Wotan placed a hard heart in my breast," says an old Scandinavian Saga: it is thus rightly expressed from the soul of a proud Viking. Such a type of man is even proud of *not* being made for sympathy; the hero of the Saga therefore adds warningly "He who has not a hard heart when young, will never have one." The noble and brave who think thus are the furthest removed from the morality which sees precisely in sympathy, or in acting for the good of others, or in *désintéressement,* the characteristic of the moral; faith in oneself, pride in oneself, a radical enmity and irony toward "selflessness," belong as definitely to noble morality, as do a careless scorn and precaution in presence of sympathy and the "warm heart."—It is the powerful who *know* how to honour, it is their art, their doman for invention. The profound reverence for age and for tradition—all law rests on this double reverence,—the belief and prejudice in favour of ancestors and unfavourable to newcomers, is typical in the morality of the powerful; and if, reversely, men of "modern ideas" believe almost instinctively in "progress" and the "future," and are more and more lacking in respect for old age, the ignoble origin of these "ideas" has complacently betrayed itself thereby. A morality of the ruling class, however, is more especially foreign and irritating to present-day taste in the sternness of its principle that one has duties only to one's equals; that one may act toward beings of a lower rank, toward all that is foreign, just as seems good to one, or "as the heart desires," and in any case "beyond good and evil": it is here that sympathy and similar sentiments can have a place. The ability and obligation to exercise prolonged gratitude and prolonged revenge—both only within the circle of equals,—artfulness in retaliation, *raffinement* of the idea in friendship, a certain necessity to have enemies (as outlets for the emotions of envy, quarrelsomeness, arrogance—in fact, in order to be a good *friend*): all these are typical characteristics of the noble morality, which, as has been pointed out, is not the morality of "modern ideas," and is therefore at present difficult to realise and also to unearth and disclose.—It is otherwise with the second type of morality, *slave-morality.* Supposing that the abused, the oppressed, the suffering, the unemancipated, the weary, and those uncertain of themselves, should moralise, what will be the common element in their moral estimates? Probably a pessimistic suspicion with regard to the entire situation of man will find expression, perhaps a condemnation of man, together with his situation. The slave has an unfavourable eye for the virtues of the powerful; he has a skepticism and distrust, a *refinement* of distrust of everything "good" that is there honoured—he would fain persuade himself that the very happiness there is not genuine. On the other hand, *those* qualities which serve to alleviate the existence of sufferers are brought into prominence and flooded with light; it is here that sympathy, the kind, helping hand, the warm heart, patience, diligence, humility, and friendliness attain to honour; for here these are the most useful qualities, and almost the only means of supporting the burden of existence. Slave-morality is essentially the morality of utility. Here is the seat of the origin of the famous antithesis "good" and "evil":—power and dangerousness are assumed to reside in the evil, a certain dreadfulness, subtlety, and strength, which do not admit of being despised. According to slave-morality, therefore, the "evil" man arouses fear; according to master-morality, it is precisely the "good" man who arouses fear and seeks to arouse it, while the bad man is regarded as the despicable being. The contrast attains its maximum when, in accordance with the logical consequences of slave-morality, a shade of depreciation—it may be slight and well-intentioned—at last attaches itself to the "good" man of this morality; because, according to the servile mode of thought, the good man must in any case be the *safe* man: he is good-natured, easily deceived, perhaps a little stupid, *un bonhomme.* Everywhere that slave-morality gains the ascendancy, language shows a tendency to approximate the significations of the words "good" and "stupid."—A last fundamental difference: the desire for *freedom,* the instinct for happiness and the refinements of the feeling of liberty belong as necessarily to slave-morals and morality, as artifice and enthusiasm in reverence and devotion are the regular symptoms of an aristocratic mode of thinking and estimating.—Hence we can understand without further detail why love *as a passion*—it is our European specialty—must absolutely be of noble origin; as is well known, its invention is due to the Provençal poet-cavaliers, those brilliant, ingenious men of the "*gai saber*," to whom Europe owes so much, and almost owes itself. . . .

There is an *instinct for rank,* which more than anything else is already the sign of a *high* rank; there is a *delight* in the *nuances* of reverence which leads one to infer noble origin and habits. The refinement, goodness, and loftiness of a soul are put to a perilous test when something passes by that is of the highest rank, but is not yet protected by the awe of authority from obtrusive touches and incivilities: something that goes its way like a living touchstone, undistinguished, undiscovered, and tentative, perhaps voluntarily veiled and disguised. He whose task and practice it is to investigate souls, will avail himself of many varieties of this very art to determine the ultimate value of a soul, the unalterable, innate order of rank to which it belongs; he will test it by its *instinct for reverence. Difference engendre haine* [Difference engenders hate.—ED.]: the vulgarity of many a nature spurts up suddenly like dirty water, when any holy vessel, any jewel from closed shrines, any book bearing the marks of great destiny, is brought before it; while on the other hand, there is an involuntary silence, a hesitation of the eye, a cessation of all gestures, by which *it* is indicated that a soul *feels* the nearness of what is worthiest of respect. . . .

The revolt of the slaves in morals begins in the very principle of *resentment* becoming creative and giving birth to values—a resentment experienced by creatures who, deprived as they are of the proper outlet of action, are forced to find their compensation in an imaginary revenge. While every aristocratic morality springs from a triumphant affirmation of its own demands, the slave morality says "no" from the very outset to what is "outside itself," "different from itself," and "not itself": and this "no" is its creative deed. This reversal of the valuing standpoint—this *inevitable* gravitation to the objective instead of back to the subjective—is typical of "resentment": the slave-morality requires as the condition of its existence an external and objective world, to employ physiological terminology, it requires objective stimuli to be capable of action at all—its action is fundamentally a reaction. The contrary is the case when we come to the aristocrat's system of values: it acts and grows spontaneously, it merely seeks its antithesis in order to pronounce a more grateful and exultant "yes" to its own self;—its negative conception, "low," "vulgar," "bad," is merely a pale late-born foil in comparison with its positive and fundamental conception (saturated as it is with life and passion), of "we aristocrats, we good ones, we beautiful ones, we happy ones."

When the aristocratic morality goes astray and commits sacrilege on reality, this is limited to that particular sphere with which it is *not* sufficiently acquainted—a sphere, in fact, from the real knowledge of which it disdainfully defends itself. It misjudges, in some cases, the sphere which it despises, the sphere of the common vulgar man and the low people: on the other hand, due weight should be given to the consideration that in any case the mood of contempt, of disdain, of superciliousness, even on the supposition that it *falsely* portrays the object of its contempt, will always be far removed from that degree of falsity which will always characterise the attacks—in effigy, of course—of the vindictive hatred and revengefulness of the weak in onslaughts on their enemies. In point of fact, there is in contempt too strong an admixture of nonchalance, of casualness, of boredom, of impatience, even of personal exultation, for it to be capable of distorting its victim into a

real caricature or a real monstrosity. Attention again should be paid to the almost benevolent *nuances* which, for instance, the Greek nobility imports into all the words by which it distinguishes the common people from itself; note how continuously a kind of pity, care, and consideration imparts its honeyed *flavour*, until at last almost all the words which are applied to the vulgar man survive finally as expressions for "unhappy," "worthy of pity" . . .—and how, conversely, "bad," "low," "unhappy" have never ceased to ring in the Greek ear with a tone in which "unhappy" is the predominant note: this is a heritage of the old noble aristocratic morality, which remains true to itself even in contempt. . . . The "well-born" simply *felt* themselves the "happy"; they did not have to manufacture their happiness artificially through looking at their enemies, or in cases to talk and lie themselves into happiness (as is the custom with all resentful men); and similarly, complete men as they were, exuberant with strength, and consequently *necessarily* energetic, they were too wise to dissociate happiness from action—activity becomes in their minds necessarily counted as happiness (that is the etymology of ευ πράττειν)—all in sharp contrast to the "happiness" of the weak and the oppressed, with their festering venom and malignity, among whom happiness appears essentially as a narcotic, a deadening, a quietude, a peace, a "Sabbath," an enervation of the mind and relaxation of the limbs,—in short, a purely *passive* phenomenon. While the aristocratic man lived in confidence and openness with himself (γευ–ναίος, "noble-born," emphasises the nuance "sincere," and perhaps also "naïf"), the resentful man, on the other hand, is neither sincere nor naïf, nor honest and candid with himself. His soul *squints;* his mind loves hidden crannies, tortuous paths and back doors, everything secret appeals to him as *his* world, *his* safety, *his* balm; he is past master in silence, in not forgetting, in waiting, in provisional self-deprecation and self-abasement. A race of such *resentful* men will of necessity eventually prove more *prudent* than any aristocratic race, it will honour prudence on quite a distinct scale, as, in fact, a paramount condition of existence, while prudence among aristocratic men is apt to be tinged with a delicate flavour of luxury and refinement; so among them it plays nothing like so integral a part as that complete certainty of function of the governing *unconscious* instincts, or as indeed a certain lack of prudence, such as a vehement and valiant charge, whether against danger or the enemy, or as those ecstatic bursts of rage, love, reverence, gratitude, by which at all times noble souls have recognised each other. When the resentment of the aristocratic man manifests itself, it fulfills and exhausts itself in an immediate reaction, and consequently instills no *venom:* on the other hand, it never manifests itself at all in countless instances, when in the case of the feeble and weak it would be inevitable. An inability to take seriously for any length of time their enemies, their disasters, their *misdeeds*—that is the sign of the full strong natures who possess a superfluity of moulding plastic force, that heals completely and produces forgetfulness: a good example of this in the modern world is Mirabeau, who had no memory for any insults and meannesses which were practised on him, and who was only incapable of forgiving because he forgot. Such a man indeed shakes off with a shrug many a worm which would have buried itself in another; it is only in characters like these that we see the possibility (supposing, of course, that there is such a possibility in the world) of the real "*love* of one's enemies." What respect for his enemies is found, forsooth, in an aristocratic man—and such a reverence is already a bridge to love! He insists on having his enemy to himself as his distinction. He tolerates no other enemy but a man in whose character there is nothing to despise and *much* to honour! On the other hand, imagine the "enemy" as the resentful man conceives him—and it is here exactly that we see his work, his creativeness; he has conceived "the evil enemy," the "evil one," and indeed that is the root idea from which he now evolves as a contrasting and corresponding figure a "good one," himself—his very self!

The method of this man is quite contrary to that of the aristocratic man, who conceives the root idea "good" spontaneously and straight away, that is to say, out of himself, and from that material then creates for himself a concept of "bad"! This "bad" of aristocratic origin and that "evil" out of the cauldron of unsatisfied hatred—the former an imitation, an "extra," and additional nuance; the latter, on the other hand, the original, the beginning, the essential act in the conception of a slave-morality—these two words "bad" and "evil," how great a difference do they mark, in spite of the fact that they have an identical contrary in the idea "good." But the idea "good" is *not* the same: much rather let the question be asked, "Who is really evil according to the meaning of the morality of resentment?" In all sternness let it be answered thus:—*just* the good man of the other morality, just the aristocrat, the powerful one, one who rules, but who is distorted by the venomous eye of resentfulness, into a new colour, a new signification, a new appearance. This particular point we would be the last to deny: the man who learnt to know those "good" ones only as enemies, learnt at the same time not to know them only as "*evil enemies*" and the same men who . . . were kept so rigorously in bounds through convention, respect, custom, and gratitude, though much more through mutual vigilance and jealousy, . . . these men who in their relations with each other find so many new ways of manifesting consideration, self-control, delicacy, loyalty, pride, and friendship, these men are in reference to what is outside their circle (where the foreign element, a *foreign* country, begins), not much better than beasts of prey, which have been let loose. They enjoy there freedom from all social control, they feel that in the wilderness they can give vent with impunity to that tension which is produced by enclosure and imprisonment in the peace of society, they *revert* to the innocence of the beast-of-prey conscience, like jubilant monsters, who perhaps come from a ghostly bout of murder, arson, rape, and torture, with bravado and a moral equanimity, as though merely some wild student's prank had been played, perfectly convinced that the poets have now an ample theme to sing and celebrate. It is impossible not to recognise at the core of all these aristocratic races the beast of prey; the magnificent *blonde brute,* avidly rampant for spoil and victory; this hidden core needed an outlet from time to time, the beast must get loose again, must return into the wilderness—the Roman, Arabic, German, and Japanese nobility, the Homeric heroes, the Scandinavian Vikings, are all alike in this need. It is the aristocratic races who have left the idea "Barbarian" on all the tracks in which they have marched; nay, a consciousness of this very barbarianism, and even a pride in it, manifests itself even in their highest civilisation (for example, when Pericles says to his Athenians in that celebrated funeral oration, "Our audacity has forced a way over every land and sea, rearing everywhere imperishable memorials of self for *good* and for *evil*"). This audacity of aristocratic races, mad, absurd, and spasmodic as may be its expression; the incalculable and fantastic nature of their enterprises, . . . their nonchalance and contempt for safety, body, life, and comfort, their awful joy and intense delight in all destruction, in all the ecstasies of victory and cruelty,—all these features become crystallised, for those who suffered thereby in the picture of the "barbarian," of the "evil enemy," perhaps of the "Goth" and of the "Vandal." The profound, icy mistrust which the German provokes, as soon as he arrives at power,—even at the present time,—is always still an aftermath of that inextinguishable horror with which for whole centuries Europe has regarded the wrath of the blonde Teuton beast. . . .

. . . One may be perfectly justified in being always afraid of the blonde beast that lies at the core of all aristocratic races, and in being on one's guard: but who would not a hundred times prefer to be afraid, when one at the same time admires, than to be immune from fear, at the cost of being perpetually obsessed with the loathsome spectacle of the distorted, the dwarfed, the stunted, the envenomed? And is that not our fate? What produces today our repulsion towards "man"?—for we *suffer* from "man," there is no doubt about it. It is not fear; it is rather that we have nothing more to fear from men; it is that the worm "man" is in the foreground and pullulates; it is that the "tame man," the wretched mediocre and unedifying creature, has learnt to consider himself a goal and a pinnacle, an inner meaning, an historic principle, a "higher man"; yes, it is that he has a certain right so to consider himself, in so far as he feels that in contrast to that excess of deformity, disease, exhaustion, and effeteness whose odour is beginning to pollute present-day Europe, he at any rate has achieved a relative success, he at any rate still says "yes" to life.

Goodness and the Will to Power

What is good?—All that enhances the feeling of power, the Will to Power, and the power itself in man. What is bad?—All that proceeds from weakness. What is happiness?—The feeling that power is increasing—that resistance has been overcome.

Not contentment, but more power; not peace at any price but war; not virtue, but competence (virtue in the Renaissance sense, *virtu,* free from all moralistic acid). The first principle of our humanism: The weak and the failures shall perish. They ought even to be helped to perish.

What is more harmful than any vice?—Practical sympathy and pity for all the failures and all the weak: Christianity.

Christianity is the religion of pity. Pity opposes the noble passions which heighten our vitality. It has a depressing effect, depriving us of strength. As we multiply the instances of pity we gradually lose our strength of nobility. Pity makes suffering contagious and under certain conditions it may cause a total loss of life and vitality out of all proportion to the magnitude of the cause. . . . Pity is the practice of nihilism.

15

The Good Is Not Natural

G. E. MOORE

George Edward Moore (1873–1958) was a British philosopher who spent much of his career at Cambridge University, where he worked with other great philosophers including Bertrand Russell and Ludwig Wittgenstein. He did work of lasting importance on philosophical methodology, epistemology, metaphysics, and moral philosophy. The present selection is taken from the early pages of his book Principia Ethica *(1902), which ranks among the most influential books on moral theory of the twentieth century. In this selection Moore famously argues that "the Good" is not reducible to any natural property or properties; instead, it is sui generis—something altogether unique in kind.*

1. It is very easy to point out some among our every-day judgments, with the truth of which Ethics is undoubtedly concerned. Whenever we say, 'So and so is a good man,' or 'That fellow is a villain'; whenever we ask, 'What ought I to do?' or 'Is it wrong for me to do like this?'; whenever we hazard such remarks as 'Temperance is a virtue and drunkenness a vice'—it is undoubtedly the business of Ethics to discuss such questions and such statements; to argue what is the true answer when we ask what it is right to do, and to give reasons for thinking that our statements about the character of persons or the morality of actions are true or false. In the vast majority of cases, where we make statements involving any of the terms 'virtue,' 'vice,' 'duty,' 'right,' 'ought,' 'good,' 'bad,' we are making ethical judgments; and if we wish to discuss their truth, we shall be discussing a point of Ethics.

So much as this is not disputed; but it falls very far short of defining the province of Ethics. That province may indeed be defined as the whole truth about that which is at the same time common to all such judgments and peculiar to them. But we have still to ask the question: What is it that is thus common and peculiar? And this is a question to which very different answers have been given by ethical philosophers of acknowledged reputation, and none of them, perhaps, completely satisfactory.

2. If we take such examples as those given above, we shall not be far wrong in saying that they are all of them concerned with the question of 'conduct'—with the question, what, in the conduct of us, human beings, is good, and what is bad, what is right, and what is wrong. For when we say that a man is good, we commonly mean that he acts rightly; when we say that drunkenness is a vice, we commonly mean that to get drunk is a wrong or wicked action. And this discussion of human conduct is, in fact, that with which the name 'Ethics' is most intimately associated. It is so associated by derivation; and conduct is undoubtedly by far the commonest and most generally interesting object of ethical judgments.

Accordingly, we find that many ethical philosophers are disposed to accept as an adequate definition of 'Ethics' the statement that it deals with the question what is good or bad in human conduct. They hold that its enquiries are properly confined to 'conduct' or to 'practice'; they hold that the name 'practical philosophy' covers all the matter with which it has to do. Now, without discussing the proper meaning of the word (for verbal questions are properly left to the writers of dictionaries and other persons interested in literature; philosophy, as we shall see, has no concern with them), I may say that I intend to use 'Ethics' to cover more than this—a usage, for which there is, I think, quite sufficient authority. I am using it to cover an enquiry for which, at all events, there is no other word: the general enquiry into what is good.

Ethics is undoubtedly concerned with the question what good conduct is; but, being concerned with this, it obviously does not start at the beginning, unless it is prepared to tell us what is good as well as what is conduct. For 'good conduct' is a complex notion: all conduct is not good; for some is certainly bad and some may be indifferent. And on the other hand, other things, beside conduct, may be good; and if they are so, then, 'good' denotes some property, that is common to them and conduct; and if we examine good conduct alone of all good things, then we shall be in danger of mistaking for this property, some property which is not shared by those other things: and thus we shall have made a mistake about Ethics even in this limited sense; for we shall not know what good conduct really is. This is a mistake which many writers have actually made, from limiting their enquiry to conduct. And hence I shall try to avoid it by considering first what is good in general; hoping, that if we can arrive at any certainty about this, it will be much easier to settle the question of good conduct: for we all know pretty well what 'conduct' is. This, then, is our first question: What is good? and What is bad? and to the discussion of this question (or these questions) I give the name of Ethics, since that science must, at all events, include it.

3. But this is a question which may have many meanings. If, for example, each of us were to say 'I am doing good now' or 'I had a good dinner yesterday,' these statements would each of them be some sort of answer to our question, although perhaps a false one. So, too, when A asks B what school he ought to send his son to, B's answer will certainly be an ethical judgment. And similarly all distribution of praise or blame to any

personage or thing that has existed, now exists, or will exist, does give some answer to the question 'What is good?' In all such cases some particular thing is judged to be good or bad: the question 'What?' is answered by 'This.' But this is not the sense in which a scientific Ethics asks the question. Not one, of all the many million answers of this kind, which must be true, can form a part of an ethical system; although that science must contain reasons and principles sufficient for deciding on the truth of all of them. There are far too many persons, things and events in the world, past, present, or to come, for a discussion of their individual merits to be embraced in any science. Ethics, therefore, does not deal at all with facts of this nature, facts that are unique, individual, absolutely particular; facts with which such studies as history, geography, astronomy, are compelled, in part at least, to deal. And, for this reason, it is not the business of the ethical philosopher to give personal advice or exhortation.

4. But there is another meaning which may be given to the question 'What is good?' 'Books are good' would be an answer to it, though an answer obviously false; for some books are very bad indeed. And ethical judgments of this kind do indeed belong to Ethics; though I shall not deal with many of them. Such is the judgment 'Pleasure is good'—a judgment, of which Ethics should discuss the truth, although it is not nearly as important as that other judgment, with which we shall be much occupied presently—'Pleasure *alone* is good.' It is judgments of this sort, which are made in such books on Ethics as contain a list of 'virtues'—in Aristotle's 'Ethics' for example. But it is judgments of precisely the same kind, which form the substance of what is commonly supposed to be a study different from Ethics, and one much less respectable— the study of Casuistry. We may be told that Casuistry differs from Ethics, in that it is much more detailed and particular, Ethics much more general. But it is most important to notice that Casuistry does not deal with anything that is

absolutely particular—particular in the only sense in which a perfectly precise line can be drawn between it and what is general. It is not particular in the sense just noticed, the sense in which this book is a particular book, and A's friend's advice particular advice. Casuistry may indeed be *more* particular and Ethics *more* general; but that means that they differ only in degree and not in kind. And this is universally true of 'particular' and 'general,' when used in this common, but inaccurate, sense. So far as Ethics allows itself to give lists of virtues or even to name constituents of the Ideal, it is indistinguishable from Casuistry. Both alike deal with what is general, in the sense in which physics and chemistry deal with what is general. Just as chemistry aims at discovering what are the properties of oxygen, *wherever it occurs*, and not only of this or that particular specimen of oxygen; so Casuistry aims at discovering what actions are good, *whenever they occur*. In this respect Ethics and Casuistry alike are to be classed with such sciences as physics, chemistry and physiology, in their absolute distinction from those of which history and geography are instances. And it is to be noted that, owing to their detailed nature, casuistical investigations are actually nearer to physics and to chemistry than are the investigations usually assigned to Ethics. For just as physics cannot rest content with the discovery that light is propagated by waves of ether, but must go on to discover the particular nature of the ether-waves corresponding to each several colour; so Casuistry, not content with the general law that charity is a virtue, must attempt to discover the relative merits of every different form of charity. Casuistry forms, therefore, part of the ideal of ethical science: Ethics cannot be complete without it. The defects of Casuistry are not defects of principle; no objection can be taken to its aim and object. It has failed only because it is far too difficult a subject to be treated adequately in our present state of knowledge. The casuist has been unable to distinguish, in the cases which

he treats, those elements upon which their value depends. Hence he often thinks two cases to be alike in respect of value, when in reality they are alike only in some other respect. It is to mistakes of this kind that the pernicious influence of such investigations has been due. For Casuistry is the goal of ethical investigation. It cannot be safely attempted at the beginning of our studies, but only at the end.

5. But our question 'What is good?' may have still another meaning. We may, in the third place, mean to ask, not what thing or things are good, but how 'good' is to be defined. This is an enquiry which belongs only to Ethics, not to Casuistry; and this is the enquiry which will occupy us first.

It is an enquiry to which most special attention should be directed; since this question, how 'good' is to be defined, is the most fundamental question in all Ethics. That which is meant by 'good' is, in fact, except its converse 'bad,' the *only* simple object of thought which is peculiar to Ethics. Its definition is, therefore, the most essential point in the definition of Ethics; and moreover a mistake with regard to it entails a far larger number of erroneous ethical judgments than any other. Unless this first question be fully understood, and its true answer clearly recognised, the rest of Ethics is as good as useless from the point of view of systematic knowledge. True ethical judgments, of the two kinds last dealt with, may indeed be made by those who do not know the answer to this question as well as by those who do; and it goes without saying that the two classes of people may lead equally good lives. But it is extremely unlikely that the *most general* ethical judgments will be equally valid, in the absence of a true answer to this question: I shall presently try to shew that the gravest errors have been largely due to beliefs in a false answer. And, in any case, it is impossible that, till the answer to this question be known, any one should know *what is the evidence* for any ethical judgment whatsoever. But the main object of Ethics, as a systematic science, is to give correct *reasons* for thinking that this or that is good; and, unless this question be answered, such reasons cannot be given. Even, therefore, apart from the fact that a false answer leads to false conclusions, the present enquiry is a most necessary and important part of the science of Ethics.

6. What, then, is good? How is good to be defined? Now, it may be thought that this is a verbal question. A definition does indeed often mean the expressing of one word's meaning in other words. But this is not the sort of definition I am asking for. Such a definition can never be of ultimate importance in any study except lexicography. If I wanted that kind of definition I should have to consider in the first place how people generally used the word 'good'; but my business is not with its proper usage, as established by custom. I should, indeed, be foolish, if I tried to use it for something which it did not usually denote: if, for instance, I were to announce that, whenever I used the word 'good,' I must be understood to be thinking of that object which is usually denoted by the word 'table.' I shall, therefore, use the word in the sense in which I think it is ordinarily used; but at the same time I am not anxious to discuss whether I am right in thinking that it is so used. My business is solely with that object or idea, which I hold, rightly or wrongly, that the word is generally used to stand for. What I want to discover is the nature of that object or idea, and about this I am extremely anxious to arrive at an agreement.

But, if we understand the question in this sense, my answer to it may seem a very disappointing one. If I am asked 'What is good?' my answer is that good is good, and that is the end of the matter. Or if I am asked 'How is good to be defined?' my answer is that it cannot be defined, and that is all I have to say about it. But disappointing as these answers may appear, they are of the very last importance. To readers who are familiar with philosophic terminology, I can express their importance by saying that they

amount to this: That propositions about the good are all of them synthetic and never analytic; and that is plainly no trivial matter. And the same thing may be expressed more popularly, by saying that, if I am right, then nobody can foist upon us such an axiom as that 'Pleasure is the only good' or that 'The good is the desired' on the pretence that this is 'the very meaning of the word.'

7. Let us, then, consider this position. My point is that 'good' is a simple notion, just as 'yellow' is a simple notion; that, just as you cannot, by any manner of means, explain to any one who does not already know it, what yellow is, so you cannot explain what good is. Definitions of the kind that I was asking for, definitions which describe the real nature of the object or notion denoted by a word, and which do not merely tell us what the word is used to mean, are only possible when the object or notion in question is something complex. You can give a definition of a horse, because a horse has many different properties and qualities, all of which you can enumerate. But when you have enumerated them all, when you have reduced a horse to his simplest terms, then you can no longer define those terms. They are simply something which you think of or perceive, and to any one who cannot think of or perceive them, you can never, by any definition, make their nature known. It may perhaps be objected to this that we are able to describe to others, objects which they have never seen or thought of. We can, for instance, make a man understand what a chimaera is, although he has never heard of one or seen one. You can tell him that it is an animal with a lioness's head and body, with a goat's head growing from the middle of its back, and with a snake in place of a tail. But here the object which you are describing is a complex object; it is entirely composed of parts, with which we are all perfectly familiar—a snake, a goat, a lioness; and we know, too, the manner in which those parts are to be put together, because we know what is

meant by the middle of a lioness's back, and where her tail is wont to grow. And so it is with all objects, not previously known, which we are able to define: they are all complex; all composed of parts, which may themselves, in the first instance, be capable of similar definition, but which must in the end be reducible to simplest parts, which can no longer be defined. But yellow and good, we say, are not complex: they are notions of that simple kind, out of which definitions are composed and with which the power of further defining ceases.

8. When we say, as Webster says, 'The definition of horse is "A hoofed quadruped of the genus Equus,"' we may, in fact, mean three different things. (1) We may mean merely: 'When I say "horse," you are to understand that I am talking about a hoofed quadruped of the genus Equus.' This might be called the arbitrary verbal definition: and I do not mean that good is indefinable in that sense. (2) We may mean, as Webster ought to mean: 'When most English people say "horse," they mean a hoofed quadruped of the genus Equus.' This may be called the verbal definition proper, and I do not say that good is indefinable in this sense either; for it is certainly possible to discover how people use a word: otherwise, we could never have known that 'good' may be translated by 'gut' in German and by 'bon' in French. But (3) we may, when we define horse, mean something much more important. We may mean that a certain object, which we all of us know, is composed in a certain manner: that it has four legs, a head, a heart, a liver, etc., etc., all of them arranged in definite relations to one another. It is in this sense that I deny good to be definable. I say that it is not composed of any parts, which we can substitute for it in our minds when we are thinking of it. We might think just as clearly and correctly about a horse, if we thought of all its parts and their arrangement instead of thinking of the whole: we could, I say, think how a horse differed from a donkey just as well, just as truly, in

this way, as now we do, only not so easily; but there is nothing whatsoever which we could so substitute for good; and that is what I mean, when I say that good is indefinable.

9. But I am afraid I have still not removed the chief difficulty which may prevent acceptance of the proposition that good is indefinable. I do not mean to say that *the* good, that which is good, is thus indefinable; if I did think so, I should not be writing on Ethics, for my main object is to help towards discovering that definition. It is just because I think there will be less risk of error in our search for a definition of 'the good,' that I am now insisting that *good* is indefinable. I must try to explain the difference between these two. I suppose it may be granted that 'good' is an adjective. Well 'the good,' 'that which is good,' must therefore be the substantive to which the adjective 'good' will apply: it must be the whole of that to which the adjective will apply, and the adjective must *always* truly apply to it. But if it is that to which the adjective will apply, it must be something different from that adjective itself; and the whole of that something different, whatever it is, will be our definition of *the* good. Now it may be that this something will have other adjectives, beside 'good,' that will apply to it. It may be full of pleasure, for example; it may be intelligent: and if these two adjectives are really part of its definition, then it will certainly be true, that pleasure and intelligence are good. And many people appear to think that, if we say 'Pleasure and intelligence are good,' or if we say 'Only pleasure and intelligence are good,' we are defining ' good.' Well, I cannot deny that propositions of this nature may sometimes be called definitions; I do not know well enough how the word is generally used to decide upon this point. I only wish it to be understood that that is not what I mean when I say there is no possible definition of good, and that I shall not mean this if I use the word again. I do most fully believe that some true proposition of the form 'Intelligence is good

and intelligence alone is good' can be found; if none could be found, our definition of *the* good would be impossible. As it is, I believe *the* good to be definable; and yet I still say that good itself is indefinable.

10. 'Good,' then, if we mean by it that quality which we assert to belong to a thing, when we say that the thing is good, is incapable of any definition, in the most important sense of that word. The most important sense of 'definition' is that in which a definition states what are the parts which invariably compose a certain whole; and in this sense 'good' has no definition because it is simple and has no parts. It is one of those innumerable objects of thought which are themselves incapable of definition, because they are the ultimate terms by reference to which whatever *is* capable of definition must be defined. That there must be an indefinite number of such terms is obvious, on reflection; since we cannot define anything except by an analysis, which, when carried as far as it will go, refers us to something, which is simply different from anything else, and which by that ultimate difference explains the peculiarity of the whole which we are defining: for every whole contains some parts which are common to other wholes also. There is, therefore, no intrinsic difficulty in the contention that 'good' denotes a simple and indefinable quality. There are many other instances of such qualities.

Consider yellow, for example. We may try to define it, by describing its physical equivalent; we may state what kind of light-vibrations must stimulate the normal eye, in order that we may perceive it. But a moment's reflection is sufficient to shew that those light-vibrations are not themselves what we mean by yellow. *They* are not what we perceive. Indeed we should never have been able to discover their existence, unless we had first been struck by the patent difference of quality between the different colours. The most we can be entitled to say of those vibrations is that they are what corresponds in space to the yellow which we actually perceive.

Yet a mistake of this simple kind has commonly been made about 'good.' It may be true that all things which are good are *also* something else, just as it is true that all things which are yellow produce a certain kind of vibration in the light. And it is a fact, that Ethics aims at discovering what are those other properties belonging to all things which are good. But far too many philosophers have thought that when they named those other properties they were actually defining good; that these properties, in fact, were simply not 'other,' but absolutely and entirely the same with goodness. This view I propose to call the 'naturalistic fallacy' and of it I shall now endeavour to dispose.

11. Let us consider what it is such philosophers say. And first it is to be noticed that they do not agree among themselves. They not only say that they are right as to what good is, but they endeavour to prove that other people who say that it is something else, are wrong. One, for instance, will affirm that good is pleasure, another, perhaps, that good is that which is desired; and each of these will argue eagerly to prove that the other is wrong. But how is that possible? One of them says that good is nothing but the object of desire, and at the same time tries to prove that it is not pleasure. But from his first assertion, that good just means the object of desire, one of two things must follow as regards his proof:

(1) He may be trying to prove that the object of desire is not pleasure. But, if this be all, where is his Ethics? The position he is maintaining is merely a psychological one. Desire is something which occurs in our minds, and pleasure is something else which so occurs; and our would-be ethical philosopher is merely holding that the latter is not the object of the former. But what has that to do with the question in dispute? His opponent held the ethical proposition that pleasure was the good, and although he should prove a million times over the psychological proposition that pleasure is not the object of desire, he is no nearer proving his opponent to be wrong. The position is like this. One man says a triangle is

a circle: another replies 'A triangle is a straight line, and I will prove to you that I am right; *for*' (this is the only argument) 'a straight line is not a circle.' 'That is quite true,' the other may reply; 'but nevertheless a triangle is a circle, and you have said nothing whatever to prove the contrary. What is proved is that one of us is wrong, for we agree that a triangle cannot be both a straight line and a circle: but which is wrong, there can be no earthly means of proving, since you define triangle as straight line and I define it as circle.'—Well, that is one alternative which any naturalistic Ethics has to face; if good is *defined* as something else, it is then impossible either to prove that any other definition is wrong or even to deny such definition.

(2) The other alternative will scarcely be more welcome. It is that the discussion is after all a verbal one. When A says 'Good means pleasant' and B says 'Good means desired,' they may merely wish to assert that most people have used the word for what is pleasant and for what is desired respectively. And this is quite an interesting subject for discussion: only it is not a whit more an ethical discussion than the last was. Nor do I think that any exponent of naturalistic Ethics would be willing to allow that this was all he meant. They are all so anxious to persuade us that what they call the good is what we really ought to do. 'Do, pray, act so, because the word "good" is generally used to denote actions of this nature': such, on this view, would be the substance of their teaching. And in so far as they tell us how we ought to act, their teaching is truly ethical, as they mean it to be. But how perfectly absurd is the reason they would give for it! 'You are to do this, because most people use a certain word to denote conduct such as this.' 'You are to say the thing which is not, because most people call it lying.' That is an argument just as good!—My dear sirs, what we want to know from you as ethical teachers, is not how people use a word; it is not even, what kind of actions they approve, which the use of this word 'good' may certainly imply: what we

want to know is simply what *is* good. We may indeed agree that what most people do think good, is actually so; we shall at all events be glad to know their opinions: but when we say their opinions about what *is* good, we do mean what we say; we do not care whether they call that thing which they mean 'horse' or 'table' or 'chair,' 'gut' or 'bon' or 'ἀγαθός'; we want to know what it is that they so call. When they say 'Pleasure is good,' we cannot believe that they merely mean 'Pleasure is pleasure' and nothing more than that.

12. Suppose a man says 'I am pleased'; and suppose that is not a lie or a mistake but the truth. Well, if it is true, what does that mean? It means that his mind, a certain definite mind, distinguished by certain definite marks from all others, has at this moment a certain definite feeling called pleasure. 'Pleased' *means* nothing but having pleasure, and though we may be more pleased or less pleased, and even, we may admit for the present, have one or another kind of pleasure; yet in so far as it is pleasure we have, whether there be more or less of it, and whether it be of one kind or another, what we have is one definite thing, absolutely indefinable, some one thing that is the same in all the various degrees and in all the various kinds of it that there may be. We may be able to say how it is related to other things: that, for example, it is in the mind, that it causes desire, that we are conscious of it, etc., etc. We can, I say, describe its relations to other things, but define it we can *not*. And if anybody tried to define pleasure for us as being any other natural object; if anybody were to say, for instance, that pleasure *means* the sensation of red, and were to proceed to deduce from that that pleasure is a colour, we should be entitled to laugh at him and to distrust his future statements about pleasure. Well, that would be the same fallacy which I have called the naturalistic fallacy. That 'pleased' does not mean 'having the sensation of red,' or anything else whatever, does not prevent us from understanding what it does mean. It is enough for us to know that

'pleased' does mean 'having the sensation of pleasure,' and though pleasure is absolutely indefinable, though pleasure is pleasure and nothing else whatever, yet we feel no difficulty in saying that we are pleased. The reason is, of course, that when I say 'I am pleased,' I do *not* mean that 'I' am the same thing as 'having pleasure.' And similarly no difficulty need be found in my saying that 'pleasure is good' and yet not meaning that 'pleasure' is the same thing as 'good,' that pleasure *means* good, and that good *means* pleasure. If I were to imagine that when I said 'I am pleased,' I meant that I was exactly the same thing as 'pleased,' I should not indeed call that a naturalistic fallacy, although it would be the same fallacy as I have called naturalistic with reference to Ethics. The reason of this is obvious enough. When a man confuses two natural objects with one another, defining the one by the other, if for instance, he confuses himself, who is one natural object, with 'pleased' or with 'pleasure' which are others, then there is no reason to call the fallacy naturalistic. But if he confuses 'good,' which is not in the same sense a natural object, with any natural object whatever, then there is a reason for calling that a naturalistic fallacy; its being made with regard to 'good' marks it as something quite specific, and this specific mistake deserves a name because it is so common. As for the reasons why good is not to be considered a natural object, they may be reserved for discussion in another place. But, for the present, it is sufficient to notice this: Even if it were a natural object, that would not alter the nature of the fallacy nor diminish its importance one whit. All that I have said about it would remain quite equally true: only the name which I have called it would not be so appropriate as I think it is. And I do not care about the name: what I do care about is the fallacy. It does not matter what we call it, provided we recognise it when we meet with it. It is to be met with in almost every book on Ethics; and yet it is not recognised: and that is why it is necessary to multiply illustrations of it, and

convenient to give it a name. It is a very simple fallacy indeed. When we say that an orange is yellow, we do not think our statement binds us to hold that 'orange' means nothing else than 'yellow,' or that nothing can be yellow but an orange. Supposing the orange is also sweet! Does that bind us to say that 'sweet' is exactly the same thing as 'yellow,' that 'sweet' must be defined as 'yellow'? And supposing it be recognised that 'yellow' just means 'yellow' and nothing else whatever, does that make it any more difficult to hold that oranges are yellow? Most certainly it does not: on the contrary, it would be absolutely meaningless to say that oranges were yellow, unless yellow did in the end mean just 'yellow' and nothing else whatever—unless it was absolutely indefinable. We should not get any very clear notion about things, which are yellow—we should not get very far with our science, if we were bound to hold that everything which was yellow, *meant* exactly the same thing as yellow. We should find we had to hold that an orange was exactly the same thing as a stool, a piece of paper, a lemon, anything you like. We could prove any number of absurdities; but should we be the nearer to the truth? Why, then, should it be different with 'good'? Why, if good is good and indefinable, should I be held to deny that pleasure is good? Is there any difficulty in holding both to be true at once? On the contrary, there is no meaning in saying that pleasure is good, unless good is something different from pleasure. It is absolutely useless, so far as Ethics is concerned, to prove that [. . .] increase of pleasure coincides with increase of life, unless good *means* something different from either life or pleasure. He might just as well try to prove that an orange is yellow by shewing that it always is wrapped up in paper.

13. In fact, if it is not the case that 'good' denotes something simple and indefinable, only two alternatives are possible: either it is a complex, a given whole, about the correct analysis of which there may be disagreement; or else it means nothing at all, and there is no such subject

as Ethics. In general, however, ethical philosophers have attempted to define good, without recognising what such an attempt must mean. They actually use arguments which involve one or both of the absurdities considered in § 11. We are, therefore, justified in concluding that the attempt to define good is chiefly due to want of clearness as to the possible nature of definition. There are, in fact, only two serious alternatives to be considered, in order to establish the conclusion that 'good' does denote a simple and indefinable notion. It might possibly denote a complex, as 'horse' does; or it might have no meaning at all. Neither of these possibilities has, however, been clearly conceived and seriously maintained, as such, by those who presume to define good; and both may be dismissed by a simple appeal to facts.

(1) The hypothesis that disagreement about the meaning of good is disagreement with regard to the correct analysis of a given whole, may be most plainly seen to be incorrect by consideration of the fact that, whatever definition be offered, it may be always asked, with significance, of the complex so defined, whether it is itself good. To take, for instance, one of the more plausible, because one of the more complicated, of such proposed definitions, it may easily be thought, at first sight, that to be good may mean to be that which we desire to desire. Thus if we apply this definition to a particular instance and say 'When we think that A is good, we are thinking that A is one of the things which we desire to desire,' our proposition may seem quite plausible. But, if we carry the investigation further, and ask ourselves 'Is it good to desire to desire A?' it is apparent, on a little reflection, that this question is itself as intelligible, as the original question 'Is A good?'—that we are, in fact, now asking for exactly the same information about the desire to desire A, for which we formerly asked with regard to A itself. But it is also apparent that the meaning of this second question cannot be correctly analysed into 'Is the desire to desire A one of the things which we desire to desire?': we have not before our minds anything so complicated as the question 'Do we desire to desire to desire to desire A?' Moreover any one can easily convince himself by inspection that the predicate of this proposition—'good'—is positively different from the notion of 'desiring to desire' which enters into its subject: 'That we should desire to desire A is good' is *not* merely equivalent to 'That A should be good is good.' It may indeed be true that what we desire to desire is always also good; perhaps, even the converse may be true: but it is very doubtful whether this is the case, and the mere fact that we understand very well what is meant by doubting it, shews clearly that we have two different notions before our minds.

(2) And the same consideration is sufficient to dismiss the hypothesis that 'good' has no meaning whatsoever. It is very natural to make the mistake of supposing that what is universally true is of such a nature that its negation would be self-contradictory: the importance which has been assigned to analytic propositions in the history of philosophy shews how easy such a mistake is. And thus it is very easy to conclude that what seems to be a universal ethical principle is in fact an identical proposition; that, if, for example, whatever is called 'good' seems to be pleasant, the proposition 'Pleasure is the good' does not assert a connection between two different notions, but involves only one, that of pleasure, which is easily recognised as a distinct entity. But whoever will attentively consider with himself what is actually before his mind when he asks the question 'Is pleasure (or whatever it may be) after all good?' can easily satisfy himself that he is not merely wondering whether pleasure is pleasant. And if he will try this experiment with each suggested definition in succession, he may become expert enough to recognise that in every case he has before his mind a unique object, with regard to the connection of which with any other object, a distinct question may be asked. Every one does in fact understand the question 'Is this good?' When he thinks of it, his state of

mind is different from what it would be, were he asked 'Is this pleasant, or desired, or approved?' It has a distinct meaning for him, even though he may not recognise in what respect it is distinct. Whenever he thinks of 'intrinsic value,' or 'intrinsic worth,' or says that a thing 'ought to exist,' he has before his mind the unique object—the unique property of things—which I mean by 'good.' Everybody is constantly aware of this notion, although he may never become aware at all that it is different from other notions of which he is also aware. But, for correct ethical reasoning, it is extremely important that he should become aware of this fact; and, as soon as the nature of the problem is clearly understood, there should be little difficulty in advancing so far in analysis.

16

The Experience Machine

ROBERT NOZICK

Robert Nozick (1938–2002) was Professor of Philosophy at Harvard University and the author of several important works in philosophy, especially Anarchy, State, and Utopia, *from which the present selection is taken. Nozick argues against hedonism. If pleasure were the only intrinsic value, we would have an overriding reason to be hooked up to a machine which would produce favorable sensations. Nozick discusses the reasons for rejecting the experience machine and, with it, hedonism.*

There are also substantial puzzles when we ask what matters other than how *people's* experiences feel "from the inside." Suppose there were an experience machine that would give you any experience you desired. Superduper neuropsychologists could stimulate your brain so that you would think and feel you were writing a great novel, or making a friend, or reading an interesting book. All the time you would be floating in a tank, with electrodes attached to your brain. Should you plug into this machine for life, preprogramming your life's experiences? If you are worried about missing out on desirable experiences, we can suppose that business enterprises have researched thoroughly the lives of many others. You can pick and choose from their large library or smorgasbord of such experiences, selecting your life's experiences for, say, the next two years. After two years have passed, you will have ten minutes or ten hours out of the tank, to select the experiences of your *next* two years. Of course, while in the tank you won't know that you're there; you'll think it's all actually happening. Others can also plug in to have the experiences they want, so there's no need

Reprinted from *Anarchy, State, and Utopia* (Harvard University Press, 1973), by permission of the publisher.

to stay unplugged to serve them. (Ignore problems such as who will service the machines if everyone plugs in.) Would you plug in? *What else can matter to us, other than how our lives feel from the inside?* Nor should you refrain because of the few moments of distress between the moment you've decided and the moment you're plugged. What's a few moments of distress compared to a lifetime of bliss (if that's what you choose), and why feel any distress at all if your decision *is* the best one?

What does matter to us in addition to our experiences? First, we want to *do* certain things, and not just have the experience of doing them. In the case of certain experiences, it is only because first we want to do the actions that we want the experiences of doing them or thinking we've done them. (But *why* do we want to do the activities rather than merely to experience them?) A second reason for not plugging in is that we want to *be* a certain way, to be a certain sort of person. Someone floating in a tank is an indeterminate blob. There is no answer to the question of what a person is like who has long been in the tank. Is he courageous, kind, intelligent, witty, loving? It's not merely that it's difficult to tell; there's no way he is. Plugging into the machine is a kind of suicide. It will seem to some, trapped by a picture, that nothing about what we are like can matter except as it gets reflected in our experiences. But should it be surprising that what *we are* is important to us? Why should we be concerned only with how our time is filled, but not with what we are?

Thirdly, plugging into an experience machine limits us to a man-made reality, to a world no deeper or more important than that which people can construct. There is no *actual* contact with any deeper reality, though the experience of it can be simulated. Many persons desire to leave themselves open to such contact and to a plumbing of deeper significance.[1] This clarifies the intensity of the conflict over psychoactive drugs, which some view as mere local experience machines, and others view as avenues to a deeper reality; what some view as equivalent to surrender to the experience machine, others view as following one of the reasons *not* to surrender!

We learn that something matters to us in addition to experience by imagining an experience machine and then realizing that we would not use it. We can continue to imagine a sequence of machines each designed to fill lacks suggested for the earlier machines. For example, since the experience machine doesn't meet our desire to *be* a certain way, imagine a transformation machine which transforms us into whatever sort of person we'd like to be (compatible with our staying us). Surely one would not use the transformation machine to become as one would wish, and thereupon plug into the experience machine![2] So something matters in addition to one's experiences *and* what one is like. Nor is the reason merely that one's experiences are unconnected with what one is like. For the experience machine might be limited to provide only experiences possible to the sort of person plugged in. Is it that we want to make a difference in the world? Consider then the result machine, which produces in the world any result you would produce and injects your vector input into any joint activity. We shall not pursue here the fascinating details of these or other machines. What is most disturbing about them is their living of our lives for us. Is it misguided to search for *particular* additional functions beyond the competence of machines to do for us? Perhaps what we desire is to live (an active verb) ourselves, in contact with reality. (And this,

machines cannot do *for* us.) Without elaborating on the implications of this, which I believe connect surprisingly with issues about free will and causal accounts of knowledge, we need merely note the intricacy of the question of what matters *for people* other than their experiences. Until one finds a satisfactory answer, and determines that this answer does not *also* apply to animals, one cannot reasonably claim that only the felt experiences of animals limit what we may do to them.

Notes

1. Traditional religious views differ on the *point* of contact with a transcendent reality. Some say that contact yields eternal bliss or Nirvana, but they have not distinguished this sufficiently from merely a *very* long run on the experience machine. Others think it is intrinsically desirable to do the will of a higher being which created us all, though presumably no one would think this if we discovered we had been created as an object of amusement by some superpowerful child from another galaxy or dimension. Still others imagine an eventual merging with a higher reality, leaving unclear its desirability, or where that merging leaves *us*.

2. Some wouldn't use the transformation machine at all; it seems like *cheating.* But the one-time use of the transformation machine would not remove all challenges; there would still be obstacles for the new us to overcome, a new plateau from which to strive even higher. And is this plateau any the less earned or deserved than that provided by genetic endowment and early childhood environment? But if the transformation machine could be used indefinitely often, so that we could accomplish anything by pushing a button to transform ourselves into someone who could do it easily, there would remain no limits we *need* to strain against or try to transcend. Would there be anything left *to do?* Do some theological views place God outside of time because an omniscient omnipotent being couldn't fill up his days?

Value Pluralism

W. D. ROSS

Sir William David Ross (1877–1971) was provost of Oriel College, Oxford University. His book The Right and the Good *(1930), from which the present selection is taken, is a classic treatise in ethical intuitionism. Ross agrees with Bentham that pleasure is intrinsically good but argues that other things are also good in themselves. In this selection he identifies four intrinsic goods and shows how they make up other complex values.*

What Things Are Good?

Our next step is to inquire what kinds of thing are intrinsically good. (1) The first thing for which I would claim that it is intrinsically good is virtuous disposition and action, i.e., action, or disposition to act, from any one of certain motives, of which at all events the most notable are the desire to do one's duty, the desire to bring into being something that is good, and the desire to give pleasure or save pain to others. It seems clear that we regard all such actions and dispositions as having value in themselves apart from any consequence. And if anyone is inclined to doubt this and to think that, say, pleasure alone is intrinsically good, it seems to me enough to ask the question whether, of two states of the universe holding equal amounts of pleasure, we should really think no better of one in which the actions and dispositions of all the persons in it were thoroughly virtuous than of one in which they were highly vicious. To this there can be only one answer. Most hedonists would shrink from giving the plainly false answer which their theory re-

Reprinted from W. D. Ross, *The Right and the Good,* first published by The Clarendon Press, Oxford, 1930, by permission of Hackett Publishing Company.

quires, and would take refuge in saying that the question rests on a false abstraction. Since virtue, as they conceive it, is a disposition to do just the acts which will produce most pleasure, a universe full of virtuous persons would be bound, they might say, to contain more pleasure than a universe full of vicious persons. To this two answers may be made. (*a*) Much pleasure, and much pain, do not spring from virtuous or vicious actions at all but from the operation of natural laws. Thus even if a universe filled with virtuous persons were bound to contain more of the pleasure and less of the pain that springs from human action than a universe filled with vicious persons would, that inequality of pleasantness might easily be supposed to be precisely counteracted by, for instance, a much greater incidence of disease. The two states of affairs would then, on balance, be equally pleasant; would they be equally good? And (*b*) even if we could not imagine any circumstances in which two states of the universe equal in pleasantness but unequal in virtue could exist, the supposition is a legitimate one, since it is only intended to bring before us in a vivid way what is really self-evident, that virtue is good apart from its consequences.

(2) It seems at first sight equally clear that pleasure is good in itself. Some will perhaps be helped to realize this if they make the corresponding supposition to that we have just made; if they suppose two states of the universe including equal amounts of virtue but the one including also widespread and intense pleasure and the other widespread and intense pain. Here too it might be objected that the supposition is an impossible one, since virtue always tends to promote general pleasure, and vice to promote general misery. But this objection may be answered just as we have answered the corresponding objection above.

Apart from this, however, there are two ways in which even the most austere moralists and the most antihedonistic philosophers are apt to betray the conviction that pleasure is good in itself. (*a*) One is the attitude which they, like all other normal human beings, take towards kindness and towards cruelty. If the desire to give pleasure to others is approved, and the desire to inflict pain on others condemned, this seems to imply the conviction that pleasure is good and pain bad. Some may think, no doubt, that the mere thought that a certain state of affairs would be *painful* for another person is enough to account for our conviction that the desire to produce it is bad. But I am inclined to think that there is involved the further thought that a state of affairs in virtue of being painful is *prima facie* (i.e., where other considerations do not enter into the case) one that a rational spectator would not approve, i.e., is *bad*; and that similarly our attitude towards kindness involves the thought that pleasure is good. (*b*) The other is the insistence, which we find in the most austere moralists as in other people, on the conception of merit. If virtue deserves to be rewarded by happiness (whether or not vice also deserves to be rewarded by unhappiness), this seems at first sight to imply that happiness and unhappiness are not in themselves things indifferent, but are good and bad respectively.

Kant's view on this question is not as clear as might be wished. He points out that the Latin *bonum* covers two notions, distinguished in German as *das Gute* (the good) and *das Wohl* (well-being, i.e., pleasure or happiness); and he speaks of 'good' as being properly applied only to actions,[1] i.e., he treats 'good' as equivalent to 'morally good,' and by implication denies that pleasure (even deserved pleasure) is good. It might seem then that when he speaks of the union of virtue with the happiness it deserves as the *bonum consummatum* he is not thinking of deserved happiness as good but only as *das Wohl*, a source of satisfaction to the person who has it. But if this exhausted his meaning, he would have no right to speak of virtue, as he repeatedly does, as *das oberste*

Gut; he should call it simply *das Gute*, and happiness, *das Wohl.* Further, he describes the union of virtue with happiness not merely as 'the object of the desires of rational finite beings,' but adds that it approves itself 'even in the judgment of an impartial reason' as 'the whole and perfect good,' rather than virtue alone. And he adds that 'happiness, while it is pleasant to the possessor of it, is not of itself absolutely and in all respects good, but always presupposes morally right behavior as its condition'; which implies that *when* that condition is fulfilled, happiness *is* good.[2] All this seems to point to the conclusion that in the end he had to recognize that while virtue alone is morally good, deserved happiness also is not merely a source of satisfaction to its possessor, but objectively good.

But reflection on the conception of merit does not support the view that pleasure is always good in itself and pain always bad in itself. For while this conception implies the conviction that pleasure when deserved is good, and pain when undeserved bad, it also suggests strongly that pleasure when undeserved is bad and pain when deserved good.

There is also another set of facts which casts doubt on the view that pleasure is always good and pain always bad. We have a decided conviction that there are bad pleasures and (though this is less obvious) that there are good pains. We think that the pleasure taken either by the agent or by a spectator in, for instance, a lustful or cruel action is bad; and we think it a good thing that people should be pained rather than pleased by contemplating vice or misery.

Thus the view that pleasure is always good and pain always bad, while it seems to be strongly supported by some of our convictions, seems to be equally strongly opposed by others. The difficulty can, I think, be removed by ceasing to speak simply of pleasure and pain as good or bad, and by asking more carefully what it is that we mean. Consideration of the question is aided if we adopt the view (tentatively adopted already)[3] that what is good or bad is always something properly expressed by a that-clause, i.e., an objective, or as I should prefer to call it, a *fact*. If we look at the matter thus, I think we can agree that the fact that a sentient being is in a state of pleasure is always in itself good, and the fact that a sentient being is in a state of pain always in itself bad, when this fact is not an element in a more complex fact having some other characteristic relevant to goodness or badness. And where considerations of desert or of moral good or evil do not -enter, i.e., in the case of animals, the fact that a sentient being is feeling pleasure or pain is the whole fact (or the fact sufficiently described to enable us to judge of its goodness or badness), and we need not hesitate to say that the pleasure of animals is always good, and the pain of animals always bad, in itself and apart from its consequences. But when a moral being is feeling a pleasure or pain that is deserved or undeserved, or a pleasure or pain that implies a good or a bad disposition, the total fact is quite inadequately described if we say 'a sentient being is feeling pleasure, or pain.' The total fact may be that 'a sentient and moral being is feeling a pleasure that is undeserved, or that is the realization of a vicious disposition,' and though the fact included in this, that 'a sentient being is feeling pleasure' would be good if it stood alone, that creates only a presumption that the total fact is good, and a presumption that is outweighed by the other element in the total fact.

Pleasure seems, indeed, to have a property analogous to that which we have previously recognized under the name of conditional or *prima facie* rightness. An act of promise-keeping has the property, not necessarily of being right but of being something that is right if the act has no other morally significant characteristic (such as that of causing much pain to another person). And similarly a state of pleasure has the property, not necessarily of being good, but of being something that is good if the state has no other characteristic that prevents it from being good. The two characteristics that may interfere with its being good are (*a*) that of being contrary to desert, and (*b*) that of being a state which is the realization of a bad disposition. Thus the pleasures of which we can say without doubt that they are good are (i) the pleasures of nonmoral beings (animals), (ii) the pleasures of moral beings that are deserved and are either realizations of good moral dispositions or realizations of neutral capacities (such as the pleasures of the senses).

Insofar as the goodness or badness of a particular pleasure depends on its being the realization of a virtuous or vicious disposition, this has been allowed for by our recognition of virtue as a thing good in itself. But the mere recognition of virtue as a thing good in itself, and of pleasure as a thing *prima facie* good in itself, does not do justice to the conception of merit. If we compare two imaginary states of the universe, alike in the total amounts of virtue and vice and of pleasure and pain present in the two, but in one of which the virtuous were all happy and the vicious miserable, while in the other the virtuous were miserable and the vicious happy, very few people would hesitate to say that the first was a much better state of the universe than the second. It would seem then that, besides virtue and pleasure, we must recognize (3), as a third independent good, the apportionment of pleasure and pain to the virtuous and the vicious respectively. And it is on the recognition of this as a separate good that the recognition of the duty of justice, in distinction from fidelity to promises on the one hand and from beneficence on the other, rests.

(4) It seems clear that knowledge, and in a less degree what we may for the present call 'right opinion,' are states of mind good in themselves. Here too we may, if we please, help ourselves to realize the fact by supposing two states of the universe equal in respect of virtue and of pleasure and of the allocation of pleasure to the virtuous, but such that the persons in the one had a far greater understanding of the nature and laws of the universe than those in the other. Can anyone doubt that the first would be a better state of the universe?

From one point of view it seems doubtful

whether knowledge and right opinion, no matter what it is of or about, should be considered good. Knowledge of mere matters of fact (say, of the number of stories in a building), without knowledge of their relation to other facts, might seem to be worthless; it certainly seems to be worth much less than the knowledge of general principles, or of facts as depending on general principles—what we might call insight or understanding as opposed to mere knowledge. But on reflection it seems clear that even about matters of fact right opinion is in itself a better state of mind to be in than wrong, and knowledge than right opinion.

There is another objection which may naturally be made to the view that knowledge is as such good. There are many pieces of knowledge which we in fact think it well for people *not* to have; e.g., we may think it a bad thing for a sick man to know how ill he is, or for a vicious man to know how he may most conveniently indulge his vicious tendencies. But its seems that in such cases it is not the knowledge but the consequences in the way of pain or of vicious action that we think bad.

It might perhaps be objected that knowledge is not a better state than right opinion, but merely a source of greater satisfaction to its possessor. It no doubt is a source of greater satisfaction. Curiosity is the desire to *know*, and is never really satisfied by mere opinion. Yet there are two facts which seem to show that this is not the whole truth. (*a*) While opinion recognized to be such is never thoroughly satisfactory to its possessor, there is another state of mind which is not knowledge—which may even be mistaken—yet which through lack of reflection is not distinguished from knowledge by its possessor, the state of mind which Professor Cook Wilson has called 'that of being under the impression that so-and-so is the case.'[4] Such a state of mind may be as great a source of satisfaction to its possessor as knowledge, yet we should all think it to be an inferior state of mind to knowledge. This surely points to a recognition by us that knowledge has a worth other than that of being a source of satisfaction

to its possessor. (*b*) Wrong opinion, so long as its wrongness is not discovered, may be as great a source of satisfaction as right. Yet we should agree that it is an inferior state of mind, because it is to a less extent founded on knowledge and is itself a less close approximation to knowledge; which again seems to point to our recognizing knowledge as something good in itself.

Four things, then, seem to be intrinsically good—virtue, pleasure, the allocation of pleasure to the virtuous, and knowledge (and in a less degree right opinion). And I am unable to discover anything that is intrinsically good, which is not either one of these or a combination of two or more of them. And while this list of goods has been arrived at on its own merits, by reflection on what we really think to be good, it perhaps derives some support from the fact that it harmonizes with a widely accepted classification of the elements in the life of the soul. It is usual to enumerate these as cognition, feeling, and conation. Now knowledge is the ideal state of the mind, and right opinion an approximation to the ideal, on the cognitive or intellectual side; pleasure is its ideal state on the side of feeling; and virtue is its ideal state on the side of conation; while the allocation of happiness to virtue is a good which we recognize when we reflect on the ideal relation between the conative side and the side of feeling. It might of course be objected that there are or may be intrinsic goods that are not states of mind or relations between states of mind at all, but in this suggestion I can find no plausibility. Contemplate any imaginary universe from which you suppose mind entirely absent, and you will fail to find anything in it that you can call good in itself. That is not to say, of course, that the existence of a material universe may not be a necessary condition for the existence of many things that are good in themselves. Our knowledge and our true opinions are to a large extent about the material world, and to that extent could not exist unless it existed. Our pleasures are to a large extent derived from material objects. Virtue owes many of its opportunities to the existence of material conditions of good and material hindrances to good. But the value of material things appears to be purely instrumental, not intrinsic.

Of the three elements virtue, knowledge, and pleasure are compounded all the complex states of mind that we think good in themselves. Aesthetic enjoyment, for example, seems to be a blend of pleasure with insight into the nature of the object that inspires it. Mutual love seems to be a blend of virtuous disposition of two minds towards each other, with the knowledge which each has of the character and disposition of the other, and with the pleasure which arises from such disposition and knowledge. And a similar analysis may probably be applied to all other complex goods.

Notes

1. *Kritik der pr. Vernunft,* pp. 59–60 (Akad. Ausgabe, vol. v), pp. 150–51 (Abbott's Trans., ed. 6).

2. Ibid., pp. 110–11 (Akad. Ausgabe), 206–7 (Abbott).

3. Ibid., pp. 111–13.

4. *Statement and Inference,* 1: 113.

What Makes Someone's Life Go Best?

DEREK PARFIT

Derek Parfit (1942–   ) is a Research Fellow at All Souls College, Oxford. He is the author of numerous articles on personal identity, population problems, and ethical theory. His book Reasons and Persons, *from which this selection is taken, has been hailed as one of the most original and important works in contemporary moral philosophy. In it he develops his views on personal identity and their consequences for ethical theory.*

In this essay Parfit compares three theories of the good life: hedonism, desire-fulfillment, *and* objective list. *Hedonism, such as Bentham's and Mill's theories, is centered in the idea that pleasure or happiness is what makes life go best. Desire-fulfillment theories hold that the good life is centered in actual or possible desires being satisfied. Objective list theories hold that certain good things are necessary for the good life: knowledge, rational activity, mutual love, and awareness of beauty. Parfit examines several versions of these theories and concludes by suggesting that the good life consists in a combination of a type of hedonism and the good things identified in the objective list theories.*

What would be best for someone, or would be most in this person's interests, or would make this person's life go, for him, as well as possible? Answers to this question I call *theories about self-interest.* There are three kinds of theory. On *Hedonistic Theories,* what would be best for someone is what would make his life happiest. On *Desire-Fulfillment Theories,* what would be best for someone is what, throughout his life, would best fulfill his desires. On *Objective List Theories,* certain things are good or bad for us, whether or not we want to have the good things, or to avoid the bad things.

Narrow Hedonists assume, falsely, that pleasure and pain are two distinctive kinds of experience. Compare the pleasures of satisfying an intense thirst or lust, listening to music, solving an intellectual problem, reading a tragedy, and knowing that one's child is happy. These various experiences do not contain any distinctive common quality.

What pains and pleasures have in common are their relations to our desires. On the use of 'pain' which has rational and moral significance, all pains are when experienced unwanted, and a pain is worse or greater the more it is unwanted. Similarly, all pleasures are when experienced wanted, and they are better or greater the more they are wanted. These are the claims of *Preference-Hedonism.* On this view, one of two experiences is more pleasant if it is preferred.

This theory need not follow the ordinary uses of the words 'pain' and 'pleasure.' Suppose that I could go to a party to enjoy the various pleasures of eating, drinking, laughing, dancing, and talking to my friends. I could instead stay at home and read *King Lear.* Knowing what both alternatives would be like, I prefer to read *King Lear.* It extends the ordinary use to say that this would give me more pleasure. But on Preference-Hedonism, if we add some further assumptions given below, reading *King Lear* would give me a better evening. Griffin cites a more extreme case. Near the end of his life Freud refused pain-killing drugs, preferring to think in torment than to be confusedly euphoric. Of these two mental states, euphoria is more pleasant. But on Preference-Hedonism, thinking in torment was, for Freud, a better mental state. It is clearer here not to stretch the meaning of the word 'pleasant.' A Preference-Hedonist should merely claim that, since Freud preferred to think clearly though in torment, his life went better if it went as he preferred.

Consider next Desire-Fulfillment Theories. The simplest is the *Unrestricted Theory*. This claims that what is best for someone is what would best fulfill *all* of his desires, throughout his life. Suppose that I meet a stranger who has what is believed to be a fatal disease. My sympathy is aroused, and I strongly want this stranger to be cured. Much later, when I have forgotten our meeting, the stranger is cured. On the Unrestricted Desire-Fulfillment Theory, this event is good for me, and makes my life go better. This is not plausible. We should reject this theory.

Another theory appeals only to someone's desires about his own life. I call this the *Success Theory*. This theory differs from Preference-Hedonism in only one way. The Success Theory appeals to all of our preferences about our own lives. A Preference-Hedonist appeals only to preferences about those present features of our lives that are introspectively discernible. Suppose that I strongly want not to be deceived by other people. On Preference-Hedonism it would be better for me if I believe that I am not being deceived. It would be irrelevant if my belief is false, since this makes no difference to my state of mind. On the Success Theory, it would be worse for me if my belief is false. I have a strong desire about my own life—that I should not be deceived in this way. It is bad for me if this desire is not fulfilled, even if I falsely believe that it is.

When this theory appeals only to desires that are about our own lives, it may be unclear what this excludes. Suppose that I want my life to be such that all of my desires, whatever their objects, are fulfilled. This may seem to make the Success Theory, when applied to me, coincide with the Unrestricted Desire-Fulfillment Theory. But a Success Theorist should claim that this desire is not really about my own life. This is like the distinction between a real change in some object, and a so-called *Cambridge-change*. An object undergoes a Cambridge-change if there is any change in the true statements that can be made

about this object. Suppose that I cut my cheek while shaving. This causes a real change in me. It also causes a change in Confucius. It becomes true, of Confucius, that he lived on a planet in which later one more cheek was cut. This is merely a Cambridge-change.

Suppose that I am an exile, and cannot communicate with my children. I want their lives to go well. I might claim that I want to live the life of someone whose children's lives go well. A Success Theorist should again claim that this is not really a desire about my own life. If unknown to me one of my children is killed by an avalanche, this is not bad for me, and does not make my life go worse.

A Success Theorist *would* count some similar desires. Suppose that I try to give my children a good start in life. I try to give them the right education, good habits, and psychological strength. Once again, I am now an exile, and will never be able to learn what happens to my children. Suppose that, unknown to me, my children's lives go badly. One finds that the education that I gave him makes him unemployable, another has a mental breakdown, another becomes a petty thief. If my children's lives fail in these ways, and these failures are in part the result of mistakes I made as their parent, these failures in my children's lives would be judged to be bad for me on the Success Theory. One of my strongest desires was to be a successful parent. What is now happening to my children, though it is unknown to me, shows that this desire is not fulfilled. My life failed in one of the ways in which I most wanted it to succeed. Though I do not know this fact, it is bad for me, and makes it true that I have had a worse life. This is like the case where I strongly want not to be deceived. Even if I never know, it is bad for me both if I am deceived and if I turn out to be an unsuccessful parent. These are not introspectively discernible differences in my conscious life. On Preference-Hedonism, these events are not bad for me. On the Success Theory, they are.

Because they are thought by some to need special treatment, I mention next the desires that people have about what happens after they are dead. For a Preference-Hedonist, once I am dead, nothing bad can happen to me. A Success Theorist should deny this. Return to the case where all my children have wretched lives because of the mistakes I made as their parent. Suppose that my children's lives all go badly only after I am dead. My life turns out to have been a failure, in the one of the ways I cared about most. A Success Theorist should claim that, here too, this makes it true that I had a worse life.

Some Success Theorists would reject this claim. Their theory ignores the desires of the dead. I believe this theory to be indefensible. Suppose that I was asked, 'Do you want it to be true that you were a successful parent even after you are dead?' I would answer 'Yes.' It is irrelevant to my desire whether it is fulfilled before or after I am dead. These Success Theorists count it as bad for me if my desire is not fulfilled, even if, because I am an exile, I never know this. How then can it matter whether, when my desire is not fulfilled, I am dead? All that my death does is to *ensure* that I will never know this. If we think it irrelevant that I never know about the nonfulfillment of my desire, we cannot defensibly claim that my death makes a difference.

I turn now to questions and objections which arise for both Preference-Hedonism and the Success Theory.

Should we appeal only to the desires and preferences that someone actually has? Return to my choice between going to a party or staying at home to read *King Lear*. Suppose that, knowing what both alternatives would be like, I choose to stay at home. And suppose that I never later regret this choice. On one theory, this shows that staying at home to read *King Lear* gave me a better evening. This is a mistake. It might be true that, if I had chosen to go to the party, I would never have regretted that choice. According to this theory, this would have shown that going to the party gave me a better evening. This theory thus implies that each alternative would have been better than the other. Since this theory implies such contradictions, it must be revised. The

obvious revision is to appeal not only to my actual preferences, in the alternative I choose, but also to the preferences that I would have had if I had chosen otherwise.

In this example, whichever alternative I choose, I would never regret this choice. If this is true, can we still claim that one of the alternatives would give me a better evening? On some theories, when in two alternatives I would have such contrary preferences, neither alternative is better or worse for me. This is not plausible when one of my contrary preferences would have been much stronger. Suppose that, if I choose to go to the party, I shall be only mildly glad that I made this choice, but that, if I choose to stay and read *King Lear*, I shall be extremely glad. If this is true, reading *King Lear* gives me a better evening.

Whether we appeal to Preference-Hedonism or the Success Theory, we should not appeal only to the desires or preferences that I actually have. We should also appeal to the desires and preferences that I would have had, in the various alternatives that were, at different times, open to me. One of these alternatives would be best for me if it is the one in which I would have the strongest desires and preferences fulfilled. This allows us to claim that some alternative life would have been better for me, even if throughout my actual life I am glad that I chose this life rather than this alternative.

There is another distinction which applies both to Preference-Hedonism and to the Success Theory. These theories are *Summative* if they appeal to all of someone's desires, actual and hypothetical, about his own life. In deciding which alternative would produce the greatest total net sum of desire-fulfillment, we assign some positive number to each desire that is fulfilled, and some negative number to each desire that is not fulfilled. How great these numbers are depends on the intensity of the desires in question. (In the case of the Success Theory, which appeals to past desires, it may also depend on how long these desires were had. [. . .] this may be a weakness in this theory. The issue does not arise for Preference-Hedonism, which appeals only to desires about one's present state of mind.) The total net sum of desire-fulfillment is the sum of the positive numbers minus the negative numbers. Provided that we can compare the relative strength of different desires, this calculation could in theory be performed. The choice of a unit for the numbers makes no difference to the result.

Another version of both theories does not appeal, in this way, to all of a person's desires and preferences about his own life. It appeals only to *global* rather than *local* desires and preferences. A preference is global if it is about some part of one's life considered as a whole, or is about one's whole life. The *Global* versions of these theories I believe to be more plausible.

Consider this example. Knowing that you accept a Summative theory, I tell you that I am about to make your life go better. I shall inject you with an addictive drug. From now on, you will wake each morning with an extremely strong desire to have another injection of this drug. Having this desire will be in itself neither pleasant nor painful, but if the desire is not fulfilled within an hour it would then become extremely painful. This is no cause for concern, since I shall give you ample supplies of this drug. Every morning, you will be able at once to fulfill this desire. The injection, and its after-effects, would also be neither pleasant nor painful. You will spend the rest of your days as you do now.

What would the Summative theories imply about this case? We can plausibly suppose that you would not welcome my proposal. You would prefer not to become addicted to this drug, even though I assure you that you will never lack supplies. We can also plausibly suppose that, if I go ahead, you will always regret that you became addicted to this drug. But it is likely that your initial desire not to become addicted, and your later regrets that you did, would not be as strong as the desires you have each morning for another injection. Given the facts as I described them, your reason to prefer not to become addicted would

not be very strong. You might dislike the thought of being addicted to anything. And you would regret the minor inconvenience that would be involved in remembering always to carry with you, like a diabetic, sufficient supplies. But these desires might be far weaker than the desires you would have each morning for a fresh injection.

On the Summative Theories, if I make you an addict, I would be increasing the sum-total of your desire-fulfillment. I would be causing one of your desires not to be fulfilled: your desire not to become an addict, which, after my act, becomes a desire to be cured. But I would also be giving you an indefinite series of extremely strong desires, one each morning, all of which you can fulfill. The fulfillment of all these desires would outweigh the nonfulfillment of your desires not to become an addict, and to be cured. On the Summative Theories, by making you an addict, I would be benefiting you—making your life go better.

This conclusion is not plausible. Having these desires, and having them fulfilled, are neither pleasant nor painful. We need not be Hedonists to believe, more plausibly, that it is in no way better for you to have and to fulfill this series of strong desires.

Could the Summative Theories be revised, so as to meet this objection? Is there some feature of the addictive desires which would justify the claim that we should ignore them when we calculate the sum total of your desire-fulfillment? We might claim that they can be ignored because they are desires that you would prefer not to have. But this is not an acceptable revision. Suppose that you are in great pain. You now have a very strong desire not to be in the state that you are in. On our revised theory, a desire does not count if you would prefer not to have this desire. This must apply to your intense desire not to be in the state you are in. You would prefer not to have this desire. If you did not dislike the state you are in, it would not be painful. Since our revised theory does not count desires that you would prefer not to have, it implies, absurdly, that it cannot be bad for you to be in great pain.

There may be other revisions which could meet these objections. But it is simpler to appeal to the Global versions of both Preference-Hedonism and the Success Theory. These appeal only to someone's desires about some part of his life, considered as a whole, or about his whole life. The Global Theories give us the right answer in the case where I make you an addict. You would prefer not to become addicted, and you would later prefer to cease to be addicted. These are the only preferences to which the Global Theories appeal. They ignore your particular desires each morning for a fresh injection. This is because you have yourself taken these desires into account in forming your Global preference.

This imagined case of addiction is in its essentials similar to countless other cases. There are countless cases in which it is true both (1) that, if someone's life goes in one of two ways, this would increase the sum total of his local desire-fulfillment, but (2) that the other alternative is what he would globally prefer, *whichever* way his actual life goes.

Rather than describing another of the countless actual cases, I shall mention an imaginary case. . . . Suppose that I could have either fifty of years of life of an extremely high quality, or an indefinite number of years that are barely worth living. In the first alternative, my fifty years would, on any theory, go extremely well. I would be very happy, would achieve great things, do much good, and love and be loved by many people. In the second alternative my life would always be, though not by much, worth living. There would be nothing bad about this life, and it would each day contain a few small pleasures.

On the Summative Theories, if the second life was long enough, it would be better for me. In each day within this life I have some desires about my life that are fulfilled. In the fifty years of the first alternative, there would be a very great sum of local desire-fulfillment. But this would be a fi-

nite sum, and in the end it would be outweighed by the sum of desire-fulfillment in my indefinitely long second alternative. A simpler way to put this point is this. The first alternative would be good. In the second alternative, since my life is worth living, living each extra day is good for me. If we merely add together whatever is good for me, some number of these extra days would produce the greatest total sum.

I do not believe that the second alternative would give me a better life. I therefore reject the Summative Theories. It is likely that, in both alternatives, I would globally prefer the first. Since the Global Theories would then imply that the first alternative gives me a better life, these theories seem to me more plausible.

Turn now to the third kind of Theory that I mentioned: the *Objective List Theory*. According to this theory, certain things are good or bad for people, whether or not these people would want to have the good things, or to avoid the bad things. The good things might include moral goodness, rational activity, the development of one's abilities, having children and being a good parent, knowledge, and the awareness of true beauty. The bad things might include being betrayed, manipulated, slandered, deceived, being deprived of liberty or dignity, and enjoying either sadistic pleasure, or aesthetic pleasure in what is in fact ugly.

An Objective List Theorist might claim that his theory coincides with the Global version of the Success Theory. On this theory, what would make my life go best depends on what I would prefer, now and in the various alternatives, if I knew all of the relevant facts about these alternatives. An Objective List Theorist might say that the most relevant facts are what his theory claims—what would in fact be good or bad for me. And he might claim that anyone who knew these facts would want what is truly good for him, and want to avoid what would be bad for him.

If this was true, though the Objective List

Theory would coincide with the Success Theory, the two theories would remain distinct. A Success Theorist would reject this description of the coincidence. On his theory, nothing is good or bad for people, whatever their preferences are. Something is bad for someone only if, knowing the facts, he wants to avoid it. And the relevant facts do not include the alleged facts cited by the Objective List Theorist. On the Success Theory it is, for instance, bad for someone to be deceived if and because this is not what he wants. The Objective List Theorist makes the reverse claim. People want not to be deceived because this is bad for them.

As these remarks imply, there is one important difference between on the one hand Preference-Hedonism and the Success Theory, and on the other hand the Objective List Theory. The first two kinds of theory give an account of self-interest which is entirely factual, or which does not appeal to facts about value. The account appeals to what a person does and would prefer, given full knowledge of the purely nonevaluative facts about the alternatives. In contrast, the Objective List Theory appeals directly to facts about value.

In choosing between these theories, we must decide how much weight to give to imagined cases in which someone's fully informed preferences would be bizarre. If we can appeal to these cases, they cast doubt on both Preference-Hedonism and the Success Theory. Consider the man that Rawls imagined who wants to spend his life counting the numbers of blades of grass in different lawns. Suppose that this man knows that he could achieve great progress if instead he worked in some especially useful part of Applied Mathematics. Though he could achieve such significant results, he prefers to go on counting blades of grass. On the Success Theory, if we allow this theory to cover all imaginable cases, it could be better for this person if he counts his blades of grass rather than achieves great and beneficial results in Mathematics.

The counterexample might be more offensive.

Suppose that what someone would most prefer, knowing the alternatives, is a life in which, without being detected, he causes as much pain as he can to other people. On the Success Theory, such a life would be what is best for this person.

We may be unable to accept these conclusions. Ought we therefore to abandon this theory? This is what Sidgwick did, though those who quote him seldom notice this. He suggests that 'a man's future good on the whole is what he would now desire and seek on the whole if all the consequences of all the different lines of conduct open to him were accurately foreseen and adequately realised in imagination at the present point of time.' As he comments: 'The notion of "Good" thus attained has an ideal element: it is something that *is* not always actually desired and aimed at by human beings: but the ideal element is entirely interpretable in terms of *fact,* actual or hypothetical, and does not introduce any judgment of value.' Sidgwick then rejects this account, claiming that what is ultimately good for someone is what this person *would* desire if his desires were in harmony with reason. This last phrase is needed, Sidgwick thought, to exclude the cases where someone's desires are irrational. He assumes that there are some things that we have good reason to desire, and others that we have good reason not to desire. These might be the things which are held to be good or bad for us by Objective List Theories.

Suppose we agree that, in some imagined cases, what someone would most want both now and later, fully knowing about the alternatives, would *not* be what would be best for him. If we accept this conclusion, it may seem that we must reject both Preference-Hedonism and the Success Theory. Perhaps, like Sidgwick, we must put constraints on what can be rationally desired.

It might be claimed instead that we can dismiss the appeal to such imagined cases. It might be claimed that what people would in fact prefer, if they knew the relevant facts, would always be something that we could accept as what is really good for them. Is this a good reply? If we agree that in the imagined cases what someone would prefer might be something that is bad for him, in these cases we have abandoned our theory. If this is so, can we defend our theory by saying that, in the actual cases, it would not go astray? I believe that this is not an adequate defence. But I shall not pursue this question here.

This objection may apply with less force to Preference-Hedonism. On this theory, what can be good or bad for someone can only be discernible features of his conscious life. These are the features that, at the time, he either wants or does not want. I asked above whether it is bad for people to be deceived because they prefer not to be, or whether they prefer not to be deceived because this is bad for them. Consider the comparable question with respect to pain. Some have claimed that pain is intrinsically bad and that this is why we dislike it. As I have suggested, I doubt this claim. After taking certain kinds of drug, people claim that the quality of their sensations has not altered, but they no longer dislike these sensations. We would regard such drugs as effective analgesics. This suggests that the badness of a pain consists in its being disliked, and that it is not disliked because it is bad. The disagreement between these views would need much more discussion. But, if the second view is better, it is more plausible to claim that whatever someone wants or does not want to experience—however bizarre we find his desires—should be counted as being for this person truly pleasant or painful, and as being for that reason good or bad for him. There may still be cases where it is plausible to claim that it would be bad for someone if he enjoys certain kinds of pleasure. This might be claimed, for instance, about sadistic pleasure. But there may be few such cases.

If instead we appeal to the Success Theory, we are not concerned only with the experienced quality of our conscious life. We are concerned with such things as whether we are achieving what we are trying to achieve, whether we are be-

ing deceived, and the like. When considering this theory, we can more often plausibly claim that, even if someone knew the facts, his preferences might go astray, and fail to correspond to what would be good or bad for him.

Which of these different theories should we accept? I shall not attempt an answer here. But I shall end by mentioning another theory, which might be claimed to combine what is most plausible in these conflicting theories. It is a striking fact that those who have addressed this question have disagreed so fundamentally. Many philosophers have been convinced Hedonists; many others have been as much convinced that Hedonism is a gross mistake.

Some Hedonists have reached their view as follows. They consider an opposing view, such as that which claims that what is good for someone is to have knowledge, to engage in rational activity, and to be aware of true beauty. These Hedonists ask, 'Would these states of mind be good, if they brought no enjoyment, and if the person in these states of mind had not the slightest desire that they continue?' Since they answer No, they conclude that the value of these states of mind must lie in their being liked, and in their arousing a desire that they continue.

This reasoning assumes that the value of a whole is just the sum of the value of its parts. If we remove the part to which the Hedonist appeals, what is left seems to have no value, hence Hedonism is the truth.

Suppose instead that we claim that the value of a whole may not be a mere sum of the value of its parts. We might then claim that what is best for people is a composite. It is not just their being in the conscious states that they want to be in. Nor is it just their having knowledge, engaging in rational activity, being aware of true beauty, and the like. What is good for someone is neither just what Hedonists claim, nor just what is claimed by Objective List Theorists. We might believe that if we had *either* of these, *without the other*, what we had would have little or no value. We might claim, for example, that what is good or bad for someone is to have knowledge, to be engaged in rational activity, to experience mutual love, and to be aware of beauty, while strongly wanting just these things. On this view, each side in this disagreement saw only half of the truth. Each put forward as sufficient something that was only necessary.

Pleasure with many other kinds of object has no value. And, if they are entirely devoid of pleasure, there is no value in knowledge, rational activity, love, or the awareness of beauty. What is of value, or is good for someone, is to have both; to be engaged in these activities, and to be strongly wanting to be so engaged.

PART V

Utilitarian Ethics

Introduction

Three common ways of evaluating actions are: (1) according to their consequences, (2) according to their internal features, and (3) according to the character traits they exhibit or reflect. These ways correspond to the three broad kinds of ethical systems that we examine in Parts V, VI, and VII.

Utilitarian ethical systems focus on the first way. They are consequentialist: that is, they imply that the moral status of actions depends *only* on their consequences. More generally they are teleological: that is, they imply that the moral status of actions depends on their relationship to the accomplishment of some end, or goal, rather than some feature of the actions themselves. Systems of virtue ethics, which focus on the third way of evaluating actions, are also teleological: however, they are not consequentialist. We examine systems of virtue ethics in Part VII. Deontological ethical systems, which focus on the second way of evaluating actions, are neither consequentialist nor teleological. We examine deontological ethical systems in Part VI.

Suppose that two men, a father and his son, have for long been stranded on a desert island. On this island is a small mountain. Sadly, the father is now dying on the island coast, at the base of the mountain. He has very little time left. "Son," he says, "I have a final favor to ask."

"Anything, Dad," says the son.

"I love the beautiful view and cool breeze of the mountain top. Promise that when I die, you will bury me up there."

"Of course, Dad," says the son.

Very soon the father passes away. Once the son is convinced that his father has died, the son pushes his father's body off of a nearby cliff into the ocean, to be devoured by sharks, and goes on about his business. After all, the son reasons, it would have been a chore to drag Dad's body all the way up that mountain. Of course I promised. But whatever solace Dad got from that promise is the end of any good it could do. Keeping the promise can do no further good. The dead cannot enjoy beautiful views or cool breezes; nor can they resent being lied to or devoured by sharks.[1]

The son in this example is apparently a committed consequentialist. He does not worry that his action is dishonest, and thus inherently wrong, as a deontologist might, or that his action exhibits viciousness of character, as a virtue ethicist might. Confronted with deontologists and virtue theorists, he might defend himself with an intuitive principle that is at the heart of much consequentialist thought: *it is irrational to prefer a worse over a better outcome*.

There are two main features of classical utilitarianism: (1) the consequentialist principle (its teleological aspect), and (2) the utility principle (its hedonic aspect). The consequentialist principle states that the rightness or wrongness of an act is determined by the results that flow from it. The utility principle states that the only thing that is good in itself is some specific type of state (e.g., pleasure, happiness, welfare, fulfillment). Hedonistic utilitarianism views pleasure as the sole good and pain as the only evil. To quote the English philosopher Jeremy

Bentham (reading IV.13), the first one to systematize classical utilitarianism: "Nature has placed mankind under the governance of two sovereign masters, pain and pleasure. It is for them alone to point out what we ought to do, as well as what we shall do."

Bentham's philosophy has often been criticized for being too simplistic. Pleasure seems either too sensuous or too ambiguous a notion. In fact, Bentham's version was in his own day referred to as the "Pig-philosophy," since a pig enjoying his life would constitute a higher moral state than a slightly dissatisfied human being. For this reason John Stuart Mill, in our first reading, sought to distinguish happiness from mere sensual pleasure "A being of higher faculties requires more to make him happy, is capable probably of more acute suffering, and certainly accessible to it at more points, than one of an inferior type," but still he is qualitatively better off than the person without these higher faculties. "It is better to be a human being dissatisfied than a pig satisfied; better to be Socrates dissatisfied than a fool satisfied." Mill's version of utilitarianism has been called 'eudaimonistic utilitarianism' (*eudaimonia* is the Greek for "happiness") in order to distinguish it from Bentham's hedonistic utilitarianism.

Utilitarians can be divided into two types: '*act*' and '*rule*.' In applying the principle of utility, act-utilitarians say that we ought ideally apply the principle to all of the alternatives open to us at any given moment. Of course, we cannot do this for each possible act, for often we must act spontaneously and quickly. So rules of thumb (e.g., in general, do not lie, keep your promises) are of practical importance. However, the right act is still that alternative which will result in the most utility.

Rule-utilitarians, by contrast, state that an act is right if it conforms to a valid rule within a system of rules that, if followed, will result in the best possible state of affairs (or least bad state of affairs, if it is a question of all the alternatives being bad). The rule-utilitarian resembles the rule-deontologist (a deontologist who holds that we ought always act according to principle rather than according to our intuition at the moment, a position to be discussed in Part VI) in that both emphasize the importance of following specific principles that are public and universal. The difference is that the deontologist sees the principles as having intrinsic value, whereas the utilitarian sees the principles as having only instrumental value. Nonetheless, it is arguable that they could have identical principles for different reasons. John Hospers defends rule-utilitarianism in our second reading.

In our third reading, "A Critique of Utilitarianism," Bernard Williams argues that utilitarianism violates personal integrity by commanding that we violate those principles that are central and deepest in our lives. "How can a man, as a utilitarian agent, come to regard as one satisfaction among others, and a dispensable one, a project or attitude round which he has built his life, just because someone else's projects have so structured the causal scene that that is how the utilitarian scheme comes out?" His conclusion is that utilitarianism leads to personal alienation and so is deeply flawed.

Our fourth reading, by Sterling Harwood, discusses eleven criticisms of utilitarianism.

In our final reading, Brad Hooker proposes and defends a rule-consequentialism according to which we should act according to the moral code that it would be best for everyone to internalize. Internalization itself has and breeds consequences that tend to bring consequentialism closer to deontological and virtue theories.

Note

1. My source for this example is Professor Charles Sayward at the University of Nebraska-Lincoln.

Utilitarianism

JOHN STUART MILL

John Stuart Mill (1806–1873) was one of the most important British philosophers in the nineteenth century, one who made a significant contribution to logic, philosophy of science, political theory, and ethics. The present essay contains parts of Chapters 2 and 4 of his Utilitarianism. *Mill seeks to distinguish happiness from mere sensual pleasure. "A being of higher faculties requires more to make him happy, is capable probably of more acute suffering, and certainly accessible to it at more points, than one of an inferior type," but still he is qualitatively better off than the person without these higher faculties. "It is better to be a human being dissatisfied than a pig satisfied; better to be Socrates dissatisfied than a fool satisfied." Mill's version of utilitarianism has been called 'eudaimonistic utilitarianism' (eudaimonia is the Greek for "happiness") to distinguish it from Bentham's hedonistic utilitarianism (see reading IV.12).*

What Utilitarianism Is

. . . The creed which accepts as the foundation of morals, Utility, or the Greatest Happiness Principle, holds that actions are right in proportion as they tend to promote happiness, wrong as they tend to produce the reverse of happiness. By happiness is intended pleasure, and the absence of pain; by unhappiness, pain, and the privation of pleasure. To give a clear view of the moral standard set up by the theory, much more requires to be said; in particular, what things it includes in the ideas of pain and pleasure; and to what extent this is left an open question. But these supplementary explanations do not affect the theory of life on which this theory of morality is grounded—namely, that pleasure, and freedom from pain, are

From John Stuart Mill, *Utilitarianism* (1861), Chapters 2 and 4.

the only things desirable as ends; and that all desirable things (which are as numerous in the utilitarian as in any other scheme) are desirable either for the pleasure inherent in themselves, or as a means to the promotion of pleasure and the prevention of pain.

Now, such a theory of life excites in many minds, and among them in some of the most estimable in feeling and purpose, inveterate dislike. To suppose that life has (as they express it) no higher end than pleasure—no better and nobler object of desire and pursuit—they designate as utterly mean and groveling; as a doctrine worthy only of swine, to whom the followers of Epicurus were, at a very early period, contemptuously likened; and modern holders of the doctrine are occasionally made the subject of equally polite comparisons by its German, French, and English assailants.

When thus attacked, the Epicureans have always answered, that it is not they, but their accusers, who represent human nature in a degrading light; since the accusation supposes human beings to be capable of no pleasures except those of which swine are capable. If this supposition were true, the charge could not be gainsaid, but would then be no longer an imputation; for if the sources of pleasure were precisely the same to human beings and to swine, the rule of life which is good enough for the one would be good enough for the other. The comparison of the Epicurean life to that of beasts is felt as degrading, precisely because a beast's pleasures do not satisfy a human being's conception of happiness. Human beings have faculties more elevated than the animal appetites, and when once made conscious of them, do not regard anything as happiness which does not include their gratification. I do not, indeed, consider the Epicureans to have been by any means faultless in drawing out their scheme of consequences from the utilitarian principle. To do this in any sufficient manner, many Stoic, as well as Christian elements require to be included. But there is no known Epicurean theory of life which does not assign to the pleasures of the intellect, of the feelings and imagination, and of the moral sentiments, a much higher value as pleasures than to those of mere sensation. It must be admitted, however, that utilitarian writers in general have placed the superiority of mental over bodily pleasures chiefly in the greater permanency, safety, uncostliness, etc., of the former—that is, in their circumstantial advantages rather than in their intrinsic nature. And on all these points utilitarians have fully proved their case; but they might have taken the other, and, as it may be called, higher ground, with entire consistency. It is quite compatible with the principle of utility to recognize the fact, that some *kinds* of pleasure are more desirable and more valuable than others. It would be absurd that while, in estimating all other things, quality is considered as well as quantity, the estimation of pleasures should be supposed to depend on quantity alone.

If I am asked, what I mean by difference of quality in pleasures, or what makes one pleasure more valuable than another, merely as a pleasure, except its being greater in amount, there is but one possible answer. Of two pleasures, if there be one which all or almost all who have experience of both give a decided preference, irrespective of any feeling of moral obligation to prefer it, that is the more desirable pleasure. If one of the two is, by those who are competently acquainted with both, placed so far above the other that they prefer it, even though knowing it to be attended with a great amount of discontent, and would not resign it for any quantity of the other pleasure which their nature is capable of, we are justified in ascribing to the preferred enjoyment a superiority in quality, so far out-weighing quantity as to render it, in comparison, of small account.

Now it is an unquestionable fact that those who are equally acquainted with, and equally capable of appreciating and enjoying, both, do give a most marked preference to the manner of existence which employs their higher faculties. Few human creatures would consent to be changed into any of the lower animals, for a promise of the fullest allowance of a beast's pleasures; no intelligent human being would consent to be a fool, no instructed person would be an ignoramus, no person of feeling and conscience would be selfish and base, even though they should be persuaded that the fool, the dunce, or the rascal is better satisfied with his lot than they are with theirs. They would not resign what they possess more than he for the most complete satisfaction of all the desires which they have in common with him. If they ever fancy they would, it is only in cases of unhappiness so extreme, that to escape from it they would exchange their lot for almost any other, however undesirable in their own eyes. A being of higher faculties requires more to make him happy, is capable probably of more acute suffering, and certainly accessible to it at more points, than one of an inferior type; but in spite of these liabilities, he can never really wish to sink into what he feels to be a lower grade of existence. We may give what explanation we please of this unwillingness; we may attribute it to pride, a name which is given indiscriminately to some of the most and to some of the least estimable feelings of which mankind are capable; we may refer it to the love of liberty and personal independence, an appeal to which was with the Stoics one of the most effective means for the inculcation of it; to the love of power, or to the love of excitement, both of which do really enter into and contribute to it: but its most appropriate appellation is a sense of dignity, which all human beings possess in one form or another, and in some, though by no means in exact, proportion to their higher faculties, and which is so essential a part of the happiness of those in whom it is strong, that nothing which conflicts with it could be, otherwise than momentarily, an object of desire to them. Whoever supposes that this preference takes place at a sacrifice of happiness—that the superior being, in anything like equal circumstances, is not happier than the inferior—confounds the two very different ideas, of happiness, and content. It is indisputable that the being whose capacities of enjoyment are low, has the greatest chance of having them fully satisfied; and a highly endowed being will always feel that any happiness which he can look for, as the world is constituted, is imperfect. But he can learn to bear its imperfections, if they are at all bearable; and they will not make him envy the being who is indeed unconscious of the imperfections, but only because he feels not at all the good which those imperfections qualify. It is better to be a human being dissatisfied than a pig satisfied; better to be Socrates dissatisfied than a fool satisfied. And if the fool, or the pig, are of a different opinion, it is because they only know their own side of the question. The other party to the comparison knows both sides.

It may be objected, that many who are capable of the higher pleasures, occasionally, under the influence of temptation, postpone them to the lower. But this is quite compatible with a full appreciation of the intrinsic superiority of the higher. Men often, from infirmity of character, make their election for the nearer good, though they know it to be the less valuable; and this no less when the choice is between two bodily pleasures, than when it is between bodily and mental. They pursue sensual indulgences to the injury of health, though perfectly aware that health is the greater good. It may be further objected, that many who begin with youthful enthusiasm for everything noble, as they advance in years sink into indolence and selfishness. But I do not believe that those who undergo this very common change, voluntarily choose the lower description of pleasures in preference to the higher. I believe that before they devote themselves exclusively to the one, they have already become incapable of the other. Capacity for the nobler feelings is in most natures a very tender plant, easily killed, not only by hostile influences, but by mere want of sustenance; and in the majority of young persons it

speedily dies away if the occupations to which their position in life has devoted them, and the society into which it has thrown them, are not favorable to keeping that higher capacity in exercise. Men lose their high aspirations as they lose their intellectual tastes, because they have not time or opportunity for indulging them; and they addict themselves to inferior pleasures, not because they deliberately prefer them, but because they are either the only ones to which they have access, or the only ones which they are any longer capable of enjoying. It may be questioned whether any one who has remained equally susceptible to both classes of pleasures, ever knowingly and calmly preferred the lower; though many, in all ages, have broken down in an ineffectual attempt to combine both.

From this verdict of the only competent judges, I apprehend there can be no appeal. On a question which is the best worth having of two pleasures, or which of two modes of existence is the most grateful to the feelings, apart from its moral attributes and from its consequences, the judgment of those who are qualified by knowledge of both, or, if they differ, that of the majority among them, must be admitted as final. And there needs to be the less hesitation to accept this judgment respecting the quality of pleasures, since there is no other tribunal to be referred to even on the question of quantity. What means are there of determining which is the acutest of two pains, or the intensest of two pleasurable sensations, except the general suffrage of those who are familiar with both? Neither pains nor pleasures are homogeneous, and pain is always heterogeneous with pleasure. What is there to decide whether a particular pleasure is worth purchasing at the cost of a particular pain, except the feelings and judgment of the experienced? When, therefore, those feelings and judgment declare the pleasures derived from the higher faculties to be preferable *in kind*, apart from the question of intensity, to those of which the animal nature, disjoined from the higher faculties, is susceptible, they are entitled on this subject to the same regard.

I have dwelt on this point, as being a necessary part of a perfectly just conception of Utility or Happiness, considered as the directive rule of human conduct. But it is by no means an indispensable condition to the acceptance of the utilitarian standard; for that standard is not the agent's own greatest happiness, but the greatest amount of happiness altogether; and if it may possibly be doubted whether a noble character is always the happier for its nobleness, there can be no doubt that it makes other people happier, and that the world in general is immensely a gainer by it. Utilitarianism, therefore, could only attain its end by the general cultivation of nobleness of character, even if each individual were only benefited by the nobleness of others, and his own, so far as happiness is concerned, were a sheer deduction from the benefit. But the bare enunciation of such an absurdity as this last, renders refutation superfluous.

According to the Greatest Happiness Principle, as above explained, the ultimate end, with reference to and for the sake of which all other things are desirable (whether we are considering our own good or that of other people), is an existence exempt as far as possible from pain, and as rich as possible in enjoyments, both in point of quantity and quality; the test of quality, and the rule for measuring it against quantity, being the preference felt by those who in their opportunities of experience, to which must be added their habits of self-consciousness and self-observation, are best furnished with the means of comparison. This, being, according to the utilitarian opinion, the end of human action, is necessarily also the standard of morality; which may accordingly be defined, the rules and precepts for human conduct, by the observance of which an existence such as has been described might be, to the greatest extent possible, secured to all mankind; and not to them only, but, so far as the nature of things admits, to the whole sentient creation. . . .

The objectors to utilitarianism cannot always be charged with representing it in a discreditable light. On the contrary, those among them who entertain anything like a just idea of its disinterested character, sometimes find fault with its standard as being too high for humanity. They say it is exacting too much to require that people shall always act from the inducement of promoting the general interests of society. But this is to mistake the very meaning of a standard of morals, and confound the rule of action with the motive of it. It is the business of ethics to tell us what are our duties, or by what test we may know them; but no system of ethics requires that the sole motive of all we do shall be a feeling of duty; on the contrary, ninety-nine hundredths of all our actions are done from other motives, and rightly so done, if the rule of duty does not condemn them. It is the more unjust to utilitarianism that this particular misapprehension should be made a ground of objection to it, inasmuch as utilitarian moralists have gone beyond almost all others in affirming that the motive has nothing to do with the morality of the action, though much with the worth of the agent. He who saves a fellow-creature from drowning does what is morally right, whether his motive be duty, or the hope of being paid for his trouble; he who betrays the friend that trusts him, is guilty of a crime, even if his object be to serve another friend to whom he is under greater obligation. But to speak only of actions done from the motive of duty, and in direct obedience to principle: it is a misapprehension of the utilitarian mode of thought, to conceive it as implying that people should fix their minds upon so wide a generality as the world, or society at large. The great majority of good actions are intended not for the benefit of the world, but for that of individuals, of which the good of the world is made up; and the thoughts of the most virtuous man need not on these occasions travel beyond the particular persons concerned, except so far as is necessary to assure himself that in benefiting them he is not violating the rights, that is, the legitimate and authorised expectations, of any one else. The multiplication of happiness is, according to the utilitarian ethics, the object of virtue: the occasions on which any person (except one in a thousand) has it in his power to do this on an extended scale, in other words to be a public benefactor, are but exceptional; and on these occasions alone is he called on to consider public utility; in every other case, private utility, the interest or happiness of some few persons, is all he has to attend to. Those alone the influence of whose actions extends to society in general, need concern themselves habitually about so large an object. In the case of abstinences indeed—of things which people forbear to do from moral considerations, though the consequences in the particular case might be beneficial—it would be unworthy of an intelligent agent not to be consciously aware that the action is of a class which, if practiced generally, would be generally injurious, and that this is the ground of the obligation to abstain from it. The amount of regard for the public interest implied in this recognition, is no greater than is demanded by every system of morals, for they all enjoin to abstain from whatever is manifestly pernicious to society. . . .

Chapter IV Of What Sort of Proof the Principle of Utility Is Susceptible

It has already been remarked, that questions of ultimate ends do not admit of proof, in the ordinary acceptation of the term. To be incapable of proof by reasoning is common to all first principles; to the first premises of our knowledge, as well as to those of our conduct. But the former, being matters of fact, may be the subject of a direct appeal to the faculties which judge of fact—namely, our senses, and our internal consciousness. Can an appeal be made to the same faculties on questions of practical ends? Or by what other faculty is cognizance taken of them?

Questions abouts ends are, in other words, questions about what things are desirable. The utilitarian doctrine is, that happiness is desirable, and the only thing desirable, as an end; all other things being only desirable as means to that end. What ought to be required of this doctrine—what conditions is it to requisite that the doctrine

should fulfil—to make good its claim to be believed?

The only proof capable of being given that an object is visible, is that people actually see it. The only proof that a sound is audible, is that people hear it: and so of the other sources of our experience. In like manner, I apprehend, the sole evidence it is possible to produce that anything is desirable, is that people do actually desire it. If the end which the utilitarian doctrine proposes to itself were not, in theory and in practice, acknowledged to be an end, nothing could ever convince any person that it was so. No reason can be given why the general happiness is desirable, except that each person, so far as he believes it to be attainable, desires his own happiness. This, however, being a fact, we have not only all the proof which the case admits of, but all which it is possible to require, that happiness is a good: that each person's happiness is a good to that person, and the general happiness, therefore, a good to the aggregate of all persons. Happiness has made out its title as *one* of the ends of conduct, and consequently one of the criteria of morality.

But it has not, by this alone, proved itself to be the sole criterion. To do that, it would seem, by the same rule, necessary to show, not only that people desire happiness, but that they never desire anything else. . . .

We have now, then, an answer to the question, of what sort of proof the principle of utility is susceptible. If the opinion which I have now stated is psychologically true—if human nature is so constituted as to desire nothing which is not either a part of happiness or a means of happiness, we can have no other proof, and we require no other, that these are the only things desirable. If so, happiness is the sole end of human action, and the promotion of it the test by which to judge of all human conduct; from whence it necessarily follows that it must be the criterion of morality, since a part is included in the whole.

And now to decide whether this is really so; whether mankind do desire nothing for itself but that which is a pleasure to them, or of which the absence is a pain; we have evidently arrived at a question of fact and experience, dependent, like all similar questions, upon evidence. It can only be determined by practised self-consciousness and self-observation, assisted by observation of others. I believe that these sources of evidence, impartially consulted, will declare that desiring a thing and finding it pleasant, aversion to it and thinking of it as painful, are phenomena entirely inseparable, or rather two parts of the same phenomenon; in strictness of language, two different modes of naming the same psychological fact: that to think of an object as desirable (unless for the sake of its consequences), and to think of it as pleasant, are one and the same thing; and that to desire anything, except in proportion as the idea of it is pleasant, is a physical and metaphysical impossibility.

Rule-Utilitarianism

JOHN HOSPERS

John Hospers (b. 1918) is the director of the School of Philosophy at the University of Southern California and the author of several works in philosophy, most notably Libertarianism and Human Conduct: An Introduction to Ethics, *from which the present selection is taken. In 1972 he ran for president of the United States on the Libertarian party ticket.*

With the use of counterexamples, Hospers rejects the act-utilitarianism defended by Bentham, Nielsen, and, perhaps, Mill. We need rules without being rigidly rule-bound or forgetting the consequentialist point of morality. Hence, Hospers opts for a version of utilitarianism that is centered in rules, which he and others have called "rule-utilitarianism."

1. In order to receive a high enough grade average to be admitted to medical school, a certain student must receive either an A or a B in one of my courses. After his final examination is in, I find, on averaging his grades, that his grade for the course comes out to a C. The student comes into my office and begs me to change the grade, on the ground that I have not read his paper carefully enough. So I reread his final exam paper, as well as some of the other papers in the class in order to get a better sense of comparison; the rechecking convinces me that his grade should be no higher than the one I have given him—if anything, it should be lower. I inform him of my opinion and he still pleads with me to change the grade, but for a different reason. "I know I didn't deserve more than a C, but I

appeal to you as a human being to change my grade, because without it I can't get into medical school, which naturally means a great deal to me." I inform him that grades are supposed to be based on achievement in the course, not on intentions or need or the worthiness of one's plans. But he pleads: "I know it's unethical to change a grade when the student doesn't deserve a higher one, but can't you please make an exception to the rule just this once?" And before I can reply, he sharpens his plea: "I appeal to you as a utilitarian. Your goal is the greatest happiness of everyone concerned, isn't it? If you give me only the grade I deserve, who will be happier? Not I, that's sure. Perhaps you will for a little while, but you have hundreds of students and you'll soon forget about it; and I will be ever so much happier for being admitted into a school that will train me for the profession I have always desired. It's true that I didn't work as hard in your course as I should have, but I realize my mistake and I wouldn't waste so much time if I had it to do over again. Anyway, you should be forward-looking rather than backward-looking in your moral judgments, and there is no doubt whatever that much more happiness will be caused (and unhappiness prevented) by your giving me the higher grade even though I fully admit that I don't deserve it."

After pondering the matter, I persist in believing that it would not be right to change the grade under these circumstances. Perhaps you agree with my decision and perhaps you don't, but *if* you agree that I should not have changed the grade, and *if* you are also a utilitarian, how are you going to reconcile such a decision with utilitarianism? *Ex hypothesi*, the greatest amount of happiness will be brought about by my changing the grade, so why shouldn't I change it?

Of course, if I changed the grade and went around telling people about it, my action would tend to have an adverse effect on the whole system of grading—and this system is useful to graduate schools and future employers to give some indication of the student's achievement in his various courses. But of course if I tell no one, nobody will know, and my action cannot set a bad example to others. This in turn raises an interesting question: If it is wrong for me to do the act publicly, is it any the less wrong for me to do it secretly?

2. A man is guilty of petty theft and is sentenced to a year in prison. Suppose he can prove to the judge's satisfaction that he would be happier out of jail, that his wife and family would too (they depend on his support), that the state wouldn't have the expense of his upkeep if he were freed, and that people won't hear about it because his case didn't hit the papers and nobody even knows that he was arrested—in short, everyone concerned would be happier and nobody would be harmed by his release. And yet, we feel, or at least many people would, that to release him would be a mistake. The sentence imposed on him is the minimum permitted by law for his offense, and he should serve out his term in accordance with the law.

3. A district attorney who has prosecuted a man for robbery chances upon information which shows conclusively that the man he has prosecuted is innocent of the crime for which he has just been sentenced. The man is a wastrel who, if permitted to go free, would almost certainly commit other crimes. Moreover, the district attorney has fairly conclusive evidence of the man's guilt in prior crimes, for which, however, the jury has failed to convict him. Should he, therefore, "sit on the evidence" and let the conviction go through in this case, in which he knows the man to be innocent? We may not be able to articulate exactly *why*, but we feel strongly that the district attorney should not sit on the evidence but that he should reveal every scrap of evidence he knows, even though the revelation means releasing the prisoner (now known to be innocent) to do more crimes and be convicted for them later.

X: It seems to me that some acts are right or wrong, not *regardless* of the consequences they produce, but *over and above* the consequences they produce. We would all agree, I suppose, that you should break a promise to save a life but not that you should break it whenever you considered it probable (even with good reason) that more good effects will come about through breaking it. Suppose you had promised someone you would do something and you didn't do it. When asked why, you replied, "Because I thought breaking it would have better results." Wouldn't the promisee condemn you for your action, and rightly? This example is quite analogous, I think, to the example of the district attorney; the district attorney might argue that more total good will be produced by keeping the prisoner's innocence secret. Besides, if he is released, people may read about it in the newspaper and say, "You see, you can get by with anything these days" and may be encouraged to violate the law themselves as a result. Still, even though it would do more total good if the man were to remain convicted, wouldn't it be wrong to do so in view of the fact that he is definitely innocent of *this* crime? The law punishes a man, not necessarily because the most good will be achieved that way, but because he has committed a crime; if we don't approve of the law, we can do our best to have it changed, but meanwhile aren't we bound to follow it? Those who execute the law are sworn to obey it; they are *not* sworn to produce certain consequences.

Y: Yes, but remember that the facts *might* always come out after their concealment and that we can never be sure they won't. If they do, keeping the man in prison will be far worse than letting the man go; it will result in a great public distrust for the law itself; nothing is more demoralizing than corruption of the law by its own supposed enforcers. Better let a hundred human derelicts go free than risk that! You see, *one* of the consequences you always have to consider is the effect of *this* action on the *general practice* of law-breaking itself; and when you bring in *this* consequence, it will surely weigh the balance in favor of divulging the information that will release the innocent man. So utilitarianism will still account quite satisfactorily for this case. I agree that the man should be released, but I do so on utilitarian grounds; I needn't abandon my utilitarianism at all to take care of this case.

X: But your view is open to one fatal objection. You say that one never can be sure that the news *won't* leak out. Perhaps so. But suppose that in a given case one *could* be sure; would that really make any difference? Suppose you are the only person that knows and you destroy the only existing evidence. Since you are not going to talk, there is simply no chance that the news will leak out, with consequent damage to public morale. Then is it all right to withhold the information? You see, I hold that if it's wrong not to reveal the truth when others might find out, then it's equally wrong not to reveal it when *nobody* will find out. You utilitarians are involved in the fatal error of making the rightness or wrongness of an act depend on whether performing it will ever be publicized. And I hold that it is immoral even to consider this condition; the district attorney should reveal the truth regardless of whether his concealing it would ever be known.

Y: But surely you aren't saying that one should *never* conceal the truth? not even if your country is at war against a totalitarian enemy and revealing truths to the people would also mean revealing them to the enemy?

X: Of course I'm not saying that—don't change the subject. I am saying that *if* in situation S it is wrong to convict an innocent man, then it is equally wrong whether or not the public knows that it is wrong; the public's knowledge will certainly have bad consequences, but the conviction would be wrong anyway even *without* these bad consequences; so you can't appeal to the consequences of the conviction's becoming public as grounds for saying that the conviction is wrong. I think that you utilitarians are really stuck here. For you, the consideration "but nobody is ever

going to know about it anyway" is a relevant consideration. It has to be; for the rightness of an act (according to you) is estimated in terms of its total consequences, and its total consequences, of course, include its effects (or lack of effects) on other acts of the same kind, and there won't be any such effects if the act is kept absolutely secret. You have to consider *all* the consequences relevant; the matter of keeping the thing quiet is one consequence; so you have to consider this one relevant too. Yet I submit to you that it isn't relevant; the suggestion "but nobody is going to know about it anyway" is not one that will help make the act permissible if it wasn't before. If anything, it's the other way round: something bad that's done publicly and openly is not as bad as if it's done secretly so as to escape detection; secret sins are the worst. . . .

Y: I deny what you say. It seems to me worse to betray a trust in public, where it may set an example to others, than to do so in secret, where it can have no bad effects on others.

X: And I submit that you would never say that if you weren't already committed to the utilitarian position. Here is a situation where you and practically everyone else would not hesitate to say that an act done in secret is no less wrong than when done in public, were it not that it flies in the face of a doctrine to which you have already committed yourself on the basis of quite different examples.

4. Here is a still different kind of example. We consider it our duty in a democracy to vote and to do so wisely and intelligently as possible, for only if we vote wisely can a democracy work successfully. But in a national election my vote is only one out of millions, and it is more and more improbable that *my* vote will have any effect upon the outcome. Nor is my failure to vote going to affect other people much, if at all. Couldn't a utilitarian argue this way: "My vote will have no effect at all—at least far, far less than other things I could be doing instead. Therefore, I shall not vote." Each and every would-be voter could argue in exactly the same way. The result would be that

nobody would vote, and the entire democratic process would be destroyed.

What conclusion emerges from these examples? If the examples point at all in the right direction, they indicate that there are some acts which it is right to perform, even though by themselves they will not have good consequences (such as my voting), and that there are some acts which it is wrong to perform, even though by themselves they would have good consequences (such as sitting on the evidence). But this conclusion is opposed to utilitarianism as we have considered it thus far. . . .

Rule-Utilitarianism and Objections to It

The batter swings, the ball flies past, the umpire yells "Strike three!" The disappointed batter pleads with the umpire, "Can't I have four strikes just this once?" We all recognize the absurdity of this example. Even if the batter could prove to the umpire's satisfaction that he would be happier for having four strikes this time, that the spectators would be happier for it (since most of the spectators are on his side), that there would be little dissatisfaction on the side of the opposition (who might have the game clinched anyway), and that there would be no effect on future baseball games, we would still consider his plea absurd. We might think, "Perhaps baseball would be a better game— i.e., contribute to the greatest total enjoyment of all concerned—if four strikes were permitted. If so, we should change the rules of the game. But until that time, we must play baseball according to the rules which are now the accepted rules of the game."

This example, though only an analogy, gives us a clue to the kind of view we are about to consider— let us call it *rule-utilitarianism*. Briefly stated (we shall amplify it gradually), rule-utilitarianism comes to this: Each act, in the moral life, falls under a *rule*; and we are to judge the rightness or wrongness of the act, not by *its* consequences, but by the consequences of its universalization—that is, by the consequences of the adoption of the *rule* under which this act falls. This . . . interpretation of Kant's categorical imperative . . . differs from Kant in being concerned with consequences, but retains the main feature which Kant introduced, that of universalizability.

Thus: The district attorney may do more good in a particular case by sitting on the evidence, but even if this case has no consequences for future cases because nobody ever finds out, still, the general policy or *practice* of doing this kind of thing is a very bad one; it uproots one of the basic premises of our legal system, namely, that an innocent person should not be condemned. Our persistent conviction that it would be wrong for him to conceal the evidence in this case comes *not* from the conviction that concealing the evidence will produce less good—we may be satisfied that it will produce more good in this case— but from the conviction that the *practice* of doing this kind of thing will have very bad consequences. In other words, "Conceal the evidence when you think that it will produce more happiness" would be a bad rule to follow, and it is because this *rule* (if adopted) would have bad consequences, not because *this* act itself has bad consequences, that we condemn the act.

The same applies in other situations: . . . perhaps I can achieve more good, in this instance, by changing the student's grade, but the consequences of the general practice of changing students' grades for such reasons as these would be very bad indeed; a graduate school or a future employer would no longer have reason to believe that the grade-transcript of the student had any reference to his real achievement in his courses; he would wonder how many of the high grades resulted from personal factors like pity, need, and irrelevant appeals by the student to the teacher. The same considerations apply also to the voting example: if Mr. Smith can reason that his vote won't make any difference to the outcome, so can Mr. Jones and Mr. Robinson and every other would-be voter; but if everyone reasoned in this way, no one would vote, and this *would* have bad effects. It is considered one's duty to vote, not because the consequences of one's not doing so are bad, but because the consequences of the general practice of not doing so are bad. To put it in Kantian language, the maxim of the action, if universalized, would have bad consequences. But the individual act of *your* not voting on a specific occasion—or of any *one* person's not voting, as long as *others* continued to vote—would probably have no bad consequences.

There are many other examples of the same kind of thing. If during a water shortage there is a regulation that water should not be used to take baths every day or to water gardens, there will be virtually no bad consequences if only *I* violate the rule. Since there will be no discernible difference to the city water supply and since my plants will remain green and fresh and pleasant to look at, why shouldn't I water my plants? But if everyone watered his plants, there would not be enough water left to drink. My act is judged wrong, not because of *its* consequences, but because the consequences of everyone doing so would be bad. If I walk on the grass where the sign says, "Do not walk on the grass," there will be no ill effects; but if everyone did so it would destroy the grass. There are some kinds of act which have little or no effect if any one person (or two, or three) does them but which have very considerable effects if everyone (or even just a large number) does them. Rule-utilitarianism is designed to take care of just such situations.

Rule-utilitarianism also takes care of situations which are puzzling in traditional utilitarianism, . . . namely, the secrecy with which an act is performed. "But no one will ever know, so my act won't have any consequences for future acts of the same kind," the utilitarian argued; and we felt that he was being somehow irrelevant, even immoral: that if something is wrong when people know about it, it is just as wrong when done in secret. Yet this condition *is* relevant according to traditional utilitarianism, for if some act with bad consequences is never known to anyone, this ignorance does mitigate the bad consequences, for it undeniably keeps the act from setting an example (except, of course, that it may start a habit

in the agent himself). Rule-utilitarianism solves this difficulty. If I change the student's grade in secret, my act is wrong, in spite of its having almost no consequences (and never being known to anyone else), because if I change the grade and don't tell anyone, how do I know how many other teachers are changing their students' grades without telling anybody? It is the result of the *practice* which is bad, not the result of my single action. The result of the practice is bad whether the act is done in secret or not: the result of the practice of changing grades in secret is just as bad as the results of the practice done in full knowledge of everyone; it would be equally deleterious to the grading system, equally a bad index of a student's actual achievement. In fact, if changing grades is done in secret, this in one way is worse; for prospective employers will not know, as they surely ought to know in evaluating their prospective employees, that their grades are not based on achievement but on other factors such as poverty, extra-curricular work load, and persuasive appeal.

Rule-utilitarianism is a distinctively twentieth-century amendment of the utilitarianism of Bentham and Mill, often called *act-utilitarianism.* . . . Since this pair of labels is brief and indicates clearly the contents of the theories referred to, we prefer these terms to a second pair of labels, which are sometimes used for the same theories: *restricted utilitarianism* as opposed to *unrestricted* (or extreme, or *traditional*) *utilitarianism.* (Whether or not Mill's theory is strictly act-utilitarianism is a matter of dispute. Mill never made the distinction between act-utilitarianism and rule-utilitarianism. . . . Some of Mill's examples, however, have to do not with individual acts but with general principles and rules of conduct. Mill and Bentham were both legislators, interested in amending the laws of England into greater conformity to the utilitarian principle; and to the extent that Mill was interested in providing a criterion of judging rules of conduct rather than individual acts, he may be said to have been a rule-utilitarian.)

Much more must be said before the full nature of the rule-utilitarian theory becomes clear. To understand it better, we shall consider some possible questions, comments, and objections that can be put to the theory as thus far stated.

1. Doesn't the . . . problem arise here . . . of *what* precisely we are to universalize? Every act can be put into a vast variety of classes of acts; or, in our present terminology, every act can be made to fall under many different general rules. Which rule among this vast variety are we to select? We can pose our problem by means of an imaginary dialogue referring back to Kant's ethics and connecting it with rule-utilitarianism:

A: Whatever may be said for Kant's ethics in general, there is one principle of fundamental importance which must be an indispensable part of every ethics—the principle of universalizability. If some act is right for me to do, it would be right for all rational beings to do it; and if it is wrong for them to do it, it would be wrong for me too.

B: If this principle simply means that nobody should make an exception in his own favor, the principle is undoubtedly true and is psychologically important in view of the fact that people constantly do make exceptions in their own favor. But as it stands I can't follow you in agreeing with Kant's principle. Do you mean that if it is wrong for Smith to get a divorce, it is also wrong for Jones to do so? But this isn't so. Smith may be hopelessly incompatible with his wife, and they may be far better off apart, whereas Jones may be reconcilable with his wife (with some mutal effort) and a divorce in his case would be a mistake. Each case must be judged on its own merits.

A: The principle doesn't mean that if it's right for one person, A, to do it, it is therefore right for B and C and D to do it. It means that if it's right for one person to do it, it is right for anyone *in those circumstances* to do it. And Jones isn't in the same circumstances as Smith. Smith and his wife would be better off apart, and Jones and his wife would be better off together.

B: I see. Do you mean *exactly* the same circumstances or *roughly* the same (similar) circumstances?

A: I think I would have to mean exactly the same circumstances for if the circumstances were not quite alike, that little difference might make the difference between a right act (done by Smith) and a wrong act (done by Jones). For instance, if in Smith's case there are no children and in Jone's case there are, this fact may make a difference.

B: Right. But I must urge you to go even further. Two men might be in exactly the same *external* circumstances, but owing to their *internal constitution* what would be right for one of them wouldn't be for the other. Jones may have the ability to be patient, impartial, and approach problems rationally, and Smith may not have this ability; here again is a relevant difference between them, although not a difference in their external circumstances. Or: Smith, after he reaches a certain point of fatigue, would do well to go fishing for a few days—this would refresh and relax him as nothing else could. But Jones dislikes fishing; it tries and irritates and bores him; so even if he were equally tired and had an equally responsible position, he would not be well advised to go fishing. Or again: handling explosives might be all right for a trained intelligent person, but not for an ignorant blunderbuss. In the light of such examples as these, you see that under the "same circumstances" you'll have to include not only the external circumstances in which they find themselves but their own internal character.

A: I grant this. So what?

B: But now your universalizability principle becomes useless. For two people never *are* in exactly the same circumstances. Nor can they be: if Smith were in exactly the same circumstances as Jones, including all his traits of character, his idiosyncracies, and his brain cells, he would *be* Jones. You see, your universalizability principle is inapplicable. It would become applicable only under conditions (two people being the same person) which are self-contradictory—and even if not self-contradictory, you'll have to admit that two exactly identical situations never occur; so once again the rule is inapplicable.

A: I see your point; but I don't think I need go along with your conclusion. Smith and Jones should do the same thing only if their situation or circumstances are the same in certain *relevant respects*. The fact that Jones is wearing a white shirt and Smith a blue one, is a difference of circumstances, but, surely, an *irrelevant* difference, a difference that for moral purposes can be ignored. But the fact that Smith and his wife are emotionally irreconcilable while Jones and his wife could work things out, would be a morally relevant circumstance.

B: Possibly. But how are you going to determine which differences are relevant and which are not?

Kant . . . never solved this problem. He assumed that "telling a lie" was morally relevant but that "telling a lie to save a life" was not; but he gave no reason for making this distinction. The rule-utilitarian has an answer.

Suppose that a red-headed man with one eye and a wart on his right cheek tells a lie on a Tuesday. What rule are we to derive from this event? Red-headed men should not tell lies? People shouldn't lie on Tuesdays? Men with warts on their cheeks shouldn't tell lies on Tuesdays? These rules seem absurd, for it seems so obvious that whether it's Tuesday or not, whether the man has a wart on his cheek or not, has nothing whatever to do with the rightness of his action—these circumstances are just *irrelevant*. But this is the problem: how are we going to establish this irrelevance? What is to be our criterion?

The criterion we tried to apply . . . was to make the rule more *specific*: instead of saying, "This is a lie and is therefore wrong," . . . we made it more specific and said, "This is a lie told to save a life and is therefore right." We could make the rule more specific still, involving the precise circumstances in which this lie is told, other than the fact that it is told to save a life. But, now it seems the use of greater specificity will not always work: instead of "Don't tell lies," suppose we say, "Don't tell lies on Tuesdays." The second is certainly more specific than the first, but is it a better rule? It seems plain that it is not—that its being a Tuesday is, in fact, wholly irrelevant. Why?

"Because," says the rule-utilitarian, "there is no difference between the effects of lies told on Tuesdays and the effects of lies told on any other day. This is simply an empirical fact, and because of this empirical fact, bringing in Tuesday is irrelevant. If lies told on Tuesdays always had good consequences and lies told on other days were disastrous, then a lie's being told on a Tuesday would be relevant to the moral estimation of the act; but in fact this is not true. Thus there is no advantage in specifying the subclass of lies, 'lies told on Tuesdays.' The same is true of 'lies told by redheads' and 'lies told by persons with warts on their cheeks.' The class of lies can be made more specific—that is no problem—but not more *relevantly* specific, at least not in the direction of Tuesdays and redheads. (However, the class can be made more relevantly specific considering certain other aspects of the situation, such as whether the lie was told to produce a good result that could not have been brought about otherwise.)"

Consider by contrast a situation in which the class of acts can easily be made relevantly more specific. A pacifist might argue as follows: "I should never use physical violence in any form against another human being, since if everyone refrained from violence, we would have a warless world." There are aspects of this example that we cannot discuss now, but our present concern with it is as follows. We can break down violence into more specific types such as violence which is unprovoked, violence in defense of one's life against attack by another, violence by a policeman in catching a lawbreaker, violence by a drunkard in response to an imaginary affront. The effects of these subclasses of violence do differ greatly in their effects upon society. Violence used by a policeman in apprehending a lawbreaker (at least under some circumstances, which could be spelled out) and violence used in preventing a would-be murderer from killing you, do on the whole have good effects; but the unprovoked violence of an aggressor or a drunkard does not. Since these subclasses do have different effects, therefore, it *is* relevant to consider them. Indeed, it is imperative to do so: the pacifist who condemns *all* violence would probably, if he thought about it, not wish to condemn the policeman who uses violent means to prevent an armed madman from killing a dozen people. In any event, the effects of the two subclasses of acts are vastly different; and, the rule-utilitarian would say, it is accordingly very important for us to consider them—to break down the general class of violent acts into more specific classes and consider separately the effects of each one until we have arrived at subclasses which cannot *relevantly* be made more specific.

How specific shall we be? Won't we get down to "acts of violence to prevent aggression, performed on Tuesdays at 11:30 P.M. in hot weather" and subclasses of that sort? And aren't these again plainly irrelevant? Of course they are, and the reason has already been given: acts of violence performed on Tuesdays, or at 11:30 P.M., or by people with blue suits, are no different in their effects from acts-of-violence-to-prevent-aggression done in circumstances other than these; and therefore these circumstances, though more specific, are not relevantly more specific. When the consequences of these more specific classes of acts differ from the consequences of the more general class, it is this specific class which should be considered; but when the consequences of the specific classes are not different from those of the more general class, the greater specificity is irrelevant and can be ignored.

The rule, then, is this: we should consider the consequences of the general performance of certain classes of actions only if that class contains within itself no subclasses, the consequences of the general practice of which would be either better or worse than the consequences of the class itself.

Let us take an actual example of how this rule applies. Many people, including Kant, have taken the principle "Thou shalt not kill" as admitting of no exceptions. But as we have just seen, such principles can be relevantly made more specific. Killing for fun is one thing, killing in self-defense another. Suppose, then, that we try to arrive at a general rule on which to base our actions in this

regard. We shall try to arrive at that rule the general following of which will have the best results. Not to kill an armed bandit who is about to shoot you if you don't shoot him first, would appear to be a bad rule by utilitarian standards; for it would tend to eliminate the good people and preserve the bad ones; moreover, if nobody resisted aggressors, the aggressors, knowing this, would go hog-wild and commit indiscriminate murder, rape, and plunder. Therefore, "Don't kill except in self-defense" (though we might improve this rule too) would be a better rule than "Never kill." But "Don't kill unless you feel angry at the victim" would be a bad rule, because the adoption of this rule would lead to no end of indiscriminate killing for no good reason. The trick is to arrive at the rule which, if adopted, would have the very best possible consequences (which includes, of course, the absolute minimum of bad consequences). Usually no simple or easily statable rule will do this, the world being as complex as it is. There will usually be subclasses of classes-of-acts which are relevantly more specific than the simple, general class with which we began. And even when we think we have arrived at a satisfactory rule, there always remains the possibility that it can relevantly be made more specific, and thus amended, with an increase in accuracy but a consequent decrease in simplicity.

To a considerable extent most people recognize this complexity. Very few people would accept the rule against killing without some qualifications. However much they may preach and invoke the rule "Thou shall not kill" in situations where it happens to suit them, they would never recommend its adoption in all circumstances: when one is defending himself against an armed killer, almost everyone would agree that killing is permissible, although he may not have formulated any theory from which this exception follows as a logical consequence. Our practical rule against killing contains within itself (often not explicitly stated) certain *classes of exceptions:* "Don't kill *except* in self-defense, in war against an aggressor nation, in carrying out the verdict of a jury recommending capital punishment." This would be a far better rule—judged by its consequences—than any simple one-line rule on the subject. Each of the classes of exceptions could be argued pro and con, of course. But such arguments would be empirical ones, hinging on whether or not the adoption of such classes of exceptions into the rule would have the maximum results in intrinsic good. (Many would argue, for example, that capital punishment achieves no good effects; on the other hand, few would contend that the man who pulls the switch at Sing Sing is committing a crime in carrying out the orders of the legal representatives of the state.) And there may always be other kinds of situations that we have not previously thought of, situations which, if incorporated into the rule, would improve the rule—that is, make it have better consequences; and thus the rule remains always open, always subject to further qualification if the addition of such qualification would improve the rule.

These qualifications of the rule are not, strictly speaking, *exceptions to* the rule. According to rule-utilitarianism, the rule, once fully stated, admits of no exceptions; but there may be, and indeed there usually are, numerous classes of exceptions *built into the* rule; a simple rule becomes through qualification a more complex rule. Thus, if a man kills someone in self-defense and we do not consider his act wrong, we are not making him an exception to the rule. Rather, his act *falls under* the rule—the rule that includes killing in self-defense as one of the classes of acts which is permissible (or, if you prefer, the rule that includes self-defense as one of the circumstances in which the rule against killing does not apply). Similarly, if a man parks in a prohibited area and the judge does not fine him because he is a physician making a professional call, the judge is not extending any favoritism to the physician; he is not making the physician an exception to the rule; rather, the rule (though it may not always be written out in black and white) includes within itself this recognized class of exceptions—or, more accurately still, the rule includes within itself a reference to just this kind of situation, so that the

action of the judge in exonerating the physician is just as much an application of the rule (not an exception to it) as another act of the same judge in imposing a fine on someone else for the same offense.

We can now see how our previous remarks about acts committed in secret fit into the rule-utilitarian scheme. On the one hand, the rule "Don't break a promise except (1) under extreme duress and (2) to promote some very great good" is admittedly somewhat vague, and perhaps it could be improved by still further qualification; but at least it is much better than the simple rule "Never break promises." On the other hand, the rule "Don't break a promise except when nobody will know about it" is a bad rule: there are many situations in which keeping promises is important . . . situations in which promises could not be relied on if this rule were adopted. That is why, among the circumstances which excuse you from keeping your word, the fact that it was broken in secret is not one of them—and for a very good reason: if this class of exceptions were incorporated into the rule, the rule's adoption would have far worse effects than if it did not contain such a clause. . . .

Rule-utilitarianism and act-utilitarianism are alike with regard to relativism. They are *not* relativistic in that they have one standard, one "rule of rules," one supreme norm, applicable to all times and situations: "Perform that act which will produce the most intrinsic good" (act-utilitarianism), "Act according to the rule whose adoption will produce the most intrinsic good" (rule-utilitarianism). But within the scope of that one standard, the recommended rules of conduct may well vary greatly from place to place. . . . In a desert area the act of wasting water will cause much harm and is therefore wrong, but it is not wrong in a region where water is plentiful. In a society where men and women are approximately equal in number, it will be best for a husband to have only one wife; but in a society in which there is great numerical disparity between the two, this arrangement may no longer be wise. So much for act-utilitarianism; the same goes for rule-utilitarianism. The rule "Never waste water" is a good rule, indeed an indispensable rule, in a desert region but not in a well-watered region. Monogamy seems to be the best possible marital system in our society but not necessarily in all societies—it depends on the conditions. What are the best acts and the best rules at a given time and place, then, depends on the special circumstances of that time and place. Some conditions, of course, are so general that the rules will be much the same everywhere: a rule against killing (at least within the society) is an indispensable condition of security and survival and therefore must be preserved in all societies.

The situation, then, is this: Rule or Act A is right in circumstances C_1, and Rule or Act B is right in circumstances C_2. In X-land circumstances C_1 prevail, so A is right; and in Y-land circumstances C_2 prevail, so B is right. Perhaps this is all the relativism that ethical relativists will demand.

4. Can't there be, in rule-utilitarianism, a conflict of rules? Suppose you have to choose between breaking a promise and allowing a human life to be lost. . . . What would the rule-utilitarian say? Which rule are we to go by?

No rule-utilitarian would hold such a rule as "Never break a promise" or "Never take a human life." Following such rigid, unqualified rules would certainly not lead to the best consequences—for example, taking Hitler's life would have had better consequences than sparing him. Since such simple rules would never be incorporated into rule-utilitarian ethics to begin with, there would be no conflict between these rules. The rule-utilitarian's rule on taking human life would be of the form, "Do not take human life except in circumstances of types A, B, C . . ." and these circumstances would be those in which taking human life *would* have the best consequences. And the same with breaking promises. Thus, when the rules in question are fully spelled out, there would be no conflict.

In any event, if there were a conflict between rules, there would have to be a second-order rule to tell us which first-order rule to adopt in cases of conflict. Only with such a rule would our rule-utilitarian ethics be *complete*, i.e., made to cover every situation that might arise. But again such a second-order rule would seldom be simple. It would not say, "In cases of conflict between preserving a life and keeping a promise, always preserve the life." For there might always be kinds of cases in which this policy would not produce the best consequences: a president who has promised something to a whole nation or who has signed a treaty with other nations which depend on that treaty being kept and base their own national policies upon it, would not be well advised to say simply, "In cases of conflict, always break your word rather than lose one human life." In cases of this kind, keeping the promise would probably produce the best results, though the particular instance would have to be decided empirically. We would have to go through a detailed empirical examination to discover which rule, among all the rules we might adopt on the matter, would have the best consequences if adopted.

5. Well, then, why not just make the whole thing simple and say, "Always keep your promises except when breaking them will produce the most good," "Always conserve human life except when taking it will produce the most good"? In other words, "In every case do what will have the best consequences"—why not make this the Rule of Rules? To do so is to have act-utilitarianism with us once again; but why not? Is there anything more obvious in ethics than that we should always try to produce the most good possible?

"No," says the rule-utilitarian, "not if this rule means that we should always do the individual *act* that produces the most good possible. We must clearly distinguish rules from acts. 'Adopt the rule which will have the best consequences' is different from 'Do the act which will have the best consequences.' (When you say, 'Always do the most good,' this is ambiguous—it could mean either one.)" The rule-utilitarian, of course, recommends the former in preference to the latter;

for if everyone were to do acts which (taken individually) had the best consequences, the result would *not* in every case be a policy having the best consequences. For example, my not voting but doing something else instead may produce better consequences than my voting (my voting may have no effect at all); your not voting will do the same; and so on for every individual, as long as most *other* people vote. But the results would be very bad, for if each individual adopted the policy of not voting, nobody would vote. In other words, the rule "Vote, except in situations where not voting will do more good" is a rule which, if followed, would *not* produce the best consequences.

Another example: The rule "Don't kill except where killing will do the most good"—which the act-utilitarian would accept—is not, the rule-utilitarian would say, as good a rule to follow as "Don't kill except in self-defense . . ." (and other classes of acts which we discussed earlier). That is, the rule to prohibit killing except under special kinds of conditions specified in advance would do more good, if followed, than the rule simply to refrain except when not refraining will do more

good. The former is better, not just because people will rationalize themselves into believing that what they want to do will produce the most good in a particular situation (though this is very important), but also because when there are certain standard classes of exceptions built into the rule, there will be a greater *predictability* of the results of such actions; the criminal will know what will happen if he is caught. If the law said, "Killing is prohibited except when it will do the most good," what could you expect? Every would-be killer would think it would do the most good in his specific situation. And would you, a potential victim, feel more secure or less secure, if such a law were enacted? Every criminal would think that he would be exonerated even if he were caught, and every victim (or would-be victim) would fear that this would be so. The effects of having such a rule, then, would be far worse than the effects of having a general rule prohibiting killing, with certain classes of qualifications built into the rule.

There is, then, it would seem, a considerable difference between act-utilitarianism and rule-utilitarianism.

21

A Critique of Utilitarianism

Bernard Williams

Bernard Williams (1929–2003) was Professor of Philosophy at Oxford University and the University of California at Berkeley. He made important contributions to philosophy of mind, as well as to moral philosophy. In this essay he argues that utilitarianism violates personal integrity by commanding that we violate those principles that are central and deepest in our lives. That is, utilitarianism often calls on us to reject conscience and compunctions and do the "lesser of evils"—even when it is loathsome to do so. He illustrates this by two examples. In one, an unemployed scientist, George, is offered a job doing research in biological warfare, to which he is opposed. Yet it turns out that on utilitarian grounds he would be obligated to take this job, for it would be even worse if an unscrupulous scientist were involved in the research. In the second example, a soldier will shoot twenty innocent Indians unless Jim, an unlucky tourist, shoots them. If Jim kills one, the rest of the Indians will be freed. Jim finds killing abhorrent. Williams examines these cases carefully and argues that because the precepts of utilitarianism cause deep alienation, utilitarianism should be rejected as a moral theory.

Reprinted with permission from *Utilitarianism: For and Against*, by Bernard Williams and J. J. C. Smart (Cambridge University Press, 1973), pp. 97–99; 101–3; 108–9; 112–16.

Negative Responsibility: And Two Examples

Consequentialism is basically indifferent to whether a state of affairs consists in what I do, or is produced by what I do, where that notion is itself wide enough to include, for instance, situations in which other people do things which I have made them do, or allowed them to do, or encouraged them to do, or given them a chance to do. All that consequentialism is interested in is the idea of these doings being *consequences* of what I do, and that is a relation broad enough to include the relations just mentioned, and many others.

Just what the relation is, is a different question, and at least as obscure as the nature of its relative, cause and effect. It is not a question I shall try to pursue; I will rely on cases where I suppose that any consequentialist would be bound to regard the situations in question as consequences of what the agent does. There are cases where the supposed consequences stand in a rather remote relation to the action, cases which are sometimes difficult to assess from a practical point of view, but which raise no very interesting question for the present enquiry. The more interesting points about consequentialism lie rather elsewhere. There are certain situations in which the causation of the situation, the relation it has to what I do, is in no way remote or problematic in itself, and entirely justifies the claim that the situation is a consequence of what I do: for instance, it is quite clear, or reasonably clear, that if I do a certain thing, this situation will come about, and if I do not, it will not. So from a consequentialist point of view it goes into the calculation of consequences along with any other state of affairs accessible to me. Yet from some, at least, non-consequentialist points of view, there is a vital difference between some such situations and others: namely, that in some a vital link in the production of the eventual outcome is provided by *someone else's* doing something. But for consequentialism, all causal connexions are on the same level, and it makes no difference, so far as that goes, whether

175

the causation of a given state of affairs lies through another agent, or not.

Correspondingly, there is no relevant difference which consists *just* in one state of affairs being brought about by me, without intervention of other agents, and another being brought about through the intervention of other agents; although some genuinely causal differences involving a difference of value may correspond to that (as when, for instance, the other agents derive pleasure or pain from the transaction), that kind of difference will already be included in the specification of the state of affairs to be produced. Granted that the states of affairs have been adequately described in causally and evaluatively relevant terms, it makes no further comprehensible difference who produces them. It is because consequentialism attaches value ultimately to states of affairs, and its concern is with what states of affairs the world contains, that it essentially involves the notion of *negative responsibility:* that if I am ever responsible for anything, then I must be just as much responsible for things that I allow or fail to prevent, as I am for things that I myself, in the more everyday restricted sense, bring about. Those things also must enter my deliberations, as a responsible moral agent, on the same footing. What matters is what states of affairs the world contains, and so what matters with respect to a given action is what comes about if it is done, and what comes about if it is not done, and those are questions not intrinsically affected by the nature of the causal linkage, in particular by whether the outcome is partly produced by other agents.

The strong doctrine of negative responsibility flows directly from consequentialism's assignment of ultimate value to states of affairs. Looked at from another point of view, it can be seen also as a special application of something that is favoured in many moral outlooks not themselves consequentialist—something which, indeed, some thinkers have been disposed to regard as the essense of morality itself: a principle of impartiality. Such a principle will claim that there can be no relevant difference from a moral point of view

which consists just in the fact, not further explicable in general terms, that benefits or harms accrue to one person rather than to another—'it's me' can never in itself be a morally comprehensible reason. [By] this principle, familiar with regard to the reception of harms and benefits, we can see consequentialism as extending to their production: from the moral point of view, there is no comprehensible difference which consists just in my bringing about a certain outcome rather than someone else's producing it. That the doctrine of negative responsibility represents in this way the extreme of impartiality, and abstracts from the identity of the agent, leaving just a locus of causal intervention in the world—that fact is not merely a surface paradox. It helps to explain why consequentialism can seem to some to express a more serious attitude than nonconsequentialist views, why part of its appeal is to a certain kind of high-mindedness. Indeed, that is part of what is wrong with it.

For a lot of the time so far we have been operating at an exceedingly abstract level. This has been necessary in order to get clearer in general terms about the differences between consequentialist and other outlooks, an aim which is important if we want to know what features of them lead to what results for our thought. Now, however, let us look more concretely at two examples, to see what utilitarianism might say about them, what we might say about utilitarianism and, most importantly of all, what would be implied by certain ways of thinking about the situations. The examples are inevitably schematized, and they are open to the objection that they beg as many questions as they illuminate. There are two ways in particular in which examples in moral philosophy tend to beg important questions. One is that, as presented, they arbitrarily cut off and restrict the range of alternative courses of action—this objection might particularly be made against the first of my two examples. The second is that they inevitably present one with the situation as a going concern, and cut off questions about how the agent got into it, and correspondingly about moral considerations which might flow from that: this objection might perhaps specially arise with regard to the second of my two situations. These difficulties, however, just have to be accepted, and if anyone finds these examples cripplingly defective in this sort of respect, then he must in his own thought rework them in richer and less question-begging form. If he feels that no presentation of any imagined situation can ever be other than misleading in morality, and that there can never be any substitute for the concrete experienced complexity of actual moral situations, then this discussion, with him, must certainly grind to a halt: but then one may legitimately wonder whether every discussion with him about conduct will not grind to a halt, including any discussion about the actual situations, since discussion about how one would think and feel about situations somewhat different from the actual (that is to say, situations to that extent imaginary) plays an important role in discussion of the actual.

(1) George, who has just taken his Ph.D. in chemistry, finds it extremely difficult to get a job. He is not very robust in health, which cuts down the number of jobs he might be able to do satisfactorily. His wife has to go out to work to keep them, which itself causes a great deal of strain, since they have small children and there are severe problems about looking after them. The results of all this, especially on the children, are damaging. An older chemist who knows about this situation says that he can get George a decently paid job in a certain laboratory which pursues research into chemical and biological warfare. [CBW] George says that he cannot accept this, since he is opposed to chemical and biological warfare. The older man replies that he is not too keen on it himself, come to that, but after all George's refusal is not going to make the job or the laboratory go away; what is more, he happens to know that if George refuses the job, it will certainly go to a contemporary of George's who is not inhibited by any such scruples and is likely if appointed to push along the research with greater zeal than George would. Indeed, it is not merely concern for George and his family, but (to speak frankly and in confidence) some alarm about this other man's excess of zeal which has led the older man to offer to use his influence to get George the job. . . . George's wife, to whom he is deeply attached, has views (the details of which need not concern us) from which it follows that at least there is nothing particularly wrong with research into CBW. What should he do?

(2) Jim finds himself in the central square of a small South American town. Tied up against the wall are a row of twenty Indians, most terrified, a few defiant, in front of them several armed men in uniform. A heavy man in a sweat-stained khaki shirt turns out to be the captain in charge and, after a good deal of questioning of Jim which establishes that he got there by accident while on a botanical expedition, explains that the Indians are a random group of the inhabitants who, after recent acts of protest against the government, are just about to be killed to remind other possible protestors of the advantages of not protesting. However, since Jim is an honoured visitor from another land, the captain is happy to offer him a guest's privilege of killing one of the Indians himself. If Jim accepts, then as a special mark of the occasion, the other Indians will be let off. Of course, if Jim refuses, then there is no special occasion, and Pedro here will do what he was about to do when Jim arrived, and kill them all. Jim, with some desperate recollection of schoolboy fiction, wonders whether if he got hold of a gun, he could hold the captain, Pedro and the rest of the soldiers to threat, but it is quite clear from the set-up that nothing of that kind is going to work: any attempt at that sort of thing will mean that all the Indians will be killed, and himself. The men against the wall, and the other villagers, understand the situation, and are obviously begging him to accept. What should he do?

To these dilemmas, it seems to me that utilitarianism replies, in the first case, that George should accept the job, and in the second, that Jim should kill the Indian. Not only does utilitarianism give these answers but, if the situations are essentially as described and there are no further special factors, it regards them, it seems to me, as *obviously* the right answers. But many of us would certainly wonder whether, in (1), that could possibly be the right answer at all; and in the case of (2), even one who came to think that perhaps that was the answer, might well wonder whether it was obviously the answer. Nor is it just a question of the rightness or obviousness of these answers. It is also a question of what sort of considerations come into finding the answer. A feature of utilitarianism is that it cuts out a kind of consideration which for some others makes a difference to what they feel about such cases: a consideration involving the idea, as we might first and very simply put it, that each of us is specially responsible for what *he* does, rather than for what other people do. This is an idea closely connected with the value of integrity. It is often suspected that utilitarianism, at least in its direct forms, makes integrity as a value more or less unintelligible. I shall try to show that this suspicion is correct. Of course, even if that is correct, it would not necessarily follow that we should reject utilitarianism; perhaps, as utilitarians sometimes suggest, we should just forget about integrity, in favour of such things as a concern for the general good. However, if I am right, we cannot merely do that, since the reason why utilitarianism cannot understand integrity is that it cannot coherently describe the relations between a man's projects and his actions.

Two Kinds of Remoter Effect

A lot of what we have to say about this question will be about the relations between my projects and other people's projects. But before we get on to that, we should first ask whether we are assuming too hastily what the utilitarian answers to the dilemmas will be. In terms of more direct effects of the possible decisions, there does not indeed seem much doubt about the answer in either case; but it might be said that in terms of more remote or less evident effects counterweights might be found to enter the utilitarian scales. Thus the ef-

fect on George of a decision to take the job might be invoked, or its effect on others who might know of his decision. The possibility of there being more beneficent labours in the future from which he might be barred or disqualified might be mentioned; and so forth. Such effects—in particular, possible effects on the agent's character, and effects on the public at large—are often invoked by utilitarian writers dealing with problems about lying or promise-breaking, and some similar considerations might be invoked here.

There is one very general remark that is worth making about arguments of this sort. The certainty that attaches to these hypotheses about possible effects is usually pretty low; in some cases, indeed, the hypothesis invoked is so implausible that it would scarcely pass if it were not being used to deliver the respectable moral answer, as in the standard fantasy that one of the effects of one's telling a particular lie is to weaken the disposition of the world at large to tell the truth. The demands on the certainty or probability of these beliefs as beliefs about particular actions are much milder than they would be on beliefs favouring the unconventional course. It may be said that this is as it should be, since the presumption must be in favour of the conventional course: but that scarcely seems a *utilitarian* answer, unless utilitarianism has already taken off in the direction of not applying the consequences to the particular act at all.

Leaving aside that very general point, I want to consider now two types of effect that are often invoked by utilitarians, and which might be invoked in connexion with these imaginary cases. The attitude or tone involved in invoking these effects may sometimes seem peculiar; but that sort of peculiarity soon becomes familiar in utilitarian discussions, and indeed it can be something of an achievement to retain a sense of it.

First, there is the psychological effect on the agent. Our descriptions of these situations have not so far taken account of how George or Jim will be after they have taken the one course or the other; and it might be said that if they take the course which seemed at first the utilitarian one, the effects on them will be in fact bad enough and extensive enough to cancel out the initial utilitarian advantages of that course. Now there is one version of this effect in which, for a utilitarian, some confusion must be involved, namely that in which the agent feels bad, his subsequent conduct and relations are crippled and so on, *because he thinks that he has done the wrong thing*—for if the balance of outcomes was as it appeared to be *before* invoking this effect, then he has not (from the utilitarian point of view) done the wrong thing. So that version of the effect, for a rational and utilitarian agent, could not possibly make any difference to the assessment of right and wrong. However, perhaps he is not a thoroughly rational agent, and is disposed to have bad feelings whichever he decided to do. Now such feelings, which are from a strictly utilitarian point of view irrational—nothing, a utilitarian can point out, is advanced by having them—cannot, consistently, have any great weight in a utilitarian calculation. I shall consider in a moment an argument to suggest that they should have no weight at all in it. But short of that, the utilitarian could reasonably say that such feelings should not be encouraged, even if we accept their existence, and that to give them a lot of weight is to encourage them. Or, at the very best, even if they are straightforwardly and without any discount to be put into the calculation, their weight must be small: they are after all (and at best) one man's feelings.

That consideration might seem to have particular force in Jim's case. In George's case, his feelings represent a larger proportion of what is to be weighed, and are more commensurate in character with other items in the calculation. In Jim's case, however, his feelings might seem to be of very little weight compared with other things that are at stake. There is a powerful and recognizable appeal that can be made on this point: as that a refusal by Jim to do what he has been invited to do would be a kind of self-indulgent squeamishness. That is an appeal which can be made by other than utilitarians—indeed, there are some uses of

it which cannot be consistently made by utilitarians, as when it essentially involves the idea that there is something dishonourable about such self-indulgence. But in some versions it is a familiar, and it must be said a powerful, weapon of utilitarianism. One must be clear, though, about what it can and cannot accomplish. The most it can do, so far as I can see, is to invite one to consider how seriously, and for what reasons, one feels that what one is invited to do is (in these circumstances) wrong, and in particular, to consider that question from the utilitarian point of view. When the agent is not seeing the situation from a utilitarian point of view, the appeal cannot force him to do so; and if he does come round to seeing it from a utilitarian point of view, there is virtually nothing left for the appeal to do. If he does not see it from a utilitarian point of view, he will not see his resistance to the invitation, and the unpleasant feelings he associates with accepting it, *just* as disagreeable experiences of his; they figure rather as emotional expressions of a thought that to accept would be wrong. He may be asked, as by the appeal, to consider whether he is right, and indeed whether he is fully serious, in thinking that. But the assertion of the appeal, that he is being self-indulgently squeamish, will not itself answer that question, or even help to answer it, since it essentially tells him to regard his feelings just as unpleasant experiences of his, and he cannot, by doing that, answer the question they pose when they are precisely not so regarded, but are regarded as indications of what he thinks is right and wrong. If he does come round fully to the utilitarian point of view, then of course he will regard these feelings just as unpleasant experiences of his. And once Jim—at least—has come to see them in that light, there is nothing left for the appeal to do, since *of course* his feelings, so regarded, are of virtually no weight at all in relation to the other things at stake. The 'squeamishness' appeal is not an argument which adds in a hitherto neglected consideration. Rather, it is an invitation to consider the situation, and one's own feelings, from a utilitarian point of view.

The reason why the squeamishness appeal can be very unsettling, and one can be unnerved by the suggestion of self-indulgence in going against utilitarian considerations, is not that we are utilitarians who are uncertain what utilitarian value to attach to our moral feelings, but that we are partially at least not utilitarians, and cannot regard our moral feelings merely as objects of utilitarian value. Because our moral relation to the world is partly given by such feelings, and by a sense of what we can or cannot 'live with,' to come to regard those feelings from a purely utilitarian point of view, that is to say, as happenings outside one's moral self, is to lose a sense of one's moral identity; to lose, in the most literal way, one's integrity. At this point utilitarianism alienates one from one's moral feelings; we shall see a little later how, more basically, it alienates one from one's actions as well.

If, then, one is really going to regard one's feelings from a strictly utilitarian point of view, Jim should give very little weight at all to his; it seems almost indecent, in fact, once one has taken that point of view, to suppose that he should give any at all. In George's case one might feel that things were slightly different. It is interesting, though, that one reason why one might think that—namely that one person principally affected is his wife—is very dubiously available to a utilitarian. George's wife has some reason to be interested in George's integrity and his sense of it; the Indians, quite properly, have no interest in Jim's. But it is not at all clear how utilitarianism would describe that difference.

There is an argument, and a strong one, that a strict utilitarian should give not merely small extra weight, in calculations of right and wrong, to feelings of this kind, but that he should give absolutely no weight to them at all. This is based on the point, which we have already seen, that if a course of action is, before taking these sorts of feelings into account, utilitarianly preferable, then bad feelings about that kind of action will be from a utilitarian point of view irrational. Now it might be thought that even if that is so, it would

not mean that in a utilitarian calculation such feelings should not be taken into account; it is after all a well-known boast of utilitarianism that it is a realistic outlook which seeks the best in the world as it is, and takes any form of happiness or unhappiness into account. While a utilitarian will no doubt seek to diminish the incidence of feelings which are utilitarianly irrational—or at least of disagreeable feelings which are so—he might be expected to take them into account while they exist. This is without doubt classical utilitarian doctrine, but there is good reason to think that utilitarianism cannot stick to it without embracing results which are startlingly unacceptable and perhaps self-defeating.

Suppose that there is in a certain society a racial minority. Considering merely the ordinary interests of the other citizens, as opposed to their sentiments, this minority does no particular harm; we may suppose that it does not confer any very great benefits either. Its presence is in those terms neutral or mildly beneficial. However, the other citizens have such prejudices that they find the sight of this group, even the knowledge of its presence, very disagreeable. Proposals are made for removing in some way this minority. If we assume various quite plausible things (as that programmes to change the majority sentiment are likely to be protracted and ineffective) then even if the removal would be unpleasant for the minority, a utilitarian calculation might well end up favouring this step, especially if the minority were a rather small minority and the majority were very severely prejudiced, that is to say, were made very severely uncomfortable by the presence of the minority.

A utilitarian might find that conclusion embarrassing; and not merely because of its nature, but because of the grounds on which it is reached. While a utilitarian might be expected to take into account certain other sorts of consequences of the prejudice, as that a majority prejudice is likely to be displayed in conduct disagreeable to the minority, and so forth, he might be made to wonder whether the unpleasant experiences of the prejudiced people should be allowed, *merely as such,* to count. If he does count them, merely as such, then he has once more separated himself from a body of ordinary moral thought which he might have hoped to accommodate; he may also have started on the path of defeating his own view of things. For one feature of these sentiments is that they are from the utilitarian point of view itself irrational, and a thoroughly utilitarian person would either not have them, or if he found that he did tend to have them, would himself seek to discount them. Since the sentiments in question are such that a rational utilitarian would discount them in himself, it is reasonable to suppose that he should discount them in his calculations about society; it does seem quite unreasonable for him to give just as much weight to feelings—considered just in themselves, one must recall, as experiences of those that have them—which are essentially based on views which are from a utilitarian point of view irrational, as to those which accord with utilitarian principles. Granted this idea, it seems reasonable for him to rejoin a body of moral thought in other respects congenial to him, and discount those sentiments, just considered in themselves, totally, on the principle that no pains or discomforts are to count in the utilitarian sum which their subjects have just because they hold views which are by utilitarian standards irrational. But if he accepts that, then in the cases we are at present considering no extra weight at all can be put in for bad feelings of George or Jim about their choices, if those choices are, leaving out those feelings, on the first round utilitarianly rational.

Integrity

The [two] situations have in common that if the agent does not do a certain disagreeable thing someone else will, and in Jim's situation at least the result, the state of affairs after the other man has acted, if he does, will be worse than after Jim has acted, if Jim does. The same, on a smaller scale, is true of George's case. I have already suggested that it is inherent in consequentialism that it offers a strong doctrine of negative responsibility: if I know that if I do X, O_1 will eventuate, and if I refrain from doing X, O_2 will, and that O_2 is worse than O_1, then I am responsible for O_2 if I refrain voluntarily from doing X. 'You could have prevented it,' as will be said, and truly, to Jim, if he refuses, by the relatives of the other Indians.

In the present cases, the situation of O_2 includes another agent bringing about results worse than O_1. So far as O_2 has been identified up to this point—merely as the worse outcome which will eventuate if I refrain from doing X—we might equally have said that what that other brings about is O_2; but that would be to underdescribe the situation. For what occurs if Jim refrains from action is not solely twenty Indians dead, but *Pedro's killing twenty Indians,* and that is not a result which Pedro brings about, though the death of the Indians is. We can say: what one does is not included in the outcome of what one does, while what another does can be included in the outcome of what one does. For that to be so, as the terms are now being used, only a very weak condition has to be satisfied: for Pedro's killing the Indians to be the outcome of Jim's refusal, it only has to be causally true that if Jim had not refused, Pedro would not have done it.

That may be enough for us to speak, in some sense, of Jim's responsibility for that outcome, if it occurs; but it is certainly not enough, it is worth noticing, for us to speak of Jim's *making* those things happen. For granted this way of their coming about, he could have made them happen only by making Pedro shoot, and there is no acceptable sense in which his refusal makes Pedro shoot. If the captain had said on Jim's refusal, 'you leave me with no alternative' he would have been lying, like most who use that phrase. While the deaths, and the killing, may be the outcome of Jim's refusal, it is misleading to think, in such a case, of Jim having an *effect* on the world through the medium (as it happens) of Pedro's acts; for this is to leave Pedro out of the picture in his essential role of one who has intentions and projects, projects for realizing which Jim's refusal would leave an opportunity. Instead of thinking in terms of supposed effects of Jim's projects on Pedro, it is more revealing to think in terms of the effects of Pedro's projects on Jim's decision.

Utilitarianism would do well then to acknowledge the evident fact that among the things that make people happy is not only making other people happy, but being taken up or involved in any of a vast range of projects, or—if we waive the evangelical and moralizing associations of the word—commitments. One can be committed to such things as a person, a cause, an institution, a career, one's own genius, or the pursuit of danger.

Now none of these is itself the *pursuit of happiness:* by an exceedingly ancient platitude, it is not at all clear that there could be anything which was just that, or at least anything that had the slightest chance of being successful. Happiness, rather, requires being involved in, or at least content with, something else. It is not impossible for utilitarianism to accept that point: it does not have to be saddled with a naïve and absurd philosophy of mind about the relation between desire and happiness. What it does have to say is that if such commitments are worthwhile, then pursuing the projects that flow from them, and realizing some of those projects, will make the person for whom they are worthwhile, happy. It may be that to claim that is still wrong: it may well be that a commitment can make sense to a man (can make sense of his life) without his supposing that it will make him *happy*. But that is not the present point, let us grant to utilitarianism that all worthwhile human projects must conduce, one way or another, to happiness. The point is that even if that is true, it does not follow, nor could it possibly be true, that those projects are themselves projects of pursuing happiness. One has to believe in, or at least want, or quite minimally be content with, other things for there to be anywhere that happiness can come from.

Utilitarianism, then, should be willing to agree that its general aim of maximizing happiness does not imply that what everyone is doing is just pursuing happiness. On the contrary, people have to be pursuing other things. What those other things may be, utilitarianism, sticking to its professed empirical stance, should be prepared just to find out. No doubt some possible projects it will want to discourage, on the grounds that their being pursued involves a negative balance of happiness to others: though even there, the unblinking accountant's eye of the strict utilitarian will have something to put in the positive column, the satisfactions of the destructive agent. Beyond that, there will be a vast variety of generally beneficent or at least harmless projects; and some no doubt will take the form not just of tastes or fancies, but of what I have called 'commitments.' It may even be that the utilitarian researcher will find that many of those with commitments, who have really identified themselves with objects outside themselves, who are thoroughly involved with other persons or institutions or activities or causes, are actually happier than those whose projects and wants are not like that. If so, that is an important piece of utilitarian empirical lore.

When I say 'happier' here, I have in mind the sort of consideration which any utilitarian would be committed to accepting: as for instance that such people are less likely to have a breakdown or commit suicide. Of course that is not all that is actually involved, but the point in this argument is to use to the maximum degree utilitarian notions in order to locate a breaking point in utilitarian thought. In appealing to this strictly utilitarian notion, I am being more consistent with utilitarianism than Smart is. In his struggles with the problem of the brain-electrode man, Smart commends the idea that 'happy' is a partly evaluative term, in the sense that we call 'happiness' those kinds of satisfaction which, as things are, we approve of. But *by what standard* is this surplus element of approval supposed, from a utilitarian point of view, to be allocated? There is no source for it, on a strictly utilitarian view, except further degrees of satisfaction, but there are none of those available, or the problem would not arise. Nor does it help to appeal to the fact that we dislike in prospect things which we like when we get there, for from a utilitarian point of view it would seem that the original dislike was merely irrational or based on an error. Smart's argument at this point seems to be embarrassed by a well-known utilitarian uneasiness which comes from a feeling that it is not respectable to ignore the 'deep,' while not having anywhere left in human life to locate it.

Let us now go back to the agent as utilitarian, and his higher-order project of maximizing desirable outcomes. At this level, he is committed only to that: what the outcome will actually consist of will depend entirely on the facts, on what persons with what projects and what potential satisfactions there are within calculable reach of the causal levers near which he finds himself. His own substantial projects and commitments come into it, but only as one lot among others—they potentially provide one set of satisfactions among those which he may be able to assist from where he happens to be. He is the agent of the satisfaction system who happens to be at a particular point at a particular time: in Jim's case, our man in South America. His own decisions as a utilitarian agent are a function of all the satisfactions which he can effect from where he is: and this means that the projects of others, to an indeterminately great extent, determine his decision.

This may be so either positively or negatively. It will be so positively if agents within the causal field of his decision have projects which are at any rate harmless, and so should be assisted. It will equally be so, but negatively, if there is an agent within the causal field whose projects are harmful, and have to be frustrated to maximize desirable outcomes. So it is with Jim and the soldier Pedro. On the utilitarian view, the undesirable projects of other people as much determine, in this negative way, one's decisions as the desirable ones do positively: if those people were not there, or had different projects, the causal nexus would be different, and it is the actual state of the causal nexus which determines the decision. The determination to an indefinite degree of my decisions by other people's projects is just another aspect of my unlimited responsibility to act for the best in a causal framework formed to a considerable extent by their projects.

The decision so determined is, for utilitarianism, the right decision. But what if it conflicts with some project of mine? This, the utilitarian will say, has already been dealt with: the satisfaction to you of fulfilling your project, and any satisfactions to others of your so doing, have already been through the calculating device and have been found inadequate. Now in the case of many sorts of projects, that is a perfectly reasonable sort of answer. But in the case of projects of the sort I have called 'commitments,' those with which one is more deeply and extensively involved and identified, this cannot just by itself be an adequate answer, and there may be no adequate answer at all. For, to take the extreme sort of case, how can a man, as a utilitarian agent, come to regard as one satisfaction among others, and a dispensable one, a project or attitude round which he has built his life, just because someone else's projects have so structured the causal scene that that is how the utilitarian sum comes out?

The point here is not, as utilitarians may hasten to say, that if the project or attitude is that central to his life, then to abandon it will be very disagreeable to him and great loss of utility will be involved. I have already argued in section 4* that it is not like that; on the contrary, once he is prepared to look at it like that, the argument in any serious case is over anyway. The point is that he is identified with his actions as flowing from projects and attitudes which in some cases he takes seriously at the deepest level, as what his life is about (or, in some cases, this section of his life—seriousness is not necessarily the same as persistence). It is absurd to demand of such a man, when the sums come in from the utility network which the projects of others have in part determined, that he should just step aside from his own project and decision and acknowledge the decision which utilitarian calculation requires. It is to alienate him in a real sense from his actions and

*Not included in this selection—Editor.

the source of his action in his own convictions. It is to make him into a channel between the input of everyone's projects, including his own, and an output of optimistic decision; but this is to neglect the extent to which *his* actions and his decisions have to be seen as the actions and decisions which flow from the projects and attitudes with which he is most closely identified. It is thus, in the most literal sense, an attack on his integrity.

These sorts of considerations do not in themselves give solutions to practical dilemmas such as those provided by our examples; but I hope they help to provide other ways of thinking about them. In fact, it is not hard to see that in George's case, viewed from this perspective, the utilitarian solution would be wrong. Jim's case is different, and harder. But if (as I suppose) the utilitarian is probably right in this case, that is not to be found out just by asking the utilitarian's questions. Discussions of it—and I am not going to try to carry it further here—will have to take seriously the distinction between my killing someone, and its coming about because of what I do that someone else kills them: a distinction based, not so much on the distinction between action and inaction, as on the distinction between my projects and someone else's projects. At least it will have to start by taking that seriously, as utilitarianism does not; but then it will have to build out from there by asking why that distinction seems to have less, or a different, force in this case than it has in George's. One question here would be how far one's powerful objection to killing people just is, in fact, an application of a powerful objection to their being killed. Another dimension of that is the issue of how much it matters that the people at risk are actual, and there, as opposed to hypothetical, or future, or merely elsewhere.

There are many other considerations that could come into such a question, but the immediate point of all this is to draw one particular contrast with utilitarianism: that to reach a grounded decision in such a case should not be regarded as a matter of just discounting one's reactions, impulses and deeply held projects in the face of the pattern of utilities, nor yet merely adding them in—but in the first instance of trying to understand them.

Of course, time and circumstances are unlikely to make a grounded decision, in Jim's case at least, possible. It might not even be decent. Instead of thinking in a rational and systematic way either about utilities or about the value of human life, the relevance of the people at risk being present, and so forth, the presence of the people at risk may just have its effect. The significance of the immediate should not be underestimated. Philosophers, not only utilitarian ones, repeatedly urge one to view the world *sub specie aeternitatis,* but for most human purposes that is not a good *species* to view it under. If we are not agents of the universal satisfaction system, we are not primarily janitors of any system of values, even our own: very often, we just act, as a possibly confused result of the situation in which we are engaged. That, I suspect, is very often an exceedingly good thing.

Utilitarianism is in more than one way an important subject; at least I hope it is, or these words, and this book, will have been wasted. One important feature of it, which I have tried to bring out, is the number of dimensions in which it runs against the complexities of moral thought: in some part because of its consequentialism, in some part because of its view of happiness, and so forth. A common element in utilitarianism's showing in all these respects, I think, is its great simple-mindedness. This is not at all the same thing as lack of intellectual sophistication: utilitarianism, both in theory and in practice, is alarmingly good at combining technical complexity with simple-mindedness. Nor is it the same as simple-heartedness, which it is at least possible (with something of an effort and in private connexions) to regard as a virtue. Simple-mindedness consists in having too few thoughts and feelings to match the world as it really is. In private life and the field of personal morality it is often possible to survive in that state—indeed, the very statement of the problem for that case is over-simple, since the question of what moral demands life makes is not independent of what one's morality demands of it. But the demands of political reality and the complexities of political thought are obstinately what they are, and in face of them the simple-mindedness of utilitarianism disqualifies it totally.

The important issues that utilitarianism raises should be discussed in contexts more rewarding than that of utilitarianism itself. The day cannot be too far off in which we hear no more of it.

22

Eleven Objections to Utilitarianism

STERLING HARWOOD

Sterling Harwood received his Ph.D. from Cornell University. He teaches communications and philosophy in San Jose, CA.

In this essay Harwood examines eleven criticisms of various forms of utilitarianism (he mentions twelve forms), arguing that the most plausible form of utilitarianism is act-utilitarianism (see reading 19), as opposed to rule-utilitarianism (see reading 20). However, act-utilitarianism is still subject to severe criticisms, including the criticisms that utilitarianism is unjust, fails to grant sufficient weight to promise keeping, enjoins going into an experience machine (see reading 16), and gives undue weight to animals.

A. Introduction

I will discuss eleven significant objections to utilitarianism, though I will not accept all eleven. My purpose is not to bury utilitarianism once and for all but to survey a large number of objections and provoke further discussion, although I may perhaps put a few more nails in utilitarianism's coffin. I start by trying to clarify the nature of utilitarianism since it has so many versions both drawing criticism and developing as responses to criticism. Here is a list of twelve versions I will at least mention below (though some of these can be combined to form still more versions): motive-utilitarianism, act-utilitarianism, rule-utilitarianism, average utilitarianism, total utilitarianism, hedonistic utilitarianism, eudaimonistic utilitarianism, negative utilitarianism, welfare-utilitarianism, preference-satisfaction utilitarianism, felt-satisfaction utilitarianism, and ideal utilitarianism. Of course these twelve versions of utilitarianism do not correspond to the eleven objections to utilitarianism I consider, but many of these versions were developed to deal with objections to other versions of utilitarianism. Indeed, many critics who thought they had finally driven a stake through the heart of utilitarianism have only seen utilitarianism live on by being transformed into another version.

Utilitarianism is a consequentialist (that is, teleological) moral principle. As a moral principle, utilitarianism tells us how we should act. Consequentialism is not itself a moral principle but a category into which some moral principles fit. Consequentialism insists that an act is determined to be morally right (or morally wrong) exclusively by particular consequences of doing that act. (Consequentialism and utilitarianism can go beyond acts to include evaluations of institutions, policies, motives, and persons, but for simplicity I shall focus on acts and deemphasize versions of utilitarianism such as motive-utilitarianism.) Some include the maximizing theory of the right as a definition of consequentialism, but this would make the definition of consequentialism under-inclusive because we can imagine moral principles that value consequences alone but do not require maximizing good consequences (because, for example, there could be two different kinds of consequences to maximize and no rule for trading off between them). The particular consequences determining the rightness (or wrongness) of the act in question are specified not by consequentialism itself but by a particular consequentialist principle. Utilitarianism is the particular consequentialist principle that specifically concerns utility. Utility is psychological satisfaction (for example, pleasure, happiness, and well-being). Since utility is utilitarianism's only value, utilitarianism is a monistic rather than a pluralistic moral principle. And it is utilitarianism's monism rather than its consequentialism that explains why utilitarianism requires maximizing utility. Because utility is the only value, there is no other value to check or limit the logical approach of requiring the gain of more and more of the only value.

Many versions of utilitarianism differ primarily according to which psychological satisfaction they emphasize. For example, hedonistic utilitarianism stresses pleasure; preference-satisfaction utilitarianism stresses satisfaction of preferences; ideal utilitarianism stresses what would be desired under ideal conditions; negative utilitarianism stresses that avoiding dissatisfaction is more important than gaining satisfaction; and welfare-utilitarianism stresses what is in the best interests of those whose well-being is in question. And of course, many of these psychological satisfactions interrelate and overlap with one another. Disutility—psychological dissatisfaction (for example, pain and unhappiness)—is the opposite of utility.

Utilitarianism essentially specifies that the consequences that determine an act's rightness (or wrongness) are the psychological satisfactions that the act causes. Utilitarianism is a monistic moral principle, since it implies that there is only one thing that has moral value, namely, psychological satisfaction. Since there is no other moral value to check or limit the value of psychological satisfaction, utilitarianism says an act is right only to the extent that it maximizes these satisfactions, that is, produces the greatest balance of satisfaction over dissatisfaction for all in the long run. If only dissatisfaction is available, then utilitarianism says an act is right to the extent that it minimizes dissatisfaction. This is not a second or separate value in utilitarianism; for we can represent utilitarianism as claiming that an act is right to the extent that its expected consequences fall as far to the right as possible on the following scale. The far left ranges to an infinite amount of dissatisfaction, the 0 represents where the amount

of satisfaction equals the amount of dissatisfaction, and the far right ranges to an infinite amount of satisfaction.

The left and right directions on the scale should not be confused with the political left or political right. Indeed, utilitarians have historically promoted governmental reforms, (for example, abolishing slavery, improving prisons, and feeding, clothing, and housing the poor) that the political left has also endorsed.

B. The Eleven Objections

1. *Utilitarianism Is Overly Demanding*

Perhaps the first objection that occurs to students is that utilitarianism appears to demand an extreme amount of self-sacrifice from us. This stems from utilitarianism's monism, its insistence that only one thing has moral value, and its insistence that we obtain more and more of that thing without limit; for there is no other value to counterbalance or limit it. Must we really sell all of our nonessential material goods (for example, musical recordings and baseball cards) and give the money to worthy charitable causes (for example, relief of famine)? Further, must we be ready to sacrifice friends and loved ones by acting impartially to maximize satisfaction? Bentham stated the utilitarian formula "Everybody to count for one, and nobody for more than one."[1] Utilitarianism's impartiality stems from its counting everyone's satisfaction as equally valuable (so long as the amount of the satisfaction is the same). Later, we will see that eudaimonistic utilitarianism seems to depart from Bentham's statement, and we will see an objection to the statement from those who believe that interpersonal comparisons of utility are impossible. Alleged counterexamples often hurled at utilitarianism include: 1) the instance where utilitarianism requires that the least useful person in a lifeboat lost at sea be killed and eaten whenever necessary to keep the other persons in the lifeboat alive long enough to be rescued; and 2) the instance where a healthy and innocent person comes in for a checkup, but his doctor can maximize satisfaction by killing him and using his organs to save the lives of five or more other people. Indeed, if the person in charge of the lifeboat or the doctor, respectively, can make these facts clear enough to us, then utilitarianism requires us to submit to being killed rather than to resist.

So we can see why a version of Objection 1, called the "objection from integrity," says that utilitarianism requires us to have a psychologically impossible (or nearly impossible) impartiality and detachment from our own lives, projects, friends, and loved ones. Of course, utilitarianism scarcely requires us to attempt the impossible, since that would be futile and would fail to maximize *expected* satisfaction; for the satisfaction expected from an act known to be impossible must be nil. The objection thus seems to be merely a complaint that morality is sometimes or oftentimes difficult to live up to. But this is hardly a conclusive objection. Nobody ever said it was going to be easy to be moral. Indeed, all or almost all moral principles require us to give up our lives under some scenarios. Even the most self-centered of moral principles, ethical egoism, which commands each person to maximize his or her own satisfaction, requires us to commit suicide the moment when the satisfaction we can expect in the rest of our lives is outweighed—even slightly—by the dissatisfaction we can expect in the rest of our lives. Every moral principle seems to require extreme actions under some scenario or other. And it would also be extreme to require this alternative: "*Never* do any extreme acts." So the objection that utilitarianism sometimes leads to extreme self-sacrifice or extreme acts is inconclusive.

Moreover, I suspect that utilitarianism is not as extremely demanding in everyday life as many think. Here is how a utilitarian could argue that utilitarianism is easy enough to pursue in every-

day life. All indications are that overpopulation and depletion of needed natural resources will get worse. Therefore, rather than give almost all of one's wealth away now, one ought to invest one's wealth wisely, probably making more wealth, and hold one's wealth in reserve for these more troubled times ahead, when charity will be needed more than ever and when the stakes will be even greater. In the meantime, one can gain satisfaction from the security of having wise investments and from the knowledge that one is self-sufficient and not a charity case oneself. Indeed, some investment activities (for example, following the business news) and investments (for example, collectibles such as baseball cards, rare musical recordings, and other art) are intrinsically satisfying for many investors. As long as the population explosion continues and needed natural resources continue to be depleted faster than they are replaced, one can maximize satisfaction by wisely investing his or her wealth to make more wealth and by holding it in reserve to help with the greater calamity likely to occur in the foreseeable future. If these trends continue through the rest of one's life, with a greater calamity always likely to occur in the foreseeable future, then one can then leave all of his or her amassed wealth to the charity one believes will maximize satisfaction. One's leaving wealth to others at one's death is no personal sacrifice at all, since "you can't take it with you when you die." But one's legal will must sacrifice some satisfaction of one's relatives if they are not needy enough. Some critics of utilitarianism will doubtless say, "How convenient!" But that misses the point here, which is that at least utilitarianism would dodge Objection 1, which claims utilitarianism is not convenient for individuals but overly demanding.

Finally, in case one thinks that utilitarianism will still be overly demanding in too many cases, consider these two arguments by Kurt Baier:

Surely, in the absence of any *special* reasons for preferring someone else's interests, *everyone's* interests are best served if *everyone* puts his own interests first. For, by and large, everyone is himself the best judge of what is in his own best interests, since everyone usually knows best what his plans, aims, ambitions, or aspirations are. Moreover, everyone is more diligent in the promotion of his own interests than that of others.[2]

2. Utilitarianism Eliminates Supererogation

Some have argued that since utilitarianism leaves no room for supererogation (that is, self-sacrifice above and beyond the call of duty), utilitarianism objectionably flies in the face of commonsense morality, which recognizes supererogation. For example, during a hasty retreat a soldier might stop to pick up and carry a fellow soldier many hazardous yards to safety, and endure being wounded. There seems to be nothing *above* or *beyond* the call of utilitarian duty, since utilitarianism says our duty is to *maximize* satisfaction. Of course, one cannot cause an amount of satisfaction above or beyond the maximum amount. So we seem to face a dilemma. Either we reject utilitarianism, or else we reject supererogation.

But this is a false dilemma, since ties are overlooked. Utilitarianism allows that the expected satisfaction of two (or even more) alternatives can be tied for the maximal amount. One of these alternatives can involve more sacrifice (dissatisfaction) for us than that expected from the other alternatives tied for the maximal amount of satisfaction. Utilitarianism cannot *require* us to make this sacrifice by choosing this alternative among those that are tied, since all of those alternatives are equally acceptable, but utilitarianism *permits* us to choose the alternative that sacrifices more of our satisfaction than the other alternatives do. So utilitarianism does allow for moral self-sacrifice that is not morally required (that is, moral self-sacrifice beyond the call of duty).

One may object that ties are so uncommon that utilitarianism still leaves too little room for supererogation, which is the main point of Objection 2. But ties are probably more common than

many of us think. For example, Raymond D. Gastil interprets James Q. Wilson's research as pointing out

that almost all recent major American studies testing hypotheses that major long-term behavior changes result from particular social policy or educational inputs have provided inconclusive or negative findings. Thus, studies have shown that the type of school or educational method makes no difference (Coleman report). . . . [Wilson] suggests, and it is probably true, that in real-life situations there is too much going on, too many cycles of reinforcement stretched over too many years, for particular interventions to get up out of the noise.[3]

This feature of ties is notorious in the so-called dismal science, economics, the social science utilitarianism has perhaps influenced most. Some joke that one can lay all the economists from end to end and never reach a definite conclusion. And some joke that the search continues for the one-armed economist, the one who cannot say "On the other hand. . . . " The serious undertone to these jokes is that utilitarianism all too often has us consider two or more alternatives which, as far as we can tell, are tied in the amount of satisfaction they will produce. Perhaps this is why some joke that economists know the price of everything but the value of nothing.

3. Utilitarianism Is Unjust

Utilitarianism is often criticized for failing to treat retributive justice (giving the guilty and only the guilty the punishment they deserve in fair proportion to the severity of their respective crimes) as having intrinsic moral importance. Familiar counterexamples to utilitarianism here include: 1) a case where a scientific genius murders his wife just as he is about to develop a cure for cancer, and giving him the punishment he justly deserves will delay the development of the cure for years or decades; 2) a case involving racial violence, where a local woman has been raped and murdered, and angry mobs are about to take the law into their own hands by executing people of the opposite race whom they suspect of being involved in the crime. The sheriff can easily prevent all this violence, which is likely to kill innocent people, by framing the useless town drunk who remembers nothing about the night in question and who has no alibi. The sheriff alone knows that he is innocent because he locked the drunk up for public drunkenness at the same time the crime was committed in the middle of the night; and 3) a case where parking offenders (or other minor offenders) are punished way out of proportion to the severity of their offenses whenever the deterrent effect of the unjustly severe punishment produces so much satisfaction from a nearly perfectly obeyed law that it maximizes satisfaction even while leading to the torture and execution of that one driver in a million or more who is foolish enough to break the law. Critics object that utilitarianism would unjustly: 1) fail to give the scientist the severe punishment he deserves; 2) frame the innocent town drunk; and 3) sometimes torture and execute people for merely parking illegally.

Critics also charge that utilitarianism violates distributive justice (giving each person his or her fair share of benefits and burdens in society). Familiar counterexamples to utilitarianism here include: 1) the case where, instead of fairly and randomly determining who should bear the burden of dying by casting lots, the occupants of a lifeboat lost at sea kill and eat the least useful occupant as a last resort to keep all others alive long enough to be rescued; 2) a case of secretly killing a healthy man just in for a routine checkup in order to maximize satisfaction by using his various organs in a number of life-saving operations; and 3) a case of neglecting to give ordinary people their fair share of benefits and instead indulging so-called utility monsters, people with nearly insatiable appetites for wealth and for whom the general economic law of diminishing marginal utility of wealth does not apply because they

are so miserly and greedy that each new unit of wealth obtained causes far more satisfaction for the utility monster than it would for those with normal human psychologies.

Utilitarians often dismiss such examples as unrealistic and thus irrelevant to our real world of troubles. Utilitarians say they have done enough to develop a moral principle that deals with the problems of real life, and need not develop a moral principle that covers every imaginable problem in every fantasy land. But the utilitarian defense that these cases are unrealistic misses the point. How realistic or unrealistic a case is surely is a matter of degree. These cases are realistic enough that some of them can and will eventually occur in real life, and when they do utilitarianism will be refuted, a refutation we can know in advance by thinking ahead.

Indeed, there have been, after all, some lifeboat cases where cannibalism has been a last resort to survive. And there have been some awfully greedy people in the history of the world. Perhaps they were utility monsters. And some would say that at least one of these situations recently occurred in California, and even one of these counterexamples is enough to refute utilitarianism. The nearly all-white jury that acquitted the police officers of nearly all criminal charges in the famous videotaped beating of motorist Rodney King has been called the jury from another planet! But of course it was a real jury. Suppose you were one of these jurors who believed there was a reasonable doubt on almost all the charges against the policemen but who also predicted, as many others did, that rioting would occur if almost all the policemen were acquitted of these charges. So, you could realistically change your vote from "not guilty beyond a reasonable doubt" to "guilty beyond a reasonable doubt" on every charge and create a mistrial, preventing the policemen from being acquitted on any charge, allowing a new trial, and probably preventing enough violence to maximize satisfaction with your vote of "guilty beyond a reasonable doubt."

I conclude that at least some of these counter-examples concerning retributive and distributive justice seem realistic enough to refute utilitarianism, especially since truth is often stranger than fiction.

4. Utilitarianism Fails to Take Promises Seriously Enough

Utilitarianism implies that keeping one's promises has no intrinsic moral value apart from any satisfaction it causes but has only instrumental and contingent moral value. Objection 4 pits utilitarianism squarely against commonsense morality, which recognizes the intrinsic moral importance of keeping promises. For example, one promises his or her dying mother to beautify her grave by always putting fresh and gorgeous flowers on her grave when her birthday arrives each year. But since an afterlife with a dissatisfied mother is unexpected, utilitarianism requires one to completely discount one's solemn pledge. After all, she will never know the difference. So utilitarianism emphasizes that life is for the living, and that one should spend his or her time, energy, and money, not putting flowers on a grave, but doing what will maximize satisfaction.

Utilitarians reply that we should not uncritically accept whatever commonsense morality dictates. Sometimes commonsense morality is wrong (for example, racist and sexist views that used to be considered commonsensical). But this reply will go only so far; for the commonsense belief in the intrinsic importance of keeping promises survives critical scrutiny that racist and sexist views cannot.

The example also seems to commit the appeal to pity. It is surely pitiful that the dying mother has such a son. But the mere fact that something is pitiful is not a conclusive reason against it. For example, it is pitiful to amputate a child's leg, but this is all too often medically necessary and for the best.

Further, some forms of utilitarianism would count the mother's preference as something to satisfy. Felt-satisfaction utilitarianism would not count her preference, since she will never feel the satisfaction. But preference-satisfaction utilitarianism can count it. Yet as Robert E. Goodin has said in objecting to a somewhat different form of utilitarianism, the closer a version of utilitarianism comes to embracing an "aesthetic ideal regardless of whether or not that is good for any living being, the less credible this analysis is as an ethical theory."[4] Keeping the promise to beautify one's mother's grave each year does seem to be a matter of aesthetics, which is presumably distinct from ethics.

There is a further problem with this type of utilitarian defense. Where do we draw the line in respecting the preferences of the dead? It seems arbitrary to limit it to those covered by promises. The other preferences were just as real and important to those now dead. Sometimes it is a fluke that one preference was covered by a promise and another was not. For example, suppose our mother is struck by lightning before we can make another promise to her. But surely we cannot cater to all the preferences the dead had. We cannot cater to all the preferences that those now dead had to live longer. Otherwise, we might have to exhaust our resources trying to put them in cryogenic freeze so that they can be thawed later when science might be able to revive them. But this seems absurd. Drawing the line at death, when preferences and satisfactions and all other psychological states presumably cease, seems less arbitrary than trying to distinguish between which preferences of the dead we will try to satisfy.

Utilitarianism cannot completely dismiss Objection 4 as requiring the impossible, namely, the satisfaction of a dead person's preference. One might think that death prevents the preference from being satisfied. But this is to assume that felt-satisfactions are the only satisfactions, which seems false. For example, a man prefers that his wife not commit adultery. But his wife is clever and decides while he is on submarine duty for months to have a secret affair with a sexually inexperienced bookworm who is a leading specialist in prevention of sexually transmitted diseases and who shyly wants only a few months more of secret sexual experience. The wife rightly expects, let us suppose, that her husband will never know the difference. He will have no felt-dissatisfaction of his preference that she not commit adultery.

Felt-satisfaction utilitarianism requires the wife to have the affair she and the bookworm want, but preference-satisfaction utilitarianism would at least count her husband's preference that she not do so (though whether there is an affair or not will make no difference to how he feels). Some critics charge that this is enough to refute felt-satisfaction utilitarianism. But again we should be concerned about whether the alleged counterexample commits the fallacy of appealing to pity. It may seem a pity that this dutiful submariner is deceived by his wife, who has broken her marriage vows (that is, promises). But mere pity is not decisive.

The error utilitarianism makes about promises is exposed by another example, though. You promise to meet me for an ordinary lunch. On your way to meet me you spot victims just emerging from a car accident in a remote area. They need your medical help immediately. So you stop to help them at the cost of making me dissatisfied with your lateness to lunch. Utilitarianism clearly requires this, and so does commonsense morality. Where they differ is in the reply you give when you come to lunch late. Commonsense morality implies, rightly I think, that you *owe* me an explanation and an expression of regret that you were sidetracked. A utilitarian cannot *simply* express sincere regret here. Once your dissatisfaction was outweighed by the prevention of more serious dissatisfaction for the accident victims, there was either nothing to be regretted or at least the expression of regret is viewed as a completely separate act, whose rightness or wrongness is determined exclusively by a separate calculation of its consequences rather than on a backward-looking expression of a genuinely felt emotion. Utilitarianism's unnecessarily complex conceptual separation of these conceptually, emotionally, and simply linked acts seems mistaken.

5. *Average and Total Utilitarianism Produce Absurdities*

Average utilitarianism states that an act is morally right only to the extent that it maximizes the amount of satisfaction per person in existence (that is, maximizes the mean of utility). Total utilitarianism states that an act is morally right only to the extent that it maximizes the aggregate amount of satisfaction (that is, maximizes the sum of satisfaction). These two forms of utilitarianism lead to different results only when population policy is involved; for, if the population is held constant, then average satisfaction and total satisfaction must rise or fall together.

Critics charge that average utilitarianism degenerates into number worship that squanders satisfaction, whereas total utilitarianism will lead us to reduce the standard of living too much and make the world barely livable. Either way, utilitarianism seems objectionable.

First, here is a counterexample to average utilitarianism. Suppose we have a person who is quite satisfied in his life but whose level of satisfaction is always consistently and predictably below the average amount of satisfaction people have. And suppose that from our experience trying to help him we know that there is no way to raise his level of satisfaction without lowering the overall average amount of satisfaction. Now, if we can raise the average of satisfaction for all by painlessly killing and disposing of this fellow who is below average, then average utilitarianism requires us to do so. But this seems absurd and contrary to a key point of utilitarianism, which is that satisfaction is the only value. Here, average utilitarianism requires us to squander an amount of net satisfaction just to raise a mere number, an average level of satisfaction. We can suppose that not one more unit of satisfaction is gained, but that the average is raised only by subtracting the below-average fellow from the population. (This would be a rather extreme case of what baseball genius Branch Rickey called "addition by subtraction"!). So average utilitarianism seems unacceptable, even to many utilitarians.

But total utilitarianism seems to err on an even more massive scale; for it requires us to bring more and more people into the world—even if this lowers the average level of satisfaction—so long as adding another person to the world adds more net satisfaction to the world than any other alternative. The worry here is that total utilitarianism will be too tolerant of the population explosion and will lead to a world where standards of living are drastically lowered and almost all of us eke out a life just barely worth living because our planet is filled to capacity. Because there will be so many of us, this will make up for the extremely low average satisfaction we will have and will maximize total satisfaction. Total satisfaction is figured by adding the amount of satisfaction each person has. Making the world barely satisfactory for everyone seems to miss a key point of utilitarianism, which is that we should try to improve the lives of everyone as much as possible. So total utilitarianism seems unacceptable, even to many utilitarians.

Since utilitarianism must take a stand on population policy, and since both its alternatives—average and total utilitarianism—seem absurd, is utilitarianism *obviously* unacceptable here? No, because total utilitarianism *might* survive. In real life, we cannot jam the planet full of people and expect to retain enough control of the situation to maximize total satisfaction. First, the more people there are to satisfy, the harder it is likely to be to satisfy them. Second, a world where everyone ekes out a life barely worth living is likely to be unstable, presenting a great danger of disease and a chain reaction of catastrophes going through the population. Given these empirically contingent facts, it is unlikely that pushing population to such extreme limits will maximize expected total satisfaction, since the catastrophes would involve so much dissatisfaction and since the chances of them occurring would be so high.

In conclusion, utilitarianism's best prospect for surviving Objection 5 is the endorsement of total utilitarianism and the rejection of average utilitarianism. But even this strategy will probably fail,

since we saw in the previous section (section 4) that utilitarianism should avoid overreliance on contingent empirical facts and avoid dismissal of hypothetical counterexamples. A world where we can maximize total satisfaction by increasing the population explosion and lowering average satisfaction is possible. It might be, for example, that our technology will improve to allow us to control the weather and the entire planet and that the more people we have the more labor power we have to enable us to keep the low average satisfaction stable and to avoid catastrophes. So utilitarianism seems unacceptable because it is woefully unprepared for this eventuality. It will yield unacceptable requirements whenever that day arrives. But we are entitled to think ahead and find utilitarianism unacceptable now.

6. Rule-Utilitarianism Is Incoherent or Redundant

Rule-utilitarianism (sometimes called restricted or indirect utilitarianism) is often distinguished from act-utilitarianism (sometimes called extreme or direct utilitarianism). R. M. Hare says:

Act-utilitarianism is the view that we have to apply the so-called 'principle of utility' [that is, maximize satisfaction] directly to individual acts. . . . Rule-utilitarianism . . . is the view that this test is not to be applied to individual actions, but to *kinds* of action. . . . Actions are to be assessed by asking whether they are forbidden or enjoined by certain moral rules or principles; and it is only when we start to ask which moral rules or principles we are to adopt for assessing actions, that we apply the utilitarian test.[5]

Rule-utilitarianism was developed to try to save utilitarianism from the sort of counterexamples we have seen from commonsense morality (for example, "do not hang the innocent," and "keep promises"). Utilitarianism recognizes that commonsense moral rules such as "Keep promises" and "do not kill" are generally useful in gaining satisfaction.

Jonathan Harrison, however, gives at least three good reasons for rejecting rule-utilitarianism. First, "It is not the case that I ought to obey a rule which has good consequences, however bad the consequences of my obeying it are."[6] For example, "Do not steal" is a rule which, if generally adopted, would seem to maximize satisfaction, but we can easily imagine a scenario where stealing a radio is necessary to warn people to evacuate before a dam bursts and kills thousands of people. If the rule-utilitarian makes an exception to the rules to cover such cases, then rule-utilitarianism would seem redundant; for it would contain rules such as "Do not kill, except to maximize satisfaction"; "Do not steal, except to maximize satisfaction"; and "Keep promises, but only if it maximizes satisfaction." These rules tell us nothing more than utilitarianism's fundamental rule "maximize satisfaction for all in the long run."

Second, following J. J. C. Smart, Harrison argues that "rule-utilitarianism is a manifestation of rule-worship."[7] Act-utilitarianism and rule-utilitarianism lead to different conclusions only if rule-utilitarianism sometimes forbids us from breaking a rule by doing an act that maximizes satisfaction. So rule-utilitarianism seems more a form of rule-worship than a form of utilitarianism, which says satisfaction—not rule following—is the only value.

Third, rule-utilitarians fail to distinguish three types of rule: 1) an actually operating social rule; 2) "a general moral *belief,* which most people in most societies have, *about* this (social) rule, to the effect that it usually or always ought to be acted upon"; and 3) "the *fact* about the social rule that it ought usually to be obeyed, whether most members of the society which has it think that it ought to be obeyed or not."[8] If rule-utilitarianism means (1) then it is still subject to the other objections above, but at least it is coherent. But if rule-utilitarianism means either (2) or (3), then it will end up referring to itself—for it is also a rule—in such a viciously circular way that it will be incoherent.

Finally, there is a fourth objection to rule-utilitarianism that Harrison does not explore. This objection uses the concept of *extensional equivalence.* Two moralities are extensionally equivalent if they always agree about what we should do in any case. Some critics argue that rule-utilitarianism is extensionally equivalent to act-utilitarianism and thus cannot coherently defend utilitarianism from familiar objections using plausible examples from commonsense morality (for example, "Do not hang the innocent") as counterexamples to utilitarianism.[9] As R. M. Hare says, "The merit of rule-utilitarianism has been said to be that it is more in accord with our common moral beliefs than is act-utilitarianism. . . ."[10] But if the two are extensionally equivalent, then rule-utilitarianism has no more merit than act-utilitarianism. Act- and rule-utilitarianism do seem to be extensionally equivalent, because if rule-utilitarianism ever disagreed with act-utilitarianism and required us to follow a rule by doing an act that failed to maximize satisfaction, then rule-utilitarianism would be rejecting the lone value of utilitarianism, satisfaction (not mere obedience to rules). Further, act- and rule-utilitarianism seem to agree and converge because the adoption of a rule is itself an act. So if a rule really were so useful that its adoption would maximize satisfaction, then act-utilitarianism would require us to do the act of adopting that rule and taking that rule to heart.

In conclusion, the best prospect for utilitarianism's surviving Objection 6 is to reject rule-utilitarianism and emphasize the strength and flexibility of act-utilitarianism, which still has its own problems, as we have seen.

7. *Utilitarianism Requires Us to Enter the Experience Machine*

I suspect that all of us are intrigued by the experimental new technology called *virtual reality.* Some models are already used as flight simulators to train pilots. But imagine programming one's own artificial universe! What wonders would it contain?! With utilitarianism, however, it seems we will be forced to have too much of a good thing here. Robert Nozick has theorized about what he calls the *experience machine*, which resembles virtual reality, though he fails to apply his example of the experience machine directly to refuting utilitarianism (see reading IV.16 in the text).[11]

We can use the experience machine to object to utilitarianism because utilitarianism will require us to spend our entire lives in the machine if that will maximize satisfaction, as it might very well do. A life spent inside the experience machine seems like one of mental masturbation, an unreal and degraded life unworthy of us, though it will seem perfectly real and satisfying to us as long as we stay inside the machine. Utilitarianism's monism, its insistence that satisfaction is the only moral value, prevents utilitarians from placing greater moral value on genuine, veridical experiences than on artificial yet credible simulations. Utilitarianism is objectionable because its monism leaves no room to place any intrinsic value on truth, knowledge, or reality, with which we lose touch once we enter the experience machine. Moreover, independent of utilitarianism's monism, utilitarianism is also objectionable because the subjective character of what utilitarianism counts as valuable—namely, the subjects' feelings or satisfactions—allows value to be radically and objectionably disconnected from how things are in the world external to the subjects.

8. Utilitarianism Wildly Overstates Our Duties to Animals

One might conceive of Objection 8 as a version of Objection 1, since animals (I use 'animals' to mean 'nonhuman animals') outnumber humans by so much that humans will be swamped with duties to maximize the satisfactions animals are psychologically capable of having. (Of course, some living things evidently have no psychology.) But Objection 8 can be made by those who refuse to object to utilitarianism as overly demanding; for they can object that what is wrong with utili-

tarianism here is not how much it demands but what utilitarianism is demanding of us, namely, the satisfaction of mere nonhuman animals. Utilitarians from Bentham to Mill to Singer have insisted on considering animals in moral deliberations. But critics charge that utilitarianism will all too often require debased or beastly satisfaction. The critics charge that utilitarianism implies that it is better to be a pig satisfied than to be Socrates dissatisfied.

In response to such criticisms, John Stuart Mill tried to develop eudaimonistic utilitarianism, which would distinguish qualities of happiness, with some types of satisfaction having more moral value than other types present in the same quantity but of lower quality. But eudaimonistic utilitarianism is incompatible with utilitarianism's monism. Since utilitarianism insists that there is only one moral value, satisfaction, there is no other value to which a utilitarian can consistently appeal in claiming that one type of satisfaction is morally better than another type of satisfaction.[12]

9. Utilitarianism Panders to Bigots and Sadists

Critics charge that utilitarianism is fundamentally mistaken in treating racist, sexist, bigoted, and sadistic satisfaction as intrinsically valuable. Since satisfaction is utilitarianism's only value, utilitarianism has no other value enabling the utilitarian to distinguish between better and worse satisfactions. Only the amount of satisfaction (or dissatisfaction) caused makes an act right (or wrong), not whether the satisfaction is noble or unbiased. Critics charge that some motivations ought not to be satisfied because they are intrinsically wrong and their satisfaction is morally bankrupt and completely without value.

But Tom L. Beauchamp and LeRoy Walters suggest that utilitarianism can dodge this objection. They say:

because 'perverse' [for example, extremely sadistic] desires have been determined on the basis of past experience to cut against the objectives of utilitarianism by creating conditions productive of unhappiness, the desires (preferences) could never even be permitted to count. We discount preferences to rape children. . . . Preferences that serve merely to frustrate the preferences of others are thus ruled out by the goal of utilitarianism. As Mill himself argued, the cultivation of certain kinds of desires is built into the 'ideal' of utilitarianism.[13]

But this defense of utilitarianism is unconvincing, since we saw in [objection]8 that Mill's eudaimonistic utilitarianism was developed to handle similar objections to the kinds of satisfactions utilitarianism would respect, and we saw that eudaimonistic utilitarianism seems inconsistent because it abandons utilitarianism's monism, its insistence that there is only one value, namely, satisfaction. As Hare suggested, "Mill's mistake was perhaps to try to incorporate ideals into a utilitarian theory, which cannot really absorb them."[14] Utilitarianism's single-minded pursuit of the maximization of only one value leaves no room for other ideals. Further, unfortunately some preferences to rape children do not serve merely to frustrate the preferences of others but also serve to satisfy the rapists. The problem for utilitarianism is not the general prohibition of rape; it surely does condemn almost all rapes. Rather, Objection 9 claims utilitarianism is pandering to sadists and bigots by counting their sadistic and bigoted satisfactions as morally valuable *at all*—even if their satisfactions are readily overridden by the dissatisfactions of others.

10. Utilitarianism Makes Interpersonal Comparisons of Utility

> I am a child.
> I last awhile.
> You can't conceive of the pleasure in my smile.
> —The Buffalo Springfield (1967)[15]

Utilitarianism requires interpersonal comparisons of utility (that is, satisfaction) because it re-quires us to maximize satisfaction for all in the long run. Thus, we must consider trade-offs, promoting the satisfaction of some at the expense of allowing the dissatisfaction of others in order to maximize the net satisfaction for everyone over the long haul. But how can we compare one person's pleasure, for example, with another's pain? Are not pleasure and pain subjective experiences? Are not thresholds and tolerances for pain highly idiosyncratic and unpredictable? Being stuck with a needle, for example, seems to bother some people much more than others. And even though sugar presumably tastes the same to everyone, some seem to have more of a sweet tooth than others and enjoy sweets immeasurably more than others. After all, critics charge, it is a well-recognized maxim that there is no accounting for or disputing matters of taste (that is, *De gustibus non est disputandum*).

Objection 10 is flashy, but there is less here than meets the eye. Objection 10 relies on what it takes to be commonsensical, namely, that people enjoy and value the same psychological experiences differently. This is true even for basic psychological experiences such as pain. Masochists sometimes seem to enjoy significant levels of pain. But there is an equivocation in Objection 10 that is illustrated by the following joke: A masochist goes up to a sadist and says, "Hit me"; the sadist prepares to hit the masochist but then, realizing the masochist will enjoy being hit, says, "No." These mind games take some surprising twists and turns for which human psychology is notorious. But the point is that pain or sweet taste should not be equated with satisfaction. Utilitarianism is fully capable of allowing individual differences in what brings about satisfaction. The bottom line is to maximize the satisfaction, not any particular experience we might misidentify as satisfaction.

Moreover, we commonsensically make interpersonal comparisons every day. For example, we build freeways even though we know that it is just a matter of time before an innocent baby who would not have died nearly so soon had the freeway never been built gets crushed in an automobile accident on the freeway. But the great convenience of the freeway and the other lives saved by allowing ambulances and other emergency vehicles to use the new freeway to speed to emergencies outweighs the harm caused to the crushed baby. So, whatever plausibility Objection 10 gains by relying on common sense is blunted by the commonsensical way we make interpersonal comparisons of satisfaction everyday.

Further, *inter*personal comparisons of satisfaction seem no more problematic than *intra*personal comparisons of satisfaction. All the same arguments for Objection 10 could be made against intrapersonal comparisons of satisfaction. After all, Objection 10 must allow that I might become a masochist or an old man with satisfactions incommensurable with those I can now have. Yet we still think that it makes good common sense to trade off some satisfaction at one stage of life (for example, exercising hard rather than enjoying more sleep) for more satisfaction later in life (for example, living longer and with fewer illnesses).

Furthermore, Objection 10 strikes me as being mathematically suspect. Even if satisfaction was as wildly unpredictable from person to person as Objection 10 states, which I doubt, would it not minimize our margin of error if we assumed that each person's satisfactions were comparable? It seems so. For if we started giving preference or extra weight to persons whose satisfaction was assumed to be weightier, then the wildly unpredictable nature of satisfaction, which Objection 10 insists upon, would imply that we are as apt to be preferring and weighting the satisfactions of the right persons (those whose satisfaction is more satisfying than others' satisfactions) as those of the wrong persons. If we chose the wrong person and thus gave extra weight, in deciding what to do, to the satisfactions of a person whose satisfactions are actually *less* satisfying than the satisfactions of others, then we have compounded any mistake we would have made by considering all satisfactions comparable, and we have extended the margin of error further than it was. For example, suppose we expect to get ten

percent more satisfaction by satisfying Pojman slightly than by satisfying Harwood slightly, but Pojman actually gets ten percent less satisfaction from being slightly satisfied than Harwood does from being slightly satisfied. Our margin of error is then twenty percent rather than the ten percent margin of error present in treating the satisfactions of Harwood and Pojman as comparable, only to learn that we could have obtained ten percent more satisfaction by satisfying Harwood slightly rather than satisfying Pojman slightly.

Finally, how can Objection 10 make sense of its claims such as, "Interpersonal comparisons of satisfaction are impossible because a slightly satisfied Harwood has immeasurably more satisfaction than a very satisfied Pojman. That's just the kind of guy Harwood is." How could we ever know such a thing unless interpersonal comparisons of satisfaction were not only possible but actually known? This very claim seems to make an interpersonal comparison of the satisfactions of Harwood and Pojman. The contradiction in claiming to know that interpersonal comparisons of satisfaction are impossible is similar to that of claiming, "My experience was impossible to describe; it was simply indescribable." Our making this very claim describes the experience. In calling our satisfactions incommensurable we make a comparison among them, namely, that they all have in common the feature for which we lack a scale by which we can accurately measure them all in the same units. But—and this is my main point—this common lack of a scale would also prevent anyone from knowing if we made a mistake in treating the satisfactions as comparable.

I conclude that rough-and-ready, short-and-snappy interpersonal comparisons of satisfaction are justified enough. Some interpersonal comparisons of utility are clearly much more plausible and defensible than others. For example, do we really have any doubt that the following claim is false: "Each time I lose a penny from my pocket change it causes me more dissatisfaction than all the dissatisfactions in human history combined"? The implications of Objection 10 are too extreme and absurd to accept.

11. *Utilitarianism Is Too Secretive, Undemocratic, and Elitist*

Since moral principles conceptually must concern how each person should live, we might think that any acceptable moral principle must be public and available for all to use in our thinking. But utilitarians often think that it would be a mistake to let most or all people directly pursue maximizing satisfaction, since too many will show bias or incompetence in calculating what will maximize satisfaction, thereby leading to too much dissatisfaction. Many critics find utilitarianism's restriction of the direct pursuit of maximizing satisfaction to a trusted utilitarian elite objectionably secretive, undemocratic, and elitist.

Utilitarians might reply that rule-utilitarianism can be more public than act-utilitarianism, since the people can be trusted as competent to follow basic and straightforward rules such as "Do not kill" and "Keep your promises." But we have already seen (in section 6) numerous reasons to doubt that rule-utilitarianism can ultimately remain distinct enough from act-utilitarianism, or to doubt that rule-utilitarianism is acceptable.

But Objection 11 fails because it accepts too uncritically the commonsense morality of public notification and use of moral rules. Indeed, it seems uncertain whether this is a requirement of commonsense morality at all. No less a champion of democracy than Winston Churchill insisted that "democracy is the worst form of Government except all those other forms that have been tried from time to time."[16] And Churchill's wisdom here is commonly quoted and accepted. So perhaps a utilitarian form of government would improve upon democracy and all the other forms of government tried so far.

C. Conclusion

In conclusion, though I reject some of the objections to utilitarianism that I still found to be worth presenting (Objections 1, 2, 10, and 11), the remaining objections collectively have enough force to convince me and many others to reject utilitarianism. But I can hardly rule out the development of a new version of utilitarianism that will dodge or withstand any silver bullets fired at utilitarianism here. I encourage those who wish to try to develop a new and improved utilitarianism.[17]

Notes

1. Quoted in J. S. Mill, *Utilitarianism* (many editions), chapter 5.

2. Kurt Baier, *The Moral Point Of View: A Rational Basis of Ethics*, abr. ed. (New York: Random House, 1965), p. 147; unabridged edition (Ithaca, N.Y.: Cornell University Press, 1958), p. 307.

3. Raymond D. Gastil, "The Moral Right Of The Majority To Restrict Obscenity And Pornography Through Law," 86 *Ethics* (1976): 231–40, pp. 235–36; reprinted in John Arthur and William H. Shaw, eds., *Readings In Philosophy Of Law* (Englewood Cliffs, N.J.: Prentice-Hall, 1984), p. 572.

4. Robert E. Goodin, "Utility And The Good," in Peter Singer, ed., *A Companion To Ethics* (Oxford: Basil Blackwell, 1991), p. 243.

5. Richard Mervyn Hare, *Freedom And Reason* (Oxford: Oxford University Press, 1963), p. 130.

6. Jonathan Harrison, "Rule Utilitarianism and Cumulative-Effect Utilitarianism," in Wesley E. Cooper, Kai Nielsen, and Steven C. Patten, eds., *New Essays on John Stuart Mill and Utilitarianism* (Guelph, Ont.: Canadian Association For Publishing In Philosophy, 1979), p. 22.

7. Harrison, "Rule-Utilitarianism and Cumulative-Effect Utilitarianism," p. 24.

8. Ibid., p. 25.

9. Hare was apparently the first in print to argue that act- and rule-utilitarianism are extensionally equivalent, though David Lyons shortly thereafter published a similar argument with much more detail and logical rigor. See, Hare, *Freedom and Reason*, p. 131 and David Lyons, *The Forms And Limits Of Utilitarianism* (Oxford: Oxford University Press, 1965).

10. Hare, *Freedom and Reason*, p. 130.

11. Robert Nozick, *Anarchy, State & Utopia* (Cambridge: Harvard University Press, 1974), pp. 42–45. Compare the idea of the experience machine with Woody Allen's 'orgasmitron' in his film "Sleeper" from

1973 and with the 'Holodeck' on the television program "Star Trek: The Next Generation."

12. For a recent attempt to rescue Mill's utilitarianism from this type of objection, see David O. Brink, "Mill's Deliberative Utilitarianism," *Philosophy & Public Affairs* 21 (1992): 67–103.

13. Tom L. Beauchamp and LeRoy Walters, eds., *Contemporary Issues In Bioethics*, 2d ed. (Belmont, Calif.: Wadsworth Publishing Co., 1982), p. 15.

14. Hare, *Freedom and Reason*, p. 121.

15. From "I Am A Child," written by Neil Young for The Buffalo Springfield. Springalo Toones/Cotillion Music, Inc.—BMI (Atco Records, 1967).

16. Winston Churchill, quoted in *The Oxford Dictionary Of Quotations*, 3d ed., s. v. "Winston Churchill."

17. I thank Louis Pojman and an anonymous reviewer for comments on this paper.

23

Ideal Code Utilitarianism

BRAD HOOKER

Brad Hooker is a professor of philosophy at the University of Reading in England. He is the author of many important articles on moral philosophy. The present selection is taken from his influential book Ideal Code, Real World: A Rule-Consequentialist Theory of Morality *(2000). In this selection Hooker proposes, and begins to develop and defend, a highly original form of rule-consequentialism, according to which actions are morally acceptable, or not, according to whether they conform to the moral code that it would have the best consequences for everyone to internalize.*

2.1 A PICTURE OF RULE-CONSEQUENTIALISM

There are many versions of rule-consequentialism. The version I favour is as follows:

RULE-CONSEQUENTIALISM. An act is wrong if and only if it is forbidden by the code of rules whose internalization by the overwhelming majority of everyone everywhere in each new generation[1] has maximum expected value in terms of well-being (with some priority for the worst off). The calculation of a code's expected value includes all costs of getting the code internalized. If in terms of expected value two or more codes are better than the rest but equal to one another, the one closest to conventional morality determines what acts are wrong.

Picture the theory like this:

TABLE 2.1. Rule-consequentialism

Wrongness determined either (1) by the code whose internalization by the overwhelming majority in each new generation has the greatest expected value or (2) if two or more codes are equally best, by the one closest to conventional morality.	*Conditions:* The people by whom rules are to be internalized (a) are the overwhelming majority in each new generation and (b) are beings with *cognitive* and *affective* limitations.	*Thus, rules* (i) whose *publicity* would have good consequences and (ii) whose internalization costs would be cost-effective.

Reprinted by permission of the publisher from Brad Hooker, *Ideal Code, Real World*, pp. 33–55. © 2000 by Oxford University Press.

2.2 Rules Are Not To Be Valued in Terms of Numbers of Acts

Before I explain what is in the picture, let me mention what is not in the picture. The version of rule-consequentialism in which I am interested evaluates rules *only* in terms of how much aggregate well-being (with some priority for the worst off) results from the internalization of these rules. It does not hold that rules should be evaluated in terms of how many acts of kindness, justice, promise-keeping, and loyalty, for example, result from the internalization of the code. Nor does it hold that rules are to be evaluated in terms of how few acts of unkindness, injustice, promise-breaking, and disloyalty result. The version of rule-consequentialism in which I am interested posits well-being (with some priority for the worse off) as the primary thing with intrinsic value. It does not posit intrinsic moral value or disvalue for any kind of act.

Note that I was careful to leave room for the idea that rule-consequentialism might hold that some acts themselves play a constitutive role in a life valuable for the person who lives it.[2] For example, if friendship and achievement are two components of well-being, and if certain acts are constitutive of friendship or achievement, then these acts can play a constitutive role in well-being. Perhaps rule-consequentialism needs to allow that acts can have intrinsic non-moral value in this way.

Consider a version of rule-consequentialism that went much further by positing positive and negative intrinsic *moral* values for different kinds of act. Such a version would hold that the positive and negative statuses of different kinds of act are beyond explanation. Admittedly, versions of rule-consequentialism positing that certain kinds of act have intrinsic moral disvalue can 'explain' why killing, wounding, robbing, promise-breaking, and so on are wrong. They are wrong because of their intrinsic disvalue, according to these versions of rule-consequentialism. Likewise, versions of rule-consequentialism attributing intrinsic moral value to certain kinds of act can 'explain'

why doing them is morally right. They are right because of their intrinsic moral value, according to these versions of rule-consequentialism.

But better will be versions of rule-consequentialism that can equally well explain why acts are wrong (or right) *without* positing intrinsic moral goodness or badness as properties of acts. For, other things being equal, a theory that does not posit intrinsic goodness or badness as properties of acts makes fewer assumptions. And if a theory making fewer assumptions can explain just as much as a theory making more assumptions, the theory making fewer assumptions is better.

There is another reason not to posit that acts can have intrinsic value or intrinsic disvalue. Some central cases of morally required actions do not plausibly have the requisite kind of value. For example, if promise keeping has intrinsic positive value, then there would be value simply in making promises so that we can keep them and thereby increase the amount of promise-keeping.[3] This implication is crazy, so crazy as to drain the assumption from which it comes of any plausibility.

What is far from crazy is the idea that certain virtues have value in and of themselves, in addition to the value of the consequences they normally produce. Do the dispositions to generosity, honesty, loyalty, and the like have intrinsic value? Are they valuable necessarily rather than contingently? Here is a test case, slightly adapted from W. D. Ross (1930: 134–5). Compare two imaginary worlds. In one, there is a certain amount of aggregate well-being, but people are highly vicious. In the other world, people are thoroughly virtuous, but this world has far fewer natural resources. Suppose that, because of the fewer natural resources, the world with virtuous people has only the same level of aggregate well-being as the other world. So our choice is between two worlds with the same level of well-being but one with virtuous people and the other with vicious people. The world with virtuous people seems clearly better. This case seems to suggest that virtue is not only instrumentally but also intrinsically valuable.

Actually, we need to go carefully here. There are other possible explanations of our ranking the virtuous world higher.

For one thing, we might be assuming we are being asked which world to bring into existence, on the supposition that we ourselves won't exist in either. We understandably feel more sympathy for the virtuous people than for the vicious ones. This makes us 'on their side', and thus inclined to rank their world higher.

Second, we might be outraged by the cosmic injustice of the vicious people being as well off as the virtuous. So our sense of justice immediately puts us on the side of the virtuous as against the vicious.

Third, we might be imagining that we are being asked in which of these worlds we ourselves would prefer to live. In this case, we have the difficulty of getting our minds around the stipulation that we would not be happier in the virtuous possible world than in the vicious one. If we are being asked to imagine possible worlds such that we would not be happier in the virtuous one than in the vicious one, are these not *very distant* possible worlds? If so, our intuitions about them may be unreliable. In particular, the explanation of our preferring the virtuous world may be that we simply fail to take to heart that we would not be happier there.

These alternative possible explanations of our reaction to Ross's example should make us pause before accepting Ross's conclusion that virtue is intrinsically valuable. Furthermore, Ross's conclusion may have implications we cannot accept. If virtue is intrinsically valuable, then presumably it is not always less important than other intrinsic values. But in that case, a loss in terms of other values could be outweighed by a gain in virtue. This threatens to imply that a world in which bad things occur to sentient beings, but where people respond virtuously to these bad things is better than a world without the bad and thus without those opportunities to respond virtuously. That is a familiar reply to the Christians' problem of explaining how there could be an all-powerful, perfectly benevolent god who creates or allows suffering and other evil.

We might be able to believe that virtue is intrinsically valuable without believing that this gives Christians a good answer to their problem. For in order for there to be opportunities for virtue, it is not necessary for bad things *really* to happen, but only for agents to *think* bad things can happen. You can exercise the virtue of kindness if you react to what you reasonably believe is my (actual or potential) suffering by trying to help me. So an all-powerful benevolent god could, while avoiding actually injecting suffering into the world, stage opportunities for people to exercise virtues.

Despite my worries about Ross's example and about his conclusion that virtue has intrinsic value, I do tentatively accept his conclusion. Does this entail abandoning rule-consequentialism? I think not. I think rule-consequentialists can agree that virtue per se is not only instrumentally but also intrinsically valuable.

For as Tom Hurka (2000: ch. 2) argues, to think virtue not only instrumentally but also intrinsically valuable is not to supply a criterion for what constitutes virtue. Nor is it to think virtue can stand alone, unconnected to other intrinsically valuable things. On the contrary, there are various ways of maintaining that what makes something a virtue is its connection with other intrinsically valuable things. Hurka's own account holds that virtue is constituted by loving the good and hating the bad.[4] On his account, virtue is thus conceptually parasitic on other values. But he holds, mainly because of the sort of example from Ross I have just outlined, that virtue is nevertheless intrinsically valuable.

Perhaps rule-consequentialism can make a similar move. Thus rule-consequentialism might hold:

(a) that, apart from virtue, well-being and perhaps some property of its distribution are the only other intrinsically valuable things;
(b) that prospective moral codes should be evaluated in terms of the effects their widespread internalization would have on aggregate well-being, and perhaps some property of its distribution;

(c) that what makes some dispositions virtues is that these dispositions are essential parts of accepting the rules prescribed by the code with the greatest expected value;

(d) and that people's having these prescribed dispositions is not only instrumentally but also intrinsically valuable.

On this form of rule-consequentialism, the virtues per se have intrinsic value, but rule-consequentialism tells us what makes something a virtue.[5]

2.3 WELL-BEING

Since the version of rule-consequentialism under consideration here evaluates rules in terms of well-being, we need to ask what exactly well-being is. Some philosophical theories about well-being point to subjective features of us. These theories hold that we benefit to the extent that we get pleasure or enjoyment, or to the extent that our desires are fulfilled. Other theories hold that there are certain objective goods whose contribution to our well-being is not exhausted by the extent to which they bring us pleasure or enjoyment or fulfil our desires.

All utilitarians have held that pleasure and the absence of pain are at least a large part of well-being. Indeed, utilitarianism is often said to maintain that pleasure and the absence of pain are the *only* things that matter in themselves. Philosophers call this view hedonism. It is normally taken to be the view of the classic utilitarians Jeremy Bentham (1789), J. S. Mill (1861), and Henry Sidgwick (1907).[6]

This view has run into enormous difficulties. First of all, there seems to be no distinctive feel that all pleasures have in common, nor any that all pains have in common (Brandt 1979: 35–42; Parfit 1984: 493; Griffin 1986: 8). Compare the pleasure of watching *King Lear* with the pleasure of satisfying an intense desire for sugar.

With this difficulty in mind, hedonism is usually modified to the equation of a person's pleasure with features of his experience that both (a) he likes or prefers and (b) are *introspectively discernible* by him.[7] On this view, something cannot affect your well-being unless there is an effect on how your life seems *from the inside.* This view has implausible implications.

Compare two lives I might have. In both of these alternatives, all the following are true: (a) I believe my 'friends' like me. (b) I believe that I have successfully completed my main aims. (c) I believe I am in control of my own life (at least to the extent people normally are). And (d) I believe I have true beliefs about other important facts. Now, in one of the lives we are comparing, all these beliefs are correct. In the other life, they are false. Suppose that, in the life in which the beliefs are false, I never find out that my 'friends' don't like me, that I fail in my main aims, that someone else is manipulating my life in a way I cannot see, and that I am deluded about other important facts. Now suppose this deluded life is a little more pleasant. This is the one and only introspectively discernible difference between the lives. So, according to the view that the sole component of well-being is the introspectively discernible quality of one's mental states, this is life in which I have greater well-being. But, looked at objectively, this seems not to be the better life (Smart 1973: 20–1; Nozick 1974: 42–5; 1989: ch. 10; Glover 1984: 92–113; Griffin 1986: 9).

Notice that we are comparing lives that are close in terms of pleasure. I do not mean to deny that *sometimes* the truth would hurt so much, be so debilitating, that the person would be better off not knowing it. A deluded life full of pleasant mental states might well be superior to an undeluded life going from one torture chamber to another. To reject the hedonistic theory of the good, we need only contend that there can be occasions on which knowing the truth makes someone better off without making her or him happier. We do not need to, and should not, contend that knowing the truth *always* makes a person better off overall.

In the face of objections such as the one about the slightly more pleasant life that involves massive delusion, most philosophers have abandoned the hedonistic theory of well-being.[8] Perhaps more common during the second half of the twentieth century has been the view that well-being is constituted by the fulfilment of people's desires, even if these desires are for things other than pleasure. Many people, even when fully informed and thinking carefully, persistently want for themselves things in addition to pleasure. They want, for example, to know important truths, to achieve valuable goals, to have close friendships, to live autonomously (by which I mean, in broad accordance with their own choices rather than always in accordance with someone else's) (Glover 1984: 95–6, 100–1, 107–8, 112–13; Griffin 1986: pt. 1; Crisp 1997: chs. 2, 3). The pleasure these things can bring is of course important. Still, human beings can care about these things in themselves, in addition to whatever pleasure they bring.

There are objections to the view that human well-being is constituted by the fulfilment of people's desires. Some of our desires seem to be about things too unconnected with us for them to play a direct role in determining our good. Consider an example of Derek Parfit's (1984: 494). You meet a stranger on the train and she tells you of her life-threatening illness. You form a strong desire that she should recover fully from her illness. She does recover, but you never find out. Now, does the fulfilment of your strong desire that she should recover make her recovery good *for you*, even if you never find out about her recovery nor indeed see or hear from her again? The question is whether the bare fulfilment of your desire that she should recover constitutes a benefit to you. Naturally, the fulfilment of such a desire would *instrumentally* benefit you if it brought you pleasure or peace of mind. But this is not to say that the bare fulfilment of your desire that the stranger should recover constitutes a benefit to you. Rather, if you get pleasure or peace of mind from the fulfilment of

this desire, this *pleasure* or *peace of mind* constitutes a benefit to you (since you doubtless also desire pleasure and peace of mind for yourself).

The view that the fulfilment of your desires itself constitutes a benefit to you—if this view is to be at all plausible—will have to limit the desires in question. The only desires the fulfilment of which constitutes a benefit to you are your desires for states of affairs that have to do with your life in some way. We might say that the states of affairs that have to do with your life in this way are ones in which you are an essential constituent, in the sense that your existing at time t is a logically necessary condition of the state of affair's obtaining at t (Overvold 1980; 1982). Examples of desires for states of affairs in which you *are* an essential constituent are your desires that *you* paint beautiful pictures, that *you* have true friends, that *you* know the truth about the origin of the universe, and that *you* bring the wicked to justice. Examples of desires for states of affairs in which you are *not* an essential constituent are your desires that the stranger on the train recover from her illness, that the innocent go free, that humanity survive forever.

Richard Brandt (1979: 330) and Gregory Kavka (1986: 41) objected that this makes irrelevant to one's own good such desires as the desire for posthumous fame. More generally, if personal success is part of one's well-being, and if personal success requires that certain states of affairs obtain after one's death, then we need to amend Overvold's criterion. We might hold that a state of affairs one desires is part of one's well-being if and only if the state of affairs logically could not exist without one's existing at *some time or other*, though not necessarily at the same time that the state of affairs exists.[9] On this criterion, some desires about events after your death could be relevant to your well-being. Still, the state of affairs in which the stranger from the train recovers is not.

There seem to be reasons for further restrictions on the desires directly relevant to personal good. Think how bizarre desires can be. When we encounter particularly bizarre ones, we might begin to wonder whether the desired things would benefit the agent simply because these things are desired. Would my desiring to count all the blades of grass in the lawns in my neighbourhood make my counting them good for me (Rawls 1971: 432; cf. Parfit 1984: 500; Crisp 1997: 56)? Whatever *pleasure* I get from the activity would be good for me. But it seems that the *desire-fulfilment as such* is worthless in this case. Intuitively, the fulfilment of my desires constitutes a benefit to me only if these desires are for the right things. Indeed, some things seem to be desired because they are perceived as valuable, not valuable merely because desired or pleasant (Brink 1989: 64, 225, 230–1; Crisp 1997: 57–62; Scanlon 1998: 124–33).

Views holding that something benefits a person if and only if it increases the person's pleasure or desire-fulfilment are in a sense 'subjectivist' theories of personal good. For these theories make something's status as a benefit depend always on the person's subjective mental states. In contrast, 'objective list' theories claim that the contributions to personal good made by such things as important knowledge, important achievement, friendship, and autonomy are not exhausted by the extent to which these things bring people pleasure or fulfil their desires.[10] These things can constitute benefits beyond the pleasure they involve and even when they don't involve pleasure. Likewise, they can constitute benefits even when they are not the objects of desire. These 'list' theories will typically add that pleasure is, of course, an objective good. List theories also typically hold that delusion, failure, friendlessness, servitude, and pain constitute objective harms.

There are also mixed views. One mixed view holds that your getting pleasure from—or at least desiring—some state of affairs is a necessary but not sufficient condition of its being beneficial to you. On this view, for something to benefit you it must not only appeal to you but also be an objectively good source of pleasure.[11]

From the point of view of list theorists, that mixed view is mistaken to claim that a state of affairs can constitute a benefit to you only if you endorse it. For example, some achievement in your life might constitute at least a small benefit to you, might have contributed at least some small meaning to your life, even if you never cared about it. From the point of view of list theorists, the mixed view is also mistaken to claim that getting pleasure from something is not a sufficient condition of its constituting at least some small benefit to you.

Many people reject the list theory because they think it has outrageously paternalistic implications: they see looming the horror of people imposing 'the good life' on others. However, the list theory identifies autonomy as one of the prudential values. It might even go so far as to give overriding importance to autonomy. Therefore, the list theory itself might prohibit what we intuitively think of as objectionable paternalism.[12]

Furthermore, even if autonomy were not one of the things on the list, paternalism would be in the offing only if *morality* requires or permits forcing things on people that they do not want. But morality might not require or permit this. For example, there may be a good moral rule telling us to keep our nose out of others' business (except in certain fairly obvious cases, like when they are drunk).

Whenever possible, in this book I will be neutral about which of the leading theories of well-being is best. When thinking about what acts are morally right, we can normally remain neutral as between the leading theories of well-being because, despite their disagreements over principle, that is, their disagreements about what *constitutes* well-being, in practice there is wide agreement among the main theories of well-being. This is because what gives people pleasure or enjoyment is normally also what satisfies their desires and involves the things that could plausibly be listed as objective goods. So in most situations we do not need to decide among these theories of personal good (Smart 1973: 26).

But sometimes we do need to decide. Suppose the ruling elite believed that quantity of pleasure is all that matters. They might believe (to take a familiar leaf from some futuristic novels) that aggregate pleasure would be maximized by deceiving the masses and even by giving the masses drugs that induce contentment but drain ambition and curiosity. In this case, the ruling elite might feel justified in establishing such practices.

Or suppose the ruling elite believed that the fulfilment of desire is all that matters. Again, the ruling elite might feel justified in manipulating the formation and development of desires such that these are easily satisfied. Or consider the case of starving people whose desires for anything beyond the most basic necessities are reduced by prolonged deprivation (Sen 1973: 15–18). These people's reduced desires might then be *completely* fulfilled. But really these people would not be flourishing.

Admittedly, wisdom might recommend that, to some extent, our desires should be modified so that there is some reasonable hope of fulfilling them. But this shaping of our desires can be pushed too far, either in the name of maximizing pleasure or in the name of maximizing desire-fulfilment. A life could be maximally pleasurable, or have maximum desire-fulfilment, and still be shallow. This would be the case if the life were

devoid of friendship, achievement, knowledge, and autonomy. While pleasure and success in one's aims are certainly important parts of well-being, these other things are important in their own right.

So, to come clean, I think the most plausible form of rule-consequentialism will involve some modest form of objective list account of well-being. Such an account will recognize the central role of autonomy. Equally, it will recognize the importance of differences in people's aptitudes, capacities, and inclinations. Still, there is more to life than pleasure, and the bare fact that some state of affairs is desired does not make it valuable.

2.4 WELL-BEING VERSUS EQUALITY

The most familiar versions of rule-consequentialism evaluate rules in terms of nothing but how much aggregate well-being they produce. Let me refer to any version of rule-consequentialism that evaluates rules solely in terms of aggregate well-being as *rule-utilitarianism*. Non-utilitarian versions of rule-consequentialism say the consequences that matter are not limited to net effects on overall well-being. Most prominently, some versions of rule-consequentialism say that what matters is not only how much well-being results but also how it is distributed.[13] Diagram 2.1 is a way of picturing the area.

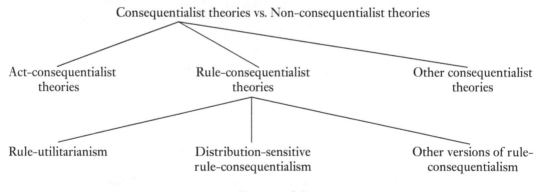

DIAGRAM 2.1

TABLE 2.2. First Code

	Units of well-being per person	per group	Total well-being for both groups
10,000 people in group A	1	10,000	
100,000 people in group B	10	1,000,000	
			1,010,000

Which version of rule-consequentialism is best? The problem with rule-*utilitarianism* is that it is ultimately insensitive to the distribution of well-being. For the sake of illustration, imagine a society with only two groups in it. One group— let us call it group A—has 10,000 people in it. The other group—group B—has 100,000 in it. Of course, this is a highly simplified example, but this is what makes it useful for bringing out certain ideas. So consider a code of rules whose internalization would leave each member of group A very badly off and each member of group B very well off (see Table 2.2).

Remember that utilitarianism (as I am using the term) is concerned with aggregate well-being, not with how equally well-being is distributed. Thus, if no alternative to the above code would provide greater net aggregate well-being, *utilitarians* would endorse this code.

Yet suppose that, from the point of view of utility, the next best code would be one with the results set out in Table 2.3. The second code results in greater equality of well-being, but less well-being in total.

In a moment, I will consider objections to the view that the second code must be better than the first. But before I do that, there is the prior question of what is attractive about the second code. The obvious answer might be that the second code contains greater equality of well-being. But the obvious answer might not be right.

To use Derek Parfit's excellent example, suppose that equality between people who are blind and people who can see could be achieved only by blinding those who could see. Such 'levelling down' would be outrageous (Parfit 1997; Gert 1998: 255; Arneson 1999b: 232–3). Anyone attracted to egalitarianism will see the point of benefiting the worse off even when this costs the better off. But careful reflection on equality suggests that a cost to the better off can be justified *only if* it benefits the worse off. The lesson is that what is important is not equality of well-being per se, but rather improvements in the well-being of the worst off. This idea has come to be called the principle of according *priority to the worst off*, or the principle of *prioritarianism* (Parfit 1997; Arneson 1999b).

Return now to our comparison of the first and second codes above. There is more equality with the second code. And the worse off are a lot better off with the second code than with the first. Parfit's work has shown us that what matters is not really equality of well-being as such but rather

TABLE 2.3. Second Code

	Units of well-being per person	per group	Total well-being for both groups
10,000 people in group A	8	80,000	
100,000 people in group B	9	900,000	
			980,000

improvements in the well-being of the worst off. So I conclude that what makes the second code more attractive than the first is that any plausible version of the principle of giving priority to the worst off will favour the second code.

2.5 Fairness, Justice, Desert

I used to think that rule-consequentialism should evaluate codes of rules in terms of aggregate well-being *and fairness,* though I was openly unsure how to characterize fairness.

On further investigation, I am not surprised I was unsure about how to characterize fairness. As Shelley Kagan (1998: 54) writes, '[T]he notion of fairness is somewhat amorphous and seems to pick out different features in different contexts. Often, indeed, to say of something that it is unfair is to say nothing more than that it is illegitimate or unjustified.' Similarly, Bernard Gert (1998: 195) observes, '"fair" is now often used as a synonym for "morally acceptable"'.[14] In this all-inclusive sense of 'fair', to say rules have to be fair is just to say that the rules have to be sensitive to all the morally relevant distinctions, as Kagan immediately goes on to remark. But this broad sense of 'fairness' invokes rather than supplies those distinctions.

Aristotle (*Nicomachean Ethics* 1130b 18–20) observed that there is a broad sense of 'justice' that subsumes all the virtues having to do with the treatment of others. This sense of 'justice' refers to whatever virtue (in our dealings with others) favours overall (Sidgwick 1907: 393). This is very close to the all-inclusive meaning of 'fairness' above.

That the terms 'fairness' and 'justice' have this meaning in common is not surprising since 'justice is often used to mean fairness' (Shaw 1999: 211). Hence the magnetism of the phrase, 'Justice as fairness.'[15]

The range of meanings for 'justice' and 'fairness' is enormous. We have already seen that they can be all-inclusive moral concepts. At the other end of the range, there is a sense of 'justice' and

of 'fairness' that equates to one of the minimal senses of impartiality. In this minimal sense, justice and fairness, like impartiality, preclude bias or inconsistency in the application or interpretation of rules. This is called *formal justice.* Thus John Rawls (1971: 58–9) wrote,

[The] impartial and consistent administration of laws and institutions, whatever their substantive principles, we may call formal justice. If we think of justice as always expressing a kind of equality, then formal justice requires that in their administration laws and institutions should apply equally (that is, in the same way) to those belonging to the classes defined by them. . . . Formal justice is adherence to principle, or as some have said, obedience to system.

However, just as rules can be impartially applied without being impartially justifiable, they can be fairly or justly applied without being fair or just. As Sidgwick (1907: 267) wrote, '[L]aws may be equally executed and yet unjust: for example, we should consider a law unjust which compelled only red-haired men to serve in the army, even thought it were applied with the strictest impartiality to all red-haired men.'

While we cannot assume that fairly applied rules are fair (or just), we also cannot assume they are not. Frederick Schauer (1991: 136–7) argues that rule-based decision-making does 'not further the aim of treating like cases alike and unalike cases differently', since rule-based decision-making can focus on morally irrelevant features and thereby treat differently cases that are actually relevantly similar. But if the rules are fair ones, then they will draw attention to, rather than overlook, relevant similarities.

What are the relevant similarities? Plato proposed that justice is 'rendering to each his due' (*Republic* Bk. 1). And Aristotle remarked, 'all men agree that what is just in distribution must be according to merit in some sense, though they do not all specify the same sort of merit' (*Nicomachean Ethics* 1131a 25–8). I call attention to these remarks because I believe that, if we read the terms 'due' and 'merit' as 'desert', we have the common view of the matter. On this view, for a rule to be morally fair it must render to each what she deserves (cf. Kagan 1998: 58).

But just as there are wide senses of 'just' and 'fair', there is a wide sense of 'desert'. So the claim that people should get what they deserve can be heard as the tautology that people should be treated as the balance of relevant moral reasons require. Here again we see a moral concept being used so broadly as to require for its application an account of all other moral reasons. If fair rules are defined as the ones that give people what they deserve, and what people deserve is to be treated as the balance of relevant moral reasons require, we have made little progress. The question is what the relevant moral reasons are.

However, I think 'desert' is normally used for a narrower class of considerations. If I am less well off than you are because I played games while you worked, then there hardly seems a good moral reason for me to be given part of what you earned. If in a competitive economy you successfully strove to be productive and I didn't bother, you deserve greater rewards. Similarly, if you are kind and trustworthy, and I am selfish and dishonest, you deserve a better life than I deserve.[16]

Sometimes there is a criterion for a just and fair outcome that is entirely independent of any procedure for reaching this outcome. But, in some kinds of case, there is no criterion for a fair outcome that is independent of a procedure for reaching this outcome (Rawls 1971: 85–6). In some cases, what people deserve is whatever the fairly conducted procedure produces. For example, in games of chance or competitions of skill, there is no criterion for a fair outcome except what is produced by the procedure, fairly conducted. These cases are known as cases of 'pure procedural fairness'.

Now to account for procedural fairness, we must take into account not only benefits and harms but also *probabilities* of and *opportunities*

for benefits. If, in a game of luck, neither of us deserves better odds, then the game is fair if and only if we each have an equal probability of success. If, in a competition, neither of us deserves more opportunities than others do, then the competition is fair only if we indeed have equal opportunities. In the context of the present discussion, we would get off track if we paused here to investigate whether anyone ever does deserve better odds in games of luck or greater opportunities in competitions of skill.

In virtually any human activity, some people are better at it than others. If you are better at some activity than I am, then you deserve that no one should say that you are not better at it. Whether your superiority is something anyone wants to comment upon is another thing. For various reasons, everyone—including you— might prefer your superiority in the activity not to be mentioned.

Of course, in many contexts we do want people to notice that we are better at some activity than others. And, in many contexts, desirable consequences will flow from the establishment of explicit rewards for demonstrated superiority in certain activities. Who wants randomly selected people running our government, or playing on our city's team, or the drawings of randomly selected people exhibited in the museums? Competition is obviously desirable in many contexts.

Many people believe that, where there are fair economic competitions, the winners deserve their rewards. Suppose the person who owns the cornfield announces in advance of the harvest that, in addition to a basic per day salary, whichever two workers gather the most corn will get a 25 per cent bonus each. If everyone has an equal opportunity to enter this competition and if the competition is run fairly, then the two who are most productive deserve their greater spoils.

Commonsense morality also holds that those who are kind and trustworthy should do better than those who are selfish or untrustworthy.

Unfortunately, often the winners of economic competitions are neither kind nor trustworthy. As Richard Arneson (1999b: 241) writes,

a competitive market responds to supply and demand, not fine-grained or for that matter coarse-grained estimations of different individuals' degrees of deservingness and responsibility. If we imagine institutions that would do better to bring about distribution of the good in accordance with people's true deservingness, but at significant cost of priority-weighted aggregate well-being, would we then be inclined to scrap the competitive market in order to institute a tolerably adequate moral meritocracy?

In any event, a common view is that to evaluate codes of rules in terms of fairness or justice is to evaluate them in terms of whether differences in the benefits (including probabilities of and opportunities for them) that individuals get correspond to differences in the individuals' desert.

This line of thinking often seems irresistible. When a kind and honest person dies of cancer in the prime of his life, this is a terrible loss not only to him but also to his family and friends. Meanwhile, many selfish and untrustworthy people enjoy long lives and unearned riches. Who could fail to be struck by such injustice?

Indeed, once we have noticed the tight conceptual connections between justice, fairness, and desert, we might also begin linking the concept of moral rights to these other concepts. A familiar line of thought is that, just as *justice* and *fairness* call for people to get what they deserve, people have a moral *right* to whatever benefits they deserve.[17]

But this may be a thought too far. Did the person cut down by cancer in the prime of his life have a moral right to a life of average length? Against whom could he have such a right?

Suppose that in the end we think there is something confused about the claim that a person has a moral right to a life of average length. But even if in this case there is no moral right that has been infringed, there is still injustice. When there is injustice for which no human is responsible, perhaps we have to call it 'cosmic injustice'. If we accept that there is this category of injustice and if we think injustice always involves the infringement of rights, we have to believe that there are rights against the cosmos. Alternatively, we could give up the idea that injustice always involves the infringement of rights.

I certainly agree that there is terrible injustice when the good die young or the wicked prosper. I also believe that at least some of these injustices are ones for which no one is responsible. But I cannot accept that there are rights against the cosmos, so I must deny that injustice always involves the infringement of rights. To deny this is not to think injustice any less awful.

Since injustice and unfairness are so awful, perhaps any proposed rules should be evaluated in terms of whether they serve justice and fairness—that is, leave people with what they deserve. To be more specific, perhaps any rules should be evaluated in terms of whether their internalization would end up rewarding only the deserving. There is the further consideration of proportionality—that is, that equals are treated equally and unequals unequally (Aristotle, *Nicomachean Ethics* 1131a 20–4). Combining the ideas of desert and proportionality, we could propose that rule-consequentialism evaluate rules either wholly or partly in terms of whether they reward people *in proportion with their desert*. If rule-consequentialism did this, it would accord desert a foundational role in the theory.

Desert, justice, and fairness seem so important that this way of constructing rule-consequentialism is difficult to resist.[18] Yet, rule-consequentialism should *not* start by helping itself to the assumption that some people deserve more than others. Rule-consequentialism does not need to assume this, because rule-consequentialism can explain why certain rules that encourage some kinds of activity and discourage others are highly desirable (cf. Kagan 1998: 55; Arneson 1999b: 238–9).

In this book, I will say only a little about punishment. Again, the rule-consequentialist rationale for rules is that their internalization has high expected value. This will be true of rules not only about how people should treat those who behave well but also about how people should react when others break the rules. If there is net value in people's internalizing a rule, there is typically net value in reinforcing conformity with that rule. So rule-consequentialism will have no trouble explaining why someone guilty of breaking its rules should be put in a more or less uncomfortable position, 'if not by law, by the opinion of his fellow creatures; if not by opinion, by the reproaches of his own conscience' (Mill 1861: ch. 5, para. 14).

Likewise, someone who has fully internalized and complied with the code should be rewarded by the combination of noninterference from the law, a good reputation in society, and a clear conscience. In addition, rules that reward those who produce what others want serve to establish further incentives. The establishment of appropriate incentives yields greater aggregate well-being than would result were there no such incentives.[19]

So rule-consequentialism can explain why rules should punish certain kinds of behaviour and reward other kinds. And it can do this without presupposing that certain kinds of behaviour inherently *deserve* to be rewarded. A moral theory is better off *explaining* why certain distinctions are morally important than simply *assuming* they are.

Return to the supposed connection between desert and fairness. If what is fair is determined by what people deserve, and if rule-consequentialism should not be formulated as evaluating rules even partly in terms of desert, then it should not be formulated as evaluating codes even partly in terms of fairness.

2.6 Fairness; Contracts, and Proportion

So far, I have discussed fairness as the unbiased application of rules, and fair or just rules as ones that allot to individuals what they deserve. But neither of these things is what I had in mind when I proposed in earlier publications that rules should be evaluated in terms of fairness as well as aggregate well-being. In those publications, I had simply taken for granted that the appropriate rules were to be fairly applied. And I had assumed that the appropriate rules would determine the principles of desert, rather than take desert as the ground of the rules. But I also assumed that, for the purposes of evaluating rules, there must be some relevant consideration other than aggregate well-being.

Consider again the case of the person who owns the cornfield and announces before the harvest that, in addition to the per day salary, the two workers who pick the most corn will get a bonus. Suppose the promise was for a 50 per cent bonus, on top of the basic per day salary. Now suppose the second most productive cornpicker picks 1,000 ears of corn and the third picks 999. Is it fair that, when the difference in their performance is so small, the second best cornpicker gets a far bigger reward than the third best cornpicker?

Consider another case. Suppose the owner of the cornfield offers only a 5 per cent bonus, beyond basic per day salary, to each of the two most productive cornpickers. And suppose the two best are really far quicker and thus more productive than all the others. So imagine that the second best picks 1,000 ears and the third best picks only 500. Is it fair that, when the difference in their performance is so large, the difference in their reward is small?

I think most people would think that if the parties were competing according to one set of reasonably fair rules—and so making decisions on the basis of one set of reasonable expectations—then fairness requires that those rules and expectations be upheld. It is striking that the *first* rule of substantive justice mentioned by Sidgwick (1907: 269) is that one should do what one has contracted to do. Moral fairness requires that a contract is binding provided all of the following.[20] (a) The contract was entered into by sane people. (b) The contract was not the result of one party's withholding information to which the other party was entitled. (c) The contract was not the result of one party's threatening to infringe someone's moral rights. (d) The contract does not itself require one or more parties to infringe moral rights (this is why, for example, contracts to commit murder or robbery are not binding). None of (a) through (d) undermine the contract which we are imagining the owner of the field made with the workers.

Contracts can of course be changed by mutual consent. But in our example there was no such change. And it is not fair for one party to a deal to change the terms of the deal unilaterally, especially after others have made decisions based on expectations created by this party.

Over the last four decades, much has been made of the principle of fair play (Hart 1955; Rawls 1971: sect. 18). But Nozick (1974: 93–5) showed that, even if you have benefited from a communal practice, and even if the benefit you received was greater than your fair share of sustaining the practice would have cost you, you may not be morally obligated to contribute to the practice. What matters is whether you *knew*, when you accepted the benefits, that you would be expected by others to contribute to the practice. If you did know, then others will take your having accepted those benefits as your having implicitly agreed to do your part in return. As Kagan (1998: 143) observes,

the more we move in the direction of requiring that benefits first be freely and knowingly accepted, the more plausible it becomes to view the agent as having made an implicit *promise* to obey the rules governing

the practice. Thus, even if there is a sound version of the principle of fair play, despite initial appearances it may not actually point to a normative factor distinct from that of promising.

Earlier we saw that fairness requires the (consistent and impartial) following of appropriate rules. Now we have to add the idea that what is fair really depends not so much on what individuals *would* have agreed to, but rather what they *actually* did agree to.

However, not all agreements are binding. For example, if I get you to agree to something by threatening to torture you, or by threatening to torture someone else, any promise you make to prevent me from carrying out this threat is not morally binding. What this shows is that to explain fully the concept of fairness we must appeal to the concept of a morally binding promise. And to explain the concept of a morally binding promise, we must appeal to the idea of a promise that was *not* made in response to a threat to infringe someone's moral rights. The concept of fairness turns out to depend on the concept of moral rights after all.

And what generates moral rights? We cannot at this point refer back to fairness, since that would be circular. One extremely plausible suggestion is that a set of moral rights is justified if their communal acceptance maximizes expected utility (Mill 1861: ch. 5; Sumner 1987). Again, perhaps we need to add a weighting so that the well-being of the worst off gets priority. I shall come back to this in a moment.

First, I want to acknowledge that many would feel some regret about the result for the cornpicker who performs far better but gets only a slightly bigger payment. Similarly, many would feel some regret about the result for the cornpicker who performs only slightly less well but gets a far smaller payment. Although proportionality is not always important, proportionality between reward and productivity in producing what others want does seem important in establishing general economic incentives.

Our conception of fairness is infused both with the idea of proportionality and with the idea that agreements between sane people should be honoured (given that the agreement was not extracted by fraud or by the threat to infringe moral rights, and given that the agreement does not itself require one or more parties to it to infringe moral rights). Since sane people can agree not to divide benefits in proportion to productivity, fairness sometimes gets into a fight with itself. Rule-utilitarianism can explain the importance of keeping your side of a deal once other parties to the deal have done their side. It can also explain the general advantages of proportional rewards. Making reward proportional to productivity seems justified in terms of creating incentives. The backbone of a system of incentives is the expectation that agreements will be honoured. So where agreements create a system of non-proportional rewards, the pressure to honour the agreements seems greater than the pressure to make rewards proportional. All this seems correct both from the point of view of rule-utilitarianism and from the point of view of our moral intuitions.

My references to fairness in earlier publications were caused partly by a worry that a code of rules whose internalization would maximize aggregate well-being might leave well-being distributed in an unacceptably unequal way. However, I thought that inequality is bad only if it is unfair (Broome 1991b: 199). I continue with questions about distribution in the next section. But first let me mention that another part of my reason for referring to fairness in earlier publications was that I thought building fairness into rule-consequentialism could help the theory answer some of the concerns about fairness that Lyons expressed in his 1965 discussion of rule-utilitarianism (Lyons 1965).

Works Cited

Aristotle. *Nicomachean Ethics*, trans. W. D. Ross, revised J. O. Urmson (Oxford: Clarendon Press, 1975).

Arneson, Richard. 1999a. 'Human Flourishing versus Desire Satisfaction', *Social Philosophy and Policy* 16: 113–42.

Bentham, J. 1789. *Introduction to the Principles of Morals and Legislation*.

Brandt, Richard B. 1959. *Ethical Theory* (Englewood Cliffs, N.J.: Prentice-Hall).

——— 1963. 'Toward a Credible Form of Utilitarianism', in H.-N. Castañeda and G. Nakhnikian, eds., *Morality and the Language of Conduct* (Detroit: Wayne State University Press), 107–43.

——— 1979. *A Theory of the Good and the Right* (Oxford: Clarendon Press).

Brink, David O. 1989. *Moral Realism and the Foundations of Ethics* (New York: Cambridge University Press).

Broad, C. D. 1930. *Five Types of Ethical Theory* (London: Routledge & Kegan Paul).

Broome, John. 1991b. *Weighing Goods* (Oxford: Blackwell).

Crisp, Roger. 1997. *Mill on Utilitarianism* (London: Routledge).

Feinberg, Joel. 1970. *Doing and Deserving* (Princeton: Princeton University, Press).

——— 1974. 'Non-Comparative Justice', *Philosophical Review* 83: 297–338.

Feldman, Fred. 1997. *Utilitarianism, Hedonism, and Desert* (Cambridge: Cambridge University Press)

Finnis, John. 1980. *Natural Law and Natural Rights* (Oxford: Clarendon Press).

Frankena, William. 1973. *Ethics*, 2nd edn. (Englewood Cliffs, N.J.: Prentice-Hall) [1st edn. 1963].

Fried, Charles. 1981. *Contract as Promise: A Theory of Contractual Obligation* (Cambridge, Mass.: Harvard University Press).

Gert, B. 1998. *Morality* (New York: Oxford University Press).

Glover, Jonathan. 1984. *What Sort of People Should There Be?* (Harmondsworth: Penguin).

Griffin, James. 1986. *Well-Being: Its Meaning, Measurement and Moral Importance* (Oxford: Clarendon Press).

——— 1992. 'The Human Good and the Ambitions of Consequentialism', *Social Philosophy and Policy* 9: 118–32.

———— 1996. *Value Judgement* (Oxford: Clarendon Press).

Hardin, Russell. 1988. *Morality Within the Limits of Reason* (Chicago: University of Chicago Press).

Hart, H. L. A. 1955. 'Are There Any Natural Rights?', *Philosophical Review* 64: 175–91.

———— 1961. *The Concept of Law* (Oxford: Clarendon Press).

Hurka, Thomas. 1993. *Perfectionism* (New York: Oxford University Press).

———— 2000. *Virtue, Vice, and Value* (New York: Oxford University Press).

Kagan, Shelly. 1998. *Normative Ethics* (Boulder, Colo.: Westview Press).

Kelly, P. J. 1990. *Utilitarianism and Distributive Justice: Bentham and the Civil Law* (Oxford: Clarendon Press).

Lyons, David. 1965. *Forms and Limits of Utilitarianism* (Oxford: Clarendon Press).

Mackie, J. L. 1977. *Ethics: Inventing Right and Wrong* (Harmondsworth: Penguin).

Mill, J. S. 1861. *Utilitarianism*.

Nagel, Thomas. 1991. *Equality and Partiality* (New York: Oxford University Press).

Nozick, Robert. 1974. *Anarchy, State, and Utopia* (Oxford: Blackwell).

———— 1981. *Philosophical Explanations* (Oxford: Clarendon Press).

Parfit, Derek. 1984. *Reasons and Persons* (Oxford: Clarendon Press).

———— 1997. 'Equality and Priority', *Ratio* 10: 202–21.

Raphael, D. D., ed. 1969. *The British Moralists* (Oxford: Clarendon Press).

Rawls, John. 1958. 'Justice as Fairness', *Philosophical Review* 67: 164–94.

———— 1971. *A Theory of Justice* (Cambridge, Mass.: Harvard University Press).

Rescher, Nicholas. 1966. *Distributive Justice* (Indianapolis: Bobbs-Merrill).

Rosen, Fred. 1998. 'Individual Sacrifice and the Greatest Happiness: Bentham on Utility and Rights', *Utilitas* 10: 129–43.

Scanlon, T. M. 1978. 'Rights, Goals, and Fairness', in S. Hampshire, ed., *Public and Private Morality* (Cambridge: Cambridge University Press, 1978), 93–111.

———— 1998. *What We Owe Each Other* (Cambridge, Mass.: Harvard University Press).

Scheffler, S. 1982. *The Rejection of Consequentialism* (Oxford: Clarendon Press).

Sen, Amartya. 1973. *On Economic Inequality* (Oxford: Clarendon Press).

———— and Williams, B. 1982. 'Introduction', in Sen and Williams, eds., *Utilitarianism and Beyond* (Cambridge: Cambridge University Press, 1982).

Shaw, William. 1999. *Contemporary Ethics: Taking Account of Utilitarianism* (Malden, Mass.: Blackwell).

Sidgwick, Henry. 1907. *Methods of Ethics*, 7th edn. (London: Macmillan).

Skorupski, John. 1995. 'Agent-Neutrality, Consequentialism, Utilitarianism . . . A Terminological Note', *Utilitas* 7: 49–54.

Smart, J. J. C. 1973. 'Outline of a System of Utilitarian Ethics', in J. J. C. Smart and Bernard Williams, *Utilitarianism: For and Against* (Cambridge: Cambridge University Press), 3–74.

Sumner, L. W. 1996. *Welfare, Happiness, and Ethics* (Oxford: Clarendon Press).

Thomson, Judith Jarvis. 1990. *The Realm of Rights* (Cambridge, Mass.: Harvard University Press).

Trianosky, Gregory. 1988. 'Rightly Ordered Appetites: How to Live Morally and Live Well', *American Philosophical Quarterly* 25: 1–12.

Wolf, Susan. 1997. 'Happiness and Meaning: Two Aspects of the Good Life', *Social Philosophy and Policy* 14: 207–25.

Notes

1. Assume that new generations are not changed genetically. If genetic engineering alters human genetic makeup, the codes that are best will probably be different.

2. Some philosophers would prefer to call such a theory teleology, rather than consequentialism. Consequentialism is said to be the kind of teleological theory that accords no intrinsic value to acts themselves—that is, no value apart from their (causal, as opposed to conceptual) consequences. See Scheffler 1982: 1 n., 2 n.; Brink 1989: 9–10, 215–16, and esp. 237; cf. Broome 1991b: ch. 1.

3. Here I am drawing on remarks by Brandt (1963: n. 2); and by Griffin (1992: 122–5). I take it that Hardin (1988: 63) takes much the same view when he writes that the value from promising '*comes from* the contribution promising makes to our actual conditions, not from any a priori rightness above such value'.

4. To loving the good and hating the bad, Hurka adds recursive principles about loving the loving of the good, hating the loving of the bad, loving the hating of the bad, and hating the hating of the good.

5. I explore the relationship between rule-consequentialism and contingency at greater length in my 2000c.

6. However, in Sidgwick's case, equality seems to have independent weight as a tie breaker (Sidgwick 1907: 417). Moreover, Fred Rosen (1998: esp. 140–3) argues that Bentham and Mill conceived of maximizing utility as favouring equality, even over aggregate utility. The security of expectations about the rewards of economic activity, for Bentham, outweighed the importance of economic equality—mainly because of the economic advantages of incentives to work. (In a forthcoming edition of Bentham's writings edited by Philip Schofield, we find Bentham stating: 'Equality in property is destructive of the very principle of subsistence; it cuts up society by its roots. Nobody would labour if no one were secure of the fruits of his labour.') Still, according to Rosen (141 n. 31), Bentham, if no issue of security arose, 'would choose 100 units of welfare equally distributed between two groups over 110 units unequally distributed, where the majority receives more at the expense of the minority'. See also Kelly 1990. But let me delay questions about equality and distribution until later.

7. I borrow the helpful term 'introspectively discernible' from Parfit 1984: 494.

8. Though compromises between hedonism and its critics are explored in Sumner 1996, 2000.

9. I am grateful to Tom Carson for suggesting this formulation to me, although I do not mean to suggest that he endorsed all its implications.

10. See Finnis 1980, 1983; Parfit 1984: Appendix I; Hurka 1993: chs. 7–10; Brink 1989: 221–36; Scanlon 1993; Griffin 1996: ch. 2; Crisp 1990, 1997: ch. 3; Bailey 1997: 7; Gert 1998: 92–4; Arneson 1999a. The chapters from Hurka 1993 present a compelling account of how to rank different kinds of knowledge and achievements.

11. Compare Wolf 1997: 211; Frankena 1973: 91; Nozick 1981: 611, 1989: 168; Parfit 1984: 502; Trianosky 1988: 3–4; Scanlon 1998: 124–5.

12. This point is made in many places, e.g. Finnis 1983: 50; Griffin 1986: 71; Hurka, 1993: 151–6.

13. The use of 'consequentialism' and 'utilitarianism' so that consequentialism allows for a concern for distribution in a way that utilitarianism does not is very common. For some examples, see Mackie 1977: 129, 149; Scanlon 1978:

esp. sect. 2; Scheffler 1982: 26–34, 70–9; Sen and Williams 1982: 3–4f; Parfit 1984: 26; Griffin 1986: 151–2; 1992: 126, 1996: 165. Examples of writers who include distributive considerations *within* utilitarianism are Brandt 1959: 404, 426, 429–31; Rescher 1966: 25; Raphael 1994: 47; Skorupski 1995: 54; and arguably Bentham (see Rosen 1998: 139–43) and Mill 1861. For writers who want to mix concern for aggregate well-being and concern for distributive matters, see not only those listed above but also Sidgwick 1907: 417; and Broad 1930: 283.

14. Gert rejects this broad use of the term 'fair' and immediately goes on to claim that 'in its basic sense, fairness is playing by the rules. To enlarge the concept by applying it to the making of the rules is to invite confusion.' (Gert 1998: 195) He denies that social practices can themselves be fair or unfair. I cannot accept this limitation on the concept. It is a further question whether fairness in the terms of a social practice is a foundational value, or instead one entirely derived from the value of aggregate well-being.

15. A phrase whose currency testifies to the impact of Rawls 1958.

16. For classic discussions of desert, see Feinberg 1970, 1974; and the writings collected together in Pojman and McLeod 1999. Attempts to fold desert into consequentialism can be found in Feldman 1997: pt. III; see also the discussions in Kagan 1999; Arneson 1999b.

17. J. S. Mill (1861: ch. 5, para. 15) claimed, 'Justice implies something which it is not only right to do, and wrong not to do, but which some individual person can claim from us as his moral right.' See also Broome's account of fairness (1991b: 194–6). Broome argues that you and I are treated fairly if the respective *duties owed to us* are satisfied in proportion to their respective strengths.

18. Hence the enormous appeal of views like those found in Feldman 1997 and Kagan 1999.

19. People have different levels of ability and different appetites for work as opposed to leisure. For these reasons, I assume any system of economic incentives will result in at least some economic inequality.

20. The claims here echo my earlier remarks about promising. Again, see Sidgwick 1907: 305–11; Hart 1961: 192–3; Fried 1981: esp. ch. 7; Thomson 1990: ch. 12; Scanlon 1998: ch. 7. One difference between a promise and a contract seems to me to be that the insane can make a morally forceful promise but not an enforceable contract. Another is that promises need not involve 'consideration', i.e. exchange.

PART VI

Deontological Ethics
Introduction

Teleological and deontological ethics take their names from ancient Greek roots. *Telos* means 'aim' or 'goal'; *deon* means 'obligation' or 'duty.' Teleological moral theories evaluate actions according to how well they promote or reflect the achievement of certain goals, such as pleasure or happiness. Thus actions are evaluated according to features extrinsic to (outside of) themselves. Deontological moral theories evaluate actions according features intrinsic to (inside of) themselves, such as whether they are of an inherently wrong kind, like lying or cheating.

Until the early modern period, Western moral philosophy was overwhelmingly teleological, although the ancient Stoics and some medievals, especially St. Thomas Aquinas, advanced deontological ideas. Since Kant, the greatest deontologist to date, deontology has become a close rival of teleology, each commanding a large following among moral philosophers.

The modern division of moral philosophy along deontological and teleological lines reflects a tension that most of us find in our everyday moral judgments. This tension is reflected in public policy, which seems to sometimes favor deontological considerations and other times favor teleological ones. For instance, most Americans would not support framing an innocent man for rape or murder in order to stop a riot (as in the famous "utilitarian sheriff" example—see reading 22), even if putting the innocent man in prison for life would save ten other people from death. Our reasons seem deontological (although they could be rule-consequentialist, instead). We think that we have a duty to respect the rights of the innocent man, whatever the consequences. Framing innocent people is a wrong kind of action, end of story. However, most Americans also seem to support singling out people who appear to be of Middle Eastern descent at airports for extra scrutiny, and thus subject them to extra inconvenience, despite the common American belief that everyone has a right to equal treatment under the law. In this case our reasons seem consequentialist, and thus teleological. We seem to regard the contribution that this policy might make towards preventing another terrorist attack like 9/11 as more important than something we usually consider fundamentally wrong: discrimination on the basis of apparent race or ethnicity.

Immanuel Kant (1724–1804) was more responsible for the importance of modern deontology than anyone. In our first reading, Kant begins by arguing for the hegemony of the right over the good. That is, he argues that goodness is a matter of promoting rightness, rather than vice versa, as teleological theories would have it. Then he proposes and begins to defend his famous *Categorical Imperative,* or ultimate criterion for the moral acceptability of all action. The Categorical Imperative is a single rule, although Kant proposes various formulations of it (ways of stating it). Our reading includes only the first two formulations, which are arguably the most important ones. The Categorical Imperative may remind you of the Golden Rule, and it may remind you of the idea that it is wrong to simply use people, as a boyfriend who dates his girlfriend only to get at her money simply uses her. You would be correct in both cases, but the Categorical Imperative goes much farther than either.

In our second reading, Melissa Bergeron and I take up the idea that Kant's Categorical Imperative is an attempt to understand rightness as fairness. We pursue and evaluate that idea, considering along the way several of the most important problems with the Categorical Imperative. We do not solve all of these problems; however we lean on the ideas of some of Kant's recent defenders, adding a few of our own, in order to argue that the problems can be solved.

W. D. Ross (1877–1971) was one of the greatest moral theorists of the twentieth century. In our third reading, he proposes a deontological theory that is often called intuitionism (although it is not the only theory that goes by that name). Ross thinks that some moral generalizations are self-evident—the "best people" understand that they are true without any need for further evidence. For instance, he thinks that "I have a prima facie duty to keep my promises" is self-evident; by a 'prima facie' duty he means an 'unless overridden by a more important duty' duty. If I promise to meet you for lunch at 11:30, I have a prima facie duty to meet you for lunch at 11:30. However, because it is only a prima facie duty it can be overridden. Suppose, for instance, that on my way to our lunch I encounter someone who needs CPR, and suppose that I know how to do CPR. I should stop and do CPR even if it means that I miss our lunch, for my duty to save the life of the person who needs CPR is more important than my duty to keep my promise to have lunch with you.

Unlike Kant, Ross thinks that every type of duty can be overridden. He is thus a moral pluralist; that is, he believes that there is no one kind of duty that always trumps every other kind of duty. Sometimes duties of beneficence trump duties of fidelity, as in my lunch/CPR example; but at other times duties go the other way. For instance, I should pay you back the fifty dollars you loaned me, because I promised to do so, even if I could do more good by giving that fifty dollars to charity (if, for instance, you would probably waste it on fleeting pleasures). In some ways Ross' pluralism makes his theory seem more plausible than Kant's. For instance, it gives Ross the flexibility to say that lies are sometimes permissible, which is what most people think. Kant's theory, on the other hand, commits him to an absolute duty to never lie (so, at least, Kant thought). However, Ross' theory has problems of its own. For instance, it makes an almost total mystery of how we should decide between conflicting duties, especially in difficult cases—the kinds of cases for which we are most in need of help from ethical theory.

In our fourth reading, William Frankena pursues Ross' project of reconciling our deontological and teleological moral judgments. However, Frankena gives our teleological judgments more credit than Ross does. Although in the final analysis Frankena remains a deontologist, he favors building teleological concerns into our conceptions of actions. He does not have us choose between deontology and teleology; he has us see the latter as the most important ingredient of the former.

T. M. Scanlon is a giant of contemporary moral theory. He is a contractualist, or contractarian: he conceives the correctness of moral principles according to whether we would accept them in certain, ideal circumstances. He is Kantian (or neo-Kantian) in the sense that he endorses Kant's view that rightness is fairness. However, he is unlike Kant in that he denies that what matters is the rationality of agents (beings capable of moral or immoral action). According to Scanlon it is instead their reasonableness that matters. In our fifth and last reading, Scanlon compares and contrasts his view, and especially his conception of reasonableness, with the views of others, including Kant.

24

The Foundations of Ethics

IMMANUEL KANT

Immanuel Kant (1724–1804), who was born in a deeply pietistic Lutheran family in Konigsberg, Germany, lived in that town his entire life and taught at the University of Konigsberg. He lived a duty-bound, methodical life, so regular that citizens were said to have set their clocks by his walks. Kant is one of the premier philosophers in the Western tradition. In his monumental work The Critique of Pure Reason *(1781) he inaugurated the equivalent of a Copernican revolution in the theory of knowledge.*

Excerpt from Kant, *Grounding for the Metaphysics of Morals*, translated by James Ellington. © 1981 by Hackett Publishing Company, Inc. Reprinted by permission of the publisher.

This selection is from his classic work Grounding for the Metaphysics of Morals *(1785), in which he outlines a rationalist ethical system centered in the notion of the* categorical imperative *as the fundamental principle of action.*

After a brief preface in which he eschews any appeal to empirical considerations, he begins his treatise by arguing that only the good will, a will to act out of a sense of duty, has unqualified moral worth.

Preface

Since I am here primarily concerned with moral philosophy, the foregoing question will be limited to a consideration of whether or not there is the utmost necessity for working out for once a pure moral philosophy that is wholly cleared of everything which can only be empirical and can only belong to anthropology. That there must be such a philosophy is evident from the common idea of duty and of moral laws. Everyone must admit that if a law is to be morally valid, i.e., is to be valid as a ground of obligation, then it must carry with it absolute necessity. He must admit that the command, "Thou shalt not lie," does not hold only for men, as if other rational beings had no need to abide by it, and so with all the other moral laws properly so called. And he must concede that the ground of obligation here must therefore be sought not in the nature of man nor in the circumstances of the world in which man is placed, but must be sought a priori solely in the concepts of pure reason; he must grant that every other precept which is founded on principles of mere experience—even a precept that may in certain respects be universal—insofar as it rests in the least on empirical grounds—perhaps only in its motive—can indeed be called a practical rule, but never a moral law.

Thus not only are moral laws together with their principles essentially different from every kind of practical cognition in which there is anything empirical, but all moral philosophy rests entirely on its pure part. When applied to man, it does not in the least borrow from acquaintance with him (anthropology) but gives a priori laws to him as a rational being. To be sure, these laws require, furthermore, a power of judgment sharpened by experience, partly in order to distinguish in what cases they are applicable, and partly to gain for them access to the human will as well as influence for putting them into practice. For man is affected by so many inclinations that, even though he is indeed capable of the idea of a pure practical reason, he is not so easily able to make that idea effective *in concreto* in the conduct of his life.

A metaphysics of morals is thus indispensably necessary, not merely because of motives of spec-

ulation regarding the source of practical principles which are present a priori in our reason, but because morals themselves are liable to all kinds of corruption as long as the guide and supreme norm for correctly estimating them are missing. For in the case of what is to be morally good, that it conforms to the moral law is not enough; it must also be done for the sake of the moral law. Otherwise that conformity is only very contingent and uncertain, since the nonmoral ground may now and then produce actions that conform with the law but quite often produces actions that are contrary to the law. Now the moral law in its purity and genuineness (which is of the utmost concern in the practical realm) can be sought nowhere but in a pure philosophy. Therefore, pure philosophy (metaphysics) must precede; without it there can be no moral philosophy at all. That philosophy which mixes pure principles with empirical ones does not deserve the name of philosophy (for philosophy is distinguished from ordinary rational knowledge by its treatment in a separate science of what the latter comprehends only confusedly). Still less does it deserve the name of moral philosophy, since by this very confusion it spoils even the purity of morals and counteracts its own end.

First Section

Transition from the Ordinary Rational Knowledge of Morality to the Philosophical

The Good Will

There is no possibility of thinking of anything at all in the world, or even out of it, which can be regarded as good without qualification, except a *good will.* Intelligence, wit, judgment, and whatever talents of the mind one might want to name are doubtless in many respects good and desirable, as are such qualities of temperament as courage, resolution, perseverance. But they can also become extremely bad and harmful if the will, which is to make use of these gifts of nature and which in its special constitution is called character, is not good. The same holds with gifts of fortune; power, riches, honor, even health, and that complete well-being and contentment with one's condition which is called happiness make for pride and often hereby even arrogance, unless there is a good will to correct their influence on the mind and herewith also to rectify the whole principle of action and make it universally conformable to its end. The sight of a being who is not graced by any touch of a pure and good will but who yet enjoys an uninterrupted prosperity can never delight a rational and impartial spectator. Thus a good will seems to constitute the indispensable condition of being even worthy of happiness.

Some qualities are even conducive to this good will itself and can facilitate its work. Nevertheless, they have no intrinsic unconditional worth; but they always presuppose, rather, a good will, which restricts the high esteem in which they are otherwise rightly held, and does not permit them to be regarded as absolutely good. Moderation in emotions and passions, self-control, and calm deliberation are not only good in many respects but even seem to constitute part of the intrinsic worth of a person. But they are far from being rightly called good without qualification (however unconditionally they were commended by the ancients). For without the principles of a good will, they can become extremely bad; the coolness of a villain makes him not only much more dangerous but also immediately more abominable in our eyes than he would have been regarded by us without it.

A good will is good not because of what it effects or accomplishes, nor because of its fitness to attain some proposed end; it is good only through its willing, i.e., it is good in itself. When it is considered in itself, then it is to be esteemed very much higher than anything which it might ever bring about merely in order to favor some inclination, or even the sum total of all inclinations. Even if, by some especially unfortunate fate or by the niggardly provision of stepmotherly nature, this will should be wholly lacking in the power to accomplish its purpose; if with the greatest effort it should yet achieve nothing, and only the good will should remain (not, to be sure, as a mere wish but as the summoning of all the means in our power), yet would it, like a jewel, still shine by its own light as something which has its full value in itself. Its usefulness or fruitlessness can neither augment nor diminish this value. Its usefulness would be, as it were, only the setting to enable us to handle it in ordinary dealings or to attract to it the attention of those who are not yet experts, but not to recommend it to real experts or to determine its value.

Nature's Purpose in Making Reason the Guide of the Will

But there is something so strange in this idea of the absolute value of a mere will, in which no account is taken of any useful results, that in spite of all the agreement received even from ordinary reason, yet there must arise the suspicion that such an idea may perhaps have as its hidden basis merely some high-flown fancy, and that we may have misunderstood the purpose of nature in assigning to reason the governing of our will. Therefore, this idea will be examined from this point of view.

In the natural constitution of an organized being, i.e., one suitably adapted to the purpose of life, let there be taken as a principle that in such a being no organ is to be found for any end unless it be the most fit and the best adapted for that end. Now if that being's preservation, welfare, or in a word its happiness, were the real end of nature in the case of a being having reason and will, then nature would have hit upon a very poor arrangement in having the reason of the creature carry out this purpose. For all the actions which such a creature has to perform with this purpose in view, and the whole rule of his conduct would have been prescribed much more exactly by instinct; and the purpose in question could have been attained much more certainly by instinct than it ever can be by reason. And if in addition reason had been imparted to this favored creature, then it would have had to serve him only to contemplate the happy constitution of his nature, to admire that nature, to rejoice in it, and to feel grateful to the cause that bestowed it; but reason would not have served him to subject his faculty of desire to its weak and delusive guidance nor would it have served him to meddle incompetently with the purpose of nature. In a word, nature would have taken care that reason did not strike out into a practical use nor presume, with its weak insight, to think out for itself a plan for happiness and the means for attaining it. Nature would have taken upon herself not only the choice of ends but also that of the means, and would with wise foresight have entrusted both to instinct alone.

And, in fact, we find that the more a cultivated reason devotes itself to the aim of enjoying life and happiness, the further does man get away from true contentment. Because of this there arises in many persons, if only they are candid enough to admit it, a certain degree of misology, i.e., hatred of reason. This is especially so in the case of those who are the most experienced in the use of reason, because after calculating all the advantages they derive, I say not from the invention of all the arts of common luxury, but even from the sciences (which in the end seem to them to be also a luxury of the understanding), they yet find that they have in fact only brought more trouble on their heads than they have gained in happiness. Therefore, they come to envy, rather than despise, the more common run of men who are closer to the guidance of mere natural instinct and who do not allow their reason much influence on their conduct. And we must admit that the judgment of those who would temper, or even reduce below zero, the boastful eulogies on behalf of the advantages which reason is supposed to provide as regards the happiness and contentment of life is by no means morose or ungrateful to the goodness with which the world is governed: There lies at the root of such judgments, rather, the idea that existence has another and much more worthy purpose, for which, and

not for happiness, reason is quite properly intended, and which must, therefore, be regarded as the supreme condition to which the private purpose of men must, for the most part, defer.

Reason, however, is not competent enough to guide the will safely as regards its objects and the satisfaction of all our needs (which it in part even multiplies); to this end would an implanted natural instinct have led much more certainly. But inasmuch as reason has been imparted to us as a practical faculty, i.e., as one which is to have influence on the will, its true function must be to produce a will which is not merely good as a means to some further end, but is good in itself. To produce a will good in itself reason was absolutely necessary, inasmuch as nature in distributing her capacities has everywhere gone to work in a purposive manner. While such a will may not indeed be the sole and complete good, it must, nevertheless, be the highest good and the condition of all the rest, even of the desire for happiness. In this case there is nothing inconsistent with the wisdom of nature that the cultivation of reason, which is requisite for the first and unconditioned purpose, may in many ways restrict, at least in this life, the attainment of the second purpose, viz., happiness, which is always conditioned. Indeed happiness can even be reduced to less than nothing, without nature's failing thereby in her purpose; for reason recognizes as its highest practical function the establishment of a good will, whereby in the attainment of this end reason is capable only of its own kind of satisfaction, viz., that of fulfilling a purpose which is in turn determined only by reason, even though such fulfilment were often to interfere with the purposes of inclination.

The First Proposition: An Act Must Be Done from a Sense of Duty to Have Moral Worth

The concept of a will estimable in itself and good without regard to any further end must now be developed. This concept already dwells in the natural sound understanding and needs not so much to be taught as merely to be elucidated. It always holds first place in estimating the total worth of our actions and constitutes the condition of all the rest. Therefore, we shall take up the concept of *duty*, which includes that of a good will, though with certain subjective restrictions and hindrances, which far from hiding a good will or rendering it unrecognizable, rather bring it out by contrast and make it shine forth more brightly.

I here omit all actions already recognized as contrary to duty, even though they may be useful for this or that end; for in the case of these the question does not arise at all as to whether they might be done from duty, since they even conflict with duty. I also set aside those actions which are really in accordance with duty, yet to which men have no immediate inclination, but perform them because they are impelled thereto by some other inclination. For in this [second] case to decide whether the action which is in accord with duty has been done from duty or from some selfish purpose is easy. This difference is far more difficult to note in the [third] case where the action accords with duty and the subject has in addition an immediate inclination to do the action. For example, that a dealer should not overcharge an inexperienced purchaser certainly accords with duty; and where there is much commerce, the prudent merchant does not overcharge but keeps to a fixed price for everyone in general, so that a child may buy from him just as well as everyone else may. Thus customers are honestly served, but this is not nearly enough for making us believe that the merchant has acted this way from duty and from principles of honesty; his own advantage required him to do it. He cannot, however, be assumed to have in addition [as in the third case] an immediate inclination toward his buyers, causing him, as it were, out of love to give no one as far as price is concerned any advantage over another. Hence the action was done neither from duty nor from immediate inclination, but merely for a selfish purpose.

On the other hand, to preserve one's life is a duty; and, furthermore, everyone has also an immediate inclination to do so. But on this account the often anxious care taken by most men for it has no intrinsic worth, and the maxim of their action has no moral content. They preserve their lives, to be sure, in accordance with duty, but not from duty. On the other hand, if adversity and hopeless sorrow have completely taken away the taste for life, if an unfortunate man, strong in soul and more indignant at his fate than despondent or dejected, wishes for death and yet preserves his life without loving it—not from inclination or fear, but from duty—then his maxim indeed has a moral content.

To be beneficent where one can is a duty; and besides this, there are many persons who are so sympathetically constituted that, without any further motive of vanity or self-interest, they find an inner pleasure in spreading joy around them and can rejoice in the satisfaction of others as their own work. But I maintain that in such a case an action of this kind, however dutiful and amiable it may be, has nevertheless no true moral worth. It is on a level with such actions as arise from other inclinations, e.g., the inclination for honor, which if fortunately directed to what is in fact beneficial and accords with duty and is thus honorable, deserves praise and encouragement, but not esteem; for its maxim lacks the moral content of an action done not from inclination but from duty. Suppose then the mind of this friend of mankind to be clouded over with his own sorrow so that all sympathy with the lot of others is extinguished, and suppose him still to have the power to benefit others in distress, even though he is not touched by their trouble because he is sufficiently absorbed with his own; and now suppose that, even though no inclination moves him any longer, he nevertheless tears himself from this deadly insensibility and performs the action without any inclination at all, but solely from duty—then for the first time his action has genuine moral worth. Further still, if nature has put little sympathy in this or that man's heart, if (while being an honest man in other respects) he is by temperament cold and indifferent to the sufferings of others, perhaps because as regards his own sufferings he is endowed with the special gift of patience and fortitude and expects or even requires that others should have the same; if such a man (who would truly not be nature's worst product) had not been exactly fashioned by her to be a philanthropist, would he not yet find in himself a source from which he might give himself a worth far higher than any that a good-natured temperament might have? By all means, because just here does the worth of the character come out; this worth is moral and incomparably the highest of all, viz., that he is beneficent, not from inclination, but from duty.

To secure one's own happiness is a duty (at least indirectly); for discontent with one's condition under many pressing cares and amid unsatisfied wants might easily become a great temptation to transgress one's duties. But here also do men of themselves already have, irrespective of duty, the strongest and deepest inclination toward happiness, because just in this idea are all inclinations combined into a sum total. But the precept of happiness is often so constituted as greatly to interfere with some inclinations, and yet men cannot form any definite and certain concept of the sum of satisfaction of all inclinations that is called happiness. Hence there is no wonder that a single inclination which is determinate both as to what it promises and as to the time within which it can be satisfied may outweigh a fluctuating idea; and there is no wonder that a man, e.g., a gouty patient, can choose to enjoy what he likes and to suffer what he may, since by his calculation he has here at least not sacrificed the enjoyment of the present moment to some possibly groundless expectations of the good fortune that is supposed to be found in health. But even in this case, if the universal inclination to happiness did not determine his will and if health, at least for him, did not figure as so necessary an element in his calculations; there still remains here, as in all other cases, a law, viz., that he should promote his happiness not from inclination but from duty, and thereby for the first time does his conduct have real moral worth.

Undoubtedly in this way also are to be understood those passages of Scripture which command us to love our neighbor and even our enemy. For love as an inclination cannot be commanded; but beneficence from duty, when no inclination impels us and even when a natural and unconquerable aversion opposes such beneficence, is practical, and not pathological, love. Such love resides in the will and not in the propensities of feeling, in principles of action and not in tender sympathy; and only this practical love can be commanded.

The Second Proposition of Morality

The second proposition is this: An action done from duty has its moral worth, not in the purpose that is to be attained by it, but in the maxim according to which the action is determined. The moral worth depends, therefore, not on the realization of the object of the action, but merely on the principle of volition according to which, without regard to any objects of the faculty of desire, the action has been done. From what has gone before it is clear that the purposes which we may have in our actions, as well as their effects regarded as ends and incentives of the will, cannot give to actions any unconditioned and moral worth. Where, then, can this worth lie if it is not to be found in the will's relation to the expected effect? Nowhere but in the principle of the will, with no regard to the ends that can be brought about through such action. For the will stands, as it were, at a crossroads between its a priori principle, which is formal, and its a posteriori incentive, which is material; and since it must be determined by something, it must be determined by the formal principle of volition, if the action is done from duty—and in that case every material principle is taken away from it.

The Third Proposition of Morality

The third proposition, which follows from the other two, can be expressed thus: Duty is the necessity of an action done out of respect for the law. I can indeed have an inclination for an object as the effect of my proposed action; but I can never have respect for such an object, just because it is merely an effect and is not an activity of the will. Similarly, I can have no respect for inclination as such, whether my own or that of another. I can at most, if my own inclination, approve it; and, if that of another, even love it, i.e., consider it to be favorable to my own advantage. An object of respect can only be what is connected with my will solely as ground and never as effect—something that does not serve my inclination but, rather, outweighs it, or at least excludes it from consideration when some choice is made—in other words, only the law itself can be an object of respect and hence can be a command. Now an action done from duty must altogether exclude the influence of inclination and therewith every object of the will. Hence, there is nothing left which can determine the will except objectively the law and subjectively pure respect for this practical law, i.e., the will can be subjectively determined by the maxim[1] that I should follow such a law even if all my inclinations are thereby thwarted.

Thus, the moral worth of an action does not lie in the effect expected from it nor in any principle of action that needs to borrow its motive from this expected effect. For all these effects (agreeableness of one's condition and even the furtherance of other people's happiness) could have been brought about also through other causes and would not have required the will of a rational being, in which the highest and unconditioned good can alone be found. Therefore, the preeminent good which is called moral can consist in nothing but the representation of the law in itself, and such a representation can admittedly be found only in a rational being insofar as this representation, and not some expected effect, is the determining ground of will. This good is already present in the person who acts according to this representation, and such good need not be awaited merely from the effect.

The Supreme Principle of Morality: The Categorical Imperative

But what sort of law can that be the thought of which must determine the will without reference to any expected effect, so that the will can be

called absolutely good without qualification? Since I have deprived the will of every impulse that might arise for it from obeying any particular law, there is nothing left to serve the will as principle except the universal conformity of its actions to law as such, i.e., I should never act except in such a way that I can also will that my maxim should become a universal law. Here mere conformity to law as such (without having as its basis any law determining particular actions) serves the will as principle and must so serve it if duty is not to be a vain delusion and a chimerical concept. The ordinary reason of mankind in its practical judgments agrees completely with this, and always has in view the aforementioned principle.

For example, take this question. When I am in distress, may I make a promise with the intention of not keeping it? I readily distinguish here the two meanings which the question may have; whether making a false promise conforms with prudence or with duty. Doubtless the former can often be the case. Indeed, I clearly see that escape from some present difficulty by means of such a promise is not enough. In addition I must carefully consider whether from this lie there may later arise far greater inconvenience for me than from what I now try to escape. Furthermore, the consequences of my false promise are not easy to foresee, even with all my supposed cunning; loss of confidence in me might prove to be far more disadvantageous than the misfortune which I now try to avoid. The more prudent way might be to act according to a universal maxim and to make it a habit not to promise anything without intending to keep it. But that such a maxim is, nevertheless, always based on nothing but a fear of consequences becomes clear to me at once. To be truthful from duty is, however, quite different from being truthful from fear of disadvantageous consequences; in the first case the concept of the action itself contains a law for me, while in the second I must first look around elsewhere to see what are the results for me that might be connected with the action. For to deviate from the principle of duty is quite certainly bad; but to abandon my maxim of prudence can often be very advantageous for me, though to abide by it is certainly safer. The most direct and infallible way, however, to answer the question as to whether a lying promise accords with duty is to ask myself whether I would really be content if my maxim (of extricating myself from difficulty by means of a false promise) were to hold as a universal law for myself as well as for others, and could I really say to myself that everyone may promise falsely when he finds himself in a difficulty from which he can find no other way to extricate himself. Then I immediately become aware that I can indeed will the lie but can not at all will a universal law to lie. For by such a law there would really be no promises at all, since in vain would my willing future actions be professed to other people who would not believe what I professed, or if they overhastily did believe, then they would pay me back in like coin. Therefore, my maxim would necessarily destroy itself just as soon as it was made a universal law.

Therefore, I need no far-reaching acuteness to discern what I have to do in order that my will may be morally good. Inexperienced in the course of the world and incapable of being prepared for all its contingencies, I only ask myself whether I can also will that my maxim should become a universal law. If not, then the maxim must be rejected, not because of any disadvantage accruing to me or even to others, but because it cannot be fitting as a principle in a possible legislation of universal law, and reason exacts from me immediate respect for such legislation. Indeed, I have as yet no insight into the grounds of such respect (which the philosopher may investigate). But I at least understand that respect is an estimation of a worth that far outweighs any worth of what is recommended by inclination, and that the necessity of acting from pure respect for the practical law is what constitutes duty, to which every other motive must give way because duty is the condition of a will good in itself, whose worth is above all else.

Thus, within the moral cognition of ordinary human reason we have arrived at its principle. To be sure, such reason does not think of this prin-

ciple abstractly in its universal form, but does always have it actually in view and does use it as the standard of judgment. . . .

Second Section

Transition from Popular Moral Philosophy to a Metaphysics of Morals

If we have so far drawn our concept of duty from the ordinary use of our practical reason, one is by no means to infer that we have treated it as a concept of experience. On the contrary, when we pay attention to our experience of the way human beings act, we meet frequent and—as we ourselves admit—justified complaints that there cannot be cited a single certain example of the disposition to act from pure duty; and we meet complaints that although much may be done that is in accordance with what duty commands, yet there are always doubts as to whether what occurs has really been done from duty and so has moral worth. Hence there have always been philosophers who have absolutely denied the reality of this disposition in human actions and have ascribed everything to a more or less refined self-love. Yet in so doing they have not cast doubt upon the rightness of the concept of morality. Rather, they have spoken with sincere regret as to the frailty and impurity of human nature, which they think is noble enough to take as its precept an idea so worthy of respect but yet is too weak to follow this idea: reason, which should legislate for human nature, is used only to look after the interest of inclinations, whether singly or, at best, in their greatest possible harmony with one another.

In fact there is absolutely no possibility by means of experience to make out with complete certainty a single case in which the maxim of an action that may in other respects conform to duty has rested solely on moral grounds and on the representation of one's duty. It is indeed sometimes the case that after the keenest self-examination we can find nothing except the moral ground of duty that could have been strong enough to move us to this or that good action and to such great sacrifice. But there cannot with certainty be at all inferred from this that some secret impulse of self-love, merely appearing as the idea of duty, was not the actual determining cause of the will. We like to flatter ourselves with the false claim to a more noble motive; but in fact we can never, even by the strictest examination, completely plumb the depths of the secret incentives of our actions. For when moral value is being considered, the concern is not with the actions, which are seen, but rather with their inner principles, which are not seen.

Moreover, one cannot better serve the wishes of those who ridicule all morality as being a mere phantom of human imagination getting above itself because of self-conceit than by conceding to them that the concepts of duty must be drawn solely from experience (just as from indolence one willingly persuades himself that such is the case as regards all other concepts as well). For by so conceding, one prepares for them a sure triumph. I am willing to admit out of love for humanity that most of our actions are in accordance with duty; but if we look more closely at our planning and striving, we everywhere come upon the dear self, which is always turning up, and upon which the intent of our actions is based rather than upon the strict command of duty (which would often require self-denial). One need not be exactly an enemy of virtue, but only a cool observer who does not take the liveliest wish for the good to be straight off its realization, in order to become doubtful at times whether any true virtue is actually to be found in the world. Such is especially the case when years increase and one's power of judgment is made shrewder by experience and keener in observation. Because of these things nothing can protect us from a complete falling away from our ideas of duty and preserve in the soul a well-grounded respect for duty's law except the clear conviction that, even if there never have been actions springing from such pure sources, the question at issue here is not whether this or that has happened but that reason of itself and independently of all experi-

ence commands what ought to happen. Consequently, reason unrelentingly commands actions of which the world has perhaps hitherto never provided an example and whose feasibility might well be doubted by one who bases everything upon experience; for instance, even though there might never yet have been a sincere friend, still pure sincerity in friendship is nonetheless required of every man, because this duty, prior to all experience, is contained as duty in general in the idea of a reason that determines the will by means of a priori grounds.

There may be noted further that unless we want to deny to the concept of morality all truth and all reference to a possible object, we cannot but admit that the moral law is of such widespread significance that it must hold not merely for men but for all rational beings generally, and that it must be valid not merely under contingent conditions and with exceptions but must be absolutely necessary. Clearly, therefore, no experience can give occasion for inferring even the possibility of such apodictic laws. For with what right could we bring into unlimited respect as a universal precept for every rational nature what is perhaps valid only under the contingent conditions of humanity? And how could laws for the determination of our will be regarded as laws for the determination of a rational being in general and of ourselves only insofar as we are rational beings, if these laws were merely empirical and did not have their source completely a priori in pure, but practical, reason?

Moreover, worse service cannot be rendered morality than that an attempt be made to derive it from examples. For every example of morality presented to me must itself first be judged according to principles of morality in order to see whether it is fit to serve as an original example, i.e., as a model. But in no way can it authoritatively furnish the concept of morality. Even the Holy One of the gospel must first be compared with our ideal of moral perfection before he is recognized as such. Even he says of himself, "Why do you call me (whom you see) good? None is good (the archetype of the good) except God only (whom you do not see)." But whence have we the concept of God as the highest good? Solely from the idea of moral perfection, which reason frames a priori and connects inseparably with the concept of a free will. *Imitation* has no place at all in moral matters. And examples serve only for encouragement, i.e., they put beyond doubt the feasibility of what the law commands and they make visible what the practical rule expresses more generally. But examples can never justify us in setting aside their true original, which lies in reason, and letting ourselves be guided by them.

If there is then no genuine supreme principle of morality that must rest merely on pure reason, independently of all experience, I think it is unnecessary even to ask whether it is a good thing to exhibit these concepts generally (*in abstracto*), which, along with the principles that belong to them, hold a priori, so far as the knowledge involved is to be distinguished from ordinary knowledge and is to be called philosophical. But in our times it may well be necessary to do so. For if one were to take a vote as to whether pure rational knowledge separated from everything empirical, i.e., metaphysics of morals, or whether popular practical philosophy is to be preferred, one can easily guess which side would be preponderant.

This descent to popular thought is certainly very commendable once the ascent to the principles of pure reason has occurred and has been satisfactorily accomplished. That would mean that the doctrine of morals has first been grounded on metaphysics and that subsequently acceptance for morals has been won by giving it a popular character after it has been firmly established. But it is quite absurd to try for popularity in the first inquiry, upon which depends the total correctness of the principles. . . .

Imperatives: Hypothetical and Categorical
Everything in nature works according to laws. Only a rational being has the power to act according to his conception of laws, i.e., according to principles, and thereby has he a will. Since the derivation of actions from laws requires reason, the will is nothing but practical reason. If reason infallibly determines the will, then in the case of such a being actions which are recognized to be objectively necessary are also subjectively necessary, i.e., the will is a faculty of choosing only that which reason, independently of inclination, recognizes as being practically necessary, i.e., as good. But if reason of itself does not sufficiently determine the will, and if the will submits also to subjective conditions (certain incentives) which do not always agree with objective conditions; in a word, if the will does not in itself completely accord with reason (as is actually the case with men), then actions which are recognized as objectively necessary are subjectively contingent, and the determination of such a will according to objective laws is necessitation. That is to say that the relation of objective laws to a will not thoroughly good is represented as the determination of the will of a rational being by principles of reason which the will does not necessarily follow because of its own nature.

The representation of an objective principle insofar as it necessitates the will is called a *command* (of reason), and the formula of the command is called an *imperative*.

All imperatives are expressed by an *ought* and thereby indicate the relation of an objective law of reason to a will that is not necessarily determined by this law because of its subjective constitution (the relation of necessitation). Imperatives say that something would be good to do or to refrain from doing, but they say it to a will that does not always therefore do something simply because it has been represented to the will as something good to do. That is practically good which determines the will by means of representations of reason and hence not by subjective causes, but objectively, i.e., on grounds valid for every rational being as such. It is distinguished from the pleasant as that which influences the will only by means of sensation from merely subjective causes, which hold only for this or that person's senses but do not hold as a principle of reason valid for everyone.

A perfectly good will would thus be quite as much subject to objective laws (of the good), but could not be conceived as thereby necessitated to act in conformity with law, inasmuch as it can of itself, according to its subjective constitution, be determined only by the representation of the good. Therefore no imperatives hold for the divine will, and in general for a holy will; the *ought* is here out of place, because the *would* is already of itself necessarily in agreement with the law. Consequently, imperatives are only formulas for expressing the relation of objective laws of willing in general to the subjective imperfection of the will of this or that rational being, e.g., the human will.

Now, all imperatives command either hypothetically or categorically. The former represent the practical necessity of a possible action as a means for attaining something else that one wants (or may possibly want). The categorical imperative would be one which represented an action as objectively necessary in itself, without reference to another end.

Every practical law represents a possible action as good and hence as necessary for a subject who is practically determinable by reason; therefore all imperatives are formulas for determining an action which is necessary according to the principle of a will that is good in some way. Now, if the action would be good merely as a means to something else, so is the imperative hypothetical. But if the action is represented as good in itself, and hence as necessary in a will which of itself conforms to reason as the principle of the will, then the imperative is categorical.

An imperative thus says what action possible by me would be good, and it presents the practical rule in relation to a will which does not forthwith perform an action simply because it is good, partly because the subject does not always know that the action is good and partly because (even if he does know it is good) his maxims might yet be opposed to the objective principles of practical reason.

A hypothetical imperative thus says only that an action is good for some purpose, either possible or actual. In the first case it is a problematic practical principle; in the second case an assertoric one. A categorical imperative, which declares an action to be of itself objectively necessary without reference to any purpose, i.e., without any other end, holds as an apodictic practical principle. . . .

The Rational Ground of the Categorical Imperative

. . . the question as to how the imperative of morality is possible is undoubtedly the only one requiring a solution. For it is not at all hypothetical; and hence the objective necessity which it presents cannot be based on any presupposition, as was the case with the hypothetical imperatives. Only there must never here be forgotten that no example can show, i.e., empirically, whether there is any such imperative at all. Rather, care must be taken lest all imperatives which are seemingly categorical may nevertheless be covertly hypothetical. For instance, when it is said that you should not make a false promise, the assumption is that the necessity of this avoidance is no mere advice for escaping some other evil, so that it might be said that you should not make a false promise lest you ruin your credit when the falsity comes to light. But when it is asserted that an action of this kind must be regarded as bad in itself, then the imperative of prohibition is therefore categorical. Nevertheless, it cannot with certainty be shown by means of an example that the will is here determined solely by the law without any other incentive, even though such may seem to be the case. For it is always possible that secretly there is fear of disgrace and perhaps also obscure dread of other dangers; such fear and dread may have influenced the will. Who can prove by experience that a cause is not present? Experience only shows that a cause is not perceived. But in such a case the so-called moral imperative, which as such appears to be categorical and unconditioned, would actually be only a pragmatic precept which makes us pay attention to our own advantage and merely teaches us to take such advantage into consideration.

We shall, therefore, have to investigate the possibility of a categorical imperative entirely a priori, inasmuch as we do not here have the advantage of having its reality given in experience and consequently of thus being obligated merely to explain its possibility rather than to establish it. In the meantime so much can be seen for now: the categorical imperative alone purports to be a practical law, while all the others may be called principles of the will but not laws. The reason for this is that whatever is necessary merely in order to attain some arbitrary purpose can be regarded as in itself contingent, and the precept can always be ignored once the purpose is abandoned. Contrariwise, an unconditioned command does not leave the will free to choose the opposite at its own liking. Consequently, only such a command carries with it that necessity which is demanded from a law.

Secondly, in the case of this categorical imperative, or law of morality, the reason for the difficulty (of discerning its possibility) is quite serious. The categorical imperative is an a priori synthetic practical proposition, and since discerning the possibility of propositions of this sort involves so much difficulty in theoretic knowledge, there may readily be gathered that there will be no less difficulty in practical knowledge.

First Formulation of the Categorical Imperative: Universal Law

In solving this problem, we want first to inquire whether perhaps the mere concept of a categorical imperative may not also supply us with the formula containing the proposition that can alone be a categorical imperative. For even when we know the purport of such an absolute command, the question as to how it is possible will still require a special and difficult effort, which we postpone to the last section.

If I think of a hypothetical imperative in general, I do not know beforehand what it will contain until its condition is given. But if I think of a categorical imperative, I know immediately what it contains. For since, besides the law, the imperative contains only the necessity that the maxim[2] should accord with this law, while the law contains no condition to restrict it, there remains nothing but the universality of a law as such with which the maxim of the action should conform. This conformity alone is properly what is represented as necessary by the imperative.

Hence there is only one categorical imperative and it is this: Act only according to that maxim whereby you can at the same time will that it should become a universal law.[3]

Now if all imperatives of duty can be derived from this one imperative as their principle, then there can at least be shown what is understood by the concept of duty and what it means, even though there is left undecided whether what is called duty may not be an empty concept.

The universality of law according to which effects are produced constitutes what is properly called nature in the most general sense (as to form), i.e., the existence of things as far as determined by universal laws. Accordingly, the universal imperative of duty may be expressed thus: Act as if the maxim of your action were to become through your will a universal law of nature.[4]

We shall now enumerate some duties, following the usual division of them into duties to ourselves and to others and into perfect and imperfect duties.[5]

1. A man reduced to despair by a series of misfortunes feels sick of life but is still so far in possession of his reason that he can ask himself whether taking his own life would not be contrary to his duty to himself.[6] Now he asks whether the maxim of his action could become a universal law of nature. But his maxim is this: from self-love I make as my principle to shorten my life when its continued duration threatens more evil than it promises satisfaction. There only remains the question as to whether this principle of self-love can become a universal law of nature. One sees at once a contradiction in a system of nature whose law would destroy life by means of the very same

feeling that acts so as to stimulate the furtherance of life, and hence there could be no existence as a system of nature. Therefore, such a maxim cannot possibly hold as a universal law of nature and is, consequently, wholly opposed to the supreme principle of all duty.

2. Another man in need finds himself forced to borrow money. He knows well that he won't be able to repay it, but he sees also that he will not get any loan unless he firmly promises to repay it within a fixed time. He wants to make such a promise, but he still has conscience enough to ask himself whether it is not permissible and is contrary to duty to get out of difficulty in this way. Suppose, however, that he decides to do so. The maxim of his action would then be expressed as follows: when I believe myself to be in need of money, I will borrow money and promise to pay it back, although I know that I can never do so. Now this principle of self-love or personal advantage may perhaps be quite compatible with one's entire future welfare, but the question is now whether it is right.[7] I then transform the requirement of self-love into a universal law and put the question thus: how would things stand if my maxim were to become a universal law? He then sees at once that such a maxim could never hold as a universal law of nature and be consistent with itself, but must necessarily be self-contradictory. For the universality of a law which says that anyone believing himself to be in difficulty could promise whatever he pleases with the intention of not keeping it would make promising itself and the end to be attained thereby quite impossible, inasmuch as no one would believe what was promised him but would merely laugh at all such utterances as being vain pretenses.

3. A third finds in himself a talent whose cultivation could make him a man useful in many respects. But he finds himself in comfortable circumstances and prefers to indulge in pleasure rather than to bother himself about broadening and improving his fortunate natural aptitudes. But he asks himself further whether his maxim of neglecting his natural gifts, besides agreeing of itself with his propensity to indulgence, might agree also with what is called duty.[8] He then sees that a system of nature could indeed always subsist according to such a universal law, even though every man (like South Sea Islanders) should let his talents rust and resolve to devote his life entirely to idleness, indulgence, propagation, and, in a word, to enjoyment. But he cannot possibly will that this should become a universal law of nature or be implanted in us as such a law by a natural instinct. For as a rational being he necessarily wills that all his faculties should be developed, inasmuch as they are given him for all sorts of possible purposes.

4. A fourth man finds things going well for himself but sees others (whom he could help) struggling with great hardships; and he thinks: what does it matter to me? Let everybody be as happy as Heaven wills or as he can make himself; I shall take nothing from him nor even envy him; but I have no desire to contribute anything to his well-being or to his assistance when in need. If such a way of thinking were to become a universal law of nature, the human race admittedly could very well subsist and doubtless could subsist even better than when everyone prates about sympathy and benevolence, and even on occasion exerts himself to practice them but, on the other hand, also cheats when he can, betrays the rights of man, or otherwise violates them. But even though it is possible that a universal law of nature could subsist in accordance with that maxim, still it is impossible to will that such a principle should hold everywhere as a law of nature.[9] For a will which resolved in this way would contradict itself, inasmuch as cases might often arise in which one would have need of the love and sympathy of others and in which he would deprive himself, by such a law of nature springing from his own will, of all hope of the aid he wants for himself.

These are some of the many actual duties, or at least what are taken to be such, whose derivation from the single principle cited above is clear. We must be able to will that a maxim of our action become a universal law; this is the canon for morally estimating any of our actions. Some actions are so constituted that their maxims cannot without contradiction even be thought as a universal law of nature, much less be willed as what should become one. In the case of others this internal impossibility is indeed not found, but there is still no possibility of willing that their maxim should be raised to the universality of a law of nature, because such a will would contradict itself. There is no difficulty in seeing that the former kind of action conflicts with strict or narrow [perfect] (irremissible) duty, while the second kind conflicts only with broad [imperfect] (meritorious) duty. By means of these examples there has thus been fully set forth how all duties depend as regards the kind of obligation (not the object of their action) upon the one principle.

If we now attend to ourselves in any transgression of a duty, we find that we actually do not will that our maxim should become a universal law—because this is impossible for us—but rather that the opposite of this maxim should remain a law universally.[10] We only take the liberty of making an exception to the law for ourselves (or just for this one time) to the advantage of our inclination. Consequently, if we weighed up everything from one and the same standpoint, namely, that of reason, we would find a contradiction in our own will, viz., that a certain principle be objectively necessary as a universal law and yet subjectively not hold universally but should admit of exceptions. But since we at one moment regard our action from the standpoint of a will wholly in accord with reason and then at another moment regard the very same action from the standpoint of a will affected by inclination, there is really no contradiction here. Rather, there is an opposition of inclination to the precept of reason, whereby the universality of the principle is changed into a mere generality so that the practical principle of reason may meet the maxim halfway. Although this procedure cannot be justified in our own im-

partial judgment, yet it does show that we actually acknowledge the validity of the categorical imperative and (with all respect for it) merely allow ourselves a few exceptions which, as they seem to us, are unimportant and forced upon us.

The Need for an A Priori Proof
for the Categorical Imperative

We have thus at least shown that if duty is a concept which is to have significance and real legislative authority for our actions, then such duty can be expressed only in categorical imperatives but not at all in hypothetical ones. We have also—and this is already a great deal—exhibited clearly and definitely for every application what is the content of the categorical imperative, which must contain the principle of all duty (if there is such a thing at all). But we have not yet advanced far enough to prove a priori that there actually is an imperative of this kind, that there is a practical law which of itself commands absolutely and without any incentives, and that following this law is duty.

In order to attain this proof there is the utmost importance in being warned that we must not take it into our mind to derive the reality of this principle from the special characteristics of human nature. For duty has to be a practical, unconditioned necessity of action; hence it must hold for all rational beings (to whom alone an imperative is at all applicable) and for this reason only can it also be a law for all human wills. On the other hand, whatever is derived from the special natural condition of humanity, from certain feelings and propensities, or even, if such were possible, from some special tendency peculiar to human reason and not holding necessarily for the will of every rational being—all of this can indeed yield a maxim valid for us, but not a law. This is to say that such can yield a subjective principle according to which we might act if we happen to have the propensity and inclination, but cannot yield an objective principle according to which we would be directed to act even though our

every propensity, inclination, and natural tendency were opposed to it. In fact, the sublimity
and inner worth of the command are so much
the more evident in a duty, the fewer subjective
causes there are for it and the more they oppose
it; such causes do not in the least weaken the
necessitation exerted by the law or take away anything from its validity.

Here philosophy is seen in fact to be put in a
precarious position, which should be firm even
though there is neither in heaven nor on earth
anything upon which it depends or is based. Here
philosophy must show its purity as author of its
laws, and not as the herald of such laws as are
whispered to it by an implanted sense or by who
knows what tutelary nature. Such laws may be
better than nothing at all, but they can never give
us principles dictated by reason. These principles
must have an origin that is completely a priori
and must at the same time derive from such origin their authority to command. They expect
nothing from the inclination of men but, rather,
expect everything from the supremacy of the law
and from the respect owed to the law. Without
the latter expectation, these principles condemn
man to self-contempt and inward abhorrence.

Hence, everything empirical is not only quite
unsuitable as a contribution to the principle of
morality, but is even highly detrimental to the
purity of morals. For the proper and inestimable
worth of an absolutely good will consists precisely
in the fact that the principle of action is free of all
influences from contingent grounds, which only
experience can furnish. This lax or even mean
way of thinking which seeks its principle among
empirical motives and laws cannot too much or
too often be warned against, for human reason in
its weariness is glad to rest upon this pillow. In a
dream of sweet illusions (in which not Juno but a
cloud is embraced) there is substituted for morality some bastard patched up from limbs of quite
varied ancestry and looking like anything one
wants to see in it but not looking like virtue to
him who has once beheld her in her true form.[11]

Therefore, the question is this: is it a necessary
law for all rational beings always to judge their
actions according to such maxims as they can
themselves will that such should serve as universal laws? If there is such a law, then it must already be connected (completely a priori) with the
concept of a rational being in general. But in
order to discover this connection we must, however reluctantly, take a step into metaphysics, although into a region of it different from speculative philosophy, i.e., we must enter the metaphysics
of morals. In practical philosophy the concern is
not with accepting grounds for what happens but
with accepting laws of what ought to happen,
even though it never does happen—that is, the
concern is with objectively practical laws. Here
there is no need to inquire into the grounds as to
why something pleases or displeases, how the
pleasure of mere sensation differs from taste, and
whether taste differs from a general satisfaction
of reason, upon what does the feeling of pleasure
and displeasure rest, and how from this feeling
desires and inclinations arise, and how, finally,
from these there arise maxims through the cooperation of reason. All of this belongs to an empirical psychology, which would constitute the second
part of the doctrine of nature, if this doctrine is
regarded as the philosophy of nature insofar as
this philosophy is grounded on empirical laws.
But here the concern is with objectively practical
laws, and hence with the relation of a will to itself
insofar as it is determined solely by reason. In this
case everything related to what is empirical falls
away of itself, because if reason entirely by itself
determines conduct (and the possibility of such
determination we now wish to investigate), then
reason must necessarily do so a priori.

Second Formulation of the Categorical Imperative: Humanity as an End in Itself

The will is thought of as a faculty of determining
itself to action in accordance with the representation of certain laws, and such a faculty can be
found only in rational beings. Now what serves

the will as the objective ground of its self-determination is an end; and if this end is given by reason alone, then it must be equally valid for all rational beings. On the other hand, what contains merely the ground of the possibility of the action, whose effect is an end, is called the means. The subjective ground of desire is the incentive; the objective ground of volition is the motive. Hence, there arises the distinction between subjective ends, which rest on incentives, and objective ends, which depend on motives valid for every rational being. Practical principles are formal when they abstract from all subjective ends; they are material, however, when they are founded upon subjective ends, and hence upon certain incentives. The ends which a rational being arbitrarily proposes to himself as effects of this action (material ends) are all merely relative, for only their relation to a specially constituted faculty of desire in the subject gives them their worth. Consequently, such worth cannot provide any universal principles, which are valid and necessary for all rational beings and, furthermore, are valid for every volition, i.e., cannot provide any practical laws. Therefore, all such relative ends can be grounds only for hypothetical imperatives.

But let us suppose that there were something whose existence has in itself an absolute worth, something which as an end in itself could be a ground of determinate laws. In it, and in it alone, would there be the ground of a possible categorical imperative, i.e., of a practical law.

Now I say that man, and in general every rational being, exists as an end in himself and not merely as a means to be arbitrarily used by this or that will. He must in all his actions, whether directed to himself or to other rational beings, always be regarded at the same time as an end. All the objects of inclinations have only a conditioned value; for if there were not these inclinations and the needs founded on them, then their object would be without value. But the inclinations themselves, being sources of needs, are so far from having an absolute value such as to render them desirable for their own sake that the universal wish of every rational being must be, rather, to be wholly free from them. Accordingly, the value of any object obtainable by our action is always conditioned. Beings whose existence depends not on our will but on nature have, nevertheless, if they are not rational beings, only a relative value as means and are therefore called things. On the other hand, rational beings are called persons inasmuch as their nature already marks them out as ends in themselves, i.e., as something which is not to be used merely as means, and hence, there is imposed thereby a limit on all arbitrary use of such beings, which are thus objects of respect. Persons are, therefore, not merely subjective ends, whose existence as an effect of our actions has a value for us; but such beings are objective ends, i.e., exist as ends in themselves. Such an end is one for which there can be substituted no other end to which such beings should serve merely as means, for otherwise nothing at all of absolute value would be found anywhere. But if all value were conditioned and hence contingent, then no supreme practical principle could be found for reason at all.

If then there is to be a supreme practical principle and, as far as the human will is concerned, a categorical imperative, then it must be such that from the conception of what is necessarily an end for everyone because this end is an end in itself it constitutes an objective principle of the will and can hence serve as a practical law. The ground of such a principle is this: rational nature exists as an end in itself. In this way man necessarily thinks of his own existence; thus far is it a subjective principle of human actions. But in this way also does every other rational being think of his existence on the same rational ground that holds also for me; hence it is at the same time an objective principle, from which, as a supreme practical ground, all laws of the will must be able to be derived. The practical imperative will therefore be the following: Act in such a way that you treat humanity, whether in your own person or in the person of another, always at the same time as an end and never simply as a means. . . .

The Third Formulation of the Categorical Imperative: The Autonomy of the Will as Universal Legislator

This principle of humanity and of every rational nature generally as an end in itself is the supreme limiting condition of every man's freedom of action. This principle is not borrowed from experience, first, because of its universality, inasmuch as it applies to all rational beings generally, and no experience is capable of determining anything about them; and, secondly, because in experience (subjectively) humanity is not thought of as the end of men, i.e., as an object that we of ourselves actually make our end which as a law ought to constitute the supreme limiting condition of all subjective ends (whatever they may be); and hence this principle must arise from pure reason [and not from experience]. That is to say that the ground of all practical legislation lies objectively in the rule and in the form of universality, which (according to the first principle) makes the rule capable of being a law (say, for example, a law of nature). Subjectively, however, the ground of all practical legislation lies in the end; but (according to the second principle) the subject of all ends is every rational being as an end in himself. From this there now follows the third practical principle of the will as the supreme condition of the will's conformity with universal practical reason, viz., the idea of the will of every rational being as a will that legislates universal law.

According to this principle all maxims are rejected which are not consistent with the will's own legislation of universal law. The will is thus not merely subject to the law but is subject to the law in such a way that it must be regarded also as legislating for itself and only on this account as being subject to the law (of which it can regard itself as the author).

In the previous formulations of imperatives, viz., that based on the conception of the confor-

mity of actions to universal law in a way similar to a natural order and that based on the universal prerogative of rational beings as ends in themselves, these imperatives just because they were thought of as categorical excluded from their legislative authority all admixture of any interest as an incentive. They were, however, only assumed to be categorical because such an assumption had to be made if the concept of duty was to be explained. But that there were practical propositions which commanded categorically could not itself be proved, nor can it be proved anywhere in this section. But one thing could have been done, viz., to indicate that in willing from duty the renunciation of all interest is the specific mark distinguishing a categorical imperative from a hypothetical one and that such renunciation was expressed in the imperative itself by means of some determination contained in it. This is done in the present (third) formulation of the principle, namely, in the idea of the will of every rational being as a will that legislates universal law.

When such a will is thought of, then even though a will which is subject to law may be bound to this law by means of some interest, nevertheless a will that is itself a supreme lawgiver is not able as such to depend on any interest. For a will which is so dependent would itself require yet another law restricting the interest of its self-love to the condition that such interest should itself be valid as a universal law.

Thus the principle that every human will is a will that legislates universal law in all its maxims, provided it is otherwise correct, would be well suited to being a categorical imperative in the following respect: just because of the idea of legislating universal law such an imperative is not based on any interest, and therefore it alone of all possible imperatives can be unconditional. Or still better, the proposition being converted, if there is a categorical imperative (i.e., a law for the will of every rational being), then it can only command that everything be done from the maxim of such a will as could at the same time have as its object only itself regarded as legislating universal law.

For only then are the practical principle and the imperative which the will obeys unconditional, inasmuch as the will can be based on no interest at all.

When we look back upon all previous attempts that have been made to discover the principle of morality, there is no reason now to wonder why they one and all had to fail. Man was viewed as bound to laws by his duty; but it was not seen that man is subject only to his own, yet universal, legislation and that he is bound only to act in accordance with his own will, which is, however, a will purposed by nature to legislate universal laws. For when man is thought as being merely subject to a law (whatever it might be), then the law had to carry with it some interest functioning as an attracting stimulus or as a constraining force for obedience, inasmuch as the law did not arise as a law from his own will. Rather, in order that his will conform with law, it had to be necessitated by something else to act in a certain way. By this absolutely necessary conclusion, however, all the labor spent in finding a supreme ground for duty was irretrievably lost; duty was never discovered, but only the necessity of acting from a certain interest. This might be either one's own interest or another's, but either way the imperative had to be always conditional and could never possibly serve as a moral command. I want, therefore, to call my principle the principle of the autonomy of the will, in contrast with every other principle, which I accordingly count under heteronomy.

The Kingdom of Ends

The concept of every rational being as one who must regard himself as legislating universal law by all his will's maxims, so that he may judge himself and his actions from this point of view, leads to another very fruitful concept, which depends on the aforementioned one, viz., that of a kingdom of ends.

By "kingdom" I understand a systematic union of different rational beings through common laws. Now laws determine ends as regards their universal validity; therefore, if one abstracts from the personal differences of rational beings and also from all content of their private ends, then it will be possible to think of a whole of all ends in systematic connection (a whole both of rational being as ends in themselves and also of the particular ends which each may set for himself); that is, one can think of a kingdom of ends that is possible on the aforesaid principles.

For all rational beings stand under the law that each of them should treat himself and all others never merely as means but always at the same time as an end in himself. Hereby arises a systematic union of rational beings through common objective laws, i.e., a kingdom that may be called a kingdom of ends (certainly only an ideal), inasmuch as these laws have in view the very relation of such beings to one another as ends and means.

A rational being belongs to the kingdom of ends as a member when he legislates in it universal laws while also being himself subject to these laws. He belongs to it as sovereign, when as legislator he is himself subject to the will of no other.

A rational being must always regard himself as legislator in a kingdom of ends rendered possible by freedom of the will, whether as member or as sovereign. The position of the latter can be maintained not merely through the maxims of his will but only if he is a completely independent being without needs and with unlimited power adequate to his will.

Hence, morality consists in the relation of all action to that legislation whereby alone a kingdom of ends is possible. This legislation must be found in every rational being and must be able to arise from his will, whose principle then is never to act on any maxim except such as can also be a universal law and hence such as the will can thereby regard itself as at the same time the legislator of universal law. If now the maxims do not by their very nature already necessarily conform with this objective principle of rational beings as legislating universal laws, then the necessity of acting on that principle is called practical necessitation, i.e., duty. Duty does not apply to the sovereign in the kingdom of ends, but it does apply to every member and to each in the same degree.

The practical necessity of acting according to this principle, i.e., duty, does not rest at all on feelings, impulses, and inclinations, but only on the relation of rational beings to one another, a relation in which the will of a rational being must always be regarded at the same time as legislative, because otherwise he could not be thought of as an end in himself. Reason, therefore, relates every maxim of the will as legislating universal laws to every other will and also to every action toward oneself; it does so not on account of any other practical motive or future advantage but rather from the idea of the dignity of a rational being who obeys no law except what he at the same time enacts himself.

In the kingdom of ends everything has either a price or a dignity. Whatever has a price can be replaced by something else as its equivalent; on the other hand, whatever is above all price, and therefore admits of no equivalent, has a dignity.

Whatever has reference to general human inclinations and needs has a market price; whatever, without presupposing any need, accords with a certain taste, i.e., a delight in the mere unpurposive play of our mental powers, has an affective price; but that which constitutes the condition under which alone something can be an end in itself has not merely a relative worth, i.e., a price, but has an intrinsic worth, i.e., dignity.

Now morality is the condition under which alone a rational being can be an end in himself, for only thereby can he be a legislating member in the kingdom of ends. Hence morality and humanity, insofar as it is capable of morality, alone have dignity. Skill and diligence in work have a market price; wit, lively imagination, and humor have an affective price; but fidelity to promises and benevolence based on principles (not on instinct) have intrinsic worth. Neither nature nor art contain anything which in default of these could be put in their place; for their worth consists, not in the effects which arise from them, nor in the advantage and profit which they pro-

vide, but in mental dispositions, i.e., in the maxims of the will which are ready in this way to manifest themselves in action, even if they are not favored with success. Such actions also need no recommendation from any subjective disposition or taste so as to meet with immediate favor and delight; there is no need of any immediate propensity or feeling toward them. They exhibit the will performing them as an object of immediate respect; and nothing but reason is required to impose them upon the will, which is not to be cajoled into them, since in the case of duties such cajoling would be a contradiction. This estimation, therefore, lets the worth of such a disposition be recognized as dignity and puts it infinitely beyond all price, with which it cannot in the least be brought into competition or comparison without, as it were, violating its *sanctity*.

What then is it that entitles the morally good disposition, or virtue, to make such lofty claims? It is nothing less than the share which such a disposition affords the rational being of legislating universal laws, so that he is fit to be a member in a possible kingdom of ends, for which his own nature has already determined him as an end in himself and therefore as a legislator in the kingdom of ends. Thereby is he free as regards all laws of nature, and he obeys only those laws which he gives to himself. Accordingly, his maxims can belong to a universal legislation to which he at the same time subjects himself. For nothing can have any worth other than what the law determines. But the legislation itself which determines all worth must for that very reason have dignity, i.e., unconditional and incomparable worth; and the word *respect* alone provides a suitable expression for the esteem which a rational being must have for it. Hence autonomy is the ground of the dignity of human nature and of every rational nature. . . .

Notes

1. A maxim is the subjective principle of volition. The objective principle (i.e., on which would serve all rational beings also subjectively as a practical principle if

reason had full control over the faculty of desire) is the practical law.

2. A maxim is the subjective principle of acting and must be distinguished from the objective principle, viz., the practical law. A maxim contains the practical rule which reason determines in accordance with the conditions of the subject (often his ignorance or his inclinations) and is thus the principle according to which the subject does act. But the law is the objective principle valid for every rational being, and it is the principle according to which he ought to act, i.e., an imperative.

3. [This formulation of the categorical imperative is often referred to as the formula of universal law.]

4. [This is often called the formula of the law of nature.]

5. There should be noted here that I reserve the division of duties for a future *Metaphysics of Morals* [in Part II of the *Metaphysics of Morals*, entitled *The Metaphysical Principles of Virtue*, Ak. 417–474]. The division presented here stands as merely an arbitrary one (in order to arrange my examples). For the rest, I understand here by a perfect duty one which permits no exception in the interest of inclination. Accordingly, I have perfect duties which are external [to others], while other ones are internal [to oneself]. This classification runs contrary to the accepted usage of the schools, but I do not intend to justify it here, since there is no difference for my purpose whether this classification is accepted or not.

6. [Not committing suicide is an example of a perfect duty to oneself.]

7. [Keeping promises is an example of a perfect duty to others.]

8. [Cultivating one's talents is an example of an imperfect duty to oneself.]

9. [Benefiting others is an example of an imperfect duty to others.]

10. [This is to say, for example, that when you tell a lie, you do so on the condition that others are truthful and believe that what you are saying is true, because otherwise your lie will never work to get you what you want. When you tell a lie, you simply take exception to the general rule that says everyone should always tell the truth.]

11. To behold virtue in her proper form is nothing other than to present morality stripped of all admixture of what is sensuous and of every spurious adornment of reward or self-love. How much she then eclipses all else that appears attractive to the inclinations can be easily seen by everyone with the least effort of his reason, if it be not entirely ruined for all abstraction.

Rightness as Fairness: Kant's Categorical Imperative

Melissa Bergeron and Peter Tramel

Melissa Bergeron and Peter Tramel teach philosophy at the United States Military Academy, West Point. In this reading we examine Kant's Categorical Imperative in terms of its commitment to a central theme, which we call "rightness as fairness". Rightness as fairness, we argue, is an essential thread that runs through, and ultimately unifies, the Categorical Imperative. After we introduce the rightness as fairness theme, we follow it through a discussion of each of Kant's three formulations of the Categorical Imperative. Finally, we argue that it plays an essential role in unifying the formulations. In each part we take advantage of some of the recent good scholarship on Kantian ethics, of which there has been a great deal.

Kant thought that the difference between moral rightness and wrongness can be captured in a single rule, the Categorical Imperative. The Categorical Imperative is among the two or three most widely discussed ideas in the history of moral philosophy. Yet most discussions of it conclude negatively: they conclude that the Categorical Imperative is a mistake or, at best, not all that Kant claims it is.

This is not surprising when we consider the number and variety of claims Kant made about the Categorical Imperative. He made claims about how we know it; about how it motivates us; about its connections with rationality, reasonableness, and the good; about its implications concerning humanity, nature, personal ethics, war, politics, and religion. The number and importance of these claims ensures that critics may attack the Categorical Imperative from many angles. Yet it has gained rather than lost importance through centuries of criticism from all these directions. It must at least strike a nerve or two.

One of those nerves, we think, is the idea, implicit in the Categorical Imperative, that rightness is fairness. We think that this idea is one of the most interesting and defensible of Kant's ideas about the Categorical Imperative. We try to clarify it in a way that brings out what is most plausible about it. In the end we argue that it is crucial to unifying the various parts of Kant's moral theory.

We largely follow what we take to be Kant's view, as he and his interpreters explain it. However, our ultimate aim is not to discover precisely what Kant thought, but rather to make progress towards identifying the best version of his theory.

Introduction

The essence of *un*fairness is the double-standard. They who act unfairly hold themselves to a different standard than they apply to others. They "make an exception of themselves."[1] The essence of fairness is the single-standard. They who act fairly hold themselves to the same standard they apply to others. They do not make an exception of themselves. Their standard is *universalizable:* everyone capable of choosing standards could choose to follow it.

Kant thought of moral rightness and wrongness in these terms. He conceived rightness as fairness, wrongness as unfairness. He thought that there is a single moral law, "the ground of all obligation," which binds all free beings in all circumstances: the Categorical Imperative.[2] So long as we obey the Categorical Imperative, we behave permissibly—either rightly or, at least, indifferently. When we disobey it, we behave impermissibly—wrongly.[3]

Kant offers three main *formulations* of the Categorical Imperative. These are supposed to be equivalent in some sense. Below we devote a part to each of the formulations, and we conclude with a brief discussion of how to understand their equivalence in terms of rightness as fairness.

Part I. The First Formulation: FUL and FULN

I.1 Preliminaries

Nowhere is it clearer that Kant conceived rightness as fairness than in the first formulation of his Categorical Imperative, the *Formulation of Universal Law*.

FUL: *Act only according to that maxim whereby you can at the same time* [rationally] *will that it become a universal law*.[4]

A maxim is a standard, or rule. Roughly, the maxim for an action is the example that the action sets, expressed as a rule that prescribes following the example. To will that a maxim becomes a universal law, the way he means it, is to will that everyone in fact obeys the maxim, as inevitably as physical things obey the law of gravity. So the main idea is that moral rightness consists in holding to single standards rather than double standards. Rightness is fairness.

Let's consider an example. Cutting in line in order to get served faster is wrong, according to the FUL, because you cannot cut in line and at the same time will that everyone cuts in line. If everyone cuts in line there are no lines to cut. The maxim

In order to get served faster, I shall cut in line

universalized (i.e., taken as a universal law) is self-contradictory. While Kant's way of talking about this seems awkward to many at first, the idea is familiar and intuitive. The person who

cuts in line institutes a double standard: his intention both endorses (for others) and rejects (for himself) the practice of forming lines to determine the order in which people will be served. He makes an exception of himself, which is the essence of moral wrongness according to the FUL, and the essence of unfairness according to almost everyone.

The line-cutting example seems to be a good one for Kant because it seems clear how to apply the FUL to it. When we think about it, we can see that the FUL will condemn as well any intention that seeks to exploit a *practice* by both endorsing it (for others) and rejecting it (for oneself). To take one of Kant's favorite examples, if I make a lying promise to get a loan I cannot pay back, then my maxim—

In order to get a loan, I shall make a lying promise

—universalized, is self-contradictory.[5] Making lying promises is not a way to get loans in a world where everyone tries to get loans with lying promises, since in such a world such promises are never believed.[6] The maxim itself assumes that promising is a way to get a loan. However, its universalization implies that promising is not a way to get a loan. Hence, the contradiction: promising is and is not a way to get a loan.

I.2 Contradiction in the Will

Maxims that become self-contradictory when universalized are not the only ones the FUL is supposed to condemn. Kant thought, for instance, that the FUL condemns failing to give to charity, failing to develop our talents, and failing to preserve our lives. Yet these failures do not obviously involve self-contradictory maxims.

Suppose that I choose never to give to charity, although I have ample means, because I always prefer to spend my disposable income on personal pleasures—cool cars, movies, parties, fancy meals, fine wines, and so on. My maxim for this is not self-contradictory. There is a possible world (a way that the world *could* be) in which no one is ever charitable and yet I have just as much to spend on personal pleasures as I have in this world. Not every possible world fits the bill. For instance, in the possible worlds where I am a National Public Radio news anchor, my income will depend on people giving to charity. Nevertheless, in some possible worlds with no charity I would have as much to spend on personal pleasures as I do in this world. So the universalization of my maxim is not inconceivable—like the universalization of a line-cutting maxim—and therefore it is not self-contradictory.

How, then, can Kant think that the FUL condemns failing to give to charity? He writes,

Some actions [such as line cutting and making lying promises] are so constituted that their maxims cannot without contradiction even be thought as a universal law of nature, much less be willed as what should become one. In the case of others [such as failing to give to charity or failing to develop your talents] this internal impossibility is indeed not found, but there is still no possibility of willing that their maxim should be raised to the universality of a law of nature, because such a will would contradict itself.[7]

We can imagine my anti-charity maxim working out for me. It is without "internal impossibility": it is not self-contradictory. Nevertheless, Kant thinks that I cannot will the universalization of that maxim without *a contradiction in my will*.

What is a contradiction in my will? It is a matter of being at cross purposes, of pursuing incompatible goals. The problem with it is practical rather than purely logical. Kant thinks that there are some things that every being with a will *must* will. In particular every being with a will must will (a) the efficacy of its will in the pursuit of its goals and (b) the continued freedom

of its will to choose and pursue new goals.[8] FUL condemns maxims that thwart these essential purposes of every will, such as

In order to maximize my personal pleasures, I shall reject every opportunity to develop my talents.

And

In order to maximize my personal pleasures, I shall reject every opportunity to give to charity.

If everyone chooses the pursuit of personal pleasure over talent-development, in every instance, then there will be a sharp decrease in opportunities for pleasure, since those opportunities require talent to conceive, create and maintain. If there is no charity, then personal fortune will be too fickle to sustain much personal pleasure for anyone over time. So both maxims thwart their original purposes when universalized, since more personal pleasure would be possible without them.

I.3 Perfect and Imperfect Duties

Corresponding to the two kinds of contradictions by which the FUL condemns unacceptable maxims, Kant thought that there are two kinds of duties. We have *perfect*, or absolute, duties to never do what the FUL condemns by way of formal contradiction. We have *imperfect*, or selective, duties to avoid what the FUL condemns by way of contradiction in the will, alone.[9]

It is always wrong to make lying promises or, for that matter, to intentionally deceive, since any maxim that prescribes deception, universalized, undermines the very practice it depends upon and is therefore formally self-contradictory. So we have a perfect duty to refrain from deception.

However, we cannot have perfect duties to both develop our talents *and* give to charity. Suppose that I have two-hundred dollars disposable income this month. I could spend it all on developing my talents—on attending the best nearby Kant seminar, for instance—or I could spend it all on charity—giving it to the most efficient famine relief charity, for instance. I could not do both. Yet if these were perfect duties then the FUL would require that I do both. They must therefore be imperfect duties.

We can express the distinction between perfect and imperfect duties this way: if I have a perfect duty to refrain from X-ing, then *it is always wrong for me to* X. If I have an imperfect duty to refrain from Y-ing, then *it is wrong for me to always* Y. Without violating the FUL, I could intend to give all of my disposable income to charity this month and to spend all of it on the development of my talents next month. Contradiction in the will arises not from failing to try to give to charity or to develop my talents in some particular instance; it arises from failing to include both in the plan of my life, to some extent.

But to what extent? Suppose that I have inherited one billion dollars and I wish to avoid, as much as possible, talent-development and charity because I desire an ultimate playboy sort of life. Would it be enough if I gave one dollar and one minute each to talent development and charity every year? Surely not. But why not?

I.4 The (Re-) Formulation of the Universal Law of Nature

Kant offers a restatement of the first formulation, a clarifying equivalent of the FUL, that gives some further insight into these difficult questions about imperfect duties. It is the *Formulation of the Universal Law of Nature:*

FULN: *Act as if the maxim of your action were to become through your will a universal law of nature.*[10]

While the FULN will not yield a precise dollar or time amount that I, or my imaginary billionaire counterpart, owe to talent development

or charity, it points, in broad outline, to a way of achieving a generally appropriate range of answers.

It requires that I think of myself as, *through my actions*, the author of universal laws of nature. When I think of myself in this way, the question arises: to whom, or what, am I giving laws? The answer: everyone, and everything, capable of (rational) *action* and thus responsible to the Categorical Imperative. What is required for action in this sense? The capacity for *volition* (or willing), and therefore the combination: *freedom* and *rationality*. Rocks, trees, and even tigers do not qualify. Human beings—especially adults in full possession of their faculties—are the only clear qualifying examples in our common experience. However, extraterrestrial aliens, if they exist and are capable of action in the same sense, also qualify. Call all who qualify, taken as a whole, *the moral community*.[11]

As the *author* of universal laws of nature, I acquire some responsibility for the maintenance of all wills in the moral community, not merely my own. It is not enough, therefore, that my maxims fail to thwart my essential purposes, in order for me to avoid contradiction in the will. My maxims must be consistent with a plan where no one's essential purposes are essentially thwarted. Thus, I cannot will a world in which the efficacy of your will is destroyed for the sake of enhancing the efficacy of mine. I cannot will a world in which the future options for your will are fundamentally damaged for the sake of enhancing the future options of mine.

This does not precisely answer the question of how much we owe to talent-development or charity. However, it puts us on the trail of an answer. It suggests that our obligations will be commensurate with our advantages. As with the graduated income tax, "from whom [to which] much is given, much is expected."

Also, as with a graduated income tax, the FUL/N (either the FUL or the FULN, or both in combination) could allow free trade between imperfect duties, such as talent development and charity. The graduated income tax allows deductions for education, on the well-supported theory that talent development is as valuable to public well-being as large contributions through taxes. For instance, a Michelangelo could contribute more to the maintenance of a and b in the moral community at large, through developing himself as an artist, than he could contribute by becoming a well-paid advertiser, even though as a well-paid advertiser he would have more money to give to charity.

The analogies with the graduated income tax should not tempt anyone to think that we are talking here of welfare rights or political duties. Concerning those, Kantians can go various ways from here. Nevertheless, for Kantians the main difference between living in a welfare state and a non-welfare state is how much they should contribute beyond what they must pay in taxes. Also, unlike political duties in welfare states, Kantians' moral duties do not end at the borders of their countries. They extend all of the way to the borders of the moral community at large.

I.5 The Problem of the Generality of Maxims

We know of a case in which a professor, call him Dr. T, had an elective class with only four students. By student request and because he saw no harm in it, Dr. T soon moved the class meeting place to the campus coffee shop. Towards the end of the semester, another professor, call him Dr. Z, got wind of this and his sense of justice was offended. He complained to their boss. He argued that it was unfair that Dr. T always held that class in the campus coffee shop, since it was impossible for every professor to always hold every class there. The coffee shop was not big enough for that. Confronted with this argument, Dr. T argued that since the coffee shop was big enough to hold every class with four or fewer students, it was not unfair for him to always hold that particular class there. He did not hold his larger classes there.

Who was right? Both professors appealed to considerations of fairness, which the FUL/N is supposed to ultimately decide. The problem was that Dr. Z conceived Dr. T's maxim more generally than Dr. T did. Dr. Z conceived it as something like

In order to promote a happy learning environment in my class, I shall regularly hold it at the campus coffee shop,

which was, under the circumstances, non-universalizable. Dr. T, on the other hand, conceived it as something more like

In order to accomplish a happy learning environment in my class with four students, *I shall regularly hold it at the campus coffee shop,*

which was, under the circumstances, universalizable.

Whatever you think about who was right, notice that your reasons do not seem to come from the FUL/N, since that principle is neutral between these competing interpretations of Dr. T's maxim. Yet if rightness is fairness and the FUL/N is an ultimate principle of all fairness, then we should not need anything besides the FUL/N to settle the dispute. Nevertheless, if we do not decide based on anything else, then it looks like both professors were right, which is impossible.

As in the example above, the FUL/N will give different results, depending on how we describe what we are doing, and thus on how we conceive our maxims. Call this *the problem of the generality of maxims.*[12] It is often thought to be a serious problem. Some philosophers have rejected the Categorical Imperative, or at least its first formulation, because of it.[13] In the next three subsections we consider two common but inadequate responses and one better response to the problem.

I.6 Inadequate Response 1

One line of possible response to the problem of the generality of maxims is to say that universalization requires conceiving the circumstances of maxims *as generally as possible*, so that they never include particular circumstances, like that Dr. T's class had only four students. According to this response we would understand the FUL like this:

FUL1: Act only according to that maxim whereby you can at the same time [rationally] will that it [with the circumstances conceived *as generally as possible*] should become a universal law.

To some extent, this interpretation seems like a good idea. Arguably, what I have placed in brackets simply follows from thinking carefully about conceiving maxims as universal laws. If so, then the FUL alone can settle all disputes like the one between Drs. T and Z, without help from other moral principles.

Another benefit of FUL1 is that it prevents a slide into specific detail that would make every maxim permissible. If we allow just any kind of circumstantial detail into maxims, then the Categorical Imperative will condemn nothing whatsoever. For instance, the line-cutter or bank robber could save his maxim from contradiction by adding unique details like his social security number or address to the circumstances. Consider for instance the following maxim (with the blanks filled in):

In order to provide easy riches for the philosophy teacher living at my address, by his effort alone, I shall rob such and such bank.

If this could be a maxim, it would pass the test of the FUL/N, since the practices it both requires and threatens, such as ownership and banking, will survive exploitation by the only person in these circumstances. In this way, we could prevent any intention from self-defeat or contradiction in the will upon universalization; and thus we could save any intention from condemnation by the Categorical Imperative. If the Categorical Imperative condemned nothing at

all, then it would be worthless or, at least, nothing like Kant intended. FUL1 prevents this problem by preventing specific detail.

However, despite its advantages, FUL1 is not plausible. As too few things would be wrong if we allow every kind of circumstantial detail into maxims, too many things will be wrong if we allow no kind of circumstantial detail into maxims. For instance, I cannot will the maxim

In order to work comfortably, I shall sit in my study chair (now)

to be a universal law. As not every class at a given hour could fit in the campus coffee shop at Dr. T's school, even less could everyone in the world fit in my study chair (now). If we cannot include anything particular in the circumstances, the FUL will similarly condemn eating any particular bit of food, breathing any particular bit of air, and so on. Yet it is not plausible that any of these things are always wrong. Nor is it plausible to suppose that Kant meant for the Categorical Imperative to condemn them.

I.7 Inadequate Response 2

The problem with FUL1 seems to be that moral relevance is not a matter of being at some level of generality or other. Sometimes particular details are relevant. Other times they are not. Obviously my address has nothing to do with whether it would be permissible for me to rob a bank. Obviously the fact that this is my chair and I am the only person anywhere near it does have something to do with whether it is morally permissible for me to be sitting in it. Since it is really moral relevance that matters, it is tempting to just say:

FUL2: Act only according to that maxim whereby you can at the same time [rationally] will that it [conceived in terms of all and only the *morally relevant circumstances*] should become a universal law.

This will not work, for reasons that may be already be apparent. However, although no one (that I am aware of) defends FUL2, many people apply the Categorical Imperative as if this interpretation is correct. When they formulate maxims, they add all and only details that they think are morally relevant, without considering whether they are justified in adding them.

Ultimately, FUL2 is useless and implausible. It is often not obvious what is morally relevant, especially in those cases where we most want help from ethical theory. For instance, FUL2 cannot settle the debate between Drs. T and Z, since Dr. T thinks that it was morally relevant that he had only four students and Dr. Z thought that that was not morally relevant. If FUL2 was all that we had to go on, then all that Drs. T and Z could do is beg the question against one another.

The deep problem is that we apparently need another moral theory, one that can tell us which circumstances are morally relevant, in order to use FUL2 to determine what is right. So if the FUL2 is an adequate account of fairness, then it fails to establish that rightness is fairness.

I.8 A Better Response

We can combine suggestions from some recent Kantian ethicists to get a better interpretation of the FUL than either of the above.

FUL3: Act only according to that maxim whereby you can at the same time [rationally] will that it [conceived in terms of your *underlying-most intentions*, including all and only *causally relevant circumstances*] should become a universal law.

This requires some explanation.

We may distinguish *surface* from *underlying* intentions.[14] In order to be kind to you I might serve you a certain wine in a certain sort of glass. You might hate the wine and the glass. You might even infer that I am trying to be unkind to you. However, my maxim depends on my underlying

intention to be kind to you, not my surface intentions: to serve you that particular wine, in that particular glass.[15] Although my intention to be kind to you underlies my intentions to serve you that wine, in that glass, I may (or may not) have yet deeper intentions, compared with which my intention to be kind to you is a surface intention. For instance, I may intend to be kind to you because you are my boss and I plan to ask for a raise. My deepest intention(s) in the chain is my underlying-most intention(s). This is the intention that belongs to my maxim.

A problem with this is that we cannot be sure about our underlying-most intentions. We can fail to penetrate our own motives, even when we try hard. Kant was well aware of this problem. He once observed that none of us can be certain that he has ever been a true friend.[16] To put the point another way, however deep into our psychologies we delve in the search for our underlying intentions, we cannot rule out that what we take to be our underlying intentions are not really more surface intentions. We must be skeptics about whether we know our maxims. Therefore, we must be skeptics about whether we can learn what to do from the FUL.

Nevertheless, we can sometimes begin to penetrate the depths of our motives through what philosophers call "counterfactual causal analysis." This brings us to the causally relevant circumstances requirement.[17] If having a different social security number or hair color have nothing to do with my decision to rob a bank, then they do not belong to my maxim. If they do not belong to my maxim, then they cannot save my maxim from condemnation by the FUL. On the other hand, since, when Dr. T had more than four students he did not hold his classes in the coffee shop, his having only four students does belong to his maxim. So he wins the dispute with his colleague on the FUL3 interpretation.

Ultimately, since we can never be certain of our maxims, FUL3 conceives the FUL/N as an ideal that we can only strive to measure up to, rather than as an infallible decision procedure that we can confidently and straightforwardly apply to every actual action. However, as we will soon see, this may be Kant's intention or, at least, the best way to conceive the FUL/N.

Whatever inadequacies FUL3 may prove to have, they are not clear and obvious, like the problems with inadequate responses 1 and 2. FUL3 will sometimes call for more, and sometimes less, generality in maxims. Thus it can avoid the problems of inadequate response 1. Arguably, it will do this in a way that correctly captures moral relevance. Yet, unlike inadequate response 2, it does not beg the question or require another moral theory in order to capture moral relevance, since it does so in purely psychological and causal terms.

I.9 Remaining Problems

Despite the superiority of FUL3 over the other interpretations of the FUL we have considered, it still leaves FUL/N somewhat vague and somewhat unhelpful. Perhaps this is because, as many critics allege, it is too formal, and thus too insubstantial, to operate as a stand-alone guide for action.

I think that FUL3 gets none of the cases I consider above wrong. But they are only the tip of the iceberg when it comes to the range of real cases to which we want to be able to apply the Categorical Imperative. In many kinds of cases I would be hard pressed to say how FUL3 or FULN might apply. Part of the problem is the inscrutability of our real motives, and thus the unknowability of our real maxims. On the FUL3 interpretation, the Categorical Imperative can be at best a kind of ideal we try to live up to, as we try as hard as we can to fathom the depths of our motives. This sort of problem is hardly unique to the Categorical Imperative. For instance the utilitarian greatest happiness principle suffers in a similar way from our inability to know the consequences, especially long-term, of our actions.

More importantly, FUL3 does not seem helpful when it comes to how to apply the Categorical Imperative to many of the most vexing moral controversies, such as whether abortion is wrong. The abortion debate seems to depend on just what, exactly, makes something a person in the full moral sense—an equal member in the community of morally considerable beings. FUL3, although more informative than other interpretations of the FUL, is still too formal, and thus too insubstantial, to help with such questions. When we apply it to practices like lining up or holding class in the coffee shop, it is clear who the participants are: they are the people lining up and the people holding class in the coffee shop. However, in many sorts of controversial cases, we disagree about who the participants are, as when we disagree in the abortion debate about whether fetuses are people, or we disagree in some kinds of euthanasia cases about who is still alive and who is really dead. Assuming that we know our maxims, who, and what, must we include in our calculations as we universalize them? Many of the most difficult issues in applied ethics depend on the answer.

Insofar as the FUL is a statement of rightness as fairness, it looks like either fairness is ultimately inadequate for rightness, because fairness is an ultimately too formal concept to "do justice" to rightness, or FUL is an inadequate statement of rightness as fairness. However that may be, the primary problem with FUL seems to be that it is uninformative concerning who matters, morally, and how much. FULN may help. However its capacity to help depends on how we understand rationality and freedom, which are among the most notoriously difficult concepts in ethics.

Fortunately, the first formulation is not the only formulation of the Categorical Imperative—although some writers never go farther. Recently, it has become common to think that the first formulation is not even the most important formulation. As we will see in Part IV [of this reading], it is clear that Kant (usually) did not intend for the first formulation to stand alone, without the second and third. Meanwhile, we now turn to Kant's second, and then, briefly, his third formulation of the Categorical Imperative.

Part II. The Second Formulation: FH

II.1 *Necessity and Normativity*

People are capable of what Kant calls self-legislation. Natural law determines the behavior of everything in the universe, except (we think) human behavior. While certainly we are subject to such laws, we take our behavior to be at least partly constituted by what we *choose* to do. Were we purely sensuous beings, physical laws alone would determine our actions; there would be no role for "choosing" to play in determining our conduct, no mechanism for expressing the deliverances of reason. Purely sensuous beings are, essentially, slaves to their desires, to the workings of nature. And we do, in fact, deny that there is any point in demanding that, say, a tiger *ought* to do x precisely because a tiger is not really free to decide, in any rich sense, what his behavior will be.

At the other extreme, a purely rational being's actions, say that of an angel or God (should they exist), are based wholly upon reason, doing whatever reason demands. If Kant is right, morality, the judgment that someone *ought* to do such and so is no more a part of a purely rational being's existence than it is of a purely sensuous being's, though for different reasons. As we have seen in our discussion of the FUL/N, reason alone establishes our moral duties. Through reason, we discover what the moral law requires of us, and the challenge faced by every moral agent is to bring inclination into line with the demands of morality. But, for a *purely* rational being, there is no "ought," no pull of duty, because rational nature *alone* determines conduct; there is nothing for such a will to pull against. Thus, the conduct of a purely

rational being is a matter of necessity: necessarily, a being capable of acting only in accordance with reason, will act only on maxims that satisfy the FUL/N. In other words, purely rational beings cannot but respond to the demands of the moral law.

For people, things are a bit trickier. We are double aspect beings, both sensual and rational. And, we know that the moral law places demands on us. But, we also have inclinations—what one might think of as the "demands of nature"—to manage. We see that the moral law demands X but also (sometimes) desire that *not-X*. In such a situation, whether we do X or not, we see that we *ought* to do X. What this suggests, is that the "oughts" that we readily apply to human behavior emerge, somehow, out of the combination or interplay of our rational and animal natures. Only hybrids like ourselves—beings capable of experiencing the often conflicting, competing demands of *both* reason and "inclination"—can experience an ought, namely, what reason demands and desire resists.

The first step in understanding the Kantian account of the binding force of moral claims is to understand the role of freedom (or autonomy) in human conduct. The core features of autonomy are that (a) our access to the requirements of the moral law is not mediated by something outside of our selves, and (b) we—in terms of our responses to those demands, i.e., our behavior—are free, to some extent, from the otherwise invariant workings of causal law.[18] The former is straightforward: all that is necessary for appreciation of the demands of the moral law is attentiveness, which is within the control of the individual agent. There is no mystical dimension to the moral realm such that we must consult an otherworldly expert, say a high priestess, for guidance. Careful reflection (and perhaps a measure of courage) is all it takes to be a competent moral agent. (b) requires further comment.

First, it should be noted that the above does not imply that we are not in any way subject to the effects of causal law; as sensuous beings, surely, we are. But, causal law alone does not exhaust the possible accounts of human behavior. Some behavior is best explained in terms of *reasons* we take for acting, something not true of animals and objects.[19] Accounts of happenings involving rocks, trees, or tigers are explicable wholly in terms of causal law. True, animals "choose" to do some things, rather than others, but this is a matter of responding to the stronger desire and not a matter of guiding one's behavior in the light of reasons for doing one thing, rather than another. People, however are different.

Familiarity with our own experience is enough to show that we do often take ourselves to act from reasons, not the mere urgings of desire (or inclination). So, unlike animals, we do not merely respond to the strongest inclination. Put in slightly more Kantian terms, one might say that while all objects in the universe—say, rocks, trees, and tigers—behave in accordance with laws, only rational beings can behave in accordance with a *conception of law*.[20] Continuing this line of thought, we might say that one who is guided by a conception of law, rather than the tug of desire, is exercising her *will*. She is acting freely (in a sense to be further articulated in what follows), rather than slavishly acquiescing to her desires. Autonomy, then, is the possession of, in the above sense, a *free* will, a will not merely responsive to the pressures of desire. And, to be free and rational just is to be autonomous. Possession of such a will constitutes the human capacity to act in accordance with the demands of reason. Kant equates this sense of the will with what he calls *practical reason,* noting that

Only a rational being has the power to act according to his conception of laws, i.e., according to principles, and thereby has he a will. Since the derivation of actions from laws requires reason, the will is nothing but practical reason.[21]

II.2 Dignity

Accruing to humanity, in virtue of the capacity to act in accordance with the demands of reason, is a special kind of worth, dignity. The capacity to adopt reasons for acting is, in the final assessment, the ultimate source of my value, what I most value in myself; it is what makes me, specifically, *me.* My conception of myself largely is constituted by this capacity, by the specific sorts of reasons that I take to be important, that I grant pride of place in determining my conduct. Indeed, the desires that I have are mine, also. But, they don't seem to be authored by me in the way that my assessment of the force of various reasons for action, and my consequent action or inaction given this assessment, is. I seem (to myself) solidly at the helm as I consider the relevance and force of reasons for acting thus and so. Yet, *authorship*—while perfectly comfortable a concept in relation to my judgments—seems wholly out of place when considering the genesis and (to a slightly lesser degree) sustenance of my desires.

Consider an example. I love coffee. I can recall with vividness my first encounter with the beverage, and (furthermore) I recall recognizing an immediate fondness for it. Did I, through my efforts, create this inclination? It does not seem so. Of course I am responsible for choosing to drink coffee (or not), but I fail to see how I am responsible for liking it to begin with. Now, if fondness for coffee were what is referred to as an "acquired taste," and, indeed, I worked to acquire it, then it would seem that I did, in a fairly straightforward way, create the fondness. But, we're thinking of those inclinations or tastes that require no cultivation. They seem to be aspects of my body, more than aspects of my person. What I am free to do, under ordinary circumstances, is to refrain from drinking, not refrain from liking.

Morality, it is commonly believed, requires freedom. That is, there seems no point in speaking of moral obligations, morality generally, unless we assume some genuine order of responsibility for our actions. But, to make sense of this sort of responsibility, we must assume that we are free in the ordinary sense of the term and that our free actions are genuine expressions of our selves. It would not be an exaggeration, I think, to claim that, whatever else personhood includes, it requires this conception of oneself as capable of responding to reasons for acting. This sensitivity to reasons is to possess a will. In short, we could not take ourselves to be *persons* were we to lack this capacity. Eliminate the free will and one, thereby, eliminates the person whose will it is.

II.3 *Formula of Humanity*

It should be obvious at this point, that the Categorical Imperative places limits on permissible maxims, on behavior. This is made stunningly clear in another formulation of the Categorical Imperative, the Formula of Humanity, according to which one must

FH: Act in such a way that you treat humanity, whether in your own person or in the person of another, always at the same time as an end and never simply as a means.[22]

According to Kant, humanity is not the same as a particular human or even (more plausibly) the set of all humans. Rather, he takes humanity to be a feature of persons, something contrasted, for instance, with our (purely) sensuous nature, our 'animality.' Humanity is best thought of as "a characteristic, or set of characteristics, of persons."[23] That characteristic, or at least its defining feature, is the capacity to set ends—it is rationality *as realized in humans*.

We know one another as persons when we know something about the life plan of the person known. For me to report, e.g., that I know Jim Bob (as a person, not a mere object of acquaintance, like I might know the Eiffel Tower) is to say that I know some things about the person he is, the things he values. This, for the simple reason that the person he is is constituted by the sorts of ends he sets for himself and the means he sanctions for securing those ends. Knowing that he is not in the habit of making an exception of himself (i.e., acting on nonuniversalizable maxims), I thereby know him to be a *fair* person. This is no minor bit of knowledge: to know that someone, fundamentally, is a fair person is to discover something deeply important about the kind of person he is, since fairness is the sort of value that, if held, permeates virtually all that we do. Part of what it is to be fair is to be committed to assessing as comparable the value of relevantly similar cases. So, I have not simply discovered a consistency in his behavior when I see that he is fair, though there is that. Rather, I have discovered something important about the means his deeper self sanctions—specifically those evincing respect of comparable values found elsewhere. A necessary condition of being fair is acknowledging the relative worth of comparable goods.[24] I am fair in my dealings with others just in case I appraise both my own and others' maxims according to the same standard. This just is to respect the ends of others as I respect my own ends.[25] And, this is just what the FH enjoins us to do, for essentially the same reasons offered in support of the FUL/N: consistency requires it. Another equally serviceable way of articulating what I know about Jim Bob is to say that he is respectful of his fellow end-setters, respectful of humanity.

Now, the FH offers some important insights regarding the FUL/N. Recall that neither the FUL nor the FULN were entirely satisfactory in our attempts to understand (a) the boundaries of our imperfect duties and (b) how best to manage the generality (i.e., scope) of maxims. To see how the FH might help here, consider the oft-lamented perfect duty to refrain from suicide. Many hold that the autonomy that warrants respect is the very same source conferring value on all decisions stemming from that autonomous agent. That is, to respect me (insofar as I am autonomous) is to respect my decisions, particularly those I make for myself. This is the sort of respect we find in Jim Bob when we discover that he is a fair person. So, the criticism goes, if I am worthy of respect as Kant insists, then my decisions regarding how to live my life, by extension, warrant respect. But, this means that the decision to forego living this life is mine to make as well, pace Kant. And this, the critic concludes, is a problem, since we seem to be committed to respecting the decisions we make regarding the disposition of our lives, and also committed to the injunction against some such dispositions, like suicide, wholesale neglect of our potential, a policy of noncharity, and the like.

II.4 Dignity: Case Study #1

By way of illustration, let us consider the Kantian injunction against suicide and the good that an agent might judge self-termination to be. Recall that the FH precludes making an exception of one's own humanity by insisting that humanity warrants respect whether "in your own person or another." In short, you are no more entitled to undermine your own humanity than you are entitled to undermine the humanity of another. Respecting the humanity of another, especially given our familiarity with the FUL/N, is fairly easy to understand: I must not exploit others, I must not fail to acknowledge others' worth as autonomous agents, as persons. But, it is not clear what it is to exploit *myself* (or if it is even possible). According to Kant, the wrongness of self-interested suicide does not inhere in its formal structure. That is, there seems no logical contradiction in universalizing a maxim like, "in order to end my intolerable suffering, I shall end my life." It seems as though this maxim is universalizable insofar as it is possible that all people suffering intolerable pain could self-terminate. So, the maxim seems to pass the FUL/N. The key to seeing

the other grounds for the Kantian objection to self-interested suicide is to attend to that which is destroyed in cases of suicide and compare its worth to that of what is gained.

It is only by remove that our interests deserve any respect; interests warrant respect only insofar as they are *someone's* interests, specifically belonging to a being of dignity. Autonomy, on the Kantian schema, is the ultimate ground of respect, and interests are of value, when they are, only in virtue of being the interests of autonomous beings. So, to attempt to justify self-termination via appeal to interests (in this case, the desire to end suffering) is to make a sort of category mistake. Independent of autonomy, interests have no value, are not really interests at all. Thus, one cannot attempt to secure one's interests via sacrificing one's autonomy just as one cannot coherently count selling oneself into slavery as an exercise of one's freedom; in both cases, the means chosen eliminate the source which confers value on the ends at issue.

In answer to the question whether it is up to me to self-terminate should I no longer value my life, the Kantian must respond negatively. Whether I value something, whether it is an interest of mine, is significant only insofar as I am an autonomous agent, an entity of dignity. And, if I am a being of dignity, then others must respect me as such, respect that dignity, which precludes destroying it in the name of interest. But, the very standard according to which I appraise others' maxims is the standard I must employ in judging my own maxims. Fairness requires this. And, if others must respect my ends because—only if—they are the ends of an autonomous agent, then I too must employ that standard in appraising whatever maxims I do, my own or others'. This is what the FUL/N requires of me. That the particular manifestation of dignity at issue resides in me is immaterial. This is exactly what the FH requires, that humanity (even in oneself) be treated as an end in itself. But, if an instance of humanity is destroyed *for the sake of securing some interest* (i.e., the cessation of suffering), then it just is being used as a means, not an end in itself. Humanity is being used in this example, destroyed, in order to secure some interest, the end of suffering. But, interests (i.e., things having a value of mere price) must never be secured at the cost of an inherently superior value, viz., dignity. The mistake here is to suppose that one has some special rights with respect to the treatment of the dignity residing in oneself. But, given the kind of value attaching to autonomy, given the nature of dignity, there can be no special right of this sort. Initial appearances to the contrary notwithstanding, my dignity—and so my life—is *not* mine to do with as I please. Autonomy, my own as well as yours, places limits on what morally I may do.

II.5 *The Limits of Consent*

The point of this discussion is to highlight the obligations we have, to one another and to ourselves, in virtue of the sort of being that we are. While intuition might seem to sanction different standards for self-directed action, reason cannot (at least not reason within the confines of a Kantian system). The question now is whether intuition and the requirements of dignity really are at odds. Most people find the FH particularly intuitive, though those same people tend to balk at the suggestion that the moral limits on self-directed action are no different from the limits the FH places on actions affecting others. The approach here is to determine whether the plausibility that we grant to a prohibition on using other people as mere means applies also to the prohibition of using one's own person as a means merely.

In part, I think the intuition has to do with consent. One way to understand of the FH is that, as Onora O'Neill[26] explains it, "[t]o use someone as a *mere means* is to involve them in a scheme of action *to which they could not in principle consent.*" And, it is not obvious that consent is a problem when it comes to self-termination.

The self-terminating agent orchestrates the act, which on the face of it seems sure evidence of consent. But, to say that one cannot *in principle* consent is not the same as claiming that one cannot sincerely utter a phrase that means, "I consent" or that one cannot do things that seem to sanction the end at issue.

Sometimes the "in principle" restriction stems from an immediate, straightforward conceptual contradiction, like consenting to being raped—the idea here is that one cannot *consent* to an act that is defined as an event *devoid of consent*. Consenting to a rape makes it no longer a case of rape. The act of consent renders the act it sanctions impossible.

A more nuanced case of the inability in principle to consent is that some necessary condition for legitimate consent is absent, unsatisfied, or defective in some way. We routinely accept that children, severely cognitively delayed adults, sometimes emotionally distraught persons, etc., are not in states fit for rendering genuine consent. Often this is explained in terms of the inability to appreciate the consequences of the events following the putative consent. A distraught person would not, in the cool light of reason, consent to that which only in the distraught state seems appropriate; a child, given full maturity, would not consent to that which only to the immature mind seems appropriate, and so forth. That is, we say that one cannot consent to x because the act of consenting lacks proper authority. I cannot sell my son, for instance; the authority simply does not exist, though there are permissible ways in which I might abdicate my parental role. (And my insistence that I fully appreciate the consequences of selling him will go no way toward establishing my right to consent to the sale.)

But also there are cases in which the act of putative consent, itself, somehow *unseats the authority* of the consent. For instance, in the case of slavery, one might say that freely choosing to eliminate one's freedom is, in a sense, incoherent. J. S. Mill argues just this, namely, that coercive paternalism is justified if necessary to prevent someone from selling himself in this manner. Specifically, the worry is that

by selling himself for a slave, he abdicates his liberty; he foregoes any future use of it beyond that single act. He therefore defeats, in his own case, the very purpose which is the justification of allowing him to dispose of himself. He is no longer free; but is thenceforth in a position which has no longer the presumption in its favour, that would be afforded by his voluntarily remaining in it. The principle of freedom cannot require that he should be free not to be free. It is not freedom, to be allowed to alienate his freedom.[27]

The idea, it seems, is that the seat of authority must remain intact throughout the act it sanctions or authorizes. One cannot consent to that which effectively eliminates that which legitimizes one's consent. A mundane illustration of this sort of incoherence: software developers employ especially powerful software applications that allow them to see and edit files that, ordinarily, are neither visible to nor editable by the user. The software, however, cannot be used to edit itself (i.e., its own executable routines) for the simple reason that the power to edit resides in those routines; editing them would eliminate the (future if not present) power of that application to edit. The attempt to do so generates a "fatal loop."

The intuition that I have special rights with respect to self-directed acts is based upon a tacit respect for my own autonomy, one I expect others to honor. I believe that others must respect my choices—the ends I set for myself—precisely because they are *my* ends, and I am an autonomous being entitled to respect of this sort; by extension, my ends warrant respect. But it is for this very reason that I cannot take as a respect-warranting interest the destruction of my own autonomy, *the very basis for my entitlement to respect.* Choosing to destroy my autonomy just is to destroy the basis for my right to so choose— a fatal loop, if ever there were one.

II.6 Dignity: Case Study #2

Let us consider another familiar challenge, the imperfect duty of charity, but this time in terms of the FH. Suppose that I entertain the maxim, *in order to keep my personal resources for my own benefit, I shall refrain always from giving to charity.* We've already noted (in Part I of this reading) that such a "no-charity" maxim is not logically flawed; that is, there is nothing obviously incoherent about a world in which all relevantly situated agents adopt this maxim. Its failure, we discovered, stems from the contradiction in the will it embodies, viz., simultaneously willing that (i) I shall have at my disposal the means necessary to my chosen ends and also that (ii) I, by my will, institute a law whereby such aid never is available. Thus, I'm willing two outcomes that pull in opposite directions, one set to eliminate the possibility of anyone receiving aid (even me, should I need it) and the other willing that I am positioned to achieve my chosen ends, which might require aid.

Let us consider this with a bit more care. If I am resolved to earn an A in my philosophy course, then I have thereby made a tacit commitment to willing all that is necessary to achieve that end. Part of what it is to be a rational agent is to appreciate our objectives within some context. It would surely strike you as irrational if, say, I told you that I planned on getting an A but I had no intention of satisfying any of the requirements stated in the syllabus: no homework, no readings, no papers. You would, quite reasonably, wonder how I could sustain my intention to secure an A while also simultaneously intending to neglect all of the events necessary for achieving an A. This objection stems from the truism that willing an end entails willing those means necessary to that end. Of course, it is possible that I am unaware of some of those requirements; maybe because I failed to read carefully the syllabus and so do not know that I must, e.g., write a paper in order to pass the course. But, part of what it is actually to intend something is to have an appropriate grasp of what such an intention entails. So, by extension, formulating an end—and, thus, formulating a maxim—requires a minimal appreciation of those means entailed by that end. Should one fail to appreciate enough of the necessary means to a given end, we are left with no alternative but to judge that such an agent simply does not understand what she is saying. That is, she cannot really understand what it means to earn an A in this course if she does not understand any of the requirements of securing that A. And, if she does not have an adequate grip on her intentions, then she cannot formulate a coherent maxim.

If, indeed, I am rationally committed to whatever means I deem necessary to my chosen ends, then part of that commitment is keeping open, to the extent that I can manage, my prospects for securing my chosen ends. Whatever my ends, there is always the *possibility* that the assistance of another person is, or will be, instrumental—*necessary*—to my securing my chosen end. It would be irrational to set a policy *ensuring* the impossibility of such assistance, given its potential role in securing my ends. In slightly more Kantian terms, one might insist that I cannot coherently will a maxim that would guarantee the frustration of my efforts to secure my chosen end (or an end I've yet to choose but, should the time come that I choose it, cannot secure because of a policy I have instituted by my own willing).

It is irrelevant to the rationality of this act of willing whether, in fact, things unfold in this manner, whether I actually need help. What is relevant to the rationality of such willing is the actual permanent and sweeping damage I thereby do to my *future prospects*. Part—again, in the workaday sense—of what it is to be rational is to keep open as many opportunities as is consistent with the ends I currently hold. Real (immediate) damage would occur with such a maxim, not merely possible (future) damage. The damage is to the prospects, the future

choices, available to one. (The same, incidentally, is true of a maxim allowing for rusting talents.) True: some opportunities would have gone unselected anyway and, so, the loss is not the specific course of action itself but, rather, the freedom, the opportunity, to have rejected or chosen that course of action. This freedom is eradicated the moment a maxim of nonbeneficence is universalized. Of course, every act of end-setting, unavoidably, seals off other prospects. But since, always, we are deciding from a position of at least partial ignorance, the closing-off of options, rationally, is to be kept to the barest minimum. A universal law of nonbeneficence, to say the least, is a gratuitous violation of this requirement of rationality.

At this point, one might object that the sense of "rational" operative here is a matter of calculating the probabilities. If so, it is possible that one might be so self-sufficient as to do the calculation and still rationally judge that a universal law of nonbeneficence (likely) will not hinder her prospects of securing her desired ends. I think that this misunderstands the sort of reasoning relevant to the matter at hand, and (more importantly) what the FH actually requires. Consider an example of the sort of calculation ordinarily employed in determining whether to take some risk.[28]

Daily on my way to post, I stop for coffee. Unlike the ubiquitous yuppie coffee shops that spring up around universities, the only place to get coffee on the outskirts of an army post is at the local diner. Diner coffee cups are not equipped with the engineering marvel that is the designer, no-spill to-go cup lid one finds at the yuppie cafés. A flat, sip-lid is standard diner to-go fare. Now, the odds of spillage while driving in the case of a flat lid are, let us say, 5 per cent. Coffee spillage, as both vender warnings and widespread lawsuits attest, is hazardous and unpleasant. In deciding whether to drink while driving, I weigh the pain associated with the odds of spilling the coffee (a stipulated 5 per cent) against the pain of waiting to drink until

I arrive at my office. For argument's sake, let us assign non-drinking a *disvalue* of *n* hedons, which is a touch *more* painful than the pain associated with the state of risk-of-spillage. So, let's suppose that it's rational, preferable all things considered, for me to drink in the car—I'm practiced at simultaneous vehicle operation and imbibing, I have an automatic transmission, I know the roads, etc. It seems, then, that it sometimes is rational to risk the pain, if the odds are in my favor. But, I don't think that this really captures all of the relevant features of my *actual* reasoning in this case. To see this, let us alter the example.

Let everything else remain the same except suppose now that I am to give a talk on the morning in question, and (something that would never, in fact, obtain) I am wearing a white suit. In this scenario, I will *not* decide to drink my coffee while driving. The odds are still in my favor, exactly the same as in the first scenario, but the cost, in the unlikely event of spillage, is greater—too great, I think, rationally to run the risk. My point is that ordinarily we do not consider *only* the probabilities, tout court; we consider the probabilities, given the nature of the risk.[29] In the second scenario, the odds are the same, but the cost is greater. This is relevant to judgments regarding the rationality of running that risk. In the case of the self-sufficient woman, whether it is rational for her to will a maxim of nonbeneficence turns on *both* the likelihood that she'll need assistance *and* the cost of not receiving it, should she, in fact, need it.

The kinds of assistance at issue in Kantian discussions of charity are not those of incidental or minor aides. "Charity" is not a matter of help in choosing the right outfit for the holiday formal. Rather, the assistance at issue regards aid central to our needs as moral agents, as human beings. Not receiving *this* sort of help is, quite likely, a matter of not being able to secure *crucial* ends, ends central to living (or continuing to live) that particular life. And, if this is right, it is hard to see how *ever* running the risk of total

(or even partial but marked) ruination, no matter how favorable the odds, could be a rational course of action. E.g., a pleasurable activity carrying mere 5 per cent chance of dumping nitric acid into my lap is not even momentarily tempting. The Kantian construes the relevance of the needs that finite beings have—and the obligation of charity to which these needs give rise—as crucial components of self-determination in the ordinary sense of that concept. The risk, no matter how miniscule, of this sort of ruination, i.e., damage to my prospects as an end-setter, seems the paradigm of *irrationality*. So, however self-sufficient one is, it simply cannot be rational to risk one's prospects of continuing to be an autonomous agent.

II.7 Respecting Humanity

What is captured by the FH is the obligation to preserve autonomy. This is not merely an appeal to prudential rationality, say, that it is in one's best interest to keep open one's options and to maximize one's prospects for electing any from among those options (though, surely, this is a happy consequence of fulfilling one's duty to perfection and beneficence). An autonomous agent who intentionally limits her capacity to set and secure rational ends or who intentionally eliminates the possibility of required assistance in securing ends she has set, thereby, willfully diminishes her own autonomy. She, in such a case, is not as free or able to pursue or attain whatever ends she might otherwise have chosen. And in this now-impoverished state, she is—by her own will—less autonomous. It is in this fact that the wrongness inheres. And to reduce one's freedom in this way is, according to the FH, not only contrary to the counsels of prudence but, in this context specifically (given its effects on one's autonomy), a moral wrong.

A universal maxim of nonbeneficence precludes assistance in procuring one's chosen ends, should such assistance be needed. A maxim of self-termination in the face of intolerable

suffering is to trade illegitimately between interests and dignity, to use humanity as a means to
the end of nonsuffering. In both cases, such
willing involves a conflict in the will, simultaneously working toward securing one's ends
and also (less directly) working against securing them. Furthermore, in both cases acting
on such a maxim is, on the Kantian schema, a
moral wrong because of the effects willing these
maxims would have on one's autonomy. It is not
a matter of mere (contingent) consequence that
determines the wrongness of so willing. Rather,
the maxims of such actions, themselves, are
contradictory insofar as the will contradicts
its very nature—its nature as an autonomous
entity, an end-setter, a thing of dignity.

Part III. The Third Formulation:
FA and FKE

Kant, and subsequent Kantians, have had less
to say about the third formulation of the Categorical Imperative than about the first two.
Nevertheless, it may be the most important formulation, given what it brings to the Kantian
attempt to conceive rightness as fairness.

As with the first formulation, Kant gives
us two variations of the third formulation: the
Formula of Autonomy and the *Formula of the
Kingdom of Ends*, respectively,

FA: [Act in accordance with] the idea *of the will of
every rational being as a will that legislates universal
law*.[30]

and

FKE: Act in accordance with the maxims of a member legislating universal laws for a merely possible
kingdom of ends.[31]

Both of these are rather like the first formulation, except the focus is on our capacity as law
makers rather than as law followers.

III.1 *The Formula of Autonomy*

This first, least-often discussed, statement of
the third formulation looks a good deal like
the FULN (Formula of the Universal Law
of Nature) statement of the first formulation.
However, the FA adds something of crucial
importance: the universal laws (of nature)
that one makes through her maxims are laws
for a community of rational, and thus equally
entitled, lawmakers. The addition is crucial in
terms of both meaning and justification, as it
does something that FULN could not: it brings
the full power of second formulation to bear.

In terms of meaning, it adds all that the second formulation implies about what it is to be
rational. In terms of justification, it adds all that
the second formulation does to justify belief in,
and motivate respect for, each rational being as
an end. Kant describes the assembly of all of
these parts in the third formulation like this:

The practical necessity of acting in accordance with
this principle, i.e., duty, does not rest at all on feelings, impulses, or inclinations, but merely on the
relation of rational beings to one another, in which
the will of one rational being must always at the same
time be considered as universally legislative, because
otherwise he could not be thought of as an end in
himself.[32]

While the FULN could only gesture vaguely
at answers to questions about imperfect duties,
such as how much I owe to talent-development,
charity, etc.; there is potential in the FA for
clearer, more precise, better justified answers.
However, we turn to Kant's more suggestive,
FKE statement of the third formulation, in
order to examine upon what lines this potential
can be developed.

III.2 *The Formula of the Kingdom of Ends*

The third formulation, particularly the FKE,
has received more attention from political
philosophers than from moral philosophers.

Indeed, the most widely discussed conception of it comes from the great political philosopher, John Rawls. I will describe Rawls's conception in broad outline, and then I will tie it back to the FKE.

Influenced by Kant's Formula of the Kingdom of Ends, Rawls argued for a theory of political justice that he called *justice as fairness*.[33] According to justice as fairness, principles of political justice are valid and binding if and only if they would be unanimously agreed to by an imaginary committee in an imaginary set of circumstances which Rawls calls the *Original Position*. It is the nature of the committee and their circumstances that Rawls thinks guarantees the fairness, and thus the justice, of their unanimous decisions.

The committee in the Original Position is made up of fully rational, wholly self-interested people attempting to find principles of justice for their political society to which they can all agree.[34] They do this behind what Rawls calls a *Veil of Ignorance*. The Veil of Ignorance keeps the members of the committee from knowing anything about themselves that could bias their decisions, such as their races, genders, talents, financial fortunes, health, and so on. It also keeps them from knowing their tastes, their developed moral attitudes (such as, for instance, whether they are utilitarians or Kantians), and even their ultimate attitudes concerning the meaning of life (such as, for instance, whether they accept any particular religion).[35]

The full rationality of the members guarantees the rationality of their choices. That they each have the same vote and are completely self-interested guarantees that "each counts for one, and none for more than one." It does not, however, translate into any selfishness in the principles that they choose, since they must all agree upon those. The Veil of Ignorance prevents all sources of bias from entering into their deliberations, and thus ensures their impartiality. They choose principles of justice which

will bind them *beyond* the Original Position, with the Veil *lifted*, so to speak. Yet outside of the Original Position they have no just basis for complaint about what they agreed to in the Original Position. Such complaint could only be special pleading: an attempt to get for themselves or their kind better, or more, than their fair share.

Rawls's theory fits especially well the FA idea that every rational being is equally an end and thus equally entitled to consideration *as a lawgiver*. It understands this, arguably in accordance with the FA, in terms of conceiving all members of a society as entitled to maximum equal freedom to make moral law. The Original Position exemplifies the FKE demand that we make moral law for a *merely possible* "kingdom" of ends. It does so by conceiving fairness, and thus justice, apart from the actual world circumstances of the moral community.

Rawls has in mind political, rather than moral, law, and in this respect his theory is markedly different from Kant's. Indeed, Rawls rejected the idea that his theory of justice is a theory of morality at large.[36]

Nevertheless, just as Rawls's theory makes sense of the idea that political government is by the consent of the governed, it has potential for making sense of Kant's idea that moral law is by the consent of the moral community. By changing a few details, we can conceive Rawls's main insight as a plausible interpretation of the third formulation, and hence as a theory of morality at large. By doing so we would move from Rawls's justice as fairness to Kant's rightness as fairness. In order to do so we would have to subtract Rawls's claims that the committee chooses merely political principles of justice and that it chooses only for a particular society. Hence, we would also have to subtract the particular knowledge of the needs, wants, etc. of a particular political society, and thus move farther in the direction of a merely possible realm of ends. Unlike justice as fairness, rightness as fairness is fairness without borders.

A Rawlsian, third-formulation-based moral theory would be *contractualist:* it would conceive rightness and wrongness in terms of what members of the moral community would agree to—or contract for—in ideal circumstances designed to preserve perfect justice. In fact, a number of recent Kantian moral philosophers, heavily influenced by Rawls, defend contractualist moral theories of the sort that we are here generally describing.[37]

III.3 Illustration: Charity and the Difference Principle

We have in several ways considered whether the Categorical Imperative implies anything precise and action-guiding concerning our duties of charity. Here we briefly examine what the third formulation, understood in broadly Rawlsian terms, can contribute. This is not the only way that someone might understand the issue. However it is a contender, and it is a good example of how we might apply the third formulation to an issue in applied ethics.

Rawls argues that one of the principles of political justice that the committee members in the Original Position would unanimously accept is this one.

The Difference Principle: "Social and economic inequalities are to be arranged so that they are both (a) to the greatest benefit of the least advantaged and (b) attached to offices and positions open to all under conditions of fair equality and opportunity."[38]

Although it might be interesting to consider the whole thing, we will here consider only

Difference Principle A: Social and economic inequalities are to be arranged so that they are to the benefit of the least advantaged.

Difference Principle A follows from the Difference Principle, so if committee members in the Original Position would unanimously accept the

Difference Principle, then they would accept Difference Principle A.

Rawls conceives the Difference Principle as a political, not a moral principle. It determines how government should distribute goods and services. Thus it determines how, and how much, government should tax the better off for the welfare of the less well off. Since members in the Original Position cannot tell how well off they are when not in the Original Position, they have no reason to vote for anything but strictly enforced equality, *unless* inequality will benefit them no matter what—even if they turn out to be among the least advantaged in their political society. It is possible that allowing inequality would make a society so well off in general that it could afford to do more for its least well off than a society of strictly enforced equality could do for any of its members. For instance, the inequalities that accompany a competitive free market could make a society so well off that it could do more for its poorest citizens than it could if it was, say, Marxist. In that case, and only in that case, a society should allow inequality. However, it still has a duty to ensure that the least well off are better off in fact, and not merely that the society is rich enough that it could make them better off if it wanted to. In any case Difference Principle A apparently implies that there should be much taxation for welfare.

Rawls's argument for Difference Principle A does not depend upon special features of the society in question, although the application of the principle does. So it is a good candidate for a moral principle on the Rawlsian interpretation of the third formulation of the Categorical Imperative. Even if we do not buy Rawls's political theory and we reject Difference Principle A as a political principle, we could still think that it determines what we owe, morally, to charity.

There is potential here for an absolutely precise, action-guiding, third-formulation-based account of our minimum duties of charity. However, its application will depend on many questions of social science that we cannot confidently answer. For instance, it depends on me knowing whether and how much my advantages benefit the least well off members of the moral community. Presumably not much, I would guess. I cannot imagine that my having a stereo or TV is doing much good for the poorest of the poor in Africa, Latin America, or South Asia.

Notice that it is the whole moral community that would matter, here. Moving Difference Principle A from a political to a moral principle dissolves the importance of borders, and thus makes it even more demanding than Rawls's political version. What it would not demand, however, is that I give more than what Difference Principle A implies is my fair share to charity. That illustrates an important practical difference between Kantian rightness as fairness and utilitarian rightness as beneficence. On a straightforward utilitarian view, if my equally or more advantaged neighbors will not contribute their fair share to charity, then my duty to contribute increases, to cover their share and mine.[39] On the other hand, the Rawlsian interpretation of the third formulation demands more charity from most of us than Kantian accounts that proceed from merely the first or second formulation.[40]

Part IV. Conclusion: Relating the Formulations in Terms of Rightness as Fairness

Kant made two kinds of *apparently* inconsistent assumptions regarding his three formulations of the Categorical Imperative. On one hand, he sometimes assumes that each formulation is an *independent*, self-sufficient account of all moral obligation, each one deducible from each of the others.[41] On the other hand, he claimed that the three formulations were *progressively inter-dependent*, each more informative than the last.[42] Our rightness-as-fairness-oriented examination of the Categorical Imperative has been

decidedly on the inter-dependence side. However, below we briefly argue that it sheds light on both sides of the apparent inconsistency.

We begin with his claim that the three formulations are inter-dependent and progressively more informative. In this vein, he claims that the three formulations are each distinct parts in an analysis of moral obligation. The first part gives the bare "form" of all moral obligation; the second part gives its "matter", or substance; and the third gives its "complete determination."[43] What he means by these distinctions is rather high-speed. He means that the first formulation expresses only the form moral obligation must take in our moral judgments and rational judgments; the second formulation expresses the "cognitive application" of moral judgment—or to put it in terms of our discussion in 1.5-6, how it determines moral relevance; and the third formulation determines the scope of the combination of the first two formulations.[44] It combines the first two in a way that sets their logical limits.

Notice that according to Kant's inter-dependence claim, the third formulation is by far the most complete and useful formulation of the Categorical Imperative. Indeed, for instance, the first two formulations can, on their own, only suggest what our duties of charity might be. The first formulation demands that we have duties of charity, if we cannot impartially will that no one has duties of charity. The second formulation says why we can owe charity to other members of the community of all rational beings, especially if we are better off than the least well off among us. However, only the third formulation—whether on the Rawlsian interpretation discussed above, or another—can be applied to the real world, in order to determine our precise obligations to charity. Even then we are limited by our abilities to understand the situation of the real world. But then every moral theory has that problem.

In terms of Kant's inter-dependence claim, it is almost obvious how rightness as fairness runs through it. The account of the three formulations in terms of progressive form, matter, and complete determination depends on each being part of the analysis of a single concept: moral obligation. Kant wants to defend each ingredient as being necessary to the concept of moral obligation. Although the phrase, "rightness as fairness" nowhere appears in his writings, so far as we know, rightness as fairness is a fair description of how he conceives moral obligation in general. That is borne out in our discussions of each of the three formulations, above, and it is particularly borne out in his ultimate, third formulation, in which the limits of rightness get understood in terms of the limits of fairness, rather than, say, how much good we might do, as utilitarianism would have it. With Kant, it is all in the end about following a single, rather than a double standard, about not making an exception of oneself. This much, he thinks, belongs to the concept of moral obligation.

Why, then, does he sometimes assume that the formulations are independent and self-sufficient? That looks inconsistent with the progressive inter-dependence account. Our best guess, based in part on our rightness as fairness interpretation, is that he thought that each formulation is independent and self-sufficient once we understand its terms, such as "maxim" and "nature" and "humanity," as we are supposed to finally understand them when all of the parts are assembled. For instance, how to formulate maxims remains unclear until we fill in with the theory of moral relevance suggested by the second formulation. No one who did not know about the first two formulations could well guess what the terms in the third formulation mean. And so on.

Kant may have thought that once we clarify the meaning of the formulations in terms of understanding them all together, for instance as a unified theory of rightness as fairness, the formulations become for us independent and self-sufficient, each implying the other two. This would make sense if we take the inter-dependence thesis to

be about *discovering* the Categorical Imperative and the independence thesis to be about *fully grasping* it. Whether he intended this or not, he saw his work on the Categorical Imperative as an analysis of the concept of moral duty itself, and when we follow the thread through the discovery phase, we find that rightness as fairness belongs to the essence of the Kantian conception of moral duty itself.

Works Cited

Bowie, Norman, *Business Ethics: A Kantian Perspective*, Malden, MA: Blackwell Publishers, Inc., 1999.

Feldman, Fred, *Introductory Ethics*, Englewood Cliffs, NJ: Prentice Hall, 1978.

Gauthier, David, *Morals by Agreement*, Oxford: Clarendon Press, 1986.

Hill, Thomas E., "Humanity as an End in Itself," *Ethics* 91, no. 1, 1980.

Kant, Immanuel, *Critique of Practical Reason*, ed. Oskar Piest, trans. Lewis White Beck, The Library of Liberal Arts, New York: The Liberal Arts Press, 1956.

———— *The Groundwork of the Metaphysics of Morals, with On a Supposed Right to Lie Because of Philanthropic Concerns*, 3rd ed., tr. by James W. Ellington, Indianapolis: Hackett Publishing Co., Inc., 1981.

Korsgaard, Christine, *Creating the Kingdom of Ends*, Cambridge: Cambridge University Press, 1996.

———— *The Sources of Normativity*, Cambridge: Cambridge University Press, 1996.

Mill, John Stuart, "Utilitarianism," in *Utilitarianism, Liberty, and Representation*, Everyman's Library: Philosophy & Theology (London: J. M. Dent & Sons Ltd., 1910.

O'Neill, Onora, *A Simplified Account of Kant's Ethics*. In J. E. White (ed.), Contemporary Moral Problems. Belmont, CA: Wadsworth, 2000.

O'Neill, Onora, *Constructions of Reason: Explorations of Kant's Practical Philosophy*, Cambridge: Cambridge University Press, 1989.

————, Reading 42, this volume.

Paton, H. J., *The Categorical Imperative: A Study in Kant's Moral Philosophy*, New York: Harper Publishing, 1967.

Potter, Nelson Jr., "How to Apply the Categorical Imperative," *Philosophia*, Vol. 5, No. 4, 1975.

Rawls, John, *A Theory of Justice*, Cambridge, MA: Belknap Press, 1971.

Regan, Tom, "The Case For Animal Rights," in *Animal Rights and Human Obligations*, 2nd ed., ed. T. Regan and P. Singer, Englewood Cliffs, NJ: Prentice Hall, 1989.

Scanlon, T. E., Reading 28, this volume.

Schneewind, J.B., "Autonomy, Obligation, and Virtue: An Overview of Kant's Moral Philosophy," in *The Cambridge Companion to Kant*, ed. Paul Guyer, Cambridge: Cambridge University Press, 1992.

Singer, Peter, reading 41, this volume.

Wood, Alan, *Kantian Ethics*, Cambridge: Cambridge University Press, 2008.

Notes

1. I owe this way of putting it to Norman Bowie. See, e.g., Bowie, 17–18.

2. Kant (1981), 29. Although he thought that there is only one Categorical Imperative, Kant sometimes speaks of categorical imperatives: absolute moral principles, like "do not lie," which he thought followed from *the* Categorical Imperative.

3. When we say "rightness as fairness," we mean 'right' in the broad sense, in which it is a synonym for 'permissible.' However, Kant's theory also gets at 'right' in its narrower sense, in which it is a synonym for 'obligatory.' Even so, the latter sense is just a special case of the former, since "X is obligatory" just means "it is not permissible not to X."

4. Kant (1981), 30.

5. Kant (1981), 31.

6. Indeed, such promises will cease to be believed, and so cease to be a way to secure loans, long before full universality is achieved. As Bowie points out vendors do not wait to stop taking checks until *all* of their customers are giving them bad checks; they stop taking checks long before that point is reached. Bowie, 19–20.

7. Kant (1981), 32.

8. Korsgaard (1996, 1), 78.

9. I add "alone" here because Kant thinks that every maxim that the FF condemns by means of formal contradiction it also condemns by means of contradiction in the will.

10. Kant (1981), 30.

11. Since in Kant's ethics non-human animals, such as tigers and cows, do not belong to the moral community,

Kant concludes that we owe *them* no moral consideration. Kant thinks that we should not treat them inhumanely; but that is because doing so harms us, not them. Many people these days are convinced that at least some non-human animals do belong to the moral community. Some of these argue for revising Kantian ethics so that the moral community includes some non-human animals. Tom Regan is a good example. *See* Regan.

12. This well-known problem goes by several names. For instance, it is sometimes called "the action description problem."

13. For instance, Feldman.

14. O'Neill (1989), 87.

15. O'Neill (1989), 87–88.

16. Kant, 20.

17. See e.g., Potter, 395–416.

18. See e.g., J. B. Schneewind, 309.

19. This way of approaching Kantian autonomy is heavily indebted to Korsgaard's interpretation.

20. Kant (1956), *xi*.

21. Kant (1981), 23.

22. Kant (1981), 36.

23. Hill, 85.

24. That is, should I see that goods, indeed, are comparable—say, my ends when compared to the ends of another person—I thus must acknowledge their relative worth, all else equal. This is *not* to say that I must be omniscient with respect to the actual value of those ends.

25. This is not to say that I must respect the specific end that, say, my brother sets for himself, maybe, squandering his time. Rather, what I must respect is the entitlement my brother and I (and all other rational animals) share, viz., the right to set for ourselves ends, the right to establish our own life plans, to be judges for ourselves what lives are worthy of our efforts.

26. O'Neill, O. (2000). In J. E. White (ed.), 49–55.

27. Mill (1910), 11.

28. Notice that this is not (or not obviously) a morally laden matter. I mean only to illustrate the process of risk assessment.

29. Note that the disvalue I assign to non-drinking (in the previous paragraph) is not weighed against the possible pain of actual spillage. Rather, the hedons measure only the actual pain of being in the anxious state of possible-spillage. Actual-spillage would drive up the hedon allocation.

30. Kant (1981), 37.
31. Kant (1981), 43.
32. Kant (1981), 40.
33. Rawls, 11.
34. Rawls, 11–22.
35. Rawls, 136–142.
36. Rawls, 17.
37. E.g., Gauthier and Scanlon.
38. Rawls, 83.
39. Peter Singer so argues in Reading 41.

40. Such as Onora O'Neill's account in Reading 42, which proceeds mostly from the second formulation.
41. E.g., Kant, 30, 36.
42. E.g., Kant, 41, 42.
43. Kant, 41, 42.
44. Wood, 2008, 68–69. Wood argues that the progressive deduction of the formulations is more plausible if understood as "something like an act of interpretation" than as "a rigorous deductive procedure."

What Makes Right Acts Right?

W. D. Ross

A biographical sketch of W. D. Ross appears at the beginning of reading 17. Ross argues against utilitarianism, asserting that optimal consequences have nothing to do with moral rightness or wrongness. We have intuitive knowledge of rightness and wrongness in terms of action-guiding principles, such as to keep promises made, to promote justice, to show gratitude for benefits rendered, and to refrain from harming others. Unlike Kant's principles, however, these principles are not absolutes, that is, duties that must never be overridden. On the contrary, putative moral duties may be overridden by more binding moral duties. Moral principles are prima facie duties. That is, while their intrinsic value is not dependent on circumstances, their application is. They can be overridden by other prima facie duties. So, for example, our prima facie duty to tell the truth will be overridden by another prima facie duty to save an innocent life in a situation in which a murderer asks us where his intended victim is hiding. Essentially, these principles are the outcomes of generations of reflection, and their holistic schema has been internalized within us, so that ultimately, as Aristotle said, the "decision lies in the perception."

. . . A . . . theory has been put forward by Professor Moore that what makes actions right is that they are productive of more *good* than could have been produced by any other action open to the agent.

This theory is in fact the culmination of all the attempts to base rightness on productivity of some sort of result. The first form this attempt takes is the attempt to base rightness on condu-

Reprinted by permission of Hackett Publishing Company from W. D. Ross, *The Right and the Good*, first published by The Clarendon Press, Oxford, 1930.

civeness to the advantage or pleasure of the agent. This theory comes to grief over the fact, which stares us in the face, that a great part of duty consists in an observance of the rights and a furtherance of the interests of others, whatever the cost to ourselves may be. Plato and others may be right in holding that a regard for the rights of others never in the long run involves a loss of happiness for the agent, that 'the just life profits a man.' But this, even if true, is irrelevant to the rightness of the act. As soon as a man does an action *because* he thinks he will promote his own interests thereby, he is acting not from a sense of its rightness but from self-interest.

To the egoistic theory hedonistic utilitarianism supplies a much-needed amendment. It points out correctly that the fact that a certain pleasure will be enjoyed by the agent is no reason why he *ought* to bring it into being, rather than an equal or greater pleasure to be enjoyed by another, though, human nature being what it is, it makes it not unlikely that he *will* try to bring it into being. But hedonistic utilitarianism in its turn needs a correction. On reflection it seems clear that pleasure is not the only thing in life that we think good in itself, that for instance we think the possession of a good character, or an intelligent understanding of the world, as good or better. A great advance is made by the substitution of 'productive of the greatest good' for 'productive of the greatest pleasure.'

Not only is this theory more attractive than hedonistic utilitarianism, but its logical relation to that theory is such that the latter could not be true unless *it* were true, while it might be true though hedonistic utilitarianism were not. It is in fact one of the logical bases of hedonistic utilitarianism. For the view that what produces the maximum pleasure is right has for its bases the views (1) that what produces the maximum good is right, and (2) that pleasure is the only thing good in itself. If they were not assuming that what produces the maximum *good* is right, the utilitarians' attempt to show that pleasure is the only thing good in itself, which is in fact the point they take most pains to establish, would have been quite irrelevant to their attempt to prove that only what produces the maximum *pleasure* is right. If, therefore, it can be shown that productivity of the maximum good is not what makes all right actions right, we shall *a fortiori* have refuted hedonistic utilitarianism.

When a plain man fulfills a promise because he thinks he ought to do so, it seems clear that he does so with no thought of its total consequences, still less with any opinion that these are likely to be the best possible. He thinks in fact much more of the past than of the future. What makes him think it right to act in a certain way is the fact that he has promised to do so—that and, usually, nothing more. That his act will produce the best possible consequences is not his reason for calling it right. What lends colour to the theory we are examining, then, is not the actions (which form probably a great majority of our actions) in which some such reflection as 'I have promised' is the only reason we give ourselves for thinking a certain action right, but the exceptional cases in which the consequences of fulfilling a promise (for instance) would be so disastrous to others that we judge it right not to do so. It must of course be admitted that such cases exist. If I have promised to meet a friend at a particular time for some trivial purpose, I should certainly think myself justified in breaking my engagement if by doing so I could prevent a serious accident or bring relief to the victims of one. And the supporters of the view we are examining hold that my thinking so is due to my thinking that I shall bring more good into existence by the one action than by the other. A different account may, however, be given of the matter, an account which will, I believe, show itself to be the true one. It may be said

that besides the duty of fulfilling promises, I have and recognize a duty of relieving distress, and that when I think it right to do the latter at the cost of not doing the former, it is not because I think I shall produce more good thereby but because I think it the duty which is in the circumstances more of a duty. This account surely corresponds much more closely with what we really think in such a situation. If, so far as I can see, I could bring equal amounts of good into being by fulfilling my promise and by helping someone to whom I had made no promise, I should not hesitate to regard the former as my duty. Yet on the view that what is right is right because it is productive of the most good I should not so regard it.

There are two theories, each in its way simple, that offer a solution of such cases of conscience. One is the view of Kant, that there are certain duties of perfect obligation, such as those of fulfilling promises, of paying debts, of telling the truth, which admit of no exception whatever in favour of duties of imperfect obligation, such as that of relieving distress. The other is the view of, for instance, Professor Moore and Dr. Rashdall, that there is only the duty of producing good, and that all 'conflicts of duties' should be resolved by asking 'By which action will most good be produced?' But it is more important that our theory fit the facts than that it be simple, and the account we have given above corresponds (it seems to me) better than either of the simpler theories with what we really think, viz. that normally promise-keeping, for example, should come before benevolence, but that when and only when the good to be produced by the benevolent act is very great and the promise comparatively trivial, the act of benevolence becomes our duty.

In fact the theory of 'ideal utilitarianism' if I may for brevity refer so to the theory of Professor Moore, seems to simplify unduly our relations to our fellows It says, in effect, that the only morally significant relation in which my neighbours stand to me is that of being possible beneficiaries by my action. They do stand in this relation to me, and this relation is morally significant. But they may also stand to me in the relation of promisee to promiser, of creditor to debtor, of wife to husband, of child to parent, of friend to friend, of fellow countryman to fellow countryman, and the like; and each of these relations is the foundation of a *prima facie* duty which is more or less incumbent on me according to the circumstances of the case. When I am in a situation, as perhaps I always am, in which more than one of these *prima facie* duties is incumbent on me, what I have to do is to study the situation as fully as I can until I form the considered opinion (it is never more) that in the circumstances one of them is more incumbent than any other; then I am bound to think that to do this *prima facie* duty is my duty *sans phrase* in the situation.

I suggest '*prima facie* duty' or 'conditional duty' as a brief way of referring to the characteristic (quite distinct from that of being a duty proper) which an act has, in virtue of being of a certain kind (e.g., the keeping of a promise), of being an act which would be a duty proper if it were not at the same time of another kind which is morally significant. Whether an act is a duty proper or actual duty depends on *all* the morally significant kinds it is an instance of. The phrase '*prima facie* duty' must be apologized for, since (1) it suggests that what we are speaking of is a certain kind of duty, whereas it is in fact not a duty but something related in a special way to duty. Strictly speaking, we want not a phrase in which duty is qualified by an adjective, but a separate noun. (2) '*Prima*' facie suggests that one is speaking only of an appearance which a moral situation presents at first sight, and which may turn out to be illusory; whereas what I am speaking of is an objective fact involved in the nature of the situation, or more strictly in an element of its nature, though not, as duty proper does, arising from its *whole* nature. I can, however, think of no term which fully meets the case. 'Claim' has been suggested by Professor Prichard. The word 'claim' has the advantage of being quite a familiar one in

this connexion, and it seems to cover much of the ground. It would be quite natural to say, 'a person to whom I have made a promise has a claim on me,' and also, 'a person whose distress I could relieve (at the cost of breaking the promise) has a claim on me.' But (1) while 'claim' is appropriate from *their* point of view, we want a word to express the corresponding fact from the agent's point of view—the fact of his being subject to claims that can be made against him; and ordinary language provides us with no such correlative to 'claim.' And (2) (what is more important) 'claim' seems inevitably to suggest two persons, one of whom might make a claim on the other; and while this covers the ground of social duty, it is inappropriate in the case of that important part of duty which is the duty of cultivating a certain kind of character in oneself. It would be artificial, I think, and at any rate metaphorical, to say that one's character has a claim on oneself.

There is nothing arbitrary about these *prima facie* duties. Each rests on a definite circumstance which cannot seriously be held to be without moral significance. Of *prima facie* duties I suggest, without claiming completeness or finality for it, the following division.

(1) Some duties rest on previous acts of my own. These duties seem to include two kinds, (*a*) those resting on a promise or what may fairly be called an implicit promise, such as the implicit undertaking not to tell lies which seems to be implied in the act of entering into conversation (at any rate by civilized men), or of writing books that purport to be history and not fiction. These may be called the duties of fidelity. (*b*) Those resting on a previous wrongful act. These may be called the duties of reparation. (2) Some rest on previous acts of other men, i.e. services done by them to me. These may be loosely described as the duties of gratitude. (3) Some rest on the fact or possibility of a distribution of pleasure or happiness (or of the means thereto) which is not in accordance with the merit of the persons concerned; in such cases there arises a duty to upset

or prevent such a distribution. These are the duties of justice. (4) Some rest on the mere fact that there are other beings in the world whose condition we can make better in respect of virtue, or of intelligence, or of pleasure. These are the duties of beneficence. (5) Some rest on the fact that we can improve our own condition in respect of virtue or of intelligence. These are the duties of self-improvement. (6) I think that we should distinguish from (4) the duties that may be summed up under the title of 'not injuring others.' No doubt to injure others is incidentally to fail to do them good; but it seems to me clear that non-maleficence is apprehended as a duty distinct from that of beneficence, and as a duty of a more stringent character. It will be noticed that this alone among the types of duty has been stated in a negative way. An attempt might no doubt be made to state this duty, like the others, in a positive way. It might be said that it is really the duty to prevent ourselves from acting either from an inclination to harm others or from an inclination to seek our own pleasure, in doing which we should incidentally harm them. But on reflection it seems clear that the primary duty here is the duty not to harm others, this being a duty whether or not we have an inclination that if followed would lead to our harming them; and that when we have such an inclination the primary duty not to harm others gives rise to a consequential duty to resist the inclination. The recognition of this duty of non-maleficence is the first step on the way to the recognition of the duty of beneficence; and that accounts for the prominence of the commands 'thou shalt not kill,' 'thou shalt not commit adultery,' 'thou shalt not steal,' 'thou shalt not bear false witness,' in so early a code as the Decalogue. But even when we have come to recognize the duty of beneficence, it appears to me that the duty of non-maleficence is recognized as a distinct one, and as *prima facie* more binding. We should not in general consider it justifiable to kill one person in order to keep another alive, or to steal from one in order to give alms to another.

The essential defect of the 'ideal utilitarian' theory is that it ignores, or at least does not do full justice to, the highly personal character of duty. If the only duty is to produce the maximum of good, the question who is to have the good—whether it is myself, or my benefactor, or a person to whom I have made a promise to confer that good on him, or a mere fellow man to whom I stand in no such special relation—should make no difference to my having a duty to produce that good. But we are all in fact sure that it makes a vast difference.

One or two other comments must be made on this provisional list of the divisions of duty. (1) The nomenclature is not strictly correct. For by 'fidelity' or 'gratitude' we mean, strictly, certain states of motivation; and, as I have urged, it is not our duty to have certain motives, but to do certain acts. By 'fidelity,' for instance, is meant, strictly, the disposition to fulfill promises and implicit promises *because we have made them.* We have no general word to cover the actual fulfillment of promises and implicit promises *irrespective of motive;* and I use 'fidelity,' loosely but perhaps conveniently, to fill this gap. So too I use 'gratitude' for the returning of services, irrespective of motive. The term 'justice' is not so much confined, in ordinary usage, to a certain state of motivation, for we should often talk of a man as acting justly even when we did not think his motive was the wish to do what was just simply for the sake of doing so. Less apology is therefore needed for our use of 'justice' in this sense. And I have used the word 'beneficence' rather than 'benevolence,' in order to emphasize the fact that it is our duty to do certain things, and not to do them from certain motives.

(2) If the objection be made that this catalogue of the main types of duty is an unsystematic one resting on no logical principle, it may be replied, first, that it makes no claim to being ultimate. It is a *prima facie* classification of the duties which reflection on our moral convictions seems actually to reveal. And if these convictions are, as I would

claim that they are, of the nature of knowledge, and if I have not misstated them, the list will be a list of authentic conditional duties, correct as far as it goes though not necessarily complete. The list of *goods* put forward by the rival theory is reached by exactly the same method—the only sound one in the circumstances—viz. that of direct reflection on what we really think. Loyalty to the facts is worth more than a symmetrical architectonic or a hastily reached simplicity. If further reflection discovers a perfect logical basis for this or for a better classification, so much the better.

(3) It may, again, be objected that our theory that there are these various and often conflicting types of *prima facie* duty leaves us with no principle upon which to discern what is our actual duty in particular circumstances. But this objection is not one which the rival theory is in a position to bring forward. For when we have to choose between the production of two heterogeneous goods, say knowledge and pleasure, the 'ideal utilitarian' theory can only fall back on an opinion, for which no logical basis can be offered, that one of the goods is the greater; and this is no better than a similar opinion that one of two duties is the more urgent. And again, when we consider the infinite variety of the effects of our actions in a way of pleasure, it must surely be admitted that the claim which *hedonism* sometimes makes, that it offers a readily applicable criterion of right conduct, is quite illusory.

I am unwilling, however, to content myself with an *argumentum ad hominem*, and I would contend that in principle there is no reason to anticipate that every act that is our duty is so for one and the same reason. Why should two sets of circumstances, or one set of circumstances, *not* possess different characteristics, any one of which makes a certain act our *prima facie* duty? When I ask what it is that makes me in certain cases sure that I have a *prima facie* duty to do so and so, I find that it lies in the fact that I have made a promise; when I ask the same question in another case, I find the answer lies in the fact that I have done a wrong.

And if on reflection I find (as I think I do) that neither of these reasons is reducible to the other, I must not on any *a priori* ground assume that such a reduction is possible.

It is necessary to say something by way of clearing up the relation between *prima facie* duties and the actual or absolute duty to do one particular act in particular circumstances. If, as almost all moralists except Kant are agreed and as most plain men think, it is sometimes right to tell a lie or to break a promise, it must be maintained that there is a difference between *prima facie* duty and actual or absolute duty. When we think ourselves justified in breaking, and indeed morally obliged to break, a promise in order to relieve someone's distress, we do not for a moment cease to recognize a *prima facie* duty to keep our promise, and this leads us to feel, not indeed shame or repentance, but certainly compunction, for behaving as we do; we recognize, further, that it is our duty to make up somehow to the promise for the breaking of the promise. We have to distinguish from the characteristic of being our duty that of tending to be our duty. Any act that we do contains various elements in virtue of which it falls under various categories. In virtue of being the breaking of a promise, for instance, it tends to be wrong; in virtue of being an instance of relieving distress it tends to be right. Tendency to be one's duty may be called a parti-resultant attribute, i.e. one which belongs to an act in virtue of some one component in its nature. *Being* one's duty is a toti-resultant attribute, one which belongs to an act in virtue of its whole nature and of nothing less than this.

Something should be said of the relation between our apprehension of the *prima facie* rightness of certain types of acts and our mental attitude toward particular acts. It is proper to use the word 'apprehension' in the former case and not in the latter. That an act, *qua* fulfilling a promise, or *qua* effecting a just distribution of good, or *qua* returning services rendered, or *qua* promoting the good of others, or *qua* promoting the virtue or insight of the agent, is *prima facie* right, is self-evident; not in the sense that it is evident from the beginning of our lives, or as soon as we attend to the proposition for the first time, but in the sense that when we have reached sufficient mental maturity and have given sufficient attention to the proposition it is evident without any need of proof, or of evidence beyond itself. It is self-evident, just as a mathematical axiom, or the validity of a form of inference, is evident. The moral order expressed in these propositions is just as much part of the fundamental nature of the universe (and, we may add, of any possible universe in which there were moral agents at all) as is the spatial or numerical structure expressed in the axioms of geometry or arithmetic. In our confidence that these propositions are true there is involved the same trust in our reason that is involved in our confidence in mathematics; and we should have no justification for trusting it in the latter sphere and distrusting it in the former. In both cases we are dealing with propositions that cannot be proved, but that just as certainly need no proof.

Supposing it to be agreed, as I think on reflection it must, that no one *means* by 'right' just 'productive of the best possible consequences,' or 'optimific,' the attributes 'right' and 'optimific' might stand in either of two kinds of relation to each other. (1) They might be so related that we could apprehend *a priori*, either immediately or deductively, that any act that is optimific is right and any that is right is optimific, as we can apprehend that any triangle that is equilateral is equiangular and *vice versa*. Professor Moore's view is, I think, that the coextensiveness of 'right' and 'optimific' is apprehended immediately. He rejects the possibility of any proof of it. Or (2) the two attributes might be such that the question whether they are invariably connected had to be answered by means of an inductive inquiry. Now at first sight it might seem as if the constant connexion of the two attributes could be immediately

apprehended. It might seem absurd to suggest that it could be right for anyone to do an act which would produce consequences less good than those which would be produced by some other act in his power. Yet a little thought will convince us that this is not absurd. The type of case in which it is easiest to see that this is so is, perhaps, that in which one has made a promise. In such a case we all think that *prima facie* it is our duty to fulfill the promise irrespective of the precise goodness of the total consequences. And though we do not think it is necessarily our actual or absolute duty to do so, we are far from thinking that any, even the slightest, gain in the value of the total consequences will necessarily justify us in doing something else instead. Suppose, to simplify the case by abstraction, that the fulfillment of a promise to *A* would produce 1,000 units of good for him, but that by doing some other act I could produce 1,001 units of good for *B*, to whom I have made no promise, the other consequences of the two acts being of equal value; should we really think it self-evident that it was our duty to do the second act and not the first? I think not. We should, I fancy, hold that only a much greater disparity of value between the total consequences would justify us in failing to discharge our *prima facie* duty to *A*. After all, a promise is a promise, and is not to be treated so lightly as the theory we are examining would imply. What, exactly, a promise is, is not so easy to determine, but we are surely agreed that it constitutes a serious moral limitation to our freedom of action. To produce the 1,001 units of good for *B* rather than fulfill our promise to *A* would be to take, not perhaps our duty as philanthropists too seriously, but certainly our duty as makers of promises too lightly.

Or consider another phase of the same problem. If I have promised to confer on *A* a particular benefit containing 1,000 units of good, is it self-evident that if by doing some different act I could produce 1,001 units of good for *A* himself (the other consequences of the two acts being supposed equal in value), it would be right for me to do so? Again, I think not. Apart from my general *prima facie* duty to do *A* what good I can, I have another *prima facie* duty to do him the particular service I have promised to do him, and this is not to be set aside in consequence of a disparity of good of the order of 1,001 to 1,000, though a much greater disparity might justify me in so doing.

Or again, suppose that *A* is a very good and *B* a very bad man, should I then, even when I have made no promise, think it self-evidently right to produce 1,001 units of good for *B* rather than 1,000 for *A?* Surely not. I should be sensible of a *prima facie* duty of justice, i.e., of producing a distribution of goods in proportion to merit, which is not outweighed by such a slight disparity in the total goods to be produced.

Such instances—and they might easily be added to—make it clear that there is no self-evident connexion between the attributes 'right' and 'optimific.' The theory we are examining has a certain attractiveness when applied to our decision that a particular act is our duty (though I have tried to show that it does not agree with our actual moral judgments even here). But it is not even plausible when applied to our recognition of *prima facie* duty. For if it were self-evident that the right coincides with the optimific, it should be self-evident that what is *prima facie* right is *prima facie* optimific. But whereas we are certain that keeping a promise is *prima facie* right, we are not certain that it is *prima facie* optimific (though we are perhaps certain that it is *prima facie* bonific). Our certainty that it is *prima facie* right depends not on its consequences but on its being the fulfillment of a promise. The theory we are examining involves too much difference between the evident ground of our conviction about *prima facie* duty and the alleged ground of our conviction about actual duty.

The coextensiveness of the right and the optimific is, then, not self-evident. And I can see no way of proving it deductively; nor, so far as I know, has anyone tried to do so. There remains the question whether it can be established inductively. Such an inquiry, to be conclusive, would

have to be very thorough and extensive. We should have to take a large variety of the acts which we, to the best of our ability, judge to be right. We should have to trace as far as possible their consequences, not only for the persons directly affected but also for those indirectly affected, and to these no limit can be set. To make our inquiry thoroughly conclusive, we should have to do what we cannot do, viz. trace these consequences into an unending future. And even to make it reasonably conclusive, we should have to trace them far into the future. It is clear that the most we could possibly say is that a large variety of typical acts that are judged right appear, so far as we can trace their consequences, to produce more good than any other acts possible to the agents in the circumstances. And such a result falls far short of proving the constant connexion of the two attributes. But it is surely clear that no inductive inquiry justifying even this result has ever been carried through. The advocates of utilitarian systems have been so much persuaded either of the identity or of the self-evident connexion of the attributes 'right' and 'optimific' (or 'felicific') that they have not attempted even such an inductive inquiry as is possible. And in view of the enormous complexity of the task and the inevitable inconclusiveness of the result, it is worth no one's while to make the attempt. What, after all, would be gained by it? If, as I have tried to show, for an act to be right and to be optimific are not the same thing, and an act's being optimific is not even the ground of its being right, then if we could ask ourselves (though the question is really unmeaning) which we ought to do, right acts because they are right or optimific acts because they are optimific, our answer must be 'the former.' If they are optimific as well as right, that is interesting but not morally important; if not, we still ought to do them (which is only another way of saying that they *are* the right acts), and the question whether they are optimific has no importance for moral theory.

There is one direction in which a fairly serious attempt has been made to show the connexion of the attributes 'right' and 'optimific.' One of the most evident facts of our moral consciousness is the sense which we have of the sanctity of promises, a sense which does not, on the face of it, involve the thought that one will be bringing more good into existence by fulfilling the promise than by breaking it. It is plain, I think, that in our normal thought we consider that the fact that we have made a promise is in itself sufficient to create a duty of keeping it, the sense of duty resting on remembrance of the past promise and not on thoughts of the future consequences of its fulfillment. Utilitarianism tries to show that this is not so, that the sanctity of promises rests on the good consequences of the fulfillment of them and the bad consequences of their nonfulfillment. It does so in this way: it points out that when you break a promise you not only fail to confer a certain advantage on your promise but you diminish his confidence, and indirectly the confidence of others, in the fulfillment of promises. You thus strike a blow at one of the devices that have been found most useful in the relations between man and man—the device on which, for example, the whole system of commercial credit rests—and you tend to bring about a state of things wherein each man, being entirely unable to rely on the keeping of promises by others, will have to do everything for himself, to the enormous impoverishment of human well-being.

To put the matter otherwise, utilitarians say that when a promise ought to be kept it is because the total good to be produced by keeping it is greater than the total good to be produced by breaking it, the former including as its main element the maintenance and strengthening of general mutual confidence, and the latter being greatly diminished by a weakening of this confidence. They say, in fact, that the case I put some pages back never arises—the case in which by fulfilling a promise I shall bring into being 1,000 units of good for my promisee, and by breaking it 1,001 units of good for someone else, the other effects of the two acts being of equal value. The other effects, they say, never are of equal value. By

keeping my promise I am helping to strengthen the system of mutual confidence; by breaking it I am helping to weaken this; so that really the first act produces $1,000 + x$ units of good, and the second $1,001 - y$ units, and the difference between $+x$ and $-y$ is enough to outweigh the slight superiority in the immediate effects of the second act. In answer to this it may be pointed out that there must be *some* amount of good that exceeds the difference between $+x$ and $-y$ (i.e. exceeds $x + y$); say, $x + y + z$. Let us suppose the *immediate* good effects of the second act to be assessed not at 1,001 but at $1,000 + x + y + z$. Then its *net* good effects are $1,000 + x + z$, i.e. greater than those of the fulfillment of the promise; and the utilitarian is bound to say forthwith that the promise should be broken. Now, we may ask whether that is really the way we think about promises. Do we really think that the production of the slightest balance of good, no matter who will enjoy it, by the breach of a promise frees us from the obligation to keep our promise? We need not doubt that a system by which promises are made and kept is one that has great advantages for the general well-being. But that is not the whole truth. To make a promise is not merely to adapt an ingenious device for promoting the general well-being; it is to put oneself in a new relation to one person in particular, a relation which creates a specifically new *prima facie* duty to him, not reducible to the duty of promoting the general well-being of society. By all means let us try to foresee the net good effects of keeping one's promise and the net good effects of breaking it, but even if we assess the first at $1,000 + x$ and the second at $1,000 + x + z$, the question still remains whether it is not our duty to fulfill the promise. It may be suspected, too, that the effect of a single keeping or breaking of a promise in strengthening or weakening the fabric of mutual confidence is greatly exaggerated by the theory we are examining. And if we suppose two men dying together alone, do we think that the duty of one to fulfill before he dies a promise he has made to the other would be extinguished by the fact that neither act would have any effect on the general confidence? Anyone who holds this may be suspected of not having reflected on what a promise is.

I conclude that the attributes 'right' and 'optimific' are not identical, and that we do not know either by intuition, by deduction, or by induction that they coincide in their application, still less that the latter is the foundation of the former. It must be added, however, that if we are ever under no special obligation such as that of fidelity to a promisee or of gratitude to a benefactor, we ought to do what will produce most good; and that even when we are under a special obligation the tendency of acts to promote general good is one of the main factors in determining whether they are right.

In what has preceded, a good deal of use has been made of 'what we really think' about moral questions; a certain theory has been rejected because it does not agree with what we really think. It might be said that this is in principle wrong; that we should not be content to expound what our present moral consciousness tells us but should aim at a criticism of our existing moral consciousness in the light of theory. Now I do not doubt that the moral consciousness of men has in detail undergone a good deal of modification as regards the things we think right, at the hands of moral theory. But if we are told, for instance, that we should give up our view that there is a special obligatoriness attaching to the keeping of promises because it is self-evident that the only duty is to produce as much good as possible, we have to ask ourselves whether we really, when we reflect, *are* convinced that this is self-evident, and whether we really *can* get rid of our view that promise-keeping has a bindingness independent of productiveness of maximum good. In my own experience I find that I cannot, in spite of a very genuine attempt to do so; and I venture to think that most people will find the same, and that just because they cannot lose the sense of special obligation, they cannot accept as self-evident, or even as true, the theory which would require

them to do so. In fact it seems, on reflection, self-evident that a promise, simply as such, is something that *prima facie* ought to be kept, and it does *not*, on reflection, seem self-evident that production of maximum good is the only thing that makes an act obligatory. And to ask us to give up at the bidding of a theory our actual apprehension of what is right and what is wrong seems like asking people to repudiate their actual experience of beauty, at the bidding of a theory which says 'only that which satisfies such and such conditions can be beautiful.' If what I have called our actual apprehension is (as I would maintain that it is) truly an apprehension, i.e. an instance of knowledge, the request is nothing less than absurd.

I would maintain, in fact, that what we are apt to describe as 'what we think' about moral questions contains a considerable amount that we do not think but know, and that this forms the standard by reference to which the truth of any moral theory has to be tested, instead of having itself to be tested by reference to any theory. I hope that I have in what precedes indicated what in my view these elements of knowledge are that are involved in our ordinary moral consciousness.

It would be a mistake to found a natural science on 'what we really think,' i.e. on what reasonably thoughtful and well-educated people think about the subjects of the science before they have studied them scientifically. For such opinions are interpretations, and often misinterpretations, of sense-experience; and the man of science must appeal from these to sense-experience itself, which furnishes his real data. In ethics no such appeal is possible. We have no more direct way of access to the facts about rightness and goodness and about what things are right or good, than by thinking about them; the moral convictions of thoughtful and well-educated people are the data of ethics just as sense-perceptions are the data of a natural science. Just as some of the latter have to be rejected as illusory, so have some of the former; but as the latter are rejected only when they are in conflict with other more accurate sense-perceptions, the former are rejected only when they are in conflict with other convictions which stand better the test of reflection. The existing body of moral convictions of the best people is the cumulative product of the moral reflection of many generations, which has developed an extremely delicate power of appreciation of moral distinctions; and this the theorist cannot afford to treat with anything other than the greatest respect. The verdicts of the moral consciousness of the best people are the foundation on which he must build; though he must first compare them with one another and eliminate any contradictions they may contain.

A Reconciliation of Ethical Theories

WILLIAM FRANKENA

William Frankena (1908–1994) was a professor of philosophy at the University of Michigan, where he distinguished himself as one of the premier moral philosophers in the nation. He is the author of several works in ethical theory, including Ethics *(1963), from which the following reading is taken.*

Frankena argues that both utilitarianism and deontological ethics have strengths and weaknesses. Utilitarianism, among other problems, makes the mistake of not respecting rights or giving adequate weight to the principle of justice. Deontological theories often fail to see that "morality is made for man, not man for morality," and becomes rigidly rule bound. Frankena opts for a compromise system with two principles: beneficence and justice, thus producing a system that is essentially deontological but preserving what is valuble in utilitarianism.

I. My Proposed Theory of Obligation

So far in this chapter I have been trying to show that we cannot be satisfied with the principle of utility as our sole basic standard of right and wrong in morality, whether it is applied in AU, GU, or RU* style. In particular, I have contended that we should recognize a principle of justice to guide our distribution of good and evil that is independent of any principle about maximizing the balance of good over evil in the world. It may still be, of course, that we should recognize other independent principles as well, as deontologists like Ross think, e.g., that of keeping promises.

Now I shall try to present the theory of obligation that seems to me most satisfactory from the moral point of view.

What precedes suggests that perhaps we should recognize two basic principles of obligation, the principle of utility and some principle of justice. The resulting theory would be a deontological one, but it would be much closer to utilitarianism than most deontological theories; we might call it a *mixed deontological theory.* It might maintain that all of our more specific rules of obligation, like that of keeping promises, and all of our judgments about what to do in particular situations can be derived, directly or indirectly, from its two principles. It might even insist that we are to determine what is right or wrong in particular situations, normally at least, by consulting rules such as we usually associate with morality, but add that the way to tell what rules to live by is to see which rules best fulfill the joint requirements of utility and justice (not, as in RU, the requirements of utility alone). This view is still faced with the problem of measuring and balancing amounts of good and evil, and, since it recognizes two basic principles, it must also face the problem of possible conflict between them. This means that it must regard its two principles as principles of prima facie, not of actual duty; and it must, if our above argument is correct, allow that the principle of justice may take precedence over that of utility, at least on some occasions, though perhaps not always. However, it may not be able to provide any formula saying when justice takes precedence and when it does not.

Should we adopt this theory of obligation? To my mind, it is close to the truth but not quite right. Let us begin, however, by asking whether we should recognize the principle of utility at all.

It seems to me we must at least recognize something like it as one of our basic premises. Whether we have even a prima facie obligation to maximize the balance of good over evil depends, in part, on whether it makes sense to talk about good and evil in quantitative terms. Assuming that it makes at least rough sense, it is not easy to deny, as pure deontologists do, that one of the things we ought to do, other things being equal, is to bring about as much of a balance of good over evil as we can, which even Ross, Garritt, and perhaps Butler, allow. I find it hard to believe that any action or rule can be right, wrong, or obligatory in the moral sense, if there is no good or evil connected with it in any way, directly or indirectly. This does not mean that there are no other factors affecting their rightness or wrongness, or that our only duty is to pile up the biggest possible stockpile of what is good, as utilitarians think; but it does imply that we do have, at least as one of our prima facie obligations, that of doing something about the good and evil in the world.

In fact, I wish to contend that we do not have any moral obligations, prima facie or actual, to do anything that does not, directly or indirectly, have some connection with what makes somebody's life good or bad, better or worse. If not our particular actions, then at least our rules must have some bearing on the increase of good or decrease of evil or on their distribution. Morality was made for man, not man for morality. Even justice is concerned about the distribution *of good and evil.* In other words, all of our duties, even that of justice, *presuppose* the existence of good and evil and some kind of concern about their existence and incidence. To this extent, and only to this extent, is the old dictum that love is what underlies and unifies the rules of morality correct. It is the failure to recognize the importance of this point that makes so many deontological systems unsatisfactory.

To say this is to say not only that we have no obligations except when some improvement or impairment of someone's life is involved but also that we have a prima facie obligation *whenever*

this is involved. To quote William James's inimitable way of putting it:

Take any demand, however slight, which any creature, however weak, may make. Ought it not, for its own sole sake, to be satisfied? If not, prove why not.[1]

II. The Principle of Beneficence

If this is so, then we must grant that the utilitarians have hold of an important part of the truth, and that we must recognize something like the principle of utility as one of our basic premises. Still, I do not think that we can regard the principle of utility itself as a basic premise, and my reason is that something more basic underlies it. By the principle of utility I have meant and shall continue to mean, quite strictly, the principle that we ought to do the act or follow the practice or rule that will or probably will bring about *the greatest possible balance of good over evil* in the universe. It seems clear, however, that this principle presupposes another one that is more basic, namely, that we ought to do good and to prevent or avoid doing harm. If we did not have this more basic obligation, we could have no duty to try to realize the greatest balance of good over evil. In fact, the principle of utility represents a compromise with the ideal. The ideal is to do only good and not to do any harm (omitting justice for the moment). But this is often impossible, and then we seem forced to try to bring about the best possible balance of good over evil. If this is so, then the principle of utility presupposes a more basic principle—that of producing good as such and preventing evil. We have a prima facie obligation to maximize the balance of good over evil only if we have a *prior* prima facie obligation to do good and prevent harm. I shall call this prior principle the *principle of beneficence.* The reason I call it the principle of *benificence* and not the principle of *benevolence* is to underline the fact that it asks us actually to do good and not evil, not merely to want or will to do so.

It might be thought that the principle of utility not only presupposes the principle of beneficence but follows from it. This, however, is not the case. The principle of utility is stated in quantitative terms and presupposes that goods and evils can be measured and balanced in some way. The principle of beneficence does not deny this, of course, but neither does it imply this. In applying it in practice one hopes that goods and evils can to a considerable extent at least be measured and balanced, but the principle of beneficence does not itself require that this be always possible; it is, for example, compatible with Mill's insistence that pleasures and pains, and hence goods and evils, differ in quality as well as quantity. I take this to be an advantage of the principle of beneficence over that of utility as I have stated it. There is another advantage. Suppose we have two acts, A and B, and that A produces 99 units of good and no evil, while B produces both good and evil but has a net balance of 100 units of good over evil. In this case, act-utilitarianism requires us to say that B is the right thing to do. But some of us would surely think that act A is the right one, and the principle of beneficence permits one to say this, though it does not require us to do so.

I propose, then, that we take as the basic premises of our theory of right and wrong two principles, that of beneficence and some principle of just distribution. To this proposal it might be objected that, although the principle of justice cannot be derived from that of beneficence, it is possible to derive the principle of beneficence from that of justice. For, if one does not increase the good of others and decrease evil for them when one can do so and when no conflicting obligations are present, then one is being unjust. Hence, justice implies beneficence (when possible and not ruled out by other considerations). In reply, I want to agree that in some sense beneficence is *right* and failure to be beneficent *wrong* under the conditions specified, but I want to deny that they are, respectively, just or unjust, properly speaking. Not everything that is right is just, and not everything that is wrong is unjust. Incest, even if it is wrong, can hardly be called unjust. Cruelty to children may be unjust, if it involves treating them differently from adults, but it is surely wrong anyway. Giving another person pleasure may be right, without its being properly called just at all. The area of justice is a part of morality but not the whole of it. Beneficence, then, may belong to the other part of morality, and this is just what seems to me to be the case. Even Mill makes a distinction between justice and the other obligations of morality, and puts charity or beneficence among the latter. So does Portia when she says to Shylock,

And earthly power doth then show likest God's
When mercy seasons justice.

It has been contended, nevertheless, that we do not have, properly speaking, a duty or obligation to be beneficent. From this point of view, being beneficent is considered praiseworthy and virtuous, but is beyond the call of moral *duty*. All that morality can demand of us is justice, keeping promises, and the like, not beneficence. There is some truth in this. It is not always strictly wrong not to perform an act of beneficence even when one can, for example, not giving someone else one's concert ticket. Not giving him the ticket is only strictly wrong if he has a *right* to my beneficence, and this he does not always have. It may still be, however, that in some wider sense of "ought," I ought to be beneficent, perhaps even to give my ticket to another who needs it more. Kant made a similar point by saying that beneficence is an "imperfect" duty; one ought to be beneficent, he thought, but one has some choice about the occasions on which to do good. In any case, it is certainly wrong, at least prima facie, to inflict evil or pain on anyone, and to admit this is to admit that the principle of beneficence is partly correct.

A point about our use of terms may help here. The terms "duty," "obligation," and "ought to be done" are often used interchangeably, especially by philosophers, for example, in this book. This is true even to some extent in ordinary discourse. But in our more careful ordinary discourse we tend to use "duty" when we have in mind some rule like "Tell the truth" or some role or office like that of a father or secretary, and to use "obligation" when we have in mind the law or some agreement or promise. In these cases we tend to think that one person has a duty or obligation and another has a correlative right. The expression "ought to do," however, is used in a wider sense to cover things we would not regard as strict duties or obligations or think another person has a right to. Thus, it is natural to say that one ought to go the second mile, not so natural to say one has a duty or obligation to do this, and quite unnatural to say that the other person has a right to expect one to do it. This will help to explain why some assert and others deny that beneficence is a requirement of morality. The matter, it should be observed, is made all the more difficult by two further facts: on the one hand, that "right" sometimes means "ought to be done" and sometimes means only "not wrong," and on the other, that "wrong" is used as the opposite of all the other expressions mentioned, and so has somewhat different forces in different contexts.

One more remark is worth making. Even if one holds that beneficence is not a *requirement* of morality but something supererogatory and morally *good*, one is still regarding beneficence as an important part of morality—as desirable if not required.

What does the principle of beneficence say? Four things, I think:

1. One ought not to inflict evil or harm (what is bad).
2. One ought to prevent evil or harm.
3. One ought to remove evil.
4. One ought to do or promote good.

These four things are different, but they may appropriately be regarded as parts of the principle of beneficence. Of the four, it is most plausible to say that (4) is not a duty in the strict sense. In

fact, one is inclined to say that in some sense (1) takes precedence over (2), (2) over (3), and (3) over (4), other things being equal. But all are, at any rate, principles of prima facie duty. By adding "to or for anyone" at the end of each of them one makes the principle of beneficence universalistic, by adding "to or for others" one makes it altruistic. What one does here depends on whether he is willing to say that one has moral duties to oneself or not. For example, does one have a moral duty not to sacrifice any of one's own happiness for that of another?

It is tempting to think that, since the first four parts of the principle of beneficence may come into conflict with one another in choice situations, say, between actions both of which do some good and some evil, we should regard it as having a fifth part that instructs us, in such cases, to do what will bring about the greatest balance of good over evil. This would, however, presuppose that good and evil can always be measured in some way and lose the advantages ascribed to the principle of beneficence over the principle of utility; in fact, it would make the former equivalent to the latter in practice, since we are always choosing between two courses of action, even if one of them is called "inaction." Even so, we may perhaps follow this instruction—or the principle of utility—as a heuristic maxim in conflict situations involving only the principle of beneficence, at least insofar as the goods and evils involved are susceptible to some kind of measuring and balancing, though remembering its limitations.

There are many rules of prima facie right, wrong, or obligation, to be used in determining our actual duties, which can be derived from the principle of beneficence. Wherever one can form a general statement about what affects the lives of people for better or for worse, there one has a valid principle of prima facie duty, for example, "One ought not to kick people in the shin" or "We ought to promote knowledge." Most of the usual rules—keeping promises, telling the truth, showing gratitude, making reparation, not interfering with liberty, etc.—can be seen on this basis to be valid prima facie rules. For instance, given the principle of beneficence and the fact that knowing the truth is a good (in itself or as a means), it follows that telling the truth is a prima facie duty.

Thus, some of our rules of prima facie duty follow directly from the principle of beneficence. The rule of telling the truth can probably be defended also (perhaps with certain built-in exceptions) on the ground that its adoption makes for the greatest general good—as rule-utilitarians hold.

However, not all of our prima facie obligations can be derived from the principle of beneficence any more than from that of utility. For the principle of beneficence does not tell us how we are to distribute goods and evils; it only tells us to produce the one and prevent the other. When conflicting claims are made upon us, the most it could do (and we saw it cannot strictly even do this) is to instruct us to promote the greatest balance of good over evil and, as we have already seen, we need something more. This is where a principle of justice must come in.

III. The Principle of Justice: Equality

We have seen that we must recognize a basic principle of justice. But which one? What is justice? We cannot go into the whole subject of social justice here, but we must at least complete our outline of a normative theory of moral obligation, in which the principle of justice plays a crucial role. We are talking here about *distributive justice*, justice in the distribution of good and evil. There is also *retributive justice* (punishment, etc.). . . . Distributive justice is a matter of the *comparative treatment* of individuals. The paradigm case of injustice is that in which there are two similar individuals in similar circumstances and one of them is treated better or worse than the other. In this case, the cry of injustice rightly goes up against the responsible agent or group; and unless that agent or group can establish that

there is some relevant dissimilarity after all between the individuals concerned and their circumstances, he or they will be guilty as charged. This is why Sidgwick suggested his formula, according to which justice is the similar and injustice the dissimilar treatment of similar cases. This formula does give a necessary condition of justice; similar cases are to be treated similarly so far as the requirements of justice are concerned, although these requirements may be outweighed by other considerations. But Sidgwick's formula is not sufficient. All it really says is that we must act according to rules if we mean to be just. Although this formula is correct as far as it goes, it tells us nothing about what the rules are to be, and this is what we want to know, since we have already seen that rules themselves may be unjust. If this were not so, there could be no unjust laws or practices, for laws and practices are rules. Much depends, as we shall see, on which similarities and dissimilarities of individuals are taken as the basis for similarity or dissimilarity of treatment.

The question remaining to be answered is how we are to tell what rules of distribution or comparative treatment we are to act on. We have seen that these rules cannot be determined on the basis of beneficence alone (as I think the rules of not injuring anyone and of keeping covenants can be). A number of criteria have been proposed by different thinkers: (1) that justice is dealing with people according to their *deserts* or *merits;* (2) that it is treating human beings as *equals* in the sense of distributing good and evil equally among them, excepting perhaps in the case of punishment; (3) that it is treating people according to their *needs,* their *abilities,* or both. An example of the first is the classical *meritarian* criterion of justice as found in Aristotle and Ross. According to this view, the criterion of desert or merit is virtue, and justice is distributing the good (e.g., happiness) in accordance with virtue. One might, of course, adopt some other criterion of merit, for example, ability, contribution, intelligence, blood, color, social rank, or wealth, and then justice would consist in distributing good and evil in accordance with this criterion. The second criterion is the *equalitarian* one that is characteristic of modern democratic theory. The third is also a modern view, and may take various forms; its most prominent form today is the Marxist dictum, "From each according to his ability, to each according to his needs." I shall argue for the second view.

Some of the criteria of merit mentioned seem to be palpably nonmoral or even unjust, for example, the use of blood, color, intelligence, sex, social rank, or wealth as a basis for one's rules of distribution. Use of ability as a basis would give us a form of the third view. This leaves moral and/or nonmoral virtue as possible criteria of merit. Should we adopt a meritarian theory of this Aristotle-Ross sort? It seems to me that virtue, moral or nonmoral, cannot be our basic criterion in matters of distributive justice, because a recognition of any kind of virtue as a basis of distribution if justified only if every individual has an equal chance of achieving all the virtue of that kind he is capable of (and it must not be assumed that they have all had this chance, for they have not). If the individuals competing for goods, positions, and the like have not had an equal chance to achieve all the virtue they are capable of, then virtue is not a fair basis for distributing such things among them. If this is so, then, before virtue can reasonably be adopted as a basis of distribution, there must first be a prior *equal* distribution of the conditions for achieving virtue, at least insofar as this is within the control of human society. This is where equality of opportunity, equality before the law, and equality of access to the means of education come in. In other words, recognition of virtue as a basis of distribution is reasonable only against the background of an acknowledgment of the principle of equality. The primary criterion of distributive justice, then, is not merit in the form of virtue of some kind or other, but equality.

One might object here that there is another kind of merit, namely, effort, and that effort made should be taken as a basis of distribution in at least certain kinds of cases. This is true, but

again, it does seem to me that effort cannot serve as our *basic* criterion of distribution, and that recognition of it in any defensible way presupposes the general notion that we should all be treated equally.

We certainly must consider abilities and needs in determining how we are to treat others. This is required by the principle of beneficence, for it asks us to be concerned about the goodness of their lives, which involves catering to their needs and fostering and making use of their abilities. But is it required by the principle of justice? More particularly, does the principle of justice require us to help people in proportion to their needs or to call on them in proportion to their abilities? It is wrong to ask more of people than they can do or to assign them tasks out of proportion to their ability, but this is because "ought" implies "can." Justice asks us to do something about cases of special need; for example, it asks us to give special attention to people with certain kinds of handicaps, because only with such attention can they have something comparable to an equal chance with others of enjoying a good life. But does it always ask us, at least prima facie, to *proportion* our help to their needs and our demands to their abilities? Are we always prima facie unjust if we help A in proportion to his needs but not B, or if we make demands of C in proportion to his abilities but not of D? It seems to me that the basic question is whether or not in so doing we are showing an equal concern for the goodness of the lives of A and B or of C and D. Whether we should treat them in proportion to their needs and abilities depends, as far as *justice* is concerned, on whether doing so helps or hinders them equally in the achievement of the best lives they are capable of. If helping them in proportion to their needs is necessary for making an equal contribution to the goodness of their lives, then and only then is it unjust to do otherwise. If asking of them in proportion to their abilities is necessary for keeping their chances of a good life equal, then and only then is it unjust to do otherwise. In other words, the basic standard of distributive justice is *equality* of treatment. That, for instance, is why justice calls for giving extra attention to handicapped people.

If this is correct, then we must adopt the equalitarian view of distributive justice. In other words, the principle of justice lays upon us the prima facie obligation of treating people equally. Here we have the answer to our question. This does not mean that it is prima facie unjust to treat people of the same color differently or to treat people of different heights similarly. Color and height are not morally relevant similarities or dissimilarities. Those that are relevant are the ones that bear on the goodness or badness of people's lives, for example, similarities or dissimilarities in ability, interest, or need. Treating people equally does not mean treating them identically; justice is not so monotonous as all that. It means making the same relative contribution to the goodness of their lives (this is equal help or helping according to need) or asking the same relative sacrifice (this is asking in accordance with ability).

Treating people equally in this sense does not mean making their lives equally good or maintaining their lives at the same level of goodness. It would be a mistake to think that justice requires this. For, though people are equally capable of some kind of good life (or least bad one), the kinds of life of which they are capable are not equally good. The lives of which some are capable simply are better, nonmorally as well as morally, than those of which others are capable. In this sense men are not equal, since they are not equal in their capacities. They are equal only in the sense that they ought prima facie to be treated equally, and they ought to be treated equally only in the sense that we ought prima facie to make proportionally the same contribution to the goodness of their lives, once a certain minimum has been achieved by all. This is what is meant by the equal intrinsic dignity or value of the individual that is such an important concept in our culture.

We must remember that this equality of treatment, though it is a basic obligation, is only a prima facie one, and that it may on occasion (and there is no formula for determining the occasions) be overruled by the principle of beneficence. We may claim, however, that in distributing goods and evils, help, tasks, roles, and so forth, people are to be treated equally in the sense indicated, except when unequal treatment can be justified by considerations of beneficence (including utility) or on the ground that it will promote greater equality in the long run. Unequal treatment always requires justification and only certain kinds of justification suffice.

It is in the light of the preceding discussion, it seems to me, that we must try to solve such social problems as education, economic opportunity, racial integration, and aid to underdeveloped countries, remembering always that the principle of beneficence requires us to respect the liberty of others. Our discussion provides only the most general guidelines for solving such problems, of course, but most of what is needed in addition is good will, clarity of thought, and knowledge of the relevant facts.

Summary of My Theory of Obligation

We have now arrived at a mixed deontological theory of obligation somewhat different from the one tentatively sketched earlier. It takes as basic the principle of beneficence (not that of utility) and the principle of justice, not identified as equal treatment. Must we recognize any other basic principle of right and wrong? It seems to me that we need not. As far as I can see, we can derive all of the things we may wish to recognize as duties from our two principles, either directly as the crow flies or indirectly as the rule-utilitarian does. From the former follow various more specific rules of prima facie obligation, for example those of not injuring anyone, and of not interfering with anyone's liberty. From the latter follow others like equality of consideration and equality before the law. Some, like telling the truth or not being cruel to children, may follow separately from both principles, which may give them a kind of priority they might not otherwise have. Others, like keeping promises and not crossing university lawns, may perhaps be justified in rule-utilitarian fashion on the basis of the two principles taken jointly, as being rules whose general acceptance and obedience is conducive to a state of affairs in which a maximal balance of good over evil is as equally distributed as possible (the greatest good of the greatest number).

The Problem of Conflict

Several problems facing this theory remain to be discussed. One is the problem of possible conflict between its two principles. I see no way out of this. It does seem to me that the two principles may come into conflict, both at the level of individual action and at that of social policy, and I know of no formula that will always tell us how to solve such conflicts or even how to solve conflicts between their corollaries. It is tempting to say that the principle of justice always takes precedence over that of beneficence: do justice though the heavens fall. But is a small injustice never to be preferred to a great evil? Perhaps we should lean over backwards to avoid committing injustice, but are we never justified in treating people unequally? One might contend that the principle of equal treatment always has priority at least over the fourth or positive part of the principle of beneficence, but is it never right to treat people unequally when a considerable good is at stake? The answer to these questions, I regret to say, does not seem to me to be clearly negative, and I am forced to conclude that the problem of conflict that faced the pluralistic deontological theories discussed earlier is still with us. One can only hope that, if we take the moral point of view, become clearheaded, and come to know all that is relevant, we will also come to agree on ways of acting that are satisfactory to all concerned.

The following reflection may be encouraging in this respect. It seems to me that everyone who takes the moral point of view can agree that the ideal state of affairs is one in which everyone has the best life he or she is capable of. Now, in such a state of affairs, it is clear that the concerns of both the principle of justice or equality and the principle of beneficence will be fulfilled. If so, then we can see that the two principles are in some sense ultimately consistent, and this seems to imply that increasing insight may enable us to know more and more how to solve the conflicts that trouble us now when we know so little about realizing the ideal state of affairs in which the principles are at one. Then, while Ross is right in saying that we must finally appeal to "perception," we can at least give an outline of what that perception is supposed to envision.

Notes

*[Act-Utilitarianism, General Utilitarianism, and Rule-Utilitarianism—ED.]

1. *Essays in Pragmatism,* A. Castell, ed. (New York: Hafner Publishing Co., 1948), p. 73.

28

A Contractarian Ethics

T. M. SCANLON

Thomas M. Scanlon, Jr. is the Alford Professor of Natural Religion, Moral Philosophy, and Civil Polity at Harvard University. His importance in contemporary moral and political philosophy would be difficult to exaggerate. The present selection is from his highly acclaimed and influential book What We Owe to Each Other *(1998), in which he defends a contractualist moral theory according to which we should act only according to principles that others, insofar as they share our aims, "could not reasonably reject." In this selection Scanlon explains and defends some key differences between his and other contractualist moral theories.*

1. Introduction

The idea that an act is right if and only if it can be justified to others is one that even a noncontractualist might accept. Utilitarians, for example, who hold that an act is right only if it would produce a greater balance of happiness than any alternative available to the agent at the time, presumably also believe that an act is justifiable to others just in case it satisfies this utilitarian formula, so they too will hold that an act is right if and only if it is justifiable to others on terms they could not reasonably reject. For utilitarians, however, what makes an action right is having the best consequences; justifiability is merely a consequence of this.

What is distinctive about my version of contractualism is that it takes the idea of justifiability to be basic in two ways: this idea provides both the normative basis of the morality of right and wrong and the most general characterization of its content. According to contractualism, when we address our minds to a question of right and wrong, what we are trying to decide is, first and foremost, whether certain principles are ones that no one, if suitably motivated, could reasonably reject. In order to make the content of my view clearer I need to say more about the ideas of justifiability and reasonable rejection on which it rests.

Many theories have been offered that are like mine in suggesting that we can understand the content of morality (or of justice) by considering what principles people would (perhaps under special conditions) have reason to agree to, or what principles could be willed (from a certain point of view) to hold universally. These include, to mention only a few well-known examples, Kant's view and the theories offered more recently by David Gauthier, Jürgen Habermas, R. M. Hare, and John Rawls. Most of these theories appeal to some idea of rationality or of what it would be rational to choose (perhaps under special conditions). In Gauthier's case, rationality is identified, initially, with doing or choosing what conduces to the fulfillment of one's aims, and his aim is to show how we could have good reason to comply with principles that it would be rational, in this sense, for all to agree to. Hare identifies the rational action with the action that would maximize the satisfaction of one's present preferences as they would be if purged of logical error and modified by exposure to the facts. Since he takes moral principles to be universal imperatives (applying not only to things as they are but also to the possible worlds in which one occupies the position of any of the other people performing or affected by actions of the kind in question), a rational decision about which principles to accept must take into account not only one's present preferences but also the preferences one would have in any of these other positions. Rationally defensible moral principles will thus be those that lead to maximum satisfaction of the rational preferences of all affected parties.

Kant famously held that an action is morally permissible if it would be allowed by a principle that one could rationally will to hold "as a universal law." Rawls maintains, as one part of his theory, that the principles of justice (standards for determining the legitimacy of basic social institutions) are those that it would be rational for parties to accept if they were to choose with the aim of doing as well as they can for those they represent but under conditions in which they lacked any information about their social position, their natural advantages, and their distinctive values and commitments (that is to say, if they were to choose behind a "veil of ignorance" that obscures these facts).

Each of the theories I have mentioned proposes that we can reach conclusions about the content of morality by asking certain questions about what it would be rational to do or choose or will. In each case these questions are understood in a way that requires us, in one way or another, to take the interests of others into account in answering it. In the case of Gauthier's theory, we must take account of what others have reason to do because we are trying to gain the benefits of cooperative arrangements and it would not be rational for others to accept a plan of action if doing so would not advance their interests. In Hare's theory, and in the part of Rawls's that I have mentioned, the rational choice in question is defined in a way that makes the fates of others relevant in a different way. In Hare's theory

this is accomplished by adding information and motivation: information about other people's preferences, which then shapes our own preferences about how we would want to be treated if we were in their position. In Rawls's theory it is done by subtracting information (imposing a veil of ignorance) and by focusing on motivation of one particular kind—the desire of mutually disinterested parties to do as well as they can for themselves and those whom they represent. Contracting parties are moved to protect the interests of the least advantaged and of cultural and religious minorities because, for all they know, they may belong to these groups themselves.

According to the version of contractualism that I am advancing here our thinking about right and wrong is structured by a different kind of motivation, namely the aim of finding principles that others, insofar as they too have this aim, could not reasonably reject. This gives us a direct reason to be concerned with other people's points of view: not because we might, for all we know, actually *be* them, or because we might occupy their position in some other possible world, but in order to find principles that they, as well as we, have reason to accept. . . . There is on this view a strong continuity between the reasons that lead us to act in the way that the conclusions of moral thought require and the reasons that shape the process through which we arrive at those conclusions. My version of contractualism is distinguished from these otherwise similar theories, then, by its particular motivational claim and by its appeal to the notion of reasonableness rather than rationality.

2. Reasonableness

This second feature, in particular, may seem questionable. Why speak of "principles which no one could reasonably reject" rather than "principles which no one could rationally reject"? The "reasonableness" formulation seems more obscure. Why use it, then, especially in view of the fact that I add the rider "given the aim of finding principles which others, insofar as they share this aim, could not reasonably reject"? Why not rely upon the idea of what would be *rational* for a person who has this aim?

. . . "Rationality" can be understood in a number of different ways. But in recent years "the (most) rational thing to do" has most commonly been taken to mean "what most conduces to the fulfillment of the agent's aims." The primacy of this usage is indicated by the contemporary theories I have just discussed, which despite their differences almost all make use of the idea of rationality in more or less this same sense. As I have indicated, I believe that this conception of rationality is mistaken, but it is so familiar that it is what any unqualified use of the term is likely to call to mind.

"Reasonable" also has an established meaning, which is much closer to what I take to be basic to moral thinking. A claim about what it is reasonable for a person to do presupposes a certain body of information and a certain range of reasons which are taken to be relevant, and goes on to make a claim about what these reasons, properly understood, in fact support. In the contractualist analysis of right and wrong, what is presupposed first and foremost is the aim of finding principles that others who share this aim could not reasonably reject. This aim then brings other reasons in its train. Given this aim, for example, it would be unreasonable to give the interests of others no weight in deciding which principles to accept. For why should they accept principles arrived at in this way? This then leads to further, more complicated questions about how, more exactly, we can be asked to "take others' interests into account" in various situations.

The distinction between what it would be reasonable to do in this sense and what it would be rational to do is not a technical one, but a familiar distinction in ordinary language. Suppose, for example, that we are negotiating about water rights in our county, and that there is one landowner who already controls most of the water in the vicinity. This person has no need for our cooperation. He can do as he pleases, and what he chooses to do will largely determine the outcome of the negotiations. Suppose also that while he is not ungenerous (he would probably provide water from his own wells for anyone who desperately needed it) he is extremely irritable and does not like to have the legitimacy of his position questioned. In such a situation, it would not be unreasonable for one of us to maintain that each person is entitled to at least a minimum supply of water, and to reject any principle of allocation which does not guarantee this. But it might not be rational to make this claim or to reject such principles, since this is very likely to enrage the large landholder and lead to an outcome that is worse for almost everyone. Moreover, it is natural to say that it would be unreasonable of the large landholder to reject our request for principles guaranteeing minimum water rights. What it would be rational for him to do (in the most common understanding of that term) is a different question, and depends on what his aims are.

There is, then, a familiar distinction between reasonableness and rationality. It might be objected that in calling attention to this distinction I have concentrated exclusively on what would be rational *simpliciter*, and have not considered what would be rational given the particular aim I have specified. Why not, it might be asked, take rightness to be determined by the principles no one could *rationally* reject given the aim of finding principles which others, who share this aim, could also not rationally reject? This seems to offer a way of capturing the idea that I have in mind while avoiding the obscure notion of reasonableness in favor of the clearer and better-understood idea of rationality.

My first reason for not formulating the contractualist account of right and wrong in this way is that so formulated it is most likely to be understood as a question of strategy, of how best to bring about the desired end of agreement on principles. So interpreted, it is unlikely to have a determinate answer, in light of the fact, noted above, that what it is rational to do will depend on what others can be expected to do in response. If there is one principle which would make everyone better off than he or she would be under any other, then it may be obvious that it is rational for everyone to choose this principle, and the question "What principle could no one rationally reject given the aim of finding principles that others, who share this aim, could not rationally reject?" may therefore have a determinate answer. But in more common situations we must choose among principles each of which would benefit some at the expense of others. In such cases, there may be no determinate answer, in the abstract, to the question whether a given principle is or is not one that no one with the aim in question could rationally reject.

The answer to this question in a given situation may become determinate once the details of that situation—the psychologies of the individuals involved and the options open to them—are fully specified. In the water rights case mentioned above, for example, even if all of us (the large landowner included) share the aim of finding principles which no one else could rationally reject, it remains true that none of us has reason to reject the terms which he prefers. Adding the aim of rational agreement makes little difference in this case, since the landowner is in a position to make it rational for his neighbors to accept whatever principle he chooses. In this example the answer, though determinate, carries little moral weight. If we rule out the features of this example which make it morally objectionable—by requiring, for example, that there be full information and a no-agreement point which leaves everyone in a position that is at least minimally acceptable—then determinateness may be lost again, since the outcome may depend on the individual psychologies of the parties, and their relations and loyalties. One familiar strategy is to impose further constraints on the agreement in question, with the aim of preserving both determinateness and moral relevance. This strategy may well succeed in particular cases. My present aim is not to argue against theories employing this strategy but rather to distinguish it from the strategy that I am pursuing.

According to my version of contractualism, deciding whether an action is right or wrong requires a substantive judgment on our part about whether certain objections to possible moral principles would be reasonable. In the argument over water rights, for example, our judgment that it would not be unreasonable for the neighbors to demand better terms than the large landowner is offering reflects a substantive judgment about the merits of their claims. It is not a judgment about what would be most likely to advance their interests or to produce agreement in their actual circumstances or in any more idealized situation, but rather a judgment about the suitability of certain principles to serve as the basis of mutual recognition and accommodation.

If my analysis is correct then the idea of what would be reasonable in this sense is one that underlies and guides our ordinary thinking about right and wrong. It is thus an idea with moral content. This moral content makes it inviting as a component in moral theory, but also invites the charge of circularity. By basing itself on reasonableness, it may be charged, a theory builds in moral elements at the start. This makes it easy to produce a theory which *sounds* plausible, but such a theory will tell us very little, since everything we are to get out of it at the end we must put in at the beginning as part of the moral content of reasonableness. A strategy which relies on the idea of rationality (together, perhaps, with structural features of an ideal situation in which the rational choices are to be made) therefore seems to promise a more successful theory, or at least an account of right and wrong which is less threatened with circularity. Before responding to this objection,

I will describe my version of contractualism in somewhat greater detail. By making clearer the ways in which judgments about reasonable rejection "have moral content" I hope to clarify both the force of the charge of circularity and my way of responding to it.

Before turning to this task, however, I want to say more about how the idea of reasonableness figures in the process of deciding whether or not an action is wrong. According to contractualism, in order to decide whether it would be wrong to do X in circumstances C, we should consider possible principles governing how one may act in such situations, and ask whether any principle that permitted one to do X in those circumstances could, for that reason, reasonably be rejected. In order to decide whether this is so, we need first to form an idea of the burdens that would be imposed on some people in such a situation if others were permitted to do X. Call these the objections to permission. We then need, in order to decide whether these objections provide grounds for reasonably rejecting the proposed principle, to consider the ways in which others would be burdened by a principle forbidding one to do X in these circumstances. Suppose that, compared to the objections to permission, the objections to prohibition are not significant, and that it is therefore reasonable to reject any principle that would permit one to do X in the circumstances in question. This means that this action is wrong, according to the contractualist formula. Alternatively, if there were some principle for regulating behavior in such situations that would permit one to do X and that it would not be reasonable to reject, then doing X would not be wrong: it could be justified to others on grounds that they could not reasonably refuse to accept.

Returning to the former case for the moment, if it would be reasonable to reject any principle that permitted one to do X in circumstances C, then it would seem that there must be some principle that it would not be reasonable to reject that would disallow doing X in these circumstances. One would expect this to be true because of the comparative nature of the question of reasonable rejection. If the objections to permission are strong enough, *compared to the objections to prohibition*, to make it reasonable to reject any principle permitting doing X in C, then one would not expect the objections to prohibition to be strong enough, *compared to the objections to permission*, to make it reasonable to reject any principle that forbids doing X in C.

But it may seem that there could be cases in which this might be true. Consider, for example, the case of two people swimming from a sinking ship, one of whom finds a life jacket floating in the water. May the other person take the jacket by force? It might seem that, even though any principle that permitted this could reasonably be rejected, any principle forbidding it could also be rejected, since taking the jacket is the only way for the other person to avoid drowning. Put in a general form, the idea might be that there is a threshold of reasonable rejection: a level of cost such that it is reasonable to reject any principle that would lead to one's suffering a cost that great, and reasonable to do this no matter what objections others might have to alternative principles. It does not seem to me that there is such a threshold. It does not seem, for example, that the fact that a principle would forbid one to do something that was necessary in order to save one's life always makes it reasonable to reject that principle. The reasonableness of rejecting such a principle will depend not only on the costs that alternative principles would impose on others but also on how those costs would be imposed. This reflects the general fact, which I will discuss later in this chapter, that the strength of a person's objection to a principle is not determined solely by the difference that the acceptance of that principle would make to that person's welfare. In the shipwreck case, for example, the costs of the two principles to the parties may be the same (one will drown if not permitted to seize the life jacket, and the other will drown if it is taken from him). But it may still make a difference to the force of their objections that one of them now has the jacket (perhaps he has looked hard to find it) and is therefore not now at risk.

Even if the general idea of a threshold of reasonable rejection is incorrect, however, there could still be cases in which opposing parties have strong objections that are evenly balanced. Suppose, for example, that the two swimmers, one of whom is much stronger than the other, arrive at the life jacket at the same moment. May each use force to try to seize it? It might seem that if a principle permitting this could reasonably be rejected then so too could a principle forbidding it, since the considerations on the two sides are the same. This conclusion depends on an overly simple view of the alternatives. A principle permitting each to struggle for the jacket at least has the merit of recognizing the symmetry of their claims and the need for some decisive solution. It would be reasonable to reject this principle if, but only if, there were some alternative that did this better (such as a principle requiring them to take turns or, unrealistic as it may seem, to draw lots). Similarly, a principle forbidding the use of force could not reasonably be rejected if there were some other (nonrejectable) method for resolving the matter.

It thus does not follow, from the fact that the situations of the people who would suffer from an action's being permitted and those who would suffer from its being forbidden are virtually the same, that if any principle that permits the action can reasonably be rejected then so too can any principle that forbids it. The very fact that these objections are symmetrical may point the way toward a class of principles that are not rejectable.

3. Principles

I have said that an act is wrong if it would be disallowed by any *principle* that no one could reasonably reject. The aim of this section is to explain what is meant here by a principle and to say something about the role that such principles play in our thinking about right and wrong. Taking familiar controversies about act and rule utilitarianism as a background, it would be natural to ask why justification of our actions to others should proceed by way of principles at all. Why not consider individual acts instead? Put in this way, the question is misconceived. To justify an action to others is to offer reasons supporting it and to claim that they are sufficient to defeat any objections that others may have. To do this, however, is also to defend a principle, namely one claiming that such reasons are sufficient grounds for so acting under the prevailing conditions. There is a question (corresponding to the debate between act and rule utilitarianism) as to whether the justification for an action should appeal only to consequences of that act (as compared with the consequences of alternative actions available to the agent) or whether other considerations are also relevant. I will address this question in the following section. But it is a question about the form that the relevant principles should take, not about whether justification should involve principles at all.

The emphasis that contractualism places on justification, hence on reasons and principles, captures a central feature of everyday judgments of right and wrong. Typically, our intuitive judgments about the wrongness of actions are not simply judgments *that* an act is wrong but that it is wrong for some reason, or in virtue of some general characteristic. Judgments of right and wrong are in this respect quite different from many other types of evaluative judgment such as judgments that something is beautiful, or ugly, or funny. In the latter cases the evaluative judgment comes first—we "see" that the thing is beautiful or funny—and the explanation comes later, if in fact we can supply it at all. But we rarely, if ever, "see" that an action is wrong without having some idea *why* it is wrong. There may be cases in which some action "just seems wrong," even though one cannot say what the objection to it is. But these reactions have the status of "hunches" or suspicions which need to be made good: there is pressure to come up with an explanation or else withdraw the judgment if we cannot explain what our objection is.

People in different cultures regard different things as funny and have different views about what constitutes a beautiful face. They thus have "different standards" of humor and (at least some kinds of) beauty, and it is plausible to say that when a member of one of these groups makes a judgment about what is funny or good-looking, the claim that this judgment makes has to be understood as relative to the standards of that group (so that opposing assessments of the same joke, made in Omsk and Los Angeles, could both be true). But even if there are, in this sense, standards of humor and beauty, these standards do not play the same role in individual judgments that moral standards generally do. A person who regards a joke as funny, or a person or scene as beautiful, may be quite unable to articulate the standards, if any, to which his or her judgment is relative. But I cannot claim that an action is morally wrong without having some idea what objection there is to it.

Contractualism offers a natural explanation of this feature of our judgments about right and wrong. In another respect, however, the claim that moral judgments involve conscious reference to principles may seem implausible. Suppose I believe that while McCormick had a legal right to build his house where he did, it was wrong of him to put it so close to the property line, thereby ruining his neighbor's view. In this example I have a definite idea what the moral objection to McCormick's action is: insufficient consideration for his neighbor's interests. But it is unlikely that I could formulate a principle to back this up, if by a principle we mean a rule specifying what weight one is supposed to give to others' interests when they conflict with one's own interests of a similar

sort. So the claim I have been making may seem very implausible insofar as it is taken to suggest that we make decisions of this kind by invoking or "applying" a principle or rule.

This observation is quite correct. But the idea that it constitutes an objection to what I have been claiming rests on an overly narrow idea of what a principle is. If a principle is taken to be a rule that can be "applied" to settle quite a wide range of questions with little or no room left for the exercise of judgment, then there are very few moral principles at all, and it would certainly be false to claim that every judgment about right and wrong must be backed by one. If the claim that moral judgments must be backed by principles is to have any plausibility, the notion of a principle will have to be understood much more broadly. Principles, as I will understand them, are general conclusions about the status of various kinds of reasons for action. So understood, principles may rule out some actions by ruling out the reasons on which they would be based, but they also leave wide room for interpretation and judgment.

Consider, for example, moral principles concerning the taking of human life. It might seem that this is a simple rule, forbidding a certain class of actions: Thou shalt not kill. But what about self-defense, suicide, and certain acts of killing by police officers and by soldiers in wartime? And is euthanasia always strictly forbidden? The parts of this principle that are the clearest are better put in terms of reasons: the fact that a course of action can be foreseen to lead to someone's death is normally a conclusive reason against it; the fact that someone's death would be to my personal advantage is no justification for aiming at it; but one may use deadly force when this seems the only defense against a person who threatens one's life; and so on.

Much the same can be said of the principle of fidelity to promises. We are not morally required to keep a promise no matter what. The clearest part of the principle is this: the fact that keeping a promise would be inconvenient or disadvantageous is not normally a sufficient reason for breaking it, but "normally" here covers many qualifications. There are, for example, questions of proportionality (the kind of disadvantage that may not be appealed to in order to justify backing out depends on what is at stake in the promise) and questions about the conditions under which the promise was given (such as whether there was duress and whether crucial information was withheld).

So even the most familiar moral principles are not rules which can be easily applied without appeals to judgment. Their succinct verbal formulations turn out on closer examination to be mere labels for much more complex ideas. Moral principles are in this respect much like some legal ones. The constitutional formula "Congress shall make no law abridging freedom of speech, or of the press" may sound like a simple prohibition. But the underlying idea is much more complicated. There is of course considerable controversy about what, more precisely, this amendment covers. What is striking, however, and more relevant for present purposes, is the breadth and complexity of the area of agreement. Presented with a range of examples of governmental regulation of expression, people who understand freedom of expression will agree on a wide range of judgments about which of these involve violations of the First Amendment and which do not. These cases are sufficiently varied that it would be difficult to explain our convergent judgments as applications of any statable rule. How, then, do we arrive at these judgments? We do so, I believe, by appeal to a shared sense of what the point of freedom of expression is and how it is supposed to work: why restrictions on governmental power to regulate expression are necessary, what threats they are supposed to rule out, and what it is that they are trying to promote.

Similarly, it is a familiar moral principle that promises freely made must be kept, although we must add "at least in the absence of special

justification." How do we decide what forms of justification are sufficient? It is sometimes suggested that this is a matter of "balancing" the competing considerations. But this metaphor is misleading insofar as it suggests that what is involved is only a process of weighing or comparing the seriousness of conflicting interests. The costs at stake for promiser and promisee are of course among the relevant factors in deciding whether a given promise must be kept, but these must be considered within a more complex structure which the metaphor of balancing conceals. Anyone who understands the point of promising—what it is supposed to ensure and what it is to protect us against—will see that certain reasons for going back on a promise could not be allowed without rendering promises pointless, while other exceptions must be allowed if the practice is not to be unbearably costly.

For example, the point of promising would be defeated if a minor inconvenience, or even a major cost that was clearly foreseeable at the time the promise was made, counted as adequate ground for failing to perform as promised. On the other hand it would not render promises pointless to recognize, as grounds for default, a cost which is both quite unexpected and much more serious than what is at stake for the promisee. Perhaps this exception is even required in order not to make promising too risky. Factors such as whether a cost to a promisee was foreseeable, foreseen, or unexpected are made relevant by the interests to which a principle of fidelity to agreements must be responsive. But when we are deciding whether, in a particular case, these factors serve as conditions that modify the force of a given cost as a reason for not keeping a promise, rather than as further interests that are balanced against that cost.

All of this structure and more is part of what each of us knows if we understand the principle that promises ought to be kept. In making particular judgments of right and wrong we are drawing on this complex understanding, rather than applying a statable rule, and this understanding enables us to arrive at conclusions about new and difficult cases, which no rule would cover.

When we judge a person to have acted in a way that was morally wrong, we take her or him to have acted on a reason that is morally disallowed, or to have given a reason more weight than is morally permitted, or to have failed to see the relevance or weight of some countervailing reason which, morally, must take precedence. Each of these judgments involves a principle in the broad sense in which I am using that term. There may be no rule we can invoke as telling us that a certain reason is not morally sufficient (that my reason for breaking my promise is not sufficiently weighty, or that McCormick did not have good reason for disregarding his neighbor's interest in preserving his view). But we make such judgments by drawing on our understanding of why there should be a moral constraint on actions of the kind in question (why principles that left us free to do as we liked in such situations are "reasonably rejectable") and of the structure that that constraint takes (in what way we can be asked to take the relevant interests into account). When, in the light of our best understanding of this moral rationale, we make a judgment about the sufficiency of the reasons for an action in a particular case, this judgment is guided by, and expresses, our understanding of a moral principle.

How many valid moral principles are there, then? An indefinite number, I would say. This, again, may seem implausible. How are we supposed to know what principles there are? By the same kind of thinking that we use to understand the content of familiar principles like fidelity to promises and freedom of speech. That is: we can see the need for limits on certain patterns of action (patterns of justification) by seeing the ways in which we are at risk if people are left free to decide to act in these ways; and by understanding the rationale for these moral constraints we can see why it is that certain

reasons for action, and certain ways of giving some reasons priority over others, are morally inadmissible. Some familiar principles are generally learned through explicit moral teaching, but we can see, on reflection, that they have a basis of the kind I have just described. Other principles we may never have thought of until we are presented with a situation (real or hypothetical) to which they would apply; but when this happens we can see immediately that they are valid.

For example: we are all taught that it is wrong to break one's promises (although, as I have said, our understanding of this principle goes far beyond the content of any explicit teaching). But . . . there are many other ways in which one can behave wrongly in regard to other people's expectations about what one will do: one can fail to take care about the expectations one leads others to form, fail to warn them that their expectations are mistaken, or (without promising anything) intentionally lead others to form false expectations when their doing so is to one's advantage. Not every action falling under the last two descriptions is wrong, but many are. There are no familiar and widely taught principles—analogous to "Keep your promises"—that cover these cases. Yet once the question arises we are able to see the wrongness of these actions in much the same way that we see the wrongness of breaking a promise or of making a promise that one does not intend to keep. That is to say, we are able to see that principles licensing such actions would be ones that people could reasonably reject.

4. Standpoints

The aim of finding and acting on principles that no one similarly motivated could reasonably reject leads us to take other people's interests into account in deciding what principles to follow. More exactly, we have reason to consider whether there are standpoints other than our own present standpoint from which the principles we are considering could reasonably be rejected. I want now to consider what these "standpoints" are.

According to contractualism, our concern with right and wrong is based on a concern that our actions be justifiable to others on grounds that they could not reasonably reject insofar as they share this concern. "Others" figure twice in this schema: as those to whom justification is owed, and as those who might or might not be able reasonably to reject certain principles. When we think of those to whom justification is owed, we naturally think first of the specific individuals who are affected by specific actions. But when we are deciding whether a given principle is one that could reasonably be rejected we must take a broader and more abstract perspective. This perspective is broader because, when we are considering the acceptability or rejectability of a principle, we must take into account not only the consequences of particular actions, but also the consequences of general performance or nonperformance of such actions and of the other implications (for both agents and others) of having agents be licensed and directed to think in the way that that principle requires. So the points of view that the question of reasonable rejectability requires us to take into account are not limited to those of the individuals affected by a particular action. This is so for several reasons, which are worth spelling out.

First and most obviously, widespread performance of acts of a given kind can have very different effects from isolated individual instances. Slightly less obviously, perhaps, the general authorization or prohibition of a class of actions can have significance that goes beyond the consequences of the actions that are performed or not performed as a result. This can be seen both from the point of view of agents and from that of the people who may be affected by these actions. As agents, if we know that we must stand ready to perform actions of a certain kind should they be required, or that we cannot count on being able to perform acts

of another kind should we want to, because they are forbidden, these things have important effects on our planning and on the organization of our lives whether or not any occasions of the relevant sort ever actually present themselves. If, for example, I lived in a desert area and were obligated to provide food for strangers in need who came by my house, then I would have to take account of this possibility in my shopping and consumption, whether or not anyone ever asked me for this kind of help; and if I am not entitled to photocopy articles at will when they turn out to be useful in my course, then I have reason to order a more inclusive anthology to begin with, even though this may prove to have been unnecessary. The same is true from the point of view of those affected by actions. Our need for privacy, for example, is not met simply because, as a matter of fact, other people do not listen in on our phone calls and go through our personal files. In order to have the benefits of privacy we need to have assurance that this will not happen, and this is something that general acceptance of a principle can provide.

These points could be summarized by saying that general prohibitions and permissions have effects on the liberty, broadly construed, of both agents and those affected by their actions. But the acceptance of principles has other implications beyond these effects. Because principles constrain the reasons we may, or must, take into account, they can affect our relations with others and our view of ourselves in both positive and negative ways. I have already discussed some "negative" examples—cases in which principles may interfere with our entering into other relations. . . . The case of privacy offers a more positive example. The fact that others recognize reasons to restrain themselves so that I may be free from observation and inquiry when I wish to be is important in defining my standing as an independent person who can enter into relations with others as an equal. If the principles we all accepted did not recognize these reasons, this would crucially alter my relations with other people, and even my view of myself. (Principles defining my distinctive rights over my own body—rights to say who can even touch it, let alone claim its parts for other purposes—are an even clearer example.)

As this discussion of the points of view that must be considered in deciding whether a principle could reasonably be rejected brings out, an assessment of the rejectability of a principle must take into account the consequences of its acceptance in general, not merely in a particular case that we may be concerned with. Since we cannot know, when we are making this assessment, which particular individuals will be affected by it in which ways (who will be affected as an agent required to act a certain way, who as a potential victim, who as a bystander, and so on), our assessment cannot be based on the particular aims, preferences, and other characteristics of specific individuals. We must rely instead on commonly available information about what people have reason to want. I will refer to this as information about generic reasons.

Some examples: We commonly take it that people have strong reasons to want to avoid bodily injury, to be able to rely on assurances they are given, and to have control over what happens to their own bodies. We therefore think it reasonable to reject principles that would leave other agents free to act against these important interests. Similarly, as agents we typically have reason to want to give special attention to our own projects, friends, and family, and thus have reason to object to principles that would constrain us in ways that would make these concerns impossible.

Generic reasons are reasons that we can see that people have in virtue of their situation, characterized in general terms, and such things as their aims and capabilities and the conditions in which they are placed. Not everyone is affected by a given principle in the same way, and generic reasons are not limited to reasons that the majority of people have. If even a small number of people would be adversely affected by

a general permission for agents to act a certain way, then this gives rise to a potential reason for rejecting that principle. (This is a generic reason since it is one that we can see people have in virtue of certain general characteristics; it is not attributed to specific individuals.)

Whether such a reason is a ground for reasonably rejecting the principle will depend, of course, on the costs this would involve for others, and these will depend on what alternatives there are. One alternative, if a principle granting general permission to act a certain way is rejected, is a general prohibition against so acting. This may be very costly from the point of view of potential agents, and may be reasonably rejected on that account. A second possibility is a principle in which the permission is qualified, by specific exceptions or by a more open-ended requirement that there be no countervailing considerations.

There is an obvious pressure toward making principles more fine-grained, to take account of more and more specific variations in needs and circumstances. But there is also counter-pressure arising from the fact that finer-grained principles will create more uncertainty and require those in other positions to gather more information in order to know what a principle gives to and requires of them. For example, the principle of fidelity to promises protects us against being bound in ways that we do not like by specifying that only voluntary undertakings are binding. But individuals differ in their ability to foresee possible difficulties and to resist subtle pressures to enter an agreement. The protection offered by the requirement of voluntariness is therefore of different value to different people. Should we have a more limited principle? That is to say, is the broader principle reasonably rejectable from the more specific point of view of those who are more easily drawn into unwelcome agreements? To argue that it is not, we need to claim that the more limited principle places an unreasonable burden on potential promisees, to ascertain the character and potential weaknesses of those with whom they are making agreements in order to know whether the agreement they have made is morally binding.

I do not mean to be deciding this substantive question here. My purpose is rather to illustrate the general point that we bring to moral argument a conception of generic points of view and the reasons associated with them which reflects our general experience of life, and that this conception is subject to modification under the pressures of moral thought and argument. Some of the most common forms of moral bias involve failing to think of various points of view which we have not occupied, underestimating the reasons associated with them, and overestimating the costs to us of accepting principles that recognize the force of those reasons.

It is commonly said that one important role of moral theory is to provide a way of correcting these biases. In one respect this is true. The pressure to be able to justify our actions to others, on terms that they could not reasonably reject, can help to reveal biases of this kind and press us to overcome them. But the process of doing this is one of gradually refining our intuitive moral categories under conflicting pressures of the kind I have just described, drawing on our expanding experience of others' points of view. I doubt that it is possible for theory to "correct biases" in a more radical way by specifying once and for all what the outcome of this process should be—for example, by specifying in advance the terms in which all "reasonable rejections" must be defended.

5. Generality and Fairness

This description of the process of moral justification is motivated by the general contractualist framework that I am defending. I believe that it is also in accord with moral intuition. In particular, it helps to explain two familiar intuitions about the moral irrelevance of certain considerations.

If we were evaluating a moral principle simply from the point of view of a particular individual, one thing that it would be natural to take into account would be the likelihood, given that person's particular needs and circumstances, of his or her benefiting from that principle and the likelihood of his or her having to bear its various costs. For example, when we are considering a principle of mutual aid, as in Kant's famous fourth example, some people (call them the fortunate Joneses) can reliably foresee that they are not very likely to need aid themselves, or at least much less likely than others, and much more likely to be called on to give it. It might seem that this gives them less reason than others have to reject a principle that imposes no duty of mutual aid, and more reason to reject a principle requiring that we give aid when it is not too difficult to do so. So it may seem that something like a veil of ignorance is necessary in order to screen such reasons out.

There are three different responses to this question, corresponding to three ways in which the differences in the degree to which various individuals benefit from a principle might be thought relevant. First, the idea might be that those who do not expect to benefit from a principle would have no reason to take account at all of the claims of those who need its protection. So the point of imposing a veil of ignorance would be to force the fortunate Joneses to take seriously the plight of those less fortunate. But this is not necessary on the account I am offering, since the requirement of justifiability (or of nonrejectability) already requires one to take these others into account.

The second idea concerns the way in which these others might be taken into account: should the Joneses, if they are moral as well as fortunate, try to compare the net cost of this principle to them with its net costs or net benefits to various others who are more likely to need the protection it offers? The answer is that at least in most cases they should not; to do so would generally be unnecessarily complicated. At least in most cases, all we need take into account in deciding whether a principle could reasonably be rejected are such things as the following: (a) the importance of being able to get aid *should one need it;* (b) the degree of inconvenience involved in giving it, should one be called upon *to do so;* (c) the generic costs of having a standing policy of giving aid in the way this principle requires; and (d) the generic benefits of having others have this policy.

Like the degree of need referred to in (a), the burdensomeness of (b) and (c) will be specified, at least loosely, in the principle itself. That is, just as a person who understands the principle will understand how urgent a need must be in order to trigger its requirement of aid, such a person will also understand the degree to which specific performance is required, and the kinds of excusing conditions recognized (including, perhaps, the fact that one has already helped other people). In assessing the rejectability of the principle, then, we can begin by taking these values at the level specified (for example, by taking the maximum level of burdensomeness and asking whether that would give a potential agent reason to reject the principle). If even someone who was burdened to this (maximum) degree could not reasonably reject the principle, then that settles the matter.

Most of us who believe that principles of mutual aid are valid believe that they pass this test of nonrejectability. But it is at least theoretically possible that there are other principles which involve a level of sacrifice that it is reasonable to demand from a person only if he or she will also benefit from the principle, thus offsetting its high cost to them. I am not certain that there are such cases. If there are, then in these cases a principle, in order not to be reasonably rejectable, would have to exempt the class of individuals who are very unlikely to benefit from it. What is at issue here is not the likelihood that any particular individual, given all that is known about him or her, will be burdened, or benefited, or both by the principle,

but rather the likelihood that anyone who is burdened by the principle will also benefit from it. As in the arguments for excuses and ceteris *paribus* conditions, what would be claimed in such a case is that any acceptable principle must be made fine-grained in ways that will make this very likely.

I maintained above that in considering whether a principle could reasonably be rejected we should consider the weightiness of the burdens it involves, for those on whom they fall, and the importance of the benefits it offers, for those who enjoy them, leaving aside the likelihood of one's actually falling in either of these two classes. It might seem that setting aside probabilities in this way presents a problem, and a dilemma, for contractualism as I am describing it. If, on the one hand, the grounds for rejecting a principle are based simply on the burdens it involves, for those who experience them, without discounting them by the probability that there will be anyone who actually does so, then it would seem that there is just as strong a reason for rejecting a principle permitting people to engage in behavior that involves a small risk of bodily harm to others as for rejecting a principle that permits behavior which is certain to cause harms of this same magnitude. If, on the other hand, we take into account the probability of bearing these burdens, there seem to be two ways of doing this. One would be to allow each person to take into account, in assessing his or her reasons for rejecting a principle, the likelihood that he or she would benefit from or be burdened by it.

The alternative would be to say that what is relevant is not any particular person's actual probability of benefiting from or being burdened by a principle, but, rather, the likelihood that *someone* will do so, as represented by the percentage of the population that falls into these groups. This alternative also leads to unacceptable results. Consider any principle licensing us to impose very severe hardships on a tiny minority of people, chosen at random (by making them involuntary subjects of painful and dangerous medical experiments, for example), in order to benefit a much larger majority. A contractualist would want to keep open the possibility that such a principle could reasonably be rejected because of the severe burdens it involves. But this would be effectively ruled out on the proposal under consideration, according to which the weight given to these burdens, as grounds for rejecting the principle, would be sharply discounted because only a very small fraction of the population would actually suffer them.

This difficulty appears to be serious because it is intuitively obvious that the likelihood that a form of behavior will lead to harm is an important factor in determining its permissibility and because it is assumed that the only way to take this probability into account is as a factor that, in one way or another, diminishes the complaint of a person who suffers this harm. But this assumption is mistaken. The probability that a form of conduct will cause harm can be relevant not as a factor diminishing the "complaint" of the affected parties (discounting the harm by the likelihood of their suffering it) but rather as an indicator of the care that the agent has to take to avoid causing harm. Our reactions to the medical experiment case mentioned above, for example, depend heavily on whether the harm in question is directly inflicted on particular people or whether it occurs "by accident," that is to say, occurs despite the fact that reasonable precautions have been taken. In the latter case, permitting the experimentation that leads to the harm may be no more objectionable than allowing air travel despite the fact that some people on the ground are likely to be killed by falling planes. The difference between these two versions of the medical experiment example does not have to do with the cost to the victims: the harm is just as bad when suffered "by accident" as when it is inflicted. The difference lies rather in the cost of avoiding these ways of bringing harm. I believe that our reactions

to these cases reflect the view that, except for a few very unusual kinds of cases, we can accept a prohibition against intentionally inflicting serious harm on others. But the cost of avoiding all behavior that involves risk of harm would be unacceptable. Our idea of "reasonable precautions" defines the level of care that we think can be demanded: a principle that demanded more than this would be too confining, and could reasonably be rejected on that ground.

I have been assuming so far that the candidate principles we are considering are all general in form, and the positions to which the generic reasons I have mentioned attach have all been described in purely general terms: "a person in need of help," "a person who is relying on an assurance that someone else has given," and so on. But many reasons that are important from each of our personal points of view depend on a distinction that is not describable in such terms—the distinction between ourselves and others. There are therefore cases in which each of us would most prefer principles which recognized this distinction, and singled us out for special benefits or exemption from burdens. Moreover, there would seem to be cases in which this might be done at no cost to others. Most cooperative schemes, for example, do not depend on literally *everyone's* doing her or his part, so no one would be disadvantaged if one person were exempted from the principle requiring people who voluntarily accept the benefits of such schemes to do their part in providing these benefits.

It is clear, intuitively, that this is morally ruled out, but different theories exclude it in different ways. Rawls observes that the principles of justice chosen in his Original Position will be "general" in form, by which he means that they may not include proper names or "rigged definite descriptions." His explanation is that when choosing behind a veil of ignorance, the parties have no incentive to agree to principles that violate this requirement: they would have no way of knowing whether they would be favoring themselves or others. He observes, however, that while it may be clear, intuitively, what is meant by a "rigged" definite description, there are philosophical difficulties involved in spelling this out.

According to Hare, on the other hand, it is part of the concept of morality that moral principles may contain no proper names. (He calls such principles "universal," but seems to mean the same thing that Rawls means by "general.") He says, however, that there is no way of saying, on logical grounds, which definite descriptions are "rigged" and which are not. The only way to tell which descriptions may figure in moral principles is to see which principles we have reason to accept as universal imperatives. Hare's discussion of "rigged definite descriptions" may sound like a criticism of Rawls, but in fact they are in agreement on the basic point that the aptness of a definite description for use in moral argument is a substantive question to be settled by asking whether principles incorporating that description would pass the relevant test of universal acceptability. (They of course have different ideas about what this test is.) Where they disagree is in the way they exclude proper names, which Hare rules out on formal grounds but Rawls treats in the same way as definite descriptions. On this point I follow Rawls. Whether or not proper names can be ruled out on formal grounds they are ruled out of moral argument on the same substantive grounds as certain definite descriptions. But I have, again, a somewhat different view of what these grounds are.

To begin with, . . . most "principles" cannot be identified with specific rules or verbal formulae which are the separable conclusions or "theorems" of moral argument. So what is presently at issue is not just a question about the logical form of such formulae (whether they can contain certain grammatical or logical elements) but rather a question about the kinds of reasons that can figure in moral argument more generally.

Proper names provide ways of picking out specific individuals. The reasons supporting principles that rely on these devices would thus be reasons for favoring (or disfavoring) particular people. Descriptions pick out specific individuals only contingently and inexactly, since it is possible that more than one individual may satisfy a given description. But descriptions strike us intuitively as "rigged" if the only reason for including them in moral argument is the belief that this provides a way of favoring (or disfavoring) certain people. In both cases, then, the question is whether the fact that a principle would help or hurt specific individuals can be a ground for preferring it, and for reasonably rejecting alternatives that would not have this effect. I believe that the answer to this question is no, and that, on the contrary, it is always reasonable to reject principles that are supported only by such "partial" reasons. The question is why this is so.

Each of us might prefer to be exempted from the requirements of any valid moral .principle requiring people to help, or to take care not to hurt, others in certain ways. In most cases it is clear why principles granting one person such an exemption are not valid. *Ex hypothesi,* the generic reasons arising from the burdens that these principles involve for agents in general are not sufficient ground for rejecting a general requirement to aid (or not injure), given the reasons that others have for wanting this protection, and there is nothing special about my case: those who suffer from this person's noncompliance have no less reason to complain than any other victims, and no reason has been given for others to see compliance as being more burdensome for him or her than for anyone else.

There are other cases, however, in which exempting one person, or even a few, would not impose burdens on others, and these cases raise the question of "partial" reasons in a sharper form. Consider, for example, the question of contribution to cooperative schemes. We derive important benefits from such arrangements, and they are almost always vulnerable to the strong temptation to free-ride. It would therefore not be reasonable to reject a principle (Rawls's principle of fairness is an example) that would help stabilize cooperative schemes at tolerable cost, in favor of a principle that would leave people free to contribute or not as they wished. But many of these arrangements do not require, in order to produce the desired consequences, that everyone who benefits should also contribute. As long as most people vote, or refrain from walking on the grass, or observe restrictions during a drought, it does not matter if a few others do not do so.

Each of us has reason to want to add, to a principle like Rawls's, which requires that everyone who accepts the benefits of others' participation in a fair scheme should also comply with its requirements, a rider specifying that if the participation of all in a given scheme is not needed then he or she will be exempt from its requirements. This could be done by singling out that person by name, with a pronoun, or by some description that was tailored to include that person but very few others (so that the exemption does not threaten the cooperative arrangements). For each individual, i, there will be many ways of specifying such an exemption, and we may call a principle that incorporates one of these an "i-favoring" variant of the impartial principle. Each i has reason to prefer i-favoring principles, but, envy aside, it would seem that each i should be indifferent between a purely neutral policy and policies with "j-favoring" exemptions (where j is some other person), since these all make the same demands on i and bring the same benefits. So it might seem that while each of us has reason to prefer exemptions favoring us, none of us has reason to reject principles just because they include exemptions favoring others, since they are no worse from our point of view than a purely neutral policy.

I believe, however, that we do have such a reason, namely that these policies arbitrarily favor one person over others and are in this respect unfair. As I have said, each person has reason to prefer partial principles that would favor him or her. If one of these principles is made binding, with no further reason to support it, then one person's reason for wanting to be favored is given precedence over others' similar reasons, without justification. This is what makes such a choice arbitrary, and makes the principle rejectable. This substantive objection applies to principles that make essential use of proper names as well as to those relying on "rigged" descriptions.

Principles can of course turn out to favor one person without being arbitrary. The aims of a cooperative scheme may, for example, require that greater benefits be given to those who satisfy a certain description. More to the point, a scheme might build in some fair mechanism for deciding who should be released from contributing when contributions from all are not required. If, for example, compliance by only 80 percent of the participants is enough to keep a scheme going, then the rule might be that each person should roll a die before deciding whether to contribute, and would be excused if the die came up "six." In these cases we would not say that the descriptions picking out those who are favored are "rigged," because they are included for good reason: as a way of sharing fairly the burden of the cooperative scheme. They are thus not merely a way of responding to the understandable wishes of some people to benefit in this way while neglecting the similar claims of others.

6. Reasonable Rejection

In order to decide whether a principle could reasonably be rejected, we need to consider it from a number of standpoints. From the point of view of those who will be its main beneficiaries, there may be strong generic reasons to insist on the principle and to reject anything that offers less. From the point of view of the agents who will be constrained by it, or of those who would be beneficiaries of an alternative principle, there may be reason to reject it in favor of something different or less demanding. In order to decide whether the principle could reasonably be rejected we need to decide whether it would be reasonable to take any of these generic reasons against it to prevail, given the reasons on the other side and given the aim of finding principles that others also could not reasonably reject. What can we say, in general, about the kinds of considerations that count as generic reasons and about how conflicting reasons are to be assessed? The present section and the next three are devoted to this question.

If we were to appeal to a prior notion of rightness to tell us which considerations are morally relevant and which are entitled to prevail in cases of conflict, then the contractualist framework would be unnecessary, since all the work would already have been done by this prior notion. It may seem, then, that when we apply the contractualist test we need to set aside any claims of rights or entitlement, or to focus on cases in which no such claims exist. This appears to mean that the relative strength of various generic reasons for and against a principle must be a function of the effects that that principle, or its absence, would have on the well-being of people in various positions. The crucial questions then would be how this notion of well-being is to be understood, and how the strength of a reason is related to well-being in this sense: Does the strongest objection belong to those whose level of well-being would be lowest if they lose out? or to those to whom the principle would make the greatest difference? Or does it depend on more complicated factors such as some combination of difference and level of well-being?

This is an appealing line of thought, but a mistaken one. While it would be objectionably circular to make "reasonable rejection" turn on presumed entitlements of the very sort that the principle in question is supposed to establish, it is misleading to suggest that when

we are assessing the "reasonable rejectability" of a principle we must, or even can, set aside assumptions about other rights and entitlements altogether. Even in those cases that come closest to being decided on the basis of a principle's implications for the welfare of individuals in various positions, many other moral claims must be presupposed in order to provide a context in which that principle can be understood.

Suppose, for example, that we are considering a principle defining our obligations to help those in need. This would seem to be a case in which considerations of welfare are most likely to be predominant. But in order to be in a position to aid someone, an agent must be entitled to dispose of the resources that are needed, and must be free from any obligation that would prevent him or her from acting in the way required to give aid. Similarly, being in need of aid is in part a matter of not being entitled simply to take what one needs, perhaps by force if necessary. So in order to understand the scope of the proposed principle (the range of actions it might require) we need to presuppose a framework of entitlements. What this illustrates is that a sensible contractualism, like most other plausible views, will involve a holism about moral justification: in assessing one principle we must hold many others fixed. This does not mean that these other principles are beyond question, but just that they are not being questioned at the moment.

Contractualism is not based on the idea that there is a "fundamental level" of justification at which only well-being (conceived in some particular way) matters and the comparison of magnitudes of well-being is the sole basis for assessing the reasonableness of rejecting principles of right and entitlement. Even though components of well-being figure prominently as grounds for reasonable rejection, the idea of such a fundamental level is misleading on two counts. First, the claim that the possibility of suffering a loss in well-being is something that has force in moral argument is a substantive moral claim. By concealing or minimizing this fact, the idea of a fundamental level has the effect of giving these claims a privileged status over other moral considerations. In many cases, gains and losses in well-being (relief from suffering, for example) are clearly the most relevant factors determining whether a principle could or could not be reasonably rejected. And in some cases of this kind questions of responsibility—such as whether the sufferer's claim to aid might be undermined by the fact that it was his or her own fault—do not arise, either because it so obviously was not the person's fault or because it would not matter if it were. But (and this is the second way in which the idea of a fundamental level can be misleading) to identify a case as of this kind is to place it within a specific moral framework, not to view it without any moral assumptions.

It may seem that contractualism becomes viciously circular if it does not take well-being as the basic coin in which reasonable rejection is measured (if, for example, it gives independent weight to considerations such as responsibility). But this is so only if the claims of well-being are unique among moral claims in needing no further justification, and well-being is therefore uniquely suited to serve as the basis in terms of which other moral notions are explained. I believe that something like this is frequently assumed, not only by utilitarians but also by others, like me, who look to views such as contractualism specifically as ways of avoiding utilitarianism. It is therefore worth considering why this assumption should seem so plausible, especially in the context of a contractualist theory of the kind I am trying to present.

There are two directions from which one might challenge the claim that a generic reason arising from a certain standpoint is a relevant, perhaps even decisive ground for rejecting a principle. First, one might question whether the consideration in question is a generic reason at all—whether it is something that people in that situation would have reason to care about.

Second, one might question whether this reason has weight in moral argument as contractualism describes it (whether it would have to be recognized as having weight by others who shared a concern with mutual justifiability).

These two challenges correspond to two possible charges of "circularity." If, for example, I were to claim that it would be reasonable to reject a certain principle because it was unfair, this might be challenged as "circular" in two different ways. One might claim that it is circular to assume that people in the situation in question would have reason to object to unfairness per se. Why should they care about it if it does not involve some loss in well-being? Alternatively, it might be held to be circular to assume that an objection on grounds of "unfairness" would have moral force—that if anyone were to have reason to raise it, then others would have reason to accept it insofar as they are concerned with mutual justifiability.

Why might it be thought that objections arising from concerns with well-being are particularly immune to charges of circularity of these two kinds? To begin with charges of the first kind, it is no doubt particularly clear that individuals typically have strong reason to want to have certain benefits, and to want to avoid pain and injury. Perhaps this claim can be generalized to cover anything that affects "how well one's life goes." But these are not the only things that people have reason to want and to object to being deprived of. I argued above, for example, that it is reasonable to object to principles that favor others arbitrarily. A principle that favors some in this way will often deprive others of benefits and opportunities they have reason to want. But why should these concrete disadvantages be the only grounds for objecting to such a principle? It would be circular for contractualism to cite, as the reason that people have for objecting to such principles, the fact that they are wrong according to some noncontractualist standard. But we need not choose between objections of this kind and objections based on loss of well-being. We have reason to object to principles simply because they arbitrarily favor the claims of some over the identical claims of others: that is to say, because they are unfair. In the process of moral reflection that contractualism describes, this provides a perfectly understandable reason for finding partial principles objectionable, a reason that does not depend on a prior idea that such principles, or the practices they would permit, are wrong.

It seems to me an important strength of contractualism that, in contrast to utilitarianism and other views which make well-being the only fundamental moral notion, it can account for the significance of different moral notions, within a unified moral framework, without reducing all of them to a single idea. What is necessary in order to do this is to show in each case why people would have reason to insist upon principles incorporating these notions (why principles that did not do this would be ones that could reasonably be rejected). I have just indicated how this can be done in the case of fairness. . . .

Let me turn now to charges of circularity of the second kind. These claim that if we count generic reasons not arising from effects on well-being as relevant objections to a principle, this can only reflect a substantive moral judgment and is therefore objectionably circular. This challenge might be based on the idea that (apart from an appeal to some substantive moral doctrine) there *are* no generic reasons for objecting to a principle other than those arising from its effects on how well people's lives go. So understood, it is just a restatement of a challenge of the first kind, to which I have already responded. So I will take the challenge to be not to the existence of certain generic reasons for objecting to a principle but rather to the legitimacy of counting these reasons as morally significant—as relevant grounds for rejecting that principle.

Here my response is that, as I have already mentioned, the judgment that *any* consider-

ation constitutes a relevant, possibly conclusive, reason for rejecting a principle in the context of contractualist moral thinking as I am describing it is a judgment with moral content. This may be easy to overlook when the reason in question is based on the impact that a principle would typically have on "how well life would go" for a person in a certain position, but it is no less true in that case than in any other. This is made even clearer once it is realized that well-being is not a well-defined notion that moral thinking can simply take over from the outlook of a single rational individual. On the contrary, . . . from an individual's own point of view the boundaries of his or her own well-being are inevitably vague. So substantive moral choices are involved not only in giving the notion moral significance but also in defining its boundaries.

Even if it would not be uniquely immune to charges of circularity, however, a form of contractualism (what might be called "welfarist contractualism") that took a specified conception of well-being as the sole standard for assessing all putative reasons for rejecting proposed principles would represent a particularly strong claim about the nature of right and wrong. It might seem that any interesting form of contractualism would have to be similarly structured: that is, it would have to begin with a clear specification of the possible grounds for reasonably rejecting a principle (whether this is given in terms of a conception of well-being or in some other way) and with a specified method for determining the relative strength of these grounds that allow us to reach conclusions about reasonable rejectability without appeals to judgment.

The version of contractualism that I am defending does not take this form. Its first aim is to provide a unified account of the subject matter of this part of morality and of its normative basis. This account also has some clear substantive implications: the rationale it offers for taking "justifiability to others on grounds they could not reasonably reject" as the central idea of the morality of obligation supports definite conclusions about the grounds of reasonable rejection: it rules out certain considerations and identifies others as definitely relevant. I will explore these implications in the following sections. But even if they are accepted, much more is left open than under a contractualism of the kind just mentioned. Of course, even welfarist contractualism would require us to rely on our judgment as to whether a given loss of well-being would, under certain circumstances, count as grounds for reasonable rejection of a principle. On the version I am defending, however, we must sometimes exercise judgment as to whether certain considerations are or are not relevant to the reasonable rejectability of a principle, since these grounds are not completely specified in advance. There is, of course, the possibility of tightening contractualism by specifying more explicitly the grounds of reasonable rejection and the method to be used in balancing these grounds against one another. I believe that although this is a feasible aim with respect to some specific areas of morality it is not likely to succeed at the level of generality of the theory I am currently offering here—that is to say, at the level of an account that is intended to cover, if not all of "morality," then that large part of it that has to do with what we owe to each other.

PART VII

Virtue Ethics

Introduction

Systems of virtue ethics are the oldest in the Western tradition, and for long they had almost everything their own way. They date back to Plato and, especially, Aristotle, receiving support in the Epicureans, the Stoics, and some sections of the Early Christian Church. Systems of virtue ethics are teleological but not consequentialist. They find the value of actions in how they relate to the achievement of goals; but those goals are not consequences. Instead, they are the realizations of certain good character traits, or virtues, in the actor. Actions are right because they exhibit those character traits, not because they cause those character traits.

Systems of virtue ethics are sometimes called *aretaic* (from the Greek word *arete,* 'excellence' or 'virtue'). Rather than seeing the heart of ethics in actions or duties, virtue ethics centers in the heart of the agent, in the character and dispositions of persons. Whereas action–ethics emphasize *doing,* virtue or agent ethics emphasize *being,* being a certain type of person who will no doubt manifest his or her being in actions or non-actions. For traditional duty-based ethics the question is: What should I do? For virtue ethics the question is: What sort of person should I become? Virtue ethics seeks to produce excellent persons who both act well out of spontaneous goodness and serve as examples who inspire others. It seeks to create people like Socrates, Jesus, St. Francis, Gandhi, and Mother Teresa, who stand out as "jewels who shine in their own light" (to paraphrase Kant's characterization of the morally good). There is a teleological aspect in virtue ethics, but it is not the kind that is usually found in utilitarianism, which asks what sort of action will maximize happiness or utility. The virtue concept of teleology focuses, rather, on the *goals* of life, living well and achieving excellence.

Our first reading is from the first two books of Aristotle's *Nicomachean Ethics,* the classic work on the virtues, written four centuries before Christ. Virtues are simply those characteristics which enable individuals to live well in communities. In order for one to achieve a state of well-being (*eudaimonia,* often translated as 'happiness'), proper social institutions are necessary. Thus the moral person cannot really exist apart from a flourishing political setting which enables the individual to develop the requisite virtues for the good life. For this reason Aristotle considers ethics to be a branch of politics.

After locating ethics as a part of politics, Aristotle explains that the moral virtues are different from the intellectual ones. While the intellectual virtues may be taught directly, the moral ones, being nonrational, cannot be taught directly but are acquired by training and practice. They must be lived in order to be learned. By living well we acquire the right habits. These habits are in fact the virtues. The virtues are to be sought as the best guarantee of the happy life. But, again, happiness requires that one be lucky enough to live in a flourishing state. The morally virtuous life consists in living according to right reason between excessive extremes. J. O. Urmson correctly notes that for Aristotle "excellence of character is explicitly said to be an intermediate disposition toward action and not a disposition to intermediate action. Extreme action will on some occasions be appropriate and carried out by the man of excellent character."[1]

Bernard Mayo, in our second reading, "Virtue and the Moral Life," provides a contemporary expression of the Aristotelian perspective. Contrasting the ethics of "doing" of the deontologists and teleologists with the ethics of "being" or character, the morality of the saints and heroes, Mayo contends that the saints and heroes show us that it is a living example that is important in ethics, not rigid rules. We learn more about ethics by looking at the lives of such people than by learning a set of principles.

Virtue ethicists are more likely to bring ethics closer to political theory, as Aristotle himself did, and to ask what kinds of upbringing and social institutions are most likely to give rise to the good life and produce good persons. They tend to despair of arguing about objective moral principles or right and wrong action, which is the putting of the cart before the horse. Many modern virtue ethicists (e.g., Alasdair MacIntyre) urge us to go back to the Greeks and center our ethics on the quest for virtue, which is connected with happiness, rather than on questions of right and wrong, which really have their place in custom and law, not humanistic ethics. They believe that duty-based ethics have their origin and justification in religious authority, as divinely given laws which are enforced by the gods or God. Take away that authority and you have only a relativistic morass. The only way to escape chaotic relativism, where everyone does what is right in his or her own eyes, is to return to a virtue-based ethics.

Action or duty-based ethical theorists do not deny the importance of character. But they claim that the nature of the virtues can only be derived from right actions or good consequences. As William Frankena puts it in our third reading, "Traits without principles are blind." Where there is a virtue, there must be some possible action to which the virtue corresponds and from which it derives its virtuosity. For example, the character trait of truthfulness is a virtue because telling the truth, in general, is a moral duty. Likewise, conscientiousness is a virtue because we have a general duty to be morally sensitive. There

is a relation of correspondence between principles and virtues, the latter being derived from the former, as the following diagram suggests: the correspondence theory of virtues:

The Virtue		*The Principle*
Truthfulness	which	telling the truth
Conscientiousness	derives from	being sensitive to one's duty
Benevolence		being beneficent
Faithfulness		being loyal or faithful

Although derived from the right kind of actions, the virtues are, nonetheless, very important for the moral life. They provide the dispositions which generate right action. In a sense, they are motivationally indispensable. To complete the passage quoted above, "Traits without principles are blind, but principles without traits are impotent." Frankena modifies the above position, distinguishing two types of virtues: (1) the standard moral virtues which correspond to specific kinds of moral principles, and (2) nonmoral virtues, such as natural kindliness or gratefulness (I would suggest that courage fits in here), which are "morality-supporting."

For example, take a situation where you have an obligation to save a drowning child in spite of some risk to your life. The specific rule of 'Always come to the aid of drowning people' is grounded in a foundational principle of general beneficence which in turn generates the foundation virtue of benevolence. In this case, it gives rise to a tendency to try to save the drowning child, but whether or not you actually dive into the lake may depend on the enabling (nonmoral) virtue of courage. Courage itself is not a moral virtue like benevolence or justice, for it is the kind of virtue which enhances and augments both virtues and vices (e.g., the courageous murderer).

In our fourth reading, Alasdair MacIntyre carries on the Aristotelian project of grounding morality in the virtues. He asks whether there is some core conception of the virtues, some vital components that are necessary to any social endeavor or practice. He compares five different conceptions of the virtues as they appear in the works of Homer, Aristotle, Jane Austen, and Benjamin Franklin. Five different theories seem to emerge, although MacIntyre finds elements of commonality among them. Without this common core, we are in danger of relapsing into a Hobbesian state of nature. MacIntyre sees his project as carrying on the Aristotelian tradition of virtue ethics.

In our fifth reading, Jonathan Bennett's "The Conscience of Huckleberry Finn," is a radical challenge to traditional deontic ethics in that Bennett argues that sometimes the moral thing to do is to override one's obligation in favor of one's sympathies. In our final reading, Rosalind Hursthouse argues for a conception of the relationship between virtue and emotion that incorporates some Kantian insights. It is worth asking how well her conception addresses the issues raised by Bennett in our fifth reading.

Note

1. J. O. Urmson, *Aristotle's Ethics* (Oxford: Oxford University Press, 1988).

29

Virtue Ethics

ARISTOTLE

Aristotle (384–322 B.C.), Greek physician, tutor to Alexander the Great, and one of the most important philosophers who ever lived, contributed importantly to virtually every major area of philosophy. This selection is from the first two books of the Nicomachean Ethics. *After a general discussion of the nature of ethics and the nature of the end of human being, Aristotle turns to the nature of virtue. Virtues are simply those characteristics that enable individuals to live well in communities. To achieve a state of well-being (eudaimonia, happiness), both proper social institutions and good character are required. Thus, Aristotle considers ethics to be a branch of politics.*

Aristotle holds that the moral virtues are different from the intellectual ones. Whereas the intellectual virtues may be taught directly, the moral ones must be lived in order to be learned. By living well we acquire the right habits. These habits are in fact the virtues. The virtues are to be sought as the best guarantee to the happy life. But, again, happiness

Reprinted from Aristotle's *Nicomachean Ethics*, trans. Terence Irwin (Indianapolis: Hackett Publishing Company, 1985) by permission of the publisher.

requires that we be lucky enough to live in a flourishing state. The morally virtuous life is a state intermediated between two extremes in which we make wise decisions.

I. The Highest Good: Happiness

Goods Correspond to Ends

Every craft and every investigation, and likewise every action and decision, seems to aim at some good; hence the good has been well described as that at which everything aims.

However, there is an apparent difference among the ends aimed at. For the end is sometimes an activity, sometimes a product beyond the activity; and when there is an end beyond the action, the product is by nature better than the activity.

The Hierarchy of Goods Corresponds to the Hierarchy of Ends

Since there are many actions, crafts, and sciences, the ends turn out to be many as well; for health is the end of medicine, a boat of boatbuilding, victory of generalship, and wealth of household management.

But whenever any of these sciences are subordinate to some one capacity—as e.g., bridle-making and every other science producing equipment for horses are subordinate to horsemanship, while this and every action in warfare are in turn subordinate to generalship, and in the same way other sciences are subordinate to further ones—in each of these the end of the ruling science is more choiceworthy than all the ends subordinate to it, since it is the end for which those ends are also pursued. And here it does not matter whether the ends of the actions are the activities themselves, or some product beyond them, as in the sciences we have mentioned.

The Highest Good

Suppose, then, that (a) there is some end of the things we pursue in our actions which we wish for because of itself, and because of which we wish for the other things; and (b) we do not choose everything because of something else, since (c) if we do, it will go on without limit, making desire empty and futile; then clearly (d) this end will be the good, i.e., the best good.

The Importance of Finding the Science of the Highest Good

Then surely knowledge of this good is also of great importance for the conduct of our lives, and if, like archers, we have a target to aim at, we are more likely to hit the right mark. If so, we should try to grasp, in outline at any rate, what the good is, and which science or capacity is concerned with it. . . .

II. Characteristics of the Good

(1) The Good Is the End of Action

But let us return once again to the good we are looking for, and consider just what it could be, since it is apparently one thing in one action or craft, and another thing in another; for it is one thing in medicine, another in generalship, and so on for the rest.

What, then, is the good in each of these cases? Surely it is that for the sake of which the other things are done; and in medicine this is health, in generalship victory, in housebuilding a house, in another case something else, but in every action and decision it is the end, since it is for the sake of the end that everyone does the other things.

And so, if there is some end of everything that is pursued in action, this will be the good pursued in action; and if there are more ends than one, these will be the goods pursued in action.

Our argument has progressed, then, to the same conclusion [as before, that the highest end is the good]; but we must try to clarify this still more.

(2) The Good Is Complete

Though apparently there are many ends, we choose some of them, e.g., wealth, flutes, and, in general, instruments, because of something else; hence it is clear that not all ends are complete. But the best good is apparently something complete. Hence, if only one end is complete, this will be what we are looking for; and if more than one are complete, the most complete of these will be what we are looking for.

An end pursued in itself, we say, is more complete than an end pursued because of something else; and an end that is never choiceworthy because of something else is more complete than ends that are choiceworthy both in themselves and because of this end; and hence an end that is always [choiceworthy, and also] choiceworthy in itself, never because of something else, is unconditionally complete.

(3) Happiness Meets the Criteria for Completeness, but Other Goods Do Not

Now happiness more than anything else seems unconditionally complete, since we always [choose it, and also] choose it because of itself, never because of something else.

Honor, pleasure, understanding, and every virtue we certainly choose because of themselves, since we would choose each of them even if it had no further result, but we also choose them for the sake of happiness, supposing that through them we shall be happy. Happiness, by contrast, no one ever chooses for their sake, or for the sake of anything else at all.

(4) The Good Is Self-sufficient; So Is Happiness

The same conclusion [that happiness is complete] also appears to follow from self-sufficiency, since the complete good seems to be self-sufficient.

Now what we count as self-sufficient is not what suffices for a solitary person by himself, living an isolated life, but what suffices also for parents, children, wife, and in general for friends and fellow-citizens, since a human being is a naturally political [animal]. Here, however, we must impose some limit; for if we extend the good to parents' parents and children's children and to friends of friends, we shall go on without limit; but we must examine this another time.

Anyhow, we regard something as self-sufficient when all by itself it makes a life choiceworthy and lacking nothing; and that is what we think happiness does.

(5) What Is Self-sufficient Is Most Choiceworthy; So Is Happiness

Moreover, we think happiness is most choiceworthy of all goods, since it is not counted as one good among many. If it were counted as one among many, then, clearly, we think that the addition of the smallest of goods would make it more choiceworthy; for [the smallest good] that is added becomes an extra quantity of goods [so creating a good larger than the original good], and the larger of two goods is always more choiceworthy. [But we do not think any addition can make happiness more choiceworthy; hence it is most choiceworthy.]

Happiness, then, is apparently something complete and self-sufficient, since it is the end of the things pursued in action.

III. A Clearer Account of the Good: The Human Soul's Activity Expressing Virtue

But presumably the remark that the best good is happiness is apparently something [generally] agreed, and what we miss is a clearer statement of what the best good is.

(1) If Something Has a Function, Its Good Depends on Its Function

Well, perhaps we shall find the best good if we first find the function of a human being. For just as the good, i.e., [doing] well, for a flautist, a sculptor, and every craftsman, and, in general, for whatever has a function and [characteristic] action, seems to depend on its function, the same seems to be true for a human being, if a human being has some function.

(2) What Sorts of Things Have Functions?

Then do the carpenter and the leatherworker have their functions and actions, while a human being has none, and is by nature idle, without any function? Or, just as eye, hand, foot and, in general, every [bodily] part apparently has its functions, may we likewise ascribe to a human being some function besides all of theirs?

(3) The Human Function

What, then, could this be? For living is apparently shared with plants, but what we are looking for is the special function of a human being; hence we should set aside the life of nutrition and growth. The life next in order is some sort of life of sense-perception; but this too is apparently shared, with horse, ox, and every animal. The remaining possibility, then, is some sort of life of action of the [part of the soul] that has reason.

Now this [part has two parts, which have reason in different ways], one as obeying the reason [in the other part], the other as itself having reason and thinking. [We intend both.] Moreover, life is also spoken of in two ways [as capacity and as activity], and we must take [a human being's special function to be] life as activity, since this seems to be called life to a fuller extent.

(4) The Human Good Is Activity Expressing Virtue

(a) We have found, then, that the human function is the soul's activity that expresses reason [as itself having reason] or requires reason [as obeying reason]. (b) Now the function of F, e.g., of a harpist, is the same kind, so we say, as the function of an excellent F, e.g., an excellent harpist. (c) The same is true unconditionally in every case, when we add to the function the superior achievement that expresses the virtue; for a harpist's function, e.g., is to play the harp, and a good harpist's is to do it well. (d) Now we take the human function to be a certain kind of life, and take this life to be the soul's activity and actions that express reason. (e) [Hence by (c) and (d)] the excellent man's function is to do this finely and well. (f) Each function is completed well when its completion expresses the proper virtue. (g) Therefore [by (d), (e), and (f)] the human good turns out to be the soul's activity that expresses virtue.

(5) The Good Must Also Be Complete

And if there are more virtues than one, the good will express the best and most complete virtue. Moreover, it will be in a complete life. For one swallow does not make a spring, nor does one day; nor, similarly, does one day or a short time make us blessed and happy. . . .

IV. Virtues of Character in General

Virtue, then, is of two sorts, virtue of thought and virtue of character. Virtue of thought arises and grows mostly from teaching, and hence needs experience and time. Virtue of character [i.e., of *ēthos*] results from habit [*ethos*]; hence its name 'ethical', slightly varied from '*ethos*.'

Virtue Comes About, Not by a Process of Nature, but by Habituation

Hence it is also clear that none of the virtues of character arises in us naturally.

(1) What Is Natural Cannot Be Changed by Habituation

For if something is by nature [in one condition], habituation cannot bring it into another condition. A stone, e.g., by nature moves downwards, and habituation could not make it move upwards, not even if you threw it up ten thousand times to habituate it; nor could habituation make fire move downwards, or bring anything that is by nature in one condition into another condition.

Thus the virtues arise in us neither by nature nor against nature. Rather, we are by nature able to acquire them, and reach our complete perfection through habit.

(2) Natural Capacities Are Not Acquired by Habituation

Further, if something arises in us by nature, we first have the capacity for it, and later display the activity. This is clear in the case of the senses; for we did not acquire them by frequent seeing or hearing, but already had them when we exercised them, and did not get them by exercising them.

Virtues, by contrast, we acquire, just as we acquire crafts, by having previously activated them. For we learn a craft by producing the same product that we must produce when we have learned it, becoming builders, e.g., by building and harpists by playing the harp; so also, then, we become just by doing just actions, temperate by doing temperate actions, brave by doing brave actions.

(3) Legislators Concentrate on Habituation

What goes on in cities is evidence for this also. For the legislator makes the citizens good by habituating them, and this is the wish of every legislator; if he fails to do it well he misses his goal. [The right] habituation is what makes the difference between a good political system and a bad one.

(4) Virtue and Vice Are Formed by Good and Bad Actions

Further, just as in the case of a craft, the sources and means that develop each virtue also ruin it. For playing the harp makes both good and bad harpists, and it is analogous in the case of builders and all the rest; for building well makes good builders, building badly, bad ones. If it were not so, no teacher would be needed, but everyone would be born a good or a bad craftsman.

It is the same, then, with the virtues. For actions in dealings with [other] human beings make some people just, some unjust; actions in terrifying situations and the acquired habit of fear or confidence make some brave and others cowardly. The same is true of situations involving appetites and anger; for one or another sort of conduct in these situations makes some people temperate and gentle, others intemperate and irascible.

To sum up, then, in a single account: A state [of character] arises from [the repetition of] similar activities. Hence we must display the right activities, since differences in these imply corresponding differences in the states. It is not unimportant, then, to acquire one sort of habit or another, right from our youth; rather, it is very important, indeed all-important. . . .

V. But Our Claims about Habituation Raise a Puzzle: How Can We Become Good without Being Good Already?

However, someone might raise this puzzle: 'What do you mean by saying that to become just we must first do just actions and to become temperate we must first do temperate actions? For if we do what is grammatical or musical, we must already be grammarians or musicians. In the same way, then, if we do what is just or temperate, we must already be just or temperate.'

First Reply: Conformity versus Understanding

But surely this is not so even with the crafts, for it is possible to produce something grammatical by chance or by following someone else's instructions. To be a grammarian, then, we must both produce something grammatical and produce it in the way in which the grammarian produces it, i.e., expressing grammatical knowledge that is in us.

Second Reply: Crafts versus Virtues

Moreover, in any case what is true of crafts is not true of virtues. For the products of a craft determine by their own character whether they have been produced well; and so it suffices that they are in the right state when they have been produced. But for actions expressing virtue to be done temperately or justly [and hence well] it does not suffice that they are themselves in the right state. Rather, the agent must also be in the right state when he does them. First, he must know [that he is doing virtuous actions]; second, he must decide on them, and decide on them for themselves; and, third, he must also do them from a firm and unchanging state.

As conditions for having a craft these three do not count, except for the knowing itself. As a condition for having a virtue, however, the knowing counts for nothing, or [rather] for only a little, whereas the other two conditions are very important, indeed all-important. And these other two conditions are achieved by the frequent doing of just and temperate actions.

Hence actions are called just or temperate when they are the sort that a just or temperate person would do. But the just and temperate person is not the one who [merely] does these actions, but the one who also does them in the way in which just or temperate people do them.

It is right, then, to say that a person comes to

be just from doing just actions and temperate from doing temperate actions; for no one has even a prospect of becoming good from failing to do them.

Virtue Requires Habituation, and Therefore Requires Practice, Not Just Theory

The many, however, do not do these actions but take refuge in arguments, thinking that they are doing philosophy, and that this is the way to become excellent people. In this they are like a sick person who listens attentively to the doctor, but acts on none of his instructions. Such a course of treatment will not improve the state of his body; any more than will the many's way of doing philosophy improve the state of their souls.

VI. A Virtue of Character Is a State Intermediate between Two Extremes, and Involving Decision

The Genus: Feelings, Capacities, States

Next we must examine what virtue is. Since there are three conditions arising in the soul—feelings, capacities and states—virtue must be one of these.

By feelings I mean appetite, anger, fear, confidence, envy, joy, love, hate, longing, jealousy, pity, in general whatever implies pleasure or pain.

By capacities I mean what we have when we are said to be capable of these feelings—capable of, e.g., being angry or afraid or feeling pity.

By states I mean what we have when we are well or badly off in relation to feelings. If, e.g., our feeling is too intense or slack, we are badly off in relation to anger, but if it is intermediate, we are well off; and the same is true in the other cases.

Virtue Is Not a Feeling . . .

First, then, neither virtues nor vices are feelings. (a) For we are called excellent or base insofar as

we have virtues or vices, not insofar as we have feelings. (b) We are neither praised nor blamed insofar as we have feelings; for we do not praise the angry or the frightened person, and do not blame the person who is simply angry, but only the person who is angry in a particular way. But we are praised or blamed insofar as we have virtues or vices. (c) We are angry and afraid without decision; but the virtues are decisions of some kind, or [rather] require decision. (d) Besides, insofar as we have feelings, we are said to be moved; but insofar as we have virtues or vices, we are said to be in some condition rather than moved.

Or a Capacity . . .

For these reasons the virtues are not capacities either; for we are neither called good nor called bad insofar as we are simply capable of feelings. Further, while we have capacities by nature, we do not become good or bad by nature; we have discussed this before.

But a State

If, then, the virtues are neither feelings nor capacities, the remaining possibility is that they are states. And so we have said what the genus of virtue is.

The Differentia

But we must say not only, as we already have, that it is a state, but also what sort of state it is.

Virtue and the Human Function

It should be said, then, that every virtue causes its possessors to be in a good state and to perform their functions well; the virtue of eyes, e.g., makes the eyes and their functioning excellent, because it makes us see well; and similarly, the virtue of a horse makes the horse excellent, and thereby good at galloping, at carrying its rider and at standing steady in the face of the enemy. If this is true in every case, then the virtue of a human being will likewise be the state that makes a human being good and makes him perform his function well.

We have already said how this will be true, and it will also be evident from our next remarks, if we consider the sort of nature that virtue has.

The Numerical Mean and the Mean Relative to Us

In everything continuous and divisible we can take more, less, and equal, and each of them either in the object itself or relative to us; and the equal is some intermediate between excess and deficiency.

By the intermediate in the object I mean what is equidistant from each extremity; this is one and the same for everyone. But relative to us the intermediate is what is neither superfluous nor deficient; this is not one, and is not the same for everyone.

If, e.g., ten are many and two are few, we take six as intermediate in the object, since it exceeds [two] and is exceeded [by ten] by an equal amount, [four]; this is what is intermediate by numerical proportion. But that is not how we must take the intermediate that is relative to us. For if, e.g., ten pounds [of food] are a lot for someone to eat, and two pounds a little, it does not follow that the trainer will prescribe six, since this might also be either a little or a lot for the person who is to take it—for Milo [the athlete] a little, but for the beginner in gymnastics a lot; and the same is true for running and wrestling. In this way every scientific expert avoids excess and deficiency and seeks and chooses what is intermediate—but intermediate relevant to us, not in the object.

Virtue Seeks the Mean Relative to Us: Argument from Craft to Virtue

This, then, is how each science produces its product well, by focusing on what is intermediate and making the product conform to that. This, indeed, is why people regularly comment on well-made products that nothing could be added or subtracted, since they assume that excess or deficiency ruins a good [result] while the mean preserves it. Good craftsmen also, we say, focus on what is intermediate when they produce their product. And since virtue, like nature, is better and more exact than any craft, it will also aim at what is intermediate.

Arguments from the Nature of Virtue of Character

By virtue I mean virtue of character; for this [pursues the mean because] it is concerned with feelings and actions, and these admit of excess, deficiency and an intermediate condition. We can be afraid, e.g., or be confident, or have appetites, or get angry, or feel pity, in general have pleasure or pain, both too much and too little, and in both ways not well; but [having these feelings] at the right times, about the right things, towards the right people, for the right end, and in the right way, is the intermediate and best condition, and this is proper to virtue. Similarly, actions also admit of excess, deficiency, and the intermediate condition.

Now virtue is concerned with feelings and actions, in which excess and deficiency are in error and incur blame, while the intermediate condition is correct and wins praise, which are both proper features of virtue. Virtue, then, is a mean, insofar as it aims at what is intermediate.

Moreover, there are many ways to be in error, since badness is proper to what is unlimited, as the Pythagoreans pictured it, and good to what is limited; but there is only one way to be correct. That is why error is easy and correctness hard; since it is easy to miss the target and hard to hit it. And so for this reason also excess and deficiency are proper to vice, the mean to virtue; 'for we are noble in only one way, but bad in all sorts of ways.'

Definition of Virtue

Virtue, then, is (a) a state that decides, (b) [consisting] in a mean, (c) the mean relative to us, (d) which is defined by reference to reason, (e) i.e., to the reason by reference to which the intelligent person would define it. It is a mean between two vices, one of excess and one of deficiency.

It is a mean for this reason also: Some vices miss what is right because they are deficient, others because they are excessive, in feelings or in actions, while virtue finds and chooses what is intermediate.

Hence, as far as its substance and the account stating its essence are concerned, virtue is a mean; but as far as the best [condition] and the good [result] are concerned, it is an extremity.

The Definition Must Not Be Misapplied to Cases in Which There Is No Mean

But not every action or feeling admits of the mean. For the names of some automatically include baseness, e.g., spite, shamelessness, envy [among feelings], and adultery, theft, murder, among actions. All of these and similar things are called by these names because they themselves, not their excesses or deficiencies, are base.

Hence in doing these things we can never be correct, but must invariably be in error. We cannot do them well or not well—e.g., by committing adultery with the right woman at the right time in the right way; on the contrary, it is true unconditionally that to do any of them is to be in error.

[To think these admit of a mean], therefore, is like thinking that unjust or cowardly or intemperate action also admits of a mean, an excess and a deficiency. For then there would be a mean of excess, a mean of deficiency, an excess of excess and a deficiency of deficiency.

Rather, just as there is no excess or deficiency of temperance or of bravery, since the intermediate is a sort of extreme [in achieving the good], so also there is no mean of these [vicious actions] either, but whatever way anyone does them, he is in error. For in general there is no mean of excess or of deficiency, and no excess or deficiency of a mean.

VII. The Definition of Virtue as a Mean Applies to the Individual Virtues

However, we must not only state this general account but also apply it to the particular cases. For among accounts concerning actions, though the general ones are common to more cases, the specific ones are truer, since actions are about particular cases, and our account must accord with these. Let us, then, find these from the chart.

Classification of Virtues of Character: Virtues Concerned with Feelings

(1) First, in feelings of fear and confidence the mean is bravery. The excessively fearless person is nameless (and in fact many cases are nameless), while the one who is excessively confident is rash; the one who is excessively afraid and deficient in confidence is cowardly.

(2) In pleasures and pains, though not in all types, and in pains less than in pleasures, the mean is temperance and the excess intemperance. People deficient in pleasure are not often found, which is why they also lack even a name; let us call them insensible.

Virtues Concerned with External Goods

(3) In giving and taking money the mean is generosity, the excess wastefulness and the deficiency ungenerosity. Here the vicious people have contrary excesses and defects; for the wasteful person spends to excess and is deficient in taking, whereas the ungenerous person takes to excess and is deficient in spending. At the moment we are speaking in outline and summary, and that suffices; later we shall define these things more exactly.

(4) In questions of money there are also other conditions. Another mean is magnificence; for the magnificent person differs from the generous by being concerned with large matters, while the generous person is concerned with small. The

excess is ostentation and vulgarity, and the deficiency niggardliness, and these differ from the vices related to generosity in ways we shall describe later.

(5) In honor and dishonor the mean is magnanimity, the excess something called a sort of vanity, and the deficiency pusillanimity.

(6) And just as we said that generosity differs from magnificence in its concern with small matters, similarly there is a virtue concerned with small honors, differing in the same way from magnanimity, which is concerned with great honors. For honor can be desired either in the right way or more or less than is right. If someone desires it to excess, he is called an honor-lover, and if his desire is deficient he is called indifferent to honor, but if he is intermediate he has no name. The corresponding conditions have no name either, except the condition of the honor-lover, which is called honor-loving.

This is why people at the extremes claim that intermediate area. Indeed, we also sometimes call the intermediate person an honor-lover, and sometimes call him indifferent to honor; and sometimes we praise the honor-lover, sometimes the person indifferent to honor. We will mention later the reason we do this; for the moment, let us speak of the other cases in the way we have laid down.

Virtues Concerned with Social Life

(7) Anger also admits of an excess, deficiency, and mean. These are all practically nameless; but since we call the intermediate person mild, let us call the mean mildness. Among the extreme people let the excessive person be irascible, and the vice be irascibility, and let the deficient person be a sort of inirascible person, and the deficiency be inirascibility.

There are three other means, somewhat similar to one another, but different. For they are all concerned with association in conversations and actions, but differ insofar as one is concerned with truth-telling in these areas, the other two with sources of pleasure, some of which are found in amusement, and the others in daily life in general. Hence we should also discuss these states, so that we can better observe that in every case the man is praiseworthy, while the extremes are neither praiseworthy nor correct, but blameworthy. Most of these cases are also nameless, and we must try, as in the other cases also, to make names ourselves, to make things clear and easy to follow.

(8) In truth-telling, then, let us call the intermediate person truthful, and the mean truthfulness; pretense that overstates will be boastfulness, and the person who has it boastful, pretense that understates will be self-deprecation, and the person who has it self-deprecating.

(9) In sources of pleasure in amusements let us call the intermediate person witty, and the condition wit; the excess buffoonery and the person who has it a buffoon; and the deficient person a sort of boor and the state boorishness.

(10) In the other sources of pleasure, those in daily life, let us call the person who is pleasant in the right way friendly, and the mean state friendliness. If someone goes to excess with no [further] aim he will be ingratiating; if he does it for his own advantage, a flatterer. The deficient person, unpleasant in everything, will be a sort of quarrelsome and ill-tempered person.

Mean States That Are Not Virtues

(11) There are also means in feelings and concerned with feelings: shame, e.g., is not a virtue, but the person prone to shame as well as the virtuous person we have described receives praise. For here also one person is called intermediate, and another—the person excessively prone to shame, who is ashamed about everything—is called excessive; the person who is deficient in shame or never feels shame at all is said to have no sense of disgrace; and the intermediate one is called prone to shame.

(12) Proper indignation is the mean between envy and spite: these conditions are concerned with pleasure and pain at what happens to our neighbors. For the properly indignant person feels pain when someone does well undeservedly; the envious person exceeds him by feeling pain when anyone does well, while the spiteful is so deficient in feeling pain that he actually enjoys [other people's misfortunes]. . . .

VIII. The Relations between Means and Extreme

The Mean Is Opposed to Each Extreme

Among these three conditions, then, two are vices—one of excess, one of deficiency—and one—the mean—is virtue. In a way each of them is opposed to each of the others, since each extreme is contrary both to the intermediate condition and to the other extreme, while the intermediate is contrary to the extremes. For as the equal is greater in comparison to the smaller, and smaller in comparison to the greater, so also the intermediate states are excessive in comparison to the deficiencies and deficient in comparison to the excesses—both in feelings and in actions.

For the brave person, e.g., appears rash in comparison to the coward, and cowardly in comparison to the rash person; similarly, the temperate person appears intemperate in comparison to the insensible person, and insensible in comparison with the intemperate person, and the generous person appears wasteful in comparison to the ungenerous, and ungenerous in comparison to the wasteful person. That is why each of the extreme people tries to push the intermediate person to the other extreme, so that the coward, e.g., calls the brave person rash, and the rash person calls him a coward, and similarly in the other cases.

Extremes Are More Opposed to Each Other Than to the Mean

Because these conditions of soul are opposed to each other in these ways, the extremes are more contrary to each other than to the intermediate. For they are further from each other than from the intermediate, just as the large is further from the small, and the small from the large, than either is from the equal.

Moreover, sometimes one extreme, e.g., rashness or wastefulness, appears somewhat like the intermediate state, e.g., bravery or generosity; but the extremes are most unlike one another; and the things that are furthest apart from each other are defined as contraries. Hence also the things that are further apart are more contrary.

Sometimes One Extreme Is More Opposed Than the Other to the Mean

In some cases the deficiency, in others the excess, is more opposed to the intermediate condition; e.g., it is cowardice, the deficiency, not rashness, the excess, that is more opposed to bravery; on the other hand, it is intemperance, the excess, not insensibility, the deficiency, that is more opposed to temperance. This happens for two reasons.

One reason is derived from the object itself. Since sometimes one extreme is closer and more similar to the intermediate condition, we oppose the contrary extreme, more than this closer one, to the intermediate condition. Since rashness, e.g., seems to be closer and more similar to bravery, and cowardice less similar, we oppose cowardice more than rashness to bravery; for what is further from the intermediate condition seems to be more contrary to it. This, then, is one reason, derived from the object itself.

The other reason is derived from ourselves. For when we ourselves have some natural tendency to one extreme more than the other, this extreme appears more opposed to the intermediate condition; since, e.g., we have more of a natural tendency to pleasure, we drift more easily towards intemperance than towards orderliness. Hence we say that an extreme is more contrary if we naturally develop more in that direction; and this is why intemperance is more contrary to temperance, since it is the excess.

Practical Advice on Ways to Achieve the Mean

We have said enough, then, to show that virtue of character is a mean and what sort of mean it is; that it is a mean between two vices, one of excess and one of deficiency; and that it is a mean because it aims at the intermediate condition in feelings and actions.

Hence it is hard work to be excellent, since in each case it is hard work to find what is intermediate; e.g., not everyone, but only one who knows, finds the midpoint in a circle. So also getting angry, or giving and spending money, is easy and anyone can do it; but doing it to the right person, in the right amount, at the right time, for the right end, and in the right way is no longer easy, nor can everyone do it. Hence [doing these things] well is rare, praiseworthy, and fine.

Avoid the More Opposed Extreme

Hence if we aim at the intermediate condition we must first of all steer clear of the more contrary extreme, following the advice that Calypso also gives—'Hold the ship outside the spray and surge.' For since one extreme is more in error, the other less, and since it is hard to hit the intermediate extremely accurately, the second-best tack, as they say, is to take the lesser of the evils. We shall succeed best in this by the method we describe.

Avoid the Easier Extreme

We must also examine what we ourselves drift into easily. For different people have different natural tendencies towards different goals, and we shall come to know our own tendencies from the pleasure or pain that arises in us. We must drag ourselves off in the contrary direction; for if we pull far away from error, as they do in straightening bent wood, we shall reach the intermediate condition.

Be Careful with Pleasures

And in everything we must beware above all of pleasure and its sources; for we are already biased in its favor when we come to judge it. Hence we must react to it as the elders reacted to Helen, and on each occasion repeat what they said; for if we do this, and send it off, we shall be less in error.

These Rules Do Not Give Exact and Detailed Guidance

In summary, then, if we do these things we shall best be able to reach the intermediate condition. But no doubt this is hard, especially in particular cases, since it is not easy to define the way we should be angry, with whom, about what, for how long; for sometimes, indeed, we ourselves praise deficient people and call them mild, and sometimes praise quarrelsome people and call them manly. Still, we are not blamed if we deviate a little in excess or deficiency from doing well, but only if we deviate a long way, since then we are easily noticed.

But how far and how much we must deviate to be blamed is not easy to define in an account; for nothing perceptible is easily defined, and [since] these [circumstances of virtuous and vicious action] are particulars, the judgment about them depends on perception.

All this makes it clear, then, that in every case the intermediate state is praised, but we must sometimes incline towards the excess, sometimes towards the deficiency; for that is the easiest way to succeed in hitting the intermediate condition and [doing] well.

30

Virtue and the Moral Life

Bernard Mayo

Bernard Mayo (1921–2000) taught philosophy at the University of Birmingham in England until his retirement in 1968. He is the author of several works in philosophy, including Ethics and the Moral Life *(1958), from which this selection is taken. Contrasting the ethics of "doing" of the deontologists and teleologists with the ethics of "being" or character, the morality of the saints and heroes, Mayo contends that the saints and heroes show us that it is a living example that is important in ethics, not rigid rules. We learn more about ethics by looking at the lives of such people than by learning a set of principles.*

The philosophy of moral principles, which is characteristic of Kant and the post-Kantian era, is something of which hardly a trace exists in Plato. . . . Plato says nothing about rules or principles or laws, except when he is talking politics. Instead he talks about virtues and vices, and about certain types of human character. The key word in Platonic ethics is Virtue; the key word in Kantian ethics is Duty. And modern ethics is a set of footnotes, not to Plato, but to Kant. . . .

Attention to the novelists can be a welcome correction to a tendency of philosophical ethics of the last generation or two to lose contact with the ordinary life of man, which is just what the novelists, in their own way, are concerned with. Of course there are writers who can be called in to illustrate problems about Duty (Graham Greene is a good example). But there are more who perhaps never mention the words duty, obligation, or principle. Yet they are all concerned—Jane Austen, for instance, entirely and absolutely—with the moral qualities or defects of their heroes and

Reprinted from *Ethics and the Moral Life* (Macmillan & Co., 1958) by permission of the publisher.

heroines and other characters. This points to a radical one-sidedness in the philosophers' account of morality in terms of principles: it takes little or no account of qualities, of what people *are*. It is just here that the old-fashioned word Virtue used to have a place; and it is just here that the work of Plato and Aristotle can be instructive. Justice, for Plato, though it is closely connected with acting according to law, does not *mean* acting according to law: it is a quality of character, and a just action is one such as a just man would do. Telling the truth, for Aristotle, is not, as it was for Kant, fulfilling an obligation; again it is a quality of character, or, rather, a whole range of qualities of character, some of which may actually be defects, such as tactlessness, boastfulness, and so on—a point which can be brought out, in terms of principles, only with the greatest complexity and artificiality, but quite simply and naturally in terms of character.

If we wish to enquire about Aristotle's moral views, it is no use looking for a set of principles. Of course we can find *some* principles to which he must have subscribed—for instance, that one ought not to commit adultery. But what we find much more prominently is a set of character-traits, a list of certain types of person—the courageous man, the niggardly man, the boaster, the lavish spender and so on. The basic moral question, for Aristotle, is not, What shall I do? but, What shall I be?

These contrasts between doing and being, negative and positive, and modern as against Greek morality were noted by John Stuart Mill; I quote from the *Essay on Liberty:*

Christian morality (so-called) has all the characters of a reaction; it is, in great part, a protest against Paganism. Its ideal is negative rather than positive, passive rather than active; Innocence rather than Nobleness; Abstinence from Evil, rather than energetic Pursuit of the Good; in its precepts (as has been well said) "Thou shalt not" predominates unduly over "Thou shalt . . ." Whatever exists of magnanimity, highmindedness, personal dignity, even the sense of honor, is derived from the purely human, not the religious part of our education, and never could have grown out of a standard of ethics in which the only worth, professedly recognized, is that of obedience.

Of course, there are connections between being and doing. It is obvious that a man cannot just *be;* he can only be what he is by doing what he does; his moral qualities are ascribed to him because of his actions, which are said to manifest those qualities. But the point is that an ethics of Being must include this obvious fact, that Being involves Doing; whereas an ethics of Doing, such as I have been examining, may easily overlook it. As I have suggested, a morality of principles is concerned only with what people do or fail to do, since that is what rules are for. And as far as this sort of ethics goes, people might well have no moral qualities at all except the possession of principles and the will (and capacity) to act accordingly.

When we speak of a moral quality such as courage, and say that a certain action was courageous, we are not merely saying something about the action. We are referring, not so much to what is done, as to the kind of person by whom we take it to have been done. We connect, by means of imputed motives and intentions, with the character of the agent as courageous. This explains, incidentally, why both Kantians and Utilitarians encounter, in their different ways, such difficulties in dealing with motives, which their principles, on the face of it, have no room for. A Utilitarian, for example, can only praise a courageous action in some such way as this: the action is of a sort such as a person of courage is likely to perform, and courage is a quality of character the

cultivation of which is likely to increase rather than diminish the sum total of human happiness. But Aristotelians have no need of such circumlocution. For them a courageous action just is one which proceeds from and manifests a certain type of character, and is praised because such a character trait is good, or better than others, or is a virtue. An evaluative criterion is sufficient: there is no need to look for an imperative criterion as well, or rather instead, according to which it is not the character which is good, but the cultivation of the character which is right. . . .

No doubt the fundamental moral question is just "What ought I to do?" And according to the philosophy of moral principles, the answer (which must be an imperative "Do this") must be derived from a conjunction of premises consisting (in the simplest case) firstly of a rule, or universal imperative, enjoining (or forbidding) all actions of a certain type in situations of a certain type, and, secondly, a statement to the effect that this is a situation of that type, falling under that rule. In practice the emphasis may be on supplying only one of these premises, the other being assumed or taken for granted: one may answer the question "What ought I to do?" either by quoting a rule which I am to adopt, or by showing that my case is legislated for by a rule which I do adopt . . . [I]f I am in doubt whether to tell the truth about his condition to a dying man, my doubt may be resolved by showing that the case comes under a rule about the avoidance of unnecessary suffering, which I am assumed to accept. But if the case is without precedent in my moral career, my problem may be soluble only by adopting a new principle about what I am to do now and in the future about cases of this kind.

This second possibility offers a connection with moral ideas. Suppose my perplexity is not merely an unprecedented situation which I could cope with by adopting a new rule. Suppose the new rule is thoroughly inconsistent with my existing moral code. This may happen, for instance, if the moral code is one to which I only pay lipservice; if . . . its authority is not yet internalized, or if it has ceased to be so; it is ready for rejection, but its final rejection awaits a moral crisis such as we are assuming to occur. What I now need is not a rule for deciding how to act in this situation and others of its kind. I need a whole set of rules, a complete morality, new principles to live by.

Now, according to the philosophy of moral character, there is another way of answering the fundamental question "What ought I to do?" Instead of quoting a rule, we quote a quality of character, a virtue: we say "Be brave," or "Be patient" or "Be lenient." We may even say "Be a man": if I am in doubt, say, whether to take a risk, and someone says "Be a man," meaning a morally sound man, in this case a man of sufficient courage. (Compare the very different ideal invoked in "Be a gentleman." I shall not discuss whether this is a *moral* ideal.) Here, too, we have the extreme cases, where a man's moral perplexity extends not merely to a particular situation but to his whole way of living. And now the question "What ought I to do?" turns into the question "What ought I to be?"—as indeed, it was treated in the first place. ("Be brave.") It is answered, not by quoting a rule or a set of rules, but by describing a quality of character or a type of person. And here the ethics of character gains a practical simplicity which offsets the greater logical simplicity of the ethics of principles. We do not have to give a list of characteristics or virtues, as we might list a set of principles. We can give a unity to our answer.

Of course we can in theory give a unity to our principles: this is implied by speaking of a *set* of principles. But if such a set is to be a system and not merely aggregate, the unity we are looking for is a logical one, namely, the possibility that some principles are deductible from others, and ultimately from one. But the attempt to construct a deductive moral system is notoriously difficult, and in any case ill-founded. Why should we expect that all rules of conduct should be ultimately reducible to a few?

Saints and Heroes

But when we are asked "What shall I be?" we can readily give a unity to our answer, though not a logical unity. It is the unity of character. A person's character is not merely a list of dispositions; it has the organic unity of something that is more than the sum of its parts. And we can say, in answer to our morally perplexed questioner, not only "Be this" and "Be that," but also "Be like So-and-So"—where So-and-So is either an ideal type of character, or else an actual person taken as representative of the ideal, an exemplar. Examples of the first are Plato's "just man" in the *Republic;* Aristotle's man of practical wisdom, in the *Nicomachean Ethics;* Augustine's citizen of the City of God; the good Communist; the American way of life (which is a collective expression for a type of character). Examples of the second kind, the exemplar, are Socrates, Christ, Buddha, St. Francis, the heroes of epic writers and of novelists. Indeed the idea of the Hero, as well as the idea of the Saint, are very much the expression of this attitude to morality. Heroes and saints are not merely people who did things. They are people whom we are expected, and expect ourselves, to imitate. And imitating them means not merely doing what they did; it means being like them. Their status is not in the least like that of legislators whose laws we admire; for the character of a legislator is irrelevant to our judgment about his legislation. The heroes and saints did not merely give us principles to live by (though some of them did that as well): they gave us examples to follow.

Kant, as we should expect, emphatically rejects this attitude as "fatal to morality." According to him, examples serve only to render *visible* an instance of the moral principle, and thereby to demonstrate its practical feasibility. But every exemplar, such as Christ himself, must be judged by the independent criterion of the moral law, before we are entitled to recognize him as worthy of imitation. I am not suggesting that the subordination of exemplars to principles is incorrect, but that it is one-sided and fails to do justice to a large area of moral experience.

Imitation can be more or less successful. And this suggests another defect of the ethics of principles. It has no room for ideals, except the ideal of a perfect set of principles (which, as a matter of fact, is intelligible only in terms of an ideal character or way of life), and the ideal of perfect conscientiousness (which is itself a character-trait). This results, of course, from the "black-or-white" nature of moral verdicts based on rules. There are no degrees by which we approach or recede from the attainment of a certain quality or virtue; if there were not, the word "ideal" would have no meaning. Heroes and saints are not people whom we try to be *just* like, since we know that is impossible. It is precisely because it is impossible for ordinary human beings to achieve the same qualities as the saints, and in the same degree, that we do set them apart from the rest of humanity. It is enough if we try to be a little like them. . . .

A Critique of Virtue-Based Ethics

WILLIAM FRANKENA

A biographical sketch of William Frankena appears in the beginning of selection 27. Frankena, a duty-based ethical theorist, agrees with the virtue-ethicist on the importance of character. But he argues that the nature of the virtues can be derived only from right actions or good consequences. "Traites without principles are blind." For every virtue there must be some possible action to which the virtue corresponds and from which it derives its virtuosity. For example, the character trait of truthfulness is a virtue because telling the truth, in general, is a moral duty. Likewise, benevolence is a virtue because we have a general duty to be benefi-cent. There is a relation of correspondence between principles and virtues.

Morality and Cultivation of Traits

Our present interest, then, is not in moral princi-ples nor in nonmoral values, but in moral values, in what is morally good or bad. Throughout its history morality has been concerned about the cultivation of certain dispositions, or traits, among which are "character" and such "virtues" (an old-fashioned but still useful term) as honesty, kindness, and conscientiousness. Virtues are dis-positions or traits that are not wholly innate; they must all be acquired, at least in part, by teaching and practice, or, perhaps, by grace. They are also traits of "character," rather than traits of "per-sonality" like charm or shyness, and they all in-volve a tendency to do certain kinds of action in certain kinds of situations, not just to think or

From *Ethics*, Second Edition (Prentice-Hall, 1973), pp. 63-71, © 1973. Reprinted by permission of Prentice-Hall, Inc., Englewood Cliffs, New Jersey.

feel in certain ways. They are not just abilities or skills, like intelligence or carpentry, which one may have without using.

In fact, it has been suggested that morality is or should be conceived as primarily concerned, not with rules or principles as we have been suppos-ing so far, but with the cultivation of such dis-positions or traits of character. Plato and Aristo-tle seem to conceive of morality in this way, for they talk mainly in terms of virtues and the vir-tuous, rather than in terms of what is right or obligatory. Hume uses similar terms, although he mixes in some nonmoral traits like cheerfulness and wit along with moral ones like benevolence and justice. More recently, Leslie Stephen stated the view in these words:

> . . . morality is internal. The moral law . . . has to be expressed in the form, "be this," not in the form, "do this." . . . the true moral law says "hate not," instead of "kill not." . . . the only mode of stating the moral law must be as a rule of char-acter.[1]

Ethics of Virtue

Those who hold this view are advocating an *ethics of virtue* or being, in opposition to an ethics of duty, principle, or doing. . . . The notion of an ethics of virtue is worth looking at here, not only because it has a long history but also because some spokesmen of "the new morality" seem to espouse it. What would an ethics of virtue be like? It would, of course, not take deontic judg-ments or principles as basic in morality, as we have been doing; instead, it would take as basic aretaic judgments like "That was a courageous deed," "His action was virtuous," or "Courage is a virtue," and it would insist that deontic judgments are either derivative from such aretaic ones or can be dispensed with entirely. Moreover, it would regard aretaic judgments about actions as secondary and as based on aretaic judgments about agents and their motives or traits, as Hume does when he writes:

. . . when we praise any actions, we regard only the motives that produced them. . . . The external performance has no merit. . . . all virtuous actions derive their merit only from virtuous motives.[2]

For an ethics of virtue, then, what is basic in morality is judgments like "Benevolence is a good motive," "Courage is a virtue," "The morally good man is kind to everyone" or, more simply and less accurately, "Be loving!"—not judgments or principles about what our duty is or what we ought to do. But, of course, it thinks that its basic instructions will guide us, not only about what to be, but also about what to do.

It looks as if there would be three kinds of ethics of virtue, corresponding to the three kinds of ethics of duty covered earlier. The question to be answered is: What dispositions or traits are moral virtues? *Trait-egoism* replies that the virtues are the dispositions that are most conducive to one's own good or welfare, or, alternatively, that prudence or a careful concern for one's own good is the cardinal or basic moral virtue, other virtues being derivative from it. *Trait-utilitarianism* asserts that the virtues are those traits that most promote the general good, or, alternatively, that benevolence is the basic or cardinal moral virtue. These views may be called *trait-teleological*, but, of course, there are also *trait-deontological theories*, which will hold that certain traits are morally good or virtuous simply as such, and not just because of the nonmoral value they may have or promote, or, alternatively, that there are other cardinal or basic virtues besides prudence or benevolence, for example, obedience to God, honesty, or justice. If they add that there is only one

such cardinal virtue, they are monistic, otherwise pluralistic.

To avoid confusion, it is necessary to notice here that we must distinguish between *virtues* and *principles of duty* like "We ought to promote the good" and "We ought to treat people equally." A virtue is not a principle of this kind; it is a disposition, habit, quality, or trait of the person or soul, which an individual either has or seeks to have. Hence, I speak of the principle of *beneficence* and the virtue of *benevolence*, since we have two words with which to mark the difference. In the case of justice, we do not have different words, but still we must not confuse the principle of equal treatment with the disposition to treat people equally.

On the basis of our earlier discussions, we may assume at this point that views of the first two kinds are unsatisfactory, and that the most adequate ethics of virtue would be one of the third sort, one that would posit two cardinal virtues, namely, benevolence and justice, considered now as dispositions or traits of character rather than as principles of duty. By a set of cardinal virtues is meant a set of virtues that (1) cannot be derived from one another and (2) all other moral virtues can be derived from or shown to be forms of them. Plato and other Greeks thought there were four cardinal virtues in this sense: wisdom, courage, temperance, and justice. Christianity is traditionally regarded as having seven cardinal virtues: three "theological" virtues—faith, hope, and love; and four "human" virtues—prudence, fortitude, temperance, and justice. This was essentially St. Thomas Aquinas's view; since St. Augustine regarded the last four as forms of love, only the first three were really cardinal for him. However, many moralists, among them Schopenhauer, have taken benevolence and justice to be the cardinal moral virtues, as I would. It seems to me that all of the usual virtues (such as love, courage, temperance, honesty, gratitude, and considerateness), at least insofar as they are *moral* virtues, can be derived from these two. Insofar as a disposition cannot be derived from benevolence and justice, I should try to argue either that it is not a *moral* virtue (e.g., I take faith, hope, and wisdom to be religious or intellectual, not moral, virtues) or that it is not a virtue at all.

On Being and Doing: Morality of Traits vs. Morality of Principles

We may now return to the issue posed by the quotation from Stephen, though we cannot debate it as fully as we should. To be or to do, that is the question. Should we construe morality as primarily a following of certain principles or as primarily a cultivation of certain dispositions and traits? Must we choose? It is hard to see how a morality of principles can get off the ground except through the development of dispositions to act in accordance with its principles, else all motivation to act on them must be of an *ad hoc* kind, either prudential or impulsively altruistic. Moreover, morality can hardly be content with a mere conformity to rules, however willing and self-conscious it may be, unless it has no interest in the spirit of its law but only in the letter. On the other hand, one cannot conceive of traits of character except as including dispositions and tendencies to act in certain ways in certain circumstances. Hating involves being disposed to kill or harm, being just involves tending to do just acts (acts that conform to the principle of justice) when the occasion calls. Again, it is hard to see how we could know what traits to encourage or inculcate if we did not subscribe to principles, for example, to the principle of utility, or to those of benevolence and justice.

I propose therefore that we regard the morality of duty and principles and the morality of virtues or traits of character not as rival kinds of morality between which we must choose, but as two complementary aspects of the same morality. Then, for every principle there will be a morally good trait, often going by the same name, consisting of a disposition or tendency to act according to it; and for every morally good trait there will be a

principle defining the kind of action in which it is to express itself. To parody a famous dictum of Kant's, I am inclined to think that principles without traits are impotent and traits without principles are blind.

Even if we adopt this double-aspect conception of morality, in which principles are basic, we may still agree that morality does and must put a premium on *being* honest, conscientious, and so forth. If its sanctions or sources of motivation are not to be entirely external (for example, the prospect of being praised, blamed, rewarded, or punished by others) or adventitious (for example, a purely instinctive love of others), if it is to have adequate "internal sanctions," as Mill called them, then morality must foster the development of such dispositions and habits as have been mentioned. It could hardly be satisfied with a mere conformity to its principles even if it could provide us with fixed principles of actual duty. For such a conformity might be motivated entirely by extrinsic or nonmoral considerations, and would then be at the mercy of these other considerations. It could not be counted on in a moment of trial. Besides, since morality cannot provide us with fixed principles of actual duty but only with principles of prima facie duty, it cannot be content with the letter of its law, but must foster in us the dispositions that will sustain us in the hour of decision when we are choosing between conflicting principles of prima facie duty or trying to revise our working rules of right and wrong.

There is another reason why we must cultivate certain traits of character in ourselves and others, or why we must be certain sorts of persons. Although morality is concerned that we act in certain ways, it cannot take the hard line of insisting that we act in precisely those ways, even if those ways could be more clearly defined. We cannot praise and blame or apply other sanctions to an agent simply on the ground that he has or has not acted in conformity with certain principles. It would not be right. Through no fault of his own, the agent may not have known all the relevant facts. What action the principles of morality called for in the situation may not have been clear to him, again through no fault of his own, and he may have been honestly mistaken about his duty. Or his doing what he ought to have done might have carried with it an intolerable sacrifice on his part. He may even have been simply incapable of doing it. Morality must therefore recognize various sorts of excuses and extenuating circumstances. All it can really insist on, then, except in certain critical cases, is that we develop and manifest fixed dispositions to find out what the right thing is and to do it if possible. In this sense a person must "be this" rather than "do this." But it must be remembered that "being" involves at least *trying* to "do." Being without doing, like faith without works, is dead.

At least it will be clear from this discussion that an ethics of duty or principles also has an important place for the virtues and must put a premium on their cultivation as a part of moral education and development. The place it has for virtue and/or the virtues is, however, different from that accorded them by an ethics of virtue. Talking in terms of . . . an ethics of duty, we may say that, if we ask for *guidance* about what to do or not do, then the answer is contained, at least primarily, in two deontic principles and their corollaries, namely, the principles of beneficence and equal treatment. Given these two deontic principles, plus the necessary clarity of thought and factual knowledge, we can know what we morally ought to do or not do, except perhaps in cases of conflict between them. We also know that we should cultivate two virtues, a disposition to be beneficial (i.e., benevolence) and a disposition to treat people equally (justice as a trait). But the point of acquiring these virtues is not further guidance or instruction; the function of the virtues in an ethics of duty is not to tell us what to do but to ensure that we will do it willingly in whatever situations we may face. In an ethics of virtue, on the other hand, the virtues play a dual role—they must not only move us to do what we do, they

must also tell us what to do. To parody Alfred Lord Tennyson:

Theirs not (only) to do or die,
Theirs (also) to reason why.

Moral Ideals

This is the place to mention ideals again, which are among what we called the ingredients of morality. One may, perhaps, identify moral ideals with moral principles, but, more properly speaking, moral ideals are ways of being rather than of doing. Having a moral ideal is wanting to be a person of a certain sort, wanting to have a certain trait of character rather than others, for example, moral courage or perfect integrity. That is why the use of exemplary persons like Socrates, Jesus, or Martin Luther King has been such an important part of moral education and self-development, and it is one of the reasons for the writing and reading of biographies or of novels and epics in which types of moral personality are portrayed, even if they are not all heroes or saints. Often such moral ideals of personality go beyond what can be demanded or regarded as obligatory, belonging among the things to be praised rather than required, except as one may require them of oneself. It should be remembered, however, that not all personal ideals are moral ones. Achilles, Hercules, Napoleon, and Prince Charming may all be taken as ideals, but the ideals they represent are not moral ones, even though they may not be immoral ones either. Some ideals, e.g., those of chivalry, may be partly moral and partly nonmoral. There is every reason why one should pursue nonmoral as well as moral ideals, but there is no good reason for confusing them.

When one has a moral ideal, wanting to be a certain sort of moral person, one has at least some motivation to live in a certain way, but one also has something to guide him in living. Here the idea of an ethics of virtue may have a point. One may, of course, take as one's ideal that of being a good man who always does his duty from a sense of duty, perhaps gladly, and perhaps even going a second mile on occasion. Then one's guidance clearly comes entirely from one's rules and principles of duty. However, one may also have an ideal that goes beyond anything that can be regarded by others or even oneself as strict duty or obligation, a form or style of personal being that may be morally good or virtuous, but is not morally required of one. An ethics of virtue seems to provide for such an aspiration more naturally than an ethics of duty or principle, and perhaps an adequate morality should at least contain a region in which we can follow such an idea, over and beyond the region in which we are to listen to the call of duty. There certainly should be moral heroes and saints who go beyond the merely good man, if only to serve as an inspiration to others to be better and do more than they would otherwise be or do. Granted all this, however, it still seems to me that, if one's ideal is truly a moral one, there will be nothing in it that is not covered by the principles of beneficence and justice conceived as principles of what we ought to do in the wider sense referred to earlier.

Dispositions to Be Cultivated

Are there any other moral virtues to be cultivated besides benevolence and justice? No cardinal ones, of course. In this sense our answer to Socrates' question whether virtue is one or many is that it is two. We saw, however, that the principles of beneficence and equality have corollaries like telling the truth, keeping promises, etc. It follows that character traits like honesty and fidelity are virtues, though subordinate ones, and should be acquired and fostered. There will then be other such virtues corresponding to other corollaries of our main principles. Let us call all of these virtues, cardinal and noncardinal, first-order moral virtues. Besides first-order virtues like these, there are certain other moral virtues that ought also to be cultivated, which are in a way more abstract and general and may be called second-

order virtues. Conscientiousness is one such virtue; it is not limited to a certain sector of the moral life, as gratitude and honesty are, but is a virtue covering the whole of the moral life. Moral courage, or courage when moral issues are at stake, is another such second-order virtue; it belongs to all sectors of the moral life. Others that overlap with these are integrity and good-will, understanding good-will in Kant's sense of respect for the moral law.

In view of what was said in a previous chapter, we must list two other second-order traits: a disposition to find out and respect the relevant facts and a disposition to think clearly. These are not just abilities but character traits; one might have the ability to think intelligently without having a disposition to use it. They are therefore virtues, though they are intellectual virtues, not moral ones. Still, though their role is not limited to the moral life, they are necessary to it. More generally speaking, we should cultivate the virtue Plato called wisdom and Aristotle practical wisdom, which they thought of as including all of the intellectual abilities and virtues essential to the moral life.

Still other second-order qualities, which may be abilities rather than virtues, but which must be cultivated for moral living, and so may, perhaps, best be mentioned here, are moral autonomy, the ability to make moral decisions and to revise one's principles if necessary, and the ability to realize vividly, in imagination and feeling, the "inner lives" of others. Of these second-order qualities, the first two have been referred to on occasion and will be again, but something should be said about the last.

If our morality is to be more than a conformity to internalized rules and principles, if it is to include and rest on an understanding of the point of these rules and principles, and certainly if it is to involve *being* a certain kind of person and not merely *doing* certain kinds of things, then we must somehow attain and develop an ability to be aware of others as persons, as important to themselves as we are to ourselves, and to have a lively and sympathetic representation in imagination of their interests and of the effects of our actions on their lives. The need for this is particularly stressed by Josiah Royce and William James. Both men point out how we usually go our own busy and self-concerned ways, with only an external awareness of the presence of others, much as if they were things, and without any realization of their inner and peculiar worlds of personal experience; and both emphasize the need and the possibility of a "higher vision of an inner significance" which pierces this "certain blindness in human beings" and enables us to realize the existence of others in a wholly different way, as we do our own.

What then is thy neighbor? He too is a mass of states, of experiences, thoughts and desires, just as concrete, as thou art. . . . Dost thou believe this? Art thou sure what it means? This is for thee the turning-point of thy whole conduct towards him.

These are Royce's quaint old-fashioned words. Here are James's more modern ones.

This higher vision of an inner significance in what, until then, we had realized only in the dead external way, often comes over a person suddenly; and, when it does so, it makes an epoch in his history.

Royce calls this more perfect recognition of our neighbors "the moral insight" and James says that its practical consequence is "the well-known democratic respect for the sacredness of individuality." It is hard to see how either a benevolent (loving) or a just (equalitarian) disposition could come to fruition without it. To quote James again,

We ought, all of us, to realize each other in this intense, pathetic, and important way.

Doing this is part of what is involved in fully taking the moral point of view.

Two Questions

We can now deal with the question, sometimes raised, whether an action is to be judged right or wrong because of its results, because of the principle it exemplifies, or because the motive, intention, or trait of character involved is morally good or bad. The answer . . . is that an action is to be judged *right* or *wrong* by reference to a principle or set of principles. Even if we say it is right or wrong because of its effects, this means that it is right or wrong by the principle of utility or some other teleological principle. But an act may also be said to be *good* or *bad*, praiseworthy or blameworthy, noble or despicable, and so on, and then the moral quality ascribed to it will depend on the agent's motive, intention, or disposition in doing it.

Another important question here is: What is moral goodness? When is a person morally good and when are his actions, dispositions, motives, or intentions morally good? Not just when he does what is actually right, for he may do what is right from bad motives, in which case he is not morally good, or he may fail to do what is right though sincerely trying to do it, in which case he is not morally bad. Whether he and his actions are morally good or not depends, not on the rightness of what he does or on its consequences, but on his character or motives; so far the statement quoted from Hume is certainly correct. But when are his motives and dispositions morally good? Some answer that a person and his actions are morally good if and only if they are motivated wholly by a sense of duty or a desire to do what is right; the Stoics and Kant sometimes seem to take this extreme view. Others hold that a man and his actions are morally good if and only if they are motivated primarily by a sense of duty or desire to do what is right, though other motives may be present too; still others contend, with Aristotle, that they are at any rate not morally good unless they are motivated at least in part by such a sense or desire. A more reasonable view, to my mind, is that a man and his actions are morally good if it is at least true that, whatever his actual motives in acting are, his sense of duty or desire to do the right is so strong in him that it would keep him trying to do his duty anyway.

Actually, I find it hard to believe that no dispositions or motivations are good or virtuous from the moral point of view except those that include a will to do the right as such. It is more plausible to distinguish two kinds of morally good dispositions or traits of character, first, those that are usually called moral virtues and do include a will to do the right, and second, others like purely natural kindliness or gratefulness, which, while they are nonmoral, are still morality-supporting, since they dispose us to do such actions as morality requires and even to perform deeds, for example, in the case of motherly love, which are well beyond the call of duty.

It has even been alleged that conscientiousness or moral goodness in the sense of a disposition to act from a sense of duty alone is not a good thing or not a virtue—that it is more desirable to have people acting from motives like friendship, gratitude, honor, love, and the like, then from a dry or driven sense of obligation. There is something to be said for this view, though it ignores the nobility of great moral courage and of the higher reaches of moral idealism. But even if conscientiousness or good will is not the only thing that is unconditionally good, as Kant believed, or the greatest of intrinsically good things, as Ross thought, it is surely a good thing from the moral point of view. For an ethics of duty, at any rate, it must be desirable that people do what is right for its own sake, especially if they do it gladly, as a gymnast may gladly make the right move just because it is right.

Notes

1. Leslie Stephen, *The Science of Ethics* (New York: G. P. Putnam's Sons, 1882), pp. 155, 158.
2. David Hume, *Treatise of Human Nature* (1739), Book III, Part II, opening of Sec. I.

The Nature of the Virtues

ALASDAIR MACINTYRE

Alasdair MacIntyre is the O'Brien Senior Research Professor of Philosophy at the University of Notre Dame. He is the author of several works in philosophy of religion, social theory, and ethics. In this selection from his influential work After Virtue, *MacIntyre carries on the Aristotelian project of grounding morality in the virtues. He asks whether there is a core conception of the virtues, some vital components that are necessary to any social endeavor or practice. He compares five different conceptions of the virtues as they appear in the works of Homer, Aristotle, the New Testament, Jane Austen, and Benjamin Franklin.*

MacIntyre argues that in every society there must be practices in which virtues are exhibited and become defined. Even though practices may vary from society to society, so that different virtues will be highlighted differently in different societies, nevertheless a core set of virtues is necessary for the successful functioning of any practice. MacIntyre provides a penetrating description of these core virtues. He ends his essay by comparing his theory of the virtues with Aristotle's project, arguing that his work is within that tradition.

One response to the history [of Greek and medieval thought about the virtues] might well be to suggest that even within the relatively coherent tradition of thought which I have sketched, there are just too many different and incompatible conceptions of a virtue for there to be any real unity to the concept or indeed to the history. Homer, Sophocles, Aristotle, the New Testament, and medieval thinkers differ from each other in too many ways. They offer us different and incompatible lists of the virtues; they give a different rank

Reprinted from *After Virtue* (1981) by permission of the University of Notre Dame Press and the author.

order of importance to different virtues; and they have different and incompatible theories of the virtues. If we were to consider later Western writers on the virtues, the list of differences and incompatibilities would be enlarged still further; and if we extended our enquiry to Japanese, say, or American Indian cultures, the differences would become greater still. It would be all too easy to conclude that there are a number of rival and alternative conceptions of the virtues, but, even within the tradition which I have been delineating, no single core conception.

The case for such a conclusion could not be better constructed than by beginning from a consideration of the very different lists of items which different authors in different times and places have included in their catalogues of virtues. Some of these catalogues—Homer's, Aristotle's and the New Testament's—I have already noticed at greater or lesser length. Let me at the risk of some repetition recall some of their key features and then introduce for further comparison the catalogues of two later Western writers, Benjamin Franklin and Jane Austen.

The first example is that of Homer. At least some of the items in a Homeric list of the *aretai* would clearly not be counted by most of us nowadays as virtues at all, physical strength being the most obvious example. To this it might be replied that perhaps we ought not to translate the word *aretê* in Homer by our word 'virtue,' but instead by our word 'excellence'; and perhaps, if we were so to translate it, the apparently surprising difference between Homer and ourselves would at first sight have been removed. For we could allow without any kind of oddity that the possession of physical strength is the possession of an excellence. But in fact we would not have removed, but instead would merely have relocated, the difference between Homer and ourselves. For we would now seem to be saying that Homer's concept of an *aretê*, an excellence, is one thing and that our concept of a virtue is quite another, since a particular quality can be an excellence in Homer's eyes but not a virtue in ours, and *vice versa*.

But of course it is not that Homer's list of virtues differs only from our own; it also notably differs from Aristotle's. And Aristotle's of course also differs from our own. For one thing, as I noticed earlier, some Greek virtue-words are not easily translatable into English or rather out of Greek. Moreover, consider the importance of friendship as a virtue in Aristotle's list—how different from us! Or the place of *phronêsis*—how different from Homer and from us! The mind receives from Aristotle the kind of tribute which the body receives from Homer. But it is not just the case that the difference between Aristotle and Homer lies in the inclusion of some items and the omission of others in their respective catalogues. It turns out also in the way in which those catalogues are ordered, in which items are ranked as relatively central to human excellence and which marginal.

Moreover, the relationship of virtues to the social order has changed. For Homer the paradigm of human excellence is the warrior; for Aristotle it is the Athenian gentleman. Indeed according to Aristotle certain virtues are only available to those of great riches and of high social status; there are virtues which are unavailable to the poor man, even if he is a free man. And those virtues are on Aristotle's view ones central to human life; magnanimity—and once again, any translation of *megalopsuchia* is unsatisfactory—and munificence are not just virtues, but important virtues within the Aristotelian scheme.

At once it is impossible to delay the remark that the most striking contrast with Aristotle's catalogue is to be found neither in Homer's nor in our own, but in the New Testament's. For the New Testament not only praises virtues of which Aris-

totle knows nothing—faith, hope and love—and says nothing about virtues such as *phronêsis*[1] which are crucial for Aristotle, but it praises at least one quality as a virtue which Aristotle seems to count as one of the vices relative to magnanimity, namely humility. Moreover, since the New Testament quite clearly sees the rich as destined for the pains of Hell, it is clear that the key virtues cannot be available to them; yet they *are* available to slaves. And the New Testament of course differs from both Homer and Aristotle not only in the items included in its catalogue, but once again in its rank ordering of the virtues.

Turn now to compare all three lists of virtues considered so far—the Homeric, the Aristotelian, and the New Testament's—with two much later lists, one which can be compiled from Jane Austen's novels and the other which Benjamin Franklin constructed for himself. Two features stand out in Jane Austen's list. The first is the importance that she allots to the virtue which she calls 'constancy,' a virtue about which I shall say more in a later chapter. In some ways constancy plays a role in Jane Austen analogous to that of *phronêsis* in Aristotle; it is a virtue the possession of which is a prerequisite for the possession of other virtues. The second is the fact that what Aristotle treats as the virtue of agreeableness (a virtue for which he says there is no name) she treats as only the simulacrum of a genuine virtue—the genuine virtue in question is the one she calls amiability. For the man who practices agreeableness does so from considerations of honour and expediency, according to Aristotle; whereas Jane Austen thought it possible and necessary for the possessor of that virtue to have a certain real affection for people as such. (It matters here that Jane Austen is a Christian.) Remember that Aristotle himself had treated military courage as a simulacrum of true courage. Thus we find here yet another type of disagreement over the virtues; namely, one as to which human qualities are genuine virtues and which mere simulacra.

In Benjamin Franklin's list we find almost all

the types of differences from at least one of the other catalogues we have considered and one more. Franklin includes virtues which are new to our consideration such as cleanliness, silence and industry; he clearly considers the drive to acquire itself a part of virtue, whereas for most ancient Greeks this is the vice of *pleonexia;* he treats some virtues which earlier ages had considered minor as major; but he also redefines some familiar virtues. In the list of thirteen virtues which Franklin compiled as part of his system of private moral accounting, he elucidates each virtue by citing a maxim obedience to which *is* the virtue in question. In the case of chastity the maxim is 'Rarely use venery but for health or offspring— never to dullness, weakness or the injury of your own or another's peace or reputation.' This is clearly not what earlier writers had meant by 'chastity.'

We have therefore accumulated a startling number of differences and incompatibilities in the five stated and implied accounts of the virtues. So the question which I raised at the outset becomes more urgent. If different writers in different times and places, but all within the history of Western culture, include such different sets and types of items in their lists, what grounds have we for supposing that they do indeed aspire to list items of one and the same kind, that there is any shared concept at all? A second kind of consideration reinforces the presumption of a negative answer to this question. It is not just that each of these five writers lists different and differing kinds of items; it is also that each of these lists embodies, the expression of a different theory about what a virtue is.

In the Homeric poems a virtue is a quality the manifestation of which enables people to do exactly what their well-defined social role requires. The primary role is that of the warrior king, and that Homer lists those virtues which he does becomes intelligible at once when we recognise that the key virtues therefore must be those which enable a man to excel in combat and in the games. It follows that we cannot identify the Homeric virtues until we have first identified the key social roles in Homeric society and the requirements of each of them. The concept of *what anyone filling such-and-such a role ought to do* is prior to the concept of a virtue; the latter concept has application only via the former.

On Aristotle's account matters are very different. Even though some virtues are available only to certain types of people, none the less virtues attach not to men as inhabiting social roles, but to man as such. It is the *telos* of man as a species which determines what human qualities are virtues. We need to remember however that although Aristotle treats the acquisition and exercise of the virtues as means to an end, the relationship of means to end is internal and not external. I call a means internal to a given end when the end cannot be adequately characterised independently of a characterisation of the means. So it is with the virtues and the *telos* which is the good life for man on Aristotle's account. The exercise of the virtues is itself a crucial component of the good life for man. This distinction between internal and external means to an end is not drawn by Aristotle himself in the *Nicomachean Ethics,* as I noticed earlier, but it is an essential distinction to be drawn if we are to understand what Aristotle intended. The distinction *is* drawn explicitly by Aquinas in the course of his defence of St. Augustine's definition of a virtue, and it is clear that Aquinas understood that in drawing it he was maintaining an Aristotelian point of view.

The New Testament's account of the virtues, even if it differs as much as it does in content from Aristotle's—Aristotle would certainly not have admired Jesus Christ and he would have been horrified by St. Paul—does have the same logical and conceptual structure as Aristotle's account. A virtue is, as with Aristotle, a quality the exercise of which leads to the achievement of the human telos. *The* good for man is of course a supernatural and not only a natural good, but supernature redeems and completes nature. Moreover the relationship of virtues as means to the end which is human incorporation in the divine kingdom of the age to come is internal and not external, just as it is in Aristotle. It is of course this parallelism which allows Aquinas to synthesise Aristotle and the New Testament. A key feature of this parallelism is the way in which the concept of *the good life for man* is prior to the concept of a virtue in just the way in which on the Homeric account the concept of a social role was prior. Once again it is the way in which the former concept is applied which determines how the latter is to be applied. In both cases the concept of a virtue is a secondary concept.

The intent of Jane Austen's theory of the virtues is of another kind. C. S. Lewis has rightly emphasised how profoundly Christian her moral vision is and Gilbert Ryle has equally rightly emphasised her inheritance from Shaftesbury and from Aristotle. In fact her views combine elements from Homer as well, since she is concerned with social roles in a way that neither the New Testament nor Aristotle is. She is therefore important for the way in which she finds it possible to combine what are at first sight disparate theoretical accounts of the virtues. But for the moment any attempt to assess the significance of Jane Austen's synthesis must be delayed. Instead we must notice the quite different style of theory articulated in Benjamin Franklin's account of the virtues.

Franklin's account, like Aristotle's, is teleological; but unlike Aristotle's, it is utilitarian. According to Franklin in his *Autobiography* the virtues are means to an end, but he envisages the means-ends relationship as external rather than internal. The end to which the cultivation of the virtues ministers is happiness, but happiness understood as success, prosperity in Philadelphia and ultimately in heaven. The virtues are to be useful, and Franklin's account continuously stresses utility as a criterion in individual cases: 'Make no expence but to do good to others or yourself; i.e., waste nothing,' 'Speak not but what may benefit others or yourself. Avoid trifling conversation,' and, as we have already seen, 'Rarely use venery but for health or offspring. . . .' When Franklin

was in Paris he was horrified by Parisian architecture: 'Marble, porcelain and gilt are squandered without utility.'

We thus have at least three very different conceptions of a virtue to confront: a virtue is a quality which enables an individual to discharge his or her social role (Homer); a virtue is a quality which enables an individual to move toward the achievement of the specifically human *telos*, whether natural or supernatural (Aristotle, the New Testament and Aquinas); a virtue is a quality which has utility in achieving earthly and heavenly success (Franklin). Are we to take these as three rival accounts of the same thing? Or are they instead accounts of three different things? Perhaps the moral structures in archaic Greece, in fourth-century Greece, and in eighteenth-century Pennsylvania were so different from each other that we should treat them as embodying quite different concepts whose difference is initially disguised from us by the historical accident of an inherited vocabulary which misleads us by linguistic resemblance long after conceptual identity and similarity have failed. Our initial question has come back to us with redoubled force.

Yet although I have dwelt upon the *prima facie* case for holding that the differences and incompatibilities between different accounts at least suggest that there is no single, central, core conception of the virtues which might make a claim for universal allegiance, I ought also to point out that each of the five moral accounts which I have sketched so summarily does embody just such a claim. It is indeed just this feature of those accounts that makes them of more than sociological or antiquarian interest. Every one of these accounts claims not only a theoretical but also an institutional hegemony. For Odysseus the Cyclopes stand condemned because they lack agriculture, on *agora* and *themis*. For Aristotle the barbarians stand condemned because they lack the *polis* and are therefore incapable of politics. For New Testament Christians there is no salvation outside the apostolic church. And we know that Benjamin Franklin found the virtues more at home in Philadelphia than in Paris and that for Jane Austen the touchstone of the virtues is a certain kind of marriage and indeed a certain kind of naval officer (that is, a certain kind of *English* naval officer).

The question can therefore now be posed directly: are we or are we not able to disentangle from these rival and various claims a unitary core concept of the virtues of which we can give a more compelling account than any of the other accounts so far? I am going to argue that we can in fact discover such a core concept and that it turns out to provide the tradition of which I have written the history with its conceptual unity. It will indeed enable us to distinguish in a clear way those beliefs about the virtues which genuinely belong to the tradition from those which do not. Unsurprisingly perhaps it is a complex concept, different parts of which derive from different stages in the development of the tradition. Thus the concept itself in some sense embodies the history of which it is the outcome.

One of the features of the concept of a virtue which has emerged with some clarity from the argument so far is that it always requires for its application the acceptance of some prior account of certain features of social and moral life in terms of which it has to be defined and explained. So in the Homeric account the concept of a virtue is secondary to that of *a social role;* in Aristotle's account it is secondary to that of *the good life for man* conceived as the *telos* of human action; and in Franklin's much later account it is secondary to that of utility. What is it in the account which I am about to give which provides in a similar way the necessary background against which the concept of a virtue has to be made intelligible? It is in answering this question that the complex, historical, multilayered character of the core concept of virtue becomes clear. For there are no fewer than three stages in the logical development of the concept which have to be identified in order, if the core conception of a virtue is to be understood, and each of these stages has its own conceptual background. The first stage requires a background account of what I shall call a practice, the

second an account of what I have already characterised as the narrative order of a single human life, and the third an account a good deal fuller than I have given up to now of what constitutes a moral tradition. Each later stage presupposes the earlier, but not *vice versa.* Each earlier stage is both modified by and reinterpreted in the light of, but also provides an essential constituent of each later stage. The progress in the development of the concept is closely related to, although it does not recapitulate in any straightforward way, the history of the tradition of which it forms the core.

In the Homeric account of the virtues—and in heroic societies more generally—the exercise of a virtue exhibits qualities which are required for sustaining a social role and for exhibiting excellence in some well-marked area of social practice: to excel is to excel at war or in the games, as Achilles does; in sustaining a household, as Penelope does; in giving counsel in the assembly, as Nestor does; in the telling of a tale, as Homer himself does. When Aristotle speaks of excellence in human activity, he sometimes, though not always, refers to some well-defined type of human practice: flute-playing, or war, or geometry. I am going to suggest that this notion of a particular type of practice as providing the arena in which the virtues are exhibited and in terms of which they are to receive their primary, if incomplete, definition is crucial to the whole enterprise of identifying a core concept of the virtues. I hasten to add two *caveats* however.

The first is to point out that my argument will not in any way imply that virtues are exercised *only* in the course of what I am calling practices. The second is to warn that I shall be using the word 'practice' in a specially defined way which does not completely agree with current ordinary usage, including my own previous use of that word. What am I going to mean by it?

By a 'practice' I am going to mean any coherent and complex form of socially established cooperative human activity through which goods internal to that form of activity are realised in the course of trying to achieve those standards of excellence which are appropriate to, and partially definitive of, that form of activity, with the result that human powers to achieve excellence, and human conceptions of the ends and goods involved, are systematically extended. Tic-tac-toe is not an example of a practice in this sense, nor is throwing a football with skill; but the game of football is, and so is chess. Bricklaying is not a practice; architecture is. Planting turnips is not a practice; farming is. So are the enquiries of physics, chemistry, and biology, and so is the work of the historian, and so are painting and music. In the ancient and medieval worlds the creation and sustaining of human communities—of households, cities, nations—is generally taken to be a practice in the sense in which I have defined it. Thus the range of practices is wide: arts, sciences, games, politics in the Aristotelian sense, the making and sustaining of family life—all fall under the concept. But the question of the precise range of practices is not at this stage of the first importance. Instead let me explain some of the key terms involved in my definition, beginning with the notion of goods internal to a practice.

Consider the example of a highly intelligent seven-year-old child whom I wish to teach to play chess, although the child has no particular desire to learn the game. The child does however have a very strong desire for candy and little chance of obtaining it. I therefore tell the child that if the child will play chess with me once a week I will give the child 50¢ worth of candy; moreover I tell the child that I will always play in such a way that it will be difficult, but not impossible, for the child to win and that, if the child wins, the child will receive an extra 50¢ worth of candy. Thus motivated the child plays and plays to win. Notice however that, so long as it is the candy alone which provides the child with a good reason for playing chess, the child has no reason not to cheat and every reason to cheat, provided he or she can do so successfully. But, so we may hope, there will come a time when the child will find in those goods specific to chess, in the achievement of a certain highly particular kind of analytical skill,

strategic imagination, and competitive intensity, a new set of reasons, reasons now not just for winning on a particular occasion, but for trying to excel in whatever way the game of chess demands. Now if the child cheats, he or she will be defeating not me but himself or herself.

There are thus two kinds of goods possibly to be gained by playing chess. On the one hand there are those goods externally and contingently attached to chess-playing and to other practices by the accidents of social circumstance—in the case of the imaginary child candy, in the case of real adults such goods as prestige, status, and money. There are always alternative ways for achieving such goods, and their achievement is never to be had *only* by engaging in some particular kind of practice. On the other hand there are the goods internal to the practice of chess which cannot be had in any way but by playing chess or some other game of that specific kind. We call them internal for two reasons: first, as I have already suggested, because we can only specify them in terms of chess or some other game of that specific kind and by means of examples from such games (otherwise the meagerness of our vocabulary for speaking of such goods forces us into such devices as my own resort to writing of 'a certain highly particular kind of'); and secondly because they can only be identified and recognised by the experience of participating in the practice in question. Those who lack the relevant experience are incompetent thereby as judges of internal goods.

This is clearly the case with all the major examples of practices: consider for example—even if briefly and inadequately—the practice of portrait painting as developed in Western Europe from the late middle ages to the eighteenth century. The successful portrait painter is able to achieve many goods which are in the sense just defined external to the practice of portrait painting—fame, wealth, social status, even a measure of power and influence at courts upon occasion. But those external goods are not to be confused with the goods which are internal to the practice. The internal goods are those which result from an extended attempt to show how Wittgenstein's dictum 'The human body is the best picture of the human soul' (*Investigations*, p. 178e) might be made to become true by teaching us 'to regard . . . the picture on our wall as the object itself (the men, landscape, and so on) depicted there' (p. 205e) in a quite new way. What is misleading about Wittgenstein's dictum as it stands is its neglect of the truth in George Orwell's thesis 'At 50 everyone has the face he deserves.' What painters from Giotto to Rembrandt learned to show was how the face at any age may be revealed as the face that the subject of a portrait deserves.

Originally in medieval paintings of the saints the face was an icon; the question of a resemblance between the depicted face of Christ or St. Peter and the face that Jesus or Peter actually possessed at some particular age did not even arise. The antithesis to this iconography was the relative naturalism of certain fifteenth-century Flemish and German painting. The heavy eyelids, the coifed hair, the lines around the mouth undeniably represent some particular woman, either actual or envisaged. Resemblance has usurped the iconic relationship. But with Rembrandt there is, so to speak, synthesis: the naturalistic portrait is now rendered as an icon, but an icon of a new and hitherto inconceivable kind. Similarly in a very different kind of sequence mythological faces in a certain kind of seventeenth-century French painting become aristocratic faces in the eighteenth century. Within each of these sequences at least two different kinds of good internal to the painting of human faces and bodies are achieved.

There is first of all the excellence of the products, both the excellence in performance by the painters and that of each portrait itself. This excellence—the very verb 'excel' suggests it—has to be understood historically. The sequences of development find their point and purpose in a progress toward and beyond a variety of types and modes of excellence. There are of course sequences of decline as well as of progress, and progress is rarely to be understood as straightforwardly linear. But it is in participation in the attempts to sustain progress and to respond creatively to moments that the second kind of good internal to the practices of portrait painting is to be found. For what the artist discovers within the pursuit of excellence in portrait painting—and what is true of portrait painting is true of the practice of the fine arts in general—is the good of a certain kind of life. That life may not constitute the whole of life for someone who is a painter by a very long way, for it may at least for a period, Gauguin-like, absorb him or her at the expense of almost everything else. But it is the painter's living out of a greater or lesser part of his or her life *as a painter* that is the second kind of good internal to painting. And judgment upon these goods requires at the very least the kind of competence that is only to be acquired either as a painter or as someone willing to learn systematically what the portrait painter has to teach.

A practice involves standards of excellence and obedience to rules as well as the achievement of goods. To enter into a practice is to accept the authority of those standards and the inadequacy of my own performance as judged by them. It is to subject my own attitudes, choices, preferences, and tastes to the standards which currently and partially define the practice. Practices of course, as I have just noticed, have a history: games, sciences, and arts all have histories. Thus the standards are not themselves immune from criticism, but none the less we cannot be initiated into a practice without accepting the authority of the best standards realised so far. If, on starting to listen to music, I do not accept my own incapacity to judge correctly, I will never learn to hear, let alone to appreciate, Bartok's last quartets. If, on starting to play baseball, I do not accept that others know better than I when to throw a fast-ball and when not, I will never learn to appreciate good pitching, let alone to pitch. In the realm of practices the authority of both goods and standards operates in such a way as to rule out all subjectivist and emotivist analyses of judgment. De gustibus *est* disputandum.

We are now in a position to notice an important

difference between what I have called internal and what I have called external goods. It is characteristic of what I have called external goods that when achieved they are always some individual's property and possession. Moreover characteristically they are such that the more someone has of them, the less there is for other people. This is sometimes necessarily the case, as with power and fame, and sometimes the case by reason of contingent circumstance, as with money. External goods are therefore characteristically objects of competition in which there must be losers as well as winners. Internal goods are indeed the outcome of competition to excel, but it is characteristic of them that their achievement is a good for the whole community who participate in the practice. So when Turner transformed the seascape in painting or W. G. Grace advanced the art of batting in cricket in a quite new way their achievement enriched the whole relevant community.

But what does all or any of this have to do with the concept of the virtues? It turns out that we are now in a position to formulate a first, even if partial and tentative, definition of a virtue: *A virtue is an acquired human quality the possession and exercise of which tends to enable us to achieve those goods which are internal to practices and the lack of which effectively prevents us from achieving any such goods.* Later this definition will need amplification and amendment. But as a first approximation to an adequate definition it already illuminates the place of the virtues in human life. For it is not difficult to show for a whole range of key virtues that without them the goods internal to practices are barred to us, but not just barred to us generally— barred in a very particular way.

It belongs to the concept of a practice as I have outlined it—and as we are all familiar with it already in our actual lives, whether we are painters or physicists or quarterbacks or indeed just lovers of good painting or first-rate experiments or a well-thrown pass—that its goods can only be achieved by subordinating ourselves to the best standard so far achieved, and that entails subordinating ourselves within the practice in our rela-

tionship to other practitioners. We have to learn to recognise what is due to whom; we have to be prepared to take whatever self-endangering risks are demanded along the way; and we have to listen carefully to what we are told about our own inadequacies and to reply with the same carefulness for the facts. In other words we have to accept as necessary components of any practice with internal goods and standards of excellence the virtues of justice, courage, and honesty. For not to accept these, to be willing to cheat as our imagined child was willing to cheat in his or her early days at chess, so far bars us from achieving the standards of excellence or the goods internal to the practice that it renders the practice pointless except as a device for achieving external goods.

We can put the same point in another way. Every practice requires a certain kind of relationship between those who participate in it. Now the virtues are those goods by reference to which, whether we like it or not, we define our relationships to those other people with whom we share the kind of purposes and standards which inform practices. Consider an example of how reference to the virtues has to be made in certain kinds of human relationship.

A, B, C, and D are friends in that sense of friendship which Aristotle takes to be primary: they share in the pursuit of certain goods. In my terms they share in a practice. D dies in obscure circumstances, A discovers how D died and tells the truth about it to B while lying to C. C discovers the lie. What A cannot then intelligibly claim is that he stands in the same relationship of friendship to both B and C. By telling the truth to one and lying to the other he has partially defined a difference in the relationship. Of course it is open to A to explain this difference in a number of ways; perhaps he was trying to spare C pain or perhaps he is simply cheating C. But some difference in the relationship now exists as a result of the lie. For their allegiance to each other in the pursuit of common goods has been put in question.

Just as, so long as we share the standards and

purposes characteristic of practices, we define our relationships to each other, whether we acknowledge it or not, by reference to standards of truthfulness and trust, as we define them too by reference to standards of justice and of courage. If A, a professor, gives B and C the grades that their papers deserve, but grades D because he is attracted by D's blue eyes or is repelled by D's dandruff, he has defined his relationship to D differently from his relationship to the other members of the class, whether he wishes it or not. Justice requires that we treat others in respect of merit or desert according to uniform and impersonal standards; to depart from the standards of justice in some particular instance defines our relationship with the relevant person as in some way special or distinctive.

The case with courage is a little different. We hold courage to be a virtue because the care and concern for individuals, communities and causes which is so crucial to so much in practices requires the existence of such a virtue. If someone says that he cares for some individual, community or cause, but is unwilling to risk harm or danger on his, her or its own behalf, he puts in question the genuineness of his care and concern. Courage, the capacity to risk harm or danger to oneself, has its role in human life because of this connection with care and concern. This is not to say that a man cannot genuinely care and also be a coward. It is in part to say that a man who genuinely cares and has not the capacity for risking harm or danger has to define himself, both to himself and to others, as a coward.

I take it then that from the standpoint of those types of relationship without which practices cannot be sustained, truthfulness, justice, and courage—and perhaps some others—are genuine excellences, are virtues in the light of which we have to characterise ourselves and others, whatever our private moral standpoint or our society's particular codes may be. For this recognition that we cannot escape the definition of our relationships in terms of such goods is perfectly compatible with the acknowledgment that different societies have and have had different codes of truthfulness, justice, and courage. Lutheran pietists brought up their children to believe that one ought to tell the truth to everybody at all times, whatever the circumstances or consequences, and Kant was one of their children. Traditional Bantu parents brought up their children not to tell the truth to unknown strangers, since they believed that this could render the family vulnerable to witchcraft. In our culture many of us have been brought up not to tell the truth to elderly great-aunts who invite us to admire their new hats. But each of these codes embodies an acknowledgment of the virtue of truthfulness. So it is also with varying codes of justice and of courage.

Practices then might flourish in societies with very different codes; what they could not do is flourish in societies in which the virtues were not valued, although institutions and technical skills serving unified purposes might well continue to flourish. (I shall have more to say about the contrast between institutions and technical skills mobilised for a unified end, on the one hand, and practices on the other, in a moment.) For the kind of cooperation, the kind of recognition of authority and of achievement, the kind of respect for standards and the kind of risk-taking which are characteristically involved in practices demand for example fairness in judging oneself and others—the kind of fairness absent in my example of the professor, a ruthless truthfulness without which fairness cannot find application—the kind of truthfulness absent in my example of A, B, C, and D—and willingness to trust the judgments of those whose achievement in the practice give them an authority to judge which presupposes fairness and truthfulness in those judgments, and from time to time the taking of self-endangering, reputation-endangering and even achievement-endangering risks. It is no part of my thesis that great violinists cannot be vicious or great chess-players mean-spirited. Where the virtues are required, the vices also may flourish. It is just that the vicious and mean-spirited necessarily rely on the virtues of others for the practices in which they engage to flourish and also deny themselves the experience of achieving those internal goods which may reward even not very good chess-players and violinists.

To situate the virtues any further within practices it is necessary now to clarify a little further the nature of a practice by drawing two important contrasts. The discussion so far I hope makes it clear that a practice, in the sense intended, is never just a set of technical skills, even when directed toward some unified purpose and even if the exercise of those skills can on occasion be valued or enjoyed for its own sake. What is distinctive of a practice is in part the way in which conceptions of the relevant goods and ends which the technical skills serve—and every practice does require the exercise of technical skills—are transformed and enriched by these extensions of human powers and by that regard for its own internal goods which are partially definitive of each particular practice or type of practice. Practices never have a goal or goals fixed for all time— painting has no such goal nor has physics—but the goals themselves are transmuted by the history of the activity. It therefore turns out not to be accidental that every practice has its own history and a history which is more and other than that of the improvement of the relevant technical skills. This historical dimension is crucial in relation to the virtues.

To enter into a practice is to enter into a relationship not only with its contemporary practitioners, but also with those who have preceded us in the practice, particularly those whose achievements extended the reach of the practice to its present point. It is thus the achievement, and *a fortiori* the authority, of a tradition which I then confront and from which I have to learn. And for this learning and the relationship to the past which it embodies, the virtues of justice, courage, and truthfulness are prerequisite in precisely the same way and for precisely the same reasons as they are in sustaining present relationships within practices.

It is not only of course with sets of technical skills that practices ought to be contrasted. Practices must not be confused with institutions. Chess, physics, and medicine are practices; chess clubs, laboratories, universities, and hospitals are institutions. Institutions are characteristically and necessarily concerned with what I have called external goods. They are involved in acquiring money and other material goods; they are structured in terms of power and status, and they distribute money, power, and status as rewards. Nor could they do otherwise if they are to sustain not only themselves, but also the practices of which they are the bearers. For no practices can survive for any length of time unsustained by institutions. Indeed so intimate is the relationship of practices to institutions—and consequently of the goods external to the goods internal to the practices in question—that institutions and practices characteristically form a single causal order in which the ideals and the creativity of the practice are always vulnerable to the acquisitiveness of the institution, in which the cooperative care for common goods of the practice is always vulnerable to the competitiveness of the institution. In this context the essential function of the virtues is clear. Without them, without justice, courage, and truthfulness, practices could not resist the corrupting power of institutions.

Yet if institutions do have corrupting power, the making and sustaining of forms of human community—and therefore of institutions—itself has all the characteristics of a practice, and moreover of a practice which stands in a peculiarly close relationship to the exercise of the virtues in two important ways. The exercise of the virtues is itself apt to require a highly determinate attitude to social and political issues; and it is always within some particular community with its own specific institutional forms that we learn or fail to learn to exercise the virtues. There is of course a crucial difference between the way in which the relationship between moral character and political community is envisaged from the standpoint of liberal individualist modernity and the way in which that relationship was envisaged from the standpoint of the type of ancient and medieval tradition of the virtues which I have sketched. For liberal individualism a community is simply an arena in which individuals each pursue their own self-chosen conception of the good life, and political institutions exist to provide that degree of order which makes such self-determined activity possible. Government and law are, or ought to be, neutral between rival conceptions of the good life for man, and hence, although it is the task of government to promote law-abidingness, it is on the liberal view no part of the legitimate function of government to inculcate any one moral outlook.

By contrast, on the particular ancient and medieval view which I have sketched, political community not only requires the exercise of the virtues for its own sustenance, but is one of the tasks of government to make its citizens virtuous, just as it is one of the tasks of parental authority to make children grow up so as to be virtuous adults. The classical statement of this analogy is by Socrates in the *Crito*. It does not of course follow from an acceptance of the Socratic view of political community and political authority that we ought to assign to the modern state the moral function which Socrates assigned to the city and its laws. Indeed the power of the liberal individualist standpoint partly derives from the evident fact that the modern state is indeed totally unfitted to act as moral educator of any community. But the history of how the modern state emerged is of course itself a moral history. If my account of the complex relationship of virtues to practices and to institutions is correct, it follows that we shall be unable to write a true history of practices and institutions unless that history is also one of the virtues and vices. For the ability of a practice to retain its integrity will depend on the way in which the virtues can be and are exercised in sustaining the institutional forms which are the social bearers of the practice. The integrity of a practice causally requires the exercise of the virtues by at least some of the individuals who embody it in their activities; and conversely the corruption of institutions is always in part at least an effect of the vices.

The virtues are of course themselves in turn fostered by certain types of social institution and endangered by others. Thomas Jefferson thought that only in a society of small farmers could the virtues flourish; and Adam Ferguson with a good deal more sophistication saw the institutions of modern commercial society as endangering at least some traditional virtues. It is Ferguson's type of sociology which is the empirical counterpart of the conceptual account of the virtues which I have given, a sociology which aspires to lay bare the empirical, causal connection between virtues, practices, and institutions. For this kind of conceptual account has strong empirical implications; it provides an explanatory scheme which can be tested in particular cases. Moreover my thesis has empirical content in another way, it does entail that without the virtues there could be a recognition only of what I have called external goods and not at all of internal goods in the context of practices. And in any society which recognised only external goods, competitiveness would be the dominant and even exclusive feature. We have a brilliant portrait of such a society in Hobbes's account of the state of nature; and Professor Turnbull's report of the fate of the Ik suggests that social reality does in the most horrifying way confirm both my thesis and Hobbes's.

Virtues then stand in a different relationship to external and to internal goods. The possession of the virtues—and not only of their semblance and simulacra—is necessary to achieve the latter; yet the possession of the virtues may perfectly well hinder us in achieving external goods. I need to emphasise at this point that external goods genuinely are goods. Not only are they characteristic objects of human desire whose allocation is what gives point to the virtues of justice and generosity, but no one can despise them altogether without a certain hypocrisy. Yet notoriously the cultivation of truthfulness, justice, and courage will often, the world being what it contingently is, bar us from being rich or famous or powerful. Thus although we may hope that we can not only achieve the standards of excellence and the internal goods of certain practices by possessing the virtues *and* become rich, famous and powerful, the virtues are always a potential stumbling block to this comfortable ambition. We should therefore expect that, if in a particular society the pursuit of external goods were to become dominant, the concept of the virtues might suffer first attrition and then perhaps something near total effacement, although simulacra might abound.

The time has come to ask the question of how far this partial account of a core conception of the virtues—and I need to emphasise that all that I have offered so far is the first stage of such an account—is faithful to the tradition which I delineated. How far, for example, and in what ways is it Aristotelian? It is—happily—not Aristotelian in two ways in which a good deal of the rest of the tradition also dissents from Aristotle. First, although this account of the virtues is teleological, it does not require the identification of any teleology in nature, and hence it does not require any allegiance to Aristotle's metaphysical biology. And secondly, just because of the multiplicity of human practices and the consequent multiplicity of goods in the pursuit of which the virtues may be exercised—goods which will often be contingently incompatible and which will therefore make rival claims upon our allegiance—conflict will not spring solely from flaws in individual character. But it was just on these two matters that Aristotle's account of the virtues seemed most vulnerable; hence if it turns out to be the case that this socially teleological account can support Aristotle's general account of the virtues as well as does his own biologically teleological account, these differences from Aristotle himself may well be regarded as strengthening rather than weakening the case for a generally Aristotelian standpoint.

There are at least three ways in which the account that I have given *is* clearly Aristotelian. First it requires for its completion a cogent elaboration of just those distinctions and concepts which Aristotle's account requires: voluntariness, the distinction between the intellectual virtues and the virtues of character, the relationship of both to natural abilities and to the passions and the structure of practical reasoning. On every one of these topics something very like Aristotle's view has to be defended, if my own account is to be plausible.

Secondly my account can accommodate an Aristotelian view of pleasure and enjoyment, whereas it is interestingly irreconcilable with any utilitarian view and more particularly with Franklin's account of the virtues. We can approach these questions by considering how to reply to someone who, having considered my account of the differences between goods internal to and goods external to a practice required into which class, if either, does pleasure or enjoyment fall? The answer is, 'Some types of pleasure into one, some into the other.'

Someone who achieves excellence in a practice, who plays chess or football well, or who carries through an enquiry in physics or an experimental mode in painting with success, characteristically enjoys his achievement and his activity in achieving. So does someone who, although not breaking the limit of achievement, plays or thinks or acts in a way that leads toward such a breaking of limit. As Aristotle says, the enjoyment of the activity and the enjoyment of achievement are not the ends at which the agent aims, but the enjoyment supervenes upon the successful activity in such a way that the activity achieved and the activity enjoyed are one and the same state. Hence to aim at the one is to aim at the other; and hence also it is easy to confuse the pursuit of excellence with the pursuit of enjoyment *in this specific sense.* This particular confusion is harmless enough; what is not harmless is the confusion of enjoyment *in this specific sense* with other forms of pleasure.

For certain kinds of pleasure are of course external goods, along with prestige, status, power, and money. Not all pleasure is the enjoyment supervening upon achieved activity; some is the pleasure of psychological or physical states independent of all activity. Such states—for example that produced on a normal palate by the closely successive and thereby blended sensations of Colchester oyster, cayenne pepper and Veuve Cliquot—may be sought as external goods, as external rewards which may be purchased by money or received in virtue of prestige. Hence the pleasures are categorised neatly and appropriately by the classification into internal and external goods.

It is just this classification which can find no place within Franklin's account of the virtues which is formed entirely in terms of external relationships and external goods. Thus although by this stage of the argument it is possible to claim that my account does capture a conception of the virtues which is at the core of the particular ancient and medieval tradition which I have delineated, it is equally clear that there is more than one possible conception of the virtues and that Franklin's standpoint and indeed any utilitarian standpoint is such that to accept it will entail rejecting the tradition and *vice versa*.

One crucial point of incompatibility was noted long ago by D. H. Lawrence. When Franklin asserts, 'Rarely use venery but for health or offspring . . . ,' Lawrence replies, 'Never *use* venery.' It is of the character of a virtue that in order that it be effective in producing the internal goods which are the rewards of the virtues, it should be exercised without regard to consequences. For it turns out to be the case that—and this is in part at least one more empirical factual claim—although the virtues are just those qualities which tend to lead to the achievement of a certain class of goods, none the less unless we practice them irrespective of whether in any particular set of contingent circumstances they will produce those goods or not, we cannot possess them at all. We cannot be genuinely courageous or truthful and be so only on occasion. Moreover, as we have seen, cultivation of the virtues always may and often does hinder the achievement of those external goods which are the mark of worldly success. The road to success in Philadelphia and the road to heaven may not coincide after all.

Furthermore we are now able to specify one crucial difficulty for *any* version of utilitarianism—in addition to those which I noticed earlier.

Utilitarianism cannot accommodate the distinction between goods internal to and goods external to a practice. Not only is that distinction marked by none of the classical utilitarians—it cannot be found in Bentham's writings nor in those of either of the Mills or of Sidgwick—but internal goods and external goods are not commensurable with each other. Hence the notion of summing goods—and *a fortiori* in the light of what I have said about kinds of pleasure and enjoyment the notion of summing happiness—in terms of one single formula or conception of utility, whether it is Franklin's or Bentham's or Mill's, makes no sense. None the less we ought to note that although *this* distinction is alien to J. S. Mill's thought, it is plausible and in no way patronising to suppose that something like this is the distinction which he was trying to make in *Utilitarianism* when he distinguished between 'higher' and 'lower' pleasures. At the most we can say 'something like this'; for J. S. Mill's upbringing had given him a limited view of human life and powers, had unfitted him, for example, for appreciating games just because of the way it had fitted him for appreciating philosophy. None the less the notion that the pursuit of excellence in a way that extends human powers is at the heart of human life is instantly recognisable as at home in not only J. S. Mill's political and social thought but also in his and Mrs. Taylor's life. Were I to choose human exemplars of certain of the virtues as I understand them, there would of course be many names to name, those of St. Benedict and St. Francis of Assisi and St. Theresa *and* those of Frederick Engels and Eleanor Marx and Leon Trotsky among them. But that of John Stuart Mill would have to be there as certainly as any other.

Thirdly my account is Aristotelian in that it links evaluation and explanation in a characteristically Aristotelian way. From an Aristotelian standpoint to identify certain actions as manifesting or failing to manifest a virtue or virtues is never only to evaluate; it is also to take the first step toward explaining why those actions rather than some others were performed. Hence for an

Aristotelian quite as much as for a Platonist the fate of a city or an individual can be explained by citing the injustice of a tyrant or the courage of its defenders. Indeed without allusion to the place that justice and injustice, courage and cowardice play in human life, very little will be genuinely explicable. It follows that many of the explanatory projects of the modern social sciences, a methodological canon of which is the separation of 'the facts' . . . from all evaluation, are bound to fail. For the fact that someone was or failed to be courageous or just cannot be recognised as 'a fact' by those who accept that methodological canon. The account of the virtues which I have given is completely at one with Aristotle's on this point. But now the question may be raised: your account may be in many respects Aristotelian, but is it not in some respects false? Consider the following important objection.

I have defined the virtues partly in terms of their place in practices. But surely, it may be suggested, some practices—that is, some coherent human activities which answer to the description of what I have called a practice—are evil. So in discussions by some moral philosophers of this type of account of the virtues, it has been suggested that torture and sadomasochistic sexual activities might be examples of practices. But how can a disposition be a virtue if it is the kind of disposition which sustains practices and some practices issue in evil? My answer to this objection falls into two parts.

First I want to allow that there *may* be practices—in the sense in which I understand the concept—which simply *are* evil. I am far from convinced that there are, and I do not in fact believe that either torture or sadomasochistic sexuality answers to the description of a practice which my account of the virtues employs. But I do not want to rest my case on this lack of conviction, especially since it is plain that as a matter of contingent fact many types of practice may on particular occasions be productive of evil. For the range of practices includes the arts, the sciences, and certain types of intellectual and athletic games. And it is at once obvious that any of these may under certain conditions be a source of evil: the desire to excel and to win can corrupt; a man may be so engrossed by his painting that he neglects his family; what was initially an honourable resort to war can issue in savage cruelty. But what follows from this?

It certainly is not the case that my account entails *either* that we ought to excuse or condone such evils or that whatever flows from a virtue is right. I do have to allow that courage sometimes sustains injustice, that loyalty has been known to strengthen a murderous aggressor, and that generosity has sometimes weakened the capacity to do good. But to deny this would be to fly in the face of just those empirical facts which I invoked in criticising Aquinas's account of the unity of the virtues. That the virtues need initially to be defined and explained with reference to the notion of a practice thus in no way entails approval of all practices in all circumstances. That the virtues—as the objection itself presupposed—*are* defined not in terms of good and right practices, but of practices, does not entail or imply that practices as actually carried through at particular times and places do not stand in need of moral criticism. And the resources for such criticism are not lacking. There is in the first place no inconsistency in appealing to the requirements of a virtue to criticise a practice. Justice may be initially defined as a disposition which in its particular way is necessary to sustain practices; it does not follow that in pursuing the requirements of a practice violations of justice are not to be condemned. Moreover I already pointed out . . . that a morality of virtues requires as its counterpart a conception of moral law. Its requirements too have to be met by practices. But, it may be asked, does not all this imply that more needs to be said about the place of practices in some larger moral context? Does not this at least suggest that there is more to the core concept of a virtue than can be spelled out in terms of practices? I have after all emphasised that the scope of any virtue in human life extends beyond the practices in terms of which it is initially defined. What then is the place of the virtues in the larger arenas of human life?

I stressed earlier that any account of the virtues in terms of practices could be only a partial and first account. What is required to complement it? The most notable difference so far between my account and any account that could be called Aristotelian is that although I have in no way restricted the exercise of the virtues to the context of practices, it is in terms of practices that I have located their point and function, whereas Aristotle locates that point and function in terms of the notion of a type of whole human life which can be called good. And it does seem that the question 'What would a human being lack who lacked the virtues?' must be given a kind of answer which goes beyond anything which I have said so far. For such an individual would not merely fail *in a variety of particular ways* in respect of the kind of excellence which can be achieved through participation in practices and in respect of the kind of human relationship required to sustain such excellence. His own life *viewed as a whole* would perhaps be defective; it would not be the kind of life which someone would describe in trying to answer the question 'What is the best kind of life for this kind of man or woman to live?' And that question cannot be answered without at least raising Aristotle's own question, 'What is the good life for man?' Consider three ways in which a human life informed only by the conception of the virtues sketched so far would be defective.

It would be pervaded, first of all, by *too many* conflicts and *too much* arbitrariness. I argued earlier that it is a merit of an account of the virtues in terms of a multiplicity of goods that it allows for the possibility of tragic conflict in a way in which Aristotle's does not. But it may also produce even in the life of someone who is virtuous and disciplined too many occasions when one allegiance points in one direction, another in another. The claims of one practice may be incompatible with another in such a way that one may find oneself oscillating in an arbitrary way, rather than making rational choices. So it seems to have been with

T. E. Lawrence. Commitment to sustaining the kind of community in which the virtues can flourish may be incompatible with the devotion which a particular practice—of the arts, for example—requires. So there may be tensions between the claims of family life and those of the arts—the problem that Gauguin solved or failed to solve by fleeing to Polynesia; or between the claims of politics and those of the arts—the problem that Lenin solved or failed to solve by refusing to listen to Beethoven.

If the life of the virtues is continuously fractured by choices in which one allegiance entails the apparently arbitrary renunciation of another, it may seem that the goods internal to practices do after all derive their authority from our individual choices; for when different goods summon in different and in incompatible directions, 'I' have to choose between their rival claims. The modern self with its criterionless choices apparently reappears in the alien context of what was claimed to be an Aristotelian world. This accusation might be rebutted in part by returning to the question of why both goods and virtues do have authority in our lives and repeating what was said earlier in this chapter. But this reply would be only partly successful; the distinctively modern notion of choice would indeed have reappeared, even if with a more limited scope for its exercise than it has usually claimed.

Secondly without an overriding conception of the *telos* of a whole human life, conceived as a unity, our conception of certain individual virtues has to remain partial and incomplete. Consider two examples. Justice, on an Aristotelian view, is defined in terms of giving each person his or her due or desert. To deserve well is to have contributed in some substantial way to the achievement of those goods the sharing of which and the common pursuit of which provide foundations for human community. But the goods internal to practices, including the goods internal to the practice of making and sustaining forms of community, need to be ordered and evaluated in some way if we are to assess relative desert. Thus only substantive application of an Aristotelian concept of justice requires an understanding of goods and of the good that goes beyond the multiplicity of goods which inform practices. As with justice, so also with patience. Patience is the virtue of waiting attentively without complaint, but not of waiting thus for anything at all. To treat patience as a virtue presupposes some adequate answer to the question: waiting for what? Within the context of practices a partial, although for many purposes adequate, answer can be given. The patience of a craftsman with refractory material, of a teacher with a slow pupil, of a politician in negotiations, are all species of patience. But what if the material is just too refractory, the pupil too slow, the negotiations too frustrating? Ought we always at a certain point just to give up in the interests of the practice itself? The medieval exponents of the virtue of patience claimed that there are certain types of situations in which the virtue of patience requires that I do not ever give up on some person or task, situations in which, as they would have put it, I am required to embody in my attitude to that person or task something of the patient attitude of God toward his creation. But this could only be so if patience served some overriding good, some *telos* which warranted putting other goods in a subordinate place. Thus it turns out that the content of the virtue of patience depends on how we order various goods in a hierarchy and *a fortiori* on whether we are able rationally so to order these particular goods.

I have suggested so far that unless there is a *telos* which transcends the limited goods of practices by constituting the good of a whole human life, the good of a human life conceived as a unity, it will be the case *both* that a certain subversive arbitrariness will invade the moral life *and* that we shall be unable to specify the context of certain virtues adequately. These two considerations are reinforced by a third: that there is at least one virtue recognised by the tradition which cannot be specified at all except with reference to the wholeness of a human life—the virtue of integrity or constancy. 'Purity of heart,' said Kierkegaard, 'is to will one thing.' This notion of singleness of purpose in a whole life can have no application unless that of a whole life does.

Note

1. *Phronêsis* is the Greek word standing broadly for practical wisdom. [Editor]

The Conscience of Huckleberry Finn

JONATHAN BENNETT

Jonathan Bennett is professor of philosophy, emeritus, at Syracuse University. He is the author of several books, including Rationality *(1964),* Linguistic Behaviour *(1976),* A Study of Spinoza's Ethics *(1984) and* Events and Their Names *(1988).*

What is the role of sympathy in moral judgment? Bennett draws our attention to three people who dealt with their sympathies in different ways. Huckleberry Finn allowed himself to be guided by his sympathies, thereby overriding his "obligation" to turn in the runaway slave, Jim. The Nazi leader Heinrich Himmler successfully struggled against his sympathies in doing his "moral duty" in sending Jews to concentration camps. The great Puritan theologian Jonathan Edwards steeled his heart against having any sympathies for the damned, since he believed that their punishment was just. Bennett calls the morality of all three men "bad morality" and argues that sometimes our sympathies are better guides to moral action than our principles. We ought to give our sympathies great weight in deciding on our moral duty.

I

In this paper, I shall present not just the conscience of Huckleberry Finn but those of two others as well. One of them is the conscience of Heinrich Himmler. Himmler became a Nazi in 1923; he served drably and quietly, but well, and was rewarded with increasing responsibility and power. At the peak of his career he held many offices and commands, of which the most powerful was that of leader of the SS—the principal police

Reprinted from "The Conscience of Huckleberry Finn," *Philosophy* 49 (1974), by permission of Cambridge University Press.

force of the Nazi regime. In this capacity Himmler commanded the whole concentration camp system and was responsible for the execution of the so-called final solution of the Jewish problem. It is important for my purposes that this piece of social engineering should be thought of not abstractly but in concrete terms of Jewish families being marched to what they thought were bathhouses, to the accompaniment of loud-speaker renditions of extracts from *The Merry Widow* and *Tales of Hoffmann*, there to be choked to death by poisonous gases. Altogether, Himmler succeeded in murdering about four and a half million of them, as well as several million gentiles, mainly Poles and Russians.

The other conscience to be discussed is that of the Calvinist theologian and philosopher Jonathan Edwards. He lived in the first half of the eighteenth century, and has a good claim to be considered America's first serious and considerable philosophical thinker. He was for many years a widely renowned preacher and Congregationalist minister in New England; in 1748 a dispute with his congregation led him to resign (he couldn't accept their view that unbelievers should be admitted to the Lord's Supper in the hope that it would convert them); for some years after that he worked as a missionary, preaching to Indians through an interpreter; then in 1758 he accepted the presidency of what is now Princeton University, and within two months died from a smallpox inoculation. Along the way he wrote some first-rate philosophy; his book attacking the notion of free will is still sometimes read. Why I should be interested in Edwards's *conscience* will be explained in due course.

I shall use Heinrich Himmler, Jonathan Edwards, and Huckleberry Finn to illustrate different aspects of a single theme, namely the relationship between *sympathy* on the one hand and *bad morality* on the other.

II

All that I can mean by a "bad morality" is a morality whose principles I deeply disapprove of. When I call a morality bad, I cannot prove that mine is better; but when I here call any morality bad, I think you will agree with me that it is bad; and that is all I need.

There could be dispute as to whether the springs of someone's actions constitute a *morality*. I think, though, that we must admit that someone who acts in ways which conflict grossly with our morality may nevertheless have a morality of his own—a set of principles of action which he sincerely assents to, so that for him the problem of acting well or rightly or in obedience to conscience is the problem of conforming to *those* principles. The problem of conscientiousness can arise as acutely for a bad morality as for any other: Rotten principles may be as difficult to keep as decent ones.

As for "sympathy" I use this term to cover every sort of fellow-feeling, as when one feels pity over someone's loneliness, or horrified compassion over his pain, or when one feels a shrinking reluctance to act in a way which will bring misfortune to someone else. These *feelings* must not be confused with *moral judgments*. My sympathy for someone in distress may lead me to help him, or even to think that I ought to help him; but in itself it is not a judgment about what I ought to do but just a *feeling* for him in his plight. We shall get some light on the difference between feelings and moral judgments when we consider Huckleberry Finn.

Obviously, feelings can impel one to action, and so can moral judgments; and in a particular case sympathy and morality may pull in opposite directions. This can happen not just with bad moralities, but also with good ones like yours and mine. For example, a small child, sick and miserable, clings tightly to his mother and screams in terror when she tries to pass him over to the doc-

tor to be examined. If the mother gave way to her sympathy, that is to her feeling for the child's misery and fright, she would hold it close and not let the doctor come near; but don't we agree that it might be wrong for her to act on such a feeling? Quite generally, then, anyone's moral principles may apply to a particular situation in a way which runs contrary to the particular thrusts of fellow-feeling that he has in that situation. My immediate concern is with sympathy in relation to bad morality, but not because such conflicts occur only when the morality is bad.

Now, suppose that someone who accepts a bad morality is struggling to make himself act in accordance with it in a particular situation where his sympathies pull him another way. He sees the struggle as one between doing the right, conscientious thing, and acting wrongly and weakly, like the mother who won't let the doctor come near her sick, frightened baby. Since we don't accept this person's morality, we may see the situation very differently, thoroughly disapproving of the action he regards as the right one, and endorsing the action which from his point of view constitutes weakness and backsliding.

Conflicts between sympathy and bad morality won't always be like this, for we won't disagree with every single dictate of a bad morality. Still, it can happen in the way I have described, with the agent's right action being our wrong one, and vice versa. That is just what happens in a certain episode in Chapter 16 of *The Adventures of Huckleberry Finn*, an episode which brilliantly illustrates how fiction can be instructive about real life.

III

Huck Finn has been helping his slave friend Jim to run away from Miss Watson, who is Jim's owner. In their raft-journey down the Mississippi River, they are near to the place at which Jim will become legally free. Now let Huck take over the story:

Jim said it made him all over trembly and feverish to be so close to freedom. Well I can tell you it made me all over trembly and feverish, too, to hear him, because I begun to get it through my head that he *was* most free—and who was to blame for it? Why, *me.* I couldn't get that out of my conscience, no how nor no way. . . . It hadn't ever come home to me, before, what this thing was that I was doing. But now it did; and it stayed with me, and scorched me more and more. I tried to make out to myself that *I* warn't to blame, because I didn't run Jim off from his rightful owner; but it warn't no use, conscience up and say, every time: "But you knowed he was running for his freedom, and you could a paddled ashore and told somebody." That was so—I couldn't get around that, no way. That was where it pinched. Conscience says to me: "What had poor Miss Watson done to you, that you could see her nigger go off right under your eyes and never say one single word? What did that poor old woman do to you, that you could treat her so mean? . . ." I got to feeling so mean and miserable I most wished I was dead.

Jim speaks his plan to save up to buy his wife, and then his children, out of slavery; and he adds that if the children cannot be bought he will arrange to steal them. Huck is horrified:

Thinks I, this is what comes of my not thinking. Here was this nigger which I had as good as helped to run away, coming right out flat-footed and saying he would steal his children—children that belonged to a man I didn't even know; a man that hadn't ever done me no harm.

I was sorry to hear Jim say that, it was such a lowering of him. My conscience got to stirring me up hotter than ever, until at last I says to it: "Let up on me—it ain't too late, yet—I'll paddle ashore at first light, and tell." I felt easy, and happy, and light as a feather, right off. All my troubles was gone.

This is bad morality all right. In his earliest years Huck wasn't taught any principles, and the only one he has encountered since then are those of

rural Missouri, in which slave-owning is just one kind of ownership and is not subject to critical pressure. It hasn't occurred to Huck to question those principles. So the action, to us abhorrent, of turning Jim in to the authorities presents itself *clearly* to Huck as the right thing to do.

For us, both morality and sympathy would dictate helping Jim to escape. If we felt any conflict, it would have both of these on one side and something else on the other—greed for a reward, or fear of punishment. But Huck's morality conflicts with his sympathy, that is, with his unargued, natural feeling for his friend. The conflict starts when Huck sets off in the canoe toward the shore, pretending that he is going to reconnoiter, but really planning to turn Jim in:

As I shoved off, [Jim] says: "Pooty soon I'll be a-shout'n for joy, en I'll say, it's all on accounts o' Huck I's a free man . . . Jim won't ever forgit you, Huck; you's de bes' fren' Jim's ever had; en you's de *only* fren' old Jim's got now."

I was paddling off, all in a sweat to tell on him; but when he says this, it seemed to kind of take the tuck all out of me. I went along slow then, and I warn't right down certain whether I was glad I started or whether I warn't. When I was fifty yards off, Jim says:

"Dah you goes, de ole true Huck; de on'y white genlman dat ever kep' his promise to ole Jim." Well, I just felt sick. But I says, I *got* to do it—I can't get *out* of it.

In the upshot, sympathy wins over morality. Huck hasn't the strength of will to do what he sincerely thinks he ought to do. Two men hunting for runaway slaves ask him whether the man on his raft is black or white:

I didn't answer up prompt. I tried to, but the words wouldn't come. I tried, for a second or two, to brace up and out with it, but I warn't man enough—hadn't the spunk of a rabbit. I see I was weakening; so I just give up trying, and up and says: "He's white."

So Huck enables Jim to escape, thus acting weakly and wickedly—he thinks. In this conflict between sympathy and morality, sympathy wins.

One critic has cited this episode in support of the statement that Huck suffers "excruciating moments of wavering between honesty and respectability." That is hopelessly wrong, and I agree with the perceptive comment on it by another critic, who says:

The conflict waged in Huck is much more serious: He scarcely cares for respectability and never hesitates to relinquish it, but he does care for honesty and gratitude—and both honesty and gratitude require that he should give Jim up. It is not, in Huck, honesty at war with respectability but love and compassion for Jim struggling against his conscience. His decision is for Jim and hell: a right decision made in the mental chains that Huck never breaks. His concern for Jim is and remains *irrational*. Huck finds many reasons for giving Jim up and none for stealing him. To the end Huck sees his compassion for Jim as a weak, ignorant, and wicked felony.[1]

That is precisely correct—and it can have that virtue only because Mark Twain wrote the episode with such unerring precision. The crucial point concerns *reasons,* which all occur on one side of the conflict. On the side of conscience we have principles, arguments, considerations, ways of looking at things:

"It hadn't ever come home to me before what I was doing"
"I tried to make out that I warn't to blame"
"Conscience said 'But you knowed . . .'—I couldn't get around that"
"What had poor Miss Watson done to you?"
"This is what comes of my not thinking"
". . . children that belonged to a man I didn't even know"

On the other side, the side of feeling, we get nothing like that. When Jim rejoices in Huck, as his only friend, Huck doesn't consider the claims of friendship or have the situation "come home" to him in a different light. All that happens is: "When he says this, it seemed to kind of take the tuck all out of me. I went along slow then, and I warn't right down certain whether I was glad I started or whether I warn't." Again, Jim's words about Huck's "promise" to him don't give Huck any *reason* for changing his plan: In his morality promises to slaves probably don't count. Their effect on him is of a different kind: "Well, I just felt sick." And when the moment for final decision comes, Huck doesn't weigh up pros and cons: he simply *fails* to do what he believes to be right—he isn't strong enough, hasn't "the spunk of a rabbit." This passage in the novel is notable not just for its finely wrought irony, with Huck's weakness of will leading him to do the right thing, but also for its masterly handling of the difference between general moral principles and particular unreasoned emotional pulls.

IV

Consider now another case of bad morality in conflict with human sympathy: the case of the odious Himmler. Here, from a speech he made to some SS generals, is an indication of the content of his morality:

What happens to a Russian, to a Czech, does not interest me in the slightest. What the nations can offer in the way of good blood of our type, we will take, if necessary by kidnapping their children and raising them here with us. Whether nations live in prosperity or starve to death like cattle interests me only in so far as we need them as slaves to our *Kultur;* otherwise it is of no interest to me. Whether 10,000 Russian females fall down from exhaustion while digging an antitank ditch interests me only in so far as the antitank ditch for Germany is finished.[2]

But has this a moral basis at all? And if it has, was there in Himmler's own mind any conflict between morality and sympathy? Yes, there was. Here is more from the same speech:

> I also want to talk to you quite frankly on a very grave matter . . . I mean . . . the extermination of the Jewish race. . . . Most of you must know what it means when 100 corpses are lying side by side, or 500, or 1,000. To have stuck it out and at the same time—apart from exceptions caused by human weakness—to have remained decent fellows, that is what has made us hard. This is a page of glory in our history which has never been written and is never to be written.

Himmler saw his policies as being hard to implement while still retaining one's human sympathies—while still remaining a "decent fellow." He is saying that only the weak take the easy way out and just squelch their sympathies, and is praising the stronger and more glorious course of retaining one's sympathies while acting in violation of them. In the same spirit, he ordered that when executions were carried out in concentration camps, those responsible "are to be influenced in such a way as to suffer no ill effect in their character and mental attitude." A year later he boasted that the SS had wiped out the Jews

> without our leaders and their men suffering any damage in their minds and souls. The danger was considerable, for there was only a narrow path between the Scylla of their becoming heartless ruffians unable any longer to treasure life, and the Charybdis of their becoming soft and suffering nervous breakdowns.

And there really can't be any doubt that the basis of Himmler's policies was a set of principles which constituted his morality—a sick, bad, wicked *morality*. He described himself as caught in "the old tragic conflict between will and obligation." And when his physician Kersten protested at the intention to destroy the Jews, saying that the suffering involved was "not to be contemplated," Kersten reports that Himmler replied that

He knew that it would mean much suffering for the Jews. . . . "It is the curse of greatness that it must step over dead bodies to create new life. Yet we must . . . cleanse the soil or it will never bear fruit. It will be a great burden for me to bear."

This, I submit, is the language of morality.

So in this case, tragically, bad morality won out over sympathy. I am sure that many of Himmler's killers did extinguish their sympathies, becoming "heartless ruffians" rather than "decent fellows"; but not Himmler himself. Although his policies ran against the human grain to a horrible degree, he did not sandpaper down his emotional surfaces so that there was no grain there, allowing his actions to slide along smoothly and easily. He did, after all, bear his hideous burden, and even paid a price for it. He suffered a variety of nervous and physical disabilities, including nausea and stomach-convulsions, and Kersten was doubtless right in saying that these were "the expression of a psychic division which extended over his whole life."

This same division must have been present in some of those officials of the Church who ordered heretics to be tortured so as to change their theological opinions. Along with the brutes and the cold careerists, there must have been some who cared, and who suffered from the conflict between their sympathies and their bad morality.

V

In the conflict between sympathy and bad morality, then, the victory may go to sympathy as in the case of Huck Finn, or to morality as in the case of Himmler.

Another possibility is that the conflict may be avoided by giving up, or not ever having, those sympathies which might interfere with one's principles. That seems to have been the case with Jonathan Edwards. I am afraid that I shall be doing an injustice to Edwards's many virtues, and to his great intellectual energy and inventiveness; for my concern is only with the worst thing about him—namely his morality, which was worse than Himmler's.

According to Edwards, God condemns some men to an eternity of unimaginably awful pain, though he arbitrarily spares others—"arbitrarily" because none deserve to be spared:

> Natural men are held in the hand of God over the pit of hell; they have deserved the fiery pit, and are already sentenced to it; and God is dreadfully provoked, his anger is as great toward them as to those that are actually suffering the executions of the fierceness of his wrath in hell . . . ; the devil is waiting for them, hell is gaping for them, the flames gather and flash about them, and would fain lay hold on them . . . ; and . . . there are no means within reach that can be any security to them. . . . All that preserves them is the mere arbitrary will, and unconvenanted unobliged forebearance of an incensed God.[3]

Notice that he says "they have deserved the fiery pit." Edwards insists that men *ought* to be condemned to eternal pain; and his position isn't that this is right because God wants it, but rather that God wants it because it is right. For him, moral standards exist independently of God, and God can be assessed in the light of them (and of course found to be perfect). For example, he says:

> They deserve to be cast into hell; so that . . . justice never stands in the way, it makes no objection against God's using his power at any moment to destroy them. Yea, on the contrary, justice calls aloud for an infinite punishment of their sins.

Elsewhere, he gives elaborate arguments to show that God is acting justly in damning sinners. For example, he argues that a punishment should be exactly as bad as the crime being punished; God is infinitely excellent; so any crime against him is infinitely bad; and so eternal damnation is exactly right as a punishment—it is infinite, but, as Edwards is careful also to say, it is "no more than infinite."

Of course, Edwards himself didn't torment the damned; but the question still arises of whether his sympathies didn't conflict with his *approval* of eternal torment. Didn't he find it painful to contemplate any fellow-human's being tortured forever? Apparently not:

> The God that holds you over the pit of hell, much as one holds a spider or some loathsome insect over the fire, abhors you, and is dreadfully provoked . . . he is of purer eyes than to bear to have you in his sight; you are ten thousand times so abominable in his eyes as the most hateful venomous serpent is in ours.

When God is presented as being as misanthropic as that, one suspects misanthropy in the theologian. This suspicion is increased when Edwards claims that "the saints in glory will . . . understand how terrible the sufferings of the damned are; yet . . . will not be sorry for [them]."[4] He bases this partly on a view of human nature whose ugliness he seems not to notice:

> The seeing of the calamities of others tends to heighten the sense of our own enjoyments. When the saints in glory, therefore, shall see the doleful state of the damned, how will this heighten their sense of the blessedness of their own state. . . . When they shall see how miserable others of their fellow-creatures are . . . when they shall see the smoke of their torment . . . and hear their dolorous shrieks and cries, and consider that they in the mean time are in the most blissful state, and shall surely be in it to all eternity; how they will rejoice!

I hope this is less than the whole truth! His other main point about why the saints will rejoice to see the torments of the damned is that it is *right* that they should do so:

> The heavenly inhabitants . . . will have no love nor pity to the damned. . . . [This will not show] a want of spirit of love in them for the heavenly inhabitants will know that it is not fit that they should love [the damned] because they will

know then, that God has no love to them, nor pity for them.

The implication that *of course* one can adjust one's feelings of pity so that they conform to the dictates of some authority—doesn't this suggest that ordinary human sympathies played only a small part in Edwards's life?

VI

Huck Finn, whose sympathies are wide and deep, could never avoid the conflict in that way; but he is determined to avoid it, and so he opts for the only other alternative he can see—to give up morality altogether. After he has tricked the slave-hunters, he returns to the raft and undergoes a peculiar crisis:

I got aboard the raft, feeling bad and low, because I knowed very well I had done wrong, and I see it warn't no use for me to try to learn to do right; a body that don't get *started* right when he's little, ain't got no show—when the pinch comes there ain't nothing to back him up and keep him to his work, and so he gets beat. Then I thought a minute, and says to myself, hold on—s'pose you'd a done right and give Jim up; would you feel better than what you do now? No, says I, I'd feel bad—I'd feel just the same way I do now. Well, then, says I, what's the use you learning to do right, when it's troublesome to do right and ain't no trouble to do wrong, and the wages is just the same? I was stuck. I couldn't answer that. So I reckoned I wouldn't bother no more about it, but after this always do whichever come handiest at the time.

Huck clearly cannot conceive of having any morality except the one he has learned—too late, he thinks—from his society. He is not entirely a prisoner of that morality, because he does after all reject it; but for him that is a decision to relinquish morality as such; he cannot envisage revising his morality, altering its content in the face of the various pressures to which it is subject, including pressures from his sympathies. For example, he does not begin to approach the thought that slavery should be rejected on moral grounds, or the thought that what he is doing is not theft because a person cannot be owned and therefore cannot be stolen.

The basic trouble is that he cannot or will not engage in abstract intellectual operations of any sort. In Chapter 33 he finds himself "feeling to blame, somehow" for something he knows he had no hand in; he assumes that this feeling is a deliverance of conscience; and this confirms him in his belief that conscience shouldn't be listened to:

It don't make no difference whether you do right or wrong, a person's conscience ain't got no sense, and just goes for him *anyway*. If I had a yaller dog that didn't know no more than a person's conscience does, I would poison him. It takes up more than all of a person's insides, and yet ain't no good, nohow.

That brisk, incurious dismissiveness fits well with the comprehensive rejection of morality back on the raft. But this is a digression.

On the raft, Huck decides not to live by principles, but just to do whatever "comes handiest at the time"—always acting according to the mood of the moment. Since the morality he is rejecting is narrow and cruel, and his sympathies are broad and kind, the results will be good. But moral principles are good to have, because they help to protect one from acting badly at moments when one's sympathies happen to be in abeyance. On the highest possible estimate of the role one's sympathies should have, one can still allow for principles as embodiments of one's best feelings, one's broadest and keenest sympathies. On that view, principles can help one across intervals when one's feelings are at less than their best, i.e. through periods of misanthropy or meanness or self-centeredness or depression or anger.

What Huck didn't see is that one can live by principles and yet have ultimate control over their content. And one way such control can be exercised is by checking one's principles in the light of one's sympathies. This is sometimes a pretty straightforward matter. It can happen that a certain moral principle becomes untenable—meaning literally that one cannot hold it any longer—because it conflicts intolerably with the pity or revulsion or whatever that one feels when one sees what the principle leads to. One's experience may play a large part here: Experiences evoke feelings, and feelings force one to modify principles. Something like this happened to the English poet Wilfred Owen, whose experiences in the First World War transformed him from an enthusiastic soldier into a virtual pacifist. I can't document his change of conscience in detail; but I want to present something which he wrote about the way experience can put pressure on morality.

The Latin poet Horace wrote that it is sweet and fitting (or right) to die for one's country— *dulce et decorum est pro patria mori*—and Owen wrote a fine poem about how experience could lead one to relinquish that particular moral principle.[5] He describes a man who is too slow donning his gas mask during a gas attack—"As under a green sea I saw him drowning," Owen says. The poem ends like this:

In all my dreams before my helpless sight
He plunges at me, guttering, choking, drowning.
If in some smothering dreams, you too could pace
Behind the wagon that we flung him in,
And watch the white eyes writhing in his face,
His hanging face, like a devil's sick of sin;
If you could hear, at every jolt, the blood
Come gargling from the froth-corrupted lungs.
Bitter as the end
Of vile, incurable sores on innocent tongues,—
My friend, you would not tell with such high zest
To children ardent for some desperate glory,
The old Lie; Dulce et decorum est
Pro patria mori.

There is a difficulty about drawing from all this

a moral for ourselves. I imagine that we agree in our rejection of slavery, eternal damnation, genocide, and uncritical patriotic self-abnegation; so we shall agree that Huck Finn, Jonathan Edwards, Heinrich Himmler, and the poet Horace would all have done well to bring certain of their principles under severe pressure from ordinary human sympathies. But then we can say this because we can say that all those are bad moralities, whereas we cannot look at our own moralities and declare them bad. This is not arrogance; It is obviously incoherent for someone to declare the system of moral principles that he *accepts* to be *bad*, just as one cannot coherently say of anything that one *believes* it but it is *false*.

Still, although I can't point to any of my beliefs and say "That is false," I don't doubt that some of my beliefs *are* false; and so I should try to remain open to correction. Similarly, I accept every single item in my morality—that is inevitable—but I am sure that my morality could be improved, which is to say that it could undergo changes which I should be glad of once I had made them. So I must try to keep my morality open to revision, exposing it to whatever valid pressures there are—including pressures from my sympathies.

I don't give my sympathies a blank check in advance. In a conflict between principle and sympathy, principles ought sometimes to win. For example, I think it was right to take part in the Second World War on the allied side; there were many ghastly individual incidents which might have led someone to doubt the rightness of his participation in that war; and I think it would have been right for such a person to keep his sympathies in a subordinate place on those occasions, not allowing them to modify his principles in such a way as to make a pacifist of him.

Still, one's sympathies should be kept as sharp and sensitive and aware as possible, and not only because they can sometimes affect one's principles or one's conduct or both. Owen, at any rate, says that feelings and sympathies are vital even when they can do nothing but bring pain and distress.

In another poem he speaks of the blessings of being numb in one's feelings: "Happy are the men who yet before they are killed/Can let their veins run cold," he says. These are the ones who do not suffer from any compassion which, as Owen puts it, "makes their feet/Sore on the alleys cobbled with their brothers." He contrasts these "happy" ones, who "lose all imagination," with himself and others "who with a thought besmirch/Blood over all our soul." Yet the poem's verdict goes against the "happy" ones. Owen does not say that they will act worse than the others whose souls are besmirched with blood because of their keen awareness of human suffering. He merely says that they are the losers because they have cut themselves off from the human condition:

By choice they made themselves immune
To pity and whatever moans in man
Before the last sea and the hapless stars;
Whatever mourns when many leave these shores;
Whatever shares
The eternal reciprocity of tears.

Notes

1. M. J. Sidnell, "Huck Finn and Jim," *The Cambridge Quarterly*, vol. 2, pp. 205–6.

2. Quoted in William L. Shirer, *The Rise and Fall of the Third Reich* (New York, 1960), pp. 937–38. Next quotation: ibid., p. 966. All further quotations relating to Himmler are from Roger Manwell and Heinrich Fraenkel, *Heinrich Himmler* (London, 1965), pp. 132, 197, 184 (twice), 187.

3. Vergilius Ferm (ed.), *Puritan Sage: Collected Writings of Jonathan Edwards* (New York, 1953), p. 370. Next three quotations: ibid., p. 366, p. 294 ("no more than infinite"), p. 372.

4. This and the next two quotations are from "The End of the Wicked Contemplated by the Righteous: Or, The Torments of the Wicked in Hell, No Occasion of Grief to the Saints in Heaven," from *The Works of President Edwards* (London, 1817), vol. 4, pp. 507–8, 511–12, and 509 respectively.

5. We are grateful to the Executors of the Estate of Harold Owen, and to Chatto and Windus Ltd. for permission to quote from Wilfred Owen's "Dulce et Decorum Est" and "Insensibility."

Virtue and Emotion

ROSALIND HURSTHOUSE

Rosalind Hursthouse is a professor of philosophy at the University of Auckland, New Zealand. She has done influential work in applied ethics, and she is a leading champion of virtue ethics. In the present selection, from her book On Virtue Ethics *(1999), Hursthouse proposes and defends a conception of how, within the framework of a virtue ethics, practical wisdom comports with the emotions. She brings Aristotelian virtue theory closer to Kantian insights than have past conceptions. There is significant overlap between concerns addressed by Hursthouse in this selection and concerns raised by Jonathan Bennett in selection VII.33.*

Now let us turn to the role emotions play in full virtue. I begin by stating, without argument, what I think an Aristotelian ought to mean, minimally, by 'the emotions are morally significant'. This is basically made up of three claims.

(1) The virtues (and vices) are morally significant.
(2) The virtues (and vices) are all dispositions not only to act, but to feel emotions, as *reactions* as well as impulses to action. (Aristotle says again and again that the virtues are concerned with actions *and* feelings.)
(3) In the person with the virtues, these emotions will be felt on the *right* occasions, towards the *right* people or objects, for the *right* reasons, where 'right' means 'correct', as in 'The right answer to "What is the capital of New Zealand?" is "Wellington".'

Reprinted by permission of the publisher from Rosalind Hursthouse, *On Virtue Ethics*, pp. 108–120. © 1999 by Oxford University Press.

We should note immediately that the second claim really does give something like a logically proper ground for the *general* claim '*the* emotions are morally significant'. It thereby stands in marked contrast to some rather weak literature which seeks to support that general claim by a piecemeal approach which at best justifies no more than 'a few emotions (love and sympathy, or regret and pride) are morally significant'.

We should note too that the claims in combination give some cash value to the view that the feeling of certain emotions on certain occasions has intrinsic *moral* value, rather than merely instrumental value or some other sort of intrinsic value. Feeling this emotion then could be said to have 'intrinsic moral value' simply in so far as it is the manifestation of virtue. It is here, I think, that the (initially, apparently rather minor) issue about regret should figure as significant. Cases of emerging, with regret, from distressing or tragic dilemmas are, in the context of 'the moral significance of the emotions', to be thought of as but some amongst a great range of situations in which we want to say 'The way to feel here/what one should feel about this/what anyone decent would feel about this/is . . .'. Another way to describe the very same fact would be that it has intrinsic moral value in so far as the emotional response had the right, i.e. correct, rational content.

Finally and most importantly, we should note that the third claim introduces the crucial notion of feeling emotions rightly or correctly, where that is a cognitive notion. When we recall that the agent with Humean benevolence, and children with natural virtue, notably fail to feel emotions correctly on every occasion, we are in a position to see that virtue is not merely a matter of being disposed to act well with a few dispositions to feel 'nice', sympathetic (or perhaps empathetic) reactions thrown in to make up the full weight. Just as Augustine's famous instruction 'Love, and do what you will' turns out not to be a license to follow one's heart, but to embody extremely stern directions concerning what really counts as love, so the claim that full virtue involves feeling emotions correctly makes it clear that this would not be possible (in general) without the influence of reason.

What account of the emotions allows this claim to be true? One account that will *not* allow for it is one that makes the emotions no part of our rational nature. And there is indeed much in Kant to suggest that, although he shares with Aristotle the view that we have not just one, but two principles of movement, in other respects his philosophical psychology is Humean. He seems committed to the view that our emotions or inclinations are no part of our rationality. They come from the non-rational, animal side of our nature; if they happen to prompt us to act in accordance with the judgements of reason about what ought to be done we are lucky; if they incline us against them we find life difficult, but their prompting us in the right direction is no mark or indication of their rationality. The emotions are not rational in any way.

A different account, with a tradition that dates back to the Stoics, has it that the emotions are indeed part of our rational nature, for they are, or are partially constituted by, judgements, at least some of which are evaluative. On the face of it, this account marries well with the claim that emotions may be had rightly or correctly; roughly, an emotion is had correctly when the judgement (or set of judgements) which (partially) constitutes it is true (or, perhaps, reasonable given the evidence available). As an enormous literature on this topic has made clear, this 'cognitive account' faces numerous difficulties; for my present purposes, it suffices to mention just two. One is the difficulty in finding a suitable judgement (or set of judgements)

to ascribe to someone who is only too aware of the fact that her emotion is irrational in some way, but is in the grip of it notwithstanding. I know perfectly well that the insect is harmless but am still terrified of it, that the tin-opener is not defying me and did not cut my thumb on purpose but am still furious with it, that my partner is a worthless skunk but I still love him, heaven help me. The second is that, even if we allow that toddlers and the higher animals can have some beliefs, there really is something very odd about maintaining that they make judgements, especially evaluative judgements; but unless they do, then, on the cognitive account, they do not have emotions either. These two objections might be summed up as one more general one; that on the cognitive account, the emotions are *too* rational, too akin to the judgements of theoretical reason.

What seems needed is an account which avoids these two extremes—of animal/non-rational and utterly rational. On Hume's, and Kant's, picture of human nature, there is no logical space between the two. But Aristotle's division of the parts of the soul into rational and non-rational is not so hard and fast. We may classify the desiderative part of the soul with the nutritive part, as non-rational, he says— but then we must divide the non-rational part of the soul in two, distinguishing the desiderative part by saying that it participates in reason as the nutritive soul does not. Alternatively, we may classify the desiderative with the reasoning part of the soul as rational—but then we must divide the rational part of the soul in two, and say that the desiderative listens to, or obeys, the reasoning part.[1]

So the Aristotelian picture of human nature creates a space for the emotions—in what is called the desiderative part of the soul—which allows them to be, shall we say, Janus-faced; animal and/or non-rational one face; rational the other. And this allows us to be struck—as surely we should be—not only by the fact that human beings are subject to some emotions which non-rational animals are also subject to, and not only by the fact that human beings are subject to some emotions that non-rational animals notably lack (for instance, pride, shame, and regret), but, much more significantly, by the way in which reason can radically transform an emotion that human beings certainly share with animals, such as fear. How very unlike the other animals human beings are when they endure agony, and risk their lives, for justice and truth, or are terrified by the prospect of university examinations; when they are ready to die for glory, but tremble at the prospect of humiliation. The emotion that in the other animals is essentially connected to physical self-preservation or preservation of the species can be transformed in human beings into an emotion connected with the preservation of what is *best,* most worth preserving, in us and our species. And the correctness (or incorrectness) of our view of that is an aspect of our rationality.

What then is an appropriate account of the emotions? The details need not concern us here; what will suffice, I believe, is the broad claim that the emotions involve ideas or images (or thoughts or perceptions) of good and evil, taking 'good' and 'evil' in their most general, generic sense, as the formal objects of pursuit and avoidance. (Readers who find 'good' and 'evil' odd in this context may substitute 'value' and 'disvalue'.)

Many philosophers have noticed the fact that our emotions involve ideas, or thoughts, of good and evil. Some use the phrase 'of pleasure and pain' as (supposedly) interchangeable with 'of good and evil'; others distinguish the phrases. Some emphasize the fact that (most) emotions are in part constituted by, or at least generate, a desire to do something, construing these desires as themselves involving ideas or thoughts, of good and evil (pleasure and pain). Hence it may be said that fear is in part, or generates, the desire to run away from something, this desire itself involving the idea of staying put as evil or painful; that love is in part, or generates, the desire to be with the loved one, this desire itself involving

the idea of being with the loved one as good or pleasant. Some emphasize the way the causes, or objects, of the emotions are, or must be, thought of, or perceived, or construed: something we fear or hate must be thought of, perceived as, evil (painful) in some way; something we hope for or love, as good (pleasant). Some, noting that the desires characteristic of (some of) the emotions actually involve the objects (or causes), introduce further complexity: hence hatred may be said to involve the idea that evil's coming to someone thought of as evil is (or would be) itself good; anger to involve the idea that evil's coming to someone who has caused evil is (or would be) itself good . . . and so on.

In short, there is much variety and disagreement, but a discernible common ground, namely the vague remark 'our emotions involve ideas, or thoughts, or perceptions, of good and evil', taking 'good' and 'evil' in their most general, generic, sense.[2]

In his otherwise admirable paper 'Morality and the Emotions', Bernard Willliams appears to overlook this point.[3] Seeking, in 1965, to explain why 'recent' moral philosophy in Britain had neglected the emotions, Williams found part of the answer to lie in the preceding and prevailing preoccupation with 'the most general features of moral language, or . . . evaluative language' and the consequent concentration on 'such very general terms as "good", "right" and "ought"'. This concentration, he said, 'has helped to push the emotions out of the picture', for '[i]f you aim to state the most general characteristics, and connexions of moral language, you will not find much to say about the emotions; because there are few, if any, *highly general* connexions between the emotions and moral language'.

But Williams was too kind to his predecessors and contemporaries; the highly general connection between the emotions and the very general terms 'good' and 'bad/evil' was sitting there, right under their noses, *manifest* in the accounts of, at least, Plato, Aristotle, the Stoics,

Aquinas, Descartes, Locke, and Hume. They left the emotions out of the picture not for lack of any general connection between them and the terms they were obsessed with, but because they fed on a very one-sided diet of examples.

Now note that the vague remark stating the general connection falls far short of the much more explicit claim that the emotions involve, or are, evaluative *judgements*. The burnt child fears the fire and is distressed by its mother's anger long before it is of an age where we can talk of its making judgements, evaluative or otherwise. Indeed, even the claim 'the emotions involve thoughts of good and evil', when applied to small children, has to be construed with some care. It signifies the appropriateness of our talking to them in terms of generic good and evil when responding to their manifested emotions, rather than the appropriateness of the ascription of views to them.

However, the vague remark is obviously related to the more explicit one, and, vague as it is, it is sufficient to ground the claim that no emotion *in us* is just the same as it is in the other animals. For, in virtue of our reason, we, unlike the other animals, draw the distinction between what appears to us to be so, and what is really so in language. Unlike the other animals we can express our ideas or thoughts or perceptions about generic good and evil in sentences which figure, in our languages, as expressions of how things appear to us to be—as beliefs which are up for assessment as true or false, correct or erroneous, reasonable or unreasonable.

The Education of the Emotions

Another fault of Williams's predecessors and (1965) contemporaries was that, though concentrating on 'the most general features of . . . evaluative language', they failed to think about the fact that such language has to be taught, and thereby failed to think about moral education and upbringing. We are taught to use sentences which contain the words (equivalent to) 'good'

and 'evil' and their cognates and species from a very early age, at the same time as we are taught how to conduct ourselves. And a central aspect of this teaching is the training of the emotions.

The immense complexity of the ways in which the emotions are trained, and values thereby inculcated, can be called to mind by considering a paradigm case of *bad* training, namely, the inculcation of racism.[4]

Recall, firstly, how extreme racism expresses itself in emotion, the way it generates not only hatred and contempt, but fear, anger, reserve, suspicion, grief that one's offspring is going to marry a member of the rejected race, joy when evil befalls them, pity for members of one's own race who are bettered by them, pride when one succeeds in doing them down, amusement at their humiliation, surprise that one of them has shown signs of advanced humanity, horror or self-contempt at the discovery that one has felt fellow-feeling for one—it is hard to think of a single emotion that is immune to its corruption.[5] It can even extend its influence to the appetites, since the rejected race's food and drink can be found disgusting, and sexual relations with its members perversely attractive.

Recall, secondly, that no one relatively free of racism thinks that *any* of these emotional responses is in any sense natural; they all have to be inculcated, and from a very early age. Children have to be taught to fear, particularly, adults of a different race; to hate and suspect and despise its younger members; to be amused or otherwise pleased when they are hurt; to be angry or suspicious when they are friendly; to join in rejoicing when it is heard they have been done down; to admire those who have brought about their downfall; to resent, or dismiss, their doing well or being happy.

And recall, thirdly, what we are beginning to understand about how racism is inculcated and how hard it is to eliminate. The last thirty years or so have seen a growing awareness of the ways in which we are influenced by the representations of racial stereotypes, of the racism implicit in many of our myths and metaphors, our images and archetypes, and a corresponding awareness that the most dedicated and sincere concern for charity and even justice is liable to be perverted and misdirected until we have both recognized, and rooted out, the racism that expresses itself in *emotional responses* we still defend as innocent, or justified, or reasonable—or beyond our control.

When we bear this real example, of the inculcation of racism, in mind, it becomes vividly clear that 'the' way in which the training of the emotions shapes one's thoughts of generic good and evil cannot be divided neatly into the rational and the non-rational. On the one hand, it is rational, in so far as children being inculcated in it are being taught applications of the generic terms 'good' and 'evil' (such people are *dangerous, ignorant, perverted;* he tried to get you to go to his place!/to eat his food? what *cheek,* how *disgusting;* she wouldn't have anything to do with him/she pushed him over?, quite *right* too, how *brave,* how *sensible*—these are all terms whose application we pick up from those who bring us up). And it is rational, further, in so far as some explanatory or justifying putative facts will be interwoven with the training— such people are dangerous *because* they can't control their passions, *because* they hate us, *because* they are cunning and devious, are not being brave *because* they don't feel pain the way we do, do not deserve pity *because* they always make a fuss—and putative evidence given for such claims. In these two ways it is a training peculiarly appropriate to rational animals.

On the other hand, it is non-rational in so far as it proceeds, one might say, by unconscious imitation, Humean sympathy, and conditioning; the children just come to respond emotionally in the same way as those who are bringing them up, in a way that is at least akin to the way in which the young of some other species acquire their emotional responses.

Finally, it is, of course, non-rational, or *ir*rational, in the sense that the whole system

of the application of the terms, their putative explanations and justifications, is a tissue of falsehoods and inconsistencies. But, as we know to our cost, the recognition of this fact does not suffice to undo the training. Coming to realize that some of one's emotional reactions have been not only entirely stupid but wicked is no guarantee that one won't go on having them.

Is it possible to extirpate them, to undo a childhood training in racism and re-train emotional reactions, in this area, into 'complete harmony' with reason—given the presence of a dedicated concern for charity and justice? The answer to this, I think it must be said, is that we still do not know.

We do know that reason can, directly, achieve a certain amount; one can catch oneself having the emotional reactions, drag the relevant stupid thoughts about good and evil to the surface of consciousness and hammer them with rational beliefs—I have *nothing* to fear from this person; she did *not* insult or patronize me, but asked a reasonable question; I have every possible reason to trust this person, and none not to; it is not at all surprising that she should be a mathematician. And we know that familiarity, in the sense of habitual acquaintance and intimacy (once again, given the dedicated concern), far from breeding contempt, breeds fellow-feeling, and can achieve much by way of casting out fear, hatred, suspicion, and misplaced surprise.

But total re-training may nevertheless be impossible. Aristotle, acknowledging his debt to Plato, emphasizes 'the importance of having been trained in some way *from infancy* to feel joy or grief at the right things';[6] given the emotions' non-rational face, it may be that reason cannot entirely unseat bad training in childhood, and that relationships of love and trust formed in adulthood cannot entirely undo a kind of unconscious expectancy of evil which still manifests itself in racist emotional reactions.

If, sadly, that is so, what follows? It certainly does not follow that anyone subject to such reactions can shrug them off and say, 'Oh well; they are beyond my control; I just can't help reacting that way.' For since we know that some re-training is possible, and do not know when, if ever, it ceases to be effective, anyone decent must be anxiously seeking ways to control them, refusing to give up hope. But what does seem to be entailed is that those of us who had racism inculcated in us early are unlucky; through no fault of our own, and despite our greatest efforts, we may remain morally inferior (though not thereby necessarily blameworthy) to those who, in virtue of good training in childhood and rational principle, achieve complete harmony between their emotions and reason and thereby full virtue.

What would be involved in denying this entailment? We would have to insist that we can be as perfect in charity and justice as any human being can be, despite being subject to racist emotional reactions, as long as we keep them from manifesting themselves in action or omission (and, perhaps, as long as we continue to try to extirpate them). Well, someone might insist on saying that, but it sounds astonishingly arrogant, and one doubts that members of the rejected race will agree.[7] And perhaps it is examples such as racism that are needed to unseat the distaste that many people feel for what Williams has christened 'constitutive moral luck'.[8]

If we try to think of Kant's third philanthropist as 'indifferent to the sufferings' of a particular oppressed race, because of his racist upbringing [which is a great deal easier than trying to imagine someone who is genuinely indifferent to the sufferings (*any* sufferings?) of other human beings (*any* other human beings?)], we would surely not think of him as a moral exemplar just because he acts to benefit a member of the oppressed race 'out of duty', notwithstanding the indubitable fact that he had no control over his upbringing. If he has not devoted any effort to trying to undo the effects of his upbringing but is resting content with the

claim that it was not his fault and his emotions are beyond his control, then he is corrupt. If he has tried but not succeeded at all then he has not tried hard enough (for we know that some re-training is possible) and is at least suspect. What if he is still fairly young, has only recently started trying, and hence has not succeeded much? Then, naturally, he will find it harder to do what is charitable and just than someone who, with the same bad upbringing, has been trying to undo it for longer, but his finding it harder does not make him morally superior to the one who now finds it easier than it used to be—quite the contrary.[9]

Why do those of us who had racism inculcated in us think that we must strive, and continue to strive, to undo the effects of that upbringing? Not because we think it will make it easier for us to do what is charitable and just (though it will), but because we think it will make us better people, more charitable and just than we are at present. Why do we try to bring up our children differently? Not in the hope that it will make their moral lives less a matter of striving than ours have been (though, with respect to racism, it should), but in the hope that they will turn out better than we have, more charitable and just. How could we think that we ought to give our children a good upbringing, that we owed it to them, if we thought that it had no effect on whether they turned out better or worse? But whether or not we ourselves had a good upbringing is just a matter of luck.

It should be noted, in this context, where we are all (I assume) vividly aware of the fact, that the whole idea that a human agent *could* do what she should, in every particular instance, while her emotions are way out of line, is a complete fantasy. Our understanding of what will hurt, offend, damage, undermine, distress or reassure, help, succour, support, or please our fellow human beings is at least as much emotional as it is theoretical. Dedicated adherence to rules or principles of charity and justice achieves a great deal, but it is only someone arrogant and self-righteous who supposes, given a conventional upbringing in which racism is embedded, that they can apply such rules and principles with the *right* imagination and sensitivity to other groups.

And even if, *per impossibile*, such correctly imaginative and sensitive application of the rules could be written into them, the grasp of, and adherence to, the rules would *still* not take us all the way to 'what we should do'. For sometimes 'what we should do' is just, as we say, 'be there' for other people. They tell us what they have suffered, and the tears come to our eyes; they tell us what they have endured and our faces flush with indignation or anger. It is all in the past, there is nothing we can do to undo it, no comfort or assuagement we can offer in the form of action. Such comfort and assuagement as we can offer, as we should, springs solely from our emotional reactions. If we can't come up with the right ones, we fail them, and it is a moral failure.

The same remarks apply, *mutatis mutandis*, to the question of whether one can fail in full virtue because of 'natural temperament'.[10] No one who is thoroughly cold-hearted as an adult is so through no fault of his own unless he is a psychopath. One preserves a cold heart and indifference to the sufferings of others in oneself as an adult by wilfully abnegating responsibility, blaming it all, childishly, on nature or one's upbringing. Or, worse, one preserves and positively fosters it by allowing oneself to think such thoughts as that one is 'endowed with the special gift of patience and robust endurance [in one's own] suffering' and assumes 'or even demand[s]' it of others, as Kant (rather revealingly) allows.[11] It is hard to imagine a more uncharitable and unjust thought in relation to the sufferings of the innocent, the helpless, and the oppressed, but one way in which we keep ourselves uncharitable and unjust while, quite sincerely, espousing charity and justice as virtues is precisely by *not* thinking such thoughts in relation to such cases. We think

about the suffering of the feckless, dishonest, and self-indulgent, classify them as 'the underclass' and, conveniently forgetting about the sufferings of the feckful, honest, and hardworking who have been unlucky, the people who would need exceptional virtue (which we should recognize we lack) to rise above their social environment, and the *children*, we harden our hearts. And when, we do so, it is all our own fault.

Conclusion

It is, I think, true, that where Aristotle, and thereby the Aristotelians, have an edge over Kant (and, indeed, Hume) with respect to the moral significance of the emotions is in the account Aristotle gives us of human rationality, an account that allows the emotions to participate in reason and thereby play their proper role in the specification of full virtue. Much modern moral philosophy, deontological and utilitarian, has followed Kant, or Hume, rather than Aristotle, on human rationality, and thereby still suffers from the fault to which Anscombe drew attention back in 1958—it lacks 'an adequate philosophy of psychology'.[12] But although this may give the Aristotelians an edge over Kant, I do not see, offhand, any deep reason why it should give them an intrinsic edge over Kantian deontologists. The Kantians can repudiate Kant's unattractive claims about the cold-hearted, as Aristotelians discard Aristotle's unattractive claims about women and natural slaves, without dismembering the philosophy. As the recent revived interest in *The Doctrine of Virtue* reveals, there are, in fact, hints in Kant's later writings[13] that he did acknowledge some rational emotions; but even if there were not, deontological moral philosophers might still, it seems to me, be recognizably Kantian (in so far as they start with the Categorical Imperative) and add on an Aristotelian account of the emotions, just as virtue ethicists are still recognizably Aristotelian (in so far as they start with the Aristotelian account of the virtues) when they add on non-Aristotelian virtues such as charity and repudiate Aristotle's sexism. Nor do I see any immediate inconsistency in utilitarians' adding on the Aristotelian account of the emotions. Once they have noticed how optimific it would be if everyone were brought up, or trained themselves, to have the right emotions, on the right occasions, to the right extent, towards the right people or objects, should they not welcome the idea?

It might turn out that thoroughly worked-out attempts to add on the Aristotelian account of the emotions changed the deontology and utilitarianism into virtue ethics in all but name; then indeed we might claim that virtue ethics is intrinsically superior in this regard. But until we see what such attempts look like, that should remain an open question; perhaps its current pre-eminence in this area will turn out to have been an historical accident.

Notes

1. *Nicomachean Ethics* 1102b10–1103a1.

2. For the kind of discriminating detail which makes the vague remark into a plausible and illuminating thesis, the best source is still Aquinas, not just in *Summa Theologiae* Ia2ae (QQ. 22–30) on 'The Emotions', but all through IIa2ae (QQ. 1–189) on hope, fear, despair, charity (*caritas*), joy, hatred, *accidie*, envy, anger, curiosity, etc. Descartes, in *The Passions of the Soul*, gives a rather watered-down but still instructive version.

3. Reprinted in his *Problems of the Self* (1973).

4. It is a tricky question whether 'racism' connotes rejection of another race or, more particularly, rejection in the context of oppression. My first two sets of remarks about the ways in which a racist upbringing affects our emotions are, I think, fairly uncommitted on this; blacks and whites, Gentiles and Jews may be affected in the same way. But the third set tends toward the concept of racism that necessarily involves oppression. It is the oppressing race, the one that imposes the myths and metaphors, whose charity and justice are liable to be perverted by that imposition.

5. In discussion, someone optimistically suggested love. But although there are heartening examples of love's triumph over racial prejudice, there are also examples of its failure to survive the discovery that the loved one has 'tainted' blood.

6. *Nicomachean Ethics* 1104b11–12; my italics.

7. I here disassociate myself strongly from Blum's lamentable claim that a 'formerly racist man who now believes in equality', who has striven, with some success, to extirpate his racist emotional reactions, but who still has 'occasional feelings of dislike and distrust towards blacks . . . can no longer be identified with them. He is not to be criticised for having them. They are thus external to his moral self', *Friendship Altruism and Morality*, 181. It seems worth recording that, when I read out this passage to a graduate class in Stanford in 1996, its members gasped with horror.

8. Williams, 'Moral Luck' (1976).

9. It is often said, even by virtue ethicists, that justice does not involve the emotions, but the example of racism seems to me to show that this is a mistake. A white person who was not horrified and grieved by Martin Luther King's assassination and overjoyed by the eventual emergence and triumph of Nelson Mandela is far from perfect in justice, no matter how impeccable their every action.

10. For a detailed defence of this view see Gregory Trianosky, 'Natural Affections and Responsibility for Character: A Critique of Kantian Views of the Virtues' (1990), an article from which I have greatly benefited.

11. See the passage quoted at p. 93 above.

12. Anscombe, 'Modern Moral Philosophy', 26.

13. See Louden, 'Kant's Virtue Ethics'. Note, further, 'Sympathetic Feeling is Generally a Duty' (in *The Doctrine of Virtue*, § 34), where Kant commends 'the capacity and the will to share in others' feelings' as an appropriate feeling, for 'a human being [is] regarded [here] nor merely as a rational being but also as an animal endowed with reason' (204).

PART VIII

Morality and Religion

Introduction

Whether it be the impoverished Calcutta harijan accepting his degradation as his karma, the Shiite Moslem fighting a jihad in the name of Allah, the Jew circumspectly striving to keep kosher, or the Christian giving to charity in the name of Christ, religion has traditionally so dominated the moral landscape as to be virtually indistinguishable from it.

There have been exceptions to be sure. Confucianism in China is essentially a secular system; there are nontheist versions of Buddhism; and the philosophers of Greece thought of morality independently from religion; but for the most part, throughout most of our history most people have identified morality with religion, with the commands of God.

The question is whether the equation is a valid one. Is morality essentially tied to religion so that the term 'secular ethic' is an oxymoron, a contradiction? Can morality survive without religion? Is it the case, as Tolstoy thought, that separating morality from religion is like cutting a flower from its roots and transplanting it rootless into the ground? Is Dostoevsky's character Ivan Karamazov correct when he proclaims that "If God doesn't exist, everything is permissible"?

Essentially, our inquiry comes down to addressing two questions: Does morality depend on religion? and Are religious ethics essentially different from secular ethics?

Does Morality Depend on Religion?

The first question is whether moral standards themselves depend on God for their validity or whether there is an autonomy of ethics, so that even God is subject to the moral order. The question first arises in Plato's dialogue the *Euthyphro*

(our first reading) where Socrates asks the pious Euthyphro, "Do the gods love holiness because it is holy, or is it holy because the gods love it?" Changing the terms but still preserving the meaning, we want to know whether God commands what is Good because it is good or whether the Good is good because God commands it? According to one theory, called the *divine command theory*, ethical principles are simply the commands of God. They derive their validity from God's commanding them, and they *mean* 'commanded by God.' Without God, there would be no universally valid morality. Here is how the theologian, Carl F. H. Henry states this view:

Biblical ethics discredits an autonomous morality. It gives theonomous ethics its classic form—the identification of the moral law with the Divine will. In Hebrew-Christian revelation, distinctions in ethics reduce to what is good or what is pleasing, and to what is wicked or displeasing to the Creator-God alone. The biblical view maintains always a dynamic statement of values, refusing to sever the elements of morality from the will of God. . . . The good is what the Creator-Lord does and commands. He is the creator of the moral law, and defines its very nature.[1]

Morality not only originates with God, but "moral rightness" simply means "willed by God" and "moral wrongness" means "being against the will of God." Since, essentially, morality is based on divine will, not on independently existing reasons for action, no further reasons for action are necessary. As Ivan Karamazov asserts, "If God doesn't exist, everything is permissible." Nothing is forbidden or required. Without God we have moral nihilism.

The opposing viewpoint, call it the *autonomy thesis* (standing for the independence of ethics), denies the theses of the divine command theory, asserting, to the contrary, that: (1) morality does not originate with God (though the way God created us may affect the specific nature of morality); (2) rightness and wrongness are not based simply on God's will; and (3) essentially, there are reasons for acting one way or the other, which may be known independently of God's will. In sum, ethics are autonomous, and even God must obey the moral law, which exists independently of himself—as the laws of mathematics and logic do. Just as even God cannot make a three-sided square or make it the case that he never existed, so even God cannot make what is intrinsically evil good or make what is good, evil.

Theists who espouse the autonomy thesis may well admit some epistemological advantage to God. God *knows* what is right—better than we do. And since he is good, we can always learn from consulting him, but in principle, we act morally for the same reasons that God does. We both follow moral reasons that are independent of God. We are against torturing the innocent because it is cruel and unjust, just as God is against torturing the innocent because it is cruel and unjust. If there is no God, on this account, nothing is changed. Morality is left intact, and both theists and nontheists have the very same moral duties.

The attractiveness of the divine command theory lies in the fact that it seems to do justice to the omnipotence or sovereignty of God. God somehow is thought to be less sovereign or necessary to our lives if he is not the source of morality. It seems inconceivable to many believers that anything having to do with goodness or duty could be "higher" than or independent of God. He is the supreme Lord of the believer's life, and what the believer means by "morally right" is that "the Lord commands it—even if I do not fully understand it." When the believer asks what the will of God is, it is a direct appeal to a personal will, not to an independently existing rule.

There are two problems with the divine command theory that need to be faced by those who hold it. One problem is that the divine command theory would seem to make the attribution of 'goodness' to God redundant. When we say 'God is good,' we think that we are ascribing a property to God, but if 'good' simply means 'what God commands or wills,' then we are not attributing any property to God. Our statement 'God is good' merely means 'God does whatever he wills to do' or 'God practices what he preaches,' and the statement 'God commands us to do what is good' merely is the tautology 'God commands us to do what God commands us to do.'

A second problem with the divine command theory is that it seems to make morality into something arbitrary. If God's fiat is the sole arbiter of right and wrong, it would seem to be logically possible for such 'heinous' acts as rape, killing of the innocent for the fun of it, and gratuitous cruelty to become morally good actions—if God suddenly decided to command us to do these things. The radicality of the divine command theory is set forth by a classic statement of Occam:

The hatred of God, theft, adultery, and actions similar to these actions according to common law, may have an evil quality annexed, insofar as they are done by a divine command to perform the opposite act. But as far as the sheer being in the actions is concerned, they can be performed by God without any evil condition annexed; and they can even be performed meritoriously by an earthly pilgrim if they should come under divine precepts, just as now the opposite of these in fact fall under the divine command.[2]

The implications of this sort of reasoning seem far-reaching. If there are no constraints on what God can command, no independent measure or reason for moral action, then anything can become a moral duty, and our moral duties can change from moment to moment. Could there be any moral stability? The proponent of the divine command theory may object that God has revealed what is his will in his word, sacred

Scriptures. But, the fitting response is, how do you know that God is not lying? For if there is no independent criterion of right and wrong except what God happens to will, how do we know God is not willing to make lying into a duty?—in which case believers have no reason to believe the Bible!

If God could make morally good what seems morally heinous simply by willing it, wouldn't morality be reduced to the right of the powerful? Nietzsche's 'Might makes Right'? Indeed, what would be the difference between the devil and God, if morality were simply an arbitrary command?

Suppose we had two sets of commands, one from the devil and one from God. How would we know which set was which? Could they be identical? What would make them different? If there is no independent criterion by which to judge right and wrong, it is difficult to see how we could know which was which. The only basis for comparison would be who won. God is simply the biggest bully on the block (granted it is a pretty big block—covering the entire universe).

There is a second question with regard to the relationship of ethics and religion: "Does morality need the sanctions of a divine being to inspire adequate motivation for compliance?" Although Immanuel Kant (VI.24) held to the autonomy thesis, he argued that morality would not be justified if there were not a God to enforce the moral law, rewarding and punishing rational agents in the

next life. Whereas Kant did not think that this ultimate sanction should play any role in motivating us (we should be moral for its own sake), others have argued that without God there is insufficient reason to be moral. Why be moral when no one will punish us for being selfish or profiting from immoral behavior?

In our second reading, "A Free Man's Worship," Bertrand Russell argues that morality does not need God or an afterlife. Reason alone provides the adequate basis for morality.

In our third reading, James Rachels argues that, far from morality depending upon God, morality is inconsistent with theism. He argues that belief in God implies worship and worship undermines moral agency, and thus belief in God undermines the possibility of a moral life.

In our fourth reading, C. Stephen Layman advances a moral argument for the existence of God. He argues that God and human immortality are the best (although not a necessary) explanation of the way that we are bound by moral obligations. In our final reading Peter Byrne challenges Layman's argument, raising two penetrating criticisms.

Notes

1. Carl F. Henry, *Christian Personal Ethics* (Grand Rapids, Mich.: Eerdmans, 1957), p. 210.

2. William of Occam, quoted in *Divine Command Morality*, ed. J. M. Idziak (Toronto: Mellon, 1979).

The Euthyphro Problem

PLATO

Socrates is questioning the ardently religious Euthyphro, who, believing it to be his religious and moral duty, is going to court to report his father for having killed a slave, who himself had committed murder. In the course of the dialogue Socrates raises the question that has come to be known as "The Euthyphro Problem," of whether the Good is good because God loves or chooses it or whether God loves or chooses the Good because it is good.

SOCRATES: Come now, my dear Euthyphro, tell me, too, that I may become wiser, what proof you have that all the gods consider that man to have been killed unjustly who became a murderer while in your service . . . and that it is right for a son to denounce and to prosecute his father on behalf of such a man. Come, try to show me a clear sign that all the gods definitely believe this action to be right. If you can give me adequate proof of this, I shall never cease to extol your wisdom.

EUTHYPHRO: This is perhaps no light task, Socrates, though I could show you very clearly. . . .

S: Let us assume, if you will, that all the gods consider this [act of killing the servant] unjust and that they all hate it. However, is this the correction we are making in our discussion, that what all the gods hate is impious, and what they all love is pious, and that what some gods love and others hate is neither or both? Is that how you now wish us to define piety and impiety?

E: What prevents us from doing so, Socrates?

Reprinted from Plato, *The Trial and Death of Socrates*, trans. G. M. A. Grube, as revised by Richard Hogan and Donald J. Zeyl (Indianapolis: Hackett Publishing Company), by permission of the publisher.

S: For my part nothing, Euthyphro, but you look whether on your part this proposal will enable you to teach me most easily what you promised.

E: I would certainly say that the pious is what all the gods love, and the opposite, what all the gods hate, is the impious.

S: Then let us again examine whether that is a sound statement, or do we let it pass, and if one of us, or someone else, merely says that something is so, do we accept that it is so? Or should we examine what the speaker means?

E: We must examine it, but I certainly think that this is now a fine statement.

S: We shall soon know better whether it is. Consider this: Is the pious loved by the gods because it is pious, or is it pious because it is loved by the gods?

E: I don't know what you mean, Socrates.

S: I shall try to explain more clearly: we speak of something being carried and something carrying, of something being led and something leading, of something being seen and something seeing, and you understand that these things are all different from one another and how they differ?

E: I think I do.

S: So there is something being loved and something loving, and the loving is a different thing.

E: Of course.

S: Tell me then whether that which is being carried is being carried because someone carries it or for some other reason.

E: No, that is the reason.

S: And that which is being led is so because someone leads it, and that which is being seen because someone sees it?

E: Certainly.

S: It is not seen by someone because it is being seen but on the contrary it is being seen because someone sees it, nor is it because it is being led that someone leads it but because someone leads it that it is being led; nor does someone carry an object because it is being carried, but it is being carried because someone carries it. Is what I want to say clear, Euthyphro? I want to say this, namely, that if anything comes to be, or is affected, it does not come to be because it is coming to be, but it is coming to be because it comes to be; nor is it affected because it is being affected but because something affects it. Or do you not agree?

E: I do.

S: What is being loved is either something that comes to be or something that is affected by something?

E: Certainly.

S: So it is in the same case as the things just mentioned; it is not loved by those who love it because it is being loved, but it is being loved because they love it?

E: Necessarily.

S: What then do we say about the pious, Euthyphro? Surely that it is loved by all the gods, according to what you say?

E: Yes.

S: Is it loved because it is pious, or for some other reason?

E: For no other reason.

S: It is loved then because it is pious, but it is not pious because it is loved?

E: Apparently.

S: And because it is loved by the gods it is being loved and is dear to the gods?

E: Of course.

S: The god-beloved is then not the same as the pious, Euthyphro, nor the pious the same as the god-beloved, as you say it is, but one differs from the other.

E: How so, Socrates?

S: Because we agree that the pious is beloved for the reason that it is pious, but it is not pious because it is loved. Is that not so?

E: Yes.

S: And that the god-beloved, on the other hand, is so because it is loved by the gods, by the very fact of being loved, but it is not loved because it is god-beloved.

E: True.

S: But if the god-beloved and the pious were the same, my dear Euthyphro, and the pious were loved because it was pious, then the god-beloved would be loved because it was god-beloved, and if the god-beloved was god-beloved because it was loved by the gods, then the pious would also be pious because it was loved by the gods; but now you see that they are in opposite cases as being altogether different from each other: the one is of a nature to be loved because it is loved, the other is loved because it is of nature to be loved. I'm afraid, Euthyphro, that when you were asked what piety is, you did not wish to make its nature clear to me, but you told me an affect or quality of it, that the pious has the quality of being loved by all the gods, but you have not yet told me what the pious is. Now, if you will, do not hide things from me but tell me again from the beginning what piety is, whether loved by the gods or having some other quality—we shall not quarrel about—but be keen to tell me what the pious and the impious are.

A Free Man's Worship

BERTRAND RUSSELL

Bertrand Russell (1872–1970) was educated at Cambridge University, where he later taught philosophy. A writer of more than a hundred books and articles on almost every major area in philosophy, he is one of the most significant philosophers of the twentieth century. In this essay written in 1903 Russell rejects the idea that religion is necessary for morality. We can be both moral and happy without God. The world is absurd, a godless tragedy in which "Nature, omnipotent but blind, in the revolutions of her secular hurryings through the abysses of space, has brought forth at last a child, subject still to her power, but gifted with sight, with knowledge of good and evil, with the capacity of judging all the works of his unthinking Mother." It is this conscious power of moral evaluation that makes the child superior to his omnipotent Mother. He is free to think, to evaluate, to create, and to live committed to ideals. So in spite of suffering, despair, and death, humans are free and life may be meaningful.

To Dr. Faustus in his study Mephistopheles told the history of the Creation, saying:

"The endless praises of the choirs of angels had begun to grow wearisome; for, after all, did he not deserve their praise? Had he not given them endless joy? Would it not be more amusing to obtain undeserved praise, to be worshiped by beings whom he tortured? He smiled inwardly, and resolved that the great drama should be performed.

"For countless ages the hot nebula whirled aimlessly through space. At length it began to take shape, the central mass threw off planets, the planets cooled, boiling seas and burning mountains heaved and tossed, from black masses of

From *The Basic Writings of Bertrand Russell*, eds. R. Egner and L. Denonn. Copyright © 1961 by George Allen and Unwin. Reprinted by permission of Simon & Schuster, Inc.

cloud hot sheets of rain deluged the barely solid crust. And now the first germ of life grew in the depths of the ocean, and developed rapidly in the fructifying warmth into vast forest trees, huge ferns springing from the damp mold, sea monsters breeding, fighting, devouring, and passing away. And from the monsters, as the play unfolded itself, Man was born, with the power of thought, the knowledge of good and evil, and the cruel thirst for worship. And Man saw that all is passing in this mad, monstrous world, that all is struggling to snatch, at any cost, a few brief moments of life before Death's inexorable decree. And Man said: 'There is a hidden purpose, could we but fathom it, and the purpose is good; for we must reverence something, and in the visible world there is nothing worthy of reverence.' And Man stood aside from the struggle, resolving that God intended harmony to come out of chaos by human efforts. And when he followed the instincts which God had transmitted to him from his ancestry of beasts of prey, he called it Sin, and asked God to forgive him. But he doubted whether he could be justly forgiven, until he invented a divine Plan by which God's wrath was to have been appeased. And seeing the present was bad, he made it yet worse, that thereby the future might be better. And he gave God thanks for the strength that enabled him to forgo even the joys that were possible. And God smiled; and when he saw that Man had become perfect in renunciation and worship, he sent another sun through the sky, which crashed into Man's sun; and all returned again to nebula.

"'Yes,' he murmured, 'it was a good play; I will have it performed again.'"

Such, in outline, but even more purposeless, more void of meaning, is the world which Science presents for our belief. Amid such a world, if anywhere, our ideals henceforward must find a home. That Man is the product of causes which had no prevision of the end they were achieving; that his origin, his growth, his hopes and fears, his loves and his beliefs, are but the outcome of accidental collocations of atoms; that no fire, no heroism, no intensity of thought and feeling, can preserve an individual life beyond the grave; that all the labors of the ages, all the devotion, all the inspiration, all the noonday brightness of human genius, are destined to extinction in the vast death of the solar system, and that the whole temple of Man's achievement must inevitably be buried beneath the debris of a universe in ruins—all these things, if not quite beyond dispute, are yet so nearly certain, that no philosophy which rejects them can hope to stand. Only within the scaffolding of these truths, only on the firm foundation of unyielding despair, can the soul's habitation henceforth be safely built.

How, in such an alien and inhuman world, can so powerless a creature as Man preserve his aspirations untarnished? A strange mystery it is that Nature, omnipotent but blind, in the revolutions of her secular hurryings through the abysses of space, has brought forth at last a child, subject still to her power, but gifted with sight, with knowledge of good and evil, with the capacity of judging all the works of his unthinking Mother. In spite of Death, the mark and seal of the parental control, Man is yet free, during his brief years, to examine, to criticize, to know, and in imagination to create. To him alone, in the world with which he is acquainted, this freedom belongs; and in this lies his superiority to the resistless forces that control his outward life.

The savage, like ourselves, feels the oppression of his impotence before the powers of Nature; but having in himself nothing that he respects more than Power, he is willing to prostrate himself before his gods, without inquiring whether they are worthy of his worship. Pathetic and very terrible is the long history of cruelty and torture, of degradation and human sacrifice, endured in the hope of placating the jealous gods: surely, the trembling believer thinks, when what is most pre-

cious has been freely given, their lust for blood must be appeased, and more will not be required. The religion of Moloch—as such creeds may be generically called—is in essence the cringing submission of the slave, who dare not, even in his heart, allow the thought that his master deserves no adulation. Since the independence of ideals is not yet acknowledged, Power may be freely worshiped, and receive an unlimited respect, despite its wanton infliction of pain.

But gradually, as morality grows bolder, the claim of the ideal world begins to be felt; and worship, if it is not to cease, must be given to gods of another kind than those created by the savage. Some, though they feel the demands of the ideal, will still consciously reject them, still urging that naked Power is worthy of worship. Such is the attitude inculcated in God's answer to Job out of the whirlwind: the divine power and knowledge are paraded, but of the divine goodness there is no hint. Such also is the attitude of those who, in our own day, base their morality upon the struggle for survival, maintaining that the survivors are necessarily the fittest. But others, not content with an answer so repugnant to the moral sense, will adopt the position which we have become accustomed to regard as specially religious, maintaining that, in some hidden manner, the world of fact is really harmonious with the world of ideals. Thus Man creates God, all-powerful and all-good, the mystic unity of what is and what should be.

But the world of fact, after all, is not good; and, in submitting our judgment to it, there is an element of slavishness from which our thoughts must be purged. For all things it is well to exalt the dignity of Man, by freeing him as far as possible from the tyranny of nonhuman Power. When we have realized that Power is largely bad, that Man, with his knowledge of good and evil, is but a helpless atom in a world which has no such knowledge, the choice is again presented to us: Shall we worship Force, or shall we worship Goodness? Shall our God exist and be evil, or shall he be recognized as the creation of our own conscience?

The answer to this question is very momentous, and effects profoundly our whole morality. The worship of Force, to which Carlyle and Nietzsche and the creed of Militarism have accustomed us, is the result of failure to maintain our own ideals against a hostile universe: it is itself a prostrate submission to evil, a sacrifice of our best to Moloch. If strength indeed is to be respected, let us respect rather the strength of those who refuse that false 'recognition of facts' which fails to recognize that facts are often bad. Let us admit that, in the world we know, there are many things that would be better otherwise, and that the ideals to which we do and must adhere are not realized in the realm of matter. Let us preserve our respect for truth, for beauty, for the ideal of perfection which life does not permit us to attain, though none of these things meet with the approval of the unconscious universe. If Power is bad, as it seems to be, let us reject it from our hearts. In this lies Man's true freedom: in determination to worship only the God created by our own love of the good, to respect only the heaven which inspires the insight of our best moments. In action, in desire, we must submit perpetually to the tyranny of outside forces; but in thought, in aspiration, we are free, free from our fellow men, free from the petty planet on which our bodies impotently crawl, free even, while we live, from the tyranny of death. Let us learn, then, that energy of faith which enables us to live constantly in the vision of the good; and let us descend, in action, into the world of fact, with that vision always before us.

When first the opposition of fact and ideal grows fully visible, a spirit of fiery revolt, of fierce hatred of the gods, seems necessary to the assertion of freedom. To defy with Promethean constancy a hostile universe, to keep its evil always in view, always actively hated, to refuse no pain that the malice of Power can invent, appears to be the duty of all who will not bow before the inevitable. But indignation is still a bondage, for it compels our thoughts to be occupied with an evil world; and in the fierceness of desire from which rebellion springs there is a kind of self-assertion which it is necessary for the wise to overcome.

Indignation is a submission of our thoughts, but not of our desires; the Stoic freedom in which wisdom consists is found in the submission of our desires, but not of our thoughts. From the submission of our desires springs the virtue of resignation; from the freedom of our thoughts springs the whole world of art and philosophy, and the vision of beauty by which, at last, we half reconquer the reluctant world. But the vision of beauty is possible only to unfettered contemplation, to thoughts not weighted by the load of eager wishes; and thus Freedom comes only to those who no longer ask of life that it shall yield them any of those personal goods that are subject to the mutations of Time.

Although the necessity of renunciation is evidence of the existence of evil, yet Christianity, in preaching it, has shown a wisdom exceeding that of the Promethean philosophy of rebellion. It must be admitted that, of the things we desire, some, though they prove impossible, are yet real goods; others, however, as ardently longed for, do not form part of a fully purified ideal. The belief that what must be renounced is bad, though sometimes false, is far less often false than untamed passion supposes; and the creed of religion, by providing a reason for proving that it is never false, has been the means of purifying our hopes by the discovery of many austere truths.

But there is in resignation a further good element: even real goods, when they are unattainable, ought not to be fretfully desired. To every man comes, sooner or later, the great renunciation. For the young, there is nothing unattainable; a good thing desired with the whole force of a passionate will, and yet impossible, is to them not credible. Yet, by death, by illness, by poverty, or by the voice of duty, we must learn, each one of us, that the world was not made for us, and that, however beautiful may be the things we crave, Fate may nevertheless forbid them. It is the part of courage, when misfortune comes, to bear without repining the ruin of our hopes, to turn away our thoughts from vain regrets. This degree of submission to Power is not only just and right: it is the very gate of wisdom.

But passive renunciation is not the whole of wisdom; for not by renunciation alone can we build a temple for the worship of our own ideals. Haunting foreshadowings of the temple appear in the realm of imagination, in music, in architecture, in the untroubled kingdom of reason, and in the golden sunset magic of lyrics, where beauty shines and glows, remote from the touch of sorrow, remote from the fear of change, remote from the failures and disenchantments of the world of fact. In the contemplation of these things the vision of heaven will shape itself in our hearts, giving at once a touchstone to judge the world about us, and an inspiration by which to fashion to our needs whatever is not incapable of serving as a stone in the sacred temple.

Except for those rare spirits that are born without sin, there is a cavern of darkness to be traversed before that temple can be entered. The gate of the cavern is despair, and its floor is paved with the gravestones of abandoned hopes. There Self must die; there the eagerness, the greed of untamed desire must be slain, for only so can the soul be free from the empire of Fate. But out of the cavern the Gate of Renunciation leads again to the daylight of wisdom, by whose radiance a new insight, a new joy, a new tenderness, shine forth to gladden the pilgrim's heart.

When, without the bitterness of impotent rebellion, we have learnt both to resign ourselves to the outward rule of Fate and to recognize that the nonhuman world is unworthy of our worship, it becomes possible at last so to transform and refashion the unconscious universe, so to transmute it in the crucible of imagination, that a new image of shining gold replaces the old idol of clay. In all the multiform facts of the world—in the visual shapes of trees and mountains and clouds, in the events of the life of Man, even in the very omnipotence of Death—the insight of creative idealism can find the reflection of a beauty which its own thoughts first made. In this way mind asserts its subtle mastery over the thoughtless forces of Nature. The more evil the material with which it deals, the more thwarting to untrained desire, the greater is its achievement in inducing the reluctant rock to yield up its hidden treasures, the prouder its victory in compelling the opposing forces to swell the pageant of its triumph. Of all the arts, Tragedy is the proudest, the most triumphant; for it builds its shining citadel in the very center of the enemy's country, on the very summit of his highest mountain; from its impregnable watchtowers, his camps and arsenals, his columns and forts, are all revealed; within its walls the free life continues, while the legions of Death and Pain and Despair, and all the servile captains of tyrant Fate, afford the burghers of that dauntless city new spectacles of beauty. Happy those sacred ramparts, thrice happy the dwellers on that all-seeing eminence. Honor to those brave warriors who, through countless ages of warfare, have preserved for us the priceless heritage of liberty, and have kept undefiled by sacrilegious invaders the home of the unsubdued.

But the beauty of Tragedy does but make visible a quality which, in more or less obvious shapes, is present always and everywhere in life. In the spectacle of Death, in the endurance of intolerable pain, and in the irrevocableness of a vanished past, there is a sacredness, an overpowering awe, a feeling of the vastness, the depth, the inexhaustible mystery of existence, in which, as by some strange marriage of pain, the sufferer is bound to the world by bonds of sorrow. In these moments of insight, we lose all eagerness of temporary desire, all struggling and striving for petty ends, all care for the little trivial things that, to a superficial view, make up the common life of day by day; we see, surrounding the narrow raft illumined by the flickering light of human comradeship, the dark ocean on whose rolling waves we toss for a brief hour; from the great night without, a chill blast breaks in upon our refuge; all the loneliness of humanity amid hostile forces is concentrated upon the individual soul, which must struggle alone, with what of courage it can command, against the whole weight of a universe that cares nothing for its hopes and fears. Victory, in this struggle with the powers of darkness, is the true baptism into the glorious company of heroes, the true initiation into the overmastering beauty of human existence. From that awful encounter of the soul with the outer world, renunciation, wisdom, and charity are born; and with their birth a new life begins. To take into the inmost shrine of the soul the irresistible forces whose puppets we seem to be—Death and change, the irrevocableness of the past, and the powerlessness of Man before the blind hurry of the universe from vanity to vanity—to feel these things and know them is to conquer them.

This is the reason why the Past has such magical power. The beauty of its motionless and silent pictures is like the enchanted purity of late autumn, when the leaves, though one breath would make them fall, still glow against the sky in golden glory. The Past does not change or strive; like Duncan, after life's fitful fever it sleeps well; what was eager and grasping, what was petty and transitory, has faded away, the things that were beautiful and eternal shine out of it like stars in the night. Its beauty, to a soul not worthy of it, is unendurable; but to a soul which has conquered Fate it is the key of religion.

The life of Man, viewed outwardly, is but a small thing in comparison with the forces of Nature. The slave is doomed to worship Time and Fate and Death, because they are greater than anything he finds in himself, and because all his thoughts are of things which they devour. But, great as they are, to think of them greatly, to feel their passionless splendor, is greater still. And such thought makes us free men; we no longer bow before the inevitable in Oriental subjection, but we absorb it, and make it a part of ourselves. To abandon the struggle for private happiness, to expel all eagerness of temporary desire, to burn with passion for eternal things—this is emancipation, and this is the free man's worship. And this liberation is effected by a contemplation of Fate; for Fate itself is subdued by the mind which leaves nothing to be purged by the purifying fire of Time.

United with his fellow men by the strongest of all ties, the tie of a common doom, the free man finds that a new vision is with him always, shedding over every daily task the light of love. The life of Man is a long march through the night, surrounded by invisible foes, tortured by weariness and pain, toward a goal that few can hope to reach, and where none may tarry long. One by one, as they march, our comrades vanish from our sight, seized by the silent orders of omnipotent Death. Very brief is the time in which we can help them, in which their happiness or misery is decided. Be it ours to shed sunshine on their path, to lighten their sorrows by the balm of sympathy, to give them the pure joy of a never-tiring affection, to strengthen failing courage, to instill faith in hours of despair. Let us not weigh in grudging scales their merits and demerits, but let us think only of their need—of the sorrows, the difficulties, perhaps the blindnesses, that make the misery of their lives; let us remember that they are fellow sufferers in the same darkness, actors in the same tragedy with ourselves. And so, when their day is over, when their good and their evil have become eternal by the immortality of the past, be it ours to feel that, where they suffered, where they failed, no deed of ours was the cause; but wherever a spark of the divine fire kindled in their hearts, we were ready with encouragement, with sympathy, with brave words in which high courage glowed.

Brief and powerless is Man's life; on him and all his race the slow, sure doom falls pitiless and dark. Blind to good and evil, reckless of destruction, omnipotent matter rolls on its relentless way; for Man, condemned today to lose his dearest, tomorrow himself to pass through the gate of darkness, it remains only to cherish, ere yet the blow fall, the lofty thoughts that ennoble his little day; disdaining the coward terrors of the slave of Fate, to worship at the shrine that his own hands have built; undismayed by the empire of chance, to preserve a mind free from the wanton tyranny that rules his outward life; proudly defiant of the irresistible forces that tolerate, for a moment, his knowledge and his condemnation, to sustain alone, a weary but unyielding Atlas, the world that his own ideals have fashioned despite the trampling march of unconscious power.

God and Morality Are Incompatible

JAMES RACHELS

A biographical sketch of James Rachels appears at the beginning of reading 10. In the following selection, Rachels argues that belief in God implies worship, worship implies the subordination of the believer's will, and the subordination of the believer's will implies the sacrifice of the believer's moral agency. So belief in God is inconsistent with moral agency, and moral agency is a necessary condition of the moral life. This does not quite add up to a moral argument against the existence of God, since someone who accepts the argument could opt to keep her belief in God and reject the moral life. However, such a move would be inconsistent with most theological systems. Interestingly the conception of moral agency upon which Rachels bases his argument is a good deal like Kant's, with its special emphasis on the autonomy of the will. Yet Kant thought that we need God in order to make sense of the moral life.

Kneeling down or grovelling on the ground, even to express your reverence for heavenly things, is contrary to human dignity.

Kant

I.

It is necessarily true that God (if He exists) is worthy of worship.[1] Any being who is not worthy of worship cannot be God, just as any being who is not omnipotent, or who is not perfectly good, cannot be God. This is

Reprinted by permission of the author's estate and the publisher, "God and Human Attitudes," *Religious Studies*, Vol. 7, 1971, pp. 325–37. © 1971 by Cambridge University Press.

reflected in the attitudes of religious believers who recognize that, whatever else God may be, He is a being before whom men should bow down. Moreover, He is unique in this; to worship anyone or anything else is blasphemy. In this paper I shall present an *a priori* argument against the existence of God which is based on the conception of God as a fitting object of worship. The argument is that God cannot exist, because no being could ever *be* a fitting object of worship.

However, before I can present this argument, there are several preliminary matters that require attention. The chief of these, which will hopefully have some independent interest of its own, is an examination of the concept of worship. In spite of its great importance this concept has received remarkably little attention from philosophers of religion; and when it has been treated, the usual approach is by way of referring to God's awesomeness or mysteriousness: to worship is to 'bow down in silent awe' when confronted with a being that is 'terrifyingly mysterious'.[2] But neither of these notions is of much help in understanding worship. Awe is certainly not the same thing as worship; one can be awed by a performance of *King Lear*, or by witnessing an eclipse of the sun or an earthquake, or by meeting one's favourite film-star, without worshipping any of these things. And a great many things are both terrifying and mysterious that we have not the slightest inclination to worship—I suppose the Black Plague fits that description for many people. The account of worship that I will give will be an alternative to those which rely on such notions as awesomeness and mysteriousness.

II.

Consider McBlank, who worked against his country's entry into the Second World War, refused induction into the army, and was sent to jail. He was active in the 'ban the bomb' movements of the fifties; he made speeches, wrote pamphlets, led demonstrations, and went back to jail. And finally, he has been active in opposing the war in Vietnam. In all of this he has acted out of principle; he thinks that all war is evil and that no war is ever justified. I want to make three observations about McBlank's pacifist commitments. (*a*) One thing that is involved is simply his recognition that certain facts are the case. History is full of wars; war causes the massive destruction of life and property; in war men suffer on a scale hardly matched in any other way; the large nations now have weapons which, if used, could destroy the human race; and so on. These are just facts which any normally informed man will admit without argument. (*b*) But of course they are not *merely* facts, which people recognise to be the case in some indifferent manner. They are facts that have special importance to human beings. They form an ominous and threatening backdrop to people's lives—even though for most people they are a backdrop only. But not so for McBlank. He sees the accumulation of these facts as having radical implications for his conduct; he behaves in a very different way from the way he would behave were it not for these facts. His whole style of life is different; his conduct is altered, not just in its details, but in its pattern. (*c*) Not only is his overt behaviour affected; so are his ways of thinking about the world and his place in it. His *self-image* is different. He sees himself as a member of a race with an insane history of self-destruction, and his self-image becomes that of an active opponent of the forces that lead to this self-destruction. He *is* an opponent of militarism just as he is a father or a musician. When some existentialists say that we 'create ourselves' by our choices, they may have something like this in mind.

Thus, there are at least three things that determine McBlank's role as an opponent of war: first, his recognition that certain facts are the case; second his taking these facts as having important implications for his conduct; and third, his self-image as living his life (at least in part) in response to these facts. My first thesis about worship is that the worshipper has a set of beliefs about God[3] which function in the same way as McBlank's beliefs about war.

First, the worshipper believes that certain things are the case: that the world was created by an all-powerful, all-wise being who knows our every thought and action; that this being, called God, cares for us and regards us as his children; that we are made by him in order to return his love and live in accordance with his laws; and that, if we do not live in a way pleasing to him, we may be severely punished. Now these beliefs are certainly not shared by all reasonable people; on the contrary, many thoughtful persons regard them as nothing more than mere fantasy. But these beliefs are accepted by religious people, and that is what is important here. I do not say that this particular set of beliefs is definitive of religion in general, or of Judaism or Christianity in particular; it is meant only as a sample of the sorts of belief typically held by religious people in the West. They are, however, the sort of beliefs about God that are required for the business of worshipping God to make any sense.

Second, like the facts about warfare, these are not merely facts which one notes with an air of indifference; they have important implications for one's conduct. An effort must be made to discover God's will both for people generally and for oneself in particular; and to this end, the believer consults the church authorities and the theologians, reads the scripture, and prays. The degree to which this will alter his overt behaviour will depend, first, on exactly what he decides God would have him do, and second, on the extent to which his behaviour would have followed the prescribed pattern in any case.[4]

Finally, the believer's recognition of these 'facts' will influence his self-image and his way of thinking about the world and his place in it. The world will be regarded as made for the fulfilment of divine purposes; the hardships that befall men will be regarded either as 'tests' in some sense or as punishments for sin; and most important, the believer will think of himself as a 'Child of God' and of his conduct as reflecting either honour or dishonour upon his Heavenly Father.

What will be most controversial in what I have said so far (to some philosophers, though perhaps not to most religious believers) is the treatment of claims such as 'God regards us as his children' as in some sense factual. Wittgenstein[5] is reported to have thought this a total misunderstanding of religious belief; and others have followed him in this.[6] Religious utterances, it is said, do not report putative facts; instead, we should understand such utterances as revealing the speaker's *form of life*. To have a form of life is to accept a language-game; the religious believer accepts a language-game in which there is talk of God, creation, Heaven and Hell, a Last Judgment, and so forth, which the sceptic does not accept. Such language-games can only be understood on their own terms; we must not try to assimilate them to other sorts of games. To see how this particular game works we need only to examine the way the language of religion is used by actual believers—in its proper habitat the language-game will be 'in order' as it is. We find that the religious believer uses such utterances for a number of purposes, e.g. to express reasons for action, to show the significance which he attaches to various things, to express his attitudes, etc.—but not to 'state facts' in the ordinary sense. So when the believer makes a typically religious assertion, and non-believer denies the same, *they are not contradicting one another;* rather, the non-believer is simply

refusing to play the believer's (very serious) game. Wittgenstein (as recorded by his pupils) said:

'Suppose that someone believed in the Last Judgement, and I don't, does this mean that I believe the opposite to him, just that there won't be such a thing? I would say: "not at all, or not always."

Suppose I say that the body will rot, and another says "No. Particles will rejoin in a thousand years, and there will be a Resurrection of you".

If some said: "Wittgenstein, do you believe in this?" I'd say: "No." "Do you contradict the man?" I'd say: "No." [7]

Wittgenstein goes on to say that the difference between the believer and the sceptic is not that one holds something to be true that the other thinks false, but that the believer takes certain things as 'guidance for life' that the sceptic does not, e.g. that there will be a Last Judgment. He illustrates this by reference to a person who 'thinks of retribution' when he plans his conduct or assesses his condition:

'Suppose you had two people, and one of them, when he had to decide which course to take, thought of retribution, and the other did not. One person might, for instance, be inclined to take everything that happened to him as a reward or punishment, and another person doesn't think of this at all.

If he is ill, he may think: "What have I done to deserve this?" This is one way of thinking of retribution. Another way is, he thinks in a general way whenever he is ashamed of himself: "This will be punished."

Take two people, one of whom talks of his behaviour and of what happens to him in terms of retribution, the other does not. These people think entirely differently. Yet, so far, you can't say they believe different things.

Suppose someone is ill and he says: "This is punishment," and I say: "If I'm ill, I don't think of punishment at all." If you say: "Do you believe the opposite?"—you can call it believing the opposite, but it is entirely different from what we would normally call believing the opposite.

I think differently, in a different way. I say different things to myself. I have different pictures.'[8]

I will limit myself to three remarks about this very difficult view.[9] First it is not at all clear that this account is true to the intentions of those who actually engage in religious discourse. If a believer (at least, the great majority of those whom I have known or read about) says that there will be a Last Judgment, and a sceptic says that there will not, the believer certainly will think that he has been contradicted. Of course, the sceptic might not think of denying such a thing except for the fact that the believer asserts it; and in this trivial sense the sceptic might 'think differently' from the believer—but this is completely beside the point. Moreover, former believers who become sceptics frequently do so because they come to believe that religious assertions are *false;* and then, they consider themselves to be denying exactly what they previously asserted. Second, a belief does not lose its ordinary factual import simply because it occupies a central place in one's way of life. McBlank takes the facts about war as 'guidance for life' in a perfectly straightforward sense; but they remain facts. I take it that just as the man in Wittgenstein's example 'thinks of retribution' often, McBlank thinks of war often. So, we do not need to assign religious utterances a special status in order to explain their importance for one's way of life. Finally, while I realise that my account is very simple and mundane, whereas Wittgenstein's is 'deep' and difficult, nonetheless this may be an advantage, not a handicap, of my view. If the impact of religious belief on one's conduct and thinking can be explained by appeal to nothing more mysterious than putative facts and their impact on conduct and thinking, then the need for a more obscure theory will be obviated. And if a man believes that, *as a matter of fact,* his actions are subject to review by a just God who will mete out rewards and punishments on a day of final reckoning, that will explain very nicely why he 'thinks of retribution' when he reflects on his conduct.

III.

Worship is something that is *done;* but it is not clear just *what* is done when one worships. Other actions, such as throwing a ball or insulting one's neighbour, seem transparent enough. But not so with worship: when we celebrate Mass in the Roman Catholic Church, for example, what are we doing (apart from eating a wafer and drinking wine)? Or when we sing hymns in a Protestant church, what are we doing (other than merely singing songs)? What is it that makes these acts acts of *worship?* One obvious point is that these actions, and others like them, are ritualistic in character; so, before we can make any progress in understanding worship, perhaps it will help to ask about the nature of ritual.

First we need to distinguish the ceremonial form of a ritual from what is supposed to be accomplished by it. Consider, for example, the ritual of investiture for an English Prince. The Prince kneels; the Queen (or King) places a crown on his head; and he takes an oath: 'I do become your liege man of life and limb and of earthly worship, and faith and trust I will bear unto thee to live and die against all manner of folks.' By this ceremony the Prince is elevated to his new station; and by this oath he acknowledges the commitments which, as Prince, he will owe the Queen. In one sense the ceremonial form of the ritual is quite unimportant: it is possible that some other procedure might have been laid down, without the point of the ritual being affected in any way. Rather than placing a crown on his head, the Queen might break an egg into his palm (that could symbolise all sorts of things). Once this was established as the procedure to be followed, it would do as well as the other. It would still be the ritual of investiture, so long as it was understood that by the ceremony a Prince is created. The performance of a ritual, then, is in certain respects like the use of language: in speaking, sounds are uttered and, thanks to the conventions of the language, something is said, or affirmed, or done, etc.: and in a ritual performance, a ceremony is enacted and, thanks to the conventions associated with the ceremony, something is done, or affirmed, or celebrated, etc.

How are we to explain the point of the ritual of investiture? We might explain that certain parts of the ritual symbolise specific things, for example that the Prince kneeling before the Queen symbolises his subordination to her (it is not, for example, merely to make it easier for her to place the crown on his head). But it is essential that, in explaining the point of the ritual as a whole, we include that a Prince is being created, that he is henceforth to have certain rights in virtue of having been made a Prince, and that he is to have certain duties which he is now acknowledging, among which are complete loyalty and faithfulness to the Queen, and so on. If the listener already knows about the complex relations between Queens, Princes, and subjects, then all we need to tell him is that a Prince is being installed in office; but if he is unfamiliar with this social system, we must tell him a great deal if he is to understand what is going on.

So, once we understand the social system in which there are Queens, Princes, and subjects, and therefore understand the role assigned to each within that system, we can sum up what is happening in the ritual of investiture in this way: someone is being made a Prince, and he is accepting that role with all that it involves. (Exactly the same explanation could be given, *mutatis mutandis*, for the marriage ceremony.)

The question to be asked about the ritual of worship is what analogous explanation can be given of it. The ceremonial form of the ritual may vary according to the customs of the religious community; it may involve singing, drinking wine, counting beads, sitting with a solemn expression on one's face, dancing, making a sacrifice, or what-have-you. But what is the point of it?

As I have already said, the worshipper thinks of himself as inhabiting a world created by an infinitely wise, infinitely powerful, perfectly good God; and it is a world in which he, along with other men, occupies a special place in virtue of God's intentions. This gives him a certain role to play: the role of a 'Child of God'. My second thesis about worship is that in worshipping God one is acknowledging and accepting this role, and that this is the primary function of the ritual of worship. Just as the ritual of investiture derives its significance from its place within the social system of Queens, Princes, and subjects, the ritual of worship gets its significance from an assumed system of relationships between God and men. In the ceremony of investiture, the Prince assumes a role with respect to the Queen and the citizenry; and in worship, a man affirms his role with respect to God.

Worship presumes the superior status of the one worshipped. This is reflected in the logical point that there can be no such things as mutual or reciprocal worship, unless one or the other of the parties is mistaken as to his own status. We can very well comprehend people loving one another or respecting one another, but not (unless they are misled) worshipping one another. This is because the worshipper necessarily assumes his own inferiority; and since inferiority is an asymmetrical relation, so is worship. (The nature of the 'superiority' and 'inferiority' involved here is of course problematic; but on the account I am presenting it may be understood on the model of superior and inferior positions within a social system. More on this later.) This is also why *humility* is necessary on the part of the worshipper. The role to which he commits himself is that of the humble servant, 'not worthy to touch the hem of His garment'. Compared to God's gloriousness, 'all our righteousnesses are as filthy rags' (Isaiah 64:6).

So, in committing oneself to this role, one is acknowledging God's greatness and one's own relative worthlessness. This humble attitude is not a mere embellishment of the ritual: on the contrary, worship, unlike love or respect, *requires* humility. Pride is a sin, and pride before God is incompatible with worshipping him.

On the view that I am suggesting, the function of worship as 'glorifying' or 'praising' God, which is usually taken to be its primary function, may be regarded as derivative from the more fundamental nature of worship as commitment to the role of God's Child. 'Praising' God is giving him the honour and respect due to one in his position of eminence, just as one shows respect and honour in giving fealty to a King.

In short, the worshipper is in this position: He believes that there is a being, God, who is the perfectly good, perfectly powerful, perfectly wise Creator of the Universe; and he views himself as the 'Child of God,' made for God's purposes and responsible to God for his conduct. And the ritual of worship, which may have any number of ceremonial forms according to the customs of the religious community, has as its point the acceptance of, and commitment to, one's role as God's Child, with all that this involves. If this account is accepted, then there is no mystery as to the relation between the act of worship and the worshipper's other activity. Worship will be regarded not as an isolated act taking place on Sunday morning, with no necessary connection to one's behaviour the rest of the week, but as a ritualistic expression of and commitment to a role which dominates one's whole way of life.[10]

IV.

An important feature of roles is that they can be violated; we can act and think consistently with a role, or we can act and think inconsistently with it. The Prince can, for example, act inconsistently with his role as Prince by giving greater importance to his own interests and welfare than to the Queen's; in this case, he is no longer her 'liege man'. And a father who does not attend to the welfare of his children is not acting consistently with his role as a father (at least as that role is defined in our society), and so on. The question that I want to raise now is, What would count as violating the role to which one is pledged in virtue of worshipping God?

In Genesis there are two familiar stories, both concerning Abraham, that are relevant here. The first is the story of the near-sacrifice of Isaac. We are told that Abraham was 'tempted' by God, who commanded him to offer Isaac as a human sacrifice. Abraham obeyed without hesitation: he prepared an altar, bound Isaac to it, and was about to kill him until God intervened at the last moment, saying 'Lay not thine hand upon the lad, neither do thou any thing unto him: for now I know that thou fearest God, seeing thou hast not withheld thy son, thine only son from me' (Genesis 22:12). So Abraham passed the test. But how could he have failed? What was his 'temptation'? Obviously, his temptation was to disobey God; God had ordered him to do something contrary to both his wishes and his sense of what would otherwise be right and wrong. He could have defied God; but he did not—he subordinated himself, his own desires and judgments, to God's command, even when the temptation to do otherwise was strongest.

It is interesting that Abraham's record in this respect was not perfect. We also have the story of him bargaining with God over the conditions for saving Sodom and Gomorrah from destruction. God had said that he would destroy those cities because they were so wicked; but Abraham gets God to agree that if fifty righteous men can be found there, then the cities will be spared. Then he persuades God to lower the number to forty-five, then forty, then thirty, then twenty, and finally ten. Here we have a different Abraham, not servile and obedient, but willing to challenge God and bargain with him. However, even as he bargains with God,

Abraham realises that there is something radically inappropriate about it: he says, 'Behold now, I have taken upon me to speak unto the Lord, which am but dust and ashes . . . Oh let not the Lord be angry . . .' (Genesis 18:27, 30).

The fact is that Abraham could not, consistently with his role as God's subject, set his own judgment and will against God's. The author of Genesis was certainly right about this. We cannot recognise any being *as God*, and at the same time set ourselves against him. The point is not merely that it would be imprudent to defy God, since we certainly can't get away with it; rather, there is a stronger, logical point involved—namely, that if we recognise any being *as God*, then we are committed, in virtue of that recognition, to obeying him.

To see why this is so, we must first notice that 'God' is not a proper name like 'Richard Nixon' but a title like 'President of the United States' or 'King'.[11] Thus, 'Jehovah is God' is a nontautological statement in which the title 'God' is assigned to Jehovah, a particular being—just as 'Richard Nixon is President of the United States' assigns the title 'President of the United States' to a particular man. This permits us to understand how statements like 'God is perfectly wise' can be logical truths, which is highly problematic if 'God' is regarded as a proper name. Although it is not a logical truth that any particular being is perfectly wise, it nevertheless is a logical truth that if any being is God (i.e. if any being properly holds that title) then that being is perfectly wise. This is exactly analogous to saying: although it is not a logical truth that Richard Nixon has the authority to veto congressional legislation, nevertheless it is a logical truth that if Richard Nixon is President of the United States then he has that authority.

To bear the title 'God', then, a being must have certain qualifications. He must, for example, be all-powerful and perfectly good in addition to being perfectly wise. And in the same vein, to apply the title 'God' to a being is to recognise him as one to be obeyed. The same is true, to a lesser extent, of 'King'—to recognise anyone as King is to acknowledge that he occupies a place of authority and has a claim on one's allegiance as his subject. And to recognise any being as God is to acknowledge that he has *unlimited* authority, and an unlimited claim on one's allegiance.[12] Thus, we might regard Abraham's reluctance to defy Jehovah as grounded not only in his fear of Jehovah's wrath, but as a logical consequence of his acceptance of Jehovah *as God*. Camus was right to think that 'From the moment that man submits God to moral judgment, he kills Him his own heart'.[13] What a man can 'kill' by defying or even questioning God is not the being that (supposedly) *is* God, but *his own conception of that being as God*. That God is not to be judged, challenged, defied, or disobeyed, is at bottom a truth of logic; to do any of these things is incompatible with taking him as One to be worshipped.

V.

So the idea that any being could be *worthy* of worship is much more problematical than we might have at first imagined. For in admitting that a being is worthy of worship we would be recognising him as having an unqualified claim on our obedience. The question, then, is whether there could be such an unqualified claim. It should be noted that the description of a being as all-powerful, all-wise, etc., would not automatically settle the issue; for even while admitting the existence of such an awesome being we might still question whether we should recognise him as having an unlimited claim on our obedience.

In fact, there is a long tradition in moral philosophy, from Plato to Kant, according to which such a recognition could never be made by a moral agent. According to this tradition, to be a moral agent is to be an autonomous or self-directed agent; unlike the precepts of law or social custom, moral precepts are imposed by the agent upon himself, and the penalty for their violation is, in Kant's words, 'self-contempt and inner abhorrence'.[14] The virtuous man is therefore identified with the man of integrity, i.e. the man who acts according to precepts which he can, on reflection, conscientiously approve in his own heart. Although this is a highly individualistic approach to morals, it is not thought to invite anarchy because men are regarded as more or less reasonable and as desiring what we would normally think of as a decent life lived in the company of other men.

On this view, to deliver oneself over to a moral authority for directions about what to do is simply incompatible with being a moral agent. To say 'I will follow so-and-so's directions no matter what they are and no matter what my own conscience would otherwise direct me to do' is to opt out of moral thinking altogether; it is to abandon one's role as a moral agent. And it does not matter whether 'so-and-so' is the law, the customs of one's society, or God. This does not, of course, preclude one from seeking advice on moral matters, and even on occasion following that advice blindly, trusting in the good judgment of the adviser. But this is to be justified by the details of the particular case, e.g. that you cannot in that case form any reasonable judgment of your own due to ignorance or inexperience in dealing with the types of matters involved. What *is* precluded is that a man should, while in possession of his wits, adopt this style of decision-making (or perhaps we should say this style of *abdicating* decision-making) as a general strategy of living, or abandon his own best judgment in any case where he can form a judgment of which he is reasonably confident.

What we have, then, is a conflict between the role of worshipper, which by its very nature commits one to total subservience to God, and the role of moral agent, which necessarily involves autonomous decision-making. The point is that the role of worshipper takes precedence over every other role which the worshipper has—when there is any conflict, the worshipper's commitment to God has priority over any other commitments which he might have. But the first commitment of a moral agent is to do what in his own heart he thinks is right. Thus the following argument might be constructed:

(*a*) If any being is God, he must be a fitting object of worship.
(*b*) No being could possibly be a fitting object of worship, since worship requires the abandonment of one's role as an autonomous moral agent.
(*c*) Therefore, there cannot be any being who is God.

VI.

The concept of moral agency underlying this argument is complex and controversial; and, although I think it is sound, I cannot give it the detailed treatment here that it requires. Instead, I will conclude by answering some of the most obvious objections to the argument.

(1) What if God lets us go our own way, and issues no commands other than that we should live according to our own consciences? In that case there would be no incompatibility between our commitment to God and our commitments as moral agents, since God would leave us free to direct our own lives. The fact that this supposition is contrary to major religious traditions (such as the Christian tradition) doesn't matter, since these traditions could be mistaken. The answer here is that this is a mere contingency, and that even if God did not require obedience to detailed commands, the worshipper would still be committed to the abandonment of his role as a moral agent, *if* God required it.

(2) It has been admitted as a necessary truth that God is perfectly good; it follows as a corollary that He would never require us to do anything except what is right. Therefore in obeying God we would only be doing

what we should do in any case. So there is no incompatibility between obeying him and carrying out our moral commitments. Our primary commitment as moral agents is to do right, and God's commands *are* right, so that's that.

This objection rests on a misunderstanding of the assertion that (necessarily) God is perfectly good. This can be intelligibly asserted only because of the principle that *No being who is not perfectly good may bear the title 'God'*.[15] We cannot determine whether some being is God without first checking on whether he is perfectly good;[16] and we cannot decide whether he is perfectly good without knowing (among other things) whether his commands to us are right. Thus our own judgment that some actions are right, and others wrong, is logically prior to our recognition of any being as God. The upshot of this is that we cannot justify the suspension of our own judgment on the grounds that we are deferring to God's command (which, as a matter of logic, *must* be right); for if, by our own best judgment, the command is wrong, this gives us good reason to withhold the title 'God' from the commander.

(3) The following expresses a view which has always had its advocates among theologians: 'Men are sinful; their very consciences are corrupt and unreliable guides. What is taken for conscientiousness among men is nothing more than self-aggrandisement and arrogance. Therefore, we cannot trust our own judgment; we must trust God and do what he wills. Only then can we be assured of doing right.'

This view suffers from a fundamental inconsistency. It is said that we cannot know for ourselves what is right and what is wrong; and this is because our judgment is corrupt. But how do we know that our judgment is corrupt? Presumably, in order to know that, we would have to know (*a*) that some actions are morally required of us, and (*b*) that our own

judgment does not reveal that these actions are required. However, (*a*) is just the sort of thing that we can*not* know, according to this view. Now it may be suggested that while we cannot know (*a*) by our own judgment, we can know it as a result of God's revelation. But even setting aside the practical difficulties of distinguishing genuine from bogus revelation (a generous concession), there is still this problem: if we learn that God (i.e. some being that we take to be God) requires us to do a certain action, and we conclude on this account that the action is morally right, then we have *still* made at least one moral judgment of our own, namely that whatever this being requires is morally right. Therefore, it is impossible to maintain the view that we do have some moral knowledge, and that *all* of it comes from God's revelation.

(4) Many philosophers, including St. Thomas, have held that the voice of individual conscience *is* the voice of God speaking to the individual, whether he is a believer or not.[17] This would resolve the alleged conflict because in following one's conscience one would at the same time be discharging his obligation as a worshipper to obey God. However, this manoeuvre is unsatisfying, since if taken seriously it would lead to the conclusion that, in speaking to us through our 'consciences', God is merely tricking us: for he is giving us the illusion of self-governance while all the time he is manipulating our thoughts from without. Moreover, in acting from conscience we are acting under the view that our actions are right and not merely that they are decreed by a higher power. Plato's argument in the *Euthyphro* can be adapted to this point: If, in speaking to us through the voice of conscience, God is informing us of what is right, then there is no reason to think that we could not discover this for ourselves—the notion of 'God informing us' is eliminable. On the other hand, if God is only giving us arbitrary commands, which cannot be thought of as

'right' independently of his promulgating them, then the whole idea of 'conscience', as it is normally understood, is a sham.

(5) Finally, someone might object that the question of whether any being is *worthy* of worship is different from the question of whether we *should* worship him. In general, that X is worthy of our doing Y with respect to X does not entail that we should do Y with respect to X. For example, Mrs Brown, being a fine woman, may be worthy of a marriage proposal, but we ought not to propose to her since she is already married. Or, Seaman Jones may be worthy of a medal for heroism but perhaps there are reasons why we should not award it. Similarly, it may be that there is a being who is worthy of worship and yet we should not worship him since it would interfere with our lives as moral agents. Thus God, who is worthy of worship, may exist; and we should love, respect, and honour him, but not worship him in the full sense of the word. If this is correct, then the argument of section 5 is fallacious.

This rebuttal will not work because of an important disanalogy between the cases of proposing marriage and awarding the medal, on the one hand, and the case of worship on the other. It may be that Mrs Brown is worthy of a proposal, yet there are circumstances in which it would be wrong to propose to her. However, these circumstances are contrasted with others in which it would be perfectly all right. The same goes for Seaman Jones's medal: there are *some* circumstances in which awarding it would be proper. But in the case of worship—if the foregoing arguments have been sound—there are *no* circumstances under which anyone should worship God. And if one should *never* worship, then the concept of a fitting object of worship is an empty one.

The above argument will probably not persuade anyone to abandon belief in God—arguments rarely do—and there are certainly many more points which need to be worked out before it can be known whether this argument is even viable. Yet it does raise an issue which is clear enough. Theologians are already accustomed to speaking of theistic belief and commitment as taking the believer 'beyond morality', and I think they are right. The question is whether this should not be regarded as a severe embarrassment.[18]

Notes

1. Hartshorne and Pike suggest that the formula 'that than which none greater can be conceived' should be interpreted as 'that than which none more worthy of worship can be conceived'. Charles Hartshorne, *Anselm's Discovery* (LaSalle, Illinois, 1966), pp. 25–6; and Nelson Pike, *God and Timelessness* (London, 1970), pp. 149–60.

2. These phrases are from John Hick, *Philosophy of Religion* (Englewood Cliffs, New Jersey, 1963), pp. 13–14.

3. In speaking of 'beliefs about God' I have in mind those typical of Western religions. I shall construct my account of worship in these terms, although the account will be adaptable to other forms of worship such as Satan-worship (see endnote 10, below).

4. For example, one religious believer who thinks that his conduct must be very different on account of his belief is P. T. Geach: see his essay 'The Moral Law and the Law of God', in *God and the Soul* (London, 1969).

5. Ludwig Wittgenstein, *Lectures and Conversations on Aesthetics, Psychology, and Religious Belief* (Berkeley, 1967). Edited by Cyril Barrett, from notes taken by Yorick Smythies, Rush Rhees, and James Taylor.

6. For example, Rush Rhees, in *Without Answers* (London, 1969), ch. 13.

7. Wittgenstein, p. 53.

8. Wittgenstein, pp. 54–5.

9. The whole subject is explored in detail in Kai Nielsen, 'Wittgensteinian Fideism', *Philosophy*, 42 (1967), pp. 191–209.

10. This account of worship, specified here in terms of what it means to worship God, may easily be adapted to the worship of other beings such as Satan. The only changes required are (*a*) that we substitute for beliefs about God analogous beliefs about Satan, and (*b*) that we understand the ritual of worship as committing the Satan-worshipper to a role as Satan's servant in the same way that worshipping God commits theists to the role of His servant.

11. Cf. Nelson Pike, 'Omnipotence and God's Ability to Sin', *American Philosophical Quarterly*, (1969), pp. 208–9, and C. B. Martin, *Religious Belief* (Ithaca, 1964), ch. 4.

12. This suggestion might also throw some light on the much-discussed problem of how we could, even in principle, *verify* the existence of God. Sceptics have argued that, even though we might be able to confirm the existence of an all-powerful cosmic superbeing (if one existed), we still wouldn't know what it means to verify that this being is *divine*. And this, it is said, casts doubt on whether the notion of divinity, and related notions such as 'Christ and 'God', are intelligible. (Cf. Kai Nielsen, 'Eschatological Verification', *The Canadian Journal of Theology*, 9, 1963.) Perhaps this is because, in designating a being as God, we are not only describing him as having certain factual properties (such as omnipotence), but also *ascribing* to him a certain place in our devotions, and taking him as one to be obeyed, worshipped, praised, etc. If this is part of the logic of 'God', then we shouldn't be surprised if God's existence, in so far as that includes the existence of divinity, is not entirely confirmable—for only the 'factual properties' such as omnipotence will be verifiable in the usual way. But once the reason for this is understood, it no longer seems such a serious matter.

13. Albert Camus, *The Rebel*, translated by Anthony Bower (New York, 1956), p. 62.

14. Immanuel Kant, *Foundations of the Metaphysics of Morals*, translated by Lewis White Beck (New York, 1959), p. 44.

15. See above, section 4.

16. Of course we cannot ever know that such a being is *perfectly* good, since this would require an examination of *all* his actions and commands, etc., which is impossible. However, if we observed many good things about him and no evil ones, we would be justified in putting forth the hypothesis that he is perfectly good and acting accordingly. The hypothesis would be confirmed or disconfirmed by future observations in the usual way.

17. Cf. Geach: 'The rational recognition that a practice is generally undesirable and that it is best for people on the whole not even to think of resorting to it is thus *in fact* a promulgation to a man of the Divine law forbidding the practice, even if he does not realise that this is a promulgation of the Divine law, even if he does not believe there is a God.'

18. A number of people read earlier versions of this paper and made helpful comments. I have to thank especially Kai Nielsen, William Ruddick, Jack Glickman, and Steven Cahn.

God and the Moral Order

C. Stephen Layman

C. Stephen Layman is a professor of philosophy at Seattle Pacific University. He has published books on moral philosophy, logic, and the philosophy of religion. In this selection, Layman advances and defends a version of the moral argument for the existence of God. His version differs from others, like Kant's, in that he does not claim that God and immortality are necessary to explain the moral obligations that we in fact have; he claims only that God and immortality are parts of the best explanation.

I argue that three theses about the moral order are defensible, that they do not beg the question of God's existence, and that they support theism over naturalism. The three theses are:

1. In every actual case, one has most reason to do what is morally required. (One has most reason to do act x if and only if the strongest relevant reasons favor doing x.)
2. If there is no God and no life after death, then there are cases in which morality requires that one make a great sacrifice that confers relatively modest benefits (or prevents relatively modest harms).
3. If in a given situation one must make a great sacrifice in order to do what is morally required, but the sacrifice confers relatively modest benefits (or prevents relatively modest harms), then one does not have most reason to do what is morally required.

For Layman: Reprinted by permission of the publisher from C. Stephen Layman, "God and the Moral Order," *Faith and Philosophy* 19, 2002, pp. 304–16. © 2002.

("Sacrifice" is here used in a technical way to indicate a permanent and uncompensated loss of something that is in the agent's long-term best interests.) After arguing for these three theses, I claim that since theism can accommodate them and naturalism cannot, theism has a theoretical advantage over naturalism.

Skepticism about the value of moral arguments for theism is widespread among philosophers. But I maintain that there is a conjunction of theses about the moral order that increases the probability of theism. None of these theses begs the question of God's existence and each is, I believe, plausible upon reflection.

Prior to stating my argument, a number of preliminaries are in order. First, in this paper "God" means "an almighty and wholly good being." By "theism" I mean simply the view that God exists. I assume that a wholly good being is perfectly loving. I also assume that God would not order reality in such a way that being moral would disadvantage agents in the long run. And I assume that "the long term" likely involves life after death, given theism.[1]

Second, I do not think the moral argument I am advancing can stand alone. Hence, in putting it forward, I assume either that other theistic arguments provide some significant support for the existence of God or that belief in God is properly basic.[2] Thus, I claim merely that my moral argument makes a positive contribution to a larger, rational case for (or defense of) theism.

Third, the argument I wish to advance is primarily an attempt to show that a certain body of evidence supports theism over *naturalism*. By "naturalism" I mean roughly the view that

(a) whatever exists is material or dependent (causally or by supervenience) on material things and (b) material things are entirely governed by natural laws. There is no God according to the naturalist and no life after death. When we die, our bodies decay, and we cease to exist.

Fourth, my argument is designed to appeal to those who believe that there are irreducibly moral facts. I assume, for example, that it is a moral fact that *it is wrong to torture people for fun.* Some individuals or groups may deny or ignore this fact, but it remains a fact. (Analogously, it is fact that the earth is round, and this remains a fact even though it is denied by the Flat Earth Society.) In saying that there are *irreducibly* moral facts, I mean that the facts in question cannot correctly be identified with non-evaluative or non-normative facts, such as merely psychological or sociological facts. To illustrate, the fact that *murder is wrong* cannot be identified with the fact that *most humans disapprove of murder.*[3]

Fifth, my argument is meant to appeal to those who accept a fairly traditional understanding of what is morally right and wrong. I shall simply assume, for example, that lying, stealing, and killing are generally wrong, though I shall not beg any questions about cases commonly regarded as allowable exceptions. For instance, I shall assume that it is generally wrong to intentionally kill a human being, but I shall not beg any questions about the usual range of possible exceptions, e.g., killing in self-defense. Of course, some moral theorists reject what I here call a "fairly traditional understanding of what is right and wrong." To illustrate, some act-utilitarians find killing, stealing, and lying permissible in many situations in which these acts are traditionally considered wrong. In my opinion, ethical theories that justify killing, stealing, and lying in a much wider range of cases than is traditionally allowed are, for that very reason, highly problematic; but I shall not argue that case here. I can only say that those who reject a fairly traditional view about the wrongness of

killing, stealing, and lying need read no further, for this paper is unlikely to be of any interest to them.

Sixth, in this paper, locutions such as "This is a moral duty" or "This is a moral requirement" express not merely *prima facie* moral duties but *ultima facie* moral duties. That is, when I say that an act is a moral duty (or that it is morally required), I mean that, in the situation in question, the act is what one morally ought to do *all things considered.* For example, if I say that one is morally required *not to steal* in a certain situation, I do not mean simply that there are some moral considerations against stealing that may be outweighed by other moral considerations in favor of stealing; rather I mean that; taking all morally relevant factors into account, one ought not to steal in that situation.

Seventh, I shall frequently use the locution "x has most reason to do y." A person has "most reason" to do something, in my sense, when the weightiest or strongest reasons favor doing that thing. So, if an agent has most reason to do act A, then taking all relevant reasons into account (e.g., prudential, moral, and aesthetic reasons), they on balance favor performing A. And I assume that "the balance of reasons" is not a merely subjective notion; agents can make mistakes in weighing up reasons for and against an action. For example, in my view, a person who thinks that moral requirements are typically outweighed by personal whims would be making a grave mistake.

Finally, I shall use the word "sacrifice" in a somewhat technical way to indicate *a permanent, net loss of something that is in the long-term best interests of the agent.* So, for present purposes, the word "sacrifice" indicates a permanent loss to the agent, not a temporary one; moreover, it indicates a loss that is not "made up for" in the long run. Of course, as the term is ordinarily used, sacrifices are often temporary and/or compensated, so let me provide some examples of a sacrifice in my sense. Suppose, for the sake of illustration, that there is no life after death, and hence that this earthly life is the only one we've got. On this supposition, if one gave up one's eyesight permanently and this loss was not compensated in any way, then one would have made a sacrifice in my sense of the term, indeed a great sacrifice. Similarly, if a person who is not poor were to give up all of her material goods, and this loss was not compensated in any way, she would have made a sacrifice in my sense of the term, presumably a great one.

I. The Argument Briefly Stated

In this section I will state my argument. My intent is to summarize the basic intuitions that give the argument its plausibility. In the next section I will consider some important objections to the argument and amplify some key points.

My argument has three main premises.[4] Premise (1) is this: *In every actual case one has most reason to do what is morally required.* In other words, in every actual case, if a person is morally required to do some act, then (taking all relevant reasons into account) the balance of reasons favors performing that act. Why think (1) is true? Consider an actual case in which someone has performed an action that you initially find quite puzzling or odd. Then imagine that you become convinced that in performing the action the person was doing his or her moral duty. The act was morally required. Would you not assume that the action was fully justified on this basis? Most of us would and most moral theorists (theist or non-theist) would agree. If an act is my moral duty, then I have overriding reason to perform it. In short, premise (1) is part of our pre-theoretical conception of morality. And thus, if we take an Aristotelian approach to philosophy, (1) is among the appearances to be saved.

We can, however, say a bit more in favor of (1): If one does not always have most reason to do what is morally required, then why should one be moral? In a given case, considerations of prudence, aesthetics, and/or etiquette may conflict with moral considerations and one faces the question, "How should one act?", where the "should" is not moral but may be interpreted along the following lines: "Which alternative course of action is backed by the strongest or weightiest reasons?" And if we grant that a certain course of action X is backed by the strongest or weightiest reasons, then from a rational point of view X should be done. Moreover, if we agree that the best reasons sometimes favor immoral actions, and yet we give our full allegiance to morality, then our allegiance to morality is irrational in the sense that it involves acting on inferior reasons. But I presume that most of my readers give morality their full allegiance and do not regard this allegiance as involving such irrationality. So, I assume that my readers will find themselves strongly inclined to accept (1).

Before going on, however, I should point out that premise (1) is *not* the claim that one has most reason to do what is morally required in every *logically possible* case. In other words, I have not claimed that (1) is a necessary truth, I have merely claimed that it is true. And I shall soon describe some *logically possible* cases or situations in which it seems to me that the agent would not have most reason to do what is morally required. I regard these cases as *merely* logically possible—I myself do not think that cases combining all of the relevant features occur in the actual world. However, those who are convinced that there is no God and no life after death may be inclined to regard cases of the relevant type as actual, and this may raise questions about premise (1). I shall return to this matter in section II, but for now I will simply make three assertions: (a) since we are discussing an argument for God's existence, I take it that the non-existence of God is not properly assumed in evaluating the truth of my premises, (b) I hope to show that each of my three main premises is either embedded in our pre-theoretical conception of morality or defensible via argument (or both), and (c) my overall strategy is to argue that theism has a theoretical advantage over naturalism because theism can accommodate my three main premises while naturalism cannot.

Premise (2) is as follows: *If there is no God and no life after death, then there are cases in which morality requires that one make a great sacrifice that confers relatively modest benefits (or prevents relatively modest harms).* The following case— let us call it the "Ms. Poore case"—is offered in support of premise (2). Suppose Ms. Poore has lived many years in grinding poverty. She is not starving, but has only the bare necessities. She has tried very hard to get ahead by hard work, but nothing has come of her efforts. An opportunity to steal a large sum of money arises. If Ms. Poore steals the money and invests it wisely, she can obtain many desirable things her poverty has denied her: cure for a painful (but nonfatal) medical condition, a well-balanced diet, decent housing, adequate heat in the winter, health insurance, new career opportunities through education, etc. Moreover, if she steals the money, her chances of being caught are very low and she knows this. She is also aware that the person who owns the money is very wealthy and will not be greatly harmed by the theft. Let us add that Ms. Poore rationally believes that if she fails to steal the money, she will likely live in poverty for the remainder of her life. In short, Ms. Poore faces the choice of stealing the money or living in grinding poverty the rest of her life. In such a case, I think it would be *morally* wrong for Ms. Poore to steal the money; and yet, assuming there is no God and no life after death, failing to steal the money will likely deny her a large measure of personal fulfillment, i.e., a large measure of *what is in her long-term best interests.*[5]

I believe that the Ms. Poore case offers intuitive support for premise (2). However, some may reject (2) on the grounds that *virtue is its own reward*, and hence we are *necessarily* compensated for our *morally required* losses because moral virtue is a great enough benefit to those who possess it to compensate fully for any losses it entails. Now, I do not doubt that virtue is a benefit to those who possess it. But the suggestion that *perfect* virtue is *necessarily* a great enough benefit to its possessor to compensate fully for any loss it entails strikes me as highly implausible. Consider the following thought experiment.[6] Imagine two people, Mr. Gladwin and Ms. Goodwin. Mr. Gladwin is a morally lukewarm person who happens to be regarded as a paragon of virtue. He is admired by most people, prosperous, loved by his family and friends, and enjoys his life very much. Ms. Goodwin on the other hand is genuinely virtuous—honest, just, and pure in heart. Unfortunately, because of some clever enemies, Ms. Goodwin is widely regarded as wicked. She is in prison for life on false charges. Her family and friends, convinced that she is guilty, have turned against her. She subsists on a bread and water diet. Leaving God out of the picture for the moment, which of these two people is better off? Which is more fulfilled assuming there is no God? Surely it is Gladwin, not Goodwin. And note that even if virtue is of value for its own sake, it isn't the *only* thing of value.[7] In particular, freedom is valuable too. Suppose the warden agrees to release Ms. Goodwin if and only if she commits one morally wrong act. Perhaps her accounting skills enable her to help steal some money for the warden. Now, it seems to me that if there is no God and no life after death, it could easily be in Ms. Goodwin's long-term best interest to act immorally in this sort of case. The choice is roughly between life-long misery and an action that is immoral but produces relatively modest harms. So, it does not seem *necessarily* true that the rewards of *perfect* virtue compensate for the rewards of wrongdoing; nor does it seem *necessarily* true that being *perfectly* virtuous is in the agent's long-term best interest, I conclude that the cases of Ms. Poore and Ms. Goodwin provide strong intuitive support for (2).

The above cases also help to support premise (3): *If in a given case one must make a great* sacrifice in order to do what is morally required, but the sacrifice confers relatively modest benefits (or prevents relatively modest harms), then one does not have most reason to do what is morally required. Further support for this third premise comes from the fallowing principle: *It is always and necessarily prudent to act so as to promote one's long-term best interests.* And therefore, making a great sacrifice (where a sacrifice is an *uncompensated* giving-up of something that is in one's long-term best interests) is not prudent. Premise (3) makes explicit what the cases of Ms. Poore and Ms. Goodwin strongly suggest, namely, that *when considerations of prudence and morality clash, if the prudential considerations are truly momentous while the results of behaving immorally are relatively minor, then morality does not override prudence.*

There are, I recognize, multiple barriers to the acceptance of (3). I shall make two brief comments here and leave more technical issues for the next section. First, it may be helpful to note that if God exists, there will be no genuine conflicts between prudence and morality. The reason is this: to act immorally is to sin; to sin is to alienate oneself from God; and it is never in one's long-term best interests to alienate oneself from God. Accordingly, the situation, envisioned in the antecedent of premise (3) could not be actual if God exists, for in doing one's moral duty one prevents a very great harm to oneself, namely, alienation from God.

Second, it might be claimed that (a) acting immorally even just once will ruin one's character and (b) to ruin one's character is to incur a great loss; hence, one always has most reason to act morally. The problem with this objection to premise (3) is that (a) is manifestly false. For one's character can be summed up in terms of traits (e.g., being fair, being responsible, being wise, being loving, etc.), each trait being a tendency to act in a certain way. But many or even most people can do something wrong *in what they regard as a rare special case* without thereby altering significantly the basic

behavioral tendencies associated with their traits of character.[8]

We have, then, three premises, each of which is plausible on reflection and none of which begs the question of God's existence. Let us now examine the logic of the situation:

Premise 1. In every actual case, one has most reason to do what is morally required.
Premise 2. If there is no God and no life after death, then there are cases in which morality requires that one make a great sacrifice that confers relatively modest benefits (or prevents relatively modest harms).
Premise 3. If in a given case one must make a great sacrifice in order to do what is morally required, but the sacrifice confers relatively modest benefits (or prevents relatively modest harms), then one does not have most reason to do what is morally required.

Premises (2) and (3) imply the following subconclusion:

4. If there is no God and no life after death, then in some cases one does not have most reason to do what is morally required.

But (4) and (1) combine to yield:

5. "There is no God and no life after death" is false, i.e., either God exists or there is life after death (or both).

Given (5), one can still avoid the conclusion that God exists by arguing that there would be (or at least might well be) a life after death *in which the best interests of morally virtuous persons are realized* even if God does not exist. This move is not, however, open to the naturalist. So, let us consider some objections that, it correct, would prevent us from arriving at step (5).

II. Objections and Replies

Objection 1. Your argument presupposes that, on pain of irrationality, one needs some non-moral or prudential reason to do what is morally required; but this presupposition is false. In fact, to be genuinely morally virtuous, one must do the morally right thing simply because it is right. Those who do the right thing for an ulterior, prudential reason are, from a moral point of view, substandard.

Reply. My argument does not involve this presupposition. Granted, from the moral standpoint, one should do the right thing for moral reasons. But what if there are possible situations in which the weightiest reasons favor doing something *besides* what's morally required? On the assumption that agents can find themselves in such situations, it would seem that agents are rationally justified in doing something other than what's morally required. So, I'm not suggesting people should behave morally for ulterior motives, I'm raising the question whether they "should" behave morally at all in certain hypothetical situations. (The "should" in scare quotes does not express the dictates of morality, but the dictates of rationality, i.e., what one *should* do is what one has the weightiest reasons to do). Let me elaborate briefly.

Assuming that conflicts between morality and prudence occur, I agree that moral reasons *can* outweigh prudential ones. For example, suppose ten children will die a very painful death if I don't help them, but helping them will produce a very slight *net* decrease in the satisfaction of my long-term best interests. Such cases are not actual, in my view, but if they do occur, then it seems clear to me that the moral reasons would outweigh the conflicting prudential ones. And so, in such cases, I would have most reason to act morally even though prudence runs contrary to morality.

What I question is the rationality of doing what's morally required if the gains (for all affected) are relatively minor and the long-term disadvantages to the agent are momentous. In such hypothetical cases it seems to me that the strongest reasons do not back morality. Thus, my argument draws attention to the fact that certain metaphysical views are demoralizing, in

the sense that they make acting on weaker reasons the price of moral virtue in some instances. It may be useful to illustrate this point with a rather farfetched metaphysical view: Suppose a very powerful Deity is in control of the universe but the Deity particularly delights in ensuring that those who do their duty for duty's sake fare very poorly as compared to the self-serving phonies, the morally lukewarm, and the wicked. And suppose the free agents are well aware of these grim metaphysical facts. In such a situation it seems to me that the free agents would often lack overriding reason to do their moral duty. Again, my point is not that people should do the right things to get a reward; rather, my point is that in certain hypothetical situations people lack overriding reason to do the right thing.

Objection 2. The cases you describe in support of premises (2) and (3) are bound to be taken by the naturalist as evidence against premise (1). Also, by attacking or qualifying the thesis that *virtue is its own reward*, you have undermined the only ground a naturalist has for accepting (1). Thus, although your premises may be logically consistent, your argument is dialectically flawed; in effect you give the naturalist good reason to reject premise (1).[9]

Reply. First of all, my moral cases (i.e., Ms. Poore, Ms. Goodwin) provide evidence against premise (1) *only* on the assumption that there is no God and no life after death. But one can hardly make this assumption and give the argument an open-minded run for its money; it is after all an argument for God's existence! So, if the naturalist regards my moral cases as evidence against (1), the naturalist is begging the question, and the dialectical error is on the naturalist's side.

Second, I doubt that many people accept (1) on the grounds that *virtue is its own reward.* I doubt that (1) is typically accepted on the basis of an argument at all. Rather, when certain questions are posed, we simply find that we are presupposing (1). To illustrate, consider an (admittedly contrived) moral theory: *one is always morally required to do what is best for others.*[10] On this theory, the agent's interests are irrelevant to morality—the agent must do what is best for others regardless of the cost to himself. But suppose a significant sacrifice on my part would only marginally improve someone else's lot, e.g., Sue's minor headache can somehow be relieved if I give up my annual two-week vacation. This moral theory seems to demand that I give up my vacation. Well, why not accept this theory of morality? One good reason seems to be this: it fails to give self-interest its due, and thus yields a situation in which *alleged* moral requirements are overridden by self-interest. The point, of course, is not that self-interest does override morality, but rather that the overridingness of moral reasons is presupposed in our moral theorizing. And of course, we bring this presupposition to our moral theorizing because it is deeply embedded in our pre-theoretical conception of morality.[11]

Third, the appeal to *virtue is its own reward* is not the only possible defense of premise (1). As noted previously, if (1) is false, then immoral actions are sometimes backed by reasons as strong as (or stronger than) those backing the moral alternative. But if immoral actions are sometimes backed by reasons as strong as (or stronger than) those backing the moral alternative, then the institution of morality lacks rational authority. That is, the system of morality does not a have blanket endorsement from the rational point of view—only parts of it do. And even if those parts are very large, this consequence is not something most of us can readily accept.

Objection 3. Some moral theorists, in company with Kant and R.M. Hare, claim that moral reasons necessarily or by definition override all others.[12] If such views are correct, then premise (3) must be false. For if moral reasons necessarily override all other kinds of reasons, then there can be no situation in which one lacks most reason to act morally; but (3) presupposes that such situations are possible.

Reply. No dictionary defines "morality" in terms of overridingness. So, those who *define* moral reasons as overriding ones are offering a *theory* and we need evidence for the theory. Similarly, the claim that moral reasons *necessarily* override all others is not obvious, and it won't do to argue for it in an inductive fashion by citing cases. The problem with such an inductive approach is that it runs afoul of the very sorts of cases that serve as the focus of this paper. The hypothetical cases described in section I cast doubt on the claim that "It is *necessarily* true that moral reasons are overriding." So, the situation seems to be that most of us find ourselves believing that, in every actual case, moral reasons are overriding; but—unless we take for granted certain highly controversial metaphysical theses (see the response to objection 5 below)—we lack good reason to think that "Moral reasons are overriding" is a *necessary truth.*

Objection 4. Kantians argue that *whenever an agent acts immorally, she acts on a maxim that she cannot consistently will to be universal law.* But it is irrational to act on a maxim one cannot consistently will to be universal law; hence, one always has most reason to act morally; therefore, premise (3) is false.

Reply. My reply is twofold. First, the Kantian thesis is in fact highly dubious. Consider the case of Ms. Poore. How should we describe the maxim she is acting on? Presumably along the following lines: *Whenever I find myself in a circumstance in which (a) I am very poor but not destitute, (b) I can easily steal a large sum of money with impunity from a very rich person, (c) I will doom myself to enduring and wretched poverty by not stealing, and (d) I will inflict little harm by stealing. I shall steal.* Why can't Ms. Poore consistently will this maxim to be universal law? The clauses of the maxim ensure that it can be applied only rarely. And I see no conceptual difficulties regarding theft (or the institution of private property) if we contemplate a world (similar to the actual world but) in which all relevantly situated persons act in accord with the maxim. And although Ms. Poore might not *like* to have money stolen from her if she were rich, she might nevertheless be *willing* to have anyone in her current circumstances act in accord with the stated maxim, and willing to take a chance on being stolen from in the event that she herself should become rich. Perhaps a few Kantians (certainly not Kant himself) will agree with all this and adopt a revisionist morality that allows stealing (lying, etc.) in the cases I've described. But since such revisionism runs contrary to my settled judgment of the cases, I do not think it provides the naturalist with a cost-free response to my argument.

Second, suppose we grant that *if one acts immorally, one acts on a maxim one cannot consistently will to be universal law.* Does it follow logically that one has most reason to be moral? Not clearly. For one may have very strong reasons to make a special exception in one's own case. And even if making a special exception in one's own case is always immoral, it may sometimes be rational.[13] One can imagine Ms. Poore saying, "Even if I cannot consistently will that all possible agents in my situation commit theft, the fact is relatively few people will ever be in my situation and in this case there's just too much at stake for me personally in doing the moral thing."

Objection 5. Not only naturalists but many theists must reject your argument, namely, those theists, very common in the Christian tradition, who hold that God exists necessarily, is necessarily perfectly morally good, and is necessarily omnipotent. Let us call these theists "classical theists." According to classical theists, it is not logically possible for there to be a situation in which an agent makes a great sacrifice (which involves a permanent and uncompensated loss of something in the agent's long-term best interests) in order to do something morally required. For a perfectly good and omnipotent Deity would not set up a

moral order in which doing one's duty is contrary to one's long-term best interests. Moreover, such a Deity exists in every possible world and is perfectly good and omnipotent in every possible world, according to the classical theist. Hence, your argument countenances situations that are simply not possible according to the classical theist.

Reply. First, since I am arguing for God's existence, it would hardly be dialogically appropriate for me to begin by assuming that God cannot fail to exist. Moreover, the classical theist herself can grant the possibility that God doesn't exist *for the sake of the argument.* So, I don't think my argumentative strategy is necessarily in conflict with classical theism.

Second, the classical theist should accept all three of my premises: Premise (2) obviously has an impossible antecedent given classical theism ("If there is no God . . ."). Hence, by a familiar principle of modal logic, classical theists should regard (2) as a necessary truth. Premise (3) is also necessarily true given classical theism, for reasons alluded to in objection 5: A perfectly good God would never set up a moral order in which doing one's duty is contrary to one's long-term best interests and such a God exists in every possible world, according to the classical theist. Hence, the situation envisaged in the antecedent of (3) is impossible, and (3) itself is necessary. Finally, classical theists should accept premise (1), but deny my claim that (1) is contingent. Since immoral behavior is sin, sin alienates one from God, and alienation from God undermines personal fulfillment, I presume prudence never trumps morality if God exists. Hence, one always has most reason to act morally, if God exists. Moreover, God exists in every possible world according to the classical theist (and is both perfectly good and omnipotent in every possible world). Of course, this way of arguing for the *necessity* of premise (1) is not available to the naturalist or indeed to any type of non-theist.

III. Completing the Argument

If my argument up to this point is any good, then it has given some support to step (5), i.e., the thesis that either God exists or there is life after death (or both). However, (5) could be true even if God does not exist; for it may be that there is no God but there is a life after death in which the best interests of the morally virtuous are realized. So, in this section I wish to complete my moral argument for theism by defending the following premise:

> 6. It is likely that if there is a life after death in which the long-term best interests of the morally virtuous are realized, then God exists.

If premise (6) is defensible, then if it is conjoined with premises (1) through (3), we have an argument that lends positive support to theism. In defending (6), I shall rely on two assumptions. First, I shall assume that there is no life after death given naturalism. Second, I shall assume that the two best theories of the afterlife centrally involve either theism or reincarnation.

Given that reincarnation occurs, each person's soul is transferred to another body at some time after death. So, given reincarnation, there is life after death. And given the doctrine of karma, one's degree of moral virtue determines one's circumstances in the next life. Indeed, if the law of karma governs the universe, the more nearly one lives up to the demands of morality, the better one's circumstances in the next life.[14] Thus, the traditional Hindu doctrines of reincarnation and karma combine to yield a cosmic moral order.

Of course, a doctrine of reincarnation could be combined with theism, but we are here concerned with versions of reincarnation that are in logical competition with theism, i.e., views that deny the existence of any sort of personal Deity. And it seems to me that such views are self-undermining, for the complexity of the moral order they postulate provides good evidence of an Intelligent and Moral Designer. Consider: given that reincarnation and karma hold in the absence of any Deity, the universe is governed not only by physical laws but by impersonal moral laws. These moral laws must be very complicated, for they have to regulate the connection between each soul's moral record in one life and that soul's total circumstances in its next life, including which body it has and the degree of happiness (and/or misery) it experiences. Accordingly, these laws must somehow take into account every act, every intention, and every choice of every moral agent and ensure that the agent receives nothing less than his or her just deserts in the next life. Now, the degree of complexity involved here is not only extraordinarily high, it is also complexity that serves a moral end, namely, justice. Such complexity can hardly be accepted as a brute fact. *Highly complex order serving a moral end* is a phenomenon that legitimates appeal to an intelligent cause. And if the order is on a scale far surpassing what can reasonably be attributed to human intelligence, the appeal to divine intelligence is surely justified. Thus, the moral order postulated by non-theistic reincarnation provides evidence for theism.[15]

To sum up, even if reincarnation occurs in accordance with the principle of karma, the nature of the postulated moral order lends support to theism. Therefore, it seems likely that if there is a life after death in which the ultimate fulfillment of the morally virtuous is realized, then God exists. And this thesis, together with the argument of section I, provides at least some positive support for the proposition that God exists.[16]

Seattle Pacific University

Notes

1. Here is a sketch of an argument linking theism and life after death: A wholly loving God would care deeply about the fulfillment of human creatures and would not leave

human creatures frustrated and unfulfilled if he is able to provide the means of fulfillment. Yet, as virtually everyone will admit, in this earthly life, the deepest yearnings of human beings are not fulfilled, and many human beings have led lives characterized by frustration. An almighty God is surely able to provide the means of fulfillment by providing human creatures with a form or existence after death in which their deepest yearnings can be satisfied. So, if God exists, life after death seems likely.

2. A belief is *properly basic* if it does not need to be based on other beliefs in order to be rational or warranted. Note that, even if belief in God is properly basic, arguments for God's existence are not necessarily rendered pointless; for even when a proposition is already known or rationally believed, independent lines of support can still have a significant confirming role. For a defense of the thesis that belief in God can be properly basic, see Alvin Plantinga, "Reason and Belief in God," in Alvin Plantinga and Nicholas Wolterstorff, eds., *Faith and Rationality* (New York: University of Notre Dame Press, 1983), 16–93 and Alvin Plantinga, *Warranted Christian Belief* (New York: Oxford University Press, 2000), 167–198.

3. Though I shall not discuss the issue in this paper, I believe that severe problems result from the denial of moral facts. See David Brink, "Moral Realism and the Sceptical Argument from Disagreement and Queerness" *Australasian Journal of Philosophy* 62 (1984): 111–125. This article is anthologized in Louis Pojman, ed.. *Ethical Theory: Classical and Contemporary Readings*, second edition (Belmont, CA: Wadsworth, 1995), 469–476. For a well-known rejection of moral facts, see J. L. Mackie, *Ethics: Inventing Right and Wrong* (New York: Penguin Books, 1977), 15–49. I should also note that my assumption that moral facts cannot be identified with non-evaluative (or non-normative) facts is incompatible with certain (I think rather extreme) versions of the divine command theory, e.g., versions claiming that *moral wrongness* is identical with *being forbidden by an all powerful being*. On the other hand, my assumption is compatible with divine command theories that identify *moral wrongness* with *being forbidden by a morally good or loving Deity*.

4. My premises are partly inspired by a quartet of theses discussed in David O. Brink, "A Puzzle About the Rational Authority of Morality," ed. James E. Tomberlin, *Philosophical Perspectives, 6 Ethics, 1992* (Atascadero, CA: Ridgeview Publishing Company, 1992), 1–26.

5. In discussing this case with various philosophers, I have found that certain ways of elaborating the case make it more convincing to some. (A) For example, to some it might make a difference if Ms. Poore steals the money partly to enrich the lives of her children (e.g., by providing them with better clothing, food they enjoy, etc). I welcome such elaborations, but with this proviso: it is essential that the elaborations not be such as to give Ms. Poore a moral duty that plausibly overrides her duty not to steal. For example, if she steals the money to pay for expensive surgery needed to save the life of one of her children, it would be at least plausible to suppose that her duty to preserve life overrides her duty not to steal. I have presented the case simply as one in which *momentous prudential concerns compete with the moral duty not to steal.* (B) Details about Ms. Poore's emotional life can make a difference in how one responds to the case. For example, if she is going to be wracked with literally unending and intense guilt for stealing the money, then it presumably is not to her advantage to steal it. But there is no need to suppose that Ms. Poore has this type of sensitivity. We may imagine her to be a person who is clear-headed, who realizes that she is in a very special sort of moral situation, and who is not going to berate herself for performing the action that is backed by the strongest reasons.

6. This thought experiment is borrowed in its essentials from Richard Taylor, "Value and the Origin of Right and Wrong," in Louis Pojman, ed., *Ethical Theory: Classical and Contemporary Readings* (Belmont, California: Wadsworth, 1989), 115–121. For some interesting, brief reflections on the difficulty of showing that it is in everyone's best interest to be virtuous, see Bernard Williams, *Ethics and the Limits of Philosophy* (Cambridge, Massachusetts: Harvard University Press, 1985), 43–45. Also see, Peter Singer, *Practical Ethics* (London: Cambridge University Press, 1979), 201–220.

7. Thus I leave open the disputed question whether the virtues are good merely as means to an end, e.g., that being fair is not good for its own sake, but good as a means to harmonious and rewarding relationships with others.

8. For an interesting set of reflections confirming the main point of this paragraph, see Christine M. Korsgaard, *The Sources of Normativity* (New York: Cambridge University Press, 1996), 102–103. ("You may know that if you always did this sort of thing your identity would disintegrate, . . . , but you also know that you can do it just this once without any such result," p. 102.)

9. I am indebted to Eleonore Stump for helping me to phrase this objection in a clear fashion.

10. The example is borrowed from Sarah Stroud, "Moral Overridingness and Moral Theory," *Pacific Philosophical Quarterly* 79 (1998), 170–189.

11. Here perhaps is the place to note that some ethicists have rejected the thesis that moral requirements always override all other considerations. See, for example, Philippa Foot, "Are Moral Considerations Overriding?" in *Virtues and Vices* (Berkeley and Los Angeles: University of California Press, 1978), pp. 181–188. The argumentation in Foot's essay seems to me unconvincing, however. For example, Foot points out that people who care about morality will sometimes say things of this sort, "It was morally wrong to do X but I *had to* do X to avoid disaster for myself, my family, or my country." But it seems to me that this sort of statement does not prove even that the speaker believes that the moral reasons are overridden by other reasons. After all, a smoker may say, "I know that the best and strongest reasons favor not smoking, but I *had to* light up anyway." Notoriously, we humans often feel we "have to" do things that are backed by inferior reasons.

12. For a helpful discussion of conceptions of morality and overridingness, see Richard Swinburne, *Responsibility and Atonement* (Oxford: Clarendon Press, 1989), 9–33.

13. See, e.g., Philippa Foot, "Morality as a System of Hypothetical Imperatives," in *Virtues and Vices and Other Essays in Moral Philosophy* (Los Angeles, CA: University of California Press, 1978), 157–173.

14. According to traditional Hindu thought, if one is *perfectly* moral, one deserves *moksha* (salvation), i.e., deliverance from *samsara* (the cycle of birth and death). This deliverance is generally equated with a kind of oneness with ultimate reality.

15. The main point of this paragraph is borrowed from Robin Collins, "Eastern Religions," in Michael J. Murray, ed., *Reason for the Hope Within* (Grand Rapids, MI: Eerdmans, 1999), 206.

16. I wish to thank Terence Cuneo, Jeanine Diller, Paul Draper, Evan Fales, Peter Forrest, Douglas Geivett, Phillip Goggans, Kenneth Einar Himma, Daniel Howard-Snyder, Robert Koons, Mark Murphy, Stephen Porter, and Eleonore Stump for thoughtful comments on various earlier drafts of this paper.

God and the Moral Order: A Reply to Layman

Peter Byrne

Peter Byrne is a professor of ethics and the philosophy of religion at King's College, London. He has done important work on morality and religion. His book, The Moral Interpretation of Religion *(1998), contains some of the most comprehensive work to date on moral arguments for the existence of God. In this article Byrne raises two objections to Layman's argument (in selection VIII.38).*

C. Stephen Layman has argued that, if there is no God, there will be circumstances in which we have most reason not to do as morality requires. This is a *reductio* of naturalism, given that the naturalist accepts that morality is always overriding. This reply contends that Layman's *reductio* fails, because: (1) the circumstances in which morality does not override will be rare on Layman's own analysis; (2) the cases used to support his argument can be re-described as ones in which conventional moral rules are set aside, but morality is not; (3) he fails to consider from what standpoint an agent judges clashes between morality and self-interest.

I

In [selection VIII.38] C. Stephen Layman defends the thesis that, in the absence of belief in God and an after-life, morality is beset by a species of incoherence.[1] This incoherence entails that, if morality is a rational enterprise, God must exist and an afterlife must await us.

Layman summarizes his argument thus:

1. In every actual case, one has most reason to do what is morally required.

Reprinted by permission of the publisher from Peter Byrne, "God and the Moral Order: A Reply to Layman," *Faith and Philosophy* 23, 2006, pp. 201–208. © 2008.

2. If there is no God and no life after death, then there are cases in which morality requires that one make a great sacrifice that confers relatively modest benefits (or prevents relatively modest harms).

3. If in a given case one must make a great sacrifice in order to do what is morally required, but the sacrifice confers relatively modest benefits (or prevents relatively modest harms), then one does not have most reason to do what is morally required.

4. Therefore, if there is no God and no life after death, then in some cases one does not have most reason to do what is morally required.

5. Therefore, given (1) and (4), "There is no God and no life after death" is false.

(5) only entails that either there is a God or there is no life after death. Further argument is then offered for concluding that, if there is a life after death whose character supplies the grounds for the truth that one always has most reason to do what is morally required, then it is because there is a God who is responsible for the moral order thus established.

Examples support Layman's argument. A central one concerns an agent, Ms Poore, who is in deep poverty and who has the opportunity to steal money from someone else. The potential thief is in dire straits and needs funds to fulfil basic human needs (she is ill, poorly housed and so forth). The victim of the theft does not need the money and will not be substantially harmed by the loss of this sum. In the absence of God and an afterlife, Ms Poore has no overwhelming reason to obey the relevant moral rules and therefore (1) is false.

Layman is at pains to defend his argument from the following counter to his examples: it is true by definition that morality is overriding. Some might object: to note that morality tells Ms Poore not to steal *is* to note that she has greatest reason not to steal. Layman responds that, if it is true that we have overriding reasons for being guided by moral claims, then this is not true by definition—as the case of Ms Poore seems to demonstrate. Layman states that such hypothetical examples show that "we lack good reason to think that 'Moral reasons are overriding' is a *necessary truth*" (383). In truth, he does not need to say this. If it is a necessary truth that there is a God with the attributes traditionally assigned (and necessarily true that this God establishes a providential order in things), then "moral reasons are overriding" will likewise be necessary.[2] But it will be a substantive necessity and one that is derived from necessary truths about the existence and character of a deity. What Layman needs to object to is the claim that "Moral reasons are overriding" is a trivial, definitional truth.

II

Layman's argument in support of premise (1) consists in an appeal to our intuitions. If we believe that someone in doing an act was doing his/her duty would we not assume that the act was fully justified on this basis? We just take it that if an act is someone's moral duty, then (but not on definitional grounds—see above) that person has overriding reasons to do it. If we deny this, then we must be prepared to admit that in some cases the answer to the question "Why should I be moral?" is "I should not."

One strategy of response to Layman is to accept his sub-conclusion (4) but deny (1) by contending that (4) does not demonstrate that atheism provides a real threat to the moral life. Layman's reasoning is indeed limited. The characteristics of cases such as Ms Poore's which make them allegedly clear examples of

agents having good reason overall not to follow their perceptions of what is honest, right etc are just those which make them few and far between. First they are cases where there is no real victim of the wrongdoing contemplated. Ms Poore is to steal from someone who has so much that she will not be substantially harmed by the theft. Second Ms Poore is very unlikely to be caught out in her theft. So Ms Poore faces a clear clash between strong, legitimate claims of self-interest and the wrongness of theft considered in isolation from any harmful effects. From consideration of this example and others in the paper, Layman offers us this principle: *"when considerations of prudence and morality clash, if the prudential considerations are truly momentous while the results of behaving immorally are relatively minor, then morality does not override prudence"* (381, emphasis in the original). This can be styled the principle "In extreme cases morality is not overriding."

It is so far open to the atheist to accept that there are some extreme cases in which premise (1) of Layman's argument is false. "Extreme" might seem a tendentious word in the context of this discussion. Yet Layman characterizes his own argument as questioning the "the rationality of doing what's morally required if the gains (for all affected) are relatively minor and the long-term disadvantages to the agent are momentous" (382). But this very account of the force of his examples strongly suggests that abandoning the intuition that morality always overrides is a reasonable option. It is true that on the page following the above quotation he makes the atheist's case sound desperate: "if immoral actions are sometimes backed by reasons as strong as (or stronger than) those backing the moral alternative, then the institution of morality lacks rational authority" (383). I submit that this ringing declaration does not square too well with the previous quotation from p. 382. The sentence that immediately follows on p. 383 is not so ringing: "That is, the system of morality does not have a [printed text: "does not a have"] blanket endorsement from the rational point of view." This last claim is merely the modest p. 382 statement that there are some tightly specified cases where what is morally required is not rationally required.

Layman does little, in truth, to show that "in extreme cases morality is not overriding" is terribly dangerous or poses a substantive threat to the moral life. Unless he can do this, his argument is open to a simple challenge: premise (1) is false. Given that, there would be no *reductio* of unbelief to be derived from it. He does indeed criticize Philippa Foot's argument[3] for the claim that moral considerations are not always overriding. But the (alleged) badness of her argument for the conclusion does not of course show that the conclusion is false. One way of taking Layman's examples with their commentary is as a straightforward argument for the claim that moral considerations/judgements are not always overriding.

The "so what?" response of the atheist to Layman gets further strength from his paper's acceptance that there is inherent value in doing what is morally required and inherent disvalue in not doing what is morally required. Virtue, he concedes, is a benefit to those who possess it (380). He does not wish to suggest that there are no moral reasons for doing this rather than that because all reasons for action have in truth to be self-regarding (383). We can support Layman in these judgements by bringing in the Aristotelian thought that acts of virtue constitute their own ends. The good produced by virtuous action need not be wholly or mainly in its effects. Virtuous actions are not merely the means to the good, as plugging in the kettle is the means to heating the water. The good for a human being is a kind of living and acting: it is in part constituted by the acts we perform and the dispositions behind them. Virtuous, good actions are worthwhile for the sake of the activity involved in doing them. They will have ends beyond themselves. Thus an act of generosity will seek the improvement of another's lot. But

such an act also constitutes its own end. It is worthwhile doing it even if it fails in its external end. So, if a naturalist follows Aristotle, she or he can say that right action is a manifestation of the human good and as such the human good will in part exist regardless of the consequences of right action. Hence, Layman is right: there is a sense in which virtue will indeed benefit its possessor.[4]

Layman's point about the inherent good in virtuous acts thus strengthens the thought that it can only be in extreme cases that what is morally required is not rationally required, since there will always be some loss of good in doing an act contrary to the claims of right.

III

Layman's argument depends on the point that "morality is overriding" is not a definitional truth, not a trivial, linguistic necessity. Even though we can concede this for the sake of argument, there is still a problem understanding why we should not say that the example of Ms Poore is a case where someone does what is morally justified, albeit she acts in violation of a customary moral rule.

It is news from nowhere that what appear to be moral considerations do not always properly trump what appear to be non-moral ones. Moral considerations at first blush might suggest that I should currently be helping to feed children and build irrigation ditches in the Third World, rather than live the comfortable life of a Professor in southern England. But most would concede that to condemn me on this score is to ignore the fact that such self-sacrifice would be a work of supererogation rather than duty. I have an interest in my own well-being (as defined by my own projects and plans) which morality can recognize as being legitimate and as thus placing limits on the extent to which I am required to act on other moral considerations. Continuing in my profession versus selling up and going to help the indigent in Africa may look like a clash between non-moral considerations and moral ones. But at a higher level it is not, since morality grants me a legitimate interest in my good. To say that morality grants this interest is to say that my heeding to this interest is not only acceptable from a personal point of view but also from the view of what is proper and improper in the behavior of any human being as such. Judging from an impartial standpoint, there are limits to how much self-sacrifice can be *demanded* of individuals. The judgement I make about myself could be commended from that impartial standpoint and be openly recommended to all as one that they could endorse if they were in similar circumstances. Hence we have the paradoxical conclusion: morality can judge that moral considerations (narrowly defined) can be sometimes given less weight than non-moral ones (narrowly defined).

If we accept the above reflections flowing from the notion of supererogation, we can be led by intermediate examples to see Ms Poore's actions as being backed by moral reasons. The familiar Heinz dilemma from studies of moral development shows us the obvious truth: sometimes there are decisive moral reasons for disobeying customary moral rules. Heinz needs medicines to save a gravely ill dependant. He has no money to buy them. He can only steal them from the local pharmacy. He does so, backed by higher order principles of respect for persons and the value of life which trump the conventional rule "Stealing is wrong." Now why should we not describe Ms Poore's action in precisely these terms? She needs the money to be acquired via her act of theft for reasons morality would endorse. She is sick, indigent, poorly housed, and cut off from the possibility of flourishing as a human being. Ms Poore's state is not simply bad from the point of view of prudence. It is also bad from the point of view of morality. It is thus open to us to describe Ms Poore's decision to steal in these terms: it is a morally legitimate setting aside of a conventional moral rule, which holds only for the most part anyway, in favor of trumping moral considerations to do with human well-being. I suggest that the availability of this distinction is implicit in the key principle that Layman says his examples support and exemplify: *"when considerations of prudence and morality clash, if the prudential considerations are truly momentous while the results of behaving immorally are relatively minor, then morality does not override prudence"* (381). The application of the clause *"if the prudential considerations are truly momentous"* invites the invocation of the notions found in supererogation and in the Heinz dilemma. And that application is reinforced by the clause *"while the results of behaving immorally are relatively minor."*

What makes Heinz's actions not an offence against morality but a recognizable result of the application of moral reason can be brought out by considering the Kantian formula "Act only on that maxim which you can at the same time will to be a universal law." Heinz's maxim is something like: "Let me steal where this is necessary to secure the well-being of others." He can will this as a universal law. That is to say, he can imagine openly recommending this maxim to others as rule that they can follow and accept. Given the generic interests of human beings, the rule stands a very good chance of being assented to as one among the many that we could all freely accept as the basis of an impartial social order.[5] Now my suggestion is that Ms Poore's decision can also be represented in a maxim that will pass the same test. "Where stealing causes little harm to others but is necessary to ensure one's own vital interests as a human being, stealing is allowed" also stands a very good chance as a rule that could be openly recommended to others for acceptance in the same way as Heinz's maxim. It might be seen as resting on the same core intuition: the force of the rule "Do not steal" can be trumped by considerations of human well-being if they are of sufficient moment.

IV

So far we have found two problems with Layman's argument. First the atheist can accept it because its conclusion allows only of extreme cases in which we have reason to set aside the verdicts of morality. Second the atheist can respond that Layman's cases are easily described as ones in which agents have good reasons from a moral standpoint to set aside conventional moral rules. These problems stem from the fact that Layman is not running the crude moral argument for God based on the premise that moral considerations can have no weight with rational agents unless they are backed by prudential ones. Layman outlines and rejects this view (see 381–2). He states that moral reasons have their own force and that they can outweigh prudential ones (382). This entails that for prudential considerations to outweigh moral ones they have to be very strong indeed and the moral considerations they are outweighing correspondingly light. That makes the examples few and invites us to see the prudential considerations as having significance from the moral point of view.

The above paragraph is rich in the metaphor of weighing reasons on either side of a decision. So is Layman's discussion: "what one *should* do is what one has the weightiest reasons to do" (382). Layman's way of approaching his moral argument suggests the following picture: rational agents are aware of a variety of reasons for action. They see prudential reasons vying with moral reasons. They measure whether moral reasons for doing something outweigh prudential reasons for not doing it and they follow that set of reasons which is stronger overall. Now it is time to ask the question "From what standpoint does Layman's rational agent weigh or measure reasons for action?" Layman's agents, such as Ms Poore, recognize both moral and prudential reasons. They give a certain weight to reasons of both types. When the different types of reason point in different directions, they seek to determine where the balance of reason falls and act accordingly. Such a picture implies that Layman's agents are neutral as between the dictates of morality and self-interest. Their underlying commitment is to rationality. They see rational force in both impartial and partial reasons for action. They do not commit themselves to either type of reason, to either the moral or the self-interested standpoint, but only to following the greater reason.

We should find the above puzzling. By reference to what does Ms Poore decide that reasons relating to her own well-being are greater in weight than those relating to the wrongness of theft? According to Layman, she faces the choice between stealing and living in grinding poverty for the rest of her life (380). Now one way in which that choice might present itself to her is this: "I must look to my own interest. I would be a fool if I let a few moral qualms condemn me to a life of misery." That manner of representation gives our agent seeing no non-conventional harm in theft. Alternatively the choice might present itself as one between avoiding poverty at the cost of dishonoring herself: "Yes, I could steal, but that would be dishonest and even if I were never detected, I would be dishonored thereby." That manner of representation works for an agent for whom acting immorally is simply *out*. To act contrary to conscience is to suffer harm, harm which no good fortune can wipe away. The problem with Layman's talk about weightier and stronger reasons is that it does not tell us whether Ms Poore is troubled by thoughts of dishonor, or reflections to the effect that she can only avoid poverty by becoming a thief—a status which she can never lose no matter how much she prospers.

The unclarity in the language of weighing reasons for action, and of judging which reasons are stronger than others, lies in the fact that such language implies a common, neutral means of measuring the reasons. The very contrast, however, between morality and self-interest suggests that there can be no such means. The agent is faced with a choice between points of view and perspectives. From within a point of view or perspective there can be weighing. From the standpoint of prudence the agent could weigh how likely is disclosure of the theft and how costly any consequent public disgrace might be. But from this point of view there could simply [be] no sense in which the harm that consists in knowing the one is a thief could be felt and exist. From the perspective of morality the claims of self-interest can indeed be registered, but there is no question of their strength being a matter of weighing in any straightforward sense. They will either be set aside with the thought that stealing is simply "out" or enter in to a consideration of what is right from an impartial or virtues-based point of view—as discussed in section III above. What remains a mystery is how any agent could measure the relative strengths of the two kinds of consideration from neither the moral or prudential point of view but from a neutral standpoint.

The above questions are a way of returning to the theme that "morality is overriding," whilst not being analytic, may be expressive of a substantive necessity. The ground of its necessity, if we deem it be a necessity, would include this thought: moral considerations are things that call for our allegiance. If Ms Poore has given them her allegiance, then she can only cope with the clash between moral and prudential considerations in one of the two ways mentioned. She can dismiss the prudential considerations or explore the thought that her own well-being and the duties she owes to herself are of sufficient weight in this case to justify an impartial verdict that a conventional moral rule be set aside. In this latter case, her reasoning has a logic to it, that set out in section III. It is truly hard to see the logic in her reasoning on Layman's presentation of the matter.

Ms Poore could go down another route and give her allegiance to self-interest. Faced with the practical dilemma Layman describes, Ms Poore might opt for stealing in the absence of any sense that this choice could be defended from the moral point of view. Leaving aside the possibility that this decision is but an example of weakness of will, her allegiance to morality has been tested and she has decided to give it up. Such a decision is intelligible, albeit regrettable. She has done that which she concedes is bad for a human being as such to do, that which she could not expect other human beings, judging impartially and rationally, to endorse.

V

This paper has argued that Layman's argument from morality to God fails because premise (1) "In every actual case, one has most reason to do what is morally required" can be defended even though there is no God and no afterlife. The atheist who does not want to admit Layman's argument as part of a cumulative case for theism (see 377–8) has room for maneuver before accepting (5) "There is no God and no life after death' is false."

A diagnosis of Layman's failure to see the room for maneuver can be offered. He has rightly eschewed the crude argument for theism which is based on the premise that moral considerations can have no weight with a rational agent unless right conduct is clearly to the agent's long term advantage. This swift argument to a rewarding and punishing God fails because it denies the possibility of genuine allegiance to moral demands. Having allowed that moral considerations motivate independent of their coincidence with prudential ones, Layman is then unable to give a full and clear characterization of how an agent can judge that moral considerations are outweighed in a given case by prudential ones. In particular, he is not able to explain how reason can come down on the side of looking after one's own welfare in cases of apparent conflict between morality and prudence while such a decision of reason somehow remains outside the moral sphere. Further, he has not appreciated the thought that morality/virtue is something that claims the allegiance of agents. Both these points suggest a deeper necessity than mere analyticity to the claim that morality is overriding.

Even if the analysis contained in sections III and IV of the above is rejected, it remains the case the Layman's disavowal of the crude argument from morality to God leaves the atheist with a conclusion that can be accepted without embarrassment: in extreme cases morality does not override.

King's College London

Notes

1. C. Stephen Layman, "God and the Moral Order," *Faith and Philosophy* 19, 304–16. Subsequent references to Layman's paper are given in brackets in the text of this reply.

2. It will not then signify—see Layman—that we can conceive of cases in which moral reasons do not override in the absence of there being a God. This will be parallel to be our being able to conceive of triangles with internal angles adding up to 200 degrees in the absence of a knowledge of relevant geometric truths.

3. P. Foot "Are Moral Considerations Overriding?" in P. Foot *Virtues and Vices* (Berkeley and Los Angeles: University of California Press, 1978), 181–88.

4. For these thoughts about the relation between goodness and virtue see N. Sherman *The Fabric of Character*, (Oxford: Clarendon Press, 1989) 114ff. Layman's recognition that there is a good within virtuous action and not merely in its effects makes his moral argument for God's existence superior in this respect to the similar case in L. Zagzebski "Does Ethics Need God?" *Faith and Philosophy* 4,1987, 294–303.

5. This way of understanding the test within Kant's Categorical Imperative is due to R. Green *Religious Reason* (New York: Oxford University Press, 1978).

PART IX

Applied Ethics

Introduction

Some moral issues divide us and threaten to tear us apart. Abortion, euthanasia, war, homosexual marriage, preferential treatment, the death penalty, our obligation to people dying of AIDs and hunger, and so on. Can moral philosophy help?

There are reasons to be pessimistic and reasons to be optimistic. On the pessimistic side, even if we could agree about what sort of ethical system to employ, we would not agree about the relevant facts or how to apply that system to those facts: For instance there are utilitarians on every side of every issue mentioned above. So there is little chance that education in moral philosophy will soon bring us to consensus. On the optimistic side, education in moral philosophy teaches us to spot and refute all sorts of worthless moral arguments. Public debate would be much more helpful if many of us could do that. As individuals, education in moral philosophy helps us to achieve consistency and reasonableness in our views. Improvement as individuals is all that we can reasonably count on. For consensus, we may only strive and hope.

In our first reading, Judith Jarvis Thompson uses thought experiments to examine the "doctrine of doing and allowing," according to which it is worse to do than to allow a bad thing. She makes progress towards developing and defending a qualified version of the doctrine, which is at the heart of much debate about consequentialism (see for instance reading 21) and many issues in applied ethics. Think, for example, of euthanasia. If, as most people think, it can be right at some point to stop trying to save someone's life in a hopeless case, can it be wrong at

that point to kill him quickly and mercifully? That depends on whether and how the doctrine of doing and allowing is true.

Our second and third readings are concerned with world hunger. Tragically, people die of hunger, and from hunger-related illnesses and wars, every day. At the same time, many of us have the means to go well beyond just keeping ourselves fed—even to the point of selecting our food on the basis of taste. Do those of us who enjoy this and other luxuries, who can achieve a high quality of life—which might include a good education; secured retirement; relaxing hobbies and vacations; a home and automobiles (both insured); healthcare and adequate insurance to cover it—have an obligation to help the hungry? In our second reading, Peter Singer argues that those of us who have more than enough to keep ourselves fed also have an obligation to help the hungry, to the extent that we can help without ourselves joining the ranks of the hungry. Although his argument is consequentialist, it is grounded in a thought experiment that non-consequentialists cannot easily ignore. In our third reading, Onora O'Neill argues that the second formulation of Kant's Categorical Imperative implies that the non-hungry have an obligation to contribute to the maintenance of the hungry to a certain extent and in certain ways, although not to the extent that Singer champions.

The next two readings address abortion. In our fourth reading, John T. Noonan uses thought experiments to try to show that we should make public policy as if there is an 80 per cent chance that fetuses (embryos, zygotes) are persons from the moment of conception, a view that would seem to favor the conservative side in the abortion debate, with the extra merit of being based solely in secular reasons. In our fifth reading, Mary Anne Warren argues, again on the basis of thought experiments, that we are not persons in the full moral sense until well after birth. She concedes that we are potential persons from the moment of conception, but she argues that that is irrelevant.

Our last three readings are concerned with war—particularly with situations where we must choose from a list of tragedies. Such situations put extreme strain on moral theory and moral common sense alike. In our sixth reading, John Rawls argues that the atomic bombings of Hiroshima and Nagasaki were immoral. In our seventh reading, Michael Walzer argues that in rare, extreme cases we should violate the rules of war, say by resorting to terror bombing or torture. He does not concede, however, that such violations would therefore be permissible or fully excusable; they are instead how we must face true moral dilemmas, where we cannot make any permissible or excusable choice. In our final reading Thomas Nagle considers, from a deontologist's perspective, whether we should be moral absolutists, holding to our principles even if it means the end of the world, or whether deontologists must compromise with consequentialism when certain limits are reached.

40

The Trolley Problem

JUDITH JARVIS THOMPSON

Judith Jarvis Thompson is a professor emeritus at MIT, where she taught for most of her career. She has done important work in moral theory and applied ethics, and she is particularly well known for her use of thought experiments. In this influential article she uses thought experiments in order to explore whether there is anything to what ethicists call the doctrine of doing and allowing: roughly, the doctrine that it is worse to do a bad thing than to allow a bad thing to happen. This doctrine is at the center of many controversies in applied ethics. In this article Thomson works towards acceptance of a much qualified version of the doctrine.

I.

Some years ago, Philippa Foot drew attention to an extraordinarily interesting problem.[1] Suppose you are the driver of a trolley. The trolley rounds a bend, and there come into view ahead five track workmen, who have been repairing the track. The track goes through a bit of a valley at that point, and the sides are steep, so you must stop the trolley if you are to avoid running the five men down. You step on the brakes, but alas they don't work. Now you suddenly see a spur of track leading off to the right. You can turn the trolley onto it, and thus save the five men on the straight track ahead. Unfortunately, Mrs. Foot has arranged that there is one track workman on that spur of track. He can no more get off the track in time than the five can, so

you will kill him if you turn the trolley onto him. Is it morally permissible for you to turn the trolley?

Everybody to whom I have put this hypothetical case says, Yes, it is.[2] Some people say something stronger than that it is morally *permissible* for you to turn the trolley: They say that morally speaking, you *must* turn it—that morality requires you to do so. Others do not agree that morality requires you to turn the trolley, and even feel a certain discomfort at the idea of turning it. But everybody says that it is true, at a minimum, that you *may* turn it—that it would not be morally wrong in you to do so.

Now consider a second hypothetical case. This time you are to imagine yourself to be a surgeon, a truly great surgeon. Among other things you do, you transplant organs, and you are such a great surgeon that the organs you transplant always take. At the moment you have five patients who need organs. Two need one lung each, two need a kidney each, and the fifth needs a heart. If they do not get those organs today, they will all die; if you find organs for them today, you can transplant the organs and they will all live. But where to find the lungs, the kidneys, and the heart? The time is almost up when a report is brought to you that a young man who has just come into your clinic for his yearly check-up has exactly the right blood-type, and is in excellent health. Lo, you have a possible donor. All you need do is cut him up and distribute *his* parts among the five who need them. You ask, but he says, "Sorry. I deeply sympathize, but no." Would it be morally permissible for you to operate anyway? Everybody to whom I have put this second hypothetical case says, No, it would not be morally permissible for you to proceed.

Reprinted by permission of the publisher from Judith Jarvis Thompson, "The Trolley Problem," *The Yale Law Journal* 94 (1985) pp. 1395–1415. © 1985.

Here then is Mrs. Foot's problem: *Why* is it that the trolley driver may turn his trolley, though the surgeon may not remove the young man's lungs, kidneys, and heart?[3] In both cases, one will die if the agent acts, but five will live who would otherwise die—a net saving of four lives. What difference in the other facts of these cases explains the moral difference between them? I fancy that the theorists of tort and criminal law will find this problem as interesting as the moral theorist does.

II.

Mrs. Foot's own solution to the problem she drew attention to is simple, straightforward, and very attractive. She would say: Look, the surgeon's choice is between operating, in which case he kills one, and not operating, in which case he lets five die; and killing is surely worse than letting die[4]—indeed, so much worse that we can even say

(I) Killing one is worse than letting five die.

So the surgeon must refrain from operating. By contrast, the trolley driver's choice is between turning the trolley, in which case he kills one, and not turning the trolley, in which case he does not *let five die*, he positively *kills* them. Now surely we can say

(II) Killing five is worse than killing one.

But then that is why the trolley driver may turn his trolley: He would be doing what is worse if he fails to turn it, since if he fails to turn it he kills five.

I do think that that is an attractive account of the matter. It seems to me that if the surgeon fails to operate, he does not kill his five patients who need parts; he merely lets them die. By contrast, if the driver fails to turn his trolley, he does not merely let the five track workmen die; he drives his trolley into them, and thereby kills them.

But there is good reason to think that this problem is not so easily solved as that.

Let us begin by looking at a case that is in some ways like Mrs. Foot's story of the trolley driver. I will call her case *Trolley Driver;* let us now consider a case I will call *Bystander at the Switch.* In that case you have been strolling by the trolley track, and you can see the situation at a glance: The driver saw the five on the track ahead, he stamped on the brakes, the brakes failed, so he fainted. What to do? Well, here is the switch, which you can throw, thereby turning the trolley yourself. Of course you will kill one if you do. But I should think you may turn it all the same.[5]

Some people may feel a difference between these two cases. In the first place, the trolley driver is, after all, captain of the trolley. He is charged by the trolley company with responsibility for the safety of his passengers and anyone else who might be harmed by the trolley he drives. The bystander at the switch, on the other hand, is a private person who just happens to be there.

Second, the driver would be driving a trolley into the five if he does not turn it, and the bystander would not—the bystander will do the five no harm at all if he does not throw the switch.

I think it right to feel these differences between the cases.

Nevertheless, my own feeling is that an ordinary person, a mere bystander, may intervene in such a case. If you see something, a trolley, a boulder, an avalanche, heading towards five, and you can deflect it onto one, it really does seem that—other things being equal—it would be permissible for you to *take* charge, *take* responsibility, and deflect the thing, whoever you may be. Of course you run a moral risk if you do, for it might be that, unbeknownst to you, other things are not equal. It might be, that is, that there is some relevant difference between the five on the one hand, and the one on the other, which would make it morally preferable that the five be hit by the trolley than that the one be hit by it. That would be so if, for example, the five are not track workmen at all, but Mafia members in workmen's clothing, and they have tied the one workman to the right-hand track in the hope that you would turn the trolley onto him. I won't canvass all the many kinds of possibilities, for in fact the moral risk is the same whether you are the trolley driver, or a bystander at the switch.

Moreover, second, we might well wish to ask ourselves what exactly is the difference between what the driver would be doing if he failed to turn the trolley and what the bystander would be doing if he failed to throw the switch. As I said, the driver would be driving a trolley into the five; but what exactly would his driving the trolley into the five consist in? Why, just sitting there, doing nothing! If the driver does just sit there, doing nothing, then that will have been how come he drove his trolley into the five.

I do not mean to make much of that fact about what the driver's driving his trolley into the five would consist in, for it seems to me to be right to say that if he does not turn the trolley, he does drive his trolley into them, and does thereby kill them. (Though this does seem to me to be right, it is not easy to say exactly what makes it so.) By contrast, if the bystander does not throw the switch, he drives no trolley into anybody, and he kills nobody.

But as I said, my own feeling is that the bystander *may* intervene. Perhaps it will seem to some even less clear that morality requires him to turn the trolley than that morality requires the driver to turn the trolley; perhaps some will feel even more discomfort at the idea of the bystander's turning the trolley than at the idea of the driver's turning the trolley. All the same, I shall take it that he *may.*

If he may, there is serious trouble for Mrs. Foot's thesis (I). It is plain that if the bystander throws the switch, he causes the trolley to hit the one, and thus he kills the one. It is equally plain that if the bystander does not throw the switch, he does not cause the trolley to hit the

five, he does not kill the five, he merely fails to save them—he lets them die. His choice therefore is between throwing the switch, in which case he kills one, and not throwing the switch, in which case he lets five die. If thesis (I) were true, it would follow that the bystander may not throw the switch, and that I am taking to be false.

III.

I have been arguing that

(I) Killing one is worse than letting five die

is false, and a fortiori that it cannot be appealed to to explain why the surgeon may not operate in the case I shall call *Transplant.*

I think it pays to take note of something interesting which comes out when we pay close attention to

(II) Killing five is worse than killing one.

For let us ask ourselves how we would feel about *Transplant* if we made a certain addition to it. In telling you that story, I did not tell you why the surgeon's patients are in need of parts. Let us imagine that the history of their ailments is as follows. The surgeon was badly overworked last fall—some of his assistants in the clinic were out sick, and the surgeon had to take over their duties dispensing drugs. While feeling particularly tired one day, he became careless, and made the terrible mistake of dispensing chemical X to five of the day's patients. Now chemical X works differently in different people. In some it causes lung failure, in others kidney failure, in others heart failure. So these five patients who now need parts need them because of the surgeon's carelessness. Indeed, if he does not get them the parts they need, so that they die, he will have killed them. Does that make a moral difference? That is, does the fact that he will have killed the five if he does nothing make it permissible for him to cut the young man up and distribute his parts to the five who need them?

We could imagine it to have been worse. Suppose what had happened was this: The surgeon was badly overextended last fall, he had known he was named a beneficiary in his five patients' wills, and it swept over him one day to give them chemical X to kill them. Now he repents, and would save them if he could. If he does not save them, he will positively have murdered them. Does *that* fact make it permissible for him to cut the young man up and distribute his parts to the five who need them?

I should think plainly not. The surgeon must not operate on the young man. If he can find no other way of saving his five patients, he will *now* have to let them die—despite the fact that if he now lets them die, he will have killed them.

We tend to forget that some killings themselves include lettings die, and do include them where the act by which the agent kills takes time to cause death—time in which the agent can intervene but does not.

In face of these possibilities, the question arises what we should think of thesis (II), since it *looks* as if it tells us that the surgeon ought to operate, and thus that he may permissibly do so, since if he operates he kills only one instead of five.

There are two ways in which we can go here. First, we can say: (II) does tell us that the surgeon ought to operate, and that shows it is false. Second, we can say: (II) does not tell us that the surgeon ought to operate, and it is true.

For my own part, I prefer the second. If Alfred kills five and Bert kills only one, then questions of motive apart, and other things being equal, what Alfred did *is* worse than what Bert did. If the surgeon does not operate, so that he kills five, then it will later be true that he did something worse than he would have done if he had operated, killing only one—especially if his killing of the five was murder, committed out of a desire for money, and his killing of the one would have been, though misguided and wrongful, nevertheless a well-intentioned effort to save five lives. Taking this line would,

of course, require saying that assessments of which acts are worse than which other acts do not by themselves settle the question what it is permissible for an agent to do.

But it might be said that we ought to bypass (II), for perhaps what Mrs. Foot would have offered us as an explanation of why the driver may turn the trolley in *Trolley Driver* is not (II) itself, but something more complex, such as

(II′) If a person is faced with a choice between doing something *here and now* to five, by the doing of which he will kill them, and doing something else *here and now* to one, by the doing of which he will kill only the one, then (other things being equal) he ought to choose the second alternative rather than the first.

We may presumably take (II′) to tell us that the driver ought to, and hence permissibly may, turn the trolley in *Trolley Driver,* for we may presumably view the driver as confronted with a choice between here and now driving his trolley into five, and here and now driving his trolley into one. And at the same time, (II′) tells us nothing at all about what the surgeon ought to do in *Transplant,* for he is not confronted with such a choice. If the surgeon operates, he does do something by the doing of which he will kill only one; but if the surgeon does not operate, he does not do something by the doing of which he kills five; he merely fails to do something by the doing of which he would make it be the case that he has not killed five.

I have no objection to this shift in attention from (II) to (II′). But we should not overlook an interesting question that lurks here. As it might be put: *Why* should the present tense matter so much? Why should a person prefer killing one to killing five if the alternatives are wholly in front of him, but not (or anyway, not in every case) where one of them is partly behind him? I shall come back to this question briefly later.

Meanwhile, however, even if (II′) can be appealed to in order to explain why the trolley driver may turn his trolley, that would leave it entirely open why the bystander at the switch may turn *his* trolley. For he does not drive a trolley into each of five if he refrains from turning the trolley; he merely lets the trolley drive into each of them.

So I suggest we set *Trolley Driver* aside for the time being. What I shall be concerned with is a first cousin of Mrs. Foot's problem, viz.: Why is it that the bystander may turn his trolley, though the surgeon may not remove the young man's lungs, kidneys, and heart? Since *I* find it particularly puzzling that the bystander may turn his trolley, I am inclined to call this The Trolley Problem. Those who find it particularly puzzling that the surgeon may not operate are cordially invited to call it The Transplant Problem instead.

IV.

It should be clear, I think, that "kill" and "let die" are too blunt to be useful tools for the solving of this problem. We ought to be looking within killings and savings for the ways in which the agents would be carrying them out.

It would be no surprise, I think, if a Kantian idea occurred to us at this point. Kant said: "Act so that you treat humanity, whether in your own person or in that of another, always as an end and never as a means only." It is striking, after all, that the surgeon who proceeds in *Transplant* treats the young man he cuts up "as a means only": He literally uses the young man's body to save his five, and does so without the young man's consent. And perhaps we may say that the agent in *Bystander at the Switch* does not use his victim to save his five, or (more generally) treat his victim as a means only, and that that is why he (unlike the surgeon) may proceed.

But what exactly is it to treat a person as a means only, or to use a person? And why exactly is it wrong to do this? These questions do not have obvious answers.[6]

Suppose an agent is confronted with a choice between doing nothing, in which case five die, or engaging in a certain course of action, in which case the five live, but one dies. Then perhaps we can say: If the agent chooses to engage in the course of action, then he uses the one to save the five only if, had the one gone out of existence just before the agent started, the agent would have been unable to save the five. That is true of the surgeon in *Transplant*. He needs the young man if he is to save his five; if the young man goes wholly out of existence just before the surgeon starts to operate, then the surgeon cannot save his five. By contrast, the agent in *Bystander at the Switch* does not need the one track workman on the right-hand track if he is to save his five; if the one track workman goes wholly out of existence before the bystander starts to turn the trolley, then the bystander *can* all the same save his five. So here anyway is a striking difference between the cases.

It does seem to me right to think that solving this problem requires attending to the means by which the agent would be saving his five if he proceeded. But I am inclined to think that this is an overly simple way of taking account of the agent's means.

One reason for thinking so[7] comes out as follows. You have been thinking of the tracks in *Bystander at the Switch* as not merely diverging, but continuing to diverge, as in the following picture:

Consider now what I shall call "the loop variant" on this case, in which the tracks do not continue to diverge—they circle back, as in the following picture:

Let us now imagine that the five on the straight track are thin, but thick enough so that although all five will be killed if the trolley goes straight, the bodies of the five will stop it, and it will therefore not reach the one. On the other hand, the one on the right-hand track is fat, so fat that his body will by itself stop the trolley, and the trolley will therefore not reach the five. May the agent turn the trolley? Some people feel more discomfort at the idea of turning the trolley in the loop variant than in the original *Bystander at the Switch*. But we cannot really suppose that the presence or absence of that extra bit of track makes a major moral difference as to what an agent may do in these cases, and it really does seem right to think (despite the discomfort) that the agent may proceed.

On the other hand, we should notice that the agent here needs the one (fat) track workman on the right-hand track if he is to save his five. If the one goes wholly out of existence just before the agent starts to turn the trolley, then the agent cannot save his five[8]—just as the surgeon in *Transplant* cannot save his five if the young man goes wholly out of existence just before the surgeon starts to operate.

Indeed, I should think that there is no plausible account of what is involved in, or what is necessary for, the application of the notions "treating a person as a means only," or "using one to save five," under which the surgeon would be doing this whereas the agent in this variant of *Bystander at the Switch* would not be. If that is right, then appeals to these notions cannot do the work being required of them here.

V.

Suppose the bystander at the switch proceeds: He throws the switch, thereby turning the trolley onto the right-hand track, thereby causing the one to be hit by the trolley, thereby killing him—but saving the five on the straight track. There are two facts about what he does which seem to me to explain the moral difference between what he does and what the agent in *Transplant* would be doing if *he* proceeded. In the first place, the bystander saves his five by making something that threatens them instead threaten one. Second, the bystander does not do that by means which themselves constitute an infringement of any right of the one's.

As is plain, then, my hypothesis as to the source of the moral difference between the cases makes appeal to the concept of a right. My own feeling is that solving this problem requires making appeal to that concept—or to some other concept that does the same kind of work.[9] Indeed, I think it is one of the many reasons why this problem is of such interest to moral theory that it does force us to appeal to that concept; and by the same token, that we learn something from it about that concept.

Let us begin with an idea, held by many friends of rights, which Ronald Dworkin expressed crisply in a metaphor from bridge: Rights "trump" utilities.[10] That is, if one would infringe a right in or by acting, then it is not sufficient justification for acting that one would thereby maximize utility. It seems to me that something like this must be correct.

Consideration of this idea suggests the possibility of a very simple solution to the problem. That is, it might be said (i) The reason why the surgeon may not proceed in *Transplant* is that if he proceeds, he maximizes utility, for he brings about a net saving of four lives, but in so doing he would infringe a right of the young man's.

Which right? Well, we might say: The right the young man has against the surgeon that the surgeon not kill him—thus a right in the cluster of rights that the young man has in having a right to life.

Solving this problem requires being able to explain also why the bystander may proceed in *Bystander at the Switch*. So it might be said (ii) The reason why the bystander may proceed is that if he proceeds, he maximizes utility, for he brings about a net saving of four lives, and in so doing he does *not* infringe any right of the one track workman's.

But I see no way—certainly there is no easy way—of establishing that these ideas are true.

Is it clear that the bystander would infringe no right of the one track workman's if he turned the trolley? Suppose there weren't anybody on the straight track, and the bystander turned the trolley onto the right-hand track, thereby killing the one, but not saving anybody, since nobody was at risk, and thus nobody needed saving. Wouldn't that infringe a right of the one workman's, a right in the cluster of rights that he has in having a right to life?

So should we suppose that the fact that there are five track workmen on the straight track who are in need of saving makes the one lack that right—which he would have had if that had not been a fact?

But then why doesn't the fact that the surgeon has five patients who are in need of saving make the young man also lack that right?

I think some people would say there is good (excellent, conclusive) reason for thinking that the one track workman lacks the right (given there are five on the straight track) lying in the fact that (given there are five on the straight track) it is morally permissible to turn the trolley onto him. But if your reason for thinking the one lacks the right is that it is permissible to turn the trolley onto him, then you can hardly go on to explain its being permissible to turn the trolley onto him by appeal to the fact that he lacks the right. It pays to stress this point: If you want to say, as (ii) does, that the bystander may proceed because he maximizes utility and infringes no right, then you need an independent account

of what makes it be the case that he infringes no right—independent, that is, of its being the case that he may proceed.

There is *some* room for maneuver here. Any plausible theory of rights must make room for the possibility of waiving a right, and within that category, for the possibility of failing to have a right by virtue of assumption of risk; and it might be argued that that is what is involved here, i.e., that track workmen know of the risks of the job, and consent to run them when signing on for it.

But that is not really an attractive way of dealing with this difficulty. Track workmen certainly do not explicitly consent to being run down with trolleys when doing so will save five who are on some other track—certainly they are not asked to consent to this at the time of signing on for the job. And I doubt that they consciously assume the risk of it at that or any other time. And in any case, what if the six people involved had not been track workmen? What if they had been young children? What if they had been people who had been shoved out of helicopters? Wouldn't it all the same be permissible to turn the trolley?

So it is not clear what (independent) reason could be given for thinking that the bystander will infringe no right of the one's if he throws the switch.

I think, moreover, that there is *some* reason to think that the bystander will infringe a right of the one if he throws the switch, even though it is permissible for him to do so. What I have in mind issues simply from the fact that if the bystander throws the switch, then he does what will kill the one. Suppose the bystander proceeds, and that the one is now dead. The bystander's motives were, of course, excellent—he acted with a view to saving five. But the one did not volunteer his life so that the five might live; the bystander volunteered it for him. The bystander made him pay with his life for the bystander's saving of the five. This consideration seems to me to lend some weight to the idea that the bystander did do him a wrong—a wrong it was morally permissible to do him, since five were saved, but a wrong *to him* all the same.

Consider again that lingering feeling of discomfort (which, as I said, some people do feel) about what the bystander does if he turns the trolley. No doubt it is permissible to turn the trolley, but still . . . but still. . . . People who feel this discomfort also think that, although it is permissible to turn the trolley, it is not morally required to do so. My own view is that they are right to feel and think these things. We would be able to explain why this is so if we supposed that if the bystander turns the trolley, then he does do the one track workman a wrong—if we supposed, in particular, that he infringes a right of the one track workman's which is in that cluster of rights which the workman has in having a right to life.[11]

I do not for a moment take myself to have established that (ii) is false. I have wished only to draw attention to the difficulty that lies ahead of a person who thinks (ii) true, and also to suggest that there is some reason to think that the bystander would infringe a right of the one's if he proceeded, and thus some reason to think that (ii) is false. It can easily be seen that if there is some reason to think the bystander would infringe a right of the one's, then there is also some reason to think that (i) is false—since if the bystander does infringe a right of the one's if he proceeds, and may nevertheless proceed, then it cannot be the fact that the surgeon infringes a right of the young man's if *he* proceeds which makes it impermissible for *him* to do so.

Perhaps a friend of (i) and (ii) can establish that they are true. I propose that, just in case he can't, we do well to see if there isn't some other way of solving this problem than by appeal to them. In particular, I propose we grant that both the bystander and the surgeon would infringe a right of their ones, a right in the cluster of rights that the ones' have in having a right to life, and that we look for some *other* difference between the cases which could be appealed to to explain the moral difference between them.

Notice that accepting this proposal does not commit us to rejecting the idea expressed in that crisp metaphor of Dworkin's. We can still say that rights trump utilities—if we can find a further feature of what the bystander does if he turns the trolley (beyond the fact that he maximizes utility) which itself trumps the right, and thus makes it permissible to proceed.

VI.

As I said, my own feeling is that the trolley problem can be solved only by appeal to the concept of a right—but not by appeal to it in as simple a way as that discussed in the preceding section. What we were attending to in the preceding section was only the fact that the agents would be killing and saving if they proceeded; what we should be attending to is the means by which they would kill and save.[12] (It is very tempting, because so much simpler, to regard a human act as a solid nugget, without internal structure, and to try to trace its moral value to the shape of its surface, as it were. The trolley problem seems to me to bring home that that will not do.)

I said earlier that there seem to me to be two crucial facts about what the bystander does if he proceeds in *Bystander at the Switch*. In the first place, he saves his five by making something that threatens them instead threaten the one. And second, he does not do that by means which themselves constitute infringements of any right of the one's.

Let us begin with the first.

If the surgeon proceeds in *Transplant*, he plainly does not save his five by making something that threatens them instead threaten one. It is organ-failure that threatens his five, and it is not *that* which he makes threaten the young man if he proceeds.

Consider another of Mrs. Foot's cases, which I shall call *Hospital*.

Suppose [Mrs. Foot says] that there are five patients in a hospital whose lives could be saved by the manufacture of a certain gas, but that this will inevitably release lethal fumes into the room of another patient whom for some reason we are unable to move.[13]

Surely it would not be permissible for us to manufacture the gas.

In *Transplant* and *Hospital*, the five at risk are at risk from their ailments, and this might be thought to make a difference. Let us by-pass it. In a variant on *Hospital*—which I shall call *Hospital′*—all six patients are convalescing. The five at risk are at risk, not from their ailments, but from the ceiling of their room, which is about to fall on them. We can prevent this by pumping on a ceiling-support-mechanism; but doing so will inevitably release lethal fumes into the room of the sixth. Here too it is plain we may not proceed.

Contrast a case in which lethal fumes are being released by the heating system in the basement of a building next door to the hospital. They are headed towards the room of five. We can deflect them towards the room of one. Would that be permissible? I should think it would be—the case seems to be in all relevant respects like *Bystander at the Switch*.

In *Bystander at the Switch*, something threatens five, and if the agent proceeds, he saves the five by making that very thing threaten the one instead of the five. That is not true of the agents in *Hospital′* or *Hospital* or *Transplant*. In *Hospital′*, for example, what threatens the five is the ceiling, and the agent does not save them by making *it* threaten the one, he saves them by doing what will make something wholly different (some lethal fumes) threaten the one.

Why is this difference morally important? Other things being equal, to kill a man is to infringe his right to life, and we are therefore morally barred from killing. It is not enough to justify killing a person that if we do so, five others will be saved: To say that if we do so, five others will be saved is merely to say that utility will be maximized if we proceed, and that is not by itself sufficient to justify proceeding. Rights trump utilities. So if that is all that can be said in defense of killing a person, then killing that person is not permissible.

But that five others will be saved is not all that can be said in defense of killing in *Bystander at the Switch*. The bystander who proceeds does not merely minimize the number of deaths which get caused: He minimizes the number of deaths which get caused by something that already threatens people, and that will cause deaths whatever the bystander does.

The bystander who proceeds does not make something be a threat to people which would otherwise not be a threat to anyone; he makes be a threat to fewer what is already a threat to more. We might speak here of a "distributive exemption," which permits arranging that something that will do harm anyway shall be better distributed than it otherwise would be— shall (in *Bystander at the Switch*) do harm to fewer rather than more. Not just any distributive intervention is permissible: It is not in general morally open to us to make one die to save five. But other things being equal, it is not morally required of us that we let a burden descend out of the blue onto five when we can make it instead descend onto one.

I do not find it clear why there should be an exemption for, and only for, making a burden which is descending onto five descend, instead, onto one. That there is seems to me very plausible, however. On the one hand, the agent who acts under this exemption makes be a threat to one something that is *already* a threat to more, and thus something that will do harm *whatever* he does; on the other hand, the exemption seems to allow those acts which intuition tells us are clearly permissible, and to rule out those acts which intuition tells us are clearly impermissible.

VII.

More precisely, it is not morally required of us that we let a burden descend out of the blue onto five when we can make it instead descend onto one *if* we can make it descend onto the one by means which do not themselves constitute infringements of rights of the one.

Consider a case—which I shall call *Fat Man*— in which you are standing on a footbridge over the trolley track. You can see a trolley hurtling down the track, out of control. You turn around to see where the trolley is headed, and there are five workmen on the track where it exits from under the footbridge. What to do? Being an expert on trolleys, you know of one certain way to stop an out-of-control trolley: Drop a really heavy weight in its path. But where to find one? It just so happens that standing next to you on the footbridge is a fat man, a really fat man. He is leaning over the railing, watching the trolley; all you have to do is to give him a little shove, and over the railing he will go, onto the track in the path of the trolley. Would it be permissible for you to do this? Everybody to whom I have put this case says it would not be. But why?

Suppose the agent proceeds. He shoves the fat man, thereby toppling him off the footbridge into the path of the trolley, thereby causing him to be hit by the trolley, thereby killing him—but saving the five on the straight track. Then it is true of this agent, as it is true of the agent in *Bystander at the Switch,* that he saves his five by making something which threatens them instead threaten one.

But *this* agent does so by means which themselves constitute an infringement of a right of the one's. For shoving a person is infringing a right of his. So also is toppling a person off a footbridge.

I should stress that doing these things is infringing a person's rights even if doing them does not cause his death—even if doing them causes him no harm at all. As I shall put it, shoving a person, toppling a person off a footbridge,

are *themselves* infringements of rights of his. A theory of rights ought to give an account of what makes it be the case that doing either of these things is itself an infringement of a right of his. But I think we may take it to be a datum that it is, the job which confronts the theorist of rights being, not to establish that it is, but rather to explain why it is.

Consider by contrast the agent in *Bystander at the Switch.* He too, if he proceeds, saves five by making something that threatens them instead threaten one. But the means he takes to make that be the case are these: Turn the trolley onto the right-hand track. And turning the trolley onto the right-hand track is not *itself* an infringement of a right of anybody's. The agent would do the one no wrong at all if he turned the trolley onto the right-hand track, and by some miracle the trolley did not hit him.

We might of course have imagined it not necessary to shove the fat man. We might have imagined that all you need do to get the trolley to threaten him instead of the five is to wobble the handrail, for the handrail is low, and he is leaning on it, and wobbling it will cause him to fall over and off. Wobbling the handrail would be impermissible, I should think—no less so than shoving. But then there is room for an objection to the idea that the contrast I point to will help explain the moral differences among these cases. For it might be said that if you wobble the handrail, thereby getting the trolley to threaten the one instead of the five, then the means you take to get this to be the case are just these: Wobble the handrail. But doing that is not *itself* an infringement of a right of anybody's. You would do the fat man no wrong at all if you wobbled the handrail and no harm came to him in consequence of your doing so. In this respect, then, your situation seems to be exactly like that of the agent in *Bystander at the Switch.* Just as the means he would be taking to make the trolley threaten one instead of five would not constitute an infringement of a right, so also would the means you would be taking to make the trolley threaten one instead of five not constitute an infringement of a right.

What I had in mind, however, is a rather tighter notion of "means" than shows itself in this objection. By hypothesis, wobbling the handrail will cause the fat man to topple onto the track in the path of the trolley, and thus will cause the trolley to threaten him instead of the five. But the trolley will not threaten him instead of the five unless wobbling the handrail does cause him to topple. Getting the trolley to threaten the fat man instead of the five *requires* getting him into its path. You get the trolley to threaten him instead of them by wobbling the handrail only if, and only because, by wobbling the handrail you topple him into the path of the trolley.

What I had in mind, then, is a notion of "means" which comes out as follows. Suppose you get a trolley to threaten one instead of five by wobbling a handrail. The means you take to get the trolley to threaten the one instead of the five include wobbling the handrail, *and* all those further things that you have to succeed in doing by wobbling the handrail if the trolley is to threaten the one instead of the five.

So the means by which the agent in *Fat Man* gets the trolley to threaten one instead of five include toppling the fat man off the footbridge; and doing that is itself an infringement of a right of the fat man's. By contrast, the means by which the agent in *Bystander at the Switch* gets the trolley to threaten one instead of five include no more than getting the trolley off the straight track onto the right-hand track; and doing that is not itself an infringement of a right of anybody's.

VIII.

It is arguable, however, that what is relevant is not that toppling the fat man off the footbridge is itself an infringement of *a* right of the fat man's but rather that toppling him off the footbridge is itself an infringement of a particularly stringent right of his.

What I have in mind comes out in yet another variant on *Bystander at the Switch*. Here the bystander must cross (without permission) a patch of land that belongs to the one in order to get to the switch; thus in order to get the trolley to threaten the one instead of five, the bystander must infringe a right of the one's. May he proceed?

Or again, in order to get the switch thrown, the bystander must use a sharply pointed tool, and the only available sharply pointed tool is a nailfile that belongs to the one; here too the bystander must infringe a right of the one's in order to get the trolley to threaten the one instead of five. May he proceed?

For my own part, I do not find it obvious that he may. (Remember what the bystander will be doing to the one by throwing that switch.) But others tell me they think it clear the bystander may proceed in such a case. If they are right—and I guess we should agree that they are—then that must surely be because the rights which the bystander would have to infringe here are minor, trivial, non-stringent—property rights of no great importance. By contrast, the right to not be toppled off a footbridge onto a trolley track is on any view a stringent right. We shall therefore have to recognize that what is at work in these cases is a matter of degree: If the agent must infringe a stringent right of the one's in order to get something that threatens five to threaten the one (as in *Fat Man*), then he may not proceed, whereas if the agent need infringe no right of the one's (as in *Bystander at the Switch*), or only a more or less trivial right of the one's (as in these variants on *Bystander at the Switch*), in order to get something that threatens five to threaten the one, then he may proceed.

Where what is at work is a matter of degree, it should be no surprise that there are borderline cases, on which people disagree. I confess to having been greatly surprised, however, at the fact of disagreement on the following variant on *Bystander at the Switch:*

The five on the straight track are regular track workmen. The right-hand track is a dead end, unused in ten years. The Mayor, representing the City, has set out picnic tables on it, and invited the convalescents at the nearby City Hospital to have their meals there, guaranteeing them that no trolleys will ever, for any reason, be turned onto that track. The one on the right-hand track is a convalescent having his lunch there; it would never have occurred to him to do so if the Mayor had not issued his invitation and guarantee. The Mayor was out for a walk; he now stands by the switch.[14]

For the Mayor to get the trolley to threaten the one instead of the five, he must turn the trolley onto the right-hand track; but the one has a right against the Mayor that he not turn the trolley onto the right-hand track—a right generated by an official promise, which was then relied on by the one. (Contrast the original *Bystander at the Switch*, in which the one had no such right.) My own feeling is that it is plain the Mayor may not proceed. To my great surprise, I find that some people think he may. I conclude they think the right less stringent than I do.

In any case, that distributive exemption that I spoke of earlier is very conservative. It permits intervention into the world to get an object that already threatens death to those many to instead threaten death to these few, but only by acts that are not themselves gross impingements on the few. That is, the intervenor must not use means that infringe stringent rights of the few in order to get his distributive intention carried out.

It could of course be argued that the fact that the bystander of the original *Bystander at the Switch* makes threaten the one what already threatens the five, and does so by means that do not themselves constitute infringements of any right of the one's (not even a trivial right of the one's), shows that the bystander in that case infringes no right of the one's at all. That is, it

could be argued that we have here that independent ground for saying that the bystander does not infringe the one's right to life which I said would be needed by a friend of (ii).[15] But I see nothing to be gained by taking this line, for I see nothing to be gained by supposing it never permissible to infringe a right; and something is lost by taking this line, namely the possibility of viewing the bystander as doing the one a wrong if he proceeds—albeit a wrong it is permissible to do him.

IX.

What counts as "*an* object which threatens death"? What marks one threat off from another? I have no doubt that ingenious people can construct cases in which we shall be unclear whether to say that if the agent proceeds, he makes threaten the one the very same thing as already threatens the five.

Moreover, which are the interventions in which the agent gets a thing that threatens five to instead threaten one by means that themselves constitute infringements of stringent rights of the one's? I have no doubt that ingenious people can construct cases in which we shall all be unclear whether to say that the agent's means do constitute infringements of stringent rights—and cases also in which we shall be unclear whether to say the agent's means constitute infringements of any rights at all.

But it is surely a mistake to look for precision in the concepts brought to bear to solve this problem: There isn't any to be had. It would be enough if cases in which it seems to us unclear whether to say "same threat," or unclear whether to say "non-right-infringing-means," also seemed to us to be cases in which it is unclear whether the agent may or may not proceed; and if also coming to see a case as one to which these expressions do (or do not) apply involves coming to see the case as one in which the agent may (or may not) proceed.

X.

If these ideas are correct, then we have a handle on anyway some of the troublesome cases in which people make threats. Suppose a villain says to us "I will cause a ceiling to fall on five unless you send lethal fumes into the room of one." Most of us think it would not be permissible for us to accede to this threat. Why? We may think of the villain as part of the world around the people involved, a part which is going to drop a burden on the five if we do not act. On this way of thinking of him, nothing *yet* threatens the five (certainly no ceiling as yet threatens them) and a fortiori we cannot save the five by making what (already) threatens them instead threaten the one. Alternatively, we may think of the villain as himself a threat to the five. But sending the fumes in is not making *him* be a threat to the one instead of to the five. The hypothesis I proposed, then, yields what it should: We may not accede.

That is because the hypothesis I proposed says nothing at all about the source of the threat to the five. Whether the threat to the five is, or is caused by, a human being or anything else, it is not permissible to do what will kill one to save the five except by making what threatens the five itself threaten the one.

By contrast, it seems to me very plausible to think that if a villain has started a trolley towards five, we may deflect the trolley towards one—other things being equal, of course. If a trolley is headed towards five, and we can deflect it towards one, we *may*, no matter who or what caused it to head towards the five.

I think that these considerations help us in dealing with a question I drew attention to earlier. Suppose a villain says to us "I will cause a ceiling to fall on five unless you send lethal fumes into the room of one." If we refuse, so that he does what he threatens to do, then he surely does something very much worse than we would be doing if we acceded to his threat and sent the fumes in. If we accede, we do

something misguided and wrongful, but not nearly as bad as what he does if we refuse.

It should be stressed: The fact that he will do something worse if we do not send the fumes in does not entail that we ought to send them in, or even that it is permissible for us to do so.

How after all could that entail that we may send the fumes in? The fact that we would be saving five lives by sending the fumes in does not itself make it permissible for us to do so. (Rights trump utilities.) How could adding that the taker of those five lives would be doing what is worse than we would tip the balance? If we may not infringe a right of the one in order to save the five lives, it cannot possibly be thought that we may infringe the right of that one in order, not merely to save the five lives, but to make the villain's moral record better than it otherwise would be.

For my own part, I think that considerations of motives apart, and other things being equal, it does no harm to say that

(II) Killing five is worse than killing one

is, after all, true. *Of course* we shall then have to say that assessments of which acts are worse than which do not by themselves settle the question of what is permissible for a person to do. For we shall have to say that, despite the truth of (II), it is not the case that we are required to kill one in order that another person shall not kill five, or even that it is everywhere permissible for us to do this.

What is of interest is that what holds interpersonally also holds intra-personally. I said earlier that we might imagine the surgeon of *Transplant* to have caused the ailments of his five patients. Let us imagine the worst: He gave them chemical X precisely in order to cause their deaths, in order to inherit from them. Now he repents. But the fact that he would be saving five lives by operating on the one does not itself make it permissible for him to operate on the one. (Rights trump utilities.) And if he may not infringe a right of the one in order to save the five lives, it cannot possibly be thought that he may infringe the right of that one in order, not merely to save the five lives, but to make his own moral record better than it otherwise would be.

Another way to put the point is this: Assessments of which acts are worse than which have to be directly relevant to the agent's circumstances if they are to have a bearing on what he may do. If A threatens to kill five unless B kills one, then although killing five is worse than killing one, these are not the alternatives open to B. The alternatives open to B are: Kill one, thereby forestalling the deaths of five (and making A's moral record better than it otherwise would be), or let it be the case that A kills five. And the supposition that it would be worse for B to choose to kill the one is entirely compatible with the supposition that killing five is worse than killing one. Again, the alternatives open to the surgeon are: Operate on the one, thereby saving five (and making the surgeon's own moral record better than it otherwise would be), or let it be the case that he himself will have killed the five. And the supposition that it would be worse for the surgeon to choose to operate is entirely compatible with the supposition that killing five is worse than killing one.

On the other hand, suppose a second surgeon is faced with a choice between here and now giving chemical X to five, thereby killing them, and operating on, and thereby killing, only one. (It taxes the imagination to invent such a second surgeon, but let that pass. And compare *Trolley Driver*.) Then, other things being equal, it does seem he may choose to operate on the one. Some people would say something stronger, namely that he is required to make this choice. Perhaps they would say that

(II′) If a person is faced with a choice between doing something *here and now* to five, by the doing of which he will kill them, and doing something else *here and now* to one, by the doing of which he will kill only the one, then

(other things being equal) he ought to choose the second alternative rather than the first

is a quite general moral truth. Whether or not the second surgeon is morally required to make this choice (and thus whether or not (II′) is a general moral truth), it does seem to be the case that he may. But this did seem puzzling. As I put it: Why should the present tense matter so much?

It is plausible to think that the present tense matters because the question for the agent at the time of acting is about the present, viz., "What may I here and now do?," and because that question is the same as the question "Which of the alternatives here and now open to me may I choose?" The alternatives now open to the second surgeon are: kill five or kill one. If killing five is worse than killing one, then perhaps he ought to, but at any rate he may, kill the one.[16]

Notes

1. *See* P. FOOT, *The Problem of Abortion and the Doctrine of the Double Effect*, in VIRTUES AND VICES AND OTHER ESSAYS IN MORAL PHILOSOPHY 19 (1978).

2. I think it possible (though by no means certain) that John Taurek would say No, it is not permissible to (all simply) turn the trolley; what you ought to do is flip a coin. *See* Taurek, *Should the Numbers Count?*, 6 PHIL. & PUB. AFF. 293 (1977). (But he is there concerned with a different kind of case, namely that in which what is in question is not whether we may do what harms one to avoid harming five, but whether we may or ought to choose to save five in preference to saving one.) For criticism of Taurek's article, see Parfit, *Innumerate Ethics*, 7 PHIL. & PUB. AFF. 285 (1978).

3. I doubt that anyone would say, with any hope of getting agreement from others, that the surgeon ought to flip a coin. So even if you think that the trolley driver ought lo flip a coin, there would remain, for you, an analogue of Mrs. Foot's problem, namely: Why ought the trolley driver flip a coin, whereas the surgeon may not?

4. Mrs. Foot speaks more generally of causing injury and failing to provide aid; and her reason for thinking that the former is worse than the latter is that the negative duty

to refrain from causing injury is stricter than the positive duty to provide aid. *See* P. FOOT, *supra* note I, at 27–29.

5. A similar case (intended to make a point similar to the one that I shall be making) is discussed in Davis, *The Priority of Avoiding Harm,* in KILLING AND LETTING DIE 172, 194–95 (B. Steinbock ed. 1980).

6. For a sensitive discussion some of the difficulties, see Davis, *Using Persons and Common Sense,* 94 ETHICS 387 (1984). Among other things, she argues (I think rightly) that the Kantian idea is not to be identified with the common sense concept of "using a person." *Id.* at 402.

7. For a second reason to think so, see *infra* note 13.

8. It is also true that if the five go wholly out of existence just before the agent starts to turn the trolley, then the one will die whatever the agent does. Should we say, then, that the agent uses one to save five if he acts, *and* uses five to save one if he does not act? No: What follows *and* is false. If the agent does not act, he uses nobody. (I doubt that it can even be said that if he does not act, he lets them *be used.* For what is the active for which this is passive? Who or what would be using them if he does not act?).

9. I strongly suspect that giving an account of what makes it wrong to *use* a person, *see supra* text accompanying notes 6–8, would also require appeal to the concept of a right.

10. R. DWORKIN, TAKING RIGHTS SERIOUSLY ix (1977).

11. Many of the examples discussed by Bernard Williams and Ruth Marcus plainly call out for this kind of treatment. *See* B. WILLIAMS, *Ethical Consistency,* in PROBLEMS OF THE SELF 166 (1973); Marcus, *Moral Dilemmas and Consistency,* 77 J. PHIL. 121 (1980).

12. It may be worth stressing that what I suggest calls for attention is not (as some construals of "double effect" would have it) whether the agent's killing of the one is his means to something, and not (as other construals of "double effect" would have it) whether the death of the one is the agent's means to something, but rather what are the means by which the agent both kills and saves. For a discussion of "the doctrine of double effect," see P. FOOT, *supra* note 1.

13. *Id.* at 29. As Mrs. Foot says, we do not *use* the one if we proceed in *Hospital.* Yet the impermissibility of proceeding in *Hospital* seems to have a common source with the impermissibility of operating in *Transplant,* in which the surgeon *would* be using the one whose parts he takes for the five who need them. This is my second reason for thinking that an appeal to the fact that the surgeon would be using his victim is an over-simple way of taking account of the means he would be employing for the saving of his five. *See supra* note 7.

14. Notice that in this case too the agent does not *use* the one if he proceeds. (This case, along with a number of other cases I have been discussing, comes from Thomson, *Killing, Letting Die, and the Trolley Problem,* 59 THE MONIST 204 (1976). Mrs. Thomson seems to me to have been blundering around in the dark in that paper, but the student of this problem may possibly find some of the cases she discusses useful.).

15. *See supra* text accompanying notes 9–11.

16. Many people have given me helpful criticism of this essay's many successive reincarnations over the years; I cannot list them all—for want of space, not of gratitude. Most recently, it benefited from criticism by the members of the Yale Law School Civil Liability Workshop and the Legal Theory Workshop, Faculty of Law, University of Toronto.

Famine, Affluence, and Morality

Peter Singer

Peter Singer is DeCamp Professor of Bioethics, University Center for Human Values, Princeton University. His book Animal Liberation *(1975) is one of the most influential books ever written on animal rights and has converted many to the animal rights movement.*

Singer argues that we have a duty to provide aid to famine victims and others who are suffering from hunger and poverty. He proposes two principles, a strong and a moderate one, which show that we have a duty to give substantial aid to those who are starving. The strong principle is "If it is in our power to prevent something bad from happening, without thereby sacrificing anything of comparable moral importance, we ought, morally, to do it." The moderate (or weak) principle is "If it is in our power to prevent something very bad from happening, without thereby sacrificing anything morally significant, we ought, morally, to do it."

As I write this, in November, 1971, people are dying in East Bengal from lack of food, shelter, and medical care. The suffering and death that are occurring there now are not inevitable, not unavoidable in any fatalistic sense of the term. Constant poverty, a cyclone, and a civil war have turned at least nine million people into destitute refugees; nevertheless, it is not beyond the capacity of the richer nations to give enough assistance to reduce any further suffering to very small proportions. The decisions and actions of human beings can prevent this kind of suffering. Unfortunately, human beings have not made the necessary decisions. At the

Reprinted from Peter Singer, "Famine, Affluence, and Morality" by permission of the publisher, Wiley-Blackwell, from *Philosophy and Public Affairs*, Vol. 1, No. 1 (Spring 1972), pp. 123–144. © 1972.

individual level, people have, with very few exceptions, not responded to the situation in any significant way. Generally speaking, people have not given large sums to relief funds; they have not written to their parliamentary representatives demanding increased government assistance; they have not demonstrated in the streets, held symbolic fasts, or done anything else directed toward providing the refugees with the means to satisfy their essential needs. At the government level, no government has given the sort of massive aid that would enable the refugees to survive for more than a few days. Britain, for instance, has given rather more than most countries. It has, to date, given £14,750,000. For comparative purposes, Britain's share of the nonrecover-able development costs of the Anglo-French Concorde project is already in excess of £275,000,000, and on present estimates will reach £440,000,000. The implication is that the British government values a supersonic transport more than thirty times as highly as it values the lives of the nine million refugees. Australia is another country which, on a per capita basis, is well up in the "aid to Bengal" table. Australia's aid, however, amounts to less than one-twentieth of the cost of Sydney's new opera house. The total amount given, from all sources, now stands at about £65,000,000. The estimated cost of keeping the refugees alive for one year is £464,000,000. Most of the refugees have now been in the camps for more than six months. The World Bank has said that India needs a minimum of £300,000,000 in assistance from other countries before the end of the year. It seems obvious that assistance on this scale will not be forthcoming. India will be forced to choose between letting the refugees starve or diverting funds from her own development program, which will mean that more of her own people will starve in the future.[1]

These are the essential facts about the present situation in Bengal. So far as it concerns us here, there is nothing unique about this situation except its magnitude. The Bengal emergency is just the latest and most acute of a series of major emergencies in various parts of the world, arising both from natural and from man-made causes. There are also many parts of the world in which people die from malnutrition and lack of food independent of any special emergency. I take Bengal as my example only because it is the present concern, and because the size of the problem has ensured that it has been given adequate publicity. Neither individuals nor governments can claim to be unaware of what is happening there.

What are the moral implications of a situation like this? In what follows, I shall argue that the way people in relatively affluent countries react to a situation like that in Bengal cannot be justified; indeed, the whole way we look at moral issues—our moral conceptual scheme—needs to be altered, and with it, the way of life that has come to be taken for granted in our society.

In arguing for this conclusion I will not, of course, claim to be morally neutral. I shall, however, try to argue for the moral position that I take, so that anyone who accepts certain assumptions, to be made explicit, will, I hope, accept my conclusion.

I begin with the assumption that suffering and death from lack of food, shelter, and medical care are bad. I think most people will agree about this, although one may reach the same view by different routes. I shall not argue for this view. People can hold all sorts of eccentric positions, and perhaps from some of them it would not follow that death by starvation is in itself bad. It is difficult, perhaps impossible, to refute such positions, and so for brevity I will henceforth take this assumption as accepted. Those who disagree need read no further.

My next point is this: If it is in our power to prevent something bad from happening, without thereby sacrificing anything of comparable moral importance, we ought, morally, to do it. By "without sacrificing anything of comparable moral importance" I mean without causing anything else comparably bad to happen, or doing something that is wrong in itself, or failing to promote some moral good, comparable in significance to the bad thing that we can prevent. This principle seems almost as uncontroversial as the last one. It requires us only to prevent what is bad, and not to promote what is good, and it requires this of us only when we can do it without sacrificing anything that is, from the moral point of view, comparably important. I could even, as far as the application of my argument to the Bengal emergency is concerned, qualify the point so as to make it: if it is in our power to prevent something very bad from happening, without thereby sacrificing anything morally significant, we ought, morally, to do it. An application of this principle would be as follows: if I am walking past a shallow pond and see a child drowning in it, I ought to wade in and pull the child out. This will mean getting my clothes muddy, but this is insignificant, while the death of the child would presumably be a very bad thing.

The uncontroversial appearance of the principle just stated is deceptive. If it were acted upon, even in its qualified form, our lives, our society, and our world would be fundamentally changed. For the principle takes, firstly, no account of proximity or distance. It makes no moral difference whether the person I can help is a neighbor's child ten yards from me or a Bengali whose name I shall never know, ten thousand miles away. Secondly, the principle makes no distinction between cases in which I am the only person who could possibly do anything and cases in which I am just one among millions in the same position.

I do not think I need to say much in defense of the refusal to take proximity and distance into account. The fact that a person is physically near to us, so that we have personal contact with him, may make it more likely that we shall assist him, but this does not show that we ought to help him rather than another who happens to be further away. If we accept any principle of impartiality, universalizability, equality, or whatever, we cannot discriminate against someone merely because he is far away from us (or we are far away from him). Admittedly, it is possible that we are in a better position to judge what needs to be done to help a person near to us than one far away, and perhaps also to provide the assistance we judge to be necessary. If this were the case, it would be a reason for helping those near to us first. This may once have been a justification for being more concerned with the poor in one's town than with famine victims in India. Unfortunately for those who like to keep their moral responsibilities limited, instant communication and swift transportation have changed the situation. From the moral point of view, the development of the world into a "global village" has made an important, though still unrecognized, difference to our moral situation. Expert observers and supervisors, sent out by famine relief organizations or permanently stationed in famine-prone areas, can direct our aid to a refugee in Bengal almost as effectively as we could get it to someone in our own block. There would seem, therefore, to be no possible justification for discriminating on geographical grounds.

There may be a greater need to defend the second implication of my principle—that the fact that there are millions of other people in the same position, in respect to the Bengali refugees, as I am, does not make the situation significantly different from a situation in which I am the only person who can prevent something very bad from occurring. Again, of course, I admit that there is a psychological difference between the cases; one feels less guilty about doing nothing if one can point to others, similarly placed, who have also done

nothing. Yet this can make no real difference to our moral obligations.[2] Should I consider that I am less obliged to pull the drowning child out of the pond if on looking around I see other people, no further away than I am, who have also noticed the child but are doing nothing? One has only to ask this question to see the absurdity of the view that numbers lessen obligation. It is a view that is an ideal excuse for inactivity; unfortunately most of the major evils—poverty, overpopulation, pollution—are problems in which everyone is almost equally involved.

The view that numbers do make a difference can be made plausible if stated in this way: if everyone in circumstances like mine gave £5 to the Bengal Relief Fund, there would be enough to provide food, shelter, and medical care for the refugees; there is no reason why I should give more than anyone else in the same circumstances as I am; therefore I have no obligation to give more than £5. Each premise in this argument is true, and the argument looks sound. It may convince us, unless we notice that it is based on a hypothetical premise, although the conclusion is not stated hypothetically. The argument would be sound if the conclusion were: if everyone in circumstances like mine were to give £5, I would have no obligation to give more than £5. If the conclusion were so stated, however, it would be obvious that the argument has no bearing on a situation in which it is not the case that everyone else gives £5. This, of course, is the actual situation. It is more or less certain that not everyone in circumstances like mine will give £5. So there will not be enough to provide the needed food, shelter, and medical care. Therefore by giving more than £5 I will prevent more suffering than I would if I gave just £5.

It might be thought that this argument has an absurd consequence. Since the situation appears to be that very few people are likely to give substantial amounts, it follows that I and everyone else in similar circumstances ought to give as much as possible, that is, at least up to the point at which by giving more one would begin to cause serious suffering for oneself and one's dependents—perhaps even beyond this point to the point of marginal utility, at which by giving more one would cause oneself and one's dependents as much suffering as one would prevent in Bengal. If everyone does this, however, there will be more than can be used for the benefit of the refugees, and some of the sacrifice will have been unnecessary. Thus, if everyone does what he ought to do, the result will not be as good as it would be if everyone did a little less than he ought to do, or if only some do all that they ought to do.

The paradox here arises only if we assume that the actions in question—sending money to the relief funds—are performed more or less simultaneously, and are also unexpected. For if it is to be expected that everyone is going to contribute something, then clearly each is not obliged to give as much as he would have been obliged to had others not been giving too. And if everyone is not acting more or less simultaneously, then those giving later will know how much more is needed, and will have no obligation to give more than is necessary to reach this amount. To say this is not to deny the principle that people in the same circumstances have the same obligations, but to point out that the fact that others have given, or may be expected to give, is a relevant circumstance: those giving after it has become known that many others are giving and those giving before are not in the same circumstances. So the seemingly absurd consequence of the principle I have put forward can occur only if people are in error about the actual circumstances—that is, if they think they are giving even when others are not, but in fact they are giving when others are. The result of everyone doing what he really ought to do cannot be worse than the result of everyone doing less than he ought to do, although the result of everyone doing what he reasonably believes he ought to do could be.

If my argument so far has been sound, neither our distance from a preventable evil nor the number of other people who, in respect to that evil, are in the same situation as we are, lessens our obligation to mitigate or prevent that evil. I shall therefore take as established the principle I asserted earlier. As I have already said, I need to assert it only in its qualified form: if it is in our power to prevent something very bad from happening, without thereby sacrificing anything else morally significant, we ought, morally, to do it.

The outcome of this argument is that our traditional moral categories are upset. The traditional distinction between duty and charity cannot be drawn, or at least, not in the place we normally draw it. Giving money to the Bengal Relief Fund is regarded as an act of charity in our society. The bodies which collect money are known as "charities." These organizations see themselves in this way—if you send them a check, you will be thanked for your "generosity." Because giving money is regarded as an act of charity, it is not thought that there is anything wrong with not giving. The charitable man may be praised, but the man who is not charitable is not condemned. People do not feel in any way ashamed or guilty about spending money on new clothes or a new car instead of giving it to famine relief. (Indeed, the alternative does not occur to them.) This way of looking at the matter cannot be justified. When we buy new clothes not to keep ourselves warm but to look "well-dressed" we are not providing for any important need. We would not be sacrificing anything significant if we were to continue to wear our old clothes, and give the money to famine relief. By doing so, we would be preventing another person from starving. It follows from what I have said earlier that we ought to give money away, rather than spend it on clothes which we do not need to keep us warm. To do so is not charitable, or generous. Nor is it the kind of act which philosophers and theologians have called "supererogatory"—an act which it would be good to do, but not wrong not to do. On the contrary, we ought to give money away, and it is wrong not to do so.

I am not maintaining that there are no acts which are charitable, or that there are no acts which it would be good to do but not wrong not to do. It may be possible to redraw the distinction between duty and charity in some other place. All I am arguing here is that the present way of drawing the distinction, which makes it an act of charity for a man living at the level of affluence which most people in the "developed nations" enjoy to give money to save someone else from starvation, cannot be supported. It is beyond the scope of my argument to consider whether the distinction should be redrawn or abolished altogether. There would be many other possible ways of drawing the distinction—for instance, one might decide that it is good to make other people as happy as possible, but not wrong not to do so.

Despite the limited nature of the revision in our moral conceptual scheme which I am proposing, the revision would, given the extent of both affluence and famine in the world today, have radical implications. These implications may lead to further objections, distinct from those I have already considered. 1 shall discuss two of these.

One objection to the position I have taken might be simply that it is too drastic a revision of our moral scheme. People do not ordinarily judge in the way I have suggested they should. Most people reserve their moral condemnation for those who violate some moral norm, such as the norm against taking another person's property. They do not condemn those who indulge in luxury instead of giving to famine relief. But given that I did not set out to present a morally neutral description of the way people make moral judgments, the way people do in fact judge has nothing to do with the validity of my conclusion. My conclusion follows from the principle which I advanced earlier, and unless that principle is rejected, or the arguments shown to be unsound, I think the conclusion must stand, however strange it appears.

It might, nevertheless, be interesting to consider why our society, and most other societies, do judge differently from the way I have suggested they should. In a well-known article, J. O. Urmson suggests that the imperatives of duty, which tell us what we must do, as distinct from what it would be good to do but not wrong not to do, function so as to prohibit behavior that is intolerable if men are to live together in society.[3] This may explain the origin and continued existence of the present division between acts of duty and acts of charity. Moral attitudes are shaped by the needs of society, and no doubt society needs people who will observe the rules that make social existence tolerable. From the point of view of a particular society, it is essential to prevent violations of norms against killing, stealing, and so on. It is quite inessential, however, to help people outside one's own society.

If this is an explanation of our common distinction between duty and supererogation, however, it is not a justification of it. The moral point of view requires us to look beyond the interests of our own society. Previously, as I have already mentioned, this may hardly have been feasible, but it is quite feasible now. From the moral point of view, the prevention of the starvation of millions of people outside our society must be considered at least as pressing as the upholding of property norms within our society.

It has been argued by some writers, among them Sidgwick and Urmson, that we need to have a basic moral code which is not too far beyond the capacities of the ordinary man, for otherwise there will be a general breakdown of compliance with the moral code. Crudely stated, this argument suggests that if we tell people that they ought to refrain from murder and give everything they do not really need to famine relief, they will do neither, whereas if we tell them that they ought to refrain from murder and that it is good to give to famine relief but not wrong not to do so, they will at least refrain from murder. The issue here is: Where should we draw the line between conduct that is required and conduct that is good although not required, so as to get the best possible result? This would seem to be an empirical question, although a very difficult one. One objection to the Sidgwick-Urmson line of argument is that it takes insufficient account of the effect that moral standards can have on the decisions we make. Given a society in which a wealthy man who gives 5 percent of his income to famine relief is regarded as most generous, it is not surprising that a proposal that we all ought to give away half our incomes will be thought to be absurdly unrealistic. In a society which held that no man should have more than enough while others have less than they need, such a proposal might seem narrow-minded. What it is possible for a man to do and what he is likely to do are both, I think, very greatly influenced by what people around him are doing and expecting him to do. In any case, the possibility that by spreading the idea that we ought to be doing very much more than we are to relieve famine we shall bring about a general breakdown of moral behavior seems remote. If the stakes are an end to widespread starvation, it is worth the risk. Finally, it should be emphasized that these considerations are relevant only to the issue of what we should require from others, and not to what we ourselves ought to do.

The second objection to my attack on the present distinction between duty and charity is one which has from time to time been made against utilitarianism. It follows from some forms of utilitarian theory that we all ought, morally, to be working full time to increase the balance of happiness over misery. The position I have taken here would not lead to this conclusion in all circumstances, for if there were no bad occurrences that we could prevent without sacrificing something of comparable moral importance, my argument would have no application. Given the present conditions in many parts of the world, however, it does follow from my argument that we ought, morally, to be working full time to relieve great suffering of the sort that occurs as a result of famine or other disasters. Of course, mitigating circum-

stances can be adduced—for instance, that if we wear ourselves out through overwork, we shall be less effective than we would otherwise have been. Nevertheless, when all considerations of this sort have been taken into account, the conclusion remains: we ought to be preventing as much suffering as we can without sacrificing something else of comparable moral importance. This conclusion is one which we may be reluctant to face. I cannot see, though, why it should be regarded as a criticism of the position for which I have argued, rather than a criticism of our ordinary standards of behavior. Since most people are self-interested to some degree, very few of us are likely to do everything that we ought to do. It would, however, hardly be honest to take this as evidence that it is not the case that we ought to do it.

It may still be thought that my conclusions are so wildly out of line with what everyone else thinks and has always thought that there must be something wrong with the argument somewhere. In order to show that my conclusions, while certainly contrary to contemporary Western moral standards, would not have seemed so extraordinary at other times and in other places, I would like to quote a passage from a writer not normally thought of as a way-out radical, Thomas Aquinas.

Now, according to the natural order instituted by divine providence, material goods are provided for the satisfaction of human needs. Therefore the division and appropriation of property, which proceeds from human law, must not hinder the satisfaction of man's necessity from such goods. Equally, whatever a man has in superabundance is owed, of natural right, to the poor for their sustenance. So Ambrosius says, and it is also to be found in the *Decretum Gratiana*: "The bread which you withhold belongs to the hungry; the clothing you shut away, to the naked; and the money you bury in the earth is the redemption and freedom of the penniless."[4]

I now want to consider a number of points, more practical than philosophical, which are relevant to the application of the moral conclusion we have reached. These points challenge not the idea that we ought to be doing all we can to prevent starvation, but the idea that giving away a great deal of money is the best means to this end.

It is sometimes said that overseas aid should be a government responsibility, and that therefore one ought not to give to privately run charities. Giving privately, it is said, allows the government and the noncontributing members of society to escape their responsibilities.

This argument seems to assume that the more people there are who give to privately organized famine relief funds, the less likely it is that the government will take over full responsibility for such aid. This assumption is unsupported, and does not strike me as at all plausible. The opposite view—that if no one gives voluntarily, a government will assume that its citizens are uninterested in famine relief and would not wish to be forced into giving aid—seems more plausible. In any case, unless there were a definite probability that by refusing to give one would be helping to bring about massive government assistance, people who do refuse to make voluntary contributions are refusing to prevent a certain amount of suffering without being able to point to any tangible beneficial consequence of their refusal. So the onus of showing how their refusal will bring about government action is on those who refuse to give.

I do not, of course, want to dispute the contention that governments of affluent nations should be giving many times the amount of genuine, no-strings-attached aid that they are giving now. I agree, too, that giving privately is not enough, and that we ought to be campaigning actively for entirely new standards for both public and private contributions to famine relief. Indeed, I would sympathize with someone who thought that campaigning was more important than giving oneself, although I doubt whether preaching what one does not practice would be very effective. Unfortunately, for many people the idea that "it's the government's responsibility" is a reason for not giving which does not appear to entail any political action either.

Another, more serious reason for not giving to famine relief funds is that until there is effective population control, relieving famine merely postpones starvation. If we save the Bengal refugees now, others, perhaps the children of these refugees, will face starvation in a few years' time. In support of this, one may cite the now well-known facts about the population explosion and the relatively limited scope for expanded production.

This point, like the previous one, is an argument against relieving suffering that is happening now, because of a belief about what might happen in the future; it is unlike the previous point in that very good evidence can be adduced in support of this belief about the future. I will not go into the evidence here. I accept that the earth cannot support indefinitely a population rising at the present rate. This certainly poses a problem for anyone who thinks it important to prevent famine. Again, however, one could accept the argument without drawing the conclusion that it absolves one from any obligation to do anything to prevent famine. The conclusion that should be drawn is that the best means of preventing famine, in the long run, is population control. It would then follow from the position reached earlier that one ought to be doing all one can to promote population control (unless one held that all forms of population control were wrong in themselves, or would have significantly bad consequences). Since there are organizations working specifically for population control, one would then support them rather than more orthodox methods of preventing famine.

A third point raised by the conclusion reached earlier relates to the question of just how much we all ought to be giving away. One possibility, which has already been mentioned, is that we ought to give until we reach the level of marginal utility—that is, the level at which, by giving more, I would cause as much suffering to myself or my dependents as I would relieve by my gift. This would mean, of course, that one would reduce oneself to very near the material circumstances of a Bengali refugee. It will be recalled that earlier I put forward both a strong and a moderate version of the principle of preventing bad occurrences. The strong version, which required us to prevent bad things from happening unless in doing so we would be sacrificing something of comparable moral significance, does seem to require reducing ourselves to the level of marginal utility. I should also say that the strong version seems to me to be the correct one. I proposed the more moderate version—that we should prevent bad occurrences unless, to do so, we had to sacrifice something morally significant—only in order to show that even on this surely undeniable principle a great change in our way of life is required. On the more moderate principle, it may not follow that we ought to reduce ourselves to the level of marginal utility, for one might hold that to reduce oneself and one's family to this level is to cause something significantly bad to happen. Whether this is so I shall not discuss, since, as I have said, I can see no good reason for holding the moderate version of the principle rather than the strong version. Even if we accepted the principle only in its moderate form, however, it should be clear that we would have to give away enough to ensure that the consumer society, dependent as it is on people spending on trivia rather than giving to famine relief, would slow down and perhaps disappear entirely. There are several reasons why this would be desirable in itself. The value and necessity of economic growth are now being questioned not only by conservationists, but by economists as well.[5] There is no doubt, too, that the consumer society has had a distorting effect on the goals and purposes of its members. Yet looking at the matter purely from the point of view of overseas aid, there must be

a limit to the extent to which we should deliberately slow down our economy; for it might be the case that if we gave away, say, 40 percent of our Gross National Product, we would slow down the economy so much that in absolute terms we would be giving less than if we gave 25 percent of the much larger GNP that we would have if we limited our contribution to this smaller percentage.

I mention this only as an indication of the sort of factor that one would have to take into account in working out an ideal. Since Western societies generally consider one percent of the GNP an acceptable level for overseas aid, the matter is entirely academic. Nor does it affect the question of how much an individual should give in a society in which very few are giving substantial amounts.

It is sometimes said, though less often now than it used to be, that philosophers have no special role to play in public affairs, since most public issues depend primarily on an assessment of facts. On questions of fact, it is said, philosophers as such have no special expertise, and so it has been possible to engage in philosophy without committing oneself to any position on major public issues. No doubt there are some issues of social policy and foreign policy about which it can truly be said that a really expert assessment of the facts is required before taking sides or acting, but the issue of famine is surely not one of these. The facts about the existence of suffering are beyond dispute. Nor, I think, is it disputed that we can do something about it, either through orthodox methods of famine relief or through population control or both. This is therefore an issue on which philosophers are competent to take a position. The issue is one which faces everyone who has more money than he needs to support himself and his dependents, or who is in a position to take some sort of political action. These categories must include practically every teacher and student of philosophy in the universities of the Western world. If philosophy is to deal with matters that are relevant to both teachers and students, this is an issue that philosophers should discuss.

Discussion, though, is not enough. What is the point of relating philosophy to public (and personal) affairs if we do not take our conclusions seriously? In this instance, taking our conclusion seriously means acting upon it. The philosopher will not find it any easier than anyone else to alter his attitudes and way of life to the extent that, if I am right, is involved in doing everything that we ought to be doing. At the very least, though, one can make a start. The philosopher who does so will have to sacrifice some of the benefits of the consumer society, but he can find compensation in the satisfaction of a way of life in which theory and practice, if not yet in harmony, are at least coming together.

Notes

1. There was also a third possibility: that India would go to war to enable the refugees to return to their lands. Since I wrote this paper, India has taken this way out. The situation is no longer that described above, but this does not affect my argument, as the next paragraph indicates.

2. In view of the special sense philosophers often give to the term, I should say that I use "obligation" simply as the abstract noun derived from "ought," so that "I have an obligation to" means no more, and no less, than "I ought to." This usage is in accordance with the definition of "ought" given by the *Shorter Oxford English Dictionary*: "the general verb to express duty or obligation." I do not think any issue of substance hangs on the way the term is used; sentences in which I use "obligation" could all be rewritten, although somewhat clumsily, as sentences in which a clause containing "ought" replaces the term "obligation."

3. J. O. Urmson, "Saints and Heroes," in *Essays in Moral Philosophy*, ed. Abraham L. Melden (Seattle: University of Washington Press, 1958), p. 214. For a related but significantly different view see also Henry Sidgwick, *The Methods of Ethics*, 7th ed. (London: Dover Press, 1907), pp. 220–21, 492–93.

4. *Summa Theologica*, II–II, Question 66, Article 7, in Aquinas, *Selected Political Writings*, ed. A. P. d'Entreves, trans. J. G. Dawson (Oxford: Basil Blackwell, 1948), p. 171.

5. See, for instance, John Kenneth Galbraith, *The New Industrial State* (Boston: Houghton-Mifflin, 1967); and E. J. Mishan, *The Costs of Economic Growth* (New York: Praeger, 1967).

Kantian Ethics and World Hunger

ONORA O'NEILL

Onora O'Neill is a baroness and member of the House of Lords. She studied philosophy with John Rawls (author of reading 45) at Harvard and taught philosophy at the University of Essex in England and at Barnard College in New York. Until 2006 she was Principal of Newnham College, Cambridge. She is well known for her important books on international justice, bioethics, and the philosophy of Immanuel Kant (author of reading 24). In the selection that follows, she argues for an understanding of the second formulation of Kant's Categorical Imperative, according to which we have duties of charity towards the hungry of the world. At the end of the selection she compares Kantian and utilitarian approaches to the problem of world hunger.

Kant's theory is frequently and misleadingly assimilated to theories of human rights. It is, in fact, a theory of human obligations; therefore it is wider in scope than a theory of human rights. (Not all obligations have corresponding rights.) Kant does not, however, try to generate a set of precise rules defining human obligations in all possible circumstances; instead, he attempts to provide a set of *principles of obligation* that can be used as the starting points for moral reasoning in actual contexts of action. The primary focus of Kantian ethics is, then, on *action* rather than either *results*, as in utilitarian thinking, or *entitlements*, as in theories that make human

rights their fundamental category. Morality requires action of certain sorts. But to know *what* sort of action is required (or forbidden) in which circumstances, we should not look just at the expected results of action or at others' supposed entitlements but, in the first instance, at the nature of the proposed actions themselves.

When we engage in moral reasoning, we often need go no further than to refer to some quite specific principle or tradition. We may say to one another, or to ourselves, things like "It would be hypocritical to pretend that our good fortune is achieved without harm to the Third World" or "Redistributive taxation shouldn't cross national boundaries." But when these specific claims are challenged, we may find ourselves pushed to justify or reject or modify them. Such moral debate, on Kant's account, rests on appeals to what he calls the *Supreme Principle of Morality*, which can (he thinks) be used to work out more specific principles of obligation. This principle, the famous Categorical Imperative, plays the same role in Kantian thinking that the Greatest Happiness Principle plays in utilitarian thought.

A second reason why Kant's moral thought often appears difficult is that he offers a number of different versions of this principle, which he claims are equivalent but which look very different. A straightforward way in which to simplify Kantian moral thought is to concentrate on just one of these formulations of the Categorical Imperative. For present purposes I shall choose the version to which he gives the sonorous name, *The Formula of the End in Itself*.

19 The Formula of the End in Itself

The Formula of the End in Itself runs as follows:

Act in such a way that you always treat humanity, whether in your own person or in the person of any other, never simply as a means but always at the same time as an end.[1]

To understand this principle we need in the first place to understand what Kant means by the term 'maxim'. The maxim of an act or policy or activity is the *underlying principle* of the act, policy, or activity, by which other, more superficial aspects of action are guided. Very often interpretations of Kant have supposed that maxims can only be the (underlying) intentions of individual human agents. If that were the case it would limit the usefulness of Kantian modes of moral thought in dealing with world hunger and famine problems. For it is clear enough that individual action (while often important) cannot deal with all the problems of Third World poverty. A moral theory that addresses *only* individual actors does not have adequate scope for discussing famine problems. As we have seen, one of the main attractions of utilitarianism as an approach to Third World poverty is that its scope is so broad: it can be applied with equal appropriateness to the practical deliberations of individuals, of institutions and groups, and even of nation states and international agencies. Kantian ethical thinking can be interpreted (though it usually isn't) to have equally broad scope.

Since maxims are *underlying* principles of action, they may not always be obvious either to the individuals or institutions whose maxims they are, or to others. We can determine what the underlying principles of some activity or institution are only by seeing the patterns made by various more superficial aspects of acts, policies, and activities. Only those principles that would generate that pattern of activity are maxims of action. Sometimes more than one

principle might lie behind a given pattern of activity, and we may be unsure what the maxim of the act was. For example, we might wonder (as Kant does) how to tell whether somebody gives change accurately only out of concern to have an honest reputation or whether he or she would do so anyhow. In such cases we can sometimes set up an "isolation test"—for example, a situation in which it would be open to somebody to be dishonest without any chance of a damaged reputation. But quite often we can't set up any such situation and may be to some extent unsure which maxim lies behind a given act. Usually we have to rely on whatever individual actors tell us about their maxims of action and on what policymakers or social scientists may tell us about the underlying principles of institutional or group action. What they tell us may well be mistaken. While mistakes can be reduced by care and thoughtfulness, there is no guarantee that we can always work out which maxim of action should be scrutinized for purposes of judging what others do. On the other hand, there is no problem when we are trying to guide our own action: if we can find out what duty demands, we can try to meet those demands.

It is helpful to think of some examples of maxims that might be used to guide action in contexts where poverty and the risk of famine are issues. Somebody who contributes to famine-relief work or advocates development might have an underlying principle such as, "Try to help reduce the risk or severity of world hunger." This commitment might be reflected in varied surface action in varied situations. In one context a gift of money might be relevant; in another some political activity such as lobbying for or against certain types of aid and trade might express the same underlying commitment. Sometimes superficial aspects of action may seem at variance with the underlying maxim they in fact express. For example, if there is reason to think that indiscriminate food aid damages the agricultural economy of the area to which food is given, then the maxim of seeking to relieve hunger might be expressed in action aimed at *limiting* the extent of food aid. More lavish use of food aid might *seem* to treat the needy more generously, but if in fact it will damage their medium- or long-term economic prospects, then it is not (contrary to superficial appearances) aimed at improving and securing their access to subsistence. On a Kantian theory, the basis for judging action should be its *fundamental* principle or policy, and superficially similar acts may be judged morally very different. Regulating food aid in order to drive up prices and profit from them is one matter; regulating food aid in order to enable local farmers to sell their crops and to stay in the business of growing food is quite another.

When we want to work out whether a proposed act or policy is morally required we should not, on Kant's view, try to find out whether it would produce more happiness than other available acts. Rather we should see whether the act or policy is required if we are to avoid acting on maxims that use others as mere means and act on maxims that treat others as ends in themselves. These two aspects of Kantian duty can each be spelled out and shown to have determinate implications for acts and policies that may affect the persistence of hunger and the risk and course of famines.

20 Using Others as Mere Means

We use others as *mere means* if what we do reflects some maxim *to which they could not in principle consent*. Kant does not suggest that there is anything wrong about using someone as a means. Evidently every cooperative scheme of action does this. A government that agrees to provide free or subsidized food to famine-relief agencies both uses and is used by the agencies; a peasant who sells food in a local market both uses and is used by those who buy the food. In such examples each party to the transaction can and does consent to take part in that transaction. Kant would say that the parties to such transactions use one another but do not use one another as *mere means*. Each party assumes that the other has its own maxims of action and is not just a thing or prop to be used or manipulated.

But there are other cases where one party to an arrangement or transaction not only uses the other but does so in ways that could only be done on the basis of a fundamental principle or maxim to which the other could not in principle consent. If, for example, a false promise is given, the party that accepts the promise is not just used but used as a mere means, because it is *impossible* for consent to be given to the fundamental principle or project of deception that must guide every false promise, whatever its surface character. Those who accept false promises *must* be kept ignorant of the underlying principle or maxim on which the "undertaking" is based. If this isn't kept concealed, the attempted promise will either be rejected or will not be a *false* promise at all. In false promising, the deceived party becomes, as it were, a prop or tool—a *mere means*—in the false promisor's scheme. Action based on any such maxim of deception would be wrong in Kantian terms, whether it is a matter of a breach of treaty obligations, of contractual undertakings, or of accepted and relied upon modes of interaction. Maxims of deception *standardly* use others as mere means, and acts that could only be based on such maxims are unjust.

Other standard ways of using others as mere means is by violence or coercion. Here too victims have no possibility of refusing what is done to them. If a rich or powerful landowner or nation destroys a poorer or more vulnerable person, group, or nation or threatens some intolerable difficulty unless a concession is made, the more vulnerable party is denied a genuine choice between consent and dissent. While the boundary that divides violence and coercion from mere bargaining and negotiation varies and is therefore often hard to discern, we have no doubt about the clearer cases. Maxims of violence destroy or damage agents or their capabilities. Maxims of coercion may threaten physical force, seizure of possessions, destruction of opportunities, or any other harm that the coerced party is thought to be unable to absorb without grave injury or danger. For example, a grain dealer in a Third World village who threatens not to make or renew an indispensable loan without which survival until the next harvest would be impossible, unless he is sold the current crop at pitifully low prices, uses the peasant as mere means. The peasant does not have the possibility of genuinely consenting to the "offer he can't refuse." In this way the outward form of some coercive transactions may *look* like ordinary commercial dealings: but we know very well that some action that is superficially of this sort is based on maxims of coercion. To avoid coercion, action must be governed by maxims that the other party can choose to refuse and is not forced to accept. The more vulnerable the other party in any transaction or negotiation, the less that party's scope for refusal, and the more demanding it is likely to be to ensure that action is noncoercive.

In Kant's view, acts done on maxims that endanger, coerce, or deceive others, and thus cannot in principle have the consent of those others, are wrong. When individuals institutions or nation states act in ways that can only be based on such maxims, they fail in their duty. They treat the parties who are either deceived or coerced unjustly. To avoid unjust action it is not enough to observe the outward forms of free agreement, cooperation, and market disciplines; it is also essential to see that the weaker party to any arrangement has a genuine option to refuse the fundamental character of the proposal.

21 *Treating Others as Ends in Themselves*

For Kant, as for utilitarians, justice is only one part of duty. We may fail in our duty, even when we don't use anyone as mere means, if we fail to treat others as "ends in themselves." To treat others as ends in themselves we must not only avoid using them as mere means but also treat them as rational and autonomous beings with their own maxims. In doing so we must also remember that (as Kant repeatedly stressed, but later Kantians have often forgotten) human beings are *finite* rational beings in several ways. First, human beings are not ideal rational calculators. We *standardly* have neither a complete list of the actions possible in a given situation nor more than a partial view of their likely consequences. In addition, abilities to assess and to use available information are usually quite limited. Second, these cognitive limitations are *standardly* complemented by limited autonomy. Human action is limited not only by various sorts of physical barrier and inability but by further sorts of (mutual or asymmetrical) *dependence.* To treat one another as ends in themselves such beings have to base their action on principles that do not undermine but rather sustain and extend one another's capacities for autonomous action. A central requirement for doing so is to share and support one another's ends and activities to some extent. Since finite rational beings cannot generally achieve their aims without some help and support from others, a general refusal of help and support amounts to failure to treat others as rational and autonomous beings, that is, as ends in themselves. Hence Kantian principles require us not only to act justly, that is, in accordance with maxims that don't injure, coerce, or deceive others, but also to avoid manipulation and to lend some support to others' plans and activities. Since hunger, great poverty, and powerlessness all undercut the possibility of autonomous action, and the requirement of treating others as ends in themselves demands that Kantians standardly act to support the possibility of autonomous action where it is most vulnerable, Kantians are required to do what they can to avert, reduce, and remedy hunger. They cannot of course do everything to avert hunger: but they may not do nothing.

22 *Justice and Beneficence in Kant's Thought*

Kant is often thought to hold that justice is morally required, but beneficence is morally less important. He does indeed, like [John Stuart] Mill, speak of justice as a *perfect duty* and of beneficence as an *imperfect duty*. But he does not mean by this that beneficence is any less a duty; rather, he holds that it has (unlike justice) to be selective. We cannot share or even support *all* others' maxims *all* of the time. Hence support for others' autonomy is always selective. By contrast we can make all action and institutions conform fundamentally to standards of nondeception and noncoercion. Kant's understanding of the distinction between perfect and imperfect duties differs from Mill's. In a Kantian perspective justice is more than the core of beneficence, as in Mill's theory, and beneficence isn't just an attractive but optional moral embellishment of just arrangements (as tends to be assumed in most theories that take human rights as fundamental).

23 *Justice to the Vulnerable in Kantian Thinking*

For Kantians, justice requires action that conforms (at least outwardly) to what could be done in a given situation while acting on maxims that use nobody. Since anyone hungry or destitute is more than usually vulnerable to deception, violence, and coercion, the possibilities and temptations to injustice are then especially strong. They are often strongest for those who are nearest to acute poverty and hunger, so could (if they chose) exploit others' need.

Examples are easily suggested. I shall begin with some situations that might arise for somebody who happened to be part of a famine-stricken population. Where shortage of food is being dealt with by a reasonably fair rationing scheme, any mode of cheating to get more than one's allocated share involves using some others and is unjust. Equally, taking advantage of others' desperation to profiteer—for example, selling food at colossal prices or making loans on the security of others' future livelihood, when these are "offers they can't refuse"—constitutes coercion, uses others as mere means, and so is unjust. Transactions that have the outward form of normal commercial dealings may be coercive when one party is desperate. Equally, forms of corruption that work by deception—such as bribing officials to gain special benefits from development schemes, or deceiving others about these entitlements—use others unjustly. Such requirements are far from trivial and are frequently violated in hard times; acting justly in such conditions may involve risking one's own life and livelihood and may require the greatest courage.

It is not so immediately obvious what justice, Kantianly conceived, requires of agents and agencies who are remote from destitution. Might it not be sufficient to argue that those of us fortunate enough to live in the developed world are far from famine and destitution, so if we do nothing but go about our usual business will successfully avoid injustice to the destitute? This conclusion has often been reached by those who take an abstract view of rationality and forget the limits of human rationality and autonomy. To such people it seems that there is nothing more to just action than noninterference with others. But once we remember the limitations of human rationality and autonomy, and the particular ways in which they are limited for those living close to the margins of subsistence, we can see that mere "noninterfering" conformity to ordinary standards of commercial honesty and political bargaining is not enough for justice toward the destitute. If the demands of the powerful constitute "offers that cannot be refused" by the government or by the citizens of a poor country, or if the concessions required for investment by a transnational corporation or a development project reflect the desperation of recipients rather than an appropriate contribution to the project, then (however benevolent the motives of some parties) the weaker party to such agreements is used by the stronger.

In the earlier days of European colonial penetration of the now underdeveloped world it was evident enough that some of the ways in which "agreements" were made with native peoples were in fact violent, deceptive, or coercive—or all three. "Sales" of land by those who had no grasp of market practices and "cession of sovereignty" by those whose forms of life were prepolitical constitute only spurious consent to the agreements struck. But it is not only in these original forms of bargaining between powerful and powerless that injustice is frequent. There are many contemporary examples. For example, if capital investment in a poorer country requires the receiving country or some of its institutions or citizens to contribute disproportionately to the maintenance of a developed, urban "enclave" economy that offers little local employment but lavish standards of life for a small number of (possibly expatriate) "experts," while guaranteeing long-term exemption from local taxation for the investors, then we may doubt that the agreement could have been struck without the element of coercion provided by the desperation of the weaker party. Often enough the coercers in such cases are members of the local as well as the international elite. Or if a trade agreement extracts political advantages (such as military bases) that are incompatible with the fundamental political interests of the country concerned, we may judge that at least some leaders of that country have been "bought" in a sense that is not consonant with ordinary commercial practice.

Even when the actions of those who are party to an agreement don't reflect a fundamental principle of violence, coercion, or deception, the agreement may alter the life circumstances and prospects of third parties in ways to which they patently could not have not consented. For example, a system of food aid and imports agreed upon by the government of a Third World country and certain developed states or international agencies may give the elite of that Third World country access to subsidized grain.

If that grain is then used to control the urban population and also produces destitution among peasants (who used to grow food for that urban population), then those who are newly destitute probably have not been offered any opening or possibility of refusing their new and worsened conditions of life. If a policy is imposed, those affected *cannot* have been given a chance to refuse it: had the chance been there, they would either have assented (and so the policy would not have been *imposed*) or refused (and so proceeding with the policy would have been evidently coercive), or they would have been able to renegotiate the terms of trade.

24 *Beneficence to the Vulnerable in Kantian Thinking*

In Kantian moral reasoning, the basis for beneficent action is that without it we fail to treat others of limited rationality and autonomy as ends in themselves. This is not to say that Kantian beneficence won't make others happier, for it will do so whenever they would be happier if (more) capable of autonomous action, but that happiness secured by purely paternalistic means, or at the cost (for example) of manipulating others' desires, will not count as beneficent in the Kantian picture. Clearly the vulnerable position of those who lack the very means of life, and their severely curtailed possibilities for autonomous action, offer many different ways in which it might be possible for others to act beneficently. Where the means of life are meager, almost any material or organizational advance may help extend possibilities for autonomy. Individual or institutional action that aims to advance economic or social development can proceed on many routes. The provision of clean water, of improved agricultural techniques, of better grain storage systems, or of adequate means of local transport may all help transform material prospects. Equally, help in the development of new forms of social organization— whether peasant self-help groups, urban cooperatives, medical and contraceptive services, or improvements in education or in the position of women—may help to extend possibilities for autonomous action. While the central core of such development projects will be requirements of justice, their full development will also demand concern to treat others as ends in themselves, by paying attention to their particular needs and desires. Kantian thinking does not provide a means by which all possible ways of treating others as ends in themselves could be listed and ranked. But where some activity helps secure possibilities for autonomous action for more people, or is likely to achieve a permanent improvement in the position of the most vulnerable, or is one that can be done with more reliable success, this provides reason for furthering that way of treating others as ends.

Clearly the alleviation of need must rank far ahead of the furthering of happiness in other ways in the Kantian picture. I might make my friends very happy by throwing extravagant parties: but this would probably not increase anybody's possibility for autonomous action to any great extent. But the sorts of development-oriented changes that have just been mentioned may *transform* the possibilities for action of some. Since hunger and the risk of famine are always and evidently highly damaging to human autonomy, any action that helps avoid or reduce famine must have a strong claim on any Kantian who is thinking through what beneficence requires. Depending on circumstances, such action may have to take the form of individual contribution to famine relief and development organizations, of individual or collective effort to influence the trade and aid policies of developed countries, or of attempts to influence the activities of those Third World elites for whom development does not seem to be an urgent priority. Some approaches can best be undertaken by private citizens of developed countries by way of lobbying, publicity, and education; others are best approached by those who work for governments, international agencies, or transnational corporations, who can "work from

within" to influence the decisions and policies of these institutions. Perhaps the most dramatic possibilities to act for a just or an unjust, a beneficent or selfish future belongs to those who hold positions of power or influence within the Third World. But wherever we find ourselves, our duties are not, on the Kantian picture, limited to those close at hand. Duties of justice arise whenever there is some involvement between parties—and in the modern world this is never wholly lacking. Duties of beneficence arise whenever destitution puts the possibility of autonomous action in question for the more vulnerable. When famines were not only far away, but nothing could be done to relieve them, beneficence or charity legitimately began—and stayed—near home. In an interconnected world, the moral significance of distance has shrunk, and we may be able to affect the capacities for autonomous action of those who are far away.

25 The Scope of Kantian Deliberations about Hunger and Famine

In many ways Kantian moral reasoning is less ambitious than utilitarian moral reasoning. It does not propose a process of moral reasoning that can (in principle) rank *all* possible actions or all possible institutional arrangements from the happiness-maximizing "right" action or institution downward. It aims rather to offer a pattern of reasoning by which we can identify whether *proposed action or institutional arrangements* would be just or unjust, beneficent or lacking in beneficence. While *some* knowledge of causal connections is needed for Kantian reasoning, it is far less sensitive than is utilitarian reasoning to gaps in our causal knowledge. It may therefore help us reach conclusions that are broadly accurate even if they are imprecise. The conclusions reached about particular proposals for action or about institutional arrangements will not hold for all time, but be relevant for the contexts for which action is proposed. For example, if it is judged that some institution—say, the World Bank—provides, under present circumstances, a just approach to certain development problems, it will not follow that under all other circumstances such an institution would be part of a just approach. There may be other institutional arrangements that are also just; and there may be other circumstances under which the institutional structure of the World Bank would be shown to be in some ways unjust.

These points show us that Kantian deliberations about hunger can lead only to conclusions that are useful in determinate contexts. This, however, is standardly what we need to know for action, whether individual or institutional. We do not need to be able to generate a complete list of available actions in order to determine whether proposed lines of action are not unjust and whether any are beneficent. Kantian patterns of moral reasoning cannot be guaranteed to identify the optimal course of action in a situation. They provide methods neither for listing nor for ranking all possible proposals for action. But any line of action that is considered can be checked to see whether it is part of what justice and beneficence require—or of what they forbid.

The reason this pattern of reasoning will not show any action or arrangement of the most beneficent one available is that the Kantian picture of beneficence is less mathematically structured than the utilitarian one. It judges beneficence by its overall contribution to the prospects for human autonomy and not by the quantity of happiness expected to result. To the extent that the autonomous pursuit of goals is what Mill called "one of the principal ingredients of human happiness" (but only to that extent)[2] the requirements of Kantian and of utilitarian beneficence will coincide. But whenever expected happiness is not a function of the scope for autonomous action, the two accounts of beneficent action diverge. For utilitarians, paternalistic imposition of, for example, certain forms of aid and

development assistance need not be wrong and may even be required. But for Kantians, who think that beneficence should secure others' possibilities for autonomous action, the case for paternalistic imposition of aid or development projects without the recipients' involvement must always be questionable.

In terms of some categories in which development projects are discussed, utilitarian reasoning may well endorse "top-down" aid and development projects that override whatever capacities for autonomous choice and action the poor of a certain area now have in the hopes of securing a happier future. If the calculations work out in a certain way, utilitarians may even think a "generation of sacrifice"—or of forced labor or of imposed population-control policies—not only permissible but mandated. In their darkest Malthusian moments some utilitarians have thought that average happiness might best be maximized not by improving the lot of the poor but by minimizing their numbers, and so have advocated policies of harsh neglect of the poorest and most desperate. Kantian patterns of reasoning are likely to endorse less global and less autonomy-overriding aid and development projects; they are not likely to endorse neglect or abandoning of those who are most vulnerable and lacking in autonomy. If the aim of beneficence is to keep or put others in a position to act for themselves, then emphasis must be placed on "bottom-up" projects, which from the start draw on, foster, and establish indigenous capacities and practices for self-help and local action.

V. Utilitarians, Kantians, and Respect for Life

26 Respect for Life in Utilitarian Reasoning

In the contrasting utilitarian and Kantian pictures of moral reasoning and of their implications for hunger, we can also discern two sharply contrasting pictures of the value of human life.

Utilitarians, since they value happiness above all, aim in achieve the happiest possible world. If their life plans remain unclear, this is because the means to this end are often unclear. But one implication of this position is entirely clear. It is that if happiness is the supreme value, then anything may and ought to be sacrificed for the sake of a greater happiness. Lesser possibilities of happiness and even life itself ought to be sacrificed to achieve maximal happiness. Such sacrifices may be required even when those whose happiness or lives are sacrificed are not willing. Rearing the fabric of felicity may be a bloody business. It all depends on the causal connections.

As our control over the means of ending and preserving lives has increased, utilitarians have confronted many uncomfortable questions. Should life be preserved at the cost of pain when modern medicine makes this possible? Or will happiness be greater if euthanasia is permitted under certain circumstances? Should the most afflicted be left to starve in famine situations if the happiness of all, and perhaps the average happiness, will be greater if those whose recovery is not likely to be complete are absent? Should population growth be fostered so long as total (or again perhaps average) happiness is increased, even if other sorts of difficulties arise? Should forced labor and enforced redistribution of income across national boundaries be imposed for the sake of a probably happier world? How far ought utilitarians to insist on the sacrifice of comforts, liberties, and even lives in order to "rear the fabric of felicity"?

Utilitarians do not deny that their moral reasoning raises many questions of these sorts. But the imprecision of our knowledge of consequences often blurs the answers to these questions. As we peer through the blur, we can see that on a utilitarian view lives must be sacrificed to build a happier world if this is the most efficient way to do so, whether or not those who lose their lives are willing. There is nothing wrong with using another as mere means, provided that the end in view is a happier result

than could have been achieved any other way, taking account of the misery the means may have caused. In utilitarian thinking, persons are not ends in themselves. Their special moral status, such as it is, derives from their being means to the production of happiness. But they are not even necessary means for this end, since happiness can be located in nonhuman lives. It may even turn out that maximal happiness requires the sacrifice of human for the sake of animal lives.

In utilitarian thinking life has a high but derivative value, and some lives may have to be sacrificed for the sake of greater happiness or reduced misery in other lives. Nor is there a deep difference between ending others' lives by not helping (as some Malthusians suggest) and doing so as a matter of deliberate intervention or policy.

27 Respect for Life in Kantian Reasoning

Kantians reach different conclusions about human life. They see it as valuable because humans have considerable (but still quite incomplete) capacities for autonomous action. There may be other beings with more complete capacities, but we are not acquainted with them. Christian tradition speaks of angels; Kant referred to hypothetical beings he called Holy Wills; writers of science fiction have multiplied the varieties. There are certainly other beings with fewer capacities for autonomous action than humans standardly have. Whether we think that (some) animals should not be used as mere means, or should be treated as ends in themselves, is going to depend on the particular picture we have of partial autonomy and on the capacities we find that certain sorts of animals have or are capable of acquiring. This is a large question, around which I shall put some hasty brackets. It is quite an important issue in working out the famine and development implications of Kantian thinking, since development strategies have different implications for various animal species. For the moment however.

I shall consider only some implications of human capacities for (partially) autonomous action in Kantian thinking on respect for human life in contexts of acute vulnerability, such as destitution and (threatened) hunger.

The fundamental idea behind the Categorical Imperative is that the actions of a plurality of rational beings can be mutually consistent. A minimal condition for their mutual consistency is that each, in acting autonomously, not preclude others' autonomous action. This requirement can be spelled out, as in the formula of the end in itself, by insisting that each avoid action that the other could not freely join in (hence avoid violence, deception, and coercion) and that each seek to foster and secure others' capacities for autonomous action. What this actually takes will, as we have seen, vary with circumstances. But it is clear enough that the partial autonomy of human beings is undermined by life-threatening and destroying circumstances, such as hunger and destitution. Hence a fundamental Kantian commitment must be to preserve life in two senses. First, others must not be deprived of life. The dead (as well as the moribund, the gravely ill, and the famine-stricken) cannot act. Second, others' lives must be preserved in forms that offer them sufficient physical energy, psychological space, and social security for action. Partial autonomy is vulnerable autonomy, and in human life psychological and social as well as material needs must be met if any but the most meager possibility of autonomous action is to be preserved. Kantians are therefore committed to the preservation not only of biological but of biographical life. To act in the typical ways humans are capable of we must not only be alive, but have a life to lead.

On a Kantian view, we may justifiably—even nobly—risk or sacrifice our lives for others. When we do so, we act autonomously, and nobody uses us as a mere means. But we cannot justly use others (nor they us) as mere means in a scheme that could only be based on violence, deception, or coercion. Nor may we always refuse others the help they need to sustain the very possibility of autonomous action. Of course, no amount of beneficence could put anyone in the position to do all possible actions: that is not what we need to be concerned about. What we do need to be concerned about is failure to secure for others a possibility of some range of autonomous action.

Where others' possibilities for autonomous action are eroded by poverty and malnutrition, the necessary action must clearly include moves to change the picture. But these moves will not meet Kantian requirements if they provide merely calories and basic medicine; they must also seek to enable those who began to be adequately fed to act autonomously. They must foster the capabilities that human beings need to function effectively. They must therefore aim at least at minimal security and subsistence. Hence the changes that Kantians argue or work for must always be oriented to development plans that create enough economic self-sufficiency and social security for independence in action to be feasible and sustainable. There is no royal road to this result and no set of actions that is likely to be either universally or totally effective. Too many changes are needed, and we have too little understanding of the precise causal connections that limit some possibilities and guarantee others. But some broadly accurate, if imprecise indication of ranges of required action, or ranges of action from which at least some are required, is possible.

VI. Nearby Hunger and Poverty

28 Hunger and Welfare in Rich Countries

So far we have been considering how we might think about and respond to the poverty, hunger, and famine that are characteristic of parts of the developing world. However, both poverty and hunger can be found nearer home. Poverty in the developed world is nowhere so widespread or acute as to risk famine; but it is well documented.[3] Hunger in the developed world is doubly hidden. As always, it shows more in the blighting of lives and health than in literal deaths. However, in contrast to Third World poverty, poverty in rich countries is a minority problem that affects parts of the population whom not everybody meets. Perhaps the most visible aspect of this poverty-amid-wealth in the 1990s is the number of homeless people now to be found on the streets of great and once-great cities in some of the richest societies of the world. In the warmer climates of the Third World, the need for warm and decent housing is also often unmet—but homelessness is nowhere a worse experience than in the colder parts of the developed world. Although the homeless of the rich world may be able to command money that would constitute wealth in a very poor country, its purchasing power where they are is not enough for minimal housing, decent hygiene, and clothing and may not be enough for adequate food. Apart from the highly visible homeless there are many others in the richer countries who for one reason or another go hungry.

The utilitarian and Kantian ways of thinking considered in this chapter have clear implications for responses to nearby hunger. For utilitarians there will be no doubt that this hunger too produces misery, and should be ended by whatever means will add to the total of human happiness. Many of the strategies that have been used successfully to eradicate hunger in some developed countries have been strongly influenced by this utilitarian thinking. For example, in many western European states social welfare systems guarantee basic welfare, including health care for all, and minimal income. The public policies of these welfare states are funded by taxation, and there would be wide public agreement that these policies

produce a greater total happiness than would *laissez-faire* policies, which would leave the poor without a publicly funded "safety net." Opposition to welfare state policies, which can reliably reduce poverty and end hunger, is not likely to come from utilitarians. On the contrary, utilitarian activism has been one of the major forces behind the emergence of welfare states.[4]

Opposition to a welfare state has, however, been vocal among some sorts of human rights thinkers. They articulate the worry that a welfare state, like foreign aid or food aid, is unjust to those who are taxed to provide the funds, and damaging to those who become dependent on what they often disparagingly call welfare handouts.

The objection to redistributive taxation has been part of a long-standing polemic between advocates of "equality" and of "liberty" during the period of the Cold War. Some of the advocates of liberty (often called libertarians) have adopted an extreme view of the demands of liberty, and argue that unrestricted rights to property-without-taxation are a human right. They conclude that the welfare state is an attack on human liberty. Equally, some advocates of equality have argued for a very strong imposition of material equality, which would indeed make heavy inroads into individual liberty. The underlying arguments for both extreme positions, and for their favored interpretations of human rights, are quite unconvincing. In practice, societies have to strike some balance between liberty and equality. Good social welfare policies are an attractive way of accommodating liberty and equality because they ensure that nobody is so vulnerable that their liberty is wholly eroded, but they do so without a heavy reduction of liberty of those who pay the necessary taxes. The even-handed collection of just taxes leaves richer citizens very great liberty to lead their lives as they will, and enables poorer citizens to reach a minimally decent standard of living that secures their capabilities for leading their lives with dignity. The real issues for social policymakers in the area of taxation have to do with questions about the containment of costs, the fairness of taxation, and the efficiency of its collection rather than with illusory attempts to create societies that embody liberty without equality, or equality without liberty.

The second of these worries, that welfare creates dependence, is a rather implausible objection to policies that end hunger: nothing damages autonomy and creates vulnerability and dependence as much as debilitating hunger and demeaning homelessness. A lack of welfare systems perhaps guarantees that the poor do not depend on the state, but it increases rather than ends their dependence. Worries about dependence have a limited appropriate role in considering *what sort* of welfare policies to pursue. Should welfare payments be in cash or in kind? How far is means testing needed? Should support go to families or to individuals? Do some welfare systems damage the incentive to work? These detailed questions, rather than ideological defense either of unrestricted liberty or of unrestricted equality, are the real issues for social policymakers today.

The Kantian position presented here stresses the importance of not using others as mere means and of treating them as ends in themselves. This position demands commitment to institutions that enable people to become and remain autonomous agents. Hence Kantians would be particularly concerned to prevent the extremes of poverty that lead to hunger and homelessness. The hungry and homeless are particularly vulnerable to every sort of injustice, and above all to violence, coercion, and deception, all of which use people as mere means. On the other hand, this same commitment to autonomy would lead Kantians to demand that welfare policies leave welfare recipients as much in charge of their lives as possible. They would argue that welfare policies (e.g., minimum wage, health care, unemployment

pay, child benefit, and many others) can all be structured to enhance rather than restrict the autonomy of those who receive benefits or payments. Good welfare policies manifest rather than damage respect for persons. Kantians do not, of course, advocate justice alone, but also insist that beneficence is important and should be manifested in support and concern for particular others and for their projects. This commitment would also be relevant to actions to relieve poverty, hunger, and homelessness. A society that manages not to use any of its members as mere means, and funds adequate levels of welfare payment, can either succeed in treating its more vulnerable members as ends in themselves, whose particular lives and plans must be respected, or fail to do so by leaving them to the undermining and humiliating procedures of an ill-trained welfare bureaucracy. Because Kantians are concerned for justice and beneficence, they would never see beneficence alone as an adequate response to poverty, homelessness, and hunger at home or abroad. Mere charity is too capricious to secure for the poor capabilities to lead their own lives. Equally, unlike persons with rights-based sorts of ethical thinking, they would never see justice alone as a morally adequate response to human vulnerability.

Whether poverty and hunger are in the next street or far away, whether we articulate the task in utilitarian, in Kantian, or in other terms, the claims of justice and of beneficence for the two cases are similar. What may differ in the two cases are our opportunities for action. Sometimes we have far greater possibilities to affect what goes on in the next street than we do to affect what goes on on distant continents. Since nobody can do everything, we not only *may* but *must* put our efforts where they will bear fruit. This, however, provides no license for injustice to distant others. Nearby neighbors need justice, but they are not entitled to justice at the expense of those who are far away. Hence legitimate concern for justice and welfare for those who are nearby fellow-citizens has always to work with and not against the vast efforts of countless agents and institutions across the world and across the generations of mankind to put an end to world hunger. In a world in which action affects distant others, justice cannot be stopped at local or national boundaries: there is no such thing as social justice in one country. It is only our activism, and not our thinking or concern, that can legitimately be local. If we act by the ecologist's slogan "Think globally, act locally" not only in protecting vulnerable environments but in protecting vulnerable humans, we may, however, become part of the solution rather than part of the problem of world hunger.

Notes

1. Immanuel Kant, *Groundwork of the Metaphysics of Morals*, tr. H.J. Paton (London: Hutcheson, 1953) p. 430.

2. John Stuart Mill, *Utilitarianism and on Liberty: Including 'Essay on Bentham' and Selections from the Writings of Jeremy Bentham and John Austin*, ed. Mary Warnock (New York: World) 1971.

3. For the United States see Harvard School of Public Health, *Hunger in America: The Growing Epidemic* (Cambridge, Mass.: Harvard University Press, 1985) and *Hunger Reaches Blue Collar America*, same publisher, 1987.

4. For a recent approach to welfare state issues from a utilitarian perspective, see Robert Goodin, *Protecting the Vulnerable: A Reanalysis of Our Social Responsibilities* (Chicago: University of Chicago Press, 1985).

Abortion Is Morally Wrong

John T. Noonan Jr.

John T. Noonan Jr. is Professor of Law, Emeritus at the University of California, Berkeley. He has written several works on moral issues, including Contraception: A History of Its Treatment by the Catholic Theologians and Canonists *and* The Morality of Abortion, *from which this selection is taken. Noonan defends the view that an entity becomes a person at conception and that abortion, except to save the mother's life, is morally wrong. He uses an argument from probabilities to show that his criterion of humanity is objectively valid.*

The most fundamental question involved in the long history of thought on abortion is: How do you determine the humanity of a being? To phrase the question that way is to put in comprehensive humanistic terms what the theologians either dealt with as an explicitly theological question under the heading of "ensoulment" or dealt with implicitly in their treatment of abortion. The Christian position as it originated did not depend on a narrow theological or philosophical concept. It had no relation to theories of infant baptism. It appealed to no special theory of instantaneous ensoulment. It took the world's view on ensoulment as that view changed from Aristotle to Zacchia. There was, indeed, theological influence affecting the theory of ensoulment finally adopted, and, of course, ensoulment itself was a theological concept, so that the position was always explained

Reprinted by permission from *The Morality of Abortion: Legal and Historical Perspective* (Cambridge, Mass.: Harvard University Press), © 1970 by the President and Fellows of Harvard College.

in theological terms. But the theological notion of ensoulment could easily be translated into humanistic language by substituting "human" for "rational soul"; the problem of knowing when a man is a man is common to theology and humanism.

If one steps outside the specific categories used by the theologians, the answer they gave can be analyzed as a refusal to discriminate among human beings on the basis of their varying potentialities. Once conceived, the being was recognized as man because he had man's potential. The criterion for humanity, thus, was simple and all-embracing: if you are conceived by human parents, you are human.

The strength of this position may be tested by a review of some of the other distinctions offered in the contemporary controversy over legalizing abortion. Perhaps the most popular distinction is in terms of viability. Before an age of some many months, the fetus is not viable, that is, it cannot be removed from the mother's womb and live apart from her. To that extent, the life of the fetus is absolutely dependent on the life of the mother. This dependence is made the basis of denying recognition to its humanity.

There are difficulties with this distinction. One is that the perfection of artificial incubation may make the fetus viable at any time: it may be removed and artificially sustained. Experiments with animals already show that such a procedure is possible. This hypothetical extreme case relates to an actual difficulty: there is considerable elasticity to the idea of viability. Mere length of life is not an exact measure. The viability of the fetus depends on the extent of its anatomical and functional development. The weight and length of the fetus are better guides to the state of its development than age, but weight and length vary. Moreover, different racial groups have different ages at which their fetuses are viable. Some evidence, for example, suggests that Negro fetuses mature more quickly than white fetuses. If viability is the norm, the standard would vary with race and with many individual circumstances.

The most important objection to this approach is that dependence is not ended by viability. The fetus is still absolutely dependent on someone's care in order to continue existence; indeed a child of one or three or even five years of age is absolutely dependent on another's care for existence; uncared for, the older fetus or the younger child will die as surely as the early fetus detached from the mother. The unsubstantial lessening in dependence at viability does not seem to signify any special acquisition of humanity.

A second distinction has been attempted in terms of experience. A being who has had experience, has lived and suffered, who possesses memories, is more human than one who has not. Humanity depends on formation by experience. The fetus is thus "unformed" in the most basic human sense.

This distinction is not serviceable for the embryo which is already experiencing and reacting. The embryo is responsive to touch after eight weeks and at least at that point is experiencing. At an earlier stage the zygote is certainly alive and responding to its environment. The distinction may also be challenged by the rare case where aphasia has erased adult memory: has it erased humanity? More fundamentally, this distinction leaves even the older fetus or the younger child to be treated as an unformed inhuman thing. Finally, it is not clear why experience as such confers humanity. It could be argued that certain central experiences such as loving or learning are necessary to make a man human. But then human beings who have failed to love or to learn might be

excluded from the class called man.

A third distinction is made by appeal to the sentiments of adults. If a fetus dies, the grief of the parents is not the grief they would have for a living child. The fetus is an unnamed "it" till birth, and is not perceived as personality until at least the fourth month of existence when movements in the womb manifest a vigorous presence demanding joyful recognition by the parents.

Yet feeling is notoriously an unsure guide to the humanity of others. Many groups of humans have had difficulty in feeling that persons of another tongue, color, religion, sex, are as human as they. Apart from reactions to alien groups, we mourn the loss of a ten-year-old boy more than the loss of his one-day-old brother or his 90-year-old grandfather. The difference felt and the grief expressed vary with the potentialities extinguished, or the experience wiped out; they do not seem to point to any substantial difference in the humanity of baby, boy, or grandfather.

Distinctions are also made in terms of sensations by the parents. The embryo is felt within the womb only after about the fourth month. The embryo is seen only at birth. What can be neither seen nor felt is different from what is tangible. If the fetus cannot be seen or touched at all, it cannot be perceived as man.

Yet experience shows that sight is even more untrustworthy than feeling in determining humanity. By sight, color became an appropriate index for saying who was a man, and the evil of racial discrimination was given foundation. Nor can touch provide the test; a being confined by sickness, "out of touch" with others, does not thereby seem to lose his humanity. To the extent that touch still has appeal as a criterion, it appears to be a survival of the old English idea of "quickening"—a possible mistranslation of the Latin *animatus* used in the canon law. To that extent touch as a criterion seems to be dependent on the Aristotelian notion of ensoulment, and to fall when this notion is discarded.

Finally, a distinction is sought in social visibility. The fetus is not socially perceived as human. It cannot communicate with others. Thus, both subjectively and objectively, it is not a member of society. As moral rules are rules for the behavior of members of society to each other, they cannot be made for behavior toward what is not yet a member. Excluded from the society of men, the fetus is excluded from the humanity of men.

By force of the argument from the consequences, this distinction is to be rejected. It is more subtle than that founded on an appeal to physical sensation, but it is equally dangerous in its implications. If humanity depends on social recognition, individuals or whole groups may be dehumanized by being denied any status in their society. Such a fate is fictionally portrayed in *1984* and has actually been the lot of many men in many societies. In the Roman empire, for example, condemnation to slavery meant the practical denial of most human rights; in the Chinese Communist world, landlords have been classified as enemies of the people and so treated as nonpersons by the state. Humanity does not depend on social recognition, though often the failure of society to recognize the prisoner, the alien, the heterodox as human has led to the destruction of human beings. Anyone conceived by a man and a woman is human. Recognition of this condition by society follows a real event in the objective order, however imperfect and halting the recognition. Any attempt to limit humanity to exclude some group runs the risk of furnishing authority and precedent for excluding other groups in the name of the consciousness or perception of the controlling group in the society.

A philosopher may reject the appeal to the humanity of the fetus because he views "humanity" as a secular view of the soul and because he doubts the existence of anything real and objective which can be identified as humanity. One answer to such a philosopher is to ask how he reasons about moral questions without supposing that there is a sense in which he and the others of whom he speaks are human. Whatever group is taken as the society which determines who may be killed is thereby taken as human. A second answer is to ask if he does not believe that there is a right and wrong way of deciding moral questions. If there is such a difference, experience may be appealed to: to decide who is human on the basis of the sentiment of a given society has led to consequences which rational men would characterize as monstrous.

The rejection of the attempted distinctions based on viability and visibility, experience and feeling, may be buttressed by the following considerations: Moral judgments often rest on distinctions, but if the distinctions are not to appear arbitrary fiat, they should relate to some real difference in probabilities. There is a kind of continuity in all life, but the earlier stages of the elements of human life possess tiny probabilities of development. Consider for example, the spermatozoa in any normal ejaculate: there are about 200,000,000 in any single ejaculate, of which one has a chance of developing into a zygote. Consider the oocytes which may become ova: there are 100,000 to 1,000,000 oocytes in a female infant, of which a maximum of 390 are ovulated. But once spermatozoon and ovum meet and the conceptus is formed, such studies as have been made show that roughly in only 20 percent of the cases will spontaneous abortion occur. In other words, the chances are about 4 out of 5 that this new being will develop. At this stage in the life of the being there is a sharp shift in probabilities, an immense jump in potentialities. To make a distinction between the rights of spermatozoa and the rights of the fertilized ovum is to respond to an enormous shift in possibilities. For about twenty days after conception the egg may split to form twins or combine with another egg to form a chimera, but the probability of either even happening is very small.

It may be asked, What does a change in biological probabilities have to do with establishing humanity? The argument from probabilities is not aimed at establishing humanity but at establishing an objective discontinuity which may be taken into account in moral discourse. As life itself is a matter of probabilities, as most moral reasoning is an estimate of probabilities, so it seems in accord with the structure of reality and the nature of moral thought to found a moral judgment on the change in probabilities at conception. The appeal to probabilities is the most commonsensical of arguments, to a greater or smaller degree all of us base our actions on probabilities, and in morals, as in law, prudence and negligence are often measured by the account one has taken of the probabilities. If the chance is 200,000,000 to 1 that the movement in the bushes into which you shoot is a man's, I doubt if many persons would hold you careless in shooting; but if the chances are 4 out of 5 that the movement is a human being's, few would acquit you of blame. Would the argument be different if only one out of ten children conceived came to term? Of course this argument would be different. This argument is an appeal to probabilities that actually exist, not to any and all states of affairs which may be imagined.

The probabilities as they do exist do not show the humanity of the embryo in the sense of a demonstration in logic any more than the probabilities of the movement in the bush being a man demonstrate beyond all doubt that the being is a man. The appeal is a "buttressing" consideration, showing the plausibility of the standard adopted. The argument focuses on the decisional factor in any moral judgment and assumes that part of the business of a moralist is drawing lines. One evidence of the nonarbitrary character of the line drawn is the difference of probabilities on either side of it. If a spermatozoon is destroyed, one destroys a being which had a chance of far less than 1 in 200 million of developing into a reasoning being, possessed of the genetic code, a heart and other organs, and capable of pain. If a fetus is destroyed, one destroys a being already pos-

sessed of the genetic code, organs, and sensitivity to pain, and one which had an 80 percent chance of developing further into a baby outside the womb who, in time, would reason.

The positive argument for conception as the decisive moment of humanization is that at conception the new being receives the genetic code. It is this genetic information which determines his characteristics, which is the biological carrier of the possibility of human wisdom, which makes him a self-evolving being. A being with a human genetic code is man.

This review of current controversy over the humanity of the fetus emphasizes what a fundamental question the theologians resolved in asserting the inviolability of the fetus. To regard the fetus as possessed of equal rights with other humans was not, however, to decide every case where abortion might be employed. It did decide the case where the argument was that the fetus should be aborted for its own good. To say a being was human was to say it had a destiny to decide for itself which could not be taken from it by another man's decision. But human beings with equal rights often come in conflict with each other, and some decision must be made as whose claims are to prevail. Cases of conflict involving the fetus are different only in two respects: the total inability of the fetus to speak for itself and the fact that the right of the fetus regularly at stake is the right to life itself.

The approach taken by the theologians to these conflicts was articulated in terms of "direct" and "indirect." Again, to look at what they were doing from outside their categories, they may be said to have been drawing lines or "balancing values." "Direct" and "indirect" are spatial metaphors; "line-drawing" is another. "To weigh" or "to balance" values is a metaphor of a more complicated mathematical sort hinting at the process which goes on in moral judgments. All the metaphors suggest that, in the moral judgments made, comparisons were necessary, that no value completely controlled. The principle of double effect was no doctrine fallen from heaven, but a method of analysis appropriate where two relative values were being compared. In Catholic moral theology, as it developed, life even of the innocent was not taken as an absolute. Judgments on acts affecting life issued from a process of weighing. In the weighing, the fetus was always given a value greater than zero, always a value separate and independent from its parents. This valuation was crucial and fundamental in all Christian thought on the subject and marked it off from any approach which considered that only the parents' interests needed to be considered.

Even with the fetus weighed as human, one interest could be weighed as equal or superior: that of the mother in her own life. The casuists between 1450 and 1895 were willing to weigh this interest as superior. Since 1895, that interest was given decisive weight only in the two special cases of the cancerous uterus and the ectopic pregnancy. In both of these cases the fetus itself had little chance of survival even if the abortion were not performed. As the balance was once struck in favor of the mother whenever her life was endangered, it could be so struck again. The balance reached between 1895 and 1930 attempted prudentially and pastorally to forestall a multitude of exceptions for interests less than life.

The perception of the humanity of the fetus and the weighing of fetal rights against other human rights constituted the work of the moral analysts. But what spirit animated their abstract judgments? For the Christian community it was the injunction of Scripture to love your neighbor as yourself. The fetus as human was a neighbor; his life had parity with one's own. The commandment gave life to what otherwise would have been only rational calculation.

The commandment could be put in humanistic as well as theological terms: Do not injure your fellow man without reason. In these terms, once the humanity of the fetus is perceived, abortion is never right except in self-defense. When life must be taken to save life, reason alone cannot say that a mother must prefer a child's life to her own. With this exception, now of great rarity, abortion violates the rational humanist tenet of the equality of human lives.

For Christians the commandment to love had received a special imprint in that the exemplar proposed of love was the love of the Lord for his disciples. In the light given by this example, self-sacrifice carried to the point of death seemed in the extreme situations not without meaning. In the less extreme cases, preference for one's own interests to the life of another seemed to express cruelty or selfishness irreconcilable with the demands of love.

44

The Personhood Argument in Favor of Abortion Rights

MARY ANNE WARREN

Mary Anne Warren is Associate Professor of Philosophy at San Francisco State University and has written widely on feminism, including The Nature of Woman: An Encyclopedia and Guide to the Literature *(1980). In this selection she defends the view that abortion is always morally permissible. She attacks Noonan's argument on the basis of an ambiguity in the use of the term* human being, *showing that the term has both a biological and moral sense. What is important is the moral sense, which presupposes certain characteristics, such as self-consciousness and rationality, which a fetus does not have. At the end of her article (not included here), she addresses the issue of infanticide.*

The question which we must answer in order to produce a satisfactory solution to the problem of the moral status of abortion is this: How are we to define the moral community, the set of beings with full and equal moral rights, such that we can decide whether a human fetus is a member of his community or not? What sort of entity, exactly, has the inalienable rights to life, liberty, and the pursuit of happiness? Jefferson attributed these rights to all *men,* and it may or may not be fair to suggest that he intended to attribute them *only* to men. Perhaps he ought to have attributed them to all human beings. If so, then we arrive, first, at Noonan's problem of defining what makes a being human, and, second, at the equally vital question which Noonan does not consider, namely, What reason is there for identifying the moral community with the set of all human beings, in whatever way we have chosen to define that term?

Reprinted by permission from *The Monist* 57: 1 (1973).

1. On the Definition of "Human"

One reason why this vital second question is so frequently overlooked in the debate over the moral status of abortion is that the term "human" has two distinct, but not often distinguished, senses. This fact results in a slide of meaning, which serves to conceal the fallaciousness of the traditional argument that since (1) it is wrong to kill innocent human beings, and (2) fetuses are innocent human beings, then (3) it is wrong to kill fetuses. For if "human" is used in the same sense in both (1) and (2) then, whichever of the two senses is meant, one of these premises is question-begging. And if it is used in two different senses then of course the conclusion doesn't follow.

Thus, (1) is a self-evident moral truth, and avoids begging the question about abortion, only if "human being" is used to mean something like "a full-fledged member of the moral community." (It may or may not also be meant to refer exclusively to members of the species *Homo sapiens.*) We may call this the *moral* sense of "human." It is not to be confused with what we will call the *genetic* sense, i.e., the sense in which any member of the species is a human being, and no member of any other species could be. If (1) is acceptable only if the moral sense is intended, (2) is non-question-begging only if what is intended is the genetic sense.

In "Deciding Who Is Human," Noonan argues for the classification of fetuses with human beings by pointing to the presence of the full genetic code, and the potential capacity for rational thought. It is clear that what he needs to show, for his version of the traditional argument to be valid, is that fetuses are human in the moral sense, the sense in which it is analytically true that all human beings have full moral rights. But, in the absence of any argument showing that whatever is genetically human is also morally human, and he gives none, nothing more than genetic humanity can be demonstrated by the presence of the human genetic code. And, as we will see, the *potential* capacity for rational thought can at most show that an entity has the potential for *becoming* human in the moral sense.

2. Defining the Moral Community

Can it be established that genetic humanity is sufficient for moral humanity? I think that there are very good reasons for not defining the moral community in this way. I would like to suggest an alternative way of defining the moral community, which I will argue for only to the extent of explaining why it is, or should be, self-evident. The suggestion is simply that the moral community consists of all and only *people*, rather than all and only human beings; and probably the best way of demonstrating its self-evidence is by considering the concept of personhood, to see what sorts of entities are and are not persons, and what the decision that a being is or is not a person implies about its moral rights.

What characteristics entitle an entity to be considered a person? This is obviously not the place to attempt a complete analysis of the concept of personhood, but we do not need such a fully adequate analysis just to determine whether and why a fetus is or isn't a person. All we need is a rough and approximate list of the most basic criteria of personhood, and some idea of which, or how many, of these an entity must satisfy in order to properly be considered a person.

In searching for such criteria, it is useful to look beyond the set of people with whom we are acquainted, and ask how we would decide whether a totally alien being was a person or not. (For we have no right to assume that genetic humanity is necessary for personhood.) Imagine a space traveler who lands on an unknown planet and encounters a race of beings utterly unlike any he has ever seen or heard of. If he wants to be sure of behaving morally toward these beings, he has to somehow decide whether they are peo-

ple, and hence have full moral rights, or whether they are the sort of thing which he need not feel guilty about treating as, for example, a source of food.

How should he go about making this decision? If he has some anthropological background, he might look for such things as religion, art, and the manufacturing of tools, weapons, or shelters, since these factors have been used to distinguish our human from our prehuman ancestors, in what seems to be closer to the moral than the genetic sense of "human." And no doubt he would be right to consider the presence of such factors as good evidence that the alien beings were people, and morally human. It would, however, be overly anthropocentric of him to take the absence of these things as adequate evidence that they were not, since we can imagine people who have progressed beyond, or evolved without ever developing, these cultural characteristics.

I suggest that the traits which are most central to the concept of personhood, or humanity in the moral sense, are, very roughly, the following:

1. consciousness (of objects and events external and/or internal to the being), and in particular the capacity to feel pain;
2. reasoning (the *developed* capacity to solve new and relatively complex problems);
3. self-motivated activity (activity which is relatively independent of either genetic or direct external control);
4. the capacity to communicate, by whatever means, messages of an indefinite variety of types, that is, not just with an indefinite number of possible contents, but on indefinitely many possible topics;
5. the presence of self-concepts, and self-awareness, either individual or racial, or both.

Admittedly, there are apt to be a great many problems involved in formulating precise definitions of these criteria, let alone in developing universally valid behavioral criteria for deciding when they apply. But I will assume that both we and our explorer know approximately what (1)–(5) mean, and that he is also able to determine whether or not they apply. How, then, should he use his findings to decide whether or not the alien beings are people? We needn't suppose that an entity must have *all* of these attributes to be properly considered a person; (1) and (2) alone may well be sufficient for personhood, and quite probably (1)–(3) are sufficient. Neither do we need to insist that any one of these criteria is *necessary* for personhood, although once again (1) and (2) look like fairly good candidates for necessary conditions, as does (3), if "activity" is construed so as to include the activity of reasoning.

All we need to claim, to demonstrate that a fetus is not a person, is that any being which satisfies *none* of (1)–(5) is certainly not a person. I consider this claim to be so obvious that I think anyone who denied it, and claimed that a being which satisfied none of (1)–(5) was a person all the same, would thereby demonstrate that he had no notion at all of what a person is—perhaps because he had confused the concept of a person with that of genetic humanity. If the opponents of abortion were to deny the appropriateness of these five criteria, I do not know what further arguments would convince them. We would probably have to admit that our conceptual schemes were indeed irreconcilably different, and that our dispute could not be settled objectively.

I do not expect this to happen, however, since I think that the concept of a person is one which is very nearly universal (to people), and that it is common to both proabortionists and antiabortionists, even though neither group has fully realized the relevance of this concept to the resolution of their dispute. Furthermore, I think that on reflection even the antiabortionists ought to agree that (1)–(5) are central to the concept of personhood, but also that it is a part of this concept that all and only people have full moral rights. The concept of a person is in part a moral concept; once we have admitted that *x* is a person we have recognized, even if we have not agreed to respect, *x*'s right to be treated as a member of the moral community. It is true that the claim that *x is a human being* is more commonly voiced as part of an appeal to treat *x* decently than is the claim that *x* is a person, but this is either because "human being" is here used in the sense which implies personhood, or because the genetic and moral senses of "human" have been confused.

Now if (1)–(5) are indeed the primary criteria of personhood, then it is clear that genetic humanity is neither necessary nor sufficient for establishing that an entity is a person. Some human beings are not people, and there may well be people who are not human beings. A man or woman whose consciousness has been permanently obliterated but who remains alive is a human being which is no longer a person; defective human beings, with no appreciable mental capacity, are not and presumably never will be people; and a fetus is a human being which is not yet a person, and which therefore cannot coherently be said to have full moral rights. Citizens of the next century should be prepared to recognize highly advanced, self-aware robots or computers, should such be developed, and intelligent inhabitants of other worlds, should such be found, as people in the fullest sense, and to respect their moral rights. But to ascribe full moral rights to an entity which is not a person is as absurd as to ascribe moral obligations and responsibilities to such an entity.

3. Fetal Development and the Right to Life

Two problems arise in the application of these suggestions for the definition of the moral community to the determination of the precise moral status of a human fetus. Given that the paradigm example of a person is a normal adult human being, then (1) How like this paradigm, in particular how far advanced since conception, does a human being need to be before it begins to have a right to life by virtue, not of being fully a person as of yet, but of being *like* a person? and (2) To what extent, if any, does the fact that a fetus has the *potential* for becoming a person endow it with some of the same rights? Each of these questions requires some comment.

In answering the first question, we need not attempt a detailed consideration of the moral rights of organisms which are not developed enough, aware enough, intelligent enough, etc., to be considered people, but which resemble people in some respects. It does seem reasonable to suggest that the more like a person, in the relevant respects, a being is, the stronger is the case for regarding it as having a right to life, and indeed the stronger its right to life is. Thus we ought to take seriously the suggestion that, insofar as "the human individual develops biologically in a continuous fashion . . . the rights of a human person might develop in the same way." But we must keep in mind that the attributes which are relevant in determining whether or not an entity is enough like a person to be regarded as having some of the same moral rights are no different from those which are relevant to determining whether or not it is fully a person—i.e., are no different from (1)–(5) — and that being genetically human, or having recognizably human facial and other physical features, or detectable brain activity, or the capacity to survive outside the uterus, are simply not among these relevant attributes.

Thus it is clear that even though a seven- or eight-month fetus has features which make it apt to arouse in us almost the same powerful protective instinct as is commonly aroused by a small infant, nevertheless it is not significantly more personlike than is a very small embryo. It is *somewhat* more personlike; it can apparently feel and respond to pain, and it may even have a rudimentary form of consciousness, insofar as its brain is quite active. Nevertheless, it seems safe to say that it is not fully conscious, in the way that an infant of a few months is, and that it cannot reason, or communicate messages of indefinitely many sorts, does not engage in self-motivated activity, and has no self-awareness. Thus, in the *relevant* respects, a fetus, even a fully developed one, is considerably less personlike than is the average mature mammal, indeed the average fish.

And I think that a rational person must conclude that if the right to life of a fetus is to be based upon its resemblance to a person, then it cannot be said to have any more right to life than, let us say, a newborn guppy (which also seems to be capable of feeling pain), and that a right of that magnitude could never override a woman's right to obtain an abortion, at any stage of her pregnancy.

There may, of course, be other arguments in favor of placing legal limits upon the stage of pregnancy in which an abortion may be performed. Given the relative safety of the new techniques of artificially inducing labor during the third trimester, the danger to the woman's life or health is no longer such an argument. Neither is the fact that people tend to respond to the thought of abortion in the later stages of pregnancy with emotional repulsion, since mere emotional responses cannot take the place of moral reasoning in determining what ought to be permitted. Nor, finally, is the frequently heard argument that legalizing abortion, especially late in the pregnancy, may erode the level of respect for human life, leading, perhaps, to an increase in unjustified euthanasia and other crimes. For this threat, if it is a threat, can be better met by educating people to the kinds of moral distinctions which we are making here than by limiting access to abortion (which limitation may, in its disregard for the rights of women, be just as damaging to the level of respect for human rights).

Thus, since the fact that even a fully developed fetus is not personlike enough to have any significant right to life on the basis of its personlikeness shows that no legal restrictions upon the stage of pregnancy in which an abortion may be performed can be justified on the grounds that we should protect the rights of the older fetus, and since there is no apparent justification for such restrictions, we may conclude that they are entirely unjustified. Whether or not it would be *indecent* (whatever that means) for a woman in her seventh month to obtain an abortion just to avoid having to postpone a trip to Europe, it would not, in itself, be *immoral,* and therefore it ought to be permitted.

4. Potential Personhood and the Right to Life

We have seen that a fetus does not resemble a person in any way which can support the claim that it has even some of the same rights. But what about its *potential*, the fact that if nurtured and allowed to develop naturally it will very probably become a person? Doesn't that alone give it at least some right to life? It is hard to deny that the fact that an entity is a potential person is a strong prima facie reason for not destroying it; but we need not conclude from this that a potential person has a right to life, by virtue of that potential. It may be that our feeling that it is better, other things being equal, not to destroy a potential person is better explained by the fact that potential people are still (felt to be) an invaluable resource, not to be lightly squandered. Surely, if every speck of dust were a potential person, we would be much less apt to conclude that every potential person has a right to become actual.

Still, we do not need to insist that a potential person has no right to life whatever. There may well be something immoral, and not just imprudent, about wantonly destroying potential people, when doing so isn't necessary to protect anyone's rights. But even if a potential person does have some prima facie right to life, such a right could not possibly outweigh the right of a woman to obtain an abortion, since the rights of any actual person invariably outweigh those of any potential person, whenever the two conflict. Since this may not be immediately obvious in the case of a human fetus, let us look at another case.

Suppose that our space explorer falls into the hands of an alien culture, whose scientists decide to create a few hundred thousand or more human beings, by breaking his body into its component cells, and using these to create fully developed human beings, with, of course, his genetic code. We may imagine that each of these newly created men will have all of the original man's abilities, skills, knowledge, and so on, and also have an individual self-concept, in short that each of them will be a bona fide (though hardly unique) person. Imagine that the whole project will take only seconds, and that its chances of success are extremely high, and that our explorer knows all of this, and also knows that these people will be treated fairly. I maintain that in such a situation he would have every right to escape if he could, and thus to deprive all of these potential people of their potential lives; for his right to life outweighs all of theirs together, in spite of the fact that they are all genetically human, all innocent, and all have a very high probability of becoming people very soon if only he refrains from acting.

Indeed, I think he would have a right to escape even if it were not his life which the alien scientists planned to take, but only a year of his freedom, or, indeed, only a day. Nor would he be obligated to stay if he had gotten captured (thus bringing all these people-potentials into existence) because of his own carelessness, or even if he had done so deliberately, knowing the consequences. Regardless of how he got captured, he is not morally obligated to remain in captivity for *any* period of time for the sake of permitting any number of potential people to come into actuality, so great is the margin by which one actual person's right to liberty outweighs whatever right to life even a hundred thousand potential people have. And it seems reasonable to conclude that the rights of a woman will outweigh by a similar margin whatever right to life a fetus may have by virtue of its potential personhood.

Thus, neither a fetus's resemblance to a person, nor its potential for becoming a person provides any basis whatever for the claim that it has any significant right to life. Consequently, a woman's right to protect her health, happiness, freedom, and even her life, by terminating an unwanted pregnancy, will always override whatever right to life it may be appropriate to ascribe to a fetus, even a fully developed one. And thus, in the absence of any overwhelming social need for every possible child, the laws which restrict the right to obtain an abortion, or limit the period of pregnancy during which an abortion may be performed, are a wholly unjustified violation of a woman's most basic moral and constitutional rights.

Fifty Years after Hiroshima

John Rawls

John Rawls (1921–2002) was a professor of political philosophy at Harvard University. He was perhaps the greatest political philosopher of the twentieth century. His groundbreaking Theory of Justice *(1971),* Political Liberalism *(1993), and* Law of Peoples *(1999) are all modern classics. Rawls was a U.S. soldier in the Pacific at the time the bombings of Hiroshima and Nagasaki. In this essay, he argues against those bombings and considers some of the moral issues surrounding statesmanship.*

The fiftieth year since the bombing of Hiroshima is a time to reflect about what one should think of it. Is it really a great wrong, as many now think, and many also thought then, or is it perhaps justified after all? I believe that both the fire-bombing of Japanese cities beginning in the spring of 1945 and the later atomic bombing of Hiroshima on August 6 were very great wrongs, and rightly seen as such. In order to support this opinion, I set out what I think to be the principles governing the conduct of war—*jus in bello*—of democratic peoples. These peoples[1] have different ends of war than nondemocratic, especially totalitarian, states, such as Germany and Japan, which sought the domination and exploitation of subjected peoples, and in Germany's case, their enslavement if not extermination.

"Fifty Years After Hiroshima" reprinted by permission of the publishers from *John Rawls: Collected Papers,* edited by Samuel Freeman, pp. 565–572, Cambridge, Mass.: Harvard University Press, © 1999 by the President and Fellows of Harvard College. Originally published in *Dissent* (Summer 1995): 323–327.

Although I cannot properly justify them here, I begin by setting out six principles and assumptions in support of these judgments. I hope they seem not unreasonable; and certainly they are familiar, as they are closely related to much traditional thought on this subject.

1. The aim of a just war waged by a decent democratic society is a just and lasting peace between peoples, especially with its present enemy.

2. A decent democratic society is fighting against a state that is not democratic. This follows from the fact that democratic peoples do not wage war against each other;[2] and since we are concerned with the rules of war as they apply to such peoples, we assume the society fought against is nondemocratic and that its expansionist aims threatened the security and free institutions of democratic regimes and caused the war.[3]

3. In the conduct of war, a democratic society must carefully distinguish three groups: the state's leaders and officials, its soldiers, and its civilian population. The reason for these distinctions rests on the principle of responsibility: since the state fought against is not democratic, the civilian members of the society cannot be those who organized and brought on the war. This was done by its leaders and officials assisted by other elites who control and staff the state apparatus. They are responsible, they willed the war, and for doing that, they are criminals. But civilians, often kept in ignorance and swayed by state propaganda, are not.[4] And this is so even if some civilians knew better and were enthusiastic for the war. In a nation's conduct of war many such marginal cases may exist,

but they are irrelevant. As for soldiers, they, just as civilians, and leaving aside the upper ranks of an officer class, are not responsible for the war, but are conscripted or in other ways forced into it, their patriotism often cruelly and cynically exploited. The grounds on which they may be attacked directly are not that they are responsible for the war but that a democratic people cannot defend itself in any other way, and defend itself it must do. About this there is no choice.

4. A decent democratic society must respect the human rights of the members of the other side, both civilians and soldiers, for two reasons. One is because they simply have these rights by the law of peoples. The other reason is to teach enemy soldiers and civilians the content of those rights by the example of how they hold in their own case. In this way their significance is best brought home to them. They are assigned a certain status, the status of the members of some human society who possess rights as human persons.[5] In the case of human rights in war the aspect of status as applied to civilians is given a strict interpretation. This means, as I understand it here, that they can never be attacked directly except in times of extreme crisis, the nature of which I discuss below.

5. Continuing with the thought of teaching the content of human rights, the next principle is that just peoples by their actions and proclamations are to foreshadow during war the kind of peace they aim for and the kind of relations they seek between nations. By doing so, they show in an open and public way the nature of their aims and the kind of people they are. These last duties fall largely on the leaders and officials of the governments of democratic peoples, since they are in the best position to speak for the whole people and to act as the principle applies. Although all the preceding principles also specify duties of statesmanship, this is especially true of 4 and 5. The way a war is fought and the

actions ending it endure in the historical memory of peoples and may set the stage for future war. This duty of statesmanship must always be held in view.

6. Finally, we note the place of practical means-end reasoning in judging the appropriateness of an action or policy for achieving the aim of war or for not causing more harm than good. This mode of thought—whether carried on by (classical) utilitarian reasoning, or by cost-benefit analysis, or by weighing national interests, or in other ways—must always be framed within and strictly limited by the preceding principles. The norms of the conduct of war set up certain lines that bound just action. War plans and strategies, and the conduct of battles, must lie within their limits. (The only exception, I repeat, is in times of extreme crisis.)

In connection with the fourth and fifth principles of the conduct of war, I have said that they are binding especially on the leaders of nations. They are in the most effective position to represent their people's aims and obligations, and sometimes they become statesmen. But who is a statesman? There is no office of statesman, as there is of president, or chancellor, or prime minister. The statesman is an ideal, like the ideal of the truthful or virtuous individual. Statesmen are presidents or prime ministers who become statesmen through their exemplary performance and leadership in their office in difficult and trying times and manifest strength, wisdom, and courage. They guide their people through turbulent and dangerous periods for which they are esteemed always, as one of their great statesmen.

The ideal of the statesman is suggested by the saying: the politician looks to the next election, the statesman to the next generation. It is the task of the student of philosophy to look to the permanent conditions and the real interests of a just and good democratic society. It is the task of the statesman, however, to discern these conditions and interests in practice; the states-man sees deeper and further than most others and grasps what needs to be done. The statesman must get it right, or nearly so, and hold fast to it. Washington and Lincoln were statesmen. Bismarck was not. He did not see Germany's real interests far enough into the future, and his judg-ment and motives were often distorted by his class interests and his wanting himself alone to be chancellor of Germany. Statesmen need not be selfless and may have their own interests when they hold office, yet they must be selfless in their judgments and assessments of society's interests and not be swayed, especially in war and crisis, by passions of revenge and retaliation against the enemy.

Above all, they are to hold fast to the aim of gaining a just peace, and avoid the things that make achieving such a peace more difficult. Here the proclamations of a nation should make clear (the statesman must see to this) that the enemy people are to be granted an autonomous regime of their own and a decent and full life once peace is securely reestablished. Whatever they may be told by their leaders, whatever reprisals they may reasonably fear, they are not to be held as slaves or serfs after surrender,[6] or denied in due course their full liberties; and they may well achieve freedoms they did not enjoy before, as the Germans and the Japanese eventually did. The statesman knows, if others do not, that all descriptions of the enemy people (not their rulers) inconsistent with this are impulsive and false.

Turning now to Hiroshima and the fire-bombing of Tokyo, we find that neither falls under the exemption of extreme crisis. One aspect of this is that since (let's suppose) there are no abso-lute rights—rights that must be respected in all circumstances—there are occasions when civilians can be attacked directly by aerial bomb-ing. Were there times during the war when Britain could properly have bombed Hamburg and Berlin? Yes, when Britain was alone and desperately facing Germany's superior might; moreover, this period would extend until Russia had clearly beat off the first German assault in the summer and fall of 1941, and would be able to fight Germany until the end. Here the cutoff point might be placed differently, say the summer of 1942, and certainly by Stalingrad.[7] I shall not dwell on this, as the crucial matter is that under no conditions could Germany be allowed to win the war, and this for two basic reasons: first, the nature and history of consti-tutional democracy and its place in European culture; and second, the peculiar evil of Nazism and the enormous and uncalculable moral and political evil it represented for civilized society.

The peculiar evil of Nazism needs to be understood, since in some circumstances a democratic people might better accept defeat if the terms of peace offered by the adversary were reasonable and moderate, did not subject them to humiliation, and looked forward to a workable and decent political relationship. Yet characteristic of Hitler was that he accepted no possibility at all of a political relationship with his enemies. They were always to be cowed by terror and brutality, and ruled by force. From the beginning the campaign against Russia, for example, was a war of destruction against Slavic peoples, with the original inhabitants remain-ing, if at all, only as serfs. When Goebbels and others protested that the war could not be won that way, Hitler refused to listen.[8]

Yet it is clear that while the extreme crisis exemption held for Britain in the early stages of the war, it never held at any time for the United States in its war with Japan. The principles of the conduct of war were always applicable to it. Indeed, in the case of Hiroshima many involved in higher reaches of the government recognized the questionable character of the bombing and that limits were being crossed. Yet during the discussions among allied leaders in June and July 1945, the weight of the practical means-end reasoning carried the day. Under the continuing pressure of war, such moral doubts as there were failed to gain an express and articulated view. As the war progressed, the heavy fire-bombing of civilians in the capitals of Berlin and Tokyo and elsewhere was increasingly accepted on the allied side. Although after the outbreak of war Roosevelt had urged both sides not to commit the inhuman barbarism of bombing civilians, by 1945 allied leaders came to assume that Roosevelt would have used the bomb on Hiroshima.[9] The bombing grew out of what had happened before.

The practical means-end reasons to justify using the atomic bomb on Hiroshima were the following:

The bomb was dropped to hasten the end of the war. It is clear that Truman and most other allied leaders thought it would do that. Another reason was that it would save lives where the lives counted are the lives of American soldiers. The lives of Japanese, military or civilian, presumably counted for less. Here the calculations of least time and most lives saved were mutually supporting. Moreover, dropping the bomb would give the Emperor and the Japanese leaders a way to save face, an important matter given Japanese samurai culture. Indeed, at the end a few top Japanese leaders wanted to make a last sacrificial stand but were overruled by others supported by the Emperor, who ordered surrender on August 12, having received word from Washington that the Emperor could stay provided it was understood that he had to comply with the orders of the American military commander. The last reason I mention is that the bomb was dropped to impress the Russians with American power and make them more agreeable with our demands. This reason is highly disputed but is urged by some critics and scholars as important.

The failure of these reasons to reflect the limits on the conduct of war is evident, so I focus on a different matter: the failure of statesmanship on the part of allied leaders and why it might

have occurred. Truman once described the Japanese as beasts and to be treated as such; yet how foolish it sounds now to call the Germans or the Japanese barbarians and beasts![10] Of the Nazis and Tojo militarists, yes, but they are not the German and the Japanese people. Churchill later granted that he carried the bombing too far, led by passion and the intensity of the conflict.[11] A duty of statesmanship is not to allow such feelings, natural and inevitable as they may be, to alter the course a democratic people should best follow in striving for peace. The statesman understands that relations with the present enemy have special importance: for as I have said, war must be openly and publicly conducted in ways that make a lasting and amicable peace possible with a defeated enemy, and prepares its people for how they may be expected to be treated. Their present fears of being subjected to acts of revenge and retaliation must be put to rest; present enemies must be seen as associates in a shared and just future peace.

These remarks make it clear that, in my judgment, both Hiroshima and the fire-bombing of Japanese cities were great evils that the duties of statesmanship require political leaders to avoid in the absence of the crisis exemption. I also believe this could have been done at little cost in further casualties. An invasion was unnecessary at that date, as the war was effectively over. However, whether that is true or not makes no difference. Without the crisis exemption, those bombings are great evils. Yet it is clear that an articulate expression of the principles of just war introduced at that time would not have altered the outcome. It was simply too late. A president or prime minister must have carefully considered these questions, preferably long before, or at least when they had the time and leisure to think things out. Reflections on just war cannot be heard in the daily round of the pressure of events near the end of the hostilities; too many are anxious and impatient, and simply worn out.

Similarly, the justification of constitutional democracy and the basis of the rights and duties it must respect should be part of the public political culture and discussed in the many associations of civic society as part of one's education. It is not clearly heard in day-to-day ordinary politics, but must be presupposed as the background, not the daily subject of politics, except in special circumstances. In the same way, there was not sufficient prior grasp of the fundamental importance of the principles of just war for the expression of them to have blocked the appeal of practical means-end reasoning in terms of a calculus of lives, or of the least time to end the war, or of some other balancing of costs and benefits. This practical reasoning justifies too much, too easily, and provides a way for a dominant power to quiet any moral worries that may arise. If the principles of war are put forward at that time, they easily become so many more considerations to be balanced in the scales.

Another failure of statesmanship was not to try to enter into negotiations with the Japanese before any drastic steps such as the fire-bombing of cities or the bombing of Hiroshima were taken. A conscientious attempt to do so was morally necessary. As a democratic people, we owed that to the Japanese people—whether to their government is another matter. There had been discussions in Japan for some time about finding a way to end the war, and on June 26 the government had been instructed by the Emperor to do so.[12] It must surely have realized that with the navy destroyed and the outer islands taken, the war was lost. True, the Japanese were deluded by the hope that the Russians might prove to be their allies,[13] but negotiations are precisely to disabuse the other side of delusions of that kind. A statesman is not free to consider that such negotiations may lessen the desired shock value of subsequent attacks.

Truman was in many ways a good, at times a very good president. But the way he ended the war showed he failed as a statesman. For him it was an opportunity missed, and a loss to the country and its armed forces as well. It is sometimes said that questioning the bombing of Hiroshima is an insult to the American troops who fought the war. This is hard to understand. We should be able to look back and consider our faults after fifty years. We expect the Germans and the Japanese to do that— *"Vergangenheitsverarbeitung,"* as the Germans say. Why shouldn't we? It can't be that we think we waged the war without moral error!

None of this alters Germany's and Japan's responsibility for the war nor their behavior in conducting it. Emphatically to be repudiated are two nihilist doctrines. One is expressed by Sherman's remark, "War is hell," so anything goes to get it over with as soon as one can. The other says that we are all guilty so we stand on a level and no one can blame anyone else. These are both superficial and deny all reasonable distinctions; they are invoked falsely to try to excuse our misconduct or to plead that we cannot be condemned.

The moral emptiness of these nihilisms is manifest in the fact that just and decent civilized societies—their institutions and laws, their civil life and background culture and mores—all depend absolutely on making significant moral and political distinctions in all situations. Certainly war is a kind of hell, but why should that mean that all moral distinctions cease to hold? And granted also that sometimes all or nearly all may be to some degree guilty, that does not mean that all are equally so. There is never a time when we are free from all moral and political principles and restraints. These nihilisms are pretenses to be free of those principles and restraints that always apply to us fully.

Notes

1. I sometimes use the term "peoples" to mean the same as nations, especially when I want to contrast peoples with states and a state's apparatus.

2. I assume that democratic peoples do not go to war against each other. There is considerable evidence of this

important idea. See Michael Doyle's two-part article, "Kant, Liberal Legacies, and Foreign Affairs," *Philosophy and Public Affairs,* 12 (Summer/Fall 1983): 205–235, 323–353. See especially his summary of the evidence in the first part, pp. 206–232.

3. Responsibility for war rarely falls on only one side, and this must be granted. Yet some dirty hands are dirtier than others, and sometimes even with dirty hands a democratic people would still have the right and even the duty to defend itself from the other side. This is clear in World War II.

4. Here I follow Michael Walzer's *Just and Unjust Wars* (New York: Basic Books, 1977).

5. For the idea of status, I am indebted to discussions of Frances Kamm and Thomas Nagel.

6. See Churchill's remarks explaining the meaning of "unconditional surrender" in *The Hinge of Fate* (Boston: Houghton Mifflin, 1950), pp. 685–688.

7. I might add here that a balancing of interests is not involved. Rather, we have a matter of judgment as to whether certain objective circumstances are present which constitute the extreme crisis exemption. As with any other complex concept, that of such an exemption is to some degree vague. Whether or not the concept applies rests on judgment.

8. On Goebbels's and others' protests, see Alan Bullock, *Hitler: A Study in Tyranny* (London: Oldham's Press, 1952), ch. 12, sec. 5, pp. 633–644.

9. For an account of events, see David M. McCullough, *Truman* (New York: Simon and Schuster, 1992), ch. 9, sec. IV and ch. 10, pp. 390–464; and Barton Bernstein, "The Atomic Bombings Reconsidered," *Foreign Affairs,* 74 (Jan./Feb. 1995): 1.

10. See McCullough's *Truman,* p. 458, the exchange between Truman and Senator Russell of Georgia in August 1945.

11. See Martin Gilbert, *Winston Churchill: Never Despair,* vol. VIII (Boston: Houghton Mifflin, 1988), p. 259, reflecting later on Dresden.

12. See Gerhard Weinberg, *A World at Arms* (Cambridge: Cambridge University Press, 1994), pp. 886–889.

13. See ibid., p. 886.

Supreme Emergency

Michael Walzer

Michael Walzer is a professor emeritus at the Institute For Advanced Study, Princeton University. He is the author of a number of important books on political science and political philosophy. His book Just and Unjust Wars *(1977), from which this selection is taken, is the modern classic of just war theory. In the following selection, Walzer argues that in certain rare circumstances, which he calls "supreme emergency," the least wrong thing for us to do would be to fight unjustly, such as resorting to terrorism or atrocity. While he argues that we should do such things in circumstances of supreme emergency, he does not accept that we would therefore be blameless for doing them.*

Everyone's troubles make a crisis. "Emergency" and "crisis" are cant words, used to prepare our minds for acts of brutality. And yet there are such things as critical moments in the lives of men and women and in the history of states. Certainly, war is such a time: every war is an emergency, every battle a possible turning point. Fear and hysteria are always latent in combat, often real, and they press us toward fearful measures and criminal behavior. The war convention is a bar to such measures, not always effective, but there nevertheless. In principle at least, as we have seen, it resists the ordinary crises of military life. Churchill's description of Britain's predicament in 1939 as a "supreme emergency" was a piece of rhetorical heightening designed to overcome that resistance. But the phrase also contains an argument: that there is a fear beyond the ordinary fearfulness (and

Reprinted by permission of the publisher from Michael Walzer, *Just and Unjust Wars*, Chap. 16. © 1977 (3rd ed., 2000) by Basic Books.

the frantic opportunism) of war, and a danger to which that fear corresponds, and that this fear and danger may well require exactly those measures that the war convention bars. Now, a great deal is at stake here, both for the men and women driven to adopt such measures and for their victims, so we must attend carefully to the implicit argument of "supreme emergency."

Though its use is often ideological, the meaning of the phrase is a matter of common sense. It is defined by two criteria, which correspond to the two levels on which the concept of necessity works: the first has to do with the imminence of the danger and the second with its nature. The two criteria must both be applied. Neither one by itself is sufficient as an account of extremity or as a defense of the extraordinary measures extremity is thought to require. Close but not serious, serious but not close—neither one makes for a supreme emergency. But since people at war can rarely agree on the seriousness of the dangers they face (or pose for one another), the idea of closeness is sometimes made to do the job alone. Then we are offered what might best be called the back-to-the-wall argument: that when conventional means of resistance are hopeless or worn out, anything goes (anything that is "necessary" to win). Thus British Prime Minister Stanley Baldwin, writing in 1932 about the dangers of terror bombing:[1]

Will any form of prohibition of bombing, whether by convention, treaty, agreement, or anything you like, be effective in war? Frankly, I doubt it, and in doubting it, I make no reflection on the good faith of either ourselves or any other country. If a man has a potential weapon and has his back to the wall and is going to be killed, he will use that weapon, whatever it is and whatever undertaking he has given about it.

The first thing that has to be said about this statement is that Baldwin does not mean his domestic analogy to be applied literally. Soldiers and statesmen commonly say that their backs are to the wall whenever military defeat seems imminent, and Baldwin is endorsing this view of extremity. The analogy is from survival at home to victory in the international sphere. Baldwin claims that people will necessarily (inevitably) adopt extreme measures if such measures are necessary (essential) either to escape death or to avoid military defeat. But the argument is wrong at both ends. It is simply not the case that individuals will always strike out at innocent men and women rather than accept risks for themselves. We even say, very often, that it is their duty to accept risks (and perhaps to die); and here as in moral life generally, "ought" implies "can." We make the demand knowing that it is possible for people to live up to it. Can we make the same demand on political leaders, acting not for themselves but for their countrymen? That will depend upon the dangers their countrymen face. What is it that defeat entails? Is it some minor territorial adjustment, a loss of face (for the leaders), the payment of heavy indemnities, political reconstruction of this or that sort, the surrender of national independence, the exile or murder of millions of people? In such cases, one's back is always to the wall, but the dangers one confronts take very different forms, and the different forms make a difference.

If we are to adopt or defend the adoption of extreme measures, the danger must be of an unusual and horrifying kind. Such descriptions, I suppose, are common enough in time of war. One's enemies are often thought to be—at least they are often said to be—unusual and horrifying.[2] Soldiers are encouraged to fight fiercely if they believe that they are fighting for the survival of their country and their families, that freedom, justice, civilization itself are at risk. But this sort of thing is only sometimes plausible to the detached observer, and one suspects that its propagandistic character is also understood by many of the participants. War is not always a struggle over ultimate values, where the victory of one side would be a human disaster for the other. It is necessary to be skeptical about such matters, to cultivate a wary disbelief of war-time rhetoric, and then to search for some touchstone against which arguments about extremity might be judged. We need to make a map of human crises and to mark off the regions of desperation and disaster. These and only these constitute the realm of necessity, truly understood. Once again, I am going to use the experience of World War II in Europe to suggest at least the rough contours of the map. For Nazism lies at the outer limits of exigency, at a point where we are likely to find ourselves united in fear and abhorrence.

That is what I am going to assume, at any rate, on behalf of all those people who believed at the time and still believe a third of a century later that Nazism was an ultimate threat to everything decent in our lives, an ideology and a practice of domination so murderous, so degrading even to those who might survive, that the consequences of its final victory were literally beyond calculation, immeasurably awful. We see it—and I don't use the phrase lightly— as evil objectified in the world, and in a form so potent and apparent that there could never have been anything to do but fight against it. I obviously cannot offer an account of Nazism in these pages. But such an account is hardly necessary. It is enough to point to the historical experience of Nazi rule. Here was a threat to human values so radical that its imminence would surely constitute a supreme emergency; and this example can help us understand why lesser threats might not do so.

In order to get the map right, however, we must imagine a Nazi-like danger somewhat different from the one the Nazis actually posed. When Churchill said that a German victory in World War II "would be fatal, not only to ourselves, but to the independent life of every small country in Europe," he was speaking the exact truth. The danger was a general one. But suppose it had existed for Britain alone. Can a supreme emergency be constituted by a particular threat—by a threat of enslavement or extermination directed against a single nation? Can soldiers and statesmen override the rights of innocent people for the sake of their own political community? I am inclined to answer this question affirmatively, though not without hesitation and worry. What choice do they have? They might sacrifice themselves in order to uphold the moral law, but they cannot sacrifice their countrymen. Faced with some ultimate horror, their options exhausted, they will do what they must to save their own people. That is not to say that their decision is inevitable (I have no way of knowing that), but the sense of obligation and of moral urgency they are likely to feel at such a time is so overwhelming that a different outcome is hard to imagine.

Still, the question is difficult, as its domestic analogue suggests. Despite Baldwin, it is not usually said of individuals in domestic society that they necessarily will or that they morally can strike out at innocent people, even in the supreme emergency of self-defense.[3] They can only attack their attackers. But communities, in emergencies, seem to have different and larger prerogatives. I am not sure that I can account for the difference, without ascribing to communal life a kind of transcendence that I don't believe it to have. Perhaps it is only a matter of arithmetic: individuals cannot kill other individuals to save themselves, but to save a nation we can violate the rights of a determinate but smaller number of people. But then large nations and small ones would have different entitlements in such cases, and I doubt very much that that is true. We might better say that it is possible to live in a world where individuals are sometimes murdered, but a world where entire peoples are enslaved or massacred is literally unbearable. For the survival and freedom of political communities—whose members share a way of life, developed by their ancestors, to be passed on to their children—are the highest values of international society. Nazism challenged these values on a grand scale, but challenges more narrowly conceived, *if they are of the same kind,* have similar moral consequences. They bring us under the rule of necessity (and necessity knows no rules).

I want to stress again, however, that the mere recognition of such a threat is not itself coercive; it neither compels nor permits attacks on the innocent, so long as other means of fighting and winning are available. Danger makes only half the argument; imminence makes the other half. Now let us consider a time when the two halves came together: the terrible two years that followed the defeat of France, from the summer of 1940 to the summer of 1942, when Hitler's armies were everywhere triumphant.

Overriding the Rules of War

The Decision to Bomb German Cities

There have been few decisions more important than this one in the history of warfare. As a direct result of the adoption of a policy of terror bombing by the leaders of Britain, some 300,000 Germans, most of them civilians, were killed and another 780,000 seriously injured. No doubt, these figures are low when compared to the results of Nazi genocide; but they were, after all, the work of men and women at war with Nazism, who hated everything it stood for and who were not supposed to imitate its effects, even at lagging rates. And the British policy had further consequences: it was the crucial precedent for the fire-bombing of Tokyo and other Japanese cities and then for Harry Truman's decision to drop atomic bombs on Hiroshima and Nagasaki. The civilian death toll from Allied terrorism in World War II must have exceeded half a million men, women, and children. How could the initial choice of this ultimate weapon ever have been defended?

The history is a complex one, and it has already been the subject of several monographic analyses.[4] I can review it only briefly, attending especially to the arguments put forward at the time by Churchill and other British leaders, and always remembering what sort of a time it was. The decision to bomb cities was made late in 1940. A directive issued in June of that year had "specifically laid down that targets had to be identified and aimed at. Indiscriminate bombing was forbidden." In November, after the German raid on Coventry, "Bomber Command was instructed simply to aim at the center of a city." What had once been called indiscriminate bombing (and commonly condemned) was now required, and by early 1942, aiming at military or industrial targets was barred: "the aiming points are to be the built-up areas, *not*, for instance, the dockyards or aircraft factories."[5] The purpose of the raids was explicitly declared to be the destruction of civilian morale. Following the famous minute of Lord Cherwell in 1942, the means to this demoralization were specified: working-class residential areas were the prime targets. Cherwell thought it possible to render a third of the German population homeless by 1943.[6]

Before Cherwell provided his "scientific" rationale for the bombing, a number of reasons had already been offered for the British decision. From the beginning, the attacks were defended as reprisals for the German blitz. This is a very problematic defense, even if we leave aside the difficulties of the doctrine of reprisals (which I have already canvassed). First of all, it appears possible, as one scholar has recently argued, that Churchill deliberately provoked the German attacks on London—by bombing Berlin—in order to relieve pressure on R.A.F. installations, until then the major *Luftwaffe* target.[7] Nor was it Churchill's purpose, once the blitz began, to deter the German attacks or to establish a policy of mutual restraint.[8]

We ask no favor of the enemy. We seek from them no compunction. On the contrary, if tonight the people of London were asked to cast their votes whether a convention should be entered into to stop the bombing of all cities, the overwhelming majority would cry, "No, we will mete out to the Germans the measure, and more than the measure, that they have meted out to us."

Needless to say, the people of London were not in fact asked to vote on such a convention. Churchill assumed that the bombing of German cities was necessary to their morale and that they wanted to hear (what he told them in a radio broadcast of 1941) that the British air force was making "the German people taste and gulp each month a sharper dose of the miseries they have showered upon mankind."[9] This argument has been accepted by many historians: there was "a popular clamor" for revenge, one of them writes, which Churchill had to satisfy if he was to maintain a fighting spirit among his own people. It is especially interesting to note, then, that a 1941 opinion poll showed that "the most determined demand for [reprisal raids] came from Cumberland, Westmoreland, and the North Riding of Yorkshire, rural areas barely touched by bombing, where some three-quarters of the population wanted them. In central London, conversely, the proportion was only 45 percent."[10] Men and women who had experienced terror bombing were less likely to support Churchill's policy than those who had not—a heartening statistic, and one which suggests that the morale of the British people (or perhaps better, their conventional morality) allowed for political leadership of a different sort than Churchill provided. The news that Germany was being bombed was certainly glad tidings in Britain; but as late as 1944, according to other opinion surveys, the overwhelming majority of Britishers still believed that the raids were directed solely against military targets. Presumably, that is what they wanted to believe; there was by then quite a bit of evidence to the contrary. But that says something, again, about the character of British morale. (It should also be said that the campaign against terror bombing, run largely by pacifists, attracted very little popular support.)

Reprisal was a bad argument; revenge was a worse one. We must concentrate now on the military justifications for terror bombing, which were presumably paramount in Churchill's mind, whatever he said on the radio. I can discuss these only in a general way. There was a great deal of dispute at the time, some of it technical, some of it moral in character. The calculations of the Cherwell minute, for example, were sharply attacked by a group of scientists whose opposition to terrorism may well have had moral grounds, but whose position, to the best of my knowledge, was never stated in moral terms.[11] Explicit moral disagreement developed most importantly among the professional soldiers involved in the decision-making process. These disagreements are described, in characteristic fashion, by a strategic analyst and historian who has studied the British escalation: "The . . . debate had been beclouded by emotion on one side of the argument, on the part of those who as a matter of moral principle objected to making war on civilians."[12] The focus of these objections seems to have been some version of the doctrine of double effect. (The arguments had, to the mind of the strategic analyst, "a curiously scholastic flavor.") At the height of the blitz, many British officers still felt strongly that their own air attacks should be aimed only at military targets and that positive efforts should be made to minimize civilian casualties. They did not want to imitate Hitler, but to differentiate themselves from him. Even officers who accepted the desirability of killing civilians still sought to maintain their professional honor: such deaths, they insisted, were desirable "only insofar as [they] remained a by-product of the primary intention to hit a military target . . ."[13] A tendentious argument, no doubt, yet one that would drastically have limited the British offensive against cities. But all such proposals ran up against the operational limits of the bomber technology then available.

Early in the war, it became clear that British bombers could fly effectively only at night and, given the navigational devices with which they were equipped, that they could reasonably aim at no target smaller than a fairly large city. A study made in 1941 indicated that of those planes that actually succeeded in attacking their target (about two-thirds of the attacking force), only one-third dropped their bombs within five miles of the point aimed at.[14] Once this was known, it would seem dishonest to claim that the intended target was, say, this aircraft factory and that the indiscriminate destruction around it was only an unintended, if foreseeable, consequence of the justified attempt to stop the production of planes. What was really unintended but foreseeable was that the factory itself would probably escape harm. If any sort of strategic bombing offensive was to be maintained, one would have to plan for the destruction that one could and did cause. Lord Cherwell's minute was an effort at such planning. In fact, of course, navigational devices were rapidly improved as the war went on, and the bombing of specific military targets was an important part of Britain's total air offensive, receiving top priority at times (before the June 1944 invasion of France, for example) and cutting into the resources allowed for attacks on cities. Today many experts believe that the war might have ended sooner had there been a greater concentration of air power against targets such as the German oil refineries.[15] But the decision to bomb cities was made at a time when victory was not in sight and the specter of defeat ever present. And it was made when no other decision seemed possible if there was to be any sort of military offensive against Nazi Germany.

Bomber Command was the only offensive weapon available to the British in those frightening years, and I expect there is some truth to the notion that it was used simply because it was there. "It was the only force in the West," writes Arthur Harris, chief of Bomber Command from early 1942 until the end of the war, "which could take offensive action . . . against Germany, our only means of getting at the enemy in a way that would hurt at all."[16] Offensive action could have been postponed until (or in hope of) some more favorable time. That is what the war convention would require, and there was also considerable military pressure for postponement. Harris was hard-pressed to keep his Command together in the face of repeated calls for tactical air support—which would have been coordinated with ground action largely defensive in character, since the German armies were still advancing everywhere. Sometimes, in his memoirs, he sounds like a bureaucrat defending his function and his office, but obviously he was also defending a certain conception of how the war might best be fought. He did not believe that the weapons he commanded should be used because he commanded them. He believed that the tactical use of bombers could not stop Hitler and that the destruction of cities could. Later in the war, he argued that only the destruction of cities could bring the fighting to a quick conclusion. The first of these arguments, at least, deserves a careful examination. It was apparently accepted by the Prime Minister. "The bombers alone," Churchill had said as early as September 1940, "provide the means of victory."[17]

The bombers alone—that poses the issue very starkly, and perhaps wrongly, given the disputes over strategy to which I have already referred. Churchill's statement suggested a certainty to which neither he nor anyone else had any right. But the issue can be put so as to accommodate a degree of skepticism and to permit even the most sophisticated among us to indulge in a common and a morally important fantasy: suppose that I sat in the seat of power and had to decide whether to use Bomber Command (in the only way that it could be used systematically and effectively) against cities. Suppose further that unless the bombers were used in this way, the probability that Germany would eventually be defeated would be radically reduced. It makes

no sense at this point to quantify the probabilities; I have no clear notion what they actually were or even how they might be calculated given our present knowledge; nor am I sure how different figures, unless they were very different, would affect the moral argument. But it does seem to me that the more certain a German victory appeared to be in the absence of a bomber offensive, the more justifiable was the decision to launch the offensive. It is not just that such a victory was frightening, but also that it seemed in those years very close; it is not just that it was close, but also that it was so frightening. Here was a supreme emergency, where one might well be required to override the rights of innocent people and shatter the war convention.

Given the view of Nazism that I am assuming, the issue takes this form: should I wager this determinate crime (the killing of innocent people) against that immeasurable evil (a Nazi triumph)? Obviously, if there is some other way of avoiding the evil or even a reasonable chance of another way, I must wager differently or elsewhere. But I can never hope to be sure; a wager is not an experiment. Even if I wager and win, it is still possible that I was wrong, that my crime was unnecessary to victory. But I can argue that I studied the case as closely as I was able, took the best advice I could find, sought out available alternatives. And if all this is true, and my perception of evil and imminent danger not hysterical or self-serving, then surely I must wager. There is no option; the risk otherwise is too great. My own action is determinate, of course, only as to its direct consequences, while the rule that bars such acts is founded on a conception of rights that transcends all immediate considerations. It arises out of our common history; it holds the key to our common future. But I dare to say that our history will be nullified and our future condemned unless I accept the burdens of criminality here and now.

This is not an easy argument to make, and yet we must resist every effort to make it easier. Many people undoubtedly found some comfort in the fact that the cities being bombed were

German and some of the victims Nazis. In effect, they applied the sliding scale and denied or diminished the rights of German civilians so as to deny or diminish the horror of their deaths. This is a tempting procedure, as we can see most clearly if we consider again the bombing of occupied France. Allied fliers killed many Frenchmen, but they did so while bombing what were (or were thought to be) military targets. They did not deliberately aim at the "built-up areas" of French cities. Suppose such a policy had been proposed. I am sure that we would all find the wager more difficult to undertake and defend if, through some strange combination of circumstances, it required the deliberate slaughter of Frenchmen. For we had special commitments to the French; we were fighting on their behalf (and sometimes the bombers were flown by French pilots). But the status of the civilians in the two cases is no different. The theory that distinguishes combatants from noncombatants does not distinguish Allied from enemy noncombatants, at least not with regard to the question of their murder. I suppose it makes sense to say that there were more people in German than in French cities who were responsible (in some fashion) for the evil of Nazism, and we may well be reluctant to extend to them the full range of civilian rights. But even if that reluctance is justified, there is no way for the bombers to search out the right people. And for all the others, terrorism only reiterates the tyranny that the Nazis had already established. It assimilates ordinary men and women to their government as if the two really made a totality, and it judges them in a totalitarian way. If one is forced to bomb cities, it seems to me, it is best to acknowledge that one has also been forced to kill the innocent.

Once again, however, I want to set radical limits to the notion of necessity even as I have myself been using it. For the truth is that the supreme emergency passed long before the British bombing reached its crescendo. The greater number by far of the German civilians killed by terror bombing were killed without moral (and probably also without military) reason. The decisive point was made by Churchill in July of 1942:[18]

In the days when we were fighting alone, we answered the question: "How are you going to win the war?" by saying: "We will shatter Germany by bombing." Since then the enormous injuries inflicted on the German Army and manpower by the Russians, and the accession of the manpower and munitions of the United States, have rendered other possibilities open.

Surely, then, it was time to stop the bombing of cities and to aim, tactically and strategically, only at legitimate military targets. But that was not Churchill's view: "All the same, it would be a mistake to cast aside our original thought . . . that the severe, ruthless bombing of Germany on an ever-increasing scale will not only cripple her war effort . . . but will create conditions intolerable to the mass of the German population." So the raids continued, culminating in the spring of 1945—when the war was virtually won—in a savage attack on the city of Dresden in which something like 100,000 people were killed.[19] Only then did Churchill have second thoughts. "It seems to me that the moment has come when the question of bombing German cities simply for the sake of increasing the terror, though under other pretexts, should be reviewed . . . The destruction of Dresden remains a serious query against the conduct of Allied bombing."[20] Indeed it does, but so does the destruction of Hamburg and Berlin and all the other cities attacked simply for the sake of terror.

The argument used between 1942 and 1945 in defense of terror bombing was utilitarian in character, its emphasis not on victory itself but on the time and price of victory. The city raids, it was claimed by men such as Harris, would end the war sooner than it would otherwise end and, despite the large number of civilian casualties they inflicted, at a lower cost in human life.

Assuming this claim to be true (I have already indicated that precisely opposite claims are made by some historians and strategists), it is nevertheless not sufficient to justify the bombing. It is not sufficient, I think, even if we do nothing more than calculate utilities. For such calculations need not be concerned only with the preservation of life. There is much else that we might plausibly want to preserve: the quality of our lives, for example, our civilization and morality, our collective abhorrence of murder, even when it seems, as it always does, to serve some purpose. Then the deliberate slaughter of innocent men and women cannot be justified simply because it saves the lives of other men and women. I suppose it is possible to imagine situations where that last assertion might prove problematic, from a utilitarian perspective, where the number of people involved is small, the proportions are right, the events hidden from the public eye, and so on. Philosophers delight in inventing such cases in order to test out our moral doctrines. But their inventions are somehow put out of our minds by the sheer scale of the calculations necessary in World War II. To kill 278,966 civilians (the number is made up) in order to avoid the deaths of an unknown but probably larger number of civilians and soldiers is surely a fantastic, godlike, frightening, and horrendous act.*

---

*George Orwell has suggested an alternative utilitarian rationale for the bombing of German cities. In a column written for the leftist journal *Tribune* in 1944, he argued that the bombing brought the true character of contemporary combat home to all those people who supported the war, even enjoyed it, only because they never felt its effects. It shattered "the immunity of civilians, one of the things that have made war possible," and so it made war less likely in the future. See *The Collected Essays, Journalism and Letters of George Orwell*, ed. Sonia Orwell and Ian Angus, New York, 1968, Vol. 3, pp. 151–152. Orwell assumes that civilians had really been immune in the past, which is false. In any case, I doubt that his argument would lead anyone to begin bombing cities. It is an apology after the fact, and not a convincing one.

I have said that such acts can probably be ruled out on utilitarian grounds, but it is also true that utilitarianism as it is commonly understood, indeed, as Sidgwick himself understands it, encourages the bizarre accounting that makes them (morally) possible. We can recognize their horror only when we have acknowledged the personality and value of the men and women we destroy in committing them. It is the acknowledgment of rights that puts a stop to such calculations and forces us to realize that the destruction of the innocent, whatever its purposes, is a kind of blasphemy against our deepest moral commitments. (This is true even in a supreme emergency, when we cannot do anything else.) But I want to look at one more case before concluding my argument—a case where the utilitarian accounting, however bizarre, seemed so radically clear-cut to the decision-makers as to leave them, they thought, no choice but to attack the innocent.

The Limits of Calculation

Hiroshima

"They all accepted the 'assignment' and produced The Bomb," Dwight Macdonald wrote in August 1945 of the atomic scientists. "Why?" It is an important question, but Macdonald poses it badly and then gives the wrong answer. "Because they thought of themselves as specialists, technicians, and not as complete men."[21] In fact, they did not accept the assignment; they sought it out, taking the initiative, urging upon President Roosevelt the critical importance of an American effort to match the work being done in Nazi Germany. And they did this precisely because they were "complete men," many of them European refugees, with an acute sense of what a Nazi victory would mean for their native lands and for all mankind. They were driven by a deep moral anxiety, not (or not most crucially) by any kind of scientific fascination; they were certainly not servile technicians. On the other hand, they were men and women without political power or following, and once their own work was done, they could not control its use. The discovery in November 1944 that German scientists had made little progress ended their own supreme emergency, but it did not end the program they had helped to launch. "If I had known that the Germans would not succeed in constructing the atom bomb," Albert Einstein said, "I would never have lifted a finger."[22] By the time he found that out, however, the scientists had largely finished their work; now indeed technicians were in charge, and the politicians in charge of them. And in the event, the bomb was not used against Germany (or to deter its use by Hitler, which is what men like Einstein had in mind), but against the Japanese, who had never posed such a threat to peace and freedom as the Nazis had.*

Still, it was an important feature of the American decision that the President and his advisors believed the Japanese to be fighting an aggressive war and, moreover, to be fighting it unjustly. Thus Truman's address to the American people on August 12, 1945:

We have used [the bomb] against those who attacked us without warning at Pearl Harbor, against those who have starved and beaten and executed American prisoners of war, against those who have abandoned all pretense of obeying international laws of warfare. We have used it in order to shorten the agony of war . . .

Here again, the sliding scale is being used to open the way for utilitarian calculations. The Japanese have forfeited (some of) their rights, and so they cannot complain about Hiroshima so long as the destruction of the city actually does, or could reasonably be expected to, shorten the agony of war. But had the Japanese exploded an atomic bomb over an American city, killing tens of thousands of civilians and thereby shortening the agony of war, the action would clearly have been a crime, one more for Truman's list. This distinction is only plausible, however, if one renders a judgment not only against the leaders of Japan but also against the ordinary people of Hiroshima and insists at the same time that no similar judgment is possible against the people of San Francisco, say, or Denver. I can find, as I have said before, no way of defending such a procedure. How did the people of Hiroshima forfeit their rights? Perhaps their taxes paid for some of the ships and planes used in the attack on Pearl Harbor; perhaps they sent their sons into the navy and air force with prayers for their success; perhaps they celebrated the actual event, after being told that their country had won a great victory in the face of an imminent American threat. Surely there is nothing here that makes these people liable to direct attack. (It is worth noting, though the fact is not relevant in judging the Hiroshima decision, that the raid on Pearl Harbor was directed entirely against naval and army installations: only a few stray bombs fell on the city of Honolulu.)[23]

But if Truman's argument on August 12 was weak, there was a worse one underlying it. He did not intend to apply the sliding scale with any precision, for he seems to have believed that, given Japanese aggression, the Americans could do anything at all to win (and shorten the

---

* In his novel *The New Men*, C. P. Snow describes the discussions among atomic scientists as to whether or not the bomb should be used. Some of them, his narrator says, answered that question with "an absolute no," feeling that if the weapon were used. to kill hundreds of thousands of innocent people, "neither science nor the civilization of which science is bone and fibre, would be free from guilt again." But the more common view was the one I have been defending: "Many, probably the majority, gave a conditional no with much the same feeling behind it; but if there were *no other way* of saving the war against Hitler, they would be prepared to drop the bomb." *The New Men*. New York, 1954, p. 177 (Snow's emphasis).

agony of war). Along with most of his advisors, he accepted the "war is hell" doctrine; it is a constant allusion in defenses of the Hiroshima decision. Thus Henry Stimson:[24]

As I look back over the five years of my service as Secretary of War, I see too many stern and heart-rending decisions to be willing to pretend that war is anything else but what it is. The face of war is the face of death; death is an inevitable part of every order that a wartime leader gives.

And James Byrnes, Truman's friend and his Secretary of State:[25]

. . . war remains what General Sherman said it was.

And Arthur Compton, chief scientific advisor to the government:[26]

When one thinks of the mounted archers of Ghengiz Khan . . . the Thirty Years War . . . the millions of Chinese who died during the Japanese invasion . . . the mass destruction of western Russia . . . one realizes that in whatever manner it is fought, war is precisely what General Sherman called it.

And Truman himself:[27]

Let us not become so preoccupied with weapons that we lose sight of the fact that war itself is the real villain.

War itself is to blame, but also the men who begin it . . . while those who fight justly merely participate in the hell of war, choicelessly, and there are no moral decisions for which they can be called to account. This is not, or not necessarily, an immoral doctrine, but it is radically one-sided; it evades the tension between *jus ad bellum* and *jus in bello;* it undercuts the need for hard judgments; it relaxes our sense of moral restraint. When he was choosing a target for the first bomb, Truman reports, he asked Stimson which

Japanese cities were "devoted exclusively to war production."[28] The question was reflexive; Truman did not want to violate the "laws of war." But it wasn't serious. Which American cities were devoted exclusively to war production? It is possible to ask such questions only when the answer doesn't matter. If war is hell however it is fought, then what difference can it make how we fight it? And if war itself is the villain, then what risks do we run (aside from the strategic risks) when we make decisions? The Japanese, who began the war, can also end it; only they can end it, and all we can do is fight it, enduring what Truman called "the daily tragedy of bitter war." I don't doubt that that was really Truman's view; it was not a matter of convenience but of conviction. But it is a distorted view. It mistakes the actual hellishness of war, which is particular in character and open to precise definition, for the limitless pains of religious mythology. The pains of war are limitless only if we make them so—only if we move, as Truman did, beyond the limits that we and others have established. Sometimes, I think, we have to do that, but not all the time. Now we must ask whether it was necessary to do it in 1945.

The only possible defense of the Hiroshima attack is a utilitarian calculation made without the sliding scale, a calculation made, then, where there was no room for it, a claim to override the rules of war and the rights of Japanese civilians. I want to state this argument as strongly as I can. In 1945, American policy was fixed on the demand for the unconditional surrender of Japan. The Japanese had by that time lost the war, but they were by no means ready to accept this demand. The leaders of their armed forces expected an invasion of the Japanese main islands and were preparing for a last-ditch resistance. They had over two million soldiers available for the fighting, and they believed that they could make the invasion so costly that the Americans would agree to a negotiated peace. Truman's military advisors also believed that the costs would be high, though the public record does not show that they ever recommended negotiations. They thought that the war might continue late into 1946 and that there would be as many as a million additional American casualties. Japanese losses would be much higher. The capture of Okinawa in a battle lasting from April to June of 1945 had cost almost 80,000 American casualties, while virtually the entire Japanese garrison of 120,000 men had been killed (only 10,600 prisoners were taken).[29] If the main islands were defended with a similar ferocity, hundreds of thousands, perhaps millions, of Japanese soldiers would die. Meanwhile, the fighting would continue in China and in Manchuria, where a Russian attack was soon due. And the bombing of Japan would also continue, and perhaps intensify, with casualty rates no different from those anticipated from the atomic attack. For the Americans had adopted in Japan the British policy of terrorism: a massive incendiary raid on Tokyo early in March 1945 had set off a firestorm and killed an estimated 100,000 people. Against all this was set, in the minds of American decision-makers, the impact of the atomic bomb—not materially more damaging but psychologically more frightening, and holding out the promise, perhaps, of a quick end to the war. "To avert a vast, indefinite butchery . . . at the cost of a few explosions," wrote Churchill in support of Truman's decision, "seemed, after all our toils and perils, a miracle of deliverance."[30]

"A vast indefinite butchery" involving quite probably the deaths of several million people: surely this is a great evil, and if it was imminent, one could reasonably argue that extreme measures might be warranted to avert it. Secretary of War Stimson thought it was the sort of case I have already described, where one had to wager; there was no option. "No man, in our position and subject to our responsibilities, holding in his hand a weapon of such possibilities for . . . saving those lives, could have failed to use it."[31]

This is by no means an incomprehensible or, on the surface at least, an outrageous argument. But it is not the same as the argument I suggested in the case of Britain in 1940. It does not have the form: if we don't do *x* (bomb cities), they will do *y* (win the war, establish tyrannical rule, slaughter their opponents). What Stimson argued is very different. Given the actual policy of the U.S. government, it amounts to this: if we don't do *x*, *we* will do *y*. The two atomic bombs caused "many casualties," James Byrnes admitted, "but not nearly so many as there would have been had our air force continued to drop incendiary bombs on Japan's cities."[32] Our purpose, then, was not to avert a "butchery" that someone else was threatening, but one that we were threatening, and had already begun to carry out. Now, what great evil, what supreme emergency, justified the incendiary attacks on Japanese cities?

Even if we had been fighting in strict accordance with the war convention, the continuation of the struggle was not something forced upon us. It had to do with our war aims. The military estimate of casualties was based not only on the belief that the Japanese would fight almost to the last man, but also on the assumption that the Americans would accept nothing less than unconditional surrender. The war aims of the American government required either an invasion of the main islands, with enormous losses of American and Japanese soldiers and of Japanese civilians trapped in the war zones, or the use of the atomic bomb. Given that choice, one might well reconsider those aims. Even if we assume that unconditional surrender was morally desirable because of the character of Japanese militarism, it might still be morally undesirable because of the human costs it entailed. But I would suggest a stronger argument than this. The Japanese case is sufficiently different from the German so that unconditional surrender should never have been asked. Japan's rulers were engaged in a more ordinary sort of military expansion, and all that was morally required was that they be defeated, not that they be conquered and totally overthrown. Some restraint upon their war-making power might be justified, but their domestic authority was a matter of concern only to the Japanese people. In any case, if killing millions (or many thousands) of men and women was militarily necessary for their conquest and overthrow, then it was morally necessary—in order not to kill those people—to settle for something less. I have made this argument before (in chapter 7); here is a further example of its practical application. If people have a right not to be forced to fight, they also have a right not to be forced to continue fighting beyond the point when the war might justly be concluded. Beyond that point, there can be no supreme emergencies, no arguments about military necessity, no cost-accounting in human lives. To press the war further than that is to re-commit the crime of aggression. In the summer of 1945, the victorious Americans owed the Japanese people an experiment in negotiation. To use the atomic bomb, to kill and terrorize civilians, without even attempting such an experiment, was a double crime.[33]

These, then are the limits of the realm of necessity. Utilitarian calculation can force us to violate the rules of war only when we are face-to-face not merely with defeat but with a defeat likely to bring disaster to a political community. But these calculations have no similar effects when what is at stake is only the speed or the scope of victory. They are relevant only to the conflict between winning and fighting well, not to the internal problems of combat itself. Whenever that conflict is absent, calculation is stopped short by the rules of war and the rights they are designed to protect. Confronted by those rights, we are not to calculate consequences, or figure relative risks, or compute probable casualties, but simply to stop short and turn aside.

Notes

1. Quoted in George Quester, *Deterrence Before Hiroshima* (New York, 1966), p. 67.

2. See J. Glenn Gray, *The Warriors: Reflections on Men in Battle* (New York, 1967), ch. 5: "Images of the Enemy."

3. But the claim that one can never kill an innocent person abstracts from questions of coercion and consent: see the examples cited in chapter 10.

4. See Quester, *Deterrence* and F. M. Sallagar, *The Road to Total War: Escalation in World War II* (Rand Corporation Report, 1969); also the official history by Sir Charles Webster and Noble Frankland, *The Strategic Air Offensive Against Germany* (London, 1961).

5. Noble Frankland, *Bomber Offensive: The Devastation of Europe* (New York, 1970), p. 41.

6. The Story of the Cherwell minute is told, most unsympathetically, in C. P. Snow, *Science and Government* (New York, 1962).

7. Quester, pp. 117–18.

8. Quoted in Quester, p. 141.

9. Quoted in Angus Calder, *The People's War: 1939–1945* (New York, 1969), p. 491.

10. Calder, p. 229; the same poll is cited by Vera Brittain, a courageous opponent of British bombing policy: *Humiliation with Honor* (New York, 1943), p. 91.

11. ". . . it was not [Cherwell's] ruthlessness that worried us most, it was his calculations." Snow, *Science and Government*, p. 48. Cf. P. M. S. Blackett's postwar critique of the bombing, worked out in narrowly strategic terms: *Fear, War, and the Bomb* (New York, 1949), ch. 2.

12. Sallagar, p. 127.

13. Sallagar, p. 128.

14. Frankland, *Bomber Offensive*, pp. 38–39.

15. Frankland, *Bomber Offensive*, p. 134.

16. Sir Arthur Harris, *Bomber Offensive* (London, 1947), p. 74.

17. Calder, p. 229.

18. *The Hinge of Fate*, p. 770.

19. For a detailed account of this attack, see David Irving, *The Destruction of Dresden* (New York, 1963).

20. Quoted in Quester, p. 156.

21. *Memoirs of a Revolutionist* (New York, 1957), p. 178.

22. Robert C. Batchelder, *The Irreversible Decision: 1939–1950* (New York, 1965), p. 38. Batchelder's is the best historical account of the decision to drop the bomb, and the only one that treats the moral issues in a systematic way.

23. A. Russell Buchanan, *The United States and World War II* (New York, 1964), I, 75.

24. "The Decision to Use the Atomic Bomb," *Harpers Magazine* (February, 1947), repr. in *The Atomic Bomb: The Great Decision,* ed. Paul R. Baker (New York, 1968), p. 21.

25. *Speaking Frankly* (New York, 1947), p. 261.

26. *Atomic Quest* (New York, 1956), p. 247.

27. *Mr. Citizen* (New York, 1960), p. 267. I owe this group of quotations to Gerald McElroy.

28. Batchelder, p. 159.

29. Batchelder, p. 149.

30. *Triumph and Tragedy* (New York, 1962), p. 639.

31. "The Decision to Use the Bomb," p. 21.

32. *Speaking Frankly,* p. 264.

33. The case would be even worse if the bomb were used for political rather than military reasons (with the Russians rather than the Japanese in mind): on this point, see the careful analysis of Martin J. Sherwin, *A World Destroyed: The Atomic Bomb and the Grand Alliance* (New York, 1975).

47

War and Massacre[1]

Thomas Nagel

Thomas Nagel is a professor of philosophy at New York University. He is the author of many important articles and books on the philosophy of mind and moral philosophy, including Mortal Questions (1979) *and* The View From Nowhere *(1986). The present selection is an early article, inspired in part by his thought about the war in Vietnam (ongoing at the time). In this article he considers (deontological) absolutism in ethics and whether an absolutist must agree with Kant's dictum: "Do no injustice though the heavens should fall".*

From the apathetic reaction to atrocities committed in Vietnam by the United States and its allies, one may conclude that moral restrictions on the conduct of war command almost as little sympathy among the general public as they do among those charged with the formation of U.S. military policy. Even when restrictions on the conduct of warfare are defended, it is usually on legal grounds alone: their moral basis is often poorly understood. I wish to argue that certain restrictions are neither arbitrary nor merely conventional, and that their validity does not depend simply on their usefulness. There is, in other words, a moral basis for the rules of war, even though the conventions now officially in force are far from giving it perfect expression.

I

No elaborate moral theory is required to account for what is wrong in cases like the Mylai massacre, since it did not serve, and was not intended

Reprinted from Thomas Nagel, "War and Massacre," by permission of the publisher, Wiley-Blackwell, from *Philosophy and Public Affairs*, vol. 1, no. 2, (Winter 1972) pp. 229–243.

to serve, any strategic purpose. Moreover, if the participation of the United States in the Indo-Chinese war is entirely wrong to begin with, then that engagement is incapable of providing a justification for *any* measures taken in its pursuit—not only for the measures which are atrocities in every war, however just its aims.

But this war has revealed attitudes of a more general kind, that influenced the conduct of earlier wars as well. After it has ended, we shall still be faced with the problem of how warfare may be conducted, and the attitudes that have resulted in the specific conduct of this war will not have disappeared. Moreover, similar problems can arise in wars or rebellions fought for very different reasons, and against very different opponents. It is not easy to keep a firm grip on the idea of what is not permissible in warfare, because while some military actions are obvious atrocities, other cases are more difficult to assess, and the general principles underlying these judgments remain obscure. Such obscurity can lead to the abandonment of sound intuitions in favor of criteria whose rationale may be more obvious. If such a tendency is to be resisted, it will require a better understanding of the restrictions than we now have.

I propose to discuss the most general moral problem raised by the conduct of warfare: the problem of means and ends. In one view, there are limits on what may be done even in the service of an end worth pursuing—and even when adherence to the restriction may be very costly. A person who acknowledges the force of such restrictions can find himself in acute moral dilemmas. He may believe, for example, that by torturing a prisoner he can obtain information necessary to prevent a disaster, or that by obliterating one village with bombs he can halt a campaign of terrorism. If he believes that the gains from a certain measure will clearly outweigh its costs, yet still suspects that he ought not to adopt it, then he is in a dilemma produced by the conflict between two disparate categories of moral reason: categories that may be called *utilitarian* and *absolutist.*

Utilitarianism gives primacy to a concern with what will *happen.* Absolutism gives primacy to a concern with what one is *doing.* The conflict between them arises because the alternatives we face are rarely just choices between *total outcomes:* they are also choices between alternative pathways or measures to be taken. When one of the choices is to do terrible things to another person, the problem is altered fundamentally; it is no longer merely a question of which outcome would be worse.

Few of us are completely immune to either of these types of moral intuition, though in some people, either naturally or for doctrinal reasons, one type will be dominant and the other suppressed or weak. But it is perfectly possible to feel the force of both types of reason very strongly; in that case the moral dilemma in certain situations of crisis will be acute, and it may appear that every possible course of action or inaction is unacceptable for one reason or another.

II

Although it is this dilemma that I propose to explore, most of the discussion will be devoted to its absolutist component. The utilitarian component is straightforward by comparison, and has a natural appeal to anyone who is not a complete skeptic about ethics. Utilitarianism says that one should try, either individually or through institutions, to maximize good and minimize evil (the definition of these categories need not enter into the schematic formulation of the view), and that if faced with the possibility of preventing a great evil by producing a

lesser, one should choose the lesser evil. There are certainly problems about the formulation of utilitarianism, and much has been written about it, but its intent is morally transparent. Nevertheless, despite the addition of various refinements, it continues to leave large portions of ethics unaccounted for. I do not suggest that some form of absolutism can account for them all, only that an examination of absolutism will lead us to see the complexity, and perhaps the incoherence, of our moral ideas.

Utilitarianism certainly justifies *some* restrictions on the conduct of warfare. There are strong utilitarian reasons for adhering to any limitation which seems natural to most people—particularly if the limitation is widely accepted already. An exceptional measure which seems to be justified by its results in a particular conflict may create a precedent with disastrous long-term effects.[2] It may even be argued that war involves violence on such a scale that it is never justified on utilitarian grounds—the consequences of refusing to go to war will never be as bad as the war itself would be, even if atrocities were not committed. Or in a more sophisticated vein it might be claimed that a uniform policy of never resorting to military force would do less harm in the long run, if followed consistently, than a policy of deciding each case on utilitarian grounds (even though on occasion particular applications of the pacifist policy might have worse results than a specific utilitarian decision). But I shall not consider these arguments, for my concern is with reasons of a different kind, which may remain when reasons of utility and interest fail.[3]

In the final analysis, I believe that the dilemma cannot always be resolved. While not every conflict between absolutism and utilitarianism creates an insoluble dilemma, and while it is certainly right to adhere to absolutist restrictions unless the utilitarian considerations favoring violation are overpoweringly weighty and extremely certain—nevertheless, when that special condition is met, it may become impossible to adhere to an absolutist position. What I shall offer, therefore, is a somewhat qualified defense of absolutism. I believe it underlies a valid and fundamental type of moral judgment—which cannot be reduced to or overridden by other principles. And while there may be other principles just as fundamental, it is particularly important not to lose confidence in our absolutist intuitions, for they are often the only barrier before the abyss of utilitarian apologetics for large-scale murder.

III

One absolutist position that creates no problems of interpretation is pacifism: the view that one may not kill another person under any circumstances, no matter what good would be achieved or evil averted thereby. The type of absolutist position that I am going to discuss is different. Pacifism draws the conflict with utilitarian considerations very starkly. But there are other views according to which violence may be undertaken, even on a large scale, in a clearly just cause, so long as certain absolute restrictions on the character and direction of that violence are observed. The line is drawn somewhat closer to the bone, but it exists.

The philosopher who has done most to advance contemporary philosophical discussion of such a view, and to explain it to those unfamiliar with its extensive treatment in Roman Catholic moral theology, is G.E.M. Anscombe. In 1958 Miss Anscombe published a pamphlet entitled *Mr. Truman's Degree*,[4] on the occasion of the award by Oxford University of an honorary doctorate to Harry Truman. The pamphlet explained why she had opposed the decision to award that degree, recounted the story of her unsuccessful opposition, and offered some reflections on the history of Truman's decision to drop atom bombs on Hiroshima and Nagasaki, and on the difference between murder and allowable killing in warfare. She pointed out that the policy of deliberately killing large numbers of civilians either as a means or as an end in itself did not originate with Truman, and was common practice among all parties during World War II for some time before Hiroshima. The Allied area bombings of German cities by conventional explosives included raids which killed more civilians than did the atomic attacks; the same is true of certain fire-bomb raids on Japan.

The policy of attacking the civilian population in order to induce an enemy to surrender, or to damage his morale, seems to have been widely accepted in the civilized world, and seems to be accepted still, at least if the stakes are high enough. It gives evidence of a moral conviction that the deliberate killing of noncombatants—women, children, old people—is permissible if enough can be gained by it. This follows from the more general position that any means can in principle be justified if it leads to a sufficiently worthy end. Such an attitude is evident not only in the more spectacular current weapons systems but also in the day-to-day conduct of the nonglobal war in Indochina: the indiscriminate destructiveness of antipersonnel weapons, napalm, and aerial bombardment; cruelty to prisoners; massive relocation of civilians; destruction of crops; and so forth. An absolutist position opposes to this the view that certain acts cannot be justified no matter what the consequences. Among those acts is murder—the deliberate killing of the harmless: civilians, prisoners of war, and medical personnel.

In the present war such measures are sometimes said to be regrettable, but they are generally defended by reference to military necessity and the importance of the long-term consequences of success or failure in the war. I shall pass over the inadequacy of this consequentialist defense in its own terms. (That is the dominant form of moral criticism of the war, for it is part of what people mean when they ask, "Is it worth it?") I am concerned rather to account for the inappropriateness of offering any defense of that kind for such actions.

Many people feel, without being able to say much more about it, that something has gone seriously wrong when certain measures are admitted into consideration in the first place. The fundamental mistake is made there, rather than at the point where the overall benefit of some monstrous measure is judged to outweigh its disadvantages, and it is adopted. An account of absolutism might help us to understand this. If it is not allowable to *do* certain things, such as killing unarmed prisoners or civilians, then no argument about what will happen if one doesn't do them can show that doing them would be all right.

Absolutism does not, of course, require one to ignore the consequences of one's acts. It operates as a limitation on utilitarian reasoning, not as a substitute for it. An absolutist can be expected to try to maximize good and minimize evil, so long as this does not require him to transgress an absolute prohibition like that against murder. But when such a conflict occurs, the prohibition takes complete precedence over any consideration of consequences. Some of the results of this view are clear enough. It requires us to forgo certain potentially useful military measures, such as the slaughter of hostages and prisoners or indiscriminate attempts to reduce the enemy civilian population by starvation, epidemic infectious diseases like anthrax and bubonic plague, or mass incineration. It means that we cannot deliberate on whether such measures are justified by the fact that they will avert still greater evils, for as intentional measures they cannot be justified in terms of any consequences whatever.

Someone unfamiliar with the events of this century might imagine that utilitarian arguments, or arguments of national interest, would suffice to deter measures of this sort. But it has become evident that such considerations are insufficient to prevent the adoption and employment of enormous antipopulation weapons once their use is considered a serious moral possibility. The same is true of the piecemeal wiping out of rural civilian populations in airborne antiguerrilla warfare. Once the door is opened to calculations of utility and national interest, the usual speculations about the future of freedom, peace, and economic prosperity can be brought to bear to ease the consciences of those responsible for a certain number of charred babies.

For this reason alone it is important to decide what is wrong with the frame of mind which allows such arguments to begin. But it is also important to understand absolutism in the cases where it genuinely conflicts with utility. Despite its appeal, it is a paradoxical position, for it can require that one refrain from choosing the lesser of two evils when that is the only choice one has. And it is additionally paradoxical because, unlike pacifism, it permits one to do horrible things to people in some circumstances but not in others.

IV

Before going on to say what, if anything, lies behind the position, there remain a few relatively technical matters which are best discussed at this point.

First, it is important to specify as clearly as possible the kind of thing to which absolutist prohibitions can apply. We must take seriously the proviso that they concern what we deliberately do to people. There could not, for example, without incoherence, be an absolute prohibition against *bringing about* the death of an innocent person. For one may find oneself in a situation in which, no matter what one does, some innocent people will die as a result. I do not mean just that there are cases in which someone will die no matter what one does, because one is not in a position to affect the outcome one way or the other. That, it is to be hoped, is one's relation to the deaths of most innocent people. I have in mind, rather, a case in which someone is bound to die, but who it is will depend on what one does. Sometimes these situations have natural causes, as when too few resources (medicine, lifeboats) are available to rescue everyone threatened with a certain catastrophe. Sometimes the situations are manmade, as when the only way to control a campaign of terrorism is to employ terrorist tactics against the community from which it has arisen. Whatever one does in cases such as these, some innocent people will die as a result. If the absolutist prohibition forbade doing what would result in the deaths of innocent people, it would have the consequence that in such cases nothing one could do would be morally permissible.

This problem is avoided, however, because what absolutism forbids is *doing* certain things to people, rather than bringing about certain *results*. Not everything that happens to others as a result of what one does is something that one has *done* to them. Catholic moral theology seeks to make this distinction precise in a doctrine known as the law of double effect, which asserts that there is a morally relevant distinction between bringing about the death of an innocent person deliberately, either as an end in itself or as a means, and bringing it about as a side effect of something else one does deliberately. In the latter case, even if the outcome is foreseen, it is not murder, and does not fall under the absolute prohibition, though of course it may still be wrong for other reasons (reasons of utility, for example). Briefly, the principle states that one is sometimes permitted knowingly to bring about as a side effect of one's actions something which it would be absolutely impermissible to bring about deliberately as an end or as a means. In application to war or revolution, the law of double effect permits a certain amount of civilian carnage as a side effect of bombing munitions plants or attacking enemy soldiers. And even this is permissible only if the cost is not too great to be justified by one's objectives.

However, despite its importance and its usefulness in accounting for certain plausible moral judgments, I do not believe that the law of double effect is a generally applicable test for the consequences of an absolutist position. Its own application is not always clear, so that it introduces uncertainty where there need not be uncertainty.

In Indochina, for example, there is a great deal of aerial bombardment, strafing, spraying of napalm, and employment of pellet- or needle-spraying antipersonnel weapons against rural villages in which guerrillas are suspected to be hiding, or from which small-arms fire has been received. The majority of those killed and wounded in these aerial attacks are reported to be women and children, even when some combatants are caught as well. However, the government regards these civilian casualties as a regrettable side effect of what is a legitimate attack against an armed enemy.

It might be thought easy to dismiss this as sophistry: if one bombs, burns, or strafes a village containing a hundred people, twenty of whom one believes to be guerrillas, so that by killing most of them one will be statistically likely to kill most of the guerrillas, then isn't one's attack on the group of one hundred a *means* of destroying the guerrillas, pure and simple? If one makes no attempt to discriminate between guerrillas and civilians, as is impossible in a aerial attack on a small village, then one cannot regard as a mere side effect the deaths of those in the group that one would not have bothered to kill if more selective means had been available.

The difficulty is that this argument depends on one particular description of the act, and the reply might be that the means used against the guerrillas is not: killing everybody in the village—but rather: obliteration bombing of the *area* in which the twenty guerrillas are known to be located. If there are civilians in the area as well, they will be killed as a side effect of such action.[5]

Because of casuistical problems like this, I prefer to stay with the original, unanalyzed distinction between what one does to people and what merely happens to them as a result of what one does. The law of double effect provides an approximation to that distinction in many cases, and perhaps it can be sharpened to the point where it does better than that. Certainly the original distinction itself needs clarification, particularly since some of the things we do to people involve things happening to them as a result of other things we do. In a case like the one discussed, however, it is clear that by bombing the village one slaughters and maims the civilians in it. Whereas by giving the only available medicine to one of two sufferers from a disease, one does not kill the other, even if he dies as a result.

The second technical point to take up concerns a possible misinterpretation of this feature of the position. The absolutist focus on actions rather than outcomes does not merely introduce a new, outstanding item into the catalogue of evils. That is, it does not say that the worst thing in the world is the deliberate murder of an innocent person. For if that were all, then one could presumably justify one such murder on the ground that it would prevent several others, or ten thousand on the ground that they would prevent a hundred thousand more. That is a familiar argument. But if this is allowable, then there is no absolute prohibition against murder after all. Absolutism requires that we *avoid* murder at all costs, not that we *prevent* it at all costs.[6]

Finally, let me remark on a frequent criticism of absolutism that depends on a misunderstanding. It is sometimes suggested that such prohibitions depend on a kind of moral self-interest, a primary obligation to preserve one's own moral purity, to keep one's hands clean no matter what happens to the rest of the world. If this were the position, it might be exposed to the charge of self-indulgence. After all, what gives one man a right to put the purity of his soul or the cleanness of his hands above the lives or welfare of large numbers of other people? It might be argued that a public servant like Truman

has no right to put himself first in that way; therefore if he is convinced that the alternatives would be worse, he must give the order to drop the bombs, and take the burden of those deaths on himself, as he must do other distasteful things for the general good.

But there are two confusions behind the view that moral self-interest underlies moral absolutism. First, it is a confusion to suggest that the need to preserve one's moral purity might be the *source* of an obligation. For if by committing murder one sacrifices one's moral purity or integrity, that can only be because there is *already* something wrong with murder. The general reason against committing murder cannot therefore be merely that it makes one an immoral person. Secondly, the notion that one might sacrifice one's moral integrity justifiably, in the service of a sufficiently worthy end, is an incoherent notion. For if one were justified in making such a sacrifice (or even morally required to make it), then one would not be sacrificing one's moral integrity by adopting that course: one would be preserving it.

Moral absolutism is not unique among moral theories in requiring each person to do what will preserve his own moral purity in all circumstances. This is equally true of utilitarianism, or of any other-theory which distinguishes between right and wrong. Any theory which defines the right course of action in various circumstances and asserts that one should adopt that course, ipso facto asserts that one should do what will preserve one's moral purity, simply because the right course of action *is* what will preserve one's moral purity in those circumstances. Of course utilitarianism does not assert that this is *why* one should adopt that course, but we have seen that the same is true of absolutism.

V

It is easier to dispose of false explanations of absolutism than to produce a true one. A positive account of the matter must begin with the observation that war, conflict, and aggression are relations between persons. The view that it can be wrong to consider merely the overall effect of one's actions on the general welfare comes into prominence when those actions involve relations with others. A man's acts usually affect more people than he deals with directly, and those effects must naturally be considered in his decisions. But if there are special principles governing the manner in which he should *treat* people, that will require special attention to the particular persons toward whom the act is directed, rather than just to its total effect.

Absolutist restrictions in warfare appear to be of two types: restrictions on the class of persons at whom aggression or violence may be directed and restrictions on the manner of attack, given that the object falls within that class. These can be combined, however, under the principle that hostile treatment of any person must be justified in terms of something *about that person* which makes the treatment appropriate. Hostility is a personal relation, and it must be suited to its target. One consequence of this condition will be that certain persons may not be subjected to hostile treatment in war at all, since nothing about them justifies such treatment. Others will be proper objects of hostility only in certain circumstances, or when they are engaged in certain pursuits. And the appropriate manner and extent of hostile treatment will depend on what is justified by the particular case.

A coherent view of this type will hold that extremely hostile behavior toward another is compatible with treating him as a person—even perhaps as an end in himself. This is possible only if one has not automatically stopped treating him as a person as soon as one starts to fight with him. If hostile, aggressive, or combative treatment of others always violated die condition that they be treated as human beings, it would be difficult to make further distinctions on that score *within* the class of hostile actions. That point of view, on the level of international relations, leads to the position that if complete pacifism is not accepted, no holds need be barred at all, and we may slaughter and massacre to our hearts' content, if it seems advisable. Such a position is often expressed in discussions of war crimes.

But the fact is that ordinary people do not believe this about conflicts, physical or otherwise, between individuals, and there is no more reason why it should be true of conflicts between nations. There seems to be a perfectly natural conception of the distinction between fighting clean and fighting dirty. To fight dirty is to direct one's hostility or aggression not at its proper object, but at a peripheral target which may be more vulnerable, and through which the proper object can be attacked indirectly. This applies in a fist fight, an election campaign, a duel, or a philosophical argument. If the concept is general enough to apply to all these matters, it should apply to war—both to the conduct of individual soldiers and to the conduct of nations.

Suppose that you are a candidate for public office, convinced that the election of your opponent would be a disaster, that he is an unscrupulous demagogue who will serve a narrow range of interests and seriously infringe the rights of those who disagree with him; and suppose you are convinced that you cannot defeat him by conventional means. Now imagine that various unconventional means present themselves as possibilities: you possess information about his sex life which would scandalize the electorate if made public; or you learn that his wife is an alcoholic or that in his youth he was associated for a brief period with a proscribed political party, and you believe that this information could be used to blackmail him into withdrawing his candidacy; or you can have a team of your supporters flatten the tires of a crucial subset of his supporters on election day; or you are in a position to stuff the ballot boxes; or, more simply, you can have him assassinated. What is wrong with these methods, given that they will achieve an overwhelmingly desirable result?

There are, of course, many things wrong with them: some are against the law; some infringe the procedures of an electoral process to which you are presumably committed by taking part in it; very importantly, some may backfire, and it is in the interest of all political candidates to adhere to an unspoken agreement not to allow certain personal matters to intrude into a campaign. But that is not all. We have in addition the feeling that these measures, these methods of attack are *irrelevant* to the issue between you and your opponent, that in taking them up you would not be directing yourself to that which makes him an object of your opposition. You would be directing your attack not at the true target of your hostility, but at peripheral targets that happen to be vulnerable.

The same is true of a fight or argument outside the framework of any system of regulations or law. In an altercation with a taxi driver over an excessive fare, it is inappropriate to taunt him about his accent, flatten one of his tires, or smear chewing gum on his windshield; and it remains inappropriate even if he casts aspersions on your race, politics, or religion, or dumps the contents of your suitcase into the street.[7]

The importance of such restrictions may vary with the seriousness of the case; and what is unjustifiable in one case may be justified in a more extreme one. But they all derive from a single principle: that hostility or aggression should be directed at its true object. This means both that it should be directed at the person or persons who provoke it and that it should aim more specifically at what is provocative about them. The second condition will determine what form the hostility may appropriately take.

It is evident that some idea of the relation in which one should stand to other people underlies this principle, but the idea is difficult to state. I believe it is roughly this: whatever one does to another person intentionally must be aimed at him as a subject, with the intention that he receive it as a subject. It should manifest an attitude to *him* rather than just to the situation, and he should be able to recognize it and identify himself as its object. The procedures by which such an attitude is manifested need not be addressed to the person directly. Surgery, for example, is not a form of personal confrontation but part of a medical treatment that can be offered to a patient face to face and received by him as a response to his needs and the natural outcome of an attitude toward *him*.

Hostile treatment, unlike surgery, is already addressed *to* a person, and does not take its interpersonal meaning from a wider context. But hostile acts can serve as the expression or implementation of only a limited range of attitudes to the person who is attacked. Those attitudes in turn have as objects certain real or presumed characteristics or activities of the person which are thought to justify them. When this background is absent, hostile or aggressive behavior can no longer be intended for the reception of the victim as a subject. Instead it takes on the character of a purely bureaucratic operation. This occurs when one attacks someone who is not the true object of one's hostility—the true object may be someone else, who can be attacked through the victim; or one may not be manifesting a hostile attitude toward anyone, but merely using the easiest available path to some desired goal. One finds oneself not facing or addressing the victim at all, but operating on him—without this larger context of personal interaction that surrounds a surgical operation.

If absolutism is to defend its claim to priority over considerations of utility, it must hold that the maintenance of a direct interpersonal response to the people one deals with is a requirement which no advantages can justify one in abandoning. The requirement is absolute only if it rules out any calculation of what would justify its violation. I have said earlier that there may be circumstances so extreme that they render an absolutist position untenable. One may find then that one has no choice but to do something terrible. Nevertheless, even in such cases absolutism retains its force in that one cannot claim *justification* for the violation. It does not become *all right*.

As a tentative effort to explain this, let me try to connect absolutist limitations with the possibility of justifying *to the victim* what is being done to him. If one abandons a person in the course of rescuing several others from a fire or a sinking ship, one *could* say to him, "You understand, I have to leave you to save the others." Similarly, if one subjects an unwilling child to a painful surgical procedure, one can say to him, "If you could understand, you would realize that I am doing this to help you." One could *even* say, as one bayonets an enemy soldier, "It's either you or me." But one cannot really say while torturing a prisoner, "You understand, I have to pull out your fingernails because it is absolutely essential that we have the names of your confederates"; nor can one say to the victims of Hiroshima, "You understand, we have to incinerate you to provide the Japanese government with an incentive to surrender."

This does not take us very far, of course, since a utilitarian would presumably be willing to offer justifications of the latter sort to his victims, in cases where he thought they were sufficient. They are really justifications to the world at large, which the victim, as a reasonable man, would be expected to appreciate. However, there seems to me something wrong with this view, for it ignores the possibility that to treat someone else horribly puts you in a special relation to him, which may have to be defended in terms of other features of your relation to him. The suggestion needs much more development; but it may help us to understand how there may be requirements which are absolute in the sense that there can be no justification for violating them. If the justification for what one did to another person had to be such that it could be offered to him specifically, rather than just to the world at large, that would be a significant source of restraint.

If the account is to be deepened, I would hope for some results along the following lines. Absolutism is associated with a view of oneself as a small being interacting with others in a large world. The justifications it requires are primarily interpersonal. Utilitarianism is associated with a view of oneself as a benevolent bureaucrat distributing such benefits as one can control to countless other beings, with whom one may have various relations or none. The justifications it requires are primarily administrative. The argument between the two moral attitudes may depend on the relative priority of these two conceptions.[8]

VI

Some of the restrictions on methods of warfare which have been adhered to from time to time are to be explained by the mutual interests of the involved parties: restrictions on weaponry, treatment of prisoners, etc. But that is not all there is to it. The conditions of directness and relevance which I have argued apply to relations of conflict and aggression apply to war as well. I have said that there are two types of absolutist restrictions on the conduct of war: those that limit the legitimate targets of hostility and those that limit its character, even when the target is acceptable. I shall say something about each of these. As will become clear, the principle I have sketched does not yield an unambiguous answer in every case.

First let us see how it implies that attacks on some people are allowed, but not attacks on others. It may seem paradoxical to assert that to fire a machine gun at someone who is throwing hand grenades at your emplacement is to treat him as a human being. Yet the relation with him is direct and straightforward.[9] The attack is aimed specifically against the threat presented by a dangerous adversary, and not against a peripheral target through which he happens to be vulnerable but which has nothing to do with that threat. For example, you might stop him by machine-gunning his wife and children, who are standing nearby, thus distracting him from his aim of blowing you up and enabling you to capture him. But if his wife and children are not threatening your life, that would be to treat them as means with a vengeance.

This, however, is just Hiroshima on a smaller scale. One objection to weapons of mass annihilation—nuclear, thermonuclear, biological, or chemical—is that their indiscriminateness disqualifies them as direct instruments for the expression of hostile relations. In attacking the civilian population, one treats neither the military enemy nor the civilians with that minimal respect which is owed to them as human beings. This is clearly true of the direct attack on people who present no threat at all. But it is also true of the character of the attack on those who *are* threatening you, viz., the government and military forces of the enemy. Your aggression is directed against an area of vulnerability quite distinct from any threat presented by them which you may be justified in meeting. You are taking aim at them through the mundane life and survival of their countrymen, instead of aiming at the destruction of their military capacity. And of course it does not require hydrogen bombs to commit such crimes.

This way of looking at the matter also helps us to understand the importance of the distinction between combatants and noncombatants, and the irrelevance of much of the criticism offered against its intelligibility and moral significance. According to an absolutist position, deliberate killing of the innocent is murder, and in warfare the role of the innocent is filled by noncombatants. This has been thought to raise two sorts of problems: first, the widely imagined difficulty of making a division, in modern warfare, between combatants and noncombatants; second, problems deriving from the connotation of the word "innocence."

Let me take up the latter question first.[10] In the absolutist position, the operative notion of innocence is not moral innocence, and it is not opposed to moral guilt. If it were, then we would be justified in killing a wicked but noncombatant hairdresser in an enemy city who supported the evil policies of his government, and unjustified in killing a morally pure conscript who was driving a tank toward us with the profoundest regrets and nothing but love in his heart. But moral innocence has very little to do with it, for in the definition of murder "innocent" means "currently harmless," and it is opposed not to "guilty" but to "doing harm." It should be noted that such an analysis has the consequence that in war we may often be justified in killing people who do not deserve to die, and unjustified in killing people who do deserve to die, if anyone does.

So we must distinguish combatants from noncombatants on the basis of their immediate threat or harmfulness. I do not claim that the line is a sharp one, but it is not so difficult as is often supposed to place individuals on one side of it or the other. Children are not combatants even though they may join the armed forces if they are allowed to grow up. Women are not combatants just because they bear children or offer comfort to the soldiers. More problematic are the supporting personnel, whether in or out of uniform, from drivers of munitions trucks and army cooks to civilian munitions workers and farmers. I believe they can be plausibly classified by applying the condition that the prosecution of conflict must direct itself to the cause of danger, and not to what is peripheral. The threat presented by an army and its members does not consist merely in the fact that they are men, but in the fact that they are armed and are using their arms in the pursuit of certain objectives. Contributions to their arms and logistics are contributions to this threat; contributions to their mere existence as men are not. It is therefore wrong to direct an attack against those who merely serve the combatants' needs as human beings, such as farmers and food suppliers, even though survival as a human being is a necessary condition of efficient functioning as a soldier.

This brings us to the second group of restrictions: those that limit what may be done even to combatants. These limits are harder to explain clearly. Some of them may be arbitrary or conventional, and some may have to be derived from other sources; but I believe that the condition of directness and relevance in hostile relations accounts for them to a considerable extent.

Consider first a case which involves both a protected class of non-combatants and a restriction on the measures that may be used against combatants. One provision of the rules of war which is universally recognized, though it seems to be turning into a dead letter in Vietnam, is the special status of medical personnel and the wounded in warfare. It might be more efficient to shoot medical officers on sight and to let the enemy wounded die rather than be patched up to fight another day. But someone with medical insignia is supposed to be left alone and permitted to tend and retrieve the wounded. I believe this is because medical attention is a species of attention to completely general human needs, not specifically the needs of a combat soldier, and our conflict with the soldier is not with his existence as a human being.

By extending the application of this idea, one can justify prohibitions against certain particularly cruel weapons: starvation, poisoning, infectious diseases (supposing they could be inflicted on combatants only), weapons designed to maim or disfigure or torture the opponent rather than merely to stop him. It is not, I think, mere casuistry to claim that such weapons attack the men, not the soldiers. The effect of dum-dum bullets, for example, is much more extended than necessary to cope with the combat situation in which they are used. They abandon any attempt to discriminate in their effects between the combatant and the human being. For this reason the use of flamethrowers and napalm is an atrocity in all circumstances that I can imagine, whoever the target may be. Burns are both extremely painful and extremely disfiguring—far more than any other category

of wound. That this well-known fact plays no (inhibiting) part in the determination of U.S. weapons policy suggests that moral sensitivity among public officials has not increased markedly since the Spanish Inquisition.[11]

Finally, the same condition of appropriateness to the true object of hostility should limit the scope of attacks on an enemy country: its economy, agriculture, transportation system, and so forth. Even if the parties to a military conflict are considered to be not armies or governments but entire nations (which is usually a grave error), that does not justify one nation in warring against every aspect or element of another nation. That is not justified in a conflict between individuals, and nations are even more complex than individuals, so the same reasons apply. Like a human being, a nation is engaged in countless other pursuits while waging war, and it is not in those respects that it is an enemy.

The burden of the argument has been that absolutism about murder has a foundation in principles governing all one's relations to other persons, whether aggressive or amiable, and that these principles, and that absolutism, apply to warfare as well, with the result that certain measures are impermissible no matter what the consequences.[12] I do not mean to romanticize war. It is sufficiently utopian to suggest that when nations conflict they might rise to the level of limited barbarity that typically characterizes violent conflict between individuals, rather than wallowing in the moral pit where they appear to have settled, surrounded by enormous arsenals.

VII

Having described the elements of the absolutist position, we must now return to the conflict between it and utilitarianism. Even if certain types of dirty tactics become acceptable when the stakes are high enough, the most serious of the prohibited acts, like murder and torture, are not just supposed to require unusually strong justification. They are supposed *never* to be done, because no quantity of resulting benefit is thought capable of justifying such treatment of a person.

The fact remains that when an absolutist knows or believes that the utilitarian cost of refusing to adopt a prohibited course will be very high, he may hold to his refusal to adopt it, but he will find it difficult to feel that a moral dilemma has been satisfactorily resolved. The same may be true of someone who rejects an absolutist requirement and adopts instead the course yielding the most acceptable consequences. In either case, it is possible to feel that one has acted for reasons insufficient to justify violation of the opposing principle. In situations of deadly conflict, particularly where a weaker party is threatened with annihilation or enslavement by a stronger one, the argument for resorting to atrocities can be powerful, and the dilemma acute.

There may exist principles, not yet codified, which would enable us to resolve such dilemmas. But then again there may not. We must face the pessimistic alternative that these two forms of moral intuition are not capable of being brought together into a single, coherent moral system, and that the world can present us with situations in which there is no honorable or moral course for a man to take, no course free of guilt and responsibility for evil.

The idea of a moral blind alley is a perfectly intelligible one. It is possible to get into such a situation by one's own fault, and people do it all the time. If, for example, one makes two incompatible promises or commitments—becomes engaged to two people, for example—then there is no course one can take which is not wrong, for one must break one's promise to at least one of them. Making a clean breast of the whole thing will not be enough to remove one's reprehensibility. The existence of such cases is not morally disturbing, however, because we feel that the situation was not unavoidable: one had

to do something wrong in the first place to get into it. But what if the world itself, or someone else's actions, could face a previously innocent person with a choice between morally abominable courses of action, and leave him no way to escape with his honor? Our intuitions rebel at the idea, for we feel that the constructibility of such a case must show a contradiction in our moral views. But it is not in itself a contradiction to say that someone can do X or not do X, and that for him to take either course would be wrong. It merely contradicts the supposition that *ought* implies *can*—since presumably one ought to refrain from what is wrong, and in such a case it is impossible to do so.[13] Given the limitations on human action, it is naïve to suppose that there is a solution to every moral problem with which the world can face us. We have always known that the world is a bad place. It appears that it may be an evil place as well.

Notes

1. This paper grew out of discussions at the Society for Ethical and Legal Philosophy, and I am indebted to my fellow members for their help.

2. Straightforward considerations of national interest often tend in the same direction: the inadvisability of using nuclear weapons seems to be overdetermined in this way.

3. These reasons, moreover, have special importance in that they are available even to one who denies the appropriateness of utilitarian considerations in international matters. He may acknowledge limitations on what may be done to the soldiers and civilians of other countries in pursuit of his nation's military objectives, while denying that one country should in general consider the interests of nationals of other countries in determining its policies.

4. (Privately printed.) See also her essay "War and Murder," in *Nuclear Weapons and Christian Conscience*, ed. Walter Stein (London, 1963). The present paper is much indebted to these two essays throughout. These and related subjects are extensively treated by Paul Ramsey in *The Just War* (New York, 1968). Among recent writings that bear on the moral problem are Jonathan Bennett, "Whatever the Consequences," *Analysis* 26, no. 3 (1966): 83–102; and Philippa Foot, "The Problem of Abortion and the

Doctrine of the Double Effect," *The Oxford Review* 5 (1967): 5–15. Miss Anscombe's replies are "A Note on Mr. Bennett," *Analysis* 26, no. 3 (1966): 208, and "Who is Wronged?" *The Oxford Review* 5 (1967): 16–17.

5. This counterargument was suggested by Rogers Albritton.

6. Someone might of course acknowledge the *moral relevance* of the distinction between deliberate and nondeliberate killing, without being an absolutist. That is, he might believe simply that it was *worse* to bring about a death deliberately than as a secondary effect. But that would be merely a special assignment of value, and not an absolute prohibition.

7. Why, on the other hand, does it seem appropriate, rather than irrelevant, to punch someone in the mouth if he insults you? The answer is that in our culture it is an insult to punch someone in the mouth, and not just an injury. This reveals, by the way, a perfectly unobjectionable sense in which convention may play a part in determining exactly what falls under an absolutist restriction and what does not. I am indebted to Robert Fogelin for this point.

8. Finally, I should mention a different possibility, suggested by Robert Nozick: that there is a strong general presumption against benefiting from the calamity of another, whether or not it has been deliberately inflicted for that or any other reason. This broader principle may well lend its force to the absolutist position.

9. It has been remarked that according to my view, shooting at someone establishes an I-thou relationship.

10. What I say on this subject derives from Anscombe.

11. Beyond this I feel uncertain. Ordinary bullets, after all, can cause death, and nothing is more permanent than that. I am not at all sure why we are justified in trying to kill those who are trying to kill us (rather than merely in trying to stop them with force which may also result in their deaths). It is often argued that incapacitating gases are a relatively humane weapon (when not used, as in Vietnam, merely to make people easier to shoot). Perhaps the legitimacy of restrictions against them must depend on the dangers of escalation, and the great utility of maintaining *any* conventional category of restriction so long as nations are willing to adhere to it.

Let me make clear that I do not regard my argument as a defense of the moral immutability of the Hague and Geneva Conventions. Rather, I believe that they rest partly on a moral foundation, and that modifications of them should also be assessed on moral grounds.

But even this connection with the actual laws of war is not essential to my claims about what is permissible and what is not. Since completing this paper I have read an essay by Richard Wasserstrom entitled "The Laws of War" (forthcoming in *The Monist*), which argues that the existing laws and conventions do not even attempt to embody a decent moral position: that their provisions have been determined by other interests, that they are in fact immoral in substance, and that it is a grave mistake to refer to them as standards in forming moral judgments about warfare. This possibility deserves serious consideration, and I am not sure what to say about it, but it does not affect my view of the moral issues.

12. It is possible to draw a more radical conclusion, which I shall not pursue here. Perhaps the technology and organization of modern war are such as to make it impossible to wage as an acceptable form of interpersonal or even international hostility. Perhaps it is too impersonal and large-scale for that. If so, then absolutism would in practice imply pacifism, given the present state of things. On the other hand, I am skeptical about the unstated assumption that a technology dictates its own use.

13. This was first pointed out to me by Christopher Boorse.